FARRAR
STRAUS
GIROUX

FIVE GERMANYS
I HAVE KNOWN

FIVE GERMANYS
I HAVE KNOWN

★ ★ ★ ★ ★

FRITZ STERN

FARRAR, STRAUS AND GIROUX

NEW YORK

FARRAR, STRAUS AND GIROUX
19 Union Square West, New York 10003

Copyright © 2006 by Fritz Stern
All rights reserved
Distributed in Canada by Douglas & McIntyre
Printed in the United States of America
First edition, 2006

Library of Congress Cataloging-in-Publication Data
Stern, Fritz Richard, 1926–
    Five Germanys I have known / Fritz Stern.
        p.   cm.
    Includes index.
    ISBN-13: 978-0-374-15540-7 (hardcover : alk. paper)
    ISBN-10: 0-374-15540-2 (hardcover : alk. paper)
    1. Stern, Fritz Richard, 1926– .   2. Historians—Germany—History—20th century.
3. Germany—History—20th century.   I. Title.

DD86.7.S84A3 2006
943.087092—dc22

                                                          2006000060

Designed by Gretchen Achilles

www.fsgbooks.com

3   5   7   9   10   8   6   4   2

TO MY CHILDREN:

FRED AND KATHERINE

Dr. Rieux resolved to compile this chronicle, so that he should not be one of those who hold their peace but should bear witness in favor of those plague-stricken people, so that some memorial of the injustice and outrage done them might endure; and to state quite simply what we learn in time of pestilence: that there are more things to admire in men than to despise . . .

He knew what those jubilant crowds did not know but could have learned from books: that the plague bacillus never dies or disappears for good; that it can lie dormant for years and years in furniture and linen-chests; that it bides its time in bedrooms, cellars, trunks, and book-shelves; and that perhaps the day would come when, for the bane and the enlightening of men, it would rouse up its rats again and send them forth to die in a happy city.

ALBERT CAMUS, *The Plague*

CONTENTS

GERMANY, 1937

LITHUANIA

Baltic Sea

North Sea

Königsberg

Danzig

Hamburg

Stettin

Berlin

THE NETHERLANDS

Hannover

Elbe

Oder

Poznań

Warsaw

Vistula

Bug

BELGIUM

Cologne

BUCHENWALD

Weimar

Dresden

Breslau

SILESIA

Warta

P O L A N D

Rhine

Frankfurt

Prague

Spindler-mühle

Cracow

LUXEMBOURG

Nurnberg

Vltava

C Z E C H O S L O V A K I A

F R A N C E

Danube

DACHAU

Munich

Vienna

AUSTRIA

© 2006 Jeffrey L. Ward

SWITZERLAND

| 0 Miles | 100 | 200 |
| 0 Kilometers | 200 | |

THE TWO GERMANYS, 1949–1990

Baltic Sea

North Sea

Rostock

Kaliningrad [Königsberg]

EAST GERMANY

Hamburg

Hannover

Elbe

Berlin

Potsdam

POLAND

THE NETHERLANDS

Vistula

Bug

Warsaw

BELGIUM

Bonn

Halle

Leipzig

Merseburg

Wrocław [Breslau]

Oświęcim [AUSCHWITZ]

FRANCE

Rhine

Frankfurt

WEST GERMANY

Spindleruv Mlyn

Prague

Kraków [Cracow]

LUXEMBOURG

C Z E C H O S L O V A K I A

Danube

Munich

AUSTRIA

HUNGARY

© 2006 Jeffrey L. Ward

BERLIN

French Sector

British Sector

Soviet Sector

U.S. Sector

ITALY

YUGOSLAVIA

| 0 Miles | 100 | 200 |
| 0 Kilometers | 200 | |

FIVE GERMANYS
I HAVE KNOWN

INTRODUCTION

WHEN GENERAL CHARLES DE GAULLE made his first trip to Russia, in the winter of 1944–1945, he went to Stalingrad, site of the farthest advance and greatest defeat of the German army. In the First World War, de Gaulle had been wounded fighting against the Germans at Verdun and been imprisoned by them for more than two years, and in the Second he was leader of the Free French fighting them. Legend, with a proper touch of verisimilitude, has it that amid the ruins of Stalingrad he muttered to an aide, "*Quel peuple!*" The translator inquired, "You mean the Russians?" "No," said de Gaulle, "the Germans."

The general's lapidary judgment at that place of devastation says much about the German drama of the past century, which he grasped clearly. He was speaking of a "people" who between 1870 and 1939 had thrice attacked his country, whose power had corrupted and nearly destroyed historic Europe, and who were guilty of a genocidal crime unique in Europe's history. But he also knew that the German people had been prodigiously creative and that they would be indispensable for the postwar recovery of Europe. He grasped the deep ambiguity that hovers around German greatness.

This book records my experiences with the five Germanys that my generation has witnessed. I was born into the German predicament that de Gaulle understood so well; I remember my parents' dismay at the slow death of the Weimar Republic during my early childhood and the swift establishment of National Socialist tyranny thereafter, a tyranny accepted by so many and opposed by so few. I remember their friends who were defiant defenders of democracy and who were defeated, some of them murdered, incarcerated, or exiled. Though I lived in National Socialist Germany for only five years, that brief period saddled me with the burning question that I have spent my professional life trying to answer: why and how did the universal human potential for evil become an actuality in Germany?

Decades of study and experience have persuaded me that the German roads to perdition, including National Socialism, were neither accidental nor inevitable. National Socialism had deep roots, and yet its growth could have been arrested. I was born into a world on the cusp of avoidable disaster. And I came to realize that no country is immune to the temptations of pseudo-religious movements of repression such as those to which Germany succumbed. The fragility of freedom is the simplest and deepest lesson of my life and work. And when an unvarnished picture of the past, always indispensable, seemed difficult, I recalled Ernst Reuter's great credo of 1913: "The fate of democracy rests on faith in history."

In my work as a historian in the postwar years, I was only intermittently aware of the ties between my life and my studies; fully committing myself to the historian's craft, I knew that while Clio allowed for many ways of serving her, all of them demanded a measure of detachment—enlivened, one hoped, by empathy and a disciplined imagination. I studied and taught the German past with American eyes and for American students and readers. But my full American life eventually came to have a vital German component, because as an American historian of Germany, I was drawn into German controversies about the past, which were roiling a defeated and divided nation, itself the principal battleground of the cold war. Perhaps I didn't quite anticipate that when one fully lives with the upheavals of one's own time—by turns destructive and uniquely constructive—one comes to see the past in new, more complex ways. Also, I realized more and more that the lessons I had learned about German history had a frightening relevance to the United States today. And gradually I acquired another German life, parallel and subordinate to my American life. I came to live in two worlds simultaneously, learning from both. Remnants of black-and-white thinking receded, and the past became a fabric of shifting colors.

As I came to know something about my third and fourth Germanys—the extraordinary democracy that developed, not without controversy, in the Federal Republic, and the less well known dictatorship of the Soviet-dominated German Democratic Republic—luck and predisposition to civic action made me "an engaged observer," to use the phrase that Raymond Aron with much greater justification used about himself. I was intermittently drawn from my study and classroom onto the fringes of political life in both Germany and America, and counted myself lucky to be able to see and respond to historic events that were shaping the new Europe in its new relations to the United States. I still thought of this as the public work of history.

For decades, I shied away from writing about my private experiences: I wanted to keep the professional and the personal properly apart. But right after I had returned for the first time to my native city of Breslau in Germany, now Wrocław in Poland, I did write a private account of it for my children, and I called it "Homecoming 1979." Only now do I fully realize the ironic, perhaps even self-delusionary character of my title: a "Homecoming" was precisely what it was *not*. I had gone to Wrocław out of the deepest kind of curiosity; I don't think I realized then that the journey had been a quest, that somehow I needed to see that my home had been destroyed and that the country into which I was born had ceased to exist. My sense of loss was overlain by an all-pervasive gratitude for having found a second, better home in the United States. But that little essay was, indeed, my first effort to write personally about going back to where I had begun, and I offer it here as a record of my earliest retrospective impression.

The northeastern route by which we drove to Wrocław, to Breslau, was strangely unfamiliar; in the old days, we had always been lured toward the south, to the Czech-Bohemian mountains, or to the west, to Berlin and beyond. But the north-east—where the Poles had re-created their own state and their own independence in 1918—had seemed a distant, vaguely hostile land. For most Germans, the Poles were at best an object of bemusement, at worst of contempt.

Polish road signs announced approaches to Wrocław; we had no way of knowing when we had crossed the old Polish-German frontier. In 1945, after a war in which Poland had suffered the most terrible devastation (and the calcu-lated liquidation of its elites by both Germans and Russians), the Soviet Union annexed the eastern parts of the country to the Ukraine, and the Allies agreed that in compensation Poles should "administer" the German lands east of the Oder-Neisse Line; these included Silesia, with its ancient capital of Breslau. Ex-pelled from their eastern provinces, hundreds of thousands of Poles perforce moved west. They "cleansed" the lands new to them of some three million Ger-mans, and every sign of former Germanness was meticulously erased.

I had suffered too much in Breslau to have regretted that the city had passed to new masters or to feel compassion for the Germans expelled from it. My fam-ily had come too close to extermination for me to have felt sympathy for unknown

Germans, whether dead or driven out. My basic response right after the war was, so be it, the expellers have themselves been expelled. But what remained was curiosity about the place and some unreasoned, stubborn loyalty to the integrity of the past.

I had read of Breslau's fate in 1944–1945, but to see the consequences of it was something else. As German forces were retreating in the east, Hitler had ordered Breslau to become a fortress city and to hold out against the advancing Russian armies. In January 1945, the SS commander of the city ordered its immediate evacuation, forcing hundreds of thousands of men, women, and children to leave under the most horrendous wintry conditions, and trapping untold numbers of others in the desperate city. Breslau withstood a Soviet siege for forty-five days, with brutal house-to-house battles and constant Soviet shelling, along with horrific destruction initiated by its own German commanders: in the midst of the siege, and in an orgy of brutal destructiveness, Hitler's minions had ordered an airstrip to be built in the very middle of the city, presumably to allow for supplies to come in—at the cost of thousands of German and non-German lives and the devastation of whole neighborhoods. Hitler was already dead and Berlin captured when Breslau finally surrendered. This perverse defense of Breslau was madness turned against itself, a murder of self when there were no other victims left to kill. Those horrible few months were blindly sacrificial: the last-ditch defense served no purpose, save as the final instance of that unquestioned obedience to Hitler that had already turned the world into a nightmare of disaster.

Wrocław showed both the signs of the wartime destruction and the drab postwar socialist reconstruction. I recognized nothing in it until we came to the center of town and a web of one-way streets that obstructed our way to the hotel, where I instantly recognized—and by which I could instantly orient myself—the massive red-brick Polizeipräsidium, the building that had always stood as a bastion of oppression, where in early 1933 the SA Nazi storm troopers had murdered my father's friend and patient Ernst Eckstein, and where in 1938 my mother and I brought my father for "an interview" at eight in the morning, preparatory to our emigration. It was still a police headquarters, but now a Polish one.

At the Hotel Monopol—the best of Breslau's old hotels, now musty and run down—they told me that they had no double room, only a suite. In fact, it was the best suite in the hotel, with a huge balcony facing out to the old city theater across the street. Prominenz, or the old elites, usually stayed here before; when Hitler visited Breslau in July 1938, had he stayed in this very suite? I wondered. What a strange return for a native son: in style, with an American wife, with a reservation made by the American embassy in Warsaw—and with no one to return to. I felt myself an irrelevance in what had once been my city but now had Polish street names and resounded with Polish voices.

That evening we took my old streetcar, the number 8, to where our apartment house should have been, along the route I had taken daily to and from school. I had thought it was a fair distance, too long to walk; in fact, it was only four stops on the streetcar. The route had once been along streets with Breslau's best shops and elegant apartment houses and villas; now there were plenty of empty spaces between old buildings, along with drab new structures going up—the cinder blocks of socialist construction, without color or form, square, squalid, and ugly.

Our corner apartment house stood no more, though the stately office building across the wide street had survived. When we had moved to this street in 1930, and until about 1936, when I was ten, it had been called Kaiser Wilhelm Strasse, but then, a while after Hitler's purge, in 1934, of the leadership of the SA (including, as I remember well, the hated local SA leader, Edmund Heines), the street was renamed Strasse der SA, which I minded every time I had to write it.

We moved on: to my father's little clinic in a side street; that building, too, had survived and now was an old-age home. We passed a major intersection with its post office, where as a child I had so often posted letters to people abroad having to do with my family's efforts to emigrate: the all-consuming hope of those years. Then, on a parallel street, about ten minutes from where we had lived, I went looking for the Jewish hospital (Israelitisches Krankenhaus) where, because my father was a Jew who had been baptized at birth, he could serve only as a consultant but not as a regular attendant physician. It must have been hard to have been persecuted as belonging to a group that also partly repudiated you. The I.K., as we called the hospital in my childhood, was still there, with its big red-brick buildings, the back ones evidently still a hospital. We finally found a date chiseled in the wall (1902) and the letters I.K.—the sole survival of its distant German past, of a time when this had been the clinic for Breslau's flourishing Jewish population.

The next morning, I tried to navigate from the hotel to Scheitnig, an easterly part of the town between the river and a huge old park. After several false starts (near the center of town all the old landmarks were gone), I saw a familiar bridge, remembered there was a second bridge, and then headed straight for the Maria Magdalen Gymnasium, which I attended from 1936 to 1938. There it stood, just as I had remembered it, a little older, faded, but still "modern" in its late-Weimar design. We went inside—the same stone staircase, the same floors, locked classrooms, director's office.

My grandmother's house, Wardeinstrasse 13, was about three minutes from my school. It, too, had survived—with all the traces of forty years' wear and disrepair. Two youngsters let us go into the garden in the back: it was diminished, part of it having been given either to the neighbors or to a community sports field nearby, but it still had the same delicious gooseberries, the same strawberry beds, the same staircase curving up to the main floor of the house. It was in this garden, during the First World War, that my father's sister, Lotte, and Richard Kobrak were married. They died in Auschwitz.

After I had taken as many pictures and eaten as many gooseberries as I could—as if somehow to assert my right, not to the garden or to the house, but to my own past—we were about to depart when an elderly gentleman came downstairs and went out the front door, following his wife to their car. I went up and asked him—we communicated in French—whether we could go upstairs, explaining that my grandmother had once lived there and I wanted to see it again. He kindly let us in, and once I was upstairs, I recognized it all. He took us to Oma's living room, now his. The walls were covered with paintings, drawings, and prints—and before I had a chance to grasp the meaning of them, the man opened his shirt and showed us a tattoo mark on his upper chest: he had been five years at Auschwitz, Birkenau, and Buchenwald, he explained, and the pictures were of him in prison garb, of children in camps, of other camp scenes. On a table was a wooden statue of Father Kolbe, the priest who had volunteered his life in the camp to spare another's. The man, whose name was Czesław Ostankowicz, said he was a writer, and he gave my wife, Peggy, a copy of his book on his camp experiences; "anus mundi" he called the first section.

This is when the feelings returned. Here was this Polish ex-cavalry officer—largely oblivious to my being a German, a Jew—who now lived in my grandmother's house and who had gone through the very experiences that my parents and I had only narrowly escaped. That this impressively robust man now lived in my grandmother's once-handsome and so unsocialist home gave me satisfaction; I felt grateful appreciation. I asked to see an adjoining room, which had been my Tante Grete's, where a huge balcony overlooked the garden; we went out onto it, and Peggy took pictures of him and me shaking hands there—the transfer of a claim, gratefully and joyfully carried out on my part, as if suddenly, for one brief moment, all the tangled past made sense. I told him I was glad he was there. It was a sudden moment of happy acceptance: in that mad world, something had gone right. Seeing my aunt's beautiful rug still there did not disturb my feelings. Then we finally left, having long tried his wife's patience. A chapter closed.

We drove around some of the adjoining streets, looking at neighboring *houses, and then returned to my school, and to the street where Tante Grete had lived before she moved in with my grandmother. And precisely opposite my old school I saw a street sign indicating that the street was now "ulica Rosenbergow." The street on which I had been beaten up for being a Jew was now named for two American Jews, the atomic spies whose trial, conviction, and execution had made them martyrs of the European left! Perhaps the only street in Wrocław named after Jews, and my street!*

Somehow, despite it all, I still felt possessive about some corners of Breslau, though returning to a city that was built on repudiation of the past made it easier to accept the disappearance of my own past. I had to admit that in some ways, going back to a Polish city was easier than if it had still been German; Germans in Breslau, living there as if nothing had happened, would have stirred resentment. As it was, I felt none, only an occasional annoyance at the Poles for having erased all signs of the city's (and my) German past—as if at that point they could have done anything else!

On the way back from Julius and Ethel Rosenbergow, we drove along the park of Scheitnig and then back across the River Oder to where I remembered the old university clinics were. They, too, stood—nineteenth-century red-brick buildings exactly as I remembered them from my earliest childhood, when we had lived nearby. Perhaps seeing them was what most excited me—the places so closely associated with my parents and their friends, where my father had worked, and where I might have worked if fate had not dispatched me elsewhere. Peggy asked why Breslau had had such a distinguished medical faculty, where Jews especially had excelled. I didn't fully know the answer, but those few remnants of Breslau's clinics and the villas where the doctors had lived stirred up no unpleasant visions of what once must have been a happy life, with some rough harmony between achievement and reward, between hope and fulfillment.

AS I HAVE ATTEMPTED TO RECORD in this book, I was to have more and different homecomings. My work in Europe as in the United States often, perhaps too often, went off in unplanned directions, but some of them veered homeward, and my political-historical interests brought me back to the altered places of my childhood. I watched from afar, for example, when Wrocław in the 1980s acquired a new and noble importance: it became a stronghold of Solidarność, the Polish movement that led the way to the self-liberation of Eastern Europe, and the newly reunited Germany (my fifth). So in one way this book is a partial memoir of a life shaped by a country that in five different political incarnations struggled for its soul, reconciliation with which led me to an unexpected, partial homecoming.

Life and study have persuaded me of the openness of history. There is no inevitability in history. Thinking about what might have happened, what could have happened, is a necessary element in trying to understand what did happen. And if, as I believe, individual acts of decency and courage make a difference, then they need to be recorded and remembered. We deem the future in a free society, however constrained by preexisting conditions, to be open, and if this is so, then civic engagement also becomes a moral and political imperative. That, too, is a theme of this book.

Of course, much of the history I have written and taught in the United States has borne the influence of my German past. And although my principal focus here is on the five Germanys, I also write about certain of my American experiences, though I have omitted much of what has been most important to me in my American life — my discoveries and disappointments, my joys with family and friends, my sorrows. This is because I have become ever more concerned that this country's generous liberal spirit, itself ever in need of renewal and correction, has in the last half century been under attack. I opposed the radical detractors of liberalism in the 1960s, and since then I have watched pseudo-conservatives and fundamentalists undermine the nation's celebrated commitment to reason and tolerance.

In my historical work, I have recorded how the German attack on liberalism began in the nineteenth century and reached its culmination decades later, in National Socialism. In doing this work, I tried to fathom some of the sources of both the rational and demonic elements that linked Germany's sublimity to its fits of barbarism. Liberalism, Cardinal Newman wrote in the 1860s, "is scarcely now a party; it is the educated lay world . . . it is nothing else than that deep, plausible scepticism, which I spoke about as being the development of human reason, as practically exercised by the natural man." The tolerant, questioning mind Newman wrote about almost always drives extremists of the left and right to frantic hatred.

In relating here the history of the five Germanys I have known to the Germanys I have studied professionally, to my personal experiences, and to my own, often unconscious emotions, I am trying to fuse memory and history — those distant twins, supportive and destructive of each other. Memory is notoriously fallible, and for nations as for individuals it is subject to the congenial, self-serving deformations that afflict us all. I also know that there is such a thing as honest (and healthy) forgetting. Yet for all its flaws and distortions, memory does recall the drama of the past, suggests some of the feelings that enveloped facts. And I bring some professional knowledge about the reconstruction of the past along with a (surprisingly large) reservoir of documented memory in the form of troves of letters from three generations of my family; I also have my own diaries of over fifty years and other memorabilia that over the decades I have allowed to accumulate. We all seek tangible traces of a past to which we are irresistibly drawn, and we try to fill them with life. We want to see connections and meanings in the scattered remains and in the varied documents of the past. I wish I could say that what follows is a mixture of "poetry and truth"—I can only hope it contains a bit of both.

While writing this book of history and memory, at once professional and personal, I had a fleeting picture of what, I realized, some of us historians are really like. On a brief holiday on Captiva Island, on Florida's Gulf Coast, I watched a flock of pelicans diving into the waters of a channel rich in fish; they drifted down the channel on its rapid current, but unswervingly facing backward, and then, when the channel widened into a lagoon and the current slowed, they flew off to the head of the channel and dove in again. Endlessly they repeated this maneuver. Pelican-historians, I mused. We, too, live in the current of time, moving forward very fast but looking backward, our perspectives changing with every wavelet, looking for nourishment along the way. Only we can't repeat the journey; we can't ever start over again.

The Germanys I have known, however partially and fleetingly, together portray the end of a historic Europe we cannot return to, and the start of a more modest, cohesive, and peaceful era for the continent. In recent decades we have seen wondrous, miraculous reconciliations in Europe, themselves perhaps intimations of partial homecoming. So the history of these five Germanys can be read as a text for political and moral lessons, as a drama in dread and hope. We owe the victims of the last century's descent into an inferno of organized bestiality an enduring, awed memorial: a prudent vigilance—and the knowledge that the bacillus that killed them did not die with them. Camus was right.

CHAPTER 1

ANCESTRAL GERMANY

THERE HAVE BEEN FIVE GERMANYS I have known since my birth in 1926, but it is the Germany I didn't know, the Germany of the years before World War I, that I think I understand the best. That Germany I have studied in my professional life, with proper distance and a measure of detachment. Only when beginning this book did I discover the thousands of letters my parents brought with them when we immigrated to the United States in 1938: bundles of letters, neatly wrapped or placed in wooden boxes, that had been left unopened since they were brought here; letters from earlier generations of my family, from my parents' friends and colleagues, family letters written in the peaceful times of that earlier Germany; and a trove of letters written to and by my father when he was at the front in the Great War. The letters are conversations about the mundane and the unusual; they take for granted the unspoken assumptions of that earlier time. They touch on all manner of subjects, and they confirm, amplify, and modify what scholarship has taught me. They speak with a special immediacy, and even their silences bespeak the customs of their time. Many, I now realize, would have served me well as illustrative footnotes to my earlier work or prompted second thoughts.

Home to at least four generations of my family was Breslau, capital of Silesia, in eastern Germany, a city with different masters and its own disputed history. Its origins went back to medieval times, its growth favored by its location on the banks of the River Oder, which flows into the Baltic. In early centuries, it was a Polish city called Vretslaw—a fact that Germans later tended to forget. When I grew up there, I knew that it had been part of the Habsburg Empire, until the day in 1741 when the young Prussian king, Frederick II, later known as Frederick the Great, wrested all of Silesia, the jewel of the Austrian Empire, from Empress Maria Theresa, a major moment in the astounding rise of Prussia. After 1871, Breslau became part of the newly created German Empire, a federal structure that apportioned some powers to its member states and allowed the great, ancient German states such as Prussia, Bavaria, and Saxony to retain their monarchies. Prussia was preeminent in the Reich by virtue of its size and tradition, and this was symbolized by the fact that the Prussian monarchs doubled as German emperors.

The citizens of Breslau had multiple overlapping civic identities: they were Silesians, with their own dialect; Prussians with austere traditions; and Germans, heirs to an old national culture. Breslau was the second largest city in Prussia. Many of Breslau's citizens in the nineteenth century were partisans of the struggle for the twin goals of unity and freedom—that is, for a German nation-state with the basic civic freedoms guaranteed in a modern constitution. Their liberal dream was shattered with the failure of the revolution in 1848; the Prussian king granted a constitution in 1850 that reserved executive power to the monarch (still deemed of divine right), though it provided for a legislature with some budgetary powers to be elected by (almost) universal male suffrage according to a three-class voting system (depending on the amount of direct taxes paid). Skipping over the details, one need but remember that this was a blatantly plutocratic system—and of course it had unanticipated consequences. After a decade of reaction and repression, during which the German economy grew significantly, the prosperous bourgeoisie of Silesia and elsewhere sent a liberal majority to the Prussian Diet.

In the face of this liberal opposition, the king, in a desperate effort to safeguard his monarchical power, appointed Otto von Bismarck as prime minister. Bismarck, a passionate but unconventional monarchist, fought the liberals and divided them—by fulfilling their wish for national unity. Under his leadership, Prussia was victorious in three wars in a span of only eight years, culminating in the victory over France in 1871 and the concurrent establishment of a unified Germany, with its federal structure leaving important powers to the member states. Prussia's old aristocracy and army struggled to maintain political dominance, but Bismarck also provided for a German parliament, the Reichstag, to be elected by universal male suffrage. He resorted to this revolutionary principle of universal suffrage (and was consequently often labeled "a white revolutionary") because he assumed that a conservative peasantry would outnumber the detested liberal bourgeoisie. This was a miscalculation: the exuberant growth of Germany's industrial capitalism created a different society— with an ever-swelling proletariat swamping a shrinking peasantry and sending its own, socialist, deputies to the Reichstag.

Most middle-class and professional Germans rejoiced that national unity had been achieved at last—pleased about or accepting of a country that combined the rule of law with a monarchical-authoritarian order at home and ever-increasing power abroad. The deepening divisions within the new Reich—Bismarck himself began to call Socialists and politically organized Catholics "enemies of the Reich"—were partly obscured by the astounding growth in every kind of power and by the often overweening pride in seeing Germany rise to dominance in Europe. Left-liberals, with their commitment to popular sovereignty and tolerance, were a declining minority within the Reich; the discrepancy between the ever more conservative Prussian Diet, determined to preserve the anachronistic political system, and an increasingly progressive Reichstag, presaged an ultimate conflict. But only a very few contemporaries recognized the contradiction between a dynamic modern society and an anachronistic political system marked by a coalition of overlapping elites—East German landowners (Junkers), powerful industrialists, the armed forces, and high civil servants. Put differently, in a dynamically growing capitalist country an economically declining agrarian aristocracy was desperately clinging to power, while the once-liberal middle classes felt squeezed between the old rulers and the ascendant Social Democrats, an ever-growing political by-product of Germany's industrialization. There were many Germans who realized the need for political reform—a frightening prospect to the entrenched powers.

My forebears reflected the successes and the contradictions of this world. To them, "the German Question" seemed settled after 1871; they were mostly absorbed in other things than national politics. After his dismissal in 1890, Bismarck became an idol for many of them—there was a virtual cult that celebrated the "strong leader," a dangerous view to which some of my family succumbed. Municipal politics, however, were different: the voting system favored, in urban local affairs, the prosperous bourgeois class that still happened to be liberal.

My great-grandparents and their descendants participated in the prosperity and prominence of Breslau, a dynamically expanding commercial-industrial center with a large agricultural hinterland and rich coal mines to the southeast. The population of the city grew apace; between 1861 and 1910 it quadrupled, from 128,000 to half a million; of these, 60 percent were Protestant, 35 percent Catholic, and about 5 percent (20,000) Jews. Breslau had a proud civic life and a vibrant cultural one—the two closely related. German cities competed for cultural distinctiveness, with their bourgeois fathers striving to replicate for their class and era what princely courts had done before.

A key institution in Breslau's cultural life was the Schlesische Friedrich-Wilhelms-Universität, established in its modern form in 1811, during the Prussian Reform Era that had responded to the forces unleashed by the French Revolution with a carefully controlled "revolution from above." It replaced a Catholic university that had been founded in 1702 by Emperor Leopold of Austria, and it was Prussia's first nonconfessional university, with both Catholic and Protestant theological faculties. After four decades of penurious mediocrity, it became eminent—in medicine, even preeminent—and internationally renowned. The state sustained the university, while the city fathers promoted Breslau's cultural life—as evident in theater and music, in its academy of arts—attracting talent in all fields. Breslau wasn't comparable to Berlin or Munich or Vienna, but it was ambitious and successful.

Given its important industrial sector, exemplified by the Borsig engineering plant, Breslau also had a growing proletarian population. In the early 1860s, Ferdinand Lassalle, a converted Jew and son of a Breslau merchant, had become the first leader of a German working-class movement, a non-revolutionary alternative Marx. And for decades, Breslau had a strong Social Democratic Party and radical groups to the left.

The Jewish community of Breslau was as diversified as any in the German lands. Some Jewish families had lived there since Jews were first readmitted to the city in 1744; others, attracted by Breslau's urban opportunities, had moved there from smaller towns in the countryside. A few had come from farther east, so-called *Ostjuden*, who thought of Prussia as a promising haven. Breslau Jews were rich and poor, Orthodox and Reformed, traditionalist and fully assimilated; as we shall see, some Jewish men lived a full civic life while women pioneered in social work and communal responsibilities. Jews, barred from certain careers, as in the army, or hindered in others, as in the civil service, were disproportionately concentrated in trade and the professions; and they were disproportionately represented in the highest rungs of the public educational system. Also, they were disproportionately wealthy, that is, they were major taxpayers and philanthropists.

In many ways, my forebears—going back to my great-grandparents, born in the 1820s and 1830s—exemplified this commonality and diversity. My four great-grandfathers, my two grandfathers, and my father were all physicians, and their successes and setbacks were characteristic of their class—increasingly prosperous until at least 1914, and professionally innovative and eminent, with a very distinct ethos.

Of my four grandparents, who were exceptionally close friends, I knew only my maternal grandmother, Hedwig Brieger, who died in 1939 in our small flat in Queens; her husband, Oskar, had died in 1914. My paternal grandfather, Richard Stern, died in 1911, and his widow, a year later, leaving my father, Rudolf, aged seventeen, an orphan, with an older and a younger sister.

The Sterns and Briegers belonged to what we have come to call the *Bildungsbürgertum*, bourgeois citizens of some means who cherished what all Germans of their class cherished, *Bildung*, that goal of self-formation and education that sprang in part from knowing and exulting in the great works of culture, the classics, poetry, music, and the arts. It was assumed that this cultural heritage, or patrimony, molded one's code of behavior, the values one professed and tried to live by. Many Germans quietly believed that theirs was a country of *Dichter und Denker* (poets and thinkers); others wore this culture all too loudly, and by 1873 the then still obscure Friedrich Nietzsche coined for them the term *Bildungsphilister* (cultured philistines). By the late nineteenth century, this cultural heritage was more and more fused with an exuberant faith in science and progress. *Wissenschaft*, the German term for science, had a special, sanctified aura, connoting both an ordered and verifiable body of knowledge and the dedication to the pursuit of truth; *Wissenschaft* had a moral character, implying total seriousness. For many, *Bildung* and *Wissenschaft* became twin deities, a faith fortified by the continuous advance of science as a life-transforming phenomenon, made still more attractive by the austere ethos that scientists adhered to. Goethe had given a warrant to this conceit with his oft-invoked dictum: "He who possesses art and science has religion; he who does not possess them needs religion." In those years and for many people, science was still innocent, an emancipatory force as against the intimidating orthodoxies of the Christian churches.

The father of my paternal grandmother, Sigismund Asch, born in 1825, was a legendary figure in Breslau: in 1848, a newly minted medical doctor, he took a leading part in the revolutions of that year, when, incited by the uprisings in Milan and Paris, Germans went to the barricades with diverse aims, of which national unity and civic freedom were the common denominators. Asch added his own radical social goals, for he was outraged at existing injustice and poverty (he had been raised in lower-class conditions) and filled with democratic fervor; in his speeches he demanded an end to indirect taxes and the institution of the ten-hour workday, a most radical idea at that time. Asch often referred to the Silesian Weavers' Riots of 1844, early protests against capitalist power and the exploitation of individual artisans. Gerhart Hauptmann's celebrated drama of 1892, *The Weavers*, evoked the conditions of immiseration that had given rise to their futile rebellion.

The newspapers reported the doings of this tall, lean young doctor, with his impressive rhetorical powers, when he addressed various protest meetings. Once, in September 1848, amid another demonstration that threatened to storm Breslau's royal residence and thus precipitate a battle between revolutionaries and armed soldiers, Asch pushed himself to the front of the crowd, warning against violence. The soldiers, he repeatedly cried out, were "the unwilling instruments of black reaction." To harm them would be "the greatest injustice," because they were bound by oath to resist the demonstrators and they deserved "respect." That and other protests remained peaceful. By December 1848, however, Asch left the Democratic League, disappointed by the intolerance and radicalism of his allies. His earlier hopes were dashed when the old order, somewhat modified, was restored.

Since he had been involved in producing placards denouncing the huge costs for royal extravaganzas at the expense of the poor, the authorities charged Asch with lèse-majesté. After a judicial delay, in May 1851 he was sentenced to a year's arrest under especially harsh conditions. After his release and his marriage to the daughter of a prosperous Jewish merchant, he concentrated on his medical practice, gaining notice by holding office hours at dawn for indigent patients. He charged his rich patients enough so that he was able to treat the poor for nothing, and often he unobtrusively left money in the latter's homes so that they could buy the medications he had prescribed. In 1863, he was elected *Stadtverordneter*, or representative to the city council, a position he held for sixteen years, and in which he fought for various causes concerning urban improvement and public health. He became a celebrated figure, honored as the subject of various plays and known for his family connections with progressive movements throughout Germany: one of his sisters, Lina, later Lina Morgenstern, became an early feminist leader.

Asch had three children: one, Betty, converted to Protestantism at the age of fourteen; another, Toni, married a young doctor, Richard Stern, my grandfather. Asch himself died in 1901, in the city where he was affectionately known as "der Alte Asch," publicly mourned and properly buried in the Jewish cemetery. His son, Robert, also a doctor, was my mother's obstetrician at my birth. I have always delighted in this democratic ancestor!*

Der Alte Asch may have seen his revolutionary hopes defeated, but he could find satisfaction in his medical practice and in his engagement in liberal reformist work. His children, facing different conditions, felt less incentive to engage politically. Their public lives centered on their work; their private lives concentrated on family and friends but were quietly shadowed not by the "German" question, but by what became a new phase of the "Jewish" question. As we shall see, Jewishness posed the deepest quandaries, so deep that one rarely talked about them.

For centuries, Jews and Germans had been separated by visible and invisible walls. Jews had lived under various disabilities, and were scorned for their (enforced) penchant for peddling and money changing, for their strange clannish orthodoxy, and for their attachment to a primitive divine dispensation that Gentiles believed could be fulfilled only in Christianity. Jews and Christians were divided by a common God. But great changes had come at the time of the momentous flowering of German thought—the great Idealist Age identified with the German Enlightenment and classicism, when Lessing, Herder, Kant, Goethe, and Schiller transformed German culture. That is when some German Jews began to feel the attraction of emancipated European life, and began to wish for what has been called assimilation or even integration. By the end of the eighteenth century, some German states decreed the partial emancipation of Jews; Prussia followed in 1812.

The subsequent history of German Jewry—the trials, triumphs, and ultimate tragedy—which remains of surpassing importance in the history of the world, provided an ever-changing context in the lives of individual families, mine included. I have grappled with and written about this subject for all my professional life: here the barest summary must suffice.

In the late eighteenth century, Jews made their first appearance in German intellectual life. Moses Mendelssohn (1729–1786) came to Berlin in 1743, met his exact contemporary Gotthold Ephraim Lessing, in 1754, and these two philosophers, both of them interpreters of Enlightenment thought and related theological questions, became friends. Lessing was a philosopher and great dramatist, whose play *Nathan the Wise* was deemed the most compelling argu-

---

*My second cousin, the poet Dagmar Nick, wrote a carefully documented biography of our common ancestor Asch, *Jüdisches Wirken in Breslau* (Jewish Achievement in Breslau) (1998).

ment for toleration of all religions. Mendelssohn had six children, of whom two converted to Protestantism, two daughters to Catholicism; his grandson Felix was the genius composer who in his music celebrated Reformation Christianity.

Thus conversion to Christianity appears at the beginning of the modern phase of German Jewry and remained a theme in German Jewish life to the very end. Motives varied with individuals and time: Heinrich Heine converted in 1825, considering, as he said, that baptism constituted the entrance ticket to European culture. Conversion became ever more common right down to the Nazi period, but it still involved only a tiny minority of all the Jews who lived in German lands.

The legal emancipation of Jews came in stages, beginning with Prussia's decree of 1812, which removed most civil disabilities. By 1869, Jews were recognized as possessing all legal rights and duties of German citizens. However brief, the road from ghetto and exclusion to legal equality and material opportunity had been painful and precarious. Legal equality did not quash ancient prejudice, and in the new age, Jews remained tacitly banned from positions of political power, indeed from all visible identification with dignified power; in the unified Germany of post-1871, the sanctum sanctorum, the officer corps, was closed to them. There was something asymmetrical in almost every aspect of German Jewish coexistence. Barred in some fields, Jews succeeded beyond all expectations in others: disproportionately prominent in the free professions, in law, medicine, and journalism; a major presence in trade and banking; disproportionately wealthy, their children disproportionately successful in higher education. In the late nineteenth century, German Jews achieved an unprecedented preeminence in the natural sciences, fields in which Germans and Jews complemented one another and collaborated in what may well have been a singular crucible of genius. But the need to excel, instilled by tradition, was nurtured by hostility.

In retrospect the ascent of German Jewry constitutes one of the most spectacular social leaps in European history. But success bred resentment, which was newly inflamed when in the early 1870s a great economic bubble burst, involving many tales of corruption. Jewish financiers were involved in some of the scandals, and a regular hate campaign began that blamed Jews as the all-powerful agents of corruption. It was in this context that a German publicist coined the very word *anti-Semitism*. The attacks, some of them in respectable journals and petitions, demanded at least a partial revocation of the Jews' emancipation. This didn't happen, but German anti-Semitism continued, not in some steady, inexorable fashion but with ups and downs, though there was a rarely articulated, latent continuum of prejudice, as there was in every country—in other countries perhaps even more strongly than in Germany, where Jews met with an equal measure of hospitality and hostility. No wonder, then, that German Jews had a shaky sense of identity, that ambivalence was a common feeling among them—but then, Germans generally have always had difficulty with their identity, and as Heine once said, Jews are like the people they live among, only more so.

For many German Jews, Jewishness was a charged and private matter about which they spoke only rarely. Yet it marked their lives. In European life, particularly before the Great War, decorum was all-important, and one did not discuss in public subjects such as sexuality and money. Some Jews may have thought that their innermost feelings about Jewishness also deserved to be passed over in silence. But then, Jews also were great disturbers of this decorum: Heine as brilliant satirist of German sentimentality, Marx as analyst of the power of money and capital, Freud as explorer of sexuality. As Freud once put it,

> A great imaginative writer may permit himself to give expression—jokingly, at all events—to psychological truths that are severely proscribed. Thus Heine confesses: "Mine is a most peaceable disposition. My wishes are: a humble cottage with a thatched roof, but a good bed, good food, the freshest milk and butter, flowers before my window, and a few fine trees before my door; and if God wants to make my happiness complete, he will grant me the joy of seeing some six or seven of my enemies hanging from those trees. Before death I shall, moved in my heart, forgive them all the wrong they did me in their lifetime. One must, it is true, forgive one's enemies—but not before they have been hanged."

Still, many German Jews felt so genuinely at home in their German milieu, so attached to German culture, that they lived in hopes that anti-Semitism, precisely because of its pre-modern roots, would disappear in their new, bright, secular, and scientific world. Jews and Christians lived alongside one another, separate for the most part but together in prescribed realms such as schools, obligatory military service, business, municipal affairs, and in many voluntary or professional organizations, in clubs, in hobbies. But in no field did Jews enter Gentile life more intimately than as physicians—as confidants and comforters in those pre-psychotherapeutic days. In imperial Germany, the physician's white coat was the one uniform of dignity to which Jews could aspire and in which they could feel a measure of authority and grateful acceptance.

My grandparents, two doctors and their wives, and their circle of friends, colleagues, and assistants exemplified the wide range of responses to a world at once enticing and hostile. In a culture in which *Bildung* and *Wissenschaft* had profoundly altered the traditional outlook of many religions, Jews faced very special quandaries. How could one reconcile ancient rituals and proscriptions with the prevailing post-Darwinian secular-scientific outlook? Like so many educated Protestants, my grandparents arrived at a worldview that fused a distillation of Christian ethics with rational precepts and national sentiment, the whole enveloped with a proper sense of awe. For Jews like them, a further step to integration was conversion to Germany's "national" religion, Lutheran Protestantism, a step made easier by the fact that that religion had become theologically undemanding by then, having made its peace with modern life, with the spirit of capitalism, and with science. (This was in contrast to the austere Catholicism prescribed by Pope Pius IX, with his canonical denunciation of modern life.)

My great-grandparents and grandparents fully shared in this *Kulturreligion*, which gave them a self-evident commonality with non-Jews. I suspect they knew their German lyric poetry far better than their Hebrew psalms (if they knew these last at all); they felt an uneasy estrangement from Jewish rituals and practices. And this transformation had happened so swiftly! In the course of but two or three generations, German Jews had lost their particular dialect, a form of Yiddish, or *Judendeutsch*, and had become entirely Germanified, though probably they had occasional recourse to a few Yiddish words when they couldn't express something in any other way. They delighted in the German language, which in serious and playful efforts, in prose and poetry, they mastered with elegant ease. And still, they carried a memory of past apartness. I think they thought of Jewishness as both stigma and distinction.

Many Jewish families, especially prosperous ones, were steeped in this kind of civic-cultural religion, so distant from the demands of Orthodox Judaism, if more compatible with the prevalent form of Reform, Liberal Judaism. But some of them wished to go even further and, breaking with ancestral ties, convert to Christianity. What in the early nineteenth century had been primarily a philosophic-emotional step gradually acquired an all-too-practical aspect. Conversion, as it was called by many, apostasy by others, eased most forms of social and economic ascent—some of Bismarck's ministers were Protestants of Jewish descent—so while no doubt conversion had many motives, even the purest grounds for it carried a taint of opportunism.

Consider but one example from the life of a friend of my grandparents,

Fritz Haber (1868–1934), a chemist of great talent and vaulting ambition who in 1892 converted—to the dismay of his father. The conversion certainly eased Fritz's academic career, which eventually made him a towering figure in the German scientific community, with a Nobel Prize as ultimate recognition. Haber had been thirsting for a university post, denied to him because he was a Jew. This is why Gentile mentors urged their academic students to convert, though pride or filial piety or self-respect kept many—such as Haber's closest friend Richard Willstätter or the celebrated industrialist-statesman Walther Rathenau—from taking that step. Like many others, these two thought it dishonorable to take a spiritual step that would afford material advantage. Many converted Jews continued to feel an ineffable affinity with their former co-religionists, but after a generation or two, some children of Jewish descent didn't even know of their Old Testament roots. They began to feel they belonged to the "evangelical" (or, rarely, "Catholic") group to which their identity papers assigned them. They were Christian by choice and often by faith.

In the first generation at least, converts were often regarded with suspicion by both new and old co-religionists. But—and this is nowadays often forgotten—it was only during the Third Reich that, by declaring race and not religion as a determinant of a person's civic identity and worth, Christians of Jewish descent were reconverted into "non-Aryans" and made subject to the same persecution as Jews, hence Jews *tout court*. In this respect, Hitler was successful: most people today think of Felix Mendelssohn, say, or Fritz Haber as a Jew, although that is not what their status was in Germany during their lifetimes. (Israelis, too, count these "apostates" as Jews, especially if they have won Nobel Prizes or are otherwise distinguished.)

My paternal grandparents, Richard Stern and his wife, Toni, née Asch, converted as adults, and they had their children baptized at birth: Lotte, the eldest, born in 1893, my father born two years later, and Marga, born in 1900. My maternal grandparents, Oskar Brieger and his wife, Hedwig, née Lion, never converted. Their extensive correspondence, however, clearly expresses their affinity to a Christian outlook, and they baptized their children at birth, of whom my mother, Käthe, was the second, born in 1894. My grandmother Hedwig, as I remember, considered herself Christian. Put differently, the converted Sterns were more conscious of their Jewishness than the unconverted Briegers.

The two families were exceptionally close friends for decades. The fathers were colleagues, and for years the families lived virtually next door to each other. Their principal friends were fellow converts, Jews tolerant and understanding of their baptism. Jews and converts intermarried, the latter perhaps more often with Jews than with ur-Christians, though among all three groups, close friendships existed. The two families vacationed together; their children went to the same schools, even to the same, very formal, dancing classes, which mixed the young of all confessions or none.

My grandfathers attended to both their Christian and Jewish patients with equal care and worked harmoniously with their Christian colleagues. Both families had Christian nursemaids and servants, who in many instances remained with them over decades, in a trusted if unequal relationship. In all this, the two families appear to have retained a kind of silence about what we would call their identity, neither openly boastful of their German and Christian belongingness nor openly denying their Jewish roots. They adopted a certain style of life and with it a definite ethos, much of it unspoken and habitual.

My grandfathers and their colleagues had a "calling" (the German word is *Beruf*) that was at the center of their lives, and this patriarchal calling had a commanding place in the family. Among the great callings in the free professions—medicine, law, the clergy—medicine was probably most highly regarded, combining as it did welfare, sacrifice, and science. We know that German Jews flocked to medicine; at the end of the nineteenth century, nearly half of Breslau's doctors were Jews or of Jewish descent. That all my immediate male forebears were doctors may say something about the effectiveness of the patriarchal model, of the comfort of following in one's father's footsteps or of having one's footsteps followed. But there was more to it than that: by the late nineteenth century, the ancient art of healing had become even more enticing, for it was now a science as well, and its discoveries proved life-transforming.

My doctor forebears were the direct heirs of a generation of clinicians committed to creating and expanding a scientific basis for medicine. They set out to discover the microbacterial origin of disease and to seek remedies through immunology and chemotherapy. During this period, professional organizations and journals multiplied and medical research became an international enterprise. One of the earliest of these German physicians was Bernhard Naunyn, whose self-chosen motto was: "Medicine will be a science or it will be nothing." For Naunyn and all those who followed him, science—that is, ceaseless work in the laboratory—was the indispensable supplement to the physician's intuition and his unfailing solicitude for the patient. At the bedside of the sick, the physician's old virtues of trust and human empathy prevailed: medicine at its best remained an art and a science. My grandfathers, even as medicine was becoming ever more "scientific," were also, inseparably, devoted clinicians.

My grandfathers' correspondence exudes a sense of privileged duty, and their progeny continued this tradition. The two men collaborated in the clinic and in medical societies, and they lived in a world of pure science. Even their most casual correspondence shows this. In 1896, for example, on a postcard written in his tiny scrawl, Haber addressed "dear Stern" (using the familiar *du*), answering a complicated question about chemistry. Paul Ehrlich, the founder of chemotherapy and ultimately the greatest scientific luminary of Breslau, wrote letters about scientific matters to both my grandfathers, often to thank them for supplying him with samples from their clinical material for his experiments. After Richard Stern's death, Ehrlich sent his handwritten condolences to Stern's widow: "I can tell you that I always esteemed and loved the suddenly deceased to the highest degree—equally as man and character, as an eminent representative of science who mastered equally theoretical research and clinical responsibility as only the fewest do." The letter was penned in Ehrlich's idiosyncratic orthography, and without capitals, which saves time. Science was a faith, a bond, a career. The obituary of my grandfather Brieger, written by his chief assistant, put it well: "Work was for him . . . not just duty, it was what life was about [*Lebensbedürfnis*], and for him it was a pleasure."

Perhaps we have forgotten just how central work was for that generation. It gave meaning to life, and it sustained health even as overexertion damaged it. Theirs was a generation that understood Tolstoi's praise of what he called the work-cure, the *Arbeitskur*. Practitioners at the time took this ethos for granted; it deserves our respect. I suppose I feel a certain genuine as well as conventionally prescribed ambivalence about descending from this privileged if embattled class. I have to ask myself whether my unbridled admiration for their ethos is a compensatory gesture. The admiration may be, but their devotion to their calling is beyond question.

Their wives, often their cultural equals or, in aesthetic matters, their superiors, chose their own duties and responsibilities—not just at home but outside it, in community and educational work—and they had their own calling in providing for and presiding over the family home, and ensuring the moral education of the children. My quietly feminist grandmothers certainly did not conform to the stereotypical view of German women restricted to KKK (*Kinder, Küche, Kirche*: "children, kitchen, church"). And I remember that, in Breslau, my maternal grandmother shared responsibility for a quite common enterprise of the time: a *Kinderhort*, a home that provided full-time care for indigent children.

The choice of a career was taken with the greatest seriousness by both men and women in my family. An undated letter from my grandfather Richard Stern to his father, Heinrich, makes this clear. (Heinrich had an exceptional reputation; in 1862 one of Germany's foremost internists, Theodor Frerichs, who had been a professor in Breslau and was briefly to be Bismarck's physician, recommended the young Stern for a post because of his "rich experience" as "a thoroughly conscientious and experienced assistant in the All Saints' Hospital and as a doctor to the poor.") The father had counseled the son to go into medicine or law, but the son was determined to study mathematics and physics. "In the choice of a career calling," he wrote, "every person has to consider two factors: the material conditions and the inner happiness that the career might provide. Disregard of the former indicates an unthinking enthusiast [*Schwärmer*], of the latter a superficial cynic."

The son wanted to discover whether he had the requisite talent to pursue his choice, preferably at a small university, where in the end he might get an assistantship and hope for an academic career. Medicine, he added, aroused disgust in him, and in law he foresaw a life of boredom, quite aside from his lacking the rhetorical gifts that the law demanded. The fact that this letter is one of the very few the family kept from that early period could be an accident, but more likely the letter was preserved because it was exemplary. It certainly bespeaks self-critical seriousness and ambition on my grandfather's part, a respectful wager on autonomy. I don't know whether my grandfather explored these earlier interests before he, too, turned to medicine, in which field, as we shall see, he excelled.

These family letters suggest something of the nature and expected closeness of family bonds. They give us a picture of how life was lived or how the writers wanted it to be lived; they articulate what was taken for granted and what seemed quirky or exceptional. Parents and family friends offered advice and admonition, affirming basic rules of conduct. Literary allusions abounded, and a light or humorous touch softened the didactic rigor or severe tone.

I have the daily letters of Oskar Brieger, my maternal grandfather, to his fiancée, Hedwig, from the year 1889—letters on average six to eight pages long. He was in Vienna and Halle, finishing his specialization in the new field of otolaryngology, having to do with ear, nose, and throat diseases. (His father was a physician in Kosel, in Upper Silesia; hers, Dr. Lion, was a physician and co-owner of a liberal daily in Breslau.) Their letters are remarkably candid, fervent love letters that also contain ruminations about life in general. In June, Oskar wrote from Halle of his utter disgust with the Saxon dialect, which made him sick and "melancholy"—and led him to this revealing remark: "in the course of time a major conversion has come over me: I have become a passionate friend of Jews . . . I am incredibly happy at every typically crooked nose I see on the street. That reminds me of Breslau. Of course in this hovel of anti-Semites nothing but boring blondness, blown-up beer faces decorated with dueling scars." Because he himself was fair-haired, he was taken to be a Christian, and thus heard all manner of anti-Semitic talk.

The other subject referred to frequently in the letters was Richard Stern. In 1889, Oskar intimated that Richard's conduct had compromised Toni Asch — a renowned beauty, and from a family that demanded special respect—and that if he now had the gall to drop her, she would be forced to lead a life of spinsterhood forever. How Richard had offended Toni isn't clear, but circumstantial evidence suggests that he had avowed his love but then proved indecisive. He had somehow violated the moral code of the time—though it is unlikely he had compromised her physically, and Oskar had no forgiveness for such behavior; in any case, within a year or so, Richard married Toni, and relations remained unscathed and close, though for decades the solid yet sentimental Briegers would mock the ironic, brittle Sterns. I can testify to this myself.

Conventions dictated manners, the outward form of morals. And moral education and correct conduct mattered intensely: one was expected to follow a code in dress, speech, financial life—to say nothing of the more serious matters of love, marriage, truthfulness, and fidelity. Infractions reflected on the entire family. Parental admonitions, freely given, survive in some of these letters. Thus Toni Stern writing to Rudolf, her fourteen-year-old son, reaffirmed "regulations on conduct" while visiting another family, and at the same time enjoined him to be solicitous of his younger sister, who would be alone at home under the care of the trusted nursemaid. He needn't take her to a pastry shop: "more valuable for her and more difficult for you is to muster a steady kindness and readiness to help. By giving her a good example you educate her more deeply than by all manner of sermons and eternal admonitions. Doesn't some example of rising above self which you may by chance witness affect your own conduct more effectively than all the brave instructions you receive?" Rudolf's imperfect schoolwork was alluded to as well, but surely he would improve after the holidays. Characteristically, the father added two lines at the bottom to his "dearest Rudi," affirming that he subscribed completely to the mother's injunctions.

At another time, the mother explained that of course she had shown the boy's confidential letter to his father, whose judgments he should treasure, quite aside from the fact that he must always be aware that "husband and wife can't have secrets between them, least of all about matters concerning their dear children." Moreover, he would eventually feel the same "unconditional confidence" in his father that he already had in his mother. A small child's natural tie to his mother ripens into a special relationship between them, "but it is equally natural that the growing man who must enter life with all its dangers and struggles will turn for advice and support to the accomplished man, the father, who has experienced all that and very differently from the mother." You are lucky, she added, to have both your father and your mother. Many a poor child must face the world alone.

These admonitions and injunctions may sound banal, but they expressed a strong implicit bond between the generations: the advice so freely given was part of what parents could do for their children's *Bildung*. This was also an expression of a secular-rational world in which the responsibility for moral education fell on the parents, though obviously there were other voices as well. (I happen to know, for example, that the confirmation classes presided over by one Pastor Wackernagel much impressed my parents.) So parental certainty—itself mirroring the prevailing sense of a world in order—informed a young person's view. Harmony and rebellion coexisted: father-son conflicts, a great theme in German life and literature, were generally conducted openly; everyone knew the ultimate sanctions of disassociation or disinheritance. There was infinite pain in the disputes, but that, too, was a sign of their moral seriousness, so different from the parental diffidence of later times.

In the years before the Great War, my grandparents had a kind of certainty, which they felt they should transmit, about how life should be led. These were the living equivalents of the *Bildungsromane*, the novels on which young Germans had been reared for generations. Books had a central place in the two families: one began with the classics at home and continued in school (in the hours before his death, my father quoted Homer to me in Greek); in adolescence one was expected to go beyond the assigned, to live, so to speak, in the great novels and dramas. Schiller called the theater a moral institution, and the children in the Stern and Brieger families followed their elders in their awe of, if not necessarily in their taste for, great drama or acting.

My father's library, which I inherited along with part of his huge medical library, is a treasure-house of German culture: the collected works of Goethe and Heine, exacting books on philosophy and religion, with bookplates showing an idyllic snow-covered village and the date of the book's acquisition (often 1912, the year after his father's death and just before his mother's). It may be my *dé-*

formation professionelle to have excessive affection for a world in which great literature was a living presence. Perhaps this love of books didn't make those generations any wiser or more attractive than later ones, and it probably encouraged a certain pride of class, a defining superiority—yet it bore a seriousness and certainty that helped to nurture them. Of course, there could be a surfeit of entombed spirit and the danger of succumbing to *Bildungsphilistertum*.

Oskar Brieger, having served his required year in the army, finished his medical studies in the new specialty of otolaryngology; at the age of twenty-eight, he became the first head of this department at the leading municipal hospital in Breslau, All Saints', and in 1907 he was appointed professor. He published a wide range of papers, belonged to the board of the German Otological Society, founded the international journal in the field, and developed a flourishing private practice. Meanwhile, Richard Stern—who may have been exceptionally ambitious and austere but was also, I believe, fragile and uncertain—became a respected internist and outstanding diagnostician, and diagnosis in those pre–X-ray days demanded a much greater intuitive gift than in our test-equipped world. He was devoted to the many facets of his work; a sought-after clinician, he was also a researcher who in 1896 published a pioneering study of the traumatic origins of internal diseases, based on his own observations and on existing international literature. Industrial accidents were very common at the time, and since Bismarck's progressive social legislation provided for workers' compensation, doctors had to determine if a physical (or even psychic) trauma might have been responsible for debilitating, even fatal, diseases of internal organs. Richard's book became a standard international work in forensic medicine—coming as it did from the country that was the laboratory of social insurance. He became an expert witness in court cases, asked to establish whether a given trauma could have caused a subsequent disease or death. To render a medical opinion in such cases was scientifically complex and, for the victim or his family, of immense importance, as it was for the state and its fiscal responsibility.

In addition to this much-hailed pioneering work, Richard Stern made important discoveries in clinical bacteriology and the bacterial etiology of disease, then the frontiers of medical science. In 1900 he was appointed associate professor at the University of Breslau, itself a place of exceptional standing in medicine. At the same time, he was appointed head of the university *Poliklinik*, or outpatient department, a position of considerable responsibility, and made chairman of internal medicine at All Saints' Hospital, where Brieger headed the ear, nose, and throat department. The next and highest rank was *Ordina-*

rius, or full professor, a rare position for anyone to attain, and especially hard for someone of Jewish descent. In 1909, Richard Stern was offered this position at the University of Greifswald, in northern Germany, in a provincial city close to the Baltic Sea with none of the cultural advantages of Breslau, where he was meant to succeed Oskar Minkowski, a stellar internist who as a young doctor discovered in animal experiments the etiology of diabetes mellitus, the essential step that years later led to the discovery of insulin.* Minkowski had been Naunyn's prize student, but as a Jew he had been held back. He had finally received and accepted a call as *Ordinarius* in Breslau.

Richard was attracted to Greifswald—after all, it offered important teaching responsibilities and high prestige. His wife prepared the children for the move in the fall of the year. But, apparently having fallen into a state of melancholy indecision, Richard first accepted and then declined the offer. In June 1910 he wrote to his friend Fritz Haber, acknowledging the latter's solicitude about the issue and saying that he was very slowly recovering from the tumultuous nonevents of the previous fall, but "still thinking too much of past happenings." The chance that he had declined haunted him; the trauma, to use his language, had intensified his melancholic streak and plunged him into a depression, from which he was hoping to recover fully. In the same letter he mentioned that he was planning to go on holiday to the North Sea and inquired whether Haber would remain loyal to Pontresina, an idyllic Alpine village near St. Moritz. But a year later he died quite suddenly at the age of forty-five. Newspaper accounts I have found about Richard Stern's death give different stories about a long or short illness. (As a child, I had always been told that he died of influenza.) He was buried at the Maria Magdalena Cemetery in Breslau; the many obituaries in medical journals emphasized his scientific research, his clinical excellence, and—with exceptional warmth—his qualities as teacher and mentor.

His death in 1911 affected my life half a century later. In the very last days of my father's life in 1962, I was in the midst of having to decide whether to stay at Columbia University or accept an invitation to teach elsewhere. My parents remarked that at least the decision wasn't as hard as the choice between Breslau and Greifswald. Then, a few years later, my relative and good friend the physicist Otto Stern casually referred to my grandfather's *suicide*. Shocked, I immediately asked my mother what my grandfather had died of; with charac-

---

*After World War II, the Hoechst pharmaceutical company founded the annual Minkowski Prize, to be awarded to the most innovative diabetes researcher under the age of forty.

teristic honesty when confronted, she acknowledged that he had died of an overdose of sleeping pills; it was, in fact, her father who had been called to Richard's deathbed to sign the death certificate. I was troubled by my parents' secretiveness about this, and still regret their deception, though I realize how much pain my father must have felt at the loss, which the subsequent repression of the truth only emphasizes.

Perhaps Richard Stern had been anguished at having made the easier choice: Breslau, after all, was familiar turf, where he and his wife were part of a cluster of distinguished colleagues who doubled as a network of friends. Among those closest to him were not only the Briegers, but Paul Ehrlich and the dermatologist Albert Neisser, discoverer of the gonococcus, also a converted Jew and a physician's son. In 1909, Neisser was appointed full professor of dermatology, the first such chair in Germany. By all accounts, Albert and Toni Neisser enjoyed a very special social presence in Breslau, with a grand villa and garden, elaborately designed and decorated, home to a celebrated salon of artists and writers, including Gerhart Hauptmann, the architect Hans Poelzig, the painter Fritz Erler, and the musicians Adolf Busch and Artur Schnabel. Albert's brother Gustav was a lawyer, or *Justizrat*, adviser to various enterprises, a liberal city councilor, and also a close friend to several generations of Sterns and Briegers. Albert Neisser died in 1916. (His successor at the university was Joseph Jadassohn, who was later considered "the most famous dermatologist in the world." Known in my family as Sepp or Onkel Pu, Jadassohn was already a friend of the Briegers and Sterns in the 1890s, and he remained a friend of my parents until his death in 1936. I remember him vividly.)

There were Gentile friends and colleagues as well, foremost among them the outstanding psychiatrist Karl Bonhoeffer, some of whose numerous children went to dancing school with my parents. Ties to the Bonhoeffer family remained close for decades. Another fabled member of the psychiatric faculty was Alois Alzheimer, who observed and described the symptoms of dementia praecox, and was the first to relate them to pathological changes in the brain. In 1890, Johann Mikulicz, student of the incomparable Theodor Billroth in Vienna and one-time assistant of Joseph Lister, was appointed professor of surgery; he acquired a worldwide reputation for his new operative techniques carried out under new aseptic conditions; Ferdinand Sauerbruch, one of his pupils, was in turn to have Rudolf Nissen as his star assistant—a lifelong friend of my father's and of mine.

A recent history of Breslau's medical faculty records that many foreign visitors and students flocked to the university, including American doctors, such as the neurosurgeon Harvey Cushing (1869–1939) and the Mayo brothers, who in 1889 went home to Minnesota to establish their famed clinic. No wonder they had come to Breslau: it did have a galaxy of preeminent physicians!

The Briegers and the Sterns, joined by three other families, spent many summer holidays together in a small village, Krummhübel, in the mountains south of Breslau, on the Silesian border with Bohemia. The children founded a "club" there, with its own elected leaders and statutes, the principal activity being to write and perform plays, and created their own entertainment for themselves and their appreciative elders. In some way, their activities duplicated an adult Breslau club, the Akademisch-Literarischer Verein, a student organization that originally served as a primarily Jewish substitute for the Gentile university fraternities that excluded Jews. The ALV comprised alumni and students, another intergenerational effort involving men and women, and held frequent feasts with lectures and poetic, witty persiflage. For years, Gustav Neisser was its head.

This older generation, born in the 1860s, gradually established themselves, overcoming prejudices and benefiting from the scientific and material progress of the times. They came to lead comfortable, respected lives. Oskar Brieger, at some point in the early years of the new century, treated the director of the Breslau Academy of Arts, Hans Poelzig, already a well-known architect and slated to become even better known. Family legend has it that in gratitude for Brieger's having saved his life, Poelzig offered to design for the Briegers a whole range of furniture for their capacious new dwelling at Königsplatz, at once home and office. I believe Poelzig's favor was richly rewarded. That furniture has had its own history, as we shall see.

My impression is that the generation of my parents, born in the 1890s, had an easier childhood and more cheerful prospects than their parents. They started life on a calm and prosperous voyage—only to be caught in a storm of violence that their elders could not even have imagined. Perhaps that mixture of felicity and seriousness in the early years gave some of them the psychological stamina to cope with the terrors of later times.

Those two generations were not much concerned with national politics, though the wives and sisters addressed what was then called "the social question," hoping to ameliorate the lot of underprivileged children, for example, while the men were used to a world of international scientific collaboration and rivalry. They were patriots in a cosmopolitan world. Some were liberals, some conservatives, but they all thought that the *Rechtsstaat*, the rule of law, was the unassailable bedrock of civic existence. They witnessed the reign of Emperor Friedrich, Queen Victoria's son-in-law and the very embodiment of German liberal hopes, who by the time he ascended the throne in 1888 had been left speechless by cancer of the esophagus; he died after three anguished months. His son, Wilhelm II, was of a different mold: arrogant, reactionary, the very epitome of strident tactlessness, though in his own way open to scientific and technological innovation. Many in my family were bemused by, even critical of, this feckless young monarch. But awareness that politics could threaten or destroy their lives came to them, as to most Germans, only with the Great War. In 1907 my twelve-year-old father began "a newspaper," of which only the first "issue" survives, in which he noted with satisfaction that in that year's election, the democratic parties had not scored further gains: he surely came to this class-bound political view via his parents.

What mattered most to this cluster of quietly privileged people was their private life—family, career, friendship. The outside world may have seemed remote and unchanging, and yet German society—in which an ever-growing, organized, educated proletariat imbued with social-democratic hopes challenged the old elites who governed a semi-authoritarian monarchical state— was anything but stable. By 1912 the Social Democratic Party had the largest representation in the national parliament, the Reichstag, with limited but expanding powers. How long before radical reforms or revolution would threaten the social order? Imperial Germany was a strange hybrid, a magnificently disciplined modern society with an antiquated political order. As Walther Rathenau wrote in 1907, "What cultural criteria justify the fact that Germany is being governed more absolutistically than almost all other civilized countries? . . . We cannot maintain a separate climate for ourselves forever."

And what about Germany's adventurous role in the world, its much-touted entry into world affairs, its high-sea fleet built to challenge British power, its imperial ambition, and its prestige-driven policies that affronted the other major powers? Wilhelmine arrogance was mixed with pervasive anxiety that Germany's powerful neighbors were "encircling" the country, trying to throttle its legitimate growth. Germany was at the geographical center of Europe, with more neighbors at its borders than any other country. For a long time German lands had been Europe's anvil; the new Germany was the hammer.

My impression is that my forebears were among those prosperous Germans who paid but intermittent attention to the great political questions of the time. They knew important cultural innovators such as Hauptmann and Poelzig, early representatives of German modernism. But were they aware of the great cultural and emancipatory movements of the Belle Epoque? Probably not. After all, Germany was not rent by a Dreyfus Affair (there could be no Dreyfus in Germany, since a Jewish officer on the German General Staff was unimaginable), nor was it threatened by a time bomb akin to the Irish question in Britain. Confident patriotism was a birthright of the prosperous citizen; local and charitable activism was the principal civic concern.

Certainly the young had other matters on their minds. My parents were educated in Breslau; my mother, Käthe Brieger, went to a private school in the first few years and to a girls' public school later, where Lotte Stern was her classmate and best friend. This *Realgymnasium*—there were no classical gymnasia for girls—offered a practical form of higher education, emphasizing modern languages, mathematics, and science. The *Abitur*, or final school examination, allowed for automatic admission to the university, and having passed her *Abitur* in May 1912, Käthe immediately enrolled in the University of Breslau to study mathematics and physics. It was a rare pursuit for a woman at that time—the whole notion of a professional career for a woman was still suspect. But her father's ambition for her had gently encouraged her to choose this path; his confident expectations spurred her all her life.

My father attended the Johannes Gymnasium, a school founded in 1872, at the height of Germany's and Breslau's civic liberalism, with the explicit aim of being a bastion of religious tolerance; it was the only *Gymnasium* in Breslau that had Jewish teachers, and by the end of the century a quarter of the staff was Jewish. The Prussian state looked with suspicion on the school, but the strong liberal wing of the municipal council cherished it. My father passed his *Abitur* in 1913 and that spring began his medical studies in Breslau; he spent the next semesters in Munich—successively attending several universities being a German academic custom.

The year 1912 was the year my father became an orphan. He had his two sisters as both comfort and responsibility, and his father's sister, Grete, kept in touch with them. (I remember her as a somewhat humorless spinster who had begun and abandoned an academic career but kept up her literary-scientific interests.) The family had a legacy of sustaining intergenerational friendships, and among the friends who became substitute parents were the Briegers, who, for example, invited my father to join them on their Swiss holiday in Pontresina, where Haber also vacationed. Albert and Gustav Neisser also kept a protective eye on him—and in the medical world he was just entering, many internists would recognize his name. And it was precisely in the years of his parents' deaths that he built up his library—he lived with his books.

Books were part of the serious side of life, of what his family thought of as moral education. So was the advice passed on by one's elders. In congratulating my mother on having passed the *Abitur,* Toni Neisser expressed the prevailing ethos, adorning her advice with a string of pearls: "I would so much want to tell you today what for me has been most important in life: to be able to be active, to be able to do without, to be able to feel joy and to be able to suffer, to be able to love, to admire. If you are able to do this as well as you have done your studies, you'll be able to say your life was sublime [*herrlich*]." This was indeed the prescribed attitude to life, though it didn't dampen the high spirits that my mother, in particular, could enjoy.

Toni Neisser's anything-but-casual remark fastened on something that her generation, unlike ours, took for granted: in a world of abundant comfort, a high value was put on renunciation, on knowing how to do without. There was a fear of indulgent luxury, of ostentation, of excessive ease, all of which bore the danger of decline and decadence. Criticism of such self-indulgence was not so much a pragmatic counsel (fear of a rainy day) as a moral tenet, part of a now-secularized, once-Christian—more specifically Calvinist—faith. It was a secular bow to the virtues of modesty and thrift. I am reminded of *Buddenbrooks,* the novel by the twenty-six-year-old Thomas Mann that was published in 1901, with its portrait of a bourgeois family in decline. Mann gave epic expression to a pervasive fear that wealth and luxury marked the road to perdition—to say nothing of his equally pervasive disdain for ostentatious wealth. He was my father's favorite modern writer. "Decent" people feared disgrace as well; der Alte Asch had a prescription for the failed ones that has a certain piquancy: give them a revolver or a passage to America, that ultimate escape for the adventurer or the miscreant.

Everyday thrift enhanced the pleasures of family celebrations and holidays, which were major occasions marked by festive meals, in turn requiring proof of proper bearing. I don't know when the earlier generations had ceased observing the Jewish holy days, but I do know that beginning with my parents' time, Christian holidays were duly celebrated—Easter; the Advent Sundays; St. Nicholas's day, with the fearsome character with the switch; Christmas, with the tree and its lighted candles, the singing of carols, presents, and the special meal.

In equal contrast to the workaday world was the annual vacation, with or occasionally without children, the travel with heavy baggage to the sea or the mountains, the time to restore one's health after habitual overexertion, the time to read, to meet up with or make friends, often the time for cultural pilgrimages to Italy or France, to the fabled spas in the vast Dual Monarchy or to primitive inns in simple villages. Frontiers, after all, were open, visas rarely required, and the prevailing gold standard served as a kind of common currency.

For this compressed portrait of my family's life my sources are family letters and photographs and, to a lesser extent, oral tradition. I have tried to hear the varied voices of the time, and I know that they may perhaps sound implausibly idyllic, that what they preserved on paper may well already have been purged or "elevated." Certainly the scenes they describe seem idyllic compared with what came later. But they couldn't—they shouldn't—have seemed idyllic to them at the time: there was too much poverty, too much disease, too short a life span. There was hardly a family that had not experienced grave illnesses—tuberculosis, syphilis, diphtheria—and many had endured the worst ravage, an infant's death. Physicians' families knew all about this. And there were constant reminders of death everywhere, with the public expression of private grief: women in mourning dressed for at least a year in the prescribed black, men with their black armbands. Death was publicly acknowledged, while the advent of birth—pregnancy—was kept hidden or referred to only in polite circumlocutions.

Of course the outside world had always impinged on these private lives—sometimes dramatically, as at the moment of German unification, in 1871; sometimes gradually, as with the industrialization of Germany and with its increasing political discord. And there were the occasional bomb-throwers, mostly anarchists venting their rage at crowned heads and other representatives of a hated order. But I doubt that many Germans—or indeed Europeans—took a full measure of what the consequences might be of the sharpening antagonisms among the great powers. To be sure there were sudden crises—the Russian Revolution of 1905, Austria-Hungary's annexation of Bosnia-Herzegovina in 1908, a second Moroccan crisis in 1912—threatening alliances, and ever-greater military expenses; but the presumption was for continued peace, even perhaps for greater international understanding, given the Hague Convention and the Socialist International, with its pledge to oppose all war. Perhaps peace, progress, and prosperity would endure.

At first, then, few realized that the assassination in 1914 in Sarajevo of the Austrian archduke Franz Ferdinand, heir to the Habsburg throne, posed a more ominous threat. The killing, it was assumed, had been the work of someone in the Serb underground, a manifestation of nationalist fury against Austro-Hungarian rule. It took almost a month for people to grasp that Europe was on the brink of war. On July 28, Käthe Brieger, busy with her university studies, wrote her parents: "I don't want to say anything about the war because I discuss that subject all the time from right and left and without any pleasure. In short, I hope this time we shall still find a pacific way out." It was not to be: Encouraged by Germany's leaders, Austria declared war on Serbia, and Russia mobilized. Three days later, Germany declared war on Russia, then on France, and began its invasion of neutral Belgium—which in turn led Great Britain to go to war against its German challenger.

Most Germans, trusting the official line and lies, believed that the war was a "defensive" one, to protect the threatened fatherland. They greeted it with an outburst of patriotic fervor, with religious enthusiasm. Or at least the German elites did, notably the university professors, giving the war their moral and religious blessing, assuming that a great sacrifice would purify the nation and end the foul and enervating peace. The clergy joined the nationalist chorus: God had imposed this moral test on a people who must once more grasp the nobility of sacrifice and of death in defense of a righteous and endangered nation. Even the Social Democrats joined in, abandoning decades of pacifist opposition to all imperialist wars and accepting the official line that the fatherland was in danger. The external threat had at long last unified Germany and transcended all political divisions. Here at last was a release from an unheroic, humdrum existence, from self-satisfied indulgence and Mammon-worship. Out of this great test would come a national rebirth. Many Germans soon glorified the "August days" of exaltation—and only the fewest (Albert Einstein among them) realized that Europe had stumbled into an all-consuming catastrophe. None, not the most prescient of skeptics, could envision the carnage that was to follow.

The German response resembled a nationalist orgy, a morally uplifting mixture of hyperpatriotism and religious passion. The other belligerent countries experienced milder versions of this divine madness, but Germans seemed peculiarly vulnerable to mystical exaltation. The most important—and outrageous—example of this new spirit was the "Manifesto of the 93" of October 1914, a statement addressed to "The Civilized World" and signed by most of Germany's best-known artists and scientists, my grandparents' friends and intellectual heroes among them. It denied German responsibility for the outbreak of the war, defended the breach of Belgium's neutrality, and avowed the identity of German militarism and German culture. The "Manifesto" outraged the very people it was supposed to impress: elite opinion-makers in neutral countries. Was this a sign of a political autism aggravated by war?

Nineteen-year-old Rudolf Stern joined the many other young men who immediately volunteered for military service. He could have continued his medical studies or enlisted for medical service in the army, as many of his friends and fellow students did. Instead he chose the army, probably as the braver alternative and because he, too, was beguiled by the pervasive idea that the war would be a short march to victory. He left behind his older sister, Lotte, whom he cherished and admired, and younger sister, Marga, for whom he felt a special responsibility.

Two kinds of uniforms may be said to characterize the extremities of life in the first half of the twentieth century: the soldier's and the camp inmate's. The former was somehow a symbol of honor, but it also identified a break: the wearer now belonged to another world, uprooted in space and spirit, living in a state of enforced camaraderie but almost always at some point having to witness or experience unnatural death. The latter was a totally powerless victim of degradation, subject to torture and death. I see a far-off connection between the two: the brutalization that soldiers experienced in the Great War may have prepared a world that condoned the barbarism of the camps.

Rudolf arrived on the western front in March 1915, assigned at first to an artillery regiment. It was a life spent in dugouts and trenches, whether in times of heavy barrage or relative calm, with periods of recuperation in some rear position and infrequent home leaves. Boredom alternated with fear, as moods and quarters changed. One's movements were always at the command of others, often superiors one judged inferior. But one's inner life was free, and Rudolf was subject to intense, anxious self-scrutiny in these strange and dangerous surroundings, charged with thoughts about a future that might never be. The ever-present threat of death heightens the sense of life, as Freud and others have observed, and this was also true for the many who remained at home, anxious about their fighting kin, increasingly burdened with anticipatory grief.

Several sets of my father's wartime correspondence survive, including many letters between him and his close friend Käthe Brieger—the tone of their correspondence is not that of two people thinking of marriage—from his godfather (whether real or self-designated, I do not know), Gustav Neisser, and from his sisters and friends.

One of the first pieces of news exchanged was calamitous: Käthe's father, Oskar, had out of pure patriotism volunteered for service in an army hospital (he also demanded that his daughter Käthe and his prospective daughter-in-law, Käthe Friedenthal, a girl from a prosperous Breslau family of Jewish descent, should serve as nurses in his section, crowded with the injured from the eastern front). Suddenly, on October 20, 1914, he died of two massive strokes.

He had been attending to both soldiers and civilians, operating under emergency conditions and giving himself no rest. In a letter of condolence to Ernst, Oskar's eldest son, who was already in the army medical service on the western front, Albert Neisser reported that the autopsy had shown grave arteriosclerosis; it had been merciful that he never regained consciousness and thus was spared "the only truly awful moment in dying, the bidding farewell." (The remark indicated either Neisser's own fears or his wish to reassure the son that the latter's absence at the time of his father's death should not heighten his pain). Neisser admonished the young Brieger to follow the example of his father, a man whose friendship he had cherished and "who always only lived and worked for others."

All manner of evidence tells us that Oskar Brieger had been an exceptionally genial, generous person with natural charm and an immense capacity for friendship shown to many people over his twenty-five years as head of the ear, nose, and throat department at All Saints'. His chief assistant, Dr. Goerke, while treating me once for a painful middle-ear infection, talked to me of my grandfather with unforgettable love. My father had been deeply attached to him. The Briegers' had been a happy companionate marriage, and he was an adored father as well. His sudden death left the family in deepest grief.

My grandmother now had to care for the two youngest boys, who were still in school but close to being called up. Yet she also quickly assumed some of her husband's responsibilities while continuing her own work with children—and her comforting letters to those closest to her at the front. One response from Ernst, written to his mother in the spring of 1915 from Lens in France, observed, "Now we are in total quiet. That you think it odd that apparently so near the heaviest fighting there can be places of absolute quiet is not surprising. For us this incredible coexistence of war and peace appears even more incredible." His mother's life had been violently disrupted by death and grief, actual and prospective. She faced all kinds of practical challenges, not to mention uncertain finances, and the ever-worsening scarcity of food when the British blockade became more effective. Her letters suggest that at times she managed to nab some luxury, often so that she could send it on to the front or save it for men on leave. We know that relatively prosperous people such as she could successfully scrounge for more than the scant rations available to everyone: this was in fact a major source of growing discontent and divisiveness in the country.

Most of Rudolf's letters had a common refrain: regrets or reproaches at Käthe's silence. He was hungry for news, for contact with the world he had left behind, at once so close and so unimaginably distant. They exchanged family news and reported on their respective experiences—on Rudolf's side at times defensively sarcastic, on Käthe's side ever friendly, sometimes teasingly reproving. And when Rudolf's sister Lotte became engaged to Richard Kobrak, somewhat to her brother's chagrin—he had hoped for a more promising and likeable partner—a fleeting exchange seemed to rule out a similar step for them.

The Kobraks were part of the outer circle of Stern-Brieger friends. Richard was a converted Jew, but not all members of his family were. Neisser reported in a letter that Fritz Kobrak was about to enlist in the field artillery "but not without first undertaking the move to the decent state religion." This rare comment about the difficult subject becomes even stranger as it continues: "Because Jewry [*Judentum*] as we know it is not a religion but a misfortune." A photograph of Lotte's and Richard's wedding shows them standing in my grandmother's garden, with some of the men in the party dressed in resplendent uniform.

So between Rudolf and Käthe the letters continued in their fraternal way. The only indications of deeper feelings—aside from the fact of the correspondence itself—were the repeated and lamented misunderstandings between them. They often discussed literature, both classical and contemporary works, and Rudolf betrayed a slightly mocking, even condescending tone when writing to Käthe about books (though he solicited her help about specific problems in chemistry and physics). Their tastes were catholic, with frequent mention of Kant and Goethe, Schopenhauer and Nietzsche. Books by the last two Rudolf sometimes took with him when, as a member of a new air force unit in 1916, he went up in balloons to observe enemy activity behind the lines: high-altitude reading!

During the Allied offensive at the Somme, in July 1916, he wrote, "I do have to say that my position can't necessarily be regarded as life insurance and that a few times I had exceptional luck. Also in military matters I remain an optimist, I have seen our infantry move forward and the fellows laughed so that tears came to my eyes. Of course there are other types as well, but that this is still possible with us commands respect."

Sometime in 1917, he volunteered for the nascent air force, specifically as an observer of enemy position from a balloon. Occasionally a very private note was struck: in November 1917, having been ordered to another balloon unit, he traveled via Brussels, where he went shopping: "But then I recalled my contractually fixed idealism and hastened to the picture gallery where . . . I stayed till five o'clock . . . In the evening, idiot that I am, I traveled to the front and reported most obediently to Koluft 7 [headquarters of his balloon unit] the next noon, but it was too early and I could have stayed longer in Brussels."

After two years of war, other thoughts crept in. From 1916 to 1918, he repeatedly but vainly sought to get extended leave so that he could sit for his *Physikum*, a prescribed examination taken in the middle of one's medical studies. Others had received such leaves, and still others had never interrupted their studies at all, but had completed them in short order and only thereafter served in the army's medical service. Repeatedly Koluft rejected Rudolf's requests; he could have done without such signs of his indispensability.

As the war years dragged on, Käthe's career went through various successful phases: after her father's death, she returned to her physics studies, as had been her father's wish, and she briefly taught science in the upper grades of *Gymnasium* to students only a few years younger than she. By 1918, she had received her doctorate in physics, with a thesis concerning the structure of crystals, based on recent experiments by Max von Laue. Then, with her doctorate in hand, still very rare for women, she embarked on a new career, explaining to Rudolf that she much preferred to work with children: "To find work that doesn't deal with instruments but with people, and especially with children whom one can help, and where, as I hope, there won't be rocky obstacles that might threaten my talents with destruction, where in short there is no maneuvering along abysses of ignorance—for me, such work is not work but only joy." And in the spring of 1918 she gave some lectures on women's suffrage in various cities and repeatedly in the Upper Silesian city of Kattowitz.

My father's letters said relatively little about conditions at the front. This was not, I think, out of fear of censorship; he indicated quite freely where he was stationed, what French or Belgian towns or villages he had visited, to what town he rode to visit Käthe's brothers. He also wrote about some landscape, some moonlit ride that reminded him of home, that stirred up all manner of sentimental thoughts.

The deepest introspection he confided to a diary that he kept for a short time in 1916–1917, written, as he put it, when his previous life had collapsed like a house of cards. In the years just before the war, he had been in thrall to the memory of his father, wishing above all to achieve his eminence. He recalled that in 1910 he had gone through a religious crisis (this was a year after he and Käthe had been confirmed) and eventually came to accept his disbelief. Scattered though his wartime correspondence are disillusioned remarks about clergymen at the front. He thought that he needed people but that people did not need him because he was an unfriendly person. Like many soldiers, he found the war a kind of journey outward and inward, the discovery of an external world beyond the familiar and an occasional search for the self beneath the uniform.

In the spring of 1915, Gustav Neisser—Onkel Gustl, as that wise and benevolent friend was called—wrote my father, deflecting his thanks for care and gifts and acknowledging only that his own peace of mind [*Seelenruhe*] had wilted: "But even worry about you is an enrichment of my life, and I wouldn't want to miss or exchange it for indifference to your fate. In what kinds of existence you must now find yourself!! In fact it must be marvelously interesting to observe in oneself how a nervous and cultivated person accepts this return to the most primitive [*ursprünglichsten*] form of life. But I very much wish for you that these lofty experiences don't last for too long." He added that he thought they wouldn't because "old Haber [Fritz's father] told me yesterday *sottissimo voce*" that his son's secret discoveries were now being practically tested. This chilling reference was to Fritz Haber's fevered experiments with the production of poison gas weapons—which in fact were first used in April 1915. Neisser ended the letter ironically: "Heil Haber and Hindenburg!" (Hindenburg was Supreme Commander of the Army—and that coupling would have pleased Haber rather more than it would have the field marshal.)

Neisser caught the strangeness of wartime existence, aware that the rawness of life in the field prompted reflections on "normal" civilized life. He must surely have been concerned also for his own son, Hans, who was in the army as well. He sensed how the constant cycle of exhaustion and exertion, of danger and release, would affect the soldier. And he knew that the war brought together fellow soldiers from the most diverse and unexpected backgrounds, from different classes, regions, and religious faiths. For some it was a democratizing experience. My father had a superior from East Prussia, Major von Hatten, with whom he came to be on good terms—a connection that in peacetime would have been most unlikely.

Still on the western front, my father was made a noncommissioned officer and, in late 1915, received the Iron Cross second class; still later, he was awarded the Iron Cross first class for particular bravery, a much rarer decoration. After having survived the horrors of Ypres and the Somme, he volunteered for duty in the expanding air force units, specifically as a balloon observer. As a child, I loved hearing about his ascents in the gas balloons, usually tethered to the ground by ropes, to observe enemy activity. A single burst of machine gunfire sufficed to set fire to a balloon and send it crashing to the ground, and by 1918 the Allies had clear air superiority. But even before that, Gustav Neisser had warned my father: "Wouldn't such a big pear [the balloon shape] make a splendid target for the English?" Still, the new assignment was an adventure; it took him away from the trenches, and in between flights he had a more comfortable life in quarters away from the front line. By May 1917, he had been promoted to lieutenant in the reserve, a position involving new responsibilities, such as training recruits for this branch of the incipient air force, and providing new privileges, foremost among these the services of an orderly.

The letters my father received from Onkel Gustl offer an astonishing commentary on the political mood of the time, for Neisser was entrusted with various semiofficial responsibilities in Berlin and had excellent connections everywhere. No doubt he, too, had thought that the war would be won in short order, for German troops were everywhere on enemy soil and only victory eluded them. But gradually Neisser's comments reflected one overriding concern: to bring the horror to an end. His candor—about rumors of political maneuvering, about military matters—was remarkable, and over the years he became increasingly "defeatist," and then unambiguously critical of German policy. In World War II, any one of Neisser's political comments would have sufficed for a death sentence on charges of defeatism.

Neisser's reports on family and friends were regularly supplemented by political asides. He belonged to the propertied elite that had access to the governing classes, and he grasped their culpabilities. He wrote as the German patriot he felt he was—and only gradually did he come to realize that the noisy, self-appointed super-patriots represented the gravest threat to Germany. In early 1915, he was pleased with German victories, assuming that they would hasten the end of the war. He noted that Haber's weapon of poison gas had contributed to the victory at Ypres—and said not a word about the horror of the new weapon or the fact that its use violated international agreement. In April, right after Ypres, he reported on the rumor that negotiations with Britain were under way and that people in high circles were wondering whether she would have to pay fifteen or twenty billion marks in reparations. (He was right in only one respect: German leaders assumed that the defeated Allies would pay for German debts incurred during the war. The precedent for Allied reparations was the indemnity of five billion francs that Bismarck had imposed on the French in 1871.)

There were the odd lighthearted remarks: my father had failed in finding books Neisser wanted, but "Once you have marched into Paris and begun to plunder the Louvre, continue to think of me." But he turned serious in the same letter, and wondered what people in twenty years would say about the fact that for six months Europeans fought over some local position while the Japanese "in all quiet swallowed the greatest parts of Asia." He also mentioned rumors that we now know had no basis in fact—that peace with France was near, and that Germany was ready to cede some parts of Alsace-Lorraine, leaving Britain and Russia to pay for the war.

In June 1915, Neisser again reported on peace rumors—himself incredulous—but noted that the official press had toned down its hate songs while "the privileged war enthusiasts escalate their rage." By now he had come to believe that Germany bore a large share of responsibility for the war: the building of a high-sea fleet, Admiral Tirpitz's great project, had posed a mortal threat to British power. In Neisser's mind—and that of many others—Tirpitz was a "misfortune," a powerful force against all reason. Neisser reported on the many splits within the German leadership: he scorned the extremists for whom Tirpitz was a hero and sided with the civilian chancellor Theodor von Bethmann Hollweg, who doggedly tried to preserve a moderate course, arguing against the declaration of unrestricted submarine warfare. When he lost in February 1917, the predictable result was that the United States entered the war. Neisser recalled with dismay the earlier German "madness about world-mastery" [Weltüberwinderwahn], the failure to understand that Britain was unbeatable. At the height of the murderous battle of the Somme—which my father experienced at close quarters—Neisser wrote that he hoped the Germans would lose some ground because only "a bitter lesson" would suffice to subdue the annexationists. As the war dragged on, Neisser's tone became more bitter. What were Germans fighting for, what were the nation's war aims? Wartime secrecy hid the details, but people gradually learned that the military leadership, increasingly in the hands of Hindenburg and his titular subordinate but actual superior, Quarter-master General Erich Ludendorff, along with captains of industry and professional right-wing chauvinists, harbored the most extreme war aims, designed to ensure German supremacy over Europe for all time. Bethmann Hollweg, the chancellor, was a conscientious realist and moderate, but he was increasingly powerless against the others; indeed by his mere presence he served as a cover for the extremists.

Still, Neisser's letters remained high-spirited, intimate, irreverent. He once offered to write more often if Rudolf promised that the letters would never be published, even if he were to rise to still higher positions—an unlikely ascent, he added, because he was not going to give up his "anarchist" views, acquired because even the Social Democrats had become accommodationist. And as to the risk of putting pen to paper, he repeated an anecdote told him by Heinrich Dove, vice president of the Reichstag, about the rabbi whom he knew in his hometown of Rogasen who had said to him, "Material goods and money I don't have and can't leave to my children, but each receives some lesson for life." Dove asked for a similar gift, and the rabbi told him, "Never write anything in writing" [Schreiben Sie nie etwas schriftliches]. Delight in paradoxical Jewish wit was quite common, and this particular example became a favorite in subsequent letters and postwar conversation.

My father had an unappeasable hunger for Neisser's news; the letters were, he once wrote, his sole spiritual fodder. In September 1915, Neisser explained his occasional silence: "Only acute war psychosis paralyzes the expression of my thoughts. I am in such total despair about the monstrous madness that we are condemned to experience that I don't know what to write you or others." That indeed had become his deepest conviction, and it was radically different from the conventional sermonizing of the time—and probably even somewhat different from the view of the recipient, who believed in the necessity of the war for a longer time.

By the end of 1916 it became clear that the Social Democratic Party, the largest in the Reichstag, was about to split: eminent leaders from the left and right wings, outraged at their conformist colleagues' support of an imperialist war, seceded and formed a radical opposition group, the Independent Socialist Party. Even moderates recognized that if the war was to be fought successfully, internal reforms were needed. Prussian conservatives turned radical: they mobilized all their power to oppose these reforms and any effort at a reasonable peace. In 1916, Neisser was invited to become a member of the "Deutsche Gesellschaft 1914," a self-constituted important club of elite Germans ranging from conservatives to right-wing Social Democrats and including a number of prominent Jews—the industrialist Walther Rathenau, the banker Max Warburg, the great theater director Max Reinhardt among them. The members discussed politics among themselves, but some members used the club to advance reasonable policies. Neisser clearly sided with political moderates such as Ernst Troeltsch, philosopher and theologian, who demanded a reformist course. By now Neisser was recognizing Germany's superpatriots as the greatest internal danger. I believe his son Hans, also on the western front, shared his father's disillusionment, but it took my father longer to lose the faith.

In March 1918, on his twenty-fourth birthday, Rudolf was brooding over his own delayed career and uncertain life. He had been feeling moments of war weariness, and he wrote to Käthe, "My readiness to sacrifice was also timebound, and with the passage of time, personal desires come to the fore." He was more than exasperated with his superiors, whose "brutality, mendacity, and boundless stupidity" he found disgusting. Käthe may have reproved him for these remarks, for in a subsequent letter he offered this rejoinder: "You people have no inkling of what the war is really like . . . some kinds of vileness can sometimes really throw one off balance."

At that point, Rudolf apparently shared everyone's high hopes that Ludendorff's massive offensive against Allied positions on the western front would succeed, supported as it was by an added million men from the eastern front, freed because Lenin had accepted the German peace terms at Brest-Litovsk, Carthaginian as they were. The German armies did break through Allied lines, but the great prize, the capture of Paris, eluded them, in part because of pervasive weariness. This fatigue took hold of Rudolf as well. It did not take much for him to fall into melancholy contemplation—or sentimental weakness, as he called it. In late March he had to order the leveling of eight fruit trees to clear a launch pad for the balloon, "and gone were all good spirits, and I felt an incredible yearning for my childhood, for a good microscope . . ." Then the hope for peace receded, and at the end of April he mentioned, à propos of some reading he had done, "that my comrades in the first thirty years' war had a very much nicer life," though "the so-called dependents found it rather unpleasant even in comparison to our bread and meat rationing, especially if they belonged to the third religion [*Confession*]." (I was startled when I first read this implicit comment that 1914–1918 was the beginning of a *second* Thirty Years' War; decades before seeing this letter, I myself had used the phrase "second Thirty Years' War" to refer to 1914–1945. The first Thirty Years' War, 1618–1648, had ravaged the German lands, and the people had suffered from terrifying violence, hunger, and pillage; one third of Germany's population perished, so it is understandable that memory of the war haunted Germans for centuries.)

"The third religion" was a typically veiled and quite rare reference to Jewishness in my father's letters. And yet we know that at the home front, anti-Semitism was becoming virulent in the course of the war. In 1916, the War Department had ordered a confidential census of the number of Jews in the German armed forces, a response to the widespread canard that Jews were shirkers. The results, not disclosed until after the war, disproved the malicious charge, but the very institution of such a census suggests the degree to which Jews were thought separate and suspect. By 1917, the Fatherland Party had great success with its wildly pan-German and anti-Semitic program. In March 1918, Rudolf asked his younger sister for the address of the League for Combating Anti-Semitism.

In mid-July 1918, German troops were close to Paris, but then the Allies, reinforced by American troops, began a successful counteroffensive, forcing a continuous German retreat. At the end of September, General Ludendorff, virtual dictator, suddenly lost his nerve, fearing that at any moment the German army might collapse. Hence he demanded that the Kaiser instantly appoint a parliamentary government, including representatives of the democratic parties, that in turn might immediately appeal to President Woodrow Wilson for an armistice. This was a clever, cynical move to shift political responsibility for Germany's defeat: an army should be the father of victory, while civilians—and democrats at that—should shoulder the defeat and the liquidation of a lost war. Weeks passed in negotiations between Wilson and the German government; meanwhile the country was beset by strikes and massive anger at the continued fighting and dying. Yet, by late October, it was clear that an armistice—with exceedingly harsh conditions—would indeed finally end the slaughter.

Neisser, realizing that immense hardships awaited Germany, foreswore any gloating at having foreseen the disaster. However, the young should take heart, he wrote, for a new world is being born: "People everywhere want peace. And too many eyes have now been opened so that the powers that work in the dark will not soon be able to begin their deadly [*unheilvoll*] work again." He reflected on his political experience; for his generation, life had begun with

> the new glow of the German Reich, and thereafter we experienced nothing but decline. The broadest strata of the *Bürgertum* combined with the old powers of reaction to engage in the most brutal pursuit of material interests and thus wrecked every strain of true liberalism. Hypocrisy and lack of inner freedom triumphed everywhere, and year by year the split between the propertied classes and the rising fourth estate widened. How all these things affected our foreign policy will have to be a subject for the future. We are now at the lowest point, and the inner renewal will begin, not only with us but in other cultured countries of the world.

He wouldn't live to see this new world, he wrote, but perhaps, like Moses, he would at least be allowed a glimpse of the promised land. But not even that: he died suddenly in mid-December 1918, a victim of the influenza epidemic. He did not live to witness how the evil powers of the past, with still more vengeful hatred and mendacity, would poison "the promised land."

The evolution of Neisser's political views—here but briefly summarized— shows how, over time, Germans began to divine the truth beyond the veil of lies and by 1918 were clamoring for peace, some even for peace and social justice. But the subjects Neisser did not mention deserve notice as well: he wrote very little about the fierce political struggles over democratic reforms, even though his views on these were implicitly clear, and he wrote nothing about the dramatic increase in rabid political anti-Semitism that began in 1917.

The gist of Neisser's judgments was common coin among admirable moderates; in 1918–1919, Ernst Troeltsch wrote pseudonymous articles that expounded similar judgments about the imperial regime. In 1918, Rathenau published an appeal to German youth, decrying as "the most shameful and the most un-Germanic [thing] that has happened in this war . . . the reckless, shameless showering of self-praise. Nothing has so contributed to the decline of morals in this country, to the disdain for law . . . as this prolonged self-glorification." (A year earlier, he had warned Ludendorff against the continuing deception of the German people.) Many Germans expressed these views in private and in their letters but kept silent in public for fear that open German acknowledgment of guilt would feed Allied vindictiveness; they probably couldn't imagine that silence would favor nationalist mendacity at home and encourage the false myth of victorious German armies being stabbed in the back.

By August 1918, the tide of war had turned decisively: the Allies broke through German lines, and Ludendorff's fears about a possible collapse intensified. Rudolf experienced both the misery of those terrible autumn days and the precipitous decline in morale. On September 28, the very day on which Ludendorff asked the Kaiser to appoint a democratic government, Rudolf wrote to Käthe, "In the last three days I have once again seen so much misery and wretchedness that even my brutalized being can't handle it." He hoped that Käthe would have congenial work for the winter, the more so as he would take on the Sisyphean task of combating "the subversive and pro-sabotage propaganda in the army. Yes, if you could help me in this or if I had a tenth of your courage, your youthful energy and optimism, but I am suited for this role as a gravedigger is to be a life-insurance agent."

Until mid-October he preserved his faith in the cause, angered by those who espoused "defeatism." He was bitter at the loss "of cohesion . . . in broad circles in Germany," replaced as it was by what he saw as massive selfishness. He caricatured the feeling: "Never mind if Alsace goes down the drain or, for all I care, the whole German Reich, the main thing is for me to have enough to eat." German youth, he thought, was schooled in "a foolish Hurrah-Patriotism," but didn't have an inkling "of the true nature of a state and the place of its citizens." He wrote scathingly of friends and relatives who, from a left and probably so-

cialist position, had become critical of the German cause, though he acknowledged as self-evident that with Germans, too, "there has been a great deal of sin
because of stupidity, malice, and delusion." "In this time of rogues it is really
difficult to know what one should do," he added, and he would be satisfied "so
long as my active fellow soldiers [Kameraden] and those who wish to appear as
such consider me an uncertain warrior [Kantonist] and a reddish defeatist, and
my friends . . . uncle Gustav, etc., take me for a nice fellow but a narrow and pan-
German polluted militarist." Käthe wrote a few days later that she and many others believed Germany could have had a better peace in 1916 and "many lives
have been sacrificed for naught."

Until the late fall of 1918, Rudolf sought to preserve a kind of inner balance
between the dominant sense of loyalty and duty and the intermittent upsurge
of "sentimental weakness." "My father told me once some twelve years ago," he
wrote, "that the best weapon against world weariness [Weltschmerz] was work.
I should remember this, he said, even after he was gone. Because of this legacy,
I remember that conversation so vividly and it has already and repeatedly
proved to be restorative." A faith in the healing or sublimating power of work,
the Arbeitskur, may have had a special appeal to German Jews.

But as my father gradually realized that the mendacity and class egoism of
Germany's wartime leaders had senselessly prolonged the suffering, he felt angry and betrayed. He certainly emerged from the war purged of all nationalist
views and with a disillusioned, cynical attitude about German politics. Of his
wartime experiences in the trenches, he rarely thereafter talked, though he
spoke somewhat more readily of his time with the balloons, and as a very young
child in Germany, I was quietly proud of his service, rank, and decorations. But
once Germany ceased to be a home — that is, when Hitler came to power — I
thought he had fought on the wrong side, and later, as a teenager in the United
States, I even felt embarrassment about his wartime service.

By the end of October, Rudolf had suffered not only the trauma of his
country's defeat and the angry feeling that the four years of war had been senseless, but also the trauma of a very dangerous illness. In mid-July he had contracted jaundice, recovering only in early August; by September he was back
with his balloon unit. But in late October he was rushed to an army hospital
with a case of influenza — it was the beginning of the global scourge that killed
more than ten million people. The head doctor, taking note of his very high
fever, pronounced him moribundus and ordered that the family be notified at
once, perhaps allowing for a final visit.

My father heard this diagnosis from his sickbed, and rebelled against the sentence. Knowing that the greatest danger of so high a fever was to the heart, which needed stimulation to combat it, he sent his orderly in search of two bottles of champagne and some strong coffee. He imbibed the medicine and survived the crisis. What the story, now of course a family legend, may lack in medical plausibility it makes up for in testimony to a family's pleasure in celebrating great moments with champagne. Typical of the confusion of those last wartime weeks, his relatives and the Briegers received first the telegram indicating that he was out of danger and only later the summons for a final visit.

There were other communications, too. After he heard the fatal diagnosis, and when he was not at all confident that he would recover, my father wrote a farewell letter to Käthe on October 25, avowing in the face of death the feelings and expectations to which in the preceding four years he had never referred: "I must thank you because every experience of true happiness I have had since I have grown up I owe to you . . . And today you will believe me, if in the most sacred seriousness, I assure you that you wouldn't have been happy with me and that you wouldn't have made me happier than you have already. Therefore chin up and fulfill my greatest wish: achieve happiness because you have the stuff it takes as few do . . . Good night, as always, R."

CHAPTER 2

★

WEIMAR

ON NOVEMBER 9, 1918, the day of the Kaiser's ignoble abdication and of the improvised proclamation of a German Republic, my father, left at a field hospital about to fall into Allied hands, had to organize his own retreat. The day before, the doctor in charge had refused to have him evacuated because his heart was still too weak. There was something emblematic about how he entered and left army life: he had volunteered in 1914 in health and confidence; now he was enfeebled and disillusioned. He had duplicated the experience of millions.

On his homeward trek my father could see for himself that the defeated country was in revolutionary chaos. In Freiburg, the first stop back in Germany, his officer's epaulettes were torn from his shoulders, as angry groups (there were many throughout Germany) sought to strip away the symbols of an old order that they held responsible for four senseless years of war. Trains were hopelessly overcrowded: he spent his last gold piece persuading a conductor to lift him through the train window to a place inside.

Gone was the sheltered life of the prewar years, gone the feeling that public events were remote spectacles. My father had discovered, as most Germans had, that politics, or the drama of public affairs, had its inescapable hold on private life. The old certainties were gone; apprehension and insecurity about the nation and the self took their place.

Rudolf returned to Breslau exhausted from the war, depleted from influenza, and yet, after a few weeks of recuperation, ready to begin a new life.

In those early weeks, Käthe visited him daily, sat by his bedside, read to him when he was awake. He recovered, but the experience of near death and of nothing but uncertainty ahead crystallized feelings that under less dramatic circumstances might have been dissipated in doubt or irresolution.

By Christmas, he and Käthe had become engaged, and he had resumed his medical studies at the university. They were married in April 1919, first in a civil ceremony in Breslau, then in a church service in a chapel near Krummhübel, the mountain village where they had spent so many carefree summers before the war. I doubt that absent their wartime separation, absent their independent growth and their shared danger, my parents would have overcome the hesitations and inhibitions that their great temperamental differences had induced. I feel that I owe my existence to my father's survival in a world of devastation, that in some way I am a child of the Great War.

A debilitated Rudolf Stern recuperating in a much-changed Breslau probably did not have the inner peace to sort out his own feelings about the fate of Germany. In October, still clinging to some skeptical faith in the old order, he had had no sympathy for soldiers and civilians who followed socialist-pacifist demands for an immediate, unconditional end to the war. The people who had torn off his epaulettes affronted him, and I think it most unlikely that by November he had already embraced his later radical views about the class-driven blindness or worse of Germany's rulers. (Not that moderates older than my father didn't instantly recognize what had happened. The preeminent historian Friedrich Meinecke wrote in a letter of late October about his hatred for "the bestial greed of our enemies," but "equally hot is my anger and outrage about the German power politicians, who through their arrogance and stupidity have driven us into this abyss." Most "respectable" Germans would have disagreed—historians most especially!) But my father was no better prepared to grasp what had happened than most Germans, who for four years had been fed nothing but boasts of German superiority and inevitable victory. And only a few months earlier, Bolshevik Russia's acceptance of a Carthaginian peace and the Germans' almost successful offensive toward Paris had seemed to warrant new optimism.

Years of wartime exaltation and decades of faith in the state's authority had ill prepared the German people for this sudden reversal of fortune. The very swiftness of the German collapse caught them all by surprise—and allowed for mendacious explanations of what had occurred. Meanwhile the country was thrown into a dual revolution—from above and also from below: while the old rulers thrust political power on civilians, among them erstwhile critics of the imperial regime, millions of war-weary and hungry people went to the streets, radicalized by a suspicion that the war had been fought to defend class interests that were not their interests; they clamored for peace and an end to blatant inequality and political subjugation. A social and political order that had seemed unshakable suddenly broke, as sailors in Kiel mutinied rather than obey orders to engage the British navy in a last-minute, probably suicidal, battle while revolutionaries in Bavaria and elsewhere toppled thrones.

Extremists on the right and left had one portentous thought in common: the real, the immediate enemy was now at home. Soldiers' and workers' councils—the very nomenclature reminiscent of Soviet Bolshevism—sprang up, and when their most immediate demand for the abdication of the hapless Kaiser went unheeded, the crowds in the streets grew ever larger and ever more defiant, finally forcing reluctant Social Democrats to proclaim a German Republic on November 9—the very day of my father's return. The Kaiser fled to Holland, and Germany's civilian government handed over power to uncertain Social Democrats and their more radical, fiercely anti-imperialist brethren, the Independent Socialists; the new government dubbed itself the People's Commissars—again the very term struck terror in the hearts of the propertied and the privileged.

By now most Germans yearned for peace—and they speculated that President Wilson's reasonableness would prevail over Anglo-French revanchism. But they were quickly disabused: Germany's civilian leaders had to sign an armistice that for all practical purposes rendered the country defenseless, and the hopes placed in Wilson collapsed. Still, on November 11, at eleven o'clock in the morning, the guns fell silent, the slaughter ended, and most of the world rejoiced. The hungry Germans—the British blockade remained in effect—at least felt some relief. But their new and inexperienced rulers faced overwhelming tasks: to preserve order, to organize the withdrawal of German troops from enemy territory, to effect demobilization, to feed their people, to maintain themselves in power, and to prepare for a new political order.

Perhaps November witnessed a revolutionary situation that partly inhibited the drive to a full revolution. The new "commissars" were old Social Democrats fearful of radicals who might try to seize power as the Bolsheviks had done in Russia, fearful that the Russian pattern of military defeat followed by Bolshevik Revolution might be repeated. True, Soviet agents were secretly encouraging their German comrades, but the danger of the "Red specter" was exaggerated. (We know a lot today about the Red danger and about fellow travelers on the communist path; we know less than we should about the history of manipulative anti-Bolshevism and the heavily funded right-wing exploitation of people's apprehensions.) There may have been millions of Germans yearning for a leveling of class barriers; there were perhaps only thousands who wanted a Bolshevik system.

What Germans didn't and couldn't know until years later was that the head of the new Council of People's Commissars, Friedrich Ebert, himself hating "social revolution like sin," had on the very evening of November 9 concluded an agreement with the only organized force left in the country, the army, by which the latter pledged loyalty to the new regime if it steered the country to a democratic, nonrevolutionary order. The "commissars" of the Majority Socialist wing were reformist receivers of a bankrupt regime. German in temperament, they wanted order *and* change—and in that order. They wanted to establish their own legitimacy with an early popular vote and rejected a possible alternative, that is, using the soldiers and workers councils to impose radical social changes that would weaken their sworn enemies, among them Junkers and business magnates. So it turned out that the "revolution" frightened but didn't disinherit the old elites. The Social Democrats feared the latter less than they did their radical-left enemies, for there was an immediate danger of radicals commanding the streets, while their long-term enemies, the guardians of the old capitalist-military order, were for the moment quiescent. But it is important to note that the Majority Socialists opted for a democratic path—and had far greater faith in the people than did their right-wing enemies, as the former were determined to establish a democratic regime that would legitimately establish a more egalitarian society. Historians have adjudged them harshly for that.

But this new regime, split by widening disagreements between Majority and Independent Socialists, failed to establish its own armed forces, republican in spirit and organization. Hence Ebert's men relied on elements of the old army to maintain the new order. Hastily organized Free Corps composed of right-wing veterans were deployed to crush many local insurrections, and in mid-January 1919 they murdered the leaders of nascent Bolshevism, Karl Liebknecht and Rosa Luxemburg. Luxemburg, a radical proponent of the class struggle, remains a controversial figure to this day, a martyr to the left, a partisan of a proletarian dictatorship to many. One point, I think, is beyond much question: had she lived, she would have become a most effective critic, perhaps opponent, of Lenin's dictatorship.

What a difference those four war years had made! The spirit of August 1914, with its celebration of national unity—itself already elevated into a powerful myth—had been replaced by the deepest discord and suspicion. Antagonisms that had ripened during the war now burst into full consciousness, as a new divisiveness marked the defeated country. All the greater the beguiling surprise that in the national election of mid-January 1919, three quarters of the electorate (women included for the first time) voted for the three parties supporting a democratic-parliamentary order (Social Democrats, Democrats, and Catholic Center Party) even if they disagreed among themselves on major issues. The remaining quarter, supporting the conservative-nationalist parties, made up in fierce or sullen passion for their numerical inferiority. The newly elected Assembly moved from turbulent, radical Berlin to Weimar, its task the drafting of a new constitution. Its first act was to elect Ebert as the first president of the new republic. This simple man—of working-class origin, grown up as a reformist Social Democratic functionary, modest, cautious, and genuinely patriotic (he had lost a son in the war)—was in many ways the perfect opposite of the Kaiser.

Breslau had its own upheavals. When radical groups took to the streets, the propertied classes took fright and organized the *Bürgerwehr*, armed volunteers to protect property and public order. I believe some Briegers and Kobraks belonged to it, while other family members and friends belonged to the soldiers' and workers' councils. At the very end of November 1918, at the height of revolutionary disorder, my mother, who must have had a reputation as a progressive, was asked by the club "Frauenwohl" (women's well-being) to lecture on women's suffrage and women's political responsibilities. I doubt that she did, absorbed as she was in taking care of Rudolf on his return.

Breslau, given its location, felt some national grievances with particular intensity. The resurrection in October 1918 of a Polish state, with its western frontiers yet to be determined, troubled people, as did the creation, to the south, of the Czechoslovak Republic, with some three million Germans within its borders. People in Breslau began to think they were living in an exposed frontier town. Some Free Corps units sought to secure the eastern territories, and Breslau had its share of such armed transients. Again, the greater the surprise when the January elections placed Breslau to the left of the mainstream: nearly half of its electorate voted for the Social Democrats, another 15 percent for the Democratic Party, and 21 percent for the Catholic Center Party. The Weimar coalition seemed immensely strong. While my parents probably voted Democratic, my grandmother Brieger would most likely have voted for a party to the right of the Weimar coalition.

I remember my grandmother Hedwig, called Oma, as conservative by temperament: decisive, practical, and generous. In 1915 she had bought a lovely large villa abutting one of Breslau's celebrated parks and architectural monuments. The house in the Wardeinstrasse was two stories high, wonderfully comfortable for her, her mother, and her four children, with a basement for gardener and general factotum. It had a large garden in back, with fruit trees and incomparable gooseberries; the Poelzig furniture came with her from Königsplatz. She was a matriarch: family and family friends came first, and just as she had been especially close to her mother, so my mother was to her. That villa remained the family home for decades (even if in later years she rented out the ground floor). The house is at the end of a short cul-de-sac: the road ends there—and in a way, it did.

What might their feelings, their expectations have been when my parents married that spring of 1919? I can only guess. Rudolf and Käthe were bound together by a shared and revered past, by common friends, by their shared wish to construct a new life in the face of enormous devastation. (Their wedding coincided with revolutionary upheavals in Bavaria, where a brief red terror was followed by a harsher white terror.) Rudolf won a wife who was at once strong, maternal, and intuitively comprehending, who was tied to her own mother by the strongest bonds. And that mother had been a friend and substitute mother to the orphaned Rudolf for a long time. So Rudolf began anew in a familiar, affectionate home. He was especially close to Käthe's older brother, Ernst, a physician, a strong, quietly self-reliant person. (That Briegers and Sterns were cut from somewhat different cloth—the former gentler, more easy going, more conservative; the latter more intense, ambitious, and vulnerable—was clear; but the occasional family friction couldn't shake an underlying trust and harmony.) It doesn't entirely surprise me that they both wanted a spiritual, that is to say, a religious ceremony to mark the beginning of their life together—and the chapel at Krummhübel gave them a kind of private continuity at a time of violent discontinuities. For the marriage vow they chose the same text from the Gospel of St. John that they had chosen for their confirmations. After the service came a festive dinner, with the requisite poems and skits, mostly written by Ernst (who during the war had married the daughter of a prominent Breslau family of converts from Judaism).

At first my parents lived in the Wardeinstrasse, in the rooms of Käthe's recently deceased grandmother. It was not the most auspicious marital beginning, but given prevailing shortages, a practical one. (I recently discovered a single reference to a substantial dowry—it was never even hinted at in conversation. In any case, the Great Inflation was to wipe out whatever assets my parents possessed.) At the University of Breslau, Rudolf, having quickly passed the

Physikum that he had been unable to take during the war, completed his studies in July 1920, with the grade of "very good," qualifying for a position roughly equivalent to a first-year residency. He visited Berlin to consult with Fritz Haber, that year's Nobel laureate and a close friend of his and Käthe's fathers, and with Karl Bonhoeffer, the great psychiatrist-neurologist who had moved from Breslau to the capital. Rudolf was looking for a regular assistantship with future prospects in some other city. I suspect he was anxiously ambitious, eager to make up for lost time. In the end, he was appointed assistant in Oskar Minkowski's clinic in Breslau. In February 1920, their first child, my sister, was born. She was baptized Toni, in memory of Rudolf's mother. A bright and precocious child, she throve under the care of doting parents (and a nursemaid); she was a source of pride and pleasure in a world that offered neither but was instead filled with violence and resentment.

By June 1919, the Allies, having agreed among themselves on peace terms for the defeated Germany (and having excluded Germans from their deliberations), presented the treaty to the German government, which was given a deadline, June 28, by which to sign it in the Hall of Mirrors at Versailles—the very hall where in 1871 the victorious Prussians had proclaimed the German Empire. (The Allies, exceedingly conscious of history, had done this deliberately. They had excluded the Germans because at the last great peace conference, in Vienna in 1814–1815, Talleyrand, the representative of defeated France, had managed to split the Allies there; they fixed the date of June 28 because it was the fifth anniversary of the murder in Sarajevo; and now Germany would receive its comeuppance for Prussia's earlier presumption in the Hall of Mirrors.) The German government had no alternative but to accept the terms, which aroused in almost all Germans outrage and deepest resentment.

The Treaty of Versailles was meant to be harsh, but, worse perhaps, it was humiliating in style and substance. Germany's territorial losses in the east— including the "Polish corridor" that afforded the new Poland an outlet to the sea and inserted a Polish sliver of land between the Reich and East Prussia— were the most resented, though the loss of Alsace-Lorraine and of all the overseas colonies was almost equally despised. Germany's military strength was reduced to a risible minimum (though with the promise that this was in preparation for a general disarmament by the other nations—which never took place). Germans were morally outraged by the clause stipulating that Germany accept responsibility for an unspecified amount of reparations for all damages that German aggression had inflicted on the Allies. A few Germans urged rejection of the treaty and a last heroic stand, but the military repudiated such futile heroism, and prudence prevailed. Weimar politicians signed the treaty under duress, and German nationalists, who had been largely responsible for Germany's defeat, vilified them for it. The treaty was regarded as a travesty of Wilson's hope to "make the world safe for democracy," or a testimony to the fact that in 1919 people knew much less about the psychological and economic preconditions for establishing democracy than they did thirty or seventy years later.

Germans were almost as one in their outrage. Between November and June, most of them had escaped to "the dreamland of the Armistice," as Ernst Troeltsch called it, the time after November 1918 when they all came to believe that President Wilson would grant them self-determination, generously defined. The reality came as a devastating shock. Even in Allied lands some expressed their doubts about the treaty, none more eloquently or more powerfully than Lord Keynes in *The Economic Consequences of the Peace*. The fall from pride to pariahdom, from feeling strong to being defenseless, would have been hard on any people, but perhaps Germans, with their chronic bouts of intermittent self-doubt, suffered particularly grievously.

By signing the treaty, the democrats of Weimar had to pay for the recklessness of their imperial predecessors, while the diehard conservatives and nationalists who opposed them could bask in irresponsibility, branding the hapless heirs of the old regime traitors. Meanwhile the National Assembly had to hammer out a constitution for this fragile novelty. The Weimar Constitution embodied compromise: Germany's federal and economic structures were retained, private property remained inviolate, and the country remained capitalist; but there were gestures toward collective ownership, nationalization, and workers' rights. Proletarian hopes for a social republic remained unfulfilled, but at least all citizens were guaranteed the fullest panoply of civic rights and freedoms. And a parliamentary system was balanced by a popularly elected president, endowed with vast emergency powers, for it was assumed that Germans, who even before 1914 had longed for a strong leader, would require such a figure. The civil servants and, worse, the judges of the old regime could stay in their posts, provided they signified their acceptance of the new order. This was a meaningless price to pay for retaining power—in fact, a majority of the judges had contempt for the republican order and repaid its meekness with contemptuous disloyalty. The most distinguished democratic jurist of the Weimar period, Gustav Radbruch, understood what so many on the left decried: German courts in political trials meted out class justice.

Thus did Germany experience a thorough change of government without a true revolution—except in form. A constitution can't create a democratic society, and Germany in 1919 was a deeply divided country with elements at both ends of the political spectrum irreconcilably opposed to liberal democracy. On the left, large numbers longed for a social republic; on the right, the officer corps, the civil service, the Junker and agrarian and industrial magnates, the Christian clergy, the professoriate—in short, the privileged elites of the old regime—felt somehow dispossessed and disinherited; some of them gradually made their peace with Weimar, but many harbored their suspicions of the new order and waited until they could once again wrap their own power in the noble cloak of national greatness.

Before and after Versailles, political violence continued to rock the country: Communist uprisings, even when initially successful and violent, were crushed; right-wing groups murdered many republican or left-wing leaders. Germany was in a state of latent civil war, inflamed by violent demagogy.

In the revolutionary turmoil of 1918–1919, German Jews simultaneously prospered and suffered. Certainly they appeared prominently and for the first time on Germany's political stage. During the war, some Jews—Rathenau and Haber, for example—had held important but not very visible posts, but now this changed. Jews were active in the democratic and radical parties; they occupied government posts, and a few of them contributed significantly to the drafting of the new Constitution. They were, importantly, represented in journalism and publishing, in the law and the professions—and in Weimar's great outburst of cultural innovation.

The Fatherland Party of 1917 had already raised pervasive, latent anti-Semitism to an explicit political platform; after Germany's defeat and the Jews' greater public prominence—in almost equal measure accepted and vilified—anti-Semitism became a staple of right-wing thought and propaganda, in some cases *the* staple: German nationalists, despisers of the Weimar Republic, blamed Jews for all of Germany's ills. The prewar antipathy toward Jews—considered to be pushy, cunning, greedy, and all too powerful—had been widespread, but rarely and never successfully built into a political program. All this changed in the more permissive, more hate-filled atmosphere of Weimar. Barriers fell, and as Jews and Germans intermingled more than before, attacks on the former intensified. How were they to understand their new place? Many of them devotedly believed in the new democratic Germany and assumed that anti-Semitism would crest and then decline. A much smaller group turned to Zionism. But then most Germans had to endure uncertainty in those years, Jews perhaps more so.

Thomas Mann had not been free of a certain dislike of some Jews or of so-called "Jewish" traits, despite or perhaps because of the fact that he had married into a prominent family of converted Jews. He scattered a few sketches of rich, decadent Jews in his work and, during the war, wrote his anti-Western *Reflections of an Unpolitical Man*, a covert diatribe against his brother Heinrich, whose cosmopolitanism repelled him. For Thomas Mann, Heinrich represented the decadent Western life of civilization, whereas Germans nurtured a life of *Kultur*, the absolute freedom of *Innerlichkeit*. But precisely because he had dipped into this Germanic underworld of resentment, he early on recognized the political dangers on the right, and in 1922 avowed his faith in the German Republic, pleading, especially with the young, to cease thinking of their country's new order as run by "Jew-boys."

My sister was especially cosseted by parental love, perhaps to compensate for the turmoil outside. Within weeks of her birth, nationalist forces staged a long-feared counterrevolutionary coup, seized power in Berlin, and forced the democratic government to flee. Veterans made up the foot soldiers of this coup, named after its—incompetent—civilian leader, Wolfgang Kapp. For a few days during the Putsch, Breslau was in the hands of the rebels, and the Free Corps murdered Bernhard Schottländer, son of a prominent Jewish family, who had become an important figure among Independent Socialists. A general strike of all workers, not just members of the socialist unions, eventually led to the collapse of the Putsch, though the old elites and some of the industrial magnates had sympathized with the Putschists; they realized that an actual overthrow of the existing regime would bring about instant French intervention. The regular army, the Reichswehr, had taken a "neutral" position, proud of not siding with the insurgents but unwilling to take active steps to defend the legitimate government. So it was workers, and the potential threat of foreign interference, that saved the republic.

But the republic failed to reward its domestic supporters. More ominous still: in the parliamentary election of June 1920, the Weimar coalition lost its parliamentary majority, and for years thereafter the largest party, the SPD, withdrew from power, thus saddling Weimar with the need to recruit, in ever-changing compositions, coalition governments along the political center. The Democratic Party, the liberal-bourgeois party (for which, I suspect, my parents still voted), dropped most precipitously. In Breslau, its share of the vote plunged from 15 percent in 1919 to 6 percent in June 1920. The German bourgeoisie had moved to the right, in anger at Versailles, in contempt for democratic forms. In Prussia, the largest state in the Reich, political power remained in the hands of the

Weimar parties, however. In fact, in those matters that were left to the states—above all, education and public administration—Prussia was to serve as a beacon of progressivism, a neat reversal from its autocratic past.

Rudolf finished his internship, but his search for a medical assistantship proved extremely difficult. Luck helped: in January 1921, by chance, my parents met Fritz Haber in Schreiberhau, a winter vacation place in the mountains southwest of Breslau (the Riesengebirge), where they had found accommodations in a simple inn while, unbeknownst to them, Haber was in a nearby sanitarium—and not in good health. Haber's wartime responsibilities had been heady and all consuming—his position as a scientific organizer for the army was not dissimilar to J. Robert Oppenheimer's for the American army in the next war—but even at the height of his powers, he had suffered private blows: his wife had killed herself (with his army revolver), in part at least in despair over her husband's work on poison gas. And his efforts had been in vain. Germany's defeat had thrown him into a deep depression, and even the award of the Nobel Prize for Chemistry in 1920 hadn't restored his spirits, the more so as many scientists outside Germany objected to the award, thinking that Haber's wartime work had vitiated his earlier triumph of extracting nitrogen from the air. Ever since the signing of the Versailles Treaty, he feared that the Allies might indict him as a war criminal. Of a naturally volatile temperament, he had multiple reasons for depression, somehow translating his country's defeat into his own. Haber was lonely, and he turned to my parents. He sought their company, and my father and he played chess and talked politics; Haber began unburdening himself about his physical complaints; my father noted the psychosomatic symptoms. My mother sat by quietly. Haber remarked that he had never seen a wife who could be contentedly silent for so long. (He had met her before, with her parents, in Pontresina in 1913, and wrote of her affectionately as of an "adopted daughter.") They shared an enthusiasm for detective stories and for the English masters of the genre, Oscar Wallace and Philip Oppenheim. A seasoned mentor, he regretted her having abandoned a promising beginning in the physical sciences, though later did much to promote her pedagogic work. From that time on, he took a parental interest in both my parents.

Rudolf was combining clinical and scientific work at Minkowski's clinic, conducting research on the toxic effects of guanidine. When that work ended in 1921, Haber offered him a position at his Kaiser Wilhelm Institute for Physical Chemistry, in Berlin, which he had directed since its founding in 1911. My father began with an unpaid assistantship under the biochemist Carl Neuberg and quickly moved to a paid assistantship in Herbert Freundlich's division for colloloid chemistry. I believe that my father had only a medical student's basic knowledge of the physical sciences, but Haber must have thought that my mother could help him with the theoretical bases of his research. My father published research papers on blood diseases and on the effects of cholesterol; these experiments proved useful in his later medical career.

My mother was unhappy at leaving Breslau and her mother, but she understood it was a move from periphery to center—and what a center! Haber—as always, finding work a temporary release from illness—was again a commanding presence in German science, as director of his institute and, even more, as a major innovator in science policy; in 1921, he helped found the Emergency Committee for German Science to support young scientists, a grant-giving foundation with governmental and corporate money behind it. He argued that scientific achievement was the only physical pillar left of German strength, hoping as well to restore the international ties that the war had virtually destroyed. (The Allied nations had proscribed meeting German scientists, many of whom in turn wished to boycott Allied conferences.) Symptomatic of his efforts and of American generosity toward Germany was my father's receipt of a Rockefeller Foundation stipend while in Berlin. He also won a Spanish prize, amounting to five hundred pesetas—at a time of the abrupt devaluation of the German currency, this was a ticket to a vacation.

A brilliant and irreverent biochemist, Erwin Chargaff, later recalled that Haber's "marvelously Socratic skill" made Berlin "the very empyrean of science." But scientific splendor coexisted with material deprivation. Housing was scarce, and my parents' first abode was with Brieger relatives in tiny attic rooms in the Tiergarten section of the city. The growing friendship with Haber was the real reward.

Haber was surrounded by friends: his circle included his fellow Nobel laureate Richard Willstätter as well as Albert Einstein; the Oppenheim family with their salon and fabled art collection; Arnold Berliner, editor of *Naturwissenschaften*; and Wichard von Moellendorff, Walther Rathenau's assistant during the war, an engineer by training, a philosopher-economist by avocation, and a man of visionary political ideas. Haber was among those, relatively few, academics and scientists who unreservedly rallied to support the new republic. He was close to the Democratic Party and to many of Weimar's political figures. In the institute and especially at home, he remained the authoritarian German professor, but politically he had become a democrat, very much at home in Berlin.

It was a heady, trying time for my parents. My father had to satisfy two demanding chiefs, Haber and Freundlich, the first being notoriously strict and irascible. Haber drove himself without regard to health or family and expected the same of his collaborators. But when my father contracted typhoid, the municipal housing authorities finally assigned my parents their own apartment, and they could escape from the almost intolerable attic.

Berlin also marked the beginning of my mother's new career. Some parents asked her to teach their three- to six-year-olds rhythmic games according to the Dalcroze method, which she had briefly studied. She followed her interest in children's education, turning to a study of Maria Montessori's ideas. Born in 1870 in Italy, Montessori had developed early versions of progressive education as an antidote to the brainless, intellectually stifling methods of the time. She was an early feminist, defiantly independent—proud of her son born out of wedlock—but became increasingly authoritarian. She was in touch with Freud and, like him, hoped to have an international organization dedicated to the spread of her ideas. Well known in the United States and western Europe, she came to Berlin for the first time in 1922; I doubt that my mother was actually present at Montessori's only lecture there, where her uncongenial message was icily received—children in Germany, she said, were treated like property, enslaved by their families and schools—but her emancipatory message fitted into one of the great achievements of the Weimar period: a liberating, progressive trend in education. My mother studied Montessori's methods and, properly authorized, opened her own Montessori kindergarten in Berlin in 1923. It was the beginning of what became a career in pedagogy; more practical than Montessori, less academic than a professional psychologist, she learned pragmatically, benefiting, I believe, from one incalculable gift: children instantly trusted her. (I once told her I thought that her pedagogic principles were secondary to this instant rapport she had with children; she minded this remark, but in a way that indicated amused acceptance of its truth.) For her, too, then, Berlin marked a decisive step in an improvised career; she had found her intellectual niche.

But there was no escaping the political storms, the legacies of the lost war and the harbingers of new disasters to come. And among the issues that Versailles had left unresolved was the fate of Upper Silesia, inhabited by both Germans and Poles. In March 1921, the League of Nations supervised a plebiscite in which a majority voted for remaining German. A year later, the League—from which Germany was still excluded—decided to divide the region, giving the richest part with the great coal mines to Poland. Germans were outraged, and Silesians doubly so when Germans from this "lost" territory found refuge in their midst. Germans had contempt for the League, to say nothing of their disdain for Poles, whom they thought undeserving of a state of their own. The whole episode was taken as further proof of Western perfidy and reinforced existing resentment against the Weimar Republic.

Still more galling was the issue of German reparations. When the Allies finally presented the bill, in 1921, it came to a staggering 132 billion gold marks, to be paid over several decades. To Germans, this was further evidence of Allied resolve to crush their country and chain it to perpetual impoverishment. The temptation to default was great, but the certain consequence was an Allied occupation of additional parts of Germany, such as the Ruhr. Under these dire circumstances the progressive Catholic chancellor reached out to the best-known financier and political visionary in Germany, Walther Rathenau, first appointing him as minister for reconstruction, then in 1922 as foreign minister.

Rathenau was Jewish, with deeply ambivalent feelings about this heritage — pride poisoned by shame; he was also a fervent patriot with exceptional connections to the outside world. His mother as well as his friends, including Einstein, warned him against accepting the post: a Jew in Bismarck's hallowed office, in a ministry with a special nimbus, traditionally the preserve of German aristocrats? But he accepted, driven by ambition and patriotism. Never before (or after) was a Jew to have such a preeminent post in German political life.

Rathenau shared the chancellor's view that in the short run, Germany had to fulfill Allied demands in order to avoid a threatened French occupation of German lands. In the long run, he hoped, a concerted European recovery program would end German isolation. But his most spectacular, and unexpected, achievement was a treaty with the Soviet Union, signed in Rapallo, establishing normal German-Soviet diplomatic relations, with the implicit prospects of a special tie between the two countries. The practical consequences of this treaty were few, but "Rapallo" retained an ominous ring for a long time, connoting unwelcome German adventures in the East.

While Rathenau remained absorbed in dealing with reparation issues, the German right continued to vilify him; in June 1922, in a Reichstag speech, the leader of the German Nationalist Party accused him of treason. Days later, assassins from a well-financed underground organization shot Rathenau dead as he was being driven to his office in an open car. The country was in shock, for many people intuited what we have subsequently discovered: that the murder was part of a strategy to kill the republic itself. Chancellor Joseph Wirth in the Reichstag pronounced the famous and correct words: "The enemy stands on the right." The immediate response was an affirmation of the republic, and the government passed emergency decrees against defamation; millions of workers marched in mourning for the slain capitalist. Rathenau's life exemplified the partial, embattled success of German Jewry; his murder expressed the country's raging passions.

The next year, 1923, threw the republic into its deepest crisis. In January, the Allies declared Germany in default of its reparation payments, and French and Belgian troops occupied the Ruhr. The German government decreed passive resistance, ordering workers in this industrial heartland not to go into the mines and assuming all attendant costs of such an action.

Successive German administrations had already allowed inflation to creep upward: now it galloped to a unique end, as the government printed more and more money that lost more and more value. (At the end of this unprecedented hyperinflation, one dollar bought 4.2 trillion marks.) Germany was awash in paper money, its value declining by the day and hour. And a middle-class government was sanctioning the bankrupting of its own class: when·most of their savings evaporated, a people who had believed in the moral and fiduciary virtue of saving found themselves dispossessed. This was yet another incomprehensible trauma, made even worse by the sense that material and moral devaluation had gone hand in hand. Sin and corruption flourished while millions were reduced to terrifying privation and uncertainty. People knew that there were profiteers of misery and bankruptcy, and a few of them were Jews. For those on the political right, all the profiteers were Jews, all Jews profiteers. In fact, of course, Jews suffered no less than others: a few prospered, as did some German magnates who built industrial empires out of the wreckage, and some major landowners who paid off their debts in devalued currency.

My parents lost most of their money to inflation, as did their relatives and friends. At Haber's institute, in addition to his scientific work, Rudolf had some administrative responsibilities, including the distribution of wages and salaries at a time when funds paid in the morning barely sufficed to buy the essentials in the afternoon. Once more, Germans could see how public events wrought havoc with private lives and traditional values. This was a trauma without nobility, almost worse than war, and it seemed self-inflicted.

The year 1923 brought other disasters: the brief emergence of communist governments in Saxony and Thuringia threatened the unity of the Reich until the Reichswehr brutally restored order. A far more portentous disruption occurred in Munich, when Adolf Hitler made his first national appearance.

Hitler had been a failed artist in prewar Vienna who had served in the German army; after 1918 he became one of its representatives in the darkest right-wing underground, joined a *völkisch* party, and successfully claimed a leadership position by virtue of his unique rhetorical brilliance. This gifted demagogue, still a citizen of Austria, roused Bavarian beer hall audiences to orgiastic excitement with his outpouring of hatred for "the November criminals," Jews and Marxists, who had betrayed the country to its enemies. He had witnessed the Bavarian revolution and counterrevolution of 1919, he had seen Jews in moments of power, and by now he had come to believe that he was destined to save Germany from this Jewish scourge. In November he forged a coalition between his storm troopers (called the SA and identified by their brown shirts and swastika bands) and military idols of the past, specifically General Ludendorff, and called for an end to the Jew republic in Berlin. The coup in Munich quickly collapsed as regular troops shot at the demonstrators in their march to seize power; the few dead became the first martyrs of "the movement," as the National Socialists called themselves. Hitler himself fled but was quickly apprehended and charged with insurrection. A travesty of a trial followed, in which a cunningly defiant Hitler won his first national platform. He received a mild sentence, an egregious example of reactionary judicial work. Were people more alarmed by the eruption of a nationalistic plot, with its fiercely anti-Semitic message, or reassured by its quick collapse? One point should have been clear: the true beneficiaries of German traumas and humiliations were the thuggish "idealists" of the nationalist right, sworn enemies of the republic who yearned for and promised national redemption.

The republic survived these multiple crises. In August 1923, Gustav Stresemann became chancellor, presiding at first over a broad coalition, including Social Democratic ministers. He had been an ardent annexationist during the war, dubbed Ludendorff's "young man," but in his postwar role as leader of a center-right party, close to industrial interests, he had come to accept the republic. As chancellor, he was determined to restore Germany's place in Europe through peaceful means. His government ended passive resistance and presided over a quick—and, to a non-economist, puzzling—end to the financial chaos: by the end of the year a new currency was introduced, and a trillion old marks could be exchanged for one new mark. In short order, partly by severe reduction in government spending, the new currency acquired legitimacy, and within a few months, American loans gave a new impetus to the German economy.

In October 1923, at the height of the inflation, Rudolf and Käthe returned to Breslau; Berlin had been something of an adventure, but Breslau was home.

Rudolf was appointed assistant to Minkowski, at whose university clinic he now began his practice of internal medicine while also publishing a series of articles on the medical significance of various biochemical processes. In 1925 he completed his doctoral thesis [*Habilitation*] on the clinical significance of cholesterol findings in blood serum and the gallbladder. He was now a *Privatdozent* and thus had his foot on the first rung on the academic ladder, with the right to teach at the university. He combined the usual trio of duties: clinician, teacher, and researcher, and of those, the first was his real passion. In the recommendations of the time, his various qualities were duly noted, but I doubt that any meant more to him than the fact that Haber had selected him as his physician-friend, as had Minkowski. Meanwhile, Käthe, pleased to be reunited with her mother, opened a private Montessori kindergarten in Breslau. To teach young children had become her métier, to find new ways of doing it her special challenge. Given the uncertain economic prospects, she also engaged in practice teaching in early school grades in order to get a regular teacher's license.

Wife to a not undemanding husband, mother, daughter, teacher, and student preparing for a major examination—all that and pregnant. I was born on February 2, 1926, two weeks before my mother's final teacher's examination. I was named after Fritz Haber, who agreed to be my godfather; my additional names were Richard and Oskar, after my two grandfathers.* Bearing Haber's name has meant something to me all my life: a gift and a burden. Also, my first and last name signified different origins: Fritz, after all, is very Germanic, while Stern is recognizably Jewish.

I was baptized days after my birth; Haber intended to come to Breslau to take part in the ceremony, to pledge his acceptance of responsibility, but a sudden gout attack prevented his attendance. (It is only now that I wonder about my parents' kind choice: Given Haber's age, was this a likely person to look after me in case of trouble? And given his thoroughly secular outlook, why him? On second thought, perhaps his absence presaged my own later dubiety about my religious identity.)

In retrospect, I realize I appeared at what must have seemed like a fortunate time: my parents were newly successful, and the country was on the road to sta-

---

*A few weeks before my birth, Haber wrote my father that his feelings moved him to use the informal *du* address: "You and your wife will have to put up with the difficulty of talking to me and treating me as if I really and truly were a brother of your fathers, and I will not have the least consideration or sympathy if that proves awkward for you." Perhaps it did in the very beginning, but very soon he became "Onkel Fritz"—which is how I remember him.

bility—ironically and in large measure, due to an influx of American loans! The year before, Stresemann had negotiated the Locarno agreements, pledging German acceptance of its western frontiers (not, however, its eastern ones); he worked toward a Franco-German reconciliation, and in 1926 Germany became a member of the League of Nations. It was a brief, auspicious moment—which lasted all of four years.

I found an offprint of a speech Haber delivered in June 1926 to visiting American physicians, inscribed fondly "to the father of Käthe's son." He reminded the Americans of the great differences between the two republics: "You live in a country in which personal freedom is the greatest political good . . . Your state exists to serve its citizens . . . But in our past the highest political good was not personal freedom but civic order . . . our state did not serve its citizens but the citizens served the state." The German Republic was burdened, he explained, not only by a class war between worker and bourgeois that had lasted thirty years, but now also by foreign dominion and the destruction of all wealth. Three years ago, he added, visitors would have thought Germany was on the brink of collapse and perhaps a new war. Now whatever government comes to power had to heed the majority's wish to maintain peace, the rule of law, and a work ethos: "Work is the refuge of people who suffer psychically or materially."

How seamlessly the private and public merge! Haber then gave a sweeping account of recent progress in the natural sciences, the prospects for closer collaboration in chemistry, physics, and biology, the need to restore the international community of science: "But it would seem that academics [Gelehrte] find it harder to overcome wartime antagonisms than the people themselves. Old malice flourishes everywhere amid the beginnings of reconciliation. In wartime the scientist belongs to his country, but in peacetime to humanity." Haber appealed to the Americans to serve the cause of reconciliation, to which he himself devoted so much energy, battling the irreconcilables abroad and the sullen diehards at home. He had spent sixteen weeks in the United States in 1902. He quickly grasped the country's special character and extraordinary dynamism. It fascinated him, as it did so many others at the time.

The Anglo-American world was, indeed, favoring Weimar's path to reconciliation: British diplomacy had paved the way to Locarno—Britain had no great interest in having France as the preeminent country on the continent—while America exerted a huge appeal to opposing camps in Germany: entrepreneurs studied its assembly-line production that fed an ever-greater and cleverly promoted consumerism, while progressives of all stripes saw American culture as a beacon of the future, with its films, its daring lifestyle, its jazz, its realistic writers — in short, its modernity and seeming freedom. These had their Weimar devotees, some of whom a decade later emigrated to the United States and enriched its cultural life.

And American loans, most of them short term and therefore potentially dangerous, helped to finance some of the Weimar Republic's most spectacular urban developments and, more important, enabled the Reich to meet its reparation payments, which in turn allowed the French and British to repay their debts to the United States. This triangular "trade" profited a few and eventually harmed many, and it illustrated the pervasive economic illiteracy of the time. Meanwhile, Haber had his own scheme for refilling German coffers: having extracted nitrogen from the air, he now sought to extract gold from the ocean. In the mid-1920s, he equipped a floating laboratory for this purpose, an ingenious if madcap idea, because the gold content of seawater proved to be hopelessly low.

Haber became an ever-greater presence in my parents' lives. In 1926 he invited my father to accompany him to Monte Carlo over Christmas and New Year's as friend and physician, provided my father could get leave from his clinic and his family. This was another instance of everyone accepting the priority of a husband's calling, though Haber assuaged whatever faint feelings of guilt he had by sending my mother almost daily poems from Monte Carlo in his usual affectionate-humorous style. Earlier that year, my father's younger sister, Marga, had married Haber's oldest son, Hermann, a union that for divergent reasons both Haber and my father had sought to discourage. (Subsequently the young Habers and my parents developed close and affectionate relations, so in time their marriage added another tie, even as Haber's divorce from his second wife made him still more dependent on friends and on his "adopted" nephew and niece.)

In 1926, Minkowski retired from the university in Breslau, and his successor, the internist Wilhelm Stepp, was someone my father did not get on with. Hence he hoped for a position elsewhere, or perhaps he would apply for another Rockefeller grant to study for a year in the United States. In 1928, Haber urged the mayor of Berlin-Dahlem to appoint Rudolf as chief of internal medicine at "our" hospital. Haber's long letter included his views on medicine: "I know enough . . . doctors who write the most wonderful scientific works but who can't diagnose or treat an illness correctly nor have the human qualities that a doctor must have in addition to his professional competence. God forbid that I should have to be treated when sick by some famous medical researcher of this sort." Hence he relied on Stern, and told the hospital it would be fortunate to get someone who had a "special and exceptional ability as diagnostician and therapist and thus combines the soul and heart of the true physician." Rudolf didn't get the position, but perhaps the copy of the letter Haber had written for him mitigated the disappointment. Haber also inquired at the Prussian ministry about Stepp, suggesting that anti-Semitism might have been a factor in his delaying Stern's promotion to associate professor.*

In the next two years, Rudolf experienced other disappointments, and Haber explained to him, "If one is a *Privatdozent* in medicine with Jewish grandparents and strong leftist convictions then one has to put up with seeking hospital positions in vain, and one should not allow oneself to be depressed if one succeeds only on the tenth try. With patience one succeeds, but only with patience, except of course, if one settles for a hospital in Podunk [*Wurzach*] that has only twelve beds and no lab!"† I think Haber's view was shared by many Jews of the time: prejudice delayed, but true achievement would ultimately gain recognition. How "leftist" was my father? I suppose by 1928 or earlier he had begun to vote Social Democratic—hardly a radical choice, and he did not become a party member. It wasn't a matter of voting, I suspect, but of his political-intellectual leanings. Rudolf's views had turned progressive-pacifist, and he had already become convinced by then that imperial Germany's chauvinist elites had fatally misled the country. Beneath that judgment was the bitter sense of having been betrayed by those worshipers of power, of their having caused untold harm to the country, to himself, and to others.

My father relished Kurt Tucholsky's brilliant and deeply wounding satires of German (and Jewish) bourgeois life as well as George Grosz's merciless caricatures of German society. I know that he devoured the great antiwar novels of Arnold Zweig and Erich Maria Remarque, which confirmed his own cleansed views of the war. And he read the radical weeklies *Weltbühne* and *Tagebuch*, whose antimilitarist stance and exposure of the prevailing "class justice" under

---

*In 1926, Stepp published a thirteen-page, most handsome tribute to Minkowski on the occasion of his seventieth birthday. He recorded the latter's immense scientific achievements, and movingly evoked his human qualities as teacher, mentor, and clinician, lauding what he had done for Breslau, including the perfect extension of the clinic, with a fully modern auditorium. "Today [this auditorium] is embellished with Minkowski's bust, placed there by his students and friends." Stepp remained in Breslau until 1934, when he was appointed to an even more prestigious post, in Munich, which he held until 1945. That appointment confirmed what I had heard in the family: Stepp had been a Hitler sympathizer even before 1933—and what did he do when that honored bust was removed in 1933, as it surely was? Nothing!

†Minkowski had suffered slow advancement, even though his teacher Naunyn thought him the best assistant he had ever had. Minkowski was a Jew from Eastern Europe—reason enough for delay. In 1924, Naunyn published his autobiography, lamenting Minkowski's hardships but acknowledging neither the true cause of them nor his own reluctance to push him.

Weimar also appealed to him. I grew up with the catchy tunes and the subversive message of Bertolt Brecht's and Kurt Weill's *Three-Penny Opera*, that masterpiece of cynicism, which mocks the pieties of a corrupt society and hypocritical church.

The route by which my father came to embrace Weimar culture was probably not atypical. He believed in a rational, modern, scientific world and he sustained his vision with increasing doubts about prevailing capitalist power and corruption. He feared the power of the new professional army, the Reichswehr, with its antidemocratic inclinations and increasing political ambitions. He had wit and a certain penchant for irreverence. But I doubt, given his friendship with mostly "moderates" of the left, that he shared the fierce cynicism of so many Weimar intellectuals. What these bemused people didn't realize or wish to realize was that their cynicism regarding the republic helped its right-wing enemies, who had already moved from cynicism to bellicose fanaticism.

"Weimar" conjures up two contrasting visions: a time of cultural brilliance, of triumphant modernism in all the arts, of radical innovation in intellectual fields, of antibourgeois transgressions; and the reality of a modern democracy in agony. The two visions were visibly and invisibly linked: the political enemies of Weimar waged culture wars against alleged "degenerate" or decadent art, and the present-day celebration of Weimar culture often misses these linked essential points. Much of what was most impressive in Weimar culture had already been adumbrated in the avant-garde art of prewar Germany, when German artists had had an intuition of a world in decomposition, of some coming catastrophe, knowing as they did about the hollowness and fraudulence of bourgeois life, rebels as they were in a seemingly stable world. So the Expressionists anticipated much of the Weimar spirit. Weimar was genuinely innovative in other fields: in urban planning, in education, in women's rights, in health care. One of the great innovators, Walter Gropius, architect and founder of the Bauhaus, acknowledged that his own wartime experience of being buried for three days under a house destroyed by an artillery shell had converted him "from Saulus to Paulus," had convinced him that artists had to find the means for collective regeneration. In short, Weimar looked differently, built differently, dressed and talked differently from prewar Germany—and its brilliant innovation stirred anger, incomprehension, and brutish resentment, cleverly exploited by nationalist demagogues.

I have always had mixed feelings about Weimar intellectuals, the more so as for some decades now Weimar has been portrayed so often as some sort of Paradise Lost. But they were a shallow lot, with their moralizing politics and their often utopian and simplistic views, pious and fiercely polemical by turns. They were cynical, as Herbert Marcuse once put it to me about himself, because they "knew how beautiful the world could be." They lived off the bankruptcy of the old order and reveled in the crudity of their opponents, arrogantly ignoring the arguments these opponents mobilized so successfully to reject liberal principles and demand a new authoritarianism. Even in those days, such writers and publicists as Carl Schmitt or Arthur Moeller van den Bruck were called "neoconservatives."

Still, by the late 1920s the republic seemed more secure: by 1928 the German economy had reached its prewar level, and in the national election of that year the Social Democrats made significant gains, which allowed them for the first time in eight years to claim the chancellorship. Reasonable conservatives rallied to the republic as well: in 1925 the right-wing parties had succeeded in electing as president Paul von Hindenburg, the fabled field marshal of the Great War—and true to his record of disloyalty, he disappointed his supporters during his first term by discharging his duties constitutionally. Stresemann remained foreign minister and embarked on negotiations aimed at lightening Germany's reparations payments, that is, stretching them out over time, and at winning an earlier-than-envisioned withdrawal of Allied troops from the Rhineland. These were major successes amid economic recovery, but the republic lacked the capacity for self-dramatization, for any persuasive demonstration of its self-confidence. The Weimar radiance, its irrepressible innovativeness of cultural creativity, had no analogue in the political-public realm, which was a lackluster world enriched by the occasional scandal and polemical defamation.

My very earliest memories still touch the last glow of Weimar and of my parents' lives in it. I have some clear recollections of a visit in 1929 to Onkel Fritz's farm in Witzmanns, an estate in Württemberg near Lake Konstanz. What I remember are stables—I had never seen any before—and the open car (a fabled Horch, which means "listen" or "hark"—the same kind of car that Hitler made famous, a fact that after the war forced the company to Latinize the name to Audi) and the elegant chauffeur, Ewald. And I also remember—though the memory may be overlaid by countless later examples of similar moments—that I was expected to have undeviatingly correct manners and, most important, to keep absolutely quiet in the mornings because of Haber's persistent, agonized insomnia. No sound in the morning—but I was used to that regimen from home. My father had the same affliction, and I had been taught that a father's sleep was something sacrosanct, the more so as my mother instructed my sister and me to regard his insomnia (and to excuse his occasional outbursts of anger) as aftershocks of the torments of the war.* I remember Witzmanns—and half a century later, in the Einstein archives, I came across a letter from Haber to Einstein inviting him to the farm in the summer of 1929, where among the other guests would be a young *Privatdozent* from Breslau and his wife, "who is a remarkable woman."

And that she was. I think Haber admired Käthe for who she was and what she did, and he took note of her ever-expanding work. She was an avid reader. She indulged in what Germans call *schmökern*, a happy absorption usually in light reading. She had an early fondness for fairy tales from all countries. Her literary tastes mirrored her style: she had a cheerful, playful outlook when possible, and analytical powers and stubborn realism when necessary. She was the more intuitive of my parents, even-tempered if strong-willed, and sufficiently sure of herself to be content to take second place, to let her light flicker under a bushel.

By the end of the 1920s, in addition to her kindergarten, my mother opened a *Kinderklub*, an afternoon group of children already in school whose parents, often for their own professional reasons, wanted them to have post-school training. The emphasis again was on children discovering things for themselves, by special games that taught them all manner of skills. The children were to develop with as much freedom and self-taught discipline as possible; the principles, which went back to Rousseau and Pestalozzi, were at odds with the traditional German method of learning by rote. The only punishment administered—a subtly severe one—was temporary banishment to an isolated room.

A signal feature of the kindergarten was the *Leisestunde*, a period of absolute quiet, when the children were meant to focus on outside noises—the rustling of the wind, the sounds of birds or insects. From the age of two or three, I attended this kindergarten, expected, I suppose, as the principal's son, to behave in exemplary fashion. My sole achievement came on the first day. When the group was told that "all quiet" had begun, I was said to have slammed my fist down and said, "Nein." The family made much of this brief moment of defiance, I suppose because it was timely and rare. No hasn't come easily to me.

In the mid-1920s, the German Montessori society split into two factions, one loyal to the master in Rome with her new mystical ideas, the other strug-

---

*I minded these outbursts, almost always directed at my mother. On one occasion, as a four-year-old, I went to the telephone, pretended to dial the zoo, asked to speak to Mr. Lion, and requested him to come over and eat my father. A story often recalled in my childhood—and remembered to this day by my sister.

gling to establish a freer approach. My mother was active in the latter group and, with Haber's help, won a major public figure, Wichard von Moellendorff, to head the unorthodox association. In 1930, Haber urged the Prussian minister of education to support the new section of the Montessori Association and thus promote the unique benefits of preschool training. Meanwhile my mother published several articles in psychology journals and, largely at the behest of Haber, began writing two books on the philosophy and practice of preschool education. The books appeared in 1932–1933 and were appropriately dedicated to Haber, who for a decade had tirelessly, even intrusively, pushed her work. At times he admonished my father to make allowances for his wife's work, which, he would be told, was in every respect as important as his own.

Weimar's time of relative stability ended in the fall of 1929. In October, Gustav Stresemann, Weimar's one effective politician, died—at the age of fifty-one. (In Weimar, I once noted, thinking of its other stalwarts dying at a young age and of its opponents who grew very old, death itself was antirepublican.) In his six years as foreign minister Stresemann had gradually restored Germany's standing in the world. Though he scored successes abroad, at home his realistic policies encountered huge opposition on the right. His battle against the right wing of his own party was an unending struggle that took a fearful physical toll. In the last months of his life, he hoped to cap his foreign successes by reaching a new agreement concerning the payment of reparations to the Allies. A commission headed by the American banker Owen Young prepared a plan, known as the Young Plan, whereby Germany would pay lower annual installments but over a longer period of time. Simultaneously, Stresemann persuaded the Allies to accept an early end to their occupation of the Rhineland; the Versailles Treaty had stipulated 1935 as the end date, but the Allies agreed to withdraw their troops in 1930, thus restoring full national sovereignty to Germany; this was Stresemann's last success. What his further plans might have been remain conjecture, but they certainly included revisionist gains in the east at the expense of Poland, to be achieved somehow by peaceful means. At heart he remained a German nationalist but, unlike most others, a reasonable and responsible one. For that alone his opponents hated him.

The Young Plan, even while still in its negotiation stage, evoked a new radical right-wing attack on Stresemann and the republic. Alfred Hugenberg, the most powerful media czar in Germany and new head of the German Nationalist Party, organized a cabal of right-wing parties and organizations to demand a plebiscite against the Young Plan on the grounds that it prolonged Germany's "enchainment" to Versailles, that signing it would be tantamount to renewed treason. Hugenberg's despicable cabal included Hitler's National Socialists, an alliance that at last offered Hitler respectability. The campaign lost steam, but enough Germans asked for the plebiscite that it had to be held, and when it was submitted to the electorate as "the Freedom Law"—how often that word has been misused!—nearly six million Germans voted for it. A much larger number would have been required for its passage, but the campaign itself signaled a radicalization of German politics and a frightening revival of the embittered mood of the early Weimar years.

Days after Stresemann's death, the stock market in New York collapsed—twin and unrelated blows to Weimar's reasonable republicans. The panic on Wall Street led to a precipitous American flight from German investments, setting in motion that unprecedented collapse of capitalism we have come to call the Great Depression. The two countries most affected by it were the United States and Germany; in both, unemployment soared. And in traumatized Germany, the Depression produced despair that in turn fanned political extremism.

Even before the onset of the economic crisis, the National Socialists scored major gains in state elections and in student elections at most German universities. Hitler, who had used his brief imprisonment after the Munich Putsch to write *Mein Kampf* and to decide to gain power by "legal" means, had recognized that insurrections in a modern state would not succeed. His party would therefore use the democratic means at their disposal, meaning above all bombarding voters with endless propaganda based on deliberately simplistic and mendacious themes. Hitler taught his organizers that big lies, endlessly repeated, would persuade people: he put faith in their stupidity, needing popular enthusiasm psychically as well as politically. In the ensuing years of Weimar's agony, he emerged as the sole tactical genius, one of cunning ruthlessness. The Nazi promise was that it would end Germany's enslavement to Versailles, end the rule of the Marxist November criminals, liberate Germans from the Jewish yoke.

The Nazis organized armed units, as did some other parties: the SA, or storm troopers, in their brown uniforms, and the SS, the elite guard, in their black uniforms. They charged the atmosphere with a tone approaching civil war and indeed exploited the fear of civil war to rally support among all classes. After all, they promised a *völkisch* community transcending existing class divisions. Hitler actually believed that Providence had chosen him as the savior of the nation, and the party's presentation of him combined martial and church rituals. In an uneasily secularized society, especially among Protestants, this pseudoreligion had great appeal.

German students flocked to the party, demanding a "Germanic" education and future and the immediate removal of Jews. Many of their elders were disdainful of these students' uncouth manners but thought them "idealists," fighters for the great national values of Germany's past. An unholy alliance, at first unnoticed, sprang up between some of the dignitaries of the elite, in the first instance professors, and the often fatherless children of the war generation. By this time, a new group of "conservative revolutionaries," writers who thought liberalism was the country's worst enemy and who repudiated the imperial past, demanded an authoritarian government ruled by strong leaders and not by divisive parties — in short, the coming of what they termed the Third Reich. My father once witnessed a bizarre prelude to what was to come: In the medical auditorium in Breslau, while the case of a psychotic patient was being demonstrated, the patient suddenly began a nationalist harangue full of violent outbursts against Jews and other criminals — and the assembled students and some of the doctors began applauding.

But in the private realm, my family prospered, if only briefly. By 1930 my father had finished a complete revision of his father's work *The Traumatic Origins of Internal Diseases*; the book was well received.* In the same year, he was appointed associate professor in the University's *Poliklinic*, headed by Alexander Bittorf — a somewhat impatiently awaited dream come true. The very title "professor" carried weight and prestige, encouraging general practitioners to call him in on consultations. He still hoped to become head of medicine at a large university hospital, but in the meantime, he opened a private practice, which quickly flourished. It embraced people of all faiths and patients of private means and those covered by public insurance as well. An influx of people from villages in Upper Silesia kept him busy: their country dialects amused him and their occasional gifts of game and sausage pleased us all.

He had achieved what his father and father-in-law had achieved before him. And his father's friends and colleagues had helped him along the way: Haber, Minkowski, and Jadassohn. He became a physician to all of them. At age thirty-five, and despite the years lost in the war, he had achieved much, though, I suspect, less than he had hoped for.

The annual vacation that summer must have had a special aura given recent achievements. The family went to a simple country hotel in Silvaplana, a village near the appallingly posh St. Moritz in the idyllic and, for my parents,

---

*From 1926 until 1933, he would serve, as his father had, as a forensic expert in court cases, often involving veterans' claims. He argued that if a person who had been healthy prior to wartime service or before the industrial accident developed a coronary condition after it, that person probably had a right to indemnity, since exceptional stress could induce such a disease.

memory-laden Engadine Valley in Switzerland. The Engadine is an alpine glory of lakes and peaks, pristine, with sublime air, a Heidi-land without kitsch, and by the late nineteenth century it had become a magnet for German vacationers, especially German Jews. In the 1880s, Nietzsche had found the divine solitude he needed in Sils Maria, the village next to Silvaplana, saying it was "the ante-chamber of paradise." I never forgot that magnificent landscape; my parents told me that they'd asked me what I had liked best about the place, and I'd answered, "The mountains and the jam." The latter suggests that the daily diet in Breslau was rather frugal, so the great holiday moments could be especially celebrated. For my parents those weeks in Silvaplana turned out to be their last holiday while there was still peace and promising prospects ahead. For me it was the first encounter with alpine grandeur, and decades later, after years away from Europe, Sils Maria became my elective home, a German-speaking *Ersatz* home with untarnished memories.

It was dismally hard for my parents, and for many of their generation, when, as they reached a certain tranquillity in their private lives, the public realm grew ever darker. In March 1930, the German Cabinet, headed for the first time in a decade by a Social Democrat, collapsed; beneath the immediate issue of social insurance at a time of mounting unemployment was the militant determination of right-wing groups, including the leaders of the Reichswehr, to install a strong government, preferably one largely free of parliamentary control. Weimar was used to long cabinet crises; in this case, a new chancellor, long since groomed by the right, appeared instantly: the Centrist Heinrich Brüning, who planned to meet the economic depression with a deflationary policy, cutting back on government expenditures at a time of heightened needs. He, too, was skeptical about the efficacy of parliamentary government, and in his heart of hearts he was a monarchist. In a long interview I had with him in the late 1940s, he explained that his hope as chancellor had been to re-create the spirit of unity and self-sacrifice in the political realm that he had found so stirring and effective when he had been in the trenches as a machine gun captain in the Great War. I was amazed to hear him thus confirm what his critics had always said: at heart he was a monarchist living in a different, unpolitical world. Austere, rigid, and untroubled by doubt, he assumed that people would accept prescribed hardships; before long, the Communists labeled him the Hunger Chancellor. President Hindenburg, a soldier all his life, granted Brüning the use of emergency decrees for his economic policy; Parliament balked and was dissolved.

The parliamentary election of September 1930 was a disaster: the National

Socialists, two years earlier only a tiny splinter party, returned to Parliament as the second largest party. In Breslau, the party had gained 1 percent of the vote in 1928; in 1930 it won 24 percent (the national average was 18 percent). Protestant voters had switched from the traditional right-wing parties to this self-proclaimed non-party, to this uniformed movement, with its demagogic Führer and its promises of national regeneration. As for its position on Jews, it has often been argued that National Socialism was more effective in promoting anti-Semitism than its strident anti-Semitism was effective in assisting it at the polls. In the country at large, the National Socialists scored heavily in rural Protestant areas, but had gained support among the upper classes everywhere. In purely arithmetical terms, a constitutional, coalition government could still have mustered a parliamentary majority, but the time for such a union had long since passed. In Weimar, *compromise* was a dirty word, and by now any kind of cooperation was impossible between Social Democrats, with their working-class constituency, already fiercely attacked by their communist rivals as "social fascists," and right-wing parties committed to their own narrow economic interests and to a defiantly revisionist foreign policy. The Reichswehr, with its special access to Hindenburg, looked upon the National Socialist movement as a possible means for moving to a more assertive foreign policy, with a reinvigorated army, freed, as Hitler always promised, from the chains of Versailles.

Unemployment kept rising, and with it political radicalism; Brüning pursued the economic prescriptions suitable during a cyclical downturn, not during the virtual collapse of the capitalist system. He placed his hopes on possible foreign successes—on a customs union with Austria, for example—or on the formal end of reparations, but these eluded him as well. Some people, Haber included, understood that the election of 1930 marked a fundamental shift in German life; most people, however, remained imprisoned in earlier assumptions and beliefs. Many Marxists, for example, assumed that National Socialism was the product of desperate and determined capitalists, intent on finding a means of manipulating the public. Very few of them understood that the real power of the National Socialists lay in their brilliantly organized pseudo-religious emotional appeal.

Whatever my father's own perceptions may have been—and he would have been inclined to political pessimism—he now ordered his life anew. My parents found a handsome seven-room apartment in a prosperous part of town, large enough for family quarters and his medical practice: the dining room doubled as a waiting room, my father's study served as examination room, and a separate room held the large X-ray unit and laboratory equipment. But the new apartment also had to be properly furnished: my grandmother gave us some of the Poelzig furniture, while other appurtenances had to be acquired. My memories become much clearer with this move to the new apartment; my parents engaged the services of Herr Hecht, whom we would now call an interior decorator. I remember him as a not particularly appealing person, but he drove a dashing motorcycle with a sidecar, in which I once rode. One room was divided in two, the larger half going to my sister, and the front sliver going to me; this minute place had the huge advantage of possessing the tiniest balcony from which to observe the broad tree-lined street below.

And observe I did. Somehow the motorcycle and the balcony merge in my mind with the images of people on the street: so many invalids, men wearing strange contraptions because of their amputated limbs, men with disfigured faces or with yellow armbands (signaling blindness). For me the street was a strange mixture of the modern, with the motorcycle and the cars and the electric tram, and constant reminders of some earlier tragedy. That second-floor balcony and my modern bed—like a Murphy bed, it could be stored upright in daytime—which I thought of as a field cot: how these two "possessions" enriched my fantasy life! I could orate to the crowds below, I could dream of the heroic life, such as Napoleon's marshals led—I was reading about Napoleon at the time.

Herr Hecht also brought to the house three Bauhaus tables—just as later, grateful patients would give my father presents of Bauhaus design. For all the more traditional furniture, the wooden bookcases and the heavy leather armchairs in my father's study, the apartment had its modern touches: it was bright and open, letting in some of the Weimar style, and a great deal of the Weimar spirit.

New friends were messengers of that spirit. The opening of a private practice enlivened and enlarged my parents' circle of friends; patients became friends, and friends patients. The most enduring friendship developed with Ernst Hamburger and his wife (first friends, then patients). A few years older than my parents, Hamburger was Jewish, had received a doctorate in history, and before the war had taught secondary school; he was charming and amiable, though irascible and schoolmasterish when annoyed. He was a centrist Social Democrat, committed to every means of social reform, pragmatic and nonideological. By the time my parents came to know him he was a major figure in the Social Democratic Party; Breslau was both his home and constituency, and from 1925 on, he was a member of the Prussian Diet, dominated throughout Weimar by a Social Democratic and Center coalition. The remarkable leader of that coalition was Otto Braun, a man of simple origin, a Social Democrat from East Prussia and a key, if now largely forgotten, figure in Weimar politics. Hamburger developed a close relation with him and hence became himself a man of influence. Hamburger was a fierce enemy of the German Communist Party, which after 1928 had embarked on an ignominious Stalinist campaign that traduced Social Democrats as "social fascists." And he was to become an indomitable campaigner against the Nazis. As an ex-teacher, he had a special interest in education, as did many Weimar progressives, and he took an early interest in my mother's work. In the ensuing nightmare, the two families became exceptionally close, and at critical junctures helped each other to survive.

Hermann Lüdemann, the fiery Social Democratic governor of Lower Silesia, of unexceptional Aryan stock, was another friend. And then there was Siegfried Marck, again a Jew and a Social Democrat, who early on in Weimar had been appointed professor of philosophy in Breslau. A Marxist specializing in political thought who wrote occasionally for left-wing journals, Marck was a particular bête noir for right-wing colleagues and students. His wife, Claire—as I remember her both from childhood and from later times in New York—was Weimar's "new woman," defiantly modern in appearance and presumption, a cigarette dangling from her mouth; in Breslau, it was hinted that she was dangerously independent and adventurous. And there was Ernst Eckstein, the local leader of a new splinter party, the Socialist Workers, who demanded a genuinely radical Marxist program as against the sclerotic, bureaucratized Social Democrats, and thought of themselves as a dynamic alternative to the Communists with their subservience to Moscow. A Jewish intellectual, Eckstein was a people's tribune, a speaker who had an immense impact on some workers. His wife was a longtime patient of my father's, Eckstein himself a good friend. (I still have the copy of Georg Brandes's Voltaire that Eckstein inscribed to my father in grateful friendship and intellectual affinity.)

The general practitioners who regularly consulted my father were, like his patients, both Jewish and not Jewish, though the percentage of Jewish physicians in Breslau remained very high. Many of the Jewish doctors were friends, too: Jadassohn's successor, Max Jessner, and Hans Biberstein, also a dermatologist (whose physician-wife, Erna, was the sister of Edith Stein, the convert and martyred Carmelite nun who was later canonized by Pope John Paul II). And he had a regular circle of card-playing friends, cards being his principal relaxation, aside from reading. Pride of place was assigned to Skat, a German game involving three, sometimes four players. The stakes were low, the emotional involvement high when he joined his friends Alexander Gabriel, liberal director of the Johannes Gymnasium; Lauterbach, a lawyer; and Karl Hacks, also a lawyer. These *Skatbrüder* were Christian, a fact of no importance before Hitler's rise to power, when they became "Aryan." They continued to come to the house till the very end.

I suspect that my parents' liberal, overtly secular temper was characteristic for a certain milieu in Weimar. In professional Jewish and Protestant circles, religion tended to be a private matter. Prejudice against Jews persisted, of course, and not only among Gentiles. There was after all a lot of Jewish self-criticism, in harsh or joking form. Anti-Semitism was the virulent form of that prejudice, and it showed itself in various ways, often in matters of appointment. Of course, my parents knew of the anti-Semitic attacks on Einstein and of Richard Willstätter's resignation from Munich University because of anti-Semitic intrigues. They had encountered anti-Semitism in all manner of guises and through countless anecdotes. My late friend Felix Gilbert, an exceptionally perceptive witness of the 1920s, recalled in his memoirs "the arrogance and aggressivity with which the conservative and reactionary forces sought to control the academic scene." Those forces fought any supporter of Weimar—if such a supporter were Jewish, so much fiercer the attack.

But there were many varieties of anti-Semitism. Its vilest form was a staple of the nationalist right and was perhaps taken too lightly as gutter politics, unpleasant, vulgar, and, it was too easily assumed, ephemeral. Meanwhile Jews rose to new prominence in most realms of public life. The positions from which they had once been barred, most notably the officer corps, were of less public importance, as the army, no longer conscript, became a state within a state, separate from civilian life. The left was perhaps all too eager to mock and vilify the military—there was much gratuitous wounding of older national shibboleths.

In many fields, Jews and Gentiles worked together. I suspect that while many Gentile physicians called my father for consultation, some would have hesitated. The same situation, if to a lesser extent, obtained in the social realm. My father enjoyed close collegial relations with a fellow internist, Mortimer von Falkenhausen, and regaled us with stories about Georg Quabbe, a prominent Breslau lawyer, author, and patient with irrepressible wit and genuine conservative views, who lamented in an irreverent book that there were no real Tories in German politics.

Whatever silent prejudices they harbored, Christians and Jews intermingled socially. I suspect that most people, especially those in the upper strata, were conscious of religious identity, formal or lapsed; one knew who was who—who was Christian, perhaps even who was Catholic or Protestant, who a believer, who not, who a Jew or a Christian of Jewish descent. But awareness did not imply separation; professional cooperation remained high and so did social mixing. Consider but one Breslau example: Paul Ehrlich's daughter Stephanie, called Steffa, had married a highly successful Breslau yarn producer, Ernst Schwerin. The discreetly Jewish couple had a salon—akin to that of the Neissers of the previous generation—and their regular guests included Thomas Mann, Gerhart Hauptmann, Moellendorff, Adolf Busch, and other visiting artists. (Did the Schwerins visit Mann in Munich? Was there that kind of reciprocity in their acquaintanceship? But then, patrons and artists usually had an unequal relationship. One of my father's favorite anecdotes—he was an aficionado of jokes and an accomplished raconteur—was about the Busch Quartet being engaged to play for a formal occasion at a rich man's house. All is set, including the fee of a thousand marks. The host adds, a bit embarrassed, that the quartet will play before dinner and will understand if they are not asked to stay for the meal. Busch's response: "Oh, in that case, five hundred marks will do.") My mother's family was related to the Schwerins, and she and Steffa were exceptionally close friends.

My first encounter with political unpleasantness, even with some kind of tacit intimidation, came in 1931, while on a family vacation. We were in Amrum, on the North Sea, together with Hans Neisser, son of Gustav and father of Dick Neisser, who was roughly my age. At the entrance to the beach stood a uniformed SA man hawking Nazi newspapers. No doubt parental loathing informed my first response, but that figure exuding hostility, and with his rubber truncheon suggesting violence, became a lasting presence in my mind, inspiring fear and, I suppose, some kind of morbid fascination. Back in Breslau, I saw plenty of these uniformed thugs, singly or when they marched in the street with their banners and their songs. I learned to avoid them.

They were still an unfortunate aberration. Reality was elsewhere, as for example in my uncle's marriage in 1931. Peter Brieger, *Privatdozent* in art history at the University of Breslau, charming, handsome, and somewhat brittle, married one of his students, the beautiful and marvelously self-possessed Barbara Ritter, daughter of an old traditional, Christian Hamburg family, her father an executive of Germany's largest shipping company, HAPAG. The quite elaborate wedding took place in Hamburg, with my mother writing the requisite play, a perfect persiflage about the wedding pair, teasing, mildly daring, with verses from current tunes, including the best-known tune from the *Three-Penny Opera*, for the entire wedding party to perform, parents of the bride and groom included.

What of the unspoken opinions? Did my grandmother feel that the Ritters, with their impeccable ancestral roots, were in some way superior to her own family, of which only the children had been baptized? (The youngest Brieger son, Friedrich, a *Privatdozent* in genetics in Breslau, talented and uncharming, something of a black sheep, had earlier married into the Christian family of a naval officer.) Or was she merely pleased that Peter had married into "a good family"? Some sixty years later, in the 1990s, I asked Barbara about her family's response to her chosen groom. With the quick directness that characterized her whole being, she remembered that her mother had said to her, "I feel as if you have put drops of dirt into a clean glass of water." A riveting metaphor, with its strange sexual undertone, and probably not an uncommon response. Yet relations between the two families were close, and the Ritter parents supported their daughter's constancy in emigrating with her husband when that became necessary—even enabling her to smuggle a Nolde painting and a Barlach drawing out of Germany when they left for good.

Yet another vacation memory: Kampen on the North Sea, in the summer of 1932, together with Ernst Hamburger and his family, Peter and Barbara Brieger, and Barbara's younger brother Jobst. The beach now mirrored the intensified politicization of German life. Each family had its own wicker beach chair, surrounded by carefully constructed walls of sand, and most of these forts carried a flag: the republican colors, the imperial flag of the nationalists, or the swastika. Jobst, in his late teens, seeking to impress my sister and the Hamburgers' daughter, somehow catapulted me into the air, and as I landed on the hard sand, I broke my right wrist. I ended up in the local hospital, where the fracture required surgery: I remember to this day the terror of being placed under an ether mask and having to count aloud while fearing suffocation. (I sensed my father's proximity in the operating room, though, and that helped.) Back home, with my arm in a cast, my mother took me regularly to a clinic where the encased wrist was put in a primitive machine that jiggled or moved it around: the constant motion, which caused excruciating pain, was supposed to help it regain mobility. I called each trip an *Angstweg*—and this became an all too frequently invoked term. So much of life in the next few years would consist of an *Angstweg*. Was all medicine then so indifferent to pain, or did I have an early taste of a then-still-prevalent German fetish: pain as an ennobling experience? The accident had a permanently beneficial effect: as my injured

wrist made it almost impossible for me to write, I was given a dilapidated typewriter to work on, and remained addicted to typewriters for the next six decades
or more.

But there were far more serious *Angstwege* that all of Germany had to endure
in 1932—and of which I got a whiff. Less than a decade after hyperinflation,
Germany suffered from hyper-unemployment amid an economic collapse; by
the fall of 1932, about six million people were unemployed, and many more
were on short-term work. The jobless and their families faced hunger, hopeless-
ness, and shame. Most people fell into a state of collective anxiety, in despair at
politics as usual. Inevitably, the Communists proved profiteers of the capitalist
collapse, which seemingly confirmed a Leninist prognosis. And the fears aroused
by communist electoral successes made conservative *Bürger* look to National Socialism for protection—how opposing extremists aid each other! Even prosperous Jews were not immune to reactionary views.

The country went through four national elections. In the spring of 1932,
two presidential elections pitted Hitler (only recently become a German citizen) against Hindenburg—the field marshal being, this time, the candidate of
both Social Democrats and the Catholic Center. The Communists ran their
own candidate, Ernst Thälmann. For the left and for Catholic voters, the
Protestant octogenarian Hindenburg appeared to be the lesser evil. No sooner
was he reelected by them than Hindenburg dismissed Brüning, who had been
the enabler of his victory, and replaced him with old favorites, contemptuously
called the Camarilla, arming them with presidential decree powers. He was
determined to emasculate the parliamentary system. By this time, Hindenburg's fellow landowners in East Prussia were under suspicion about various
material shenanigans. Defense of privilege and greed hastened the demise of
Weimar.

Franz von Papen, the new chancellor, became the frivolous gravedigger of
what was left of German democracy. By now, the Reichswehr had become the
dominant if largely hidden force in German politics, and with its backing in reserve, Papen liquidated Otto Braun's regime in Prussia, the last democratic
bulwark in the Reich, with its republican police force and largely loyal civil service. It was a naked coup. The Social Democrats and their allies yielded, feeling too weak to call for resistance, but the militants in their own ranks were
appalled at what they viewed as fatal pusillanimity. Papen's pretext for the
Prussian coup was the breakdown of public order, and the summer of 1932 saw
bloody clashes between National Socialists and Communists or between the
former and members of the Reichsbanner, a militant formation of republicans;

I admired the Reichsbanner emblem of three arrows, standing for the great trinity of the French Revolution.

However many Germans were deluded by Hitler or frozen in their ideological commitments, there were certainly enough individuals who understood what Nazism was and in power would be. Kurt Schumacher, a young and immensely promising Social Democratic deputy, put it well: "National Socialism is nothing but the permanent appeal to the swine in man." And in that very year of 1932, Theodor Heuss, a deputy to the minute successor of the Democratic Party and a distinguished writer, warned that National Socialism in power would create a "totalitarian state." There was no dearth of such voices.

In July came another parliamentary election: my parents rented a radio to hear the results and invited friends to listen as well. I felt their gloom, for the results exceeded their worst nightmares. The National Socialists gained 37 percent of the vote, a devastating outlook that was only partially brightened by Hindenburg's refusal to appoint Hitler as chancellor unless he could obtain a parliamentary majority. Negotiations led nowhere. Even in the light of Hitler's successes, many people continued to underestimate him and the success of his Manichean message. The pageantry of Nazism, like the pageantry of Italian Fascism, a secular amalgam of church and army rituals, continued to appeal to a defeated, deprived, self-flagellating people. Hitler, the man of violence, rhetorically dissolved political complexity into a Wagnerian battle between the pure and the impure, between German heroes and Jewish-Marxist traitors.

In August, in a small town in Upper Silesia, five SA men killed a communist worker in front of his mother; when the five were apprehended and sentenced to death, Hitler telegraphed them a message of unswerving loyalty. For democrats or simply for decent people, his penchant for violence should have been obvious. Sympathizers produced extenuating excuses for such excesses, as many would after the Nazis came to power, but perhaps there was also an unacknowledged admiration of force, of the demonic in action? Violence in word and deed has its own fascination, as spectators at bullfights or viewers of Hollywood films would know.

In the fall of 1932, violence was omnipresent in Germany. Political rallies were routinely disrupted and street clashes occurred daily. At some point that fall, a bomb was thrown into Ernst Eckstein's living room, miraculously not injuring anyone. This was shocking news, and I was fearful: I knew who threw bombs—Nazis did—though I don't think I knew where babies came from. (I was treated as a precocious youth in matters political, but sexual topics remained taboo.) At roughly that time, my father brought Hamburger and Eckstein together in his study in the hope that their two parties, albeit of unequal strength, would rise above their rivalry and work together. It was not to be. Ideological differences and party interests prevailed over the need for a common front against Hitler: a microcosm of prevailing blindness.

The next election was scheduled for November. On election Sunday, my father was called to some country town for an urgent consultation. He hired a car (we didn't have one), and he wanted my company for the trip. My mother, afraid of violence and excessively protective of me, opposed my going with him—to no avail. The car had a cracked windshield, which my father pointed out—half jokingly because he didn't want to have to pay for it afterward. The driver acknowledged the fact, adding that on Election Day more car windows would be smashed, so he was going to wait and have this earlier damage fixed then. There were many moments of violent agitation in the neighboring towns, I knew, but we returned unscathed, and joked about it later; I suppose I remember the day so clearly because the whole experience had filled me with apprehension.

The November election recorded the first decline in the Nazi vote, a tumble from 37 to 33 percent (in Breslau from 43 to 40 percent), enough to cheer the party's opponents, who hoped the movement had crested. The Communists, already the third largest party, gained, their strength further alarming Social Democrats and reactionaries alike. But by now Parliament had been entirely marginalized. And the most openly political general, Kurt von Schleicher, was appointed chancellor; he had feasible plans for reducing unemployment and for eventually forging an alliance between left-wing National Socialists and right-wing trade unionists, with the Reichswehr the ultimate guarantor of an authoritarian regime. But within weeks, he fell victim to palace intrigues against him. The sheer frivolity of those months!

My own life remained sheltered. In April 1932, I was enrolled in a small private school called Weinhold, near our home; teachers were addressed as "aunts."* To get to the school, I walked past the clinic where my father placed

---

*In recent years, some of my classmates from Weinhold have written to me; most of the boys were killed in the war. An "Aryan" girl reminded me that most of our classmates were either Jewish or came from aristocratic families (including a genuinely deranged Bismarck, whom I remember picking up horse manure from the street and putting it in his mouth). Another pupil, Renate Harpprecht-Lasker, remembered that the aristocratic kids later behaved most decently when she and her sister were slave laborers having to wear a yellow star. She survived Auschwitz because her sister was a gifted cello player, drafted into the camp orchestra—and the subject of a famous film. Renate is married to Klaus Harpprecht, a one-time intimate adviser to Chancellor Willy Brandt and a prolific German writer; they live in a tiny French village on the Côte d'Azur.

some of his patients, and past the post office, which later was to become very important. My first report card claimed that I was given to "silly and unruly" behavior. At home that phrase would later often be quoted, mostly in jest, but I now wonder whether occasional naughtiness at school took the place of open defiance at home. I was on the way to becoming a spoiled and hence unhappy child, enveloped in comfortable privilege and parental adulation. I wonder what would have become of me if life had not dramatically changed.

On January 30, 1933—three days before my seventh birthday—on my way home from school I heard newsboys hawking a special edition of the newspaper. The headline: "Hitler Appointed Chancellor." I picked up the single sheet and brought it home to my father. As I gave it to him, during his habitual afternoon rest before patients came, I knew it was bad news, and he confirmed it.

That same afternoon I heard rumblings in the street and from my little balcony saw a steady stream of straggling ill-clad men, women, and children marching behind red banners and intoning "Hunger, Hunger." It was a communist demonstration—the last, I suspect, in Breslau. My sympathies were entirely with the demonstrators, who were quickly followed by a band of Nazis who marched down the middle of the street, unfurled their dread-inducing flags with their swastikas, and brandished their truncheons and daggers. The naked drama of the street is for me a scene of amazing clarity even today. Six years later, and in another country, I would be stunned when I read about the German-Soviet Pact: it was a brutal correction to an earlier childhood illusion. I suppose I would have forgotten these scenes if they had not been a prelude to an all-encompassing catastrophe.

I came to know Weimar best at its end—and that is how subsequent generations think of it too. For more than half a century, Weimar has become the synonym for political failure; a democracy foundering or a political system in crisis is quickly dubbed "Weimar," as if it were the generic name of a debilitating political disease.

Or else Weimar is remembered as a period of exuberant creativity, which it certainly was. In the popular imagination, transgressive wildness may have a special place. Germany's astounding creativity and innovation in the arts, in architecture, in film, and especially in the natural sciences marked a new and sometimes discordant culmination of what had been its cultural promise before the Great War. But this very progress—achieved in little more than a decade in the defiant aftermath of war and defeat—made millions of Germans uncomfortable; they felt threatened by modernity. They didn't read Tucholsky and probably not even Thomas Mann; they didn't thrill to jazz and the blasphemous text of the *Three-Penny Opera*, or marvel at the flat roofs and the brilliant lightness of the Bauhaus, or ponder the playful abstractions of Paul Klee. Many of them saw in the incomprehensible but much-publicized theory of relativity a Jewish fraud. They viewed all revolutionary experimentation as destructive of old customs, the godless works of alien, cosmopolitan, and Jewish manipulators. They suffered from cultural shock in one realm and from financial disaster in another, and many of them succumbed to the nostalgic sounds of *völkisch* rhetoric, coupled as it was with the promise of providential recovery and dynamic growth, a return to an authentic, unified Germany. National Socialists hated and ultimately banned something that was truly German and European in Weimar culture: the daring leap to modernity in thought and life.

By chance of birth and family inclination, I caught a glimpse of Weimar's brave political defenders, men and women who placed their ambitions in the service of old Enlightenment ideals. We shouldn't forget that this Germany struggled along through successive, terrifying, often numbing traumas: defeat, pariahdom, hyperinflation, capitalist collapse—all compressed into fourteen short years. For most of this time, Germany clung to parliamentary government, while Italy abandoned democracy in favor of fascism, and Eastern Europe (except for Masaryk's Czechoslovakia) adopted authoritarian regimes. The Germans' was a stolid, often unimaginative defense of democracy, in the face of brutal opposition coming from self-anointed patriots and the ruthless representatives of material interests who supported them, but it was a defense of democracy nonetheless.

At the end of Weimar, I caught a glimpse of the promise of its beginning— and its end was the beginning of my political education. I saw enough to know that men and women had indeed struggled hard against National Socialism, that its rise had not been inevitable. Weimar is full of lessons for all of us.

★

CHAPTER 3

THE THIRD REICH

THE THIRD REICH BEGAN IN TRIUMPH and deceit. On the night of January 30, 1933—subsequently commemorated as the day of the *Machtergreifung*, or seizure of power—a carefully orchestrated mass of uniformed storm troopers staged a torch-lit parade around the chancellory in Berlin, their thronged might and martial chants an intimation of their pent-up hunger for violence and revenge. For many, the sound of those confident goose-stepping youth, dutifully broadcast on national radio, may have recalled the days of August 1914, when the German people had reveled in a sense of unity and sacrifice. But that was only one facet of the new regime.

Among non-Nazis—who still made up the majority of Germans—and especially among the "unpolitical" ones, many may have been relieved that the terrible uncertainty about political authority seemed to be over, that the threat of some Bolshevik coup or left-wing comeback had been lifted. They may have believed what the rightist intriguers believed when they persuaded old Hindenburg to appoint Hitler as chancellor of a government that contained a mere three Nazis and nine conservatives. They may have fallen for the notion that the new government signified the conservative domestication of the populist and thuggish demagogue, that Hitler had been made a captive of responsible interests. "Those whom the gods wish to destroy they strike dumb first," and in this case the willed blindness of the old elites destroyed the innocent ones first.

But even foes and skeptics could not have had "the imagination of disaster," to use Henry James's phrase, to foresee the full horror of Nazism, let alone the speed with which the party would gain total power. After all, Hindenburg was still there as guardian of some basic decency, and so was the Constitution. And surely the *Rechtstaat*, which had existed under previous authoritarian regimes, would persist. Fritz Erler, a distinguished Social Democrat, has recalled that in those days people became "victim[s] of their own decency"; despite the Nazis' violence in speech and deed, they simply could not conceive the full inhumanity that lay ahead. Still, fears persisted: might this mean the beginning of a terrorist dictatorship? The Nazis themselves were uncertain, but they proved to be impressive improvisers, superb and ruthless tacticians on their way to absolute power, waging war against their enemies at home and abroad. They could not have anticipated the cheerful servility of so many Germans.

In dealing with any past—and this past in particular—we must remember the most elementary truth: this past did not know what we now know. It is our task to try to re-create the likely hopes and apprehensions of people at the time, and we must also remember the unprecedented swiftness of events: what some people may have believed or wished to believe during the first days of the new regime became less and less credible in subsequent weeks and months. At what point, if ever, people at home and abroad awoke to the true nature of National Socialism remains a haunting question even now.

At the very beginning of the regime, my family may have, ironically, been "fortunate" in being closer to disaster than many others. They saw sooner, and their apprehensions settled in early, especially with my father, more politically attuned than my emotionally robust and unpolitical mother. She had a cheerful temperament, was protective of her children and remarkably capable of dealing with conflicts and crises, though her amiable preference was to avoid them. And now, given the external political threat, home became ever more important—certainly for me.

In mid-February 1933, in a letter to my mother thanking her for the second volume of her work, Haber added: "The anxieties concerning the political conditions which emerge from Rudi's letters and less explicitly but no less clearly from yours can only be overcome if you accept the inevitable. At the moment when fascism grasps power, it is useless to resist particular changes and especially to allow their repercussions on one's own life to become a matter of painful suffering." But within a few weeks, his own life became unbearable.

The swiftness of what might be called the Nazi conquest of Germany remains astounding even in retrospect. At the time, it was breathtaking. A majority of the people probably welcomed the new authority and those who remained skeptical may not have realized the rapidity with which sometimes hidden lawlessness was taking root. What had taken Mussolini some three years in Italy, in Germany Hitler achieved in three months. The new government called for parliamentary elections on March 5 (the fifth national election in less than a year), and in the ensuing weeks the Nazis dominated the streets and the media, though opposition papers and rallies were still permitted, if often disrupted. Then, on February 27, the Reichstag was set on fire, and the Nazis instantly accused the Communists of responsibility for the crime, claiming it was the first signal of a planned uprising that only the harshest measures could prevent or quash. The evidence for communist culpability? A half-crazed Dutchman with some putative associations with Communists had been found in the burning building. Within hours, Hitler's government convinced Hindenburg that the nation was in imminent danger, and the latter dutifully signed emergency decrees, quickly formulated, that suspended all basic civic rights contained in the Constitution, allowing, for instance, the arrest of any "suspected" person, without indictment or right to legal counsel. These decrees provided the "legal" basis for all the terror and repression that was to follow.

The Reichstag fire ironically proved a boon to Nazis and Communists alike—to the former because it gave them the opening for this "legal" abrogation of all basic civil rights, to the latter because at the public trial of the Dutchman and his alleged "accomplices," Georgi Dimitrov, the Bulgarian Communist accused of setting it, dramatically pointed the finger at Hermann Goering, Nazi chieftain and president of the Reichstag, branding him as the perpetrator—a gesture of courageous defiance that made Dimitrov the hero of antifascism and made it plausible to think of the Communists as Nazism's most courageous enemies, thus dimming the memory of the Nazi-Communist collusion in the dying months of Weimar. Historians have remained divided as to the true perpetrator of the fire, with some credible experts insisting that the single Dutchman could have acted alone and probably did. I have come to share this revisionist view: but certainly the Nazis proved themselves masters at instantly exploiting the unforeseen opportunity.

A week later came the election: the Nazis received 43 percent of the vote, in Breslau, 50 percent. With their nationalist allies, they had a bare majority, insufficient for amending what was left of Weimar's Constitution. Public drama and private terror continued. The masters of Nazi pageantry prepared for what they called the Day of Potsdam: Hitler, attired in a black tailcoat and top hat, bowed to the aged president, attired in his Great War field marshal's uniform, adorned with all his medals, and surrounded by the principal dignitaries of the old imperial army. This was a reconciliation of old tradition and new promise, with the Prussian field marshal giving his blessing to the Austrian corporal's disciplined rabble. Historians have long debated when Prussia ceased to exist; its moral end, I believe, came on that day.

Hitler needed a two-thirds parliamentary majority to gain the legal basis for the four-year dictatorship he craved. In the most statesmanlike manner, he appealed to the Reichstag to give him this authority to rule by decree, to restore national well-being. Decorum was observed inside the hall, but outside, threats of retribution were made, as storm troopers surrounded the building clamoring for the new law "or else." All parties but one succumbed, including, most damagingly, the Catholic Center Party. The communist deputies had been arrested or prevented from attending. Only the Social Democrats—all attending ninety-seven of them—in a moment of memorable courage, opposed the law. After the vote, the true, violent Hitler gave an impromptu harangue, pouring out his hate on the Social Democrats. That vote was the bleakest moment in the history of German parliamentarianism and the most admirable in the history of the— all-too-often submissive—Social Democrats.

Despite the triumphs, and despite the growing evidence of civic passivity, the regime faced quandaries. The storm troopers longed for a genuine revolution, for a time when heads would roll, for greater violence. But the government noted uneasily the hostile responses to Nazi rule abroad, responding with angry accusations of a Jewish-sponsored "hate campaign" against the new Germany. To satisfy the rabble at home and frighten opponents abroad, the Nazis imposed an official boycott of Jewish enterprises: on April 1, SA men were posted in front of Jewish stores and professional offices, including, of course, medical ones, warning Germans—that is to say, "Aryans"—against patronizing Jewish enterprises; in some places, individual Jews were hounded. The boycott was intended to serve notice to the outside world that German Jews would be hostages, objects of reprisal, if there were foreign criticism or boycotts.

This much-publicized Nazi action was far from a popular success, however, and it was called off after only a day. The regime returned to its preferred mode, that of "the national revolution" with a pseudo-legal façade. The façade was all important: as long as everything appeared "legal" and was embodied in government decree, the myriad functionaries and civil servants whose collaboration the regime absolutely needed continued in their work. Strikingly, the German elites, for reasons of survival or advancement, out of enthusiasm or delusion, and with only a few exceptions, submitted to the new regime, perfectly fulfilling their duties to criminal rulers.

On April 7, a decree for "the restoration of the professional civil service" was promulgated; this was a cynical euphemism for an act that purged the civil service of all Jews (a Jew being defined as anyone with one Jewish grandparent, exceptions being made for war veterans) and of any citizens deemed politically unreliable. The law removed—in most cases, retired—all Jews from all public offices, from academic life, from hospitals and clinics, from the judiciary. World-renowned scientists were expelled or resigned. In countless cases, students taunted and physically abused their teachers, while colleagues, in the gesture that defined so much of German life under the Third Reich, looked the other way. Thus did the German Jews' uneasy process of emancipation come to its brutal end. The Nazi aim was to extrude Jews and persons of Jewish ancestry from the Reich. For a while, Jews working in the private sector, for example those still prominent in business and finance, deemed as yet indispensable, remained largely untouched, though they were increasingly harassed and ostracized.

Gentile professors who had openly opposed National Socialism—such as the jurist Gustav Radbruch and the theologian Paul Tillich—were also instantly suspended or dismissed. By May 1933, labor unions were abolished and their property confiscated; all other political parties were outlawed or dissolved themselves; newspapers, magazines, and the radio were placed under Nazi control.

In ninety days, a one-party state had been established and people had been stripped of rights that in the Western world had been thought inalienable for centuries: habeas corpus, for one. But Germans seemed barely to notice, and the regime relied on the double track it laid down at the start: one where the laws of the state still applied, especially in matters of property, and one where the party could follow its own intentions. The first victims of the regime— Socialists, Communists, democrats (and if any of these were Jews, they were treated with special ferocity)—had no practical means of resistance. Some Socialists and even some Jews half expected a return to the old system of exclusion and repression, perhaps no worse than it had been in much earlier times. By March, more than ten thousand men and women had been arrested and the first concentration camp, notorious Dachau, in a suburb of Munich, had been established.

Germans, who by position and their own assessment were the nation's guardians of law and of morality, were silent. Their submissiveness, perhaps servility or fervent complicity, sealed the fate of the first victims—and ultimately the fate of the country. Never before had a modern, educated, proudly civilized class so readily abandoned, betrayed, and traduced the most basic rights of citizens. Why? Fear? Willing acquiescence and complicity? Indifference? The questions haunt us still. There are no simple answers.

My father, a Jewish physician with leftist inclinations and friends, had very early intimations of the terror. Almost at once, the Nazis seized Ernst Eckstein and held him incommunicado; by early May he was reported to have died in a Nazi prison—either murdered or driven to suicide by torture, one assumed. The official explanation referred to lung disease. My parents told me of his death, and gloom and apprehension filled our house. This was but one instance of the Nazis' country-wide hunt for political opponents, who within days were being dragged to underground SA cellars, beaten, reviled, and tortured. Breslau workers marched behind Eckstein's coffin in one last defiant measure. (My mother told me, after my father's death, that he had decided after much agonizing not to march in the funeral procession; he feared the possibility of violence, also of being photographed. Perhaps there were other reasons; perhaps he sensed that a "bourgeois" doctor might not have been acceptable to the grieving workers.) Shortly thereafter, Hermann Lüdemann, another friend, was dragged through the streets of Breslau in a clown's costume, mocked and spat upon by bystanders, on the way to Duerrgoy, a nearby concentration camp. Even his tormentors were impressed by his stoic bearing. In March, the press, publishing pictures of prisoners at the concentration camp at Dachau, sardonically spoke of their "re-education."*

Another "Aryan" friend and patient of my father, Albert Wagner, a Democrat and high civil servant, removed from his office in February, was shortly thereafter incarcerated in successive concentration camps. He came to see us after his release, a changed and silent man. Political prisoners were warned that if, when released, they spoke of what they had seen or suffered, they would be hauled back.† The regime wanted known the existence of the camps, but not the terrors committed therein. In unmistakable if veiled terms, my father

---

*In subsequent decades, some Germans were upset when I insisted that you had to be a village idiot not to have known about Dachau and some of the other camps during the 1930s. Hence I was interested to read not long ago that in July 1933 the celebrated violinist Adolf Busch wrote to his brother Fritz, the conductor, that Germans nowadays prayed: "Lieber Gott, mach mich stumm, dass ich nicht nach Dachau kumm." (Lord, make me dumb [mute], so I to Dachau do not come.)

†I think of Hamlet's Ghost:
But that I am forbid
To tell the secrets of my prison-house,
I could a tale unfold whose lightest word
Would harrow up thy soul, freeze thy young blood . . .

warned Ernst Hamburger, who happened to be traveling abroad that spring, not to return to Germany. The warning probably saved his life.

How quickly fear set in. I remember that one day my father moved "dangerous" books—those by Kurt Tucholsky, or by the ardent pacifist Carl von Ossietzky, perhaps those by Arnold Zweig and Remarque's *All Quiet on the Western Front*—from his open bookshelves to less visible places behind the front row of books. People began to be careful when talking on the phone, lest it be tapped, and one knew that mail could be intercepted. We learned to speak freely only at home or with our closest friends. It became an ever more controlled life.

It is all too often forgotten that the first victims of National Socialism were its domestic political enemies, the brave people who had fought and in previous elections sometimes bested the Nazis; "Aryans" and "non-Aryans" both were rounded up, the latter no doubt treated with special sadism. We need only recall the names of a few of these first victims: Social Democratic deputies such as Ernst Reuter, Kurt Schumacher, and Gustav Dahrendorf. (An account of "life" in the concentration camps for these early victims of Nazism appeared abroad and anonymously, a book called *Die Moorsoldaten*, after a song the prisoners had composed. I read it on one of my family's foreign trips.) These men and women, officially placed in "protective custody"—the very term attests to the regime's cynical sneer—found themselves beyond the reach of justice, and only a very few people in all of Germany protested these breaches of right and law. I have long held that the first test of future German conduct is to assess how Germans treat Germans: if National Socialists didn't scruple to inflict torture on their own people, is it any wonder that they did unspeakably worse to those whom they deemed "subhuman" and mortal enemies of the race?

These outrages were intended to intimidate, and indeed both non- and anti-Nazis were conscious of living under a shroud of fear, with the suspicion of surveillance everywhere, not to mention denunciation by neighbors or malcontents. At the same time, most of the country was reveling in public order. The streets were safe, and open to the party marches of jubilant men and women in uniform. From time to time one heard the Führer's frenetic shouting, a clipped, shrieking tone that his minions from top to bottom sought to emulate. It was easy to deceive yourself into believing that order was the essence of the new regime. Or to find comfort, or an excuse, in explanations that might assuage the few misgivings about certain events: eggs need to be broken to make omelettes; the excesses would soon disappear—after all, the stolid Hindenburg disapproved of them, and perhaps the Führer himself was ignorant of them. Totalitarian regimes know how to mobilize their subjects and arouse their passionate, pseudo-involvement in public life while masking and coddling their actual impotence. Of course there were countless exceptions: public acquiescence coexisted with intensely private soul searching, and people took refuge in what Germans called "inner emigration," indicative of inner opposition and the total withdrawal from the public realm.

In the last "free" election, in March 1933, my parents went to the polling place and voted for the Social Democrats. Shortly thereafter they left on a long-planned trip to Italy (their first, I believe)—to Florence, Rome, and Sicily.* My sister and I were left in the care of our housekeeper and, from a distance, my grandmother. My parents' trip somehow captured the ambiguities of the time: we children were considered safe at home since the regime was attacking only political enemies, and "vacation" already involved plans for escape: while abroad, they arranged to spend the coming fall with my father's sister, now married to Haber's son and living in Paris. From there, they would seek a place to immigrate to. That was a clear, and realistic, plan. By the time they returned in late April, the impact of the anti-Jewish laws and spirit had become all too evident. The law purging the civil service defined much of life. My father, as a veteran, was exempt from the law's immediate application, but he discontinued his academic lectures and met some of his university students at home. His practice grew, despite the fact that some of the public insurance agencies had expelled Jewish doctors from their rolls, forcing patients who wished to stay with my father to pay out of their pockets. A good part of his work consisted of consultations, when general practitioners called him to a patient's bed for "a second opinion." Most Aryan doctors probably ceased to use him for this, but then, their non-Aryan counterparts constituted close to half of all Breslau physicians.

As a professional group, German doctors were early and enthusiastic Nazis: the competition from the exceptionally popular Jewish doctors had always been galling to them. My father told me once that an old-time colleague with whom he had been in medical school now ostentatiously crossed the street so as to avoid greeting him. My father was pained, perhaps even frightened—or he wouldn't have mentioned it, and I wouldn't have remembered it. Even if

---

*At the time, democrats distinguished between Italy—that southern paradise of beauty and culture, an apolitical tourist dream, with its humane people—and its Fascist rulers. But the resolute Mussolini fascinated people of many stripes, certainly most rightists. The well-known German Jewish writer Emil Ludwig wrote a flattering portrait of him (until 1938 Mussolini had no use for anti-Semitism), and even Winston Churchill was impressed. Full awareness of the inhumanity of Italian fascism came only with Mussolini's attack on Ethiopia, in 1935, and his massive intervention in the Spanish Civil War, a year later.

the man felt a twinge of shame, he was merely following a pervasive German habit of the time: one chose not to see, one didn't see, one didn't want to know. *Zivilcourage*—meaning civil courage, an excellent German word but not a German practice—grew ever rarer.

My mother's books, just published, were condemned to oblivion. She gave up her kindergarten and worked at home on her method for teaching arithmetic. All three of her brothers either lost their positions or had no possible prospects for the future: the eldest, Ernst, who had been running an innovative state rehabilitation center for tuberculosis patients near Breslau, found a position at a similar institution in England. The two younger brothers left for London: Peter, an art historian, found a temporary position at the Courtauld Institute and later received an appointment at the University of Toronto; the youngest, Friedrich, ended up in Brazil, as chief botanist in Piracicaba, near São Paulo, working on orchids—one hybrid was named for him—with the help of a Rockefeller Foundation grant mediated by Haber. Both men were accompanied by their Christian wives, who could with impunity return to Germany for brief family visits. The two couples were young enough to start new lives in new surroundings; they belonged to the thousands of German Jews who as instant victims of the new law were "forced to be free," forced to leave.

It was harder for the older generation, whose anguish my family could see most poignantly in Fritz Haber's fate. A pillar of the German scientific community, since its inception in 1911 head of the Kaiser Wilhelm Institute for Physical Chemistry in Berlin, and a veteran exempted from the immediate consequences of the law for "purifying" the civil service, he was left with the choice of staying at his post at the cost of dismissing his Jewish colleagues or of resigning. (In May, fearful of what might befall him and his children, he turned to his wartime collaborator, Major-General Hermann Geyer, who wrote a letter testifying to Haber's front-line courage and invaluable service. But this could not really help.) Like a few others, such as the physicists James Franck and Otto Stern, he chose to resign, though he was too old, he thought, to begin anywhere anew. He had lived for his science and his country; now he was a broken man. The deprivation and degradation induced despair. "I have lived for too long," he wrote my parents in June. He left Germany and traveled in various European countries, finally "settling" in Cambridge, where Sir William Pope and the university offered him a laboratory position, without salary. (Thus the welcome invitation came from the very people who knew the most about Haber's invention of gas warfare.) To his friend Einstein he wrote, "In my whole life I have never felt so Jewish as now."

In his final devastated months Haber found a friend and helper in Chaim Weizmann, fellow chemist and world leader of Zionism, whose vision and personality fascinated him, though he had never been sympathetic to Zionism. He confided to Weizmann in January 1934 that he thought German Jews, so staunchly attached to the German state, would, if conditions permitted, remain indifferent to Zionism. And in the same month, he wrote to my father from his exile in England: "Lucky the person who did not grow up in the German world and is not growing up there now. But the people on the far side of the Rhine will find it harder than they imagine to pay off the debts against humanity that they are now incurring, and your children and their children will benefit more from the sufferings of their parents than we benefited from the well-being of our own forebears."

Haber, a Christian convert, always remembered his Jewish roots, and somehow he had been able to fuse a nominal Christianity with a kind of civic religion, Germanness, and a private Jewish identity. To speak in his scientific language, this was not an easy compound to keep in stable solution, but somehow he had managed to do so, like thousands of other Jewish men and women who had been baptized at birth or who at some point in their lives had decided to convert—until Hitler's regime substituted race for religion as defining a person. Though racial thought had permeated European culture since the second half of the nineteenth century, only in Nazi Germany did "race" supersede religion by decree, did "blood," not baptism, become dispositive.

Before 1933, I didn't even know about my Jewish roots. But then, at some point very shortly after Hitler's accession to power, in one of my verbal fights with my sister, I dredged up some anti-Semitic epithet and threw it at her. Instantly, I was summoned to my father's study, a rare event in itself. I wish I could remember exactly what he said to me, but I know I left his study aware of our Jewish origins and ashamed of having abused my sister in that manner, my father's severe reprimand serving simultaneously as an astounding revelation. The full significance of this dawned on me only in the following weeks. My earlier fear of Nazis had come merely from my associating them with violence and power. After all, even a child could intuit that just about any decent person could fall victim to that violence: one didn't have to be Jewish. Now I saw it differently. Barely seven years old, I began to be at least partially, blessedly enlightened. I began to have some sense of who I was—and, gradually, of who I was not.

My father and mother had somewhat divergent inclinations. My mother had a genuine feeling for the Christian significance of Advent, Christmas, and

Easter, or at least she found the Protestant rites the only way of expressing her religious feelings; I suppose she was something like a Christian deist. But my father had become more defiantly secular during the Weimar years, appalled that the churches were so manifestly anti-Semitic, and he was a devotee of Jewish jokes that ridiculed with equal zest Jewish and Christian pretensions. For me these were unforgettable, and they colored my sense of things. Here is one peerless example remembered from my childhood:

Two Germans on vacation in Italy meet at their modest hotel, discover their common interests, go on long and reverential walks together—in short, delight in each other's company. On the last evening of their holiday they celebrate their chance encounter with a bottle of vintage wine. One of them says, "This has been so special! I want to tell you something now, in all candor: I'm Jewish." The other, a Christian, replies, "I, too, want to be equally candid. I'm a hunchback."*

Now I was learning that I was not Aryan, a term that meant nothing to me. At some point I may have equated *Aryan* with *Christian*, thinking of both as categories I didn't belong to. And in response to what I was now seeing around me, I began to feel I was not German. In today's language, one would say I was uncertain about my identity. I lived in a state of ambiguity, as befit someone who was officially defined negatively, that is, as non-Aryan. So the world was conspiring to make me particularly conscious of my attachment to and responsibilities for my family, at once a blessing and a burden. And then there was always a flight to fantasyland. In time I was able to form or imagine other attachments. Meanwhile, most of my cousins remained quite ignorant of their Jewish "blood," and indeed a myth arose among some of them that the reason they and their families had to leave Germany was that their aunt "Kate," my mother, had married a Jewish doctor.

As a small child, I had been taught to say prayers at night, and I had read a children's version of the Old and New Testaments. The holidays we celebrated had always been the Christian ones, Christmas and Easter, even if we noted

---

*Another classic example also concerns a holiday tale: A pastor and a rabbi are old friends and spent many vacations together. On one of these, in the mountains, they lose their way as darkness falls, stumble along, and then finally see the light of a peasant hut. They knock, enter, and explain their predicament to the peasant woman, who welcomes them. She explains that alas she has nothing to offer except some fish. In time, she comes with a plate containing one glorious, big and one scrawny, small trout. Pastor and rabbi take turns refusing to help themselves first, until finally the rabbi takes the big one. Says the pastor, "You know, I don't have an anti-Semitic bone in my body, but none of us could have done that." Rabbi: "Done what?" Pastor: "Taken the big one." "What would you have done?" asks the rabbi. "Taken the smaller one, of course," the pastor said. "But that's what you *have!*" the rabbi replied.

them more with secular glamour than with religious devotion, along with Advent, with its wreath and candles, and St. Nicholas's Day. On one or two occasions a dressed-up St. Nicholas would thump into the kids' rooms, gruffly ask my sister and me whether we had been good, and then give us nuts and apples from his big sack. By Christmas Eve, the tree would be in place in the living room, and decoration of the tree—chocolate *Kringel*, apples, and of course candles—was a family affair, with Oma and often Hanna Landmann, an "Aryan" ex-girlfriend of Uncle Peter's, participating as well. (Hanna Landmann was a bit too fervently religious for my taste, but she behaved admirably in the ever-worsening days for non-Aryans after we left.)

At this point in the pre-Christmas festivities, and before Toni and I were allowed into the living room with the lighted tree and a table of gifts for each of us, my father would take me into his study and there he would read to me: most memorably, Heine's poems. And he would read his favorite passages from *Germany: A Winter's Tale*, that lyrical, ironic account of Heine—this baptized Jew living in French exile, with his love of Germany and the German language, with his witty denunciation of Prussian oppression—returning briefly to German lands. At my request, he would read "The Two Grenadiers" over and over again, the poem about Napoleon's faithful soldiers after his defeat. I learned some of those lines by heart, and remember them still. At other times my father and I read an old family Bible, a beautiful mid-nineteenth-century Old Testament with Gustav Doré's dramatic illustrations: the one of Samson tearing down the temple left a strong impression on me. We also read the ballads of Theodor Fontane and the lyrics of Conrad Ferdinand Meyer.

After this non-Christian, male interlude, with its mockery of things German, my father would rejoin the other adults, and they would light the candles on the tree; only then were my sister and I called in. We would stand around the tree and sing the traditional carols; then my sister and I would be taken by the hands and led to the tables where our gifts had been placed: a toy or two, a book, a plate of sweets, including much-cherished marzipan. We of course had prepared presents for our parents, mostly things we made ourselves, primitively woven things or cut-out paper decorations. After all the presents had been inspected (I don't think they were wrapped), the candles were blown out (there was always a bucket of water next to the tree), and we went into the dining room for Christmas Eve supper—festive but relatively meager: the inevitable carp and usually a dessert of *Weingelée*. The Christmas goose came the next day, along with poppy seed cake and *Zitronencreme*, a lemon mousse. Once, among the Christmas gifts from grateful patients (including colleagues, whose illnesses, whether of self or family, my father regularly treated as a matter of collegial friendship), had been an entire deer, which had to be parked on the balcony; then venison took the place of goose.

Now this pleasantly ambivalent life changed radically. My parents, apprehensive, became determined to emigrate. In September my father received a letter, in somewhat stilted handwriting, from his wartime superior, Captain Hardinac von Hatten. Hatten recalled that he had become Stern's commanding officer in July 1916 at the beginning of the Battle of the Somme, and that Stern remained in his service until September 1917: "For his [Stern's] exemplary courage at the Somme and his commitment to duty, he was promoted to lieutenant of the reserve, and after the battle of Arras in the spring of 1917, I successfully recommended him for an Iron Cross, First Class. If every soldier of the German army had fulfilled his duty to the fatherland as loyally and courageously in the foremost position as Lieut. Stern did under my command 1916–1917, we would have been spared the shame of the last fourteen years," he wrote. Hatten could not have conceived of anyone *not* thinking of Weimar (or the postwar era) as a "shame" (the very word was standard Nazi rhetoric); my father and I cited the phrase time and again in the next decades, cherishing the ironic inappropriateness. Had my father asked for this testimony? It is possible, but equally possible that Hatten on his own believed that his testimonial might serve as a kind of preemptive protection for his lieutenant. This was a kind of decency—and there were decent Germans, just as there were many Jews who believed that their service in the Great War would protect them.

That same month my parents left for Paris to stay with Hermann Haber and his family. It is often forgotten that, at the time, France was uniquely hospitable to refugees from Hitler; the government's invocation of France's proud tradition of granting asylum to political exiles echoed popular sentiment. (All too soon, French attitudes changed.) My father had been encouraged to hope for a medical position in French North Africa, specifically in Tunis; Fritz Haber had told him that in June, Chaim Weizmann had talked with the French education minister, Anatole de Monzie, about the possibility of Jewish doctors who had been dismissed from their positions in Germany entering French services in Tunisia. (In the aftermath of Haber's departure from Berlin and life in exile, he and Weizmann became close friends, a tribute to Haber's self-critical realism and Weizmann's magnanimity.) On October 6, Monzie, at Weizmann's behest, received my father and Hermann Haber, assuring them that the chances of such a position in Tunis looked "very promising." On the same day, Marga Haber wrote to Weizmann to say she was "overjoyed" at this news, and my father appended a grateful note: "At a time when human meanness and brutality celebrate their greatest orgies, the efforts of true humanity and benevolence are felt with particular force. I would think myself fortunate if sometime in the future I could prove my gratitude through actual deed." While waiting for the Tunis promise to be realized, my father worked as a volunteer physician at the Hôtel Dieu, that ancient famous hospital near Notre Dame.

My sister and I were left in Breslau, under the care of our grandmother and our maid. After a normal grippe, I contracted a serious case of nephritis, and a pediatrician colleague of my father's took care of me. I remember being in bed, spoiled, reading a great deal, including an illustrated children's edition of the Old and New Testaments. I developed a great liking for the books of a particular publisher; their pleasing smell I can still recall. On several occasions, Onkel Pu Jadassohn visited, diverting me by teaching me what he called mirror writing. But then the disease suddenly reached a critical point, indicating that my kidneys were barely functioning. My parents, duly informed, instantly returned, arriving in the middle of the night.

My father quickly gave me a transfusion of his own blood that very night. He then ordered several days of strict fasting, a deprivation the other doctor had been unwilling to impose; a few days later I was made to drink buckets of light tea. (This was a procedure called a Volhard Push, after the well-known internist who had devised it; his name will reappear.) My kidneys began to function again. Gradually, I recovered. The experience of having had a serious illness from which I was saved by my own doctor father may have been the origin of my excessive veneration for the white coat or, put more precisely, for the exceptional person wearing it. But it may also have left me with an excessive anxiety about illness, encouraged by my father's worries.

My illness had a life-altering, beneficent consequence: after an interval for recuperation, we all left for Paris on the Nord-Express sleeper from Berlin to the Gare du Nord, my father and I sharing a compartment. As we cleared Brussels, we broke into singing "La Marseillaise" and the "Internationale"—the latter having been a socialist hymn of freedom before it became a communist battle song. We stayed with the Habers in Neuilly-sur-Seine, a comfortable suburb, and though still mostly confined to bed, I was happy. I enjoyed playing with my three cousins; I picked up some French and could pronounce nonsense words with a decent French accent. I learned a French card game in which speed was decisive, and remember my pleasure when a French friend of the family called me *cochon* because of some quick and successful move I had made. I most especially remember the sharp noise of Hermann cutting the baguette, a thrice-daily prelude to the family meals. My parents came to know several of Haber's friends, most notably the families of Jean Mercier, a French engineer-inventor, and of Joseph Blumenfeld, an industrial chemist, whose wife, Russian-born like him, was Chaim Weizmann's sister-in-law. The Merciers and Blumenfelds became our close family friends a few years later—in the United States.

For my parents, the Paris sojourn was grim, for the work at the Hôtel Dieu was ephemeral, and Tunis became less and less certain. In mid-December, my father's sister reported to Weizmann that various friendly persons had advised her that only the intervention of the French Foreign Office could effect a favorable response in Tunis, and she asked for his help. She added that her brother would otherwise have to "return to the horrible country . . . which I think would endanger his life." Weizmann used his good offices, but in the end, Monzie replied that the French doctors in Tunis objected to the "flood" of refugee doctors in their midst. I believe that all of three or four German Jewish physicians had already sought refuge there.

In late January 1934 my parents and the young Habers traveled from Paris to Basel to see Fritz Haber, who came to meet them from his unhappy exile in Cambridge in order to discuss everyone's plans for the future. By this time, thanks to his disillusion with assimilation, his developing close relationship with his fellow chemist Weizmann, and his confidence in Weizmann as a great leader of men, Haber was planning a trip to Palestine. They all talked together, Haber talked to each individually, and then he retired to his room. Minutes later, he called for my father: a massive heart attack ended his life—a year after Hitler's accession to power almost to the day.

The funeral took place in Basel, and Haber's best friend, Richard Willstätter, spoke at the graveside. The German press barely mentioned the death, but the news traveled quickly, and Wichard von Moellendorff immediately wrote a letter of condolence to my mother, because both he and she had been especially close to Haber. He regarded Haber's death as a kind of benign liberation. So great a man could not have survived, for he was "a victim of this time . . . at this collapse of all decency he would have had to lose his equanimity, and we who were his friends saw him even now . . . stumbling desperately. Impossible to see him . . . as the mutilated prisoner of his own nature. I for one feel he deserves the peace of complete unconsciousness." I have recently found an unpublished letter of Einstein to his first wife, Mileva, remarking that of course he knew of Haber's death: "How the pigs in Berlin have rewarded his achievements. During the war, of course, they could use him." To Hermann and Marga, Einstein wrote: "Haber was of all my friends the intellectually broadest and most stimulating and the one ever readiest to help."

Even before the families returned from Basel, my sister and I heard the shocking news. Onkel Fritz had been a central person in my own little universe, a kind of revered guardian, and I knew this was a devastating blow to both families. My bereft parents had lost a paternal friend, adviser, and protector, and we were engulfed in gloom. For the moment, all hopes vanished, and in dismay, my parents decided we should return to Breslau. (I know of other German Jews who returned from exile in 1934 assuming that the worst was over. But this was not the case of my parents, for whom it was clearly an interim step.)

Before our departure from Paris, probably on my eighth birthday, my father, ending what had been a virtual house arrest to allow for my complete recovery, took me on a tour of Paris: the Arc de Triomphe and the Champs Elysées, the Place de la Concorde, Napoleon's tomb, Notre Dame. Earlier I had been given a splendid children's book, Le grand Napoléon des petits enfans [sic], which I read with delight and still treasure. It had been the beginning of my infatuation with the Napoleonic legend, and with France.

We were still in Paris on February 6 when right-wing groups — taking advantage of public outrage at the so-called Stavisky scandal, concerning a Jewish émigré embezzler with shady links to centrist politicians — took to the streets and provoked a bloody confrontation on the Place de la Concorde, across the river from the Chamber of Deputies. Several people were killed and fifteen hundred were injured. The image of upturned buses on the Place de la Concorde and the chaos left a vivid impression. Still, the republic survived. Later in February, after we had left France to return to Breslau and when I was still afflicted with an extravagant case of Francophilia, I wrote my first political letter, a plea that we should be allowed to stay in that great and beautiful country. The letter, alas, was addressed to a member of the government named Pierre Laval. Right instinct, wrong person — to whom, needless to say, it was never delivered. (My parents did send it to the Hamburgers, who had settled in Paris.)

On our return, we faced an enormous contrast between public order and private worry. Germany had an air of uniformed normality: the political opposition had been imprisoned and silenced; economic conditions had improved; every success was pompously celebrated as public triumph. The Nazis had instituted a year-long Arbeitsdienst, or compulsory labor service, at once reducing unemployment and promoting a sense of national purpose. (The idea had been adumbrated by Walther Rathenau, and Schleicher had been close to implementing it a year earlier.) We have come to accept the term *Gleichschaltung* as meaning enforced conformity; more likely, many people, especially "unpolitical" Germans relieved to have decisions made for them, freely accommodated themselves to the new regime—and for the rest there were whispered jokes about the top Nazis, the fat, bemedalled Hermann Goering and the club-footed, promiscuous Josef Goebbels. I remember the jokes but I remember more clearly the varying degrees of unease and gloom in the house and among friends.

A few weeks after our return, my mother received a letter from Richard Willstätter that well expressed some of the different responses to German conditions. He was pleased that our family had settled back well: "We shall today be aliens in our own home [*Heimat*], as on foreign soil we would really be. But at home there is still so much connection that we can't easily be deprived of." My father's dedication to his calling as a physician, Willstätter believed, would or should become a kind of happy and complete immersion, a compensation for what had been lost. He could close himself off from "diseases of nations and the age," seeing in his "vocation in Breslau something more valuable and fulfilling than anything new in foreign countries." Willstätter's own research was progressing better and more happily than for many years past. And then he added: "It seems to me that in many places, in Nürnberg, Mannheim, Frankfurt, for example, Jews managed things badly in the last decades; affluence, opulence, also often immodesty, they often become soft. One must hope that the catastrophe of our time has its good side." (A year later he wrote to my mother again on other matters, adding that he was glad she had passed her driving test and that there was now a family car, "which in your case is no luxury and I would rather you have it than all the Aryans.")

There were no particular difficulties when I returned to school after an absence of half a year. I suspect the teachers would have understood the reasons for our prolonged stay abroad. In those early months, many German Jews (of whatever faith!) were leaving Germany; some returned, as we did. Father's practice revived rather quickly, with the same mix of Aryan and non-Aryan patients as before, if with far less contact with Aryan doctors. And oddly enough, some of my father's clinical papers continued to be published in leading medical journals. That spring he was invited to give a paper in Brussels at an international congress on some aspect of the traumatic origins of internal disease. (The rest of the German delegation, away from German soil, treated him courteously.) And my mother was invited to give a paper in Berne on her method of teaching arithmetic. Every foray abroad lifted the family mood; spiritually we already lived in exile.

At about that time, I was given two rabbits to care for; we kept them in a crate in the backyard of our apartment building. One day, I found swastikas scrawled on the crate. Terribly upset, I told my parents that my rabbits shouldn't have to live under swastikas, so they were taken to the safety of my grandmother's garden. In retrospect, I see this as an unconscious, not-so-subtle message to my parents.

Public order and tight censorship hid the ever-intensifying conflicts within the regime. The conservatives who had put Hitler in power, notably Franz von Papen, now deputy chancellor, and his friends, grew worried about the pros-pect of further radicalization of the regime. In veiled language, Papen publicly warned against a second revolution—but that was the very goal that the million-strong SA yearned for. They sought more power, hoping for a merger with the Reichswehr, which in turn desperately opposed any diminution of its authority.

On June 30, the public learned of Hitler's "solution": in "the night of the long knives," Himmler's SS, the Nazis' elite guard, liquidated the top leader-ship of the SA. Hitler took full responsibility, claiming, as he had in the case of the Reichstag fire, that he had saved the nation from a great conspiracy: he also had General von Schleicher killed (as well as his wife) and General von Bre-dow. At random, various other nonpolitical people, including Jews, were also murdered.* Within days, President Hindenburg, that much-venerated, if fee-ble, guarantor of some ultimate shred of decency, thanked Hitler for his deci-sive action. And the high command of the Reichswehr accepted the price of their seeming victory—the murder of two of their own; this was unprecedented in army history. The army believed itself to be the very embodiment of honor yet traduced that honor time and again.

By moving against his own paladins, Hitler had most startlingly demon-strated his cold-blooded ruthlessness and his ambition to achieve total power. He was duly rewarded: after Hindenburg's death at the age of eighty-seven on August 2, the army took a personal oath of loyalty to Führer and chancellor, a fateful oath to which the morally bankrupt army leadership clung to the last. And Hindenburg's funeral was a brilliantly staged evocation of past glory. Nazi pageantry was unfailingly impressive.

I remember the excitement of those days and the liquidation of the SA leaders, including the Nazi chief of police in Breslau, Edmund Heines, a par-

---

*Somehow I learned at the time that in Munich an innocent music teacher named Willy Schmid was killed, having been mistaken for an anti-Nazi journalist by the same name. During the writing of this book, the most appealing widow of the great physicist Victor Weisskopf sent me a private memoir: she is the daughter of the mistakenly murdered man!

ticularly brutal and abhorrent man. We rejoiced at his death. (My mother tried to hide newspapers from me, lest I stumble across the more or less explicit references to the fact that some of the slain chieftains had been caught at moments of homosexual indulgence.) We assumed, as did many foreigners, that this great purge, as it came to be called, was a sign of the regime's weakness. The very opposite was true: a million foot soldiers had been subordinated to the disciplined fanatics of Himmler's SS. (In its inexhaustible cynicism, the Breslau regime soon thereafter renamed our street Strasse der SA. What a compensation for the faithful, shorn of its leaders and power!)

We now know that this was the moment when Stalin fully recognized Hitler's demonic character. Felix Gilbert, a wonderfully sensitive German American historian, already then in exile, wrote anonymously in an Austrian newspaper about his return visit to Germany in the summer of 1934: "I don't know how else to put it, but it is as if a people is beginning to lose 'its soul.'" It was a melancholy diagnosis: most people didn't recognize what was happening; others, filled with disgust, rejected the very notion that such a soul even existed. I think Gilbert caught perfectly what my family felt: we were living in a soulless country.

There was another murder that year. In October, King Alexander of Yugoslavia was murdered as he disembarked in Marseilles for a visit to France. Foreign minister Louis Barthou was accidentally shot as well, and in the ensuing chaos was left to bleed to death on the street. Barthou, a man of impeccable conservative conviction, had grasped the new German threat and had been trying to build up an East European alliance against it, including the Soviet Union. Perspicacious conservatives such as he were hard to come by in the early 1930s, and his death served the fascist cause well. He should be on that long list of men and women of whom one might speculate: had they but lived . . .

I was learning about the contingency of history early on, witnessing the accidents that eased the Nazis' path to ever-greater power. I was encouraged by my father to be attuned to public drama, and the world was charged with danger and excitement. Of course I had my normal private worries, but they have faded from memory. The drama of politics impinging on our lives and the lives of our friends was dominant. I lived prematurely on the threshold of an adult world. Even in my sheltered private school, on special days we were made to listen to the radio, as in January 1935, when the people of the Saarland, in accordance with a provision of the Versailles Treaty, had to vote on whether to remain under the control of the League of Nations or return to Germany. Amid immense fanfare, the radio reported that 90 percent of the people had chosen to return to Germany, that is, to accept Nazi rule. I remember feeling sad, though I had to hide that response in public.

Every success like this one emboldened Hitler and solidified his support at home. The Saar plebiscite was the last of his "legal" victories, where he merely plucked the fruits of a prior international agreement. Two months later, he addressed the Reichstag to announce to thundering applause that in defiance of the Versailles Treaty, Germany would reintroduce military conscription; as justification he claimed that a recent Franco-Soviet treaty violated the Locarno treaties. Simultaneously he offered various peace proposals, but that this was a decisive step toward open rearmament should have been unmistakable. Germany's military preparations became obvious: I could see the army searchlights illuminating the night sky in training for some future war with attendant air raids. Later there were blackouts. One had to be blind not to see the signs of warlike activity; most people didn't wish to see. (A joke captures the moment: A class in school practices an air raid drill: when the teacher gives the pre-arranged signal, all the pupils are to crouch under the tables and desks. The signal is given, and all but Moritz, the one Jewish kid, do as they are told. Furious, the teacher asks him why he has disobeyed: "I wanted to show you that even among Jews there are heroes.")

By chance, my parents planned a spring holiday in 1935, in Orselina, a mountain village above Locarno, overlooking Lake Maggiore, where a Swiss colleague of my father's had a hospitable sanitarium. Down the lake, just south of the Italian border, was Stresa, where, in mid-April, the leaders of Italy, France, and Britain—the signatories of the Locarno treaties—deliberated on how to respond to Hitler's challenge. I heard the welcoming shots across the lake marking the arrival of the several leaders—but that great "Stresa Front," as it was dubbed at the time, came up with nothing more than an ineffectual protest, a slap on the German wrist in response to a mailed fist. The French and British hoped that Mussolini could be enlisted to check his ideological offspring to the north, but in the fall of that year he himself embarked on his long-planned conquest of Ethiopia. The democratic powers imposed mild economic sanctions on Italy, hoping to halt this aggression while trying to appease Mussolini at the same time. The dignified, hapless figure of Emperor Haile Selassie pleaded for help in the name of collective security to a self-emasculated League of Nations.

Politics intruded everywhere. Once back in Germany that spring, our close-knit family, with its inevitable tensions and a perhaps excessive amount of sibling conflict, was roiled by my sister's wish to attend confirmation class and be confirmed. Toni was fifteen at the time, with strong religious yearnings, and the only tradition she knew was Christian, though I don't think she had gone to church regularly. Normally this would have been a private matter, but on this issue, given the political conditions, the line between private and public was difficult to draw. Her wish to be confirmed brought home to us the very real (if limited) conflict between the Christian churches and the Nazi regime, which early on had decreed that the former must abide by the non-Aryan paragraphs of the Civil Service Law. This Nazi command to discriminate against Christians of Jewish descent was a key issue in the intermittent struggles between the regime and the Protestant churches, which were divided on how to respond to the National Socialists in any case. Official Protestantism had been hostile to the Weimar Republic, and many of its clergy were beset by deep-seated anti-Semitism, virulently enhanced by hatred of Weimar's "godless culture." Even before Hitler's rise to power, the Protestant churches had among them groups who called themselves "German Christians," dedicated to an extreme *völkisch* faith, clamoring for the elimination of the Old Testament from the teachings of the Church and forbidding any acknowledgment of the Judaic origins of Christianity. (This patently absurd doctrine had already arisen among some Protestant theologians in the late nineteenth century.) With Hitler in power, the German Christians' self-definition said it all: they now called themselves "the SA of Jesus Christ." Hitler hoped that the German Christians could capture the entire Protestant establishment. That effort failed, and other pastors recognized that despite features they might admire in Nazism, there were issues of theology and church autonomy that could not be compromised.

The conflict between the Nazi regime and a significant number of other Protestant pastors came into the open when Martin Niemöller, a pastor in the affluent Berlin suburb of Dahlem, founded an Emergency Union of Protestant Pastors, a forerunner of what was later called the Confessing Church. Members of the latter, which was particularly strong in Silesia, refused to abide by the non-Aryan proscription. (An oft-repeated parable was told at the time: a Breslau pastor opens his Sunday sermon by asking all non-Aryans to leave; he repeats the demand thrice, at which point the figure on the Cross disappears. These antiregime stories had a kind of momentary anesthetizing effect; they were a refuge into never-never land.) The struggle between pastors such as Niemöller and the Nazis grew more intense as the 1930s progressed. Niemöller himself, with his own ambivalent feelings about Jews and the place of the church in the state, was incarcerated in Dachau and Buchenwald until the end of the war. Thousands of Catholic priests and Protestant pastors were jailed in those years, and their stand lent hope to critics of the regime.

My mother, responding to and strongly seconding my sister's wishes, found a member of the Confessing Church, Pastor Schröter, who eagerly welcomed Toni to his confirmation class. (In fact, before the first meeting of the class and before her arrival, he told the group that a non-Aryan would be joining them, to which one responded, "Then we have to be especially nice to her.") My parents attended Toni's confirmation, but I rebelled and refused to go, despite my family's entreaties. And yet I was impressed that Pastor Schröter had been repeatedly arrested for his open defiance of the regime's orders; he even taunted the Gestapo men who listened to his sermons. I had a child's thrill at learning that Schröter communicated with next-cell prisoners by knocking on the wall in Morse code. These vivid stories bolstered my admiration for dissenters and resisters—an admiration I never lost.

But I was an unkind, uncomprehending observer of my sister's actions. I felt instinctively that this was a wrong step, a "caving in" to an institution that, I believed, was hostile to us. I couldn't clearly articulate my view, but I felt embarrassment at any effort at assimilation to German Christian life. In retrospect, I can understand her contrary impulse: she longed for and found a community and a faith—and as her notes of the time make clear (notes that her children gave me recently) she was especially grateful for Pastor Schröter's acceptance. I can now imagine what could well have been her feeling—or that of many non-Aryan Christians—that to deny one's Christian faith because of Nazi policies was to accept Hitler's dictate and surrender to racial dogma.

Our family continued to celebrate Christmas and Easter, festive occasions with all the familiar customs, which I enjoyed uneasily. But by 1935, if not before, I felt estranged from anything "formally" Christian and felt a clear identity with Jews, though I was ignorant of Jewish rites. I often went to see Jewish friends who lived around the corner from us to borrow their Jewish newspapers, still allowed under the Nazi regime, which were largely dedicated to announcements of Jewish cultural events and above all information about places for immigration.

Beyond the Christmas and Easter holidays, the other family celebrations became vividly important. On New Year's Eve, Toni and I almost always recited poems written by or to our parents and enacted plays my mother had composed for us (sometimes for our cousins as well), and again there was a special meal. Festive as these occasions were—and my mother had a special gift for making them so—the outside world in all its ominous grimness cast its shadow. Perhaps times of public threat heighten the need for reaffirming private well-being.

Books generally became ever more important, and A. A. Milne's *Winnie-the-Pooh* acquired a lasting family significance. I insisted that the book clearly depicted our own family: my mother was obviously Pooh, my father Rabbit, my sister bouncy Tigger, and I, Piglet. Within the family and among friends, the names stuck; my mother was often called Pooh-bear. My father became "Ka" for *Kaninchen*, or rabbit, a useful term when writing more or less coded mail from and to friends abroad. My mother corresponded with Milne, offering to translate into German some of his poems.

I remember a child's novel about a youth in New York who rose from selling newspapers on the street to become a tycoon. I read Sir Walter Scott's *Quentin Durward* and books about Napoleon and Clemenceau—books I still have. And reading was richly supplemented with conversations: on countless walks my father would talk of some medical crisis or cure and just as often of historical or political subjects.

The main topic in 1935 wasn't religion—it was emigration. My parents' intention had been clear from that summer in Paris, and they continued to explore—and were encouraged to explore—all possible avenues. An inquiry was made concerning the United States; the indirect reply came in March 1934 from the Emergency Committee in Aid of Displaced Foreign Physicians: "We have Dr. Stern's credentials on file and his name has been brought to the attention of medical institutions in this country." If an opportunity were to arise, the committee would notify him at once; if he wanted to immigrate to practice medicine, he would have to come in under the German immigration quota and pass the requisite examinations.

The United States seemed very remote. It was hard enough to resolve leaving your home, your language, your German past. My father hoped for a clinical position in Europe, or in a country closer to Europe than America. Negotiations were carried on by another emergency committee to assist German scholars, headed by Fritz Demuth and located in Zurich. The next likely prospect, explored by Demuth, was a professorship in Tehran. Jadassohn, whose ailing wife depended on my father's epistolary advice, had moved to Zurich and was supervising these efforts. In July, he wrote that my father's old teacher Erich Frank, now in Istanbul, had told him about his contractual arrangements there; it was information that could serve as a basis for negotiations with Tehran. He was reassuring that "from the point of view of climate, T. is good, with the exception of water." A later letter acknowledged that hygienically Tehran was rather sad, but "the roads excellent." My father took out the atlas, showed me a map of Persia, and pointed to the mountains near Tehran. Onkel Pu continued, in his necessarily telegraphic, gnomic way, "We understand perfectly how difficult the decision is for you, but no one can take it for you." I gathered that my father wasn't pursuing this possibility with all the energy that might have been necessary. In September, Jadassohn wrote again: "I am not the least bit sorry that T. is out. Following my principle, I never spoke for or against it, but I was convinced that it isn't for you."

The next major possibility focused on Ankara. The great Turkish modernizer-dictator Kemal Ataturk had decided early on to profit from Hitler's expulsionary policies and had invited leading German émigrés to positions in Turkey. Istanbul had not only an astounding circle of German economists but also great physicians, including Erich Frank and my father's old friend Rudolf Nissen, who hoped to facilitate our move to Ankara. In the end those negotiations collapsed as well. Some thought was given to posts in Pisa and in Shanghai.

Emigration was the central topic not only for my father but for many of his colleagues. And there was a steady exodus of friends and associates to all sorts of destinations. So I owe my first impressions of the vastness of the world to the terrors we were trying to leave behind. When acknowledging such a dubious gift of fate, or indeed any other unlikely, ironically burdened blessing, my father and I would invoke the Nazi slogan that we saw at construction sites or at other mundane wonders: *"Das verdanken wir dem Führer!"* (We owe that to the Führer!)

America, long known as the land of unlimited opportunities, was now dubbed by refugees the land of "unpaid opportunities." But after the disappointments with Tunisia, Persia, and Turkey, and a brief interlude of serious negotiations with the Prince of Liechtenstein about running some government sanitarium there, thoughts of emigrating to the United States intensified. In January 1936, Florence Willstätter, Richard's American sister-in-law, sent us an affidavit. Jadassohn, too, offered help, noting that "besides New York there are other cities in the U.S. which are not so overcrowded." He also wrote about contacts in Palestine—an option that was also discussed, the more so as the Nazi government, eager to get rid of Jews, made extra concessions for emigration there.

The government, which still contained some "conservatives," most notably Hjalmar Schacht as minister of economics, tried to balance the demands of its most radical elements, who wanted a final onslaught on Jewish life and property, with the conservatives' warning that Jews remained important in the German economy and that open violence would have unpleasant repercussions abroad. (The specter of world Jewry's revenge!) In May 1935, the Central Association of German Citizens of Jewish Faith estimated that 450,000 "full"— that is, unconverted—Jews remained in Germany as well as 50,000 converted ones. In September of that year, at the annual party rally—that master pageant brilliantly captured in Leni Riefenstahl's film *Triumph of the Will*—the regime opted for a "legal solution" to the problem of these half-million Jewish Germans, announcing the infamous Nürnberg decrees, which excluded Jews and non-Aryans from German citizenship, assigning them the status of "state subjects." The Nürnberg laws were a further shock, and the definition of who exactly was Jewish continued to bedevil the regime and its potential victims for years: another law "for the protection of German blood and honor" proscribed all sexual relations between Jews and Aryans; violations involving "racial defilement" were severely punished, and Jewish households were forbidden to employ any Aryan German woman younger than forty-five years of age. (The largest number of denunciations made to the Gestapo in subsequent years involved charges of "racial defilement." These, when proven, punished the Jews involved far more harshly than their Aryan partners.)

Both the intent and reception of the Nürnberg laws were complex. The regime wanted to satisfy radical anti-Jewish demands while discouraging individual acts of violence, such as had occurred before. And it certainly intended to rob Jews of their rights as citizens, casting them out of the German national community. Also, now that Hindenburg was safely dead, the thousands of Jewish war veterans were no longer exempt.

The prohibition of sexual relations between Aryan and Jew not only outlawed intermarriage but also gave official sanction to the vulgar slur that Jewish men had an innate compulsion to seduce German women. This had been a commonplace of popular German anti-Semitism even before the Nazis came to power; it was the obscene staple of Julius Streicher's pornographic weekly *Der Stürmer*, with its disgusting caricatures and lurid stories. *Der Stürmer* had its own display cases on many street corners, often close to schools.

So the new laws made the definition of Jewish and non-Aryan both more urgent and more difficult. Within a few years, life or death was to depend on the fine distinction, newly introduced, as to who was a half or quarter Jew. And the need to prove pure Aryan ancestry became a full-time German industry. To criticize, let alone to mock, this new requirement would have implied insufficient faith in the Führer and in the validity of racial determinism.

I grasped that the first part of the new laws were a clear token of further discrimination. I didn't then know the term *second-class citizen*—actually Jews didn't even have that status, though they may have thought they did—but I realized that we were endangered outcasts. I can't remember what gloss, if any, my mother might have put on the age requirement for maids, but fortunately our two household domestics—one a half-time receptionist who helped with the coming and going of my father's patients—were over forty-five years old. Our maid, Augusta, a friendly woman, lived not far from our house, in a basement apartment, and I would occasionally greet her across her barred windows, and she would give me old illustrated weeklies that we didn't have at home. (Once, much earlier and half in jest, I hit a younger female servant and immediately felt not only remorse and fear of denunciation but also the ever-present apprehension that I might have endangered my parents.)

Even for us outcasts, life alternated between normality and persecution. In 1935, my father's cousin Käthe Nick and her Aryan conductor husband left Breslau in the hope of finding a position in Berlin for him, handicapped as he was by having a non-Aryan wife. (Their daughter, Dagmar, has reminded me that for the next years, and especially during the war, her father and mother protected each other: as long as he was alive, she would not be deported, and as long as she was alive, Nazi rules didn't deem him worthy of serving in the Wehrmacht; he was in fact drafted for a few days but sent home in disgrace.) The Nicks owned a small vacation home on the slope of a modest mountain near Breslau; by this time we had acquired a secondhand car, and we rented this place for weekends. To get there we drove through five or six villages, each with its own anti-Semitic doggerel on plaques at the village entrance. I can't forget some of those slogans: TRAU NICHT DEM FUCHS AUF GRÜNER HEID, UND NICHT DEM JUD BEI SEINEM EID. (Trust not the fox on the green heath, and not the Jew when he gives his oath.) Why does this piece of filthy trash remain in my head?

One night on the way back to Breslau, we hit an oncoming car and ended up in a ditch. The fault was ours, since our car had been on the wrong side of the road, and it was our further bad luck that the other car was driven by an SS officer in civilian clothing. Papers were exchanged, and lawyers later settled the matter; but for the moment we remained in the ditch. A bus came by and stopped: a group of uniformed men poured out of it and pushed our car back onto the road. They were members of a *Kriegerverein*, a veterans' organization, returning from an outing, and they were pleased to help us.

Unlikely situations continued to characterize my father's practice. The clientele remained mixed in every sense: Aryan and Jewish, affluent and poor.

Many patients came from villages where by word of mouth his practice had become well known. These faithful, simple villagers would sometimes pay in kind, with eggs or fowl, for example, or that Christmas deer. For an affluent and critically ill Jewish patient, my father asked the well-known Frankfurt internist Professor Volhard for a consultation, and Volhard lunched with us at home, at once a normal and exceptional occasion.

Another case concerned one Frau von Roebern, who lived on a country estate that we occasionally were invited to visit, and who suddenly developed punishing headaches. My father suspected a brain tumor, the diagnosis was confirmed, and her only chance of survival was the most delicate, dangerous surgery. Several surgeons refused to take her on, but a very fine Jewish surgeon, Ludwig Guttmann, agreed to perform the operation. Her son-in-law, a high SS officer in Breslau, came in mufti to ask my father whether the operation was indeed necessary and the choice of surgeon inevitable. He accepted my father's verdict. The family tension on the day of the operation was palpable, but the operation was a success. (Days later my father had the unfortunate idea that I should visit Frau von Roebern in the hospital to cheer her up. I doubt that she even noticed my tongue-tied presence, but the sight of her completely bandaged head provoked vivid images of what it must be like to have one's skull drilled into and opened, frightening thoughts that reduced me to near silence.)*

For Christmas 1935, the Hermann Habers in Paris gave us our first radio, paying for it with their *Sperrmark*, that is to say, money in an account that could be used only within Germany. On the very first night, fiddling with the tuner, I chanced on Radio Strasbourg, broadcasting in German. I even found Radio Moscow, also broadcasting in German: "Proletarians of the world, unite!" followed by the "Internationale." Listening to such broadcasts had to be done secretively and only rarely—early efforts were already being made to jam foreign broadcasts—in bracing moments of defiance and escape. We continued to lead this kind of double life, unconsciously accepting it as if it were normal.

In 1936, the National Socialist propaganda machine—a remarkably cunning, modern operation, as one can see in retrospect—carefully prepared people for some great national event. The denouement was Hitler's speech to the Reichstag—that parody of a parliament—on March 7, 1936. I listened to this harangue—first, about the wrongs that had been inflicted on Germany,

---

*Dr. Guttmann suffered all the degradations of German Jews, tending to patients in the Jewish Hospital, until his emigration to England in March 1939. There, in 1966, he was knighted for his service to injured British soldiers and for his remarkable work in the rehabilitation of paraplegics.

second, his attack on the recently concluded Franco-Soviet alliance that allegedly violated the Locarno treaties, and finally his chilling announcement that at that very hour, German troops were marching into the demilitarized zone on the left bank of the Rhine. Hitler's style was intended to project dramatic decisiveness: unilateral, instant command as against dreary negotiations. The whole performance, frightening as it was, was audacious and impressive, including the hysterical ovation he received from the puppet deputies. Hitler offered all manner of peace proposals, but the effect was clear: this was a violent assertion of German power, which most Germans greeted joyously. Hitler had kept his promise: the last "shackle" of Versailles had been tossed off.

That night or the next, I listened to Radio Strasbourg (its German-language broadcasts were at 9:00 p.m.), with its news that French guns had been moved into position. How we hoped for a decisive response by France and Britain! After all, Hitler's move was the clearest defiance of the Western powers—and it had profound military implications.

We now know that the decision to send German troops to the French-Belgian border was a supreme gamble on Hitler's part, that some of the generals were sure that the Allies would respond with an ultimatum or perhaps by force of arms (in which case, the generals were prepared to depose Hitler). But the French were unwilling to act without full and immediate British support, and the British procrastinated—some in the government still moved by a sense of guilt about the harshness of the Versailles Treaty, some swayed by the idea that "we should not be beastly to the Germans," some somehow becalmed into thinking that after all the Germans were merely "moving into their backyard." Perhaps some believed Hitler when he claimed that this was his "last demand." In short, they wanted to be deceived. The last chance to check Hitler without grave risk, to stop the war colossus he was building up, passed. Simultaneously, Hitler's power was confirmed at home and established in Europe. His triumph prepared the way for Europe's catastrophe.

That spring, while Germany successfully pursued its militaristic defiance of the outside world and at the same time lured foreigners to the Olympic Games in Berlin, I began a new phase of life: at the age of ten, my days at the cozy private school within walking distance of home came to an end. Law and custom prescribed my entry into a *Gymnasium*, that once-hallowed, privileged route to a humanistic German education. My sister was already enrolled in a girls' *Gymnasium*, and I doubt that my parents seriously entertained the possibility of sending me to the Jewish *Gymnasium*, which in any case probably would not have accepted me. My mother put her faith in one of Breslau's oldest schools, the Maria Magdalena Gymnasium, which her brothers had attended, as had my somewhat older cousin Ernst before his emigration to England, and whose director, Dr. Konrad Linder, had been friendly in the past. (Ferdinand Lassalle and Paul Ehrlich—at that time, of course, "unpersons"—were among the school's distinguished alumni.)

Since the school was in a prosperous neighborhood at the other end of town, I had to take two streetcars and then walk quite a distance to get there: it took at least forty minutes each way, but it was only three minutes from my grandmother's villa. Classes began at eight in the morning. I felt the normal anxiety when I began my first trek to that new school, in its large brick building with a flat roof and modern design of the 1920s, but I had no idea what unpleasantness was in store for me. The school came to dominate a good part of my life, and it established a realm of my own experience that was separate from that of my parents. Yet in the event, it was hardly a road to independence.

The spirit of the school was set by traditional authoritarian discipline with an ever-increasing overlay of National Socialist conformity. Classes were relatively small, perhaps twenty-five boys or so, but the etiquette between teacher and pupil was fiercely formal. Relations between the youngest boys and those in the highest grades, aged eighteen or nineteen, were distant or bellicose, and the former held the latter in awe. Several times during the day we had to scurry from one classroom to another, and there were regular breaks in the schedule when the students had to go to the schoolyard, to play and eat snacks brought from home. We had frequent all-school assemblies in the aula, with Nazi themes predominating.

The curriculum was traditional: Latin in the first year, Greek in the third, along with German, geography, history, music, and athletics. The teachers were mixed: the Latin master, Herr Eckert, was a fierce, devoted teacher, exacting and exciting, and renowned throughout the school for his resounding slaps to the face, administered in front of the class for the least infraction—misconduct, inattention, or even dirty fingernails. This noisy punishment was administered nonracially, and I have a most pleasant memory of his slapping a fellow student who had deliberately thrown all my books on the floor, most hurtfully a cherished atlas. I gloated over that slap. I was once a recipient of one as well, but the physical assault hurt less than the anti-Semitic lessons given by the math teacher, Herr Müth. "If three Jews robbed a bank, and each got a part of the loot proportionate to their ages [details supplied], how much would each get?" Eckert was a straightforward conservative, and in his conduct to me and to the few other non-Aryans impeccably correct. Herr Müth, a little man, had been a moderate in Weimar, or so I was told, and hence now had to be a superconformist.

I spent more than two years at Maria Magdalena, beginning in April 1936, and with each passing term, it became increasingly unpleasant, and my sense of exclusion ever greater. Most of my classmates were in the Hitler Youth, and on special days (the Führer's birthday, for example) they would appear in their uniforms. Even without them, their pride in things German and Nazi and their joy in communal belonging were tangible. At times I was a target of verbal and, in the schoolyard, physical assault. Once I fought back, hitting the bully boy of the class. (I got a present from my father for that deed.) School was demanding in any case, and the added exclusions and dangers made it worse.

I have forgotten, or perhaps repressed, much of the unpleasantness, probably because it was so minor compared with the horrors visited later on others, but I do remember the indoctrinations, the celebratory assemblies, the Heil Hitlers that I neither could nor would say, the hateful songs, the party sermons. For six days a week—we had a half day of school on Saturdays—I had to keep my thoughts to myself and maintain a kind of silent antagonism. I occasionally caught myself envying my classmates, fused so unambiguously as they were in a common faith and so clearly reveling in their uniformed camaraderie. And I had to get through the formal moments of exclusion, notably when the entire class was supposed to go on a week's outing for physical toughening—some party-related exercise from which non-Aryans were excluded. I was given the option of showing up at school even though no classes would be held, but it was arranged instead that I would be apprenticed for that week to my father's cousin, who had a tree nursery near Breslau; a strict authoritarian, he fit the role of taskmaster.

The day there began at six every morning; my permanent gain was that I learned how to cut asparagus when only the white tips were visible, a skill for which, unfortunately, I have had little use in later life. As for Cousin Otto, after his arrest on the night of the November pogrom in 1938, and his Aryan wife's desertion, he came to the United States, where he invented an immensely successful plant fertilizer, Miracle-Gro.

School, far from offering a space apart from the family and a path to independence, was so unpleasant that it deepened the ties to the only safe place I knew, my home. I may have been naturally shy with children my own age, and I had a trained pleasure in the company of adults, whose card games, for example, I mastered early on. But some mixture of psychological predisposition, family dynamics, and relentless outside pressure combined to give home an exceptional centrality for me. I did have the very occasional playmate, I had books, and I had a wonderfully clever construction set to play with (Lego sets before Lego). When I was given a bicycle, I had a chance to roam around—sometimes I would deliver my parents' letters to their recipients, earning some extra pocket money. One day, when I was riding my bike on the sidewalk on a quiet street near home, some SA men stopped me, asked my name, indicated they knew just who my father was, and threatened to come to my school the next day so as to demand a public rebuke for my infraction. I skipped school for a day, but I lived with the ever-present intimation of danger—and lingering fear, even without actual persecution.

The summer of 1936 is remembered as the time of the Olympic Games in Berlin: again, Leni Riefenstahl has left us a brilliant record of sports and politics. Foreigners who saw Germany on exhibit were impressed by its prevailing order, by its bustling economy, by the endless spectacles of triumph. Once more Germany was in ascendancy, full of mechanized energy, and this at a time when most other industrial nations remained in a slump and riven by class conflict. Every success was cause for yet another celebration, another public holiday: Breslau was regularly beflagged, when the various units of the party—the SA, the SS, the Labor Front, and the Hitler Youth—staged their huge parades with martial music and the catchy "Horst Wessel" song. And everywhere were pictures of ever-smiling Nordic types enjoying their Strength-Through-Joy holidays. Politics became a great spectator sport, cunningly admixed with the pretense of participation and the demand for sacrifice—such as with the compulsory Winter Aid, where every other Sunday during the winter months, a prescribed one-pot meal was to be served at home—the savings to be collected by the party for the poor.

Bread, circuses, and mass mobilization gave most Germans a sense of certainty, of faith in present and future: they perceived the Führer as a divinely inspired commander in chief. If Hitler had died that summer of 1936, or indeed at anytime before the outbreak of the war, he would probably still, in today's Germany, be hailed as a hero—a murderer of thousands, yes, but the savior of millions, an oppressor and demonic genius. For a brief moment that summer and for the politically naïve, Germany was transformed into a bustling Potemkin village, and the armed malevolence was hidden. And this false Germany aroused much sympathy among prosperous conservatives elsewhere.

My family lived for their temporary escapes abroad to free countries. In the summer of 1936 we went to Denmark: vacations by the seaside would have been exciting in any case, but there was the added excitement of clearing the border, of the train moving from the German side, with its hated uniforms, to the other, friendly side, where uniforms exuded a sense of protective authority. First we went to Copenhagen, where, while I was parked in the institute garden, my parents consulted James Franck at the Niels Bohr Institute about plans for emigration. They returned to the garden with Franck, who in the kindest manner asked how old I was. Ten, I replied. "What an unfortunate age," he said, commiserating. "Too young to be invited to my home tonight with your parents, and old enough to stay alone in the hotel." I liked the physicist's precision. Next we traveled by train and ferry to the island of Fano (a place made famous two years earlier as the locus of an ecumenical meeting of Protestant pastors, at which accommodationists and critics of Nazi policies compromised so that at least a resolution in support of the Confessing Church was passed). Swimming in the North Sea, carefully supervised by anxious parents, was joy, and reading the forbidden newspapers in German—the *Neue Zürcher Zeitung* or the *Basler Nationalzeitung* as well as the German exile press—was an even greater thrill. We caught up on forbidden, inspiring texts, such as Thomas Mann's withering response to the University of Bonn's withdrawal of his honorary degree. On every vacation we were joined by the Hamburgers, seemingly safe exiles in Paris, and the principal topic of conversation was politics and emigration.

In the summer of 1937, we traveled to Nordwijk, on the Dutch coast, long a favorite resort of the German and German Jewish upper class, where we stayed at a modest hotel, for money was never plentiful (and was a frequent cause of parental discord). Again we were joined by the Paris contingent—the Hamburgers and Hermann and Marga Haber. Hermann, genial and seemingly insouciant, with an intriguing Citroën car I had never seen before, secretly promised to take me with them back to Paris, where I would go to school; he would tell my parents on the day of departure. But the Habers left without me; he had never been serious, and I felt cheated and angry. Still, the trip to Holland had an inestimable benefit: my parents took me to the great Mauritshuis in The Hague, where I was mesmerized by Rembrandt's *Anatomy Lesson*. Was it the contrast between the intense gaze of the living and the grisly exactness of the corpse? Picture and painter stayed in my mind; on later visits, I was even more moved by Rembrandt's *Saul and David*, the young rival trying to comfort a king sunk in melancholy.

The two weeks in Nordwijk were followed by another week in England. We took the boat from Hook van Holland to Harwich, a stormy crossing, during which I was continuously seasick. But every moment of travel was an adventure and became a treasured memory. In London we visited with my mother's brother Peter, an art historian, who had come to England from his post as professor in Toronto. From there we went to a fifteenth-century rectory in Caldecote, a small village near Cambridge, where my mother's brother Ernest (his anglicized name) had settled in a big, rambling house, cold even in summer but gloriously warm in spirit. He had found a position in nearby Papworth, a leading center for the rehabilitation of tubercular patients. Uncle Ernest was markedly different from most other members of the Brieger family: cheerfully distant and self-reliant, already deeply rooted in his new and primitive surroundings, with goats in the garden and a large plot where his exceedingly efficient wife and three children raised all manner of fruits and vegetables. Ernest ran by his own gyroscope—stubborn in small matters, habitually late, at times exasperating to his family, but a wise and wonderful uncle. At a later moment of supreme crisis, he helped us dramatically. I went to Caldecote once more before the war, and many times thereafter: it became a family home.

But the foreign havens were hospitable only for a given time; permanent residence or immigration was not granted. Inevitably the vacations and their sense of double freedom ended with the return to familiar fear, to Germany's real unpleasantness and potential terror. Eventually I was the sole "non-Aryan" at my school, and felt more and more excluded. I managed the work but was uncomfortable, never knowing when or from where the next insult would come. German schools have never been supposed to be "soft"; suffering was considered good in itself. Did some of my classmates lighten their misery by heightening mine? Toward the end of my time there, the sons of a Pastor Bunzel, in the Confessional Church, kept an eye on me, more or less undemonstrably hovering nearby and offering at the very least some psychological protection. My mother may have asked for this help, or so I thought later, but the boys were good to me on their own.

Of course there was relief: at home my mother was cheerful, self-assured, and self-deprecating, ever protective, and resourceful in creating pleasant, peaceful interludes. Once she brought the stately Wichard von Moellendorff to visit me in the schoolyard. And I spent happy hours at Oma's villa, so close to school. My father, calm and ever caring with his patients, could be irascible at home; I learned to dodge his angry outbursts and a few times even protested some stormy words he had directed against my mother. Mostly he treated me as a friend or confidant far beyond my age. Hence I came to share some of his burdens as well, and some of his justified fears.

In 1937, the Nazis began a more radical policy of "Aryanizing" property and dispossessing Jews. In the winter of that year the prosperous Breslau industrialist Ernst Schwerin, son-in-law of Paul Ehrlich, and his wife, Steffa, had to flee Germany overnight: a loyal accountant had told him that although the Finance Ministry had not found any irregularity in his business, the Gestapo was about to arrest him. The tactic at the time was to seize a person, throw him into a concentration camp, and release him after he agreed to dispose of his property at some risible price. To hear of the Schwerins' nighttime flight was a shock, but soon this was an increasingly common story.

There was disheartening news everywhere. I followed the slanted reports about the Spanish Civil War, the feeble response of the democratic countries to the fascist attack on the republic, the adoption of a nonintervention policy that the fascist powers violated at will—the Italians by sending troops, the Germans by experimenting with their fledgling Luftwaffe. Franco kept gaining ground, though in the spring of 1937 even the German papers had to report an Italian defeat at Guadalajara—to my delight. What kind of a perverted life was I living that I secretly rejoiced at the crash of the German zeppelin the *Hindenburg*, at Lakehurst, New Jersey, in May 1937? Any defeat of the seemingly ever triumphant Nazis brought us cheer. Their poisonous hatreds had infected me with a counter-hatred, which is the moral-intellectual cost of living under so inhuman a regime.

Another means of escape became ever more important. The Czech border was only some three hours by car from Breslau. In 1936, we went for a long weekend to Prague, where we visited the medieval Jewish cemetery, with its slanted, broken, crowded tombstones: I followed the ancient tradition of writing a wish on a piece of paper and placing it under a pebble on a tombstone. The wish was clear: give us a chance to escape our dreadful country. Czechoslovakia, in contrast, was the free and democratic country of Thomas Masaryk. I had read Capek's conversations with Masaryk, and I was moved to see Prague's castle, the Hradcany, imagining that it showed that political power could be benign. One night my parents insisted that I go with them to the opera, which I resisted, wishing to stay in the hotel and read a whole set of old copies of the *Prager Tageblatt*, a newspaper of liberal views. But already by the overture to *Die Fledermaus*, I was transported to a saner, happier world—a permanent gain.

We had friends in Prague, Paul and Gret Kubelka and their two children. The Nazis would have classified the Kubelkas as *Sudetendeutsche* (Aryan); they were among Czechoslovakia's three million German-speaking citizens, and they were utterly loyal to their state. They were friends of the young Habers: a spirited, lovely couple, happy and confident people. I enjoyed them, and I assumed that their disposition reflected what life was like in a free country. In the next two years we met them repeatedly on the Czech side of the Riesengebirge, in a popular German-speaking resort village called Spindlermühle, where we hiked in the summer and skied or sledded in the winter. (In the 1970s it served as a convenient secret meeting place for Václav Havel and Polish dissidents.)

We were slated to go again to Spindlermühle at the end of January 1938, but at the last minute, my father decided to stay with a critically ill patient, and my sister and I went off by ourselves. We crossed the border on January 29—I still have my sister's passport with the stamp—at the beginning of our winter break. I buried myself in the *Prager Tageblatt*, which reported on changes taking place in the Nazi government: there had been a shake-up in the army high command, and Hitler had made himself commander in chief of the armed forces; at the same time, the remaining "conservative" ministers, despite their well-practiced acquiescence, were being eliminated, replaced by super-loyal Nazis: a harbinger, so outside observers correctly thought, of a violent radicalization of Nazi policy.

The Kubelkas and I skied (how primitive skiing was in those days!) and talked, hatching a happy plan: I would come to live with them in Prague beginning that summer, and attend the French *Gymnasium* there. The fact that their fourteen-year-old daughter, Hanne, was a girl of stunning and serene beauty may have been an extra pull; the push without a doubt was my yearning to get out of Germany. My very pleasure at recollecting that plan over the decades made me wonder sometimes whether my memory might be playing tricks on me, but in 1977, I saw Hanne Kubelka again—by this time she had become a leading geneticist in Brazil. I asked her whether she had any memory of our plan. Her instant response: "But it was all set! You were going to come and live with us in Prague!" Right idea, wrong place.

On returning to Breslau and my hated school, I confronted my parents with my plan for Prague. I believe it hastened their decision to emigrate to the United States, but certainly political events impelled a sense of urgency. Within a few weeks, in the early days of March, Hitler made dramatic demands on Austria, then governed by an authoritarian Catholic regime that was trying to contain the illegal but powerful Nazi Party there. The drama intensified when, at the last moment, Chancellor Kurt von Schuschnigg defied the Nazis and suddenly called for an immediate plebiscite on whether or not Austria should remain "free and independent." I listened to his speech—so clearly defiant in the face of Hitler's demands—and wrote a note to my parents, who happened to be out that evening, telling them how marvelously moving the speech had been. They teased me for my extravagant words.

Hitler was enraged by Schuschnigg, and three days later, on March 12, German troops moved into Austria; Hitler proclaimed that Austria had "returned" to the Reich. The Nazis' frenzied reception in Austria could not have been faked, any more than the hysterical welcome that shortly afterward greeted Hitler in Linz and Vienna. (Hitler kept insisting that he was fulfilling God's will, that he was a providential instrument of God's will.) No, this was a genuine and rather spontaneous Austrian outburst, greater than anything that happened in Germany in 1933, just as in Vienna the sadistic assaults on Jews far exceeded anything that had happened so far in Germany. By then Hitler's tyrannical and murderous rule was well known, as, it must be added, were the regime's successes. The Nazis arrested Schuschnigg, and I heard at the time that he was forced, while imprisoned in a concentration camp, to listen ceaselessly to recordings of Hitler's outbursts against him. Most Germans were thrilled just as the Austrians were, and the geopolitical balance in Central Europe was alarmingly altered. German power now virtually encircled the Czech Republic.

Meanwhile anti-Jewish measures escalated within the Reich. In March, Jewish passports were either confiscated or, as in my father's case, marked "valid only within the country" (an act of intimidation: one had to reapply to have the restriction lifted). At the end of April, a law decreed that all Jewish property in whatever form needed to be registered. Between these two dates, sometime in April, my parents went on a trip to the United States to explore the possibilities of my father's practicing medicine and earning a livelihood there.* They stayed in New York, consulting colleagues and councils for refugee aid. Marga Haber wrote impassioned letters to her brother urging him to stay in the United States and escape danger, and suggesting that my mother return alone in order to prepare for the family's emigration. But they both returned—and now readied us for removal with all possible speed.

---

*My father asked several prominent doctors for letters of reference in connection with that trip. Germany's best-known surgeon, Ferdinand Sauerbruch, wrote a letter dated March 1, referring to my father's scientific publications and to patients they had jointly treated: "I can therefore say in the field of internal medicine, my colleague Stern is a well-known and highly esteemed physician" with an excellent education as one of Minkowski's pupils. This official letter carried his seal of office, with a swastika on it. To write it was an act of prudent decency, but did he or any of the other colleagues add a word of sympathy or regret? Not to my knowledge. After the war, some medical colleagues "envied" our family's good luck in escaping what they had to face during the war.

In the intervening decades, I have often wondered why my parents reached their decision so dangerously late. They had been among the first to recognize the need to emigrate, in the spring of 1933. Then came negotiations for assured positions, beginning with Tunis, and when all these failed, they scanned other possibilities, but prospects grew ever dimmer as most European countries restricted immigration, claiming, as the Swiss infamously did, that "the boat is full." Inwardly my parents may have been torn, and the disappointments may have had their depressing effect. It is desperately hard to leave all that is familiar to you for something so uncertain as to start a new life, penniless, in an utterly foreign country and language. On the other hand, their friends and relatives had taken the leap, life in Germany became ever more intolerable, and they knew I was unhappy and had no future in Germany whatsoever.

Once they returned from the United States, they moved with as much dispatch as possible. The prerequisite for everything was the American immigrant visa, and obtaining that priceless document had also become harder year by year. The United States was still digging itself out of a paralyzing depression, and American consuls abroad were instructed to be especially wary of applicants who might end up as public charges. We already had the affidavit that Florence Willstätter had signed in 1936 on our behalf—though Richard Willstätter himself had time and again counseled my parents against emigration. On February 1, 1938, he wrote my mother that an exploratory trip to the United States was no doubt a good idea: "But you will see that for us New York is hardly bearable, Boston better . . . After the trip, reflect a hundred times before leaving Breslau." A year later, he wrote to tell her that he had barely escaped arrest and had finally been able to flee to Switzerland. My father's second cousin, the physicist Otto Stern, who had found a position at the Carnegie Institute of Technology, gave us a supplemental affidavit.

A cash guarantee was also needed: the sum involved, $3,500, was a very considerable amount, and obviously the German government did not allow its own currency to be used. The Habers in Paris were the only ones who had the requisite resources, but Hermann—whose efforts at French naturalization had just failed—was resistant, even though it was clear that the money would merely be a short-term loan. He rebuffed all pleas by his wife and by Ernst Hamburger, who had become a close friend; finally Uncle Ernst went from Caldecote to Paris, where that mild, often somewhat detached person told Hermann that continued refusal to help the Sterns would precipitate a total break in their exceptionally close relations. Hermann relented. When Ernst telephoned from England with the news, I happened to be the only person at home: in somewhat Aesopian language, he told me of his success in Paris. I rejoiced.

Further obstacles remained. For one thing, my father needed a new passport. My mother and I dropped him off at police headquarters, where he had to present himself to the Gestapo. It was another day of terrible tension. The Nazis wanted to get rid of Jews, yet they placed difficulties in their efforts to leave. Officials from the Finance Ministry had to assess the value of the belongings we intended to take with us, and then an equivalent sum had to be paid to the state, the so-called *Reichsfluchtsteuer*. Once that tax was paid, all that remained was to find money for the ocean passage, for us and our belongings.

There were sudden delays at the American consulate in Berlin: our applications had been "lost" or misplaced. My mother managed to get an appointment with the American consul, Raymond Geist—who, we now know, had a far keener sense of the desperate plight of German Jews than his superiors at the State Department. She pleaded for the recovery of our papers; her tears of supplication came quite naturally. She was successful, and then at the last minute I became a potential further obstacle: I had contracted chicken pox, and American authorities forbade persons with a contagious disease from entering the country. I was half healed by the time we drove to Berlin for the final inspection, in September, and a friendly consulate doctor blinked at whatever remained of my spots. On September 16, we received our immigration visas, mine numbered 757. What a joyful return trip on the autobahn from Berlin to Breslau!

I remember that summer of 1938 vividly: Europe was on the brink of war, and we were battling all these obstacles, yet there were also bright spots, moments of anticipatory joy. On June 23, on my way to school, I heard that Joe Louis had knocked out Max Schmeling, the purebred German darling of boxing, in less than two minutes! I rejoiced. A classmate said to me belligerently, "You are happy about this outcome." I murmured some kind of false denial— yet another instance of enforced mendacity. I wasn't meant to live under that kind of regime: I gather my face is all too easy to read.

Toward the end of July, my school closed for its annual summer vacation— and thus arrived my last day in what had become a dreaded place. My mother had talked to the school director, and they had agreed that no one would make mention of the fact that I was leaving for good. But Herr Müth, that weak and wretched person, had to share the good news with his pupils, so on my last day at Maria Magdalena the blackboard in the math class bore the chalked inscription STERN IS LEAVING FOR PALESTINE! Many of my fellow students were visibly pleased that the last full-blooded non-Aryan was going. At the end of the day, I went to bid the director, Herr Linder, good-bye. To his final remark, "I hope you know that I have always tried to make your life here as good as possible," I replied, "No, I hadn't noticed." In that short exchange, all that had previously been left unsaid, all that had been bottled up within me, came bubbling out. I left with immense relief, some wonderment, and a bit of satisfaction at the last exchange.

Meanwhile the anti-Jewish campaign in Germany was growing fiercer. In July, it was decreed that by the end of September the licenses of Jewish doctors would be revoked (although some doctors would be allowed, under a different designation, to attend Jewish patients). Lawyers were equally marginalized. The Nazis were now determined to expropriate the property of all Jews and to exclude them altogether from German life; it was as if an invisible ghetto were being established, but, still, the goal remained wholesale extrusion. The Nazis speculated that forcing impoverished Jews onto other countries would fan existing anti-Semitic sentiments elsewhere, and precisely at that time, it did indeed become harder and harder to find a place of refuge.

All summer long, the German propaganda machine unleashed venomous attacks on Czechoslovakia for its alleged maltreatment of the Sudeten Germans, many of them organized in the Nazi satellite party led by the contemptible Konrad Henlein. But among them were also tens of thousands of democrats such as the Kubelkas, and many Jews. Hitler—flush with past triumphs, contemptuous of all opponents, and driven, according to some historians, by a partly unconscious sense that he had only a limited time to fulfill his destiny—wanted a war in order to gain the Sudetenland. The Czech government in May had decreed a general mobilization in response to his thunderous threats, and Hitler, enraged by this unexpected defiance, became determined to smash the state. At this precise moment, within the German army, an opposition group coalesced under General Beck, determined to remove Hitler if he were to start a war. Tied to Czechoslovakia by a military assistance pact (which in turn involved the Soviet Union), France looked to Britain for guidance and support, but that country had embarked on its course of appeasement.

The roots of that appeasement went back to the Great War and to a justified fear of any new war, and to misgivings about the Versailles Treaty, and to fears of Bolshevism. But by 1938, Hitler's massive rearmament and his relentless drive for European hegemony should have been clear—and it was to many politicians, Winston Churchill among them. More recently, the term *appeasement* has often and harmfully been used in thoughtless polemics, as if any effort at controlling conflict were somehow akin to cowardice or treason. In any case, on September 15, in an unprecedented gesture, Prime Minister Neville Chamberlain flew to Hitler's Eagle's Nest at Berchtesgaden, in the Bavarian Alps, seeking a compromise that would meet most, but not all, of Hitler's demands. The next days were filled with rumors of war, while Britain and France pressured the Czechs to surrender the disputed territory in exchange for an international guarantee of the remaining rump state. The tension was palpable. On September 22, Chamberlain returned to Germany to find that Hitler had upped his demands. Chamberlain found this unacceptable, and all signs pointed to war.

Meanwhile we waited for our immigration visas to the United States, having booked passage on a Dutch ship due to leave Rotterdam on September 30. On September 16, we returned from Berlin with our American visas in our passports. The plan now was to pack up—a huge job that had to be done quickly, in time for us to board the SS *Statendam* in Rotterdam. One night, at around 9:00 p.m.—I now reckon it must have been September 19 or 20—the doorbell rang, and when I answered it, there stood Major Edgar von Zerboni, the husband of one of my father's patients. He had come unannounced. Unprecedented. I took him to my father's study, careful not to go to bed until I had heard what it was all about. Herr von Zerboni had come to say that while he had always counseled my father against emigrating—that Hitler would pass and that his wife, with her malfunctioning kidney, needed her doctor—now, realizing we were leaving, he urged us to depart at once: his comrades on active service had told him that Hitler was determined to destroy Czechoslovakia by war if necessary. "If war were to come, you would be drafted into the medical service and then you wouldn't be able to get away," he told my father. What a memorable gesture, this act of decency prompted by a benevolent illusion about the Nazis: the Aryan officer coming to tell his Jewish doctor to leave at once lest he be drafted into the Wehrmacht!

We heeded Zerboni's warning. The plan was to leave Breslau at once and spend the interval before the *Statendam*'s departure in Caldecote. My mother had succeeded, against great odds, in sending grandmother Oma to England days before; my parents now bade their remaining relatives and many friends good-bye. My father decided that he and I would go to Berlin the very next night, for it was easier to leave Germany instantly from there, if need be. The following day was spent collecting and packing his papers, and I helped that night to empty his desk. In the midst of this work, I chanced upon a farewell letter he had written to his sister Marga on the night in 1918 when he had thought he would die. He pleaded with her not to spoil her life in excessive mourning, but to act well, "i.e., to make others happy and with all energy to become happy." So it was then that I discovered that the man who became my father had been so close to death those many years before, and it shook me. I never confronted him with my upsetting discovery. I had known about his influenza and his self-prescribed remedy, but somehow seeing his contemplation of death—and at the very moment we were leaving Germany!—was a different order of information. Just before midnight we took a taxi to the station, and went to our sleeping compartment on the overnight train to Berlin. As it pulled away from Breslau, I noticed my father had tears in his eyes. He was saying good-bye to all that he had once held dear, to all the hopes and dreams of a lifetime. I had no regrets; I felt nothing but joy.

My father and I stayed in Berlin at the home of his older sister, Lotte, a strong and deeply generous person, married to Richard Kobrak, a now-retired civil servant and a wounded veteran of the war who believed that for him the worst was over. We waited for a couple of days until my mother and sister had finished the packing (getting rid of pieces that needed to be left behind, such as the X-ray machine, at risible prices). They joined us on September 22, the day of Neville Chamberlain's second and disastrous visit to Hitler, who rejected the Anglo-French offer to surrender the Sudetenland. War seemed imminent.

On the morning of September 24, Tante Lotte accompanied us to Tempelhof Airport, which was surrounded by a ring of antiaircraft guns. I felt the desperate tension as we passed through the last of the German posts, and then the thrill of having my very first airplane ride also be my passage to freedom. The flight was supposed to be direct to Amsterdam, but suddenly the plane descended and made an unscheduled stop in Hanover—for refueling, since the Berlin authorities were hoarding their supplies. We were once more on German soil, anxious. Eventually the flight resumed, and we reached Schiphol, the Dutch airport. The ride into Amsterdam was one of boundless joy. (The next day, when we flew on to England, we discovered that by mistake we were booked on a Lufthansa plane, subject yet again—but for the last time—to German sovereignty.) We landed in Croydon, stayed long enough in London for me to see the air-raid trenches in Hyde Park, and proceeded to Caldecote, where we remained glued to the radio.

War seemed almost certain. We returned to Holland, and on September 30, we embarked from Rotterdam on the SS *Statendam*—on the very day of the Munich surrender, when France and Britain agreed to Germany's annexation of the Sudetenland, thus rendering a rump Czechoslovakia defenseless. War had been averted, and Hitler could celebrate a great victory—but he felt ag-grieved. He had wanted a war.

As the ship sailed, I felt nothing but joyous relief and wondrous excitement at being on an ocean liner, though I sensed my parents' apprehension about our uncertain future. I knew no English. My Latin and Greek seemed like poor preparation for a new life in America. I left with a loathing for that jubi-lant, Hitler-enthralled Germany. Only in retrospect did I come to understand that growing up in the Third Reich had given me my first and deepest lesson in political education. Only much later did I find in Heine the perfect epitaph for what I had gained: "The love of freedom," he wrote, "was a prison's flower." Also, I came to realize, in this formative—and, no doubt, also deforming—part of my life, that the happiest moments had been in Europe—in France, Switzerland, Denmark, Holland, Czechoslovakia, and England; so I had grown up a European *avant la lettre*. I gained much if at the price of anything resembling a real sentimental education. I rejoiced at escaping the pains of that deadening regime. I had felt the pinpricks of terror; its full and unimagin-able horror began to descend within weeks of our escape. I am left wondering at the accident of survival, the kindness of fate.

✭

CHAPTER 4

THE TERROR FROM AFAR

THE OCEAN TRIP FROM ROTTERDAM to New York was a strange, in a way anxious, interlude, still paid for with the last German money we had. My father sat in a deck chair struggling with an English phrase book, my mother brushed up her English by reading P. G. Wodehouse, while I indulged in some shipboard diversions: Ping-Pong, shuffleboard, and endlessly gazing at the ocean. I felt both short- and long-term apprehension filtering down from my parents, the immediate worry being Ellis Island—the one part of New York I knew by name!—where, we had been told, American immigration officials detained passengers with dubious papers, and there was no certainty what would happen to them. Even regular immigration visas, such as we had, didn't protect you from unpleasant detention.

As the ship neared New York Harbor, immigration officers came aboard and set up tables in the dining room, with passengers like us lining up in front of them. We passed without trouble, but having been cooped up on that line, I had missed the grand entrance into New York, though I think I caught a glimpse of the Statue of Liberty through a porthole. No matter: I knew we were safe. I also knew that only a few weeks before, America's eastern seaboard had been devastated by one of the worst hurricanes of the century. What good fortune: we had arrived just after a natural disaster in our new country and had left Germany just before that human tragedy called *Kristallnacht*.

In Hoboken, that October 9, we were met by a courtly, kind American named Bernhard Heller, Florence Willstätter's brother. On the pier, feeling liberated and responsible, I ran around the huge arrival hall trying to find our trunks and suitcases, scattered as they were not just in the piles marked S but often under the wrong initials. My parents told me later that Mr. Heller was much impressed by my assembling our belongings, but the task seemed natural to me. Was this the beginning of my playing a new role as co-protector of the family?

Mr. Heller took us to Manhattan, which with its awesome skyscrapers really did seem like an overwhelmingly new world—but free of the horrors of the past. He had decided on our first lodging, at the Hotel Washington (good name, nondescript place), on Lexington Avenue in Lower Manhattan, where Toni and I shared a small room. Looking out the window from some high floor, I was suddenly disoriented and afraid. "So this is New York," I said to her. Had I imagined it would be more welcoming or familiar?

I have few memories of the first lonely, anxious days. My parents would be away all day, making myriad contacts and arrangements, and Toni, who spoke some English, would, as I remember, go along with my mother or visit friends of friends. They left me with a dollar a day to feed myself in their absence. I wandered around the neighborhood of the hotel, unaccustomed to the tempo of the streets yet feeling perfectly safe, my greatest articulated fear having to do with the language: would I ever manage to learn English? I liked the Horn and Hardart Automats, because there you could get by mutely: Along the walls were square, windowed compartments that displayed single helpings of every kind of food. You dropped a nickel or a dime in a slot, and out came a sandwich or a slice of pie. I bought some fruit at street stands, pointing to what I wanted, amazed at the variety and affordability of the produce. One day that first week Mr. Heller took me on a tour of New York, including a lunch at the Fraunces Tavern, site of George Washington's Farewell Address. (I kept a carbon copy of my thank-you note, written from the hotel on my battered old typewriter, given to me in 1932, explaining that I was alone there attending to the telephone and to the family's German correspondence. I managed to include a few words in English.)

My father was hoping for a year's fellowship to tide us over while he took the requisite examinations for a medical license. He called on some well-known New York doctors bearing generous letters of recommendations from German physicians. At some point, he received this initial grant. Many refugee physicians had already come to New York, some of whom my father knew, and other close doctor friends arrived shortly after, all of them helped by various organizations that assisted refugees, some specializing in doctors. The closest friend was Hans Neisser, Onkel Gustl's son, now an economics professor at the New School for Social Research. And we had distant relatives in New York who had come to America decades earlier. Peter Brieger, my mother's art historian-brother, had moved to Toronto, and he came to visit us.

Meanwhile my mother, with the advice of friends, looked all over for an affordable and halfway congenial place to live, including in Washington Heights, already known as the Fourth Reich because of its aggregation of German refugees. She favored something "greener" than Manhattan, and we ended up in Jackson Heights, Queens, a leafier borough of New York. It was an appealingly quiet, middle- or lower-middle-class neighborhood, and our three-and-a-half-room apartment came with "a concession," that is, no rent for the first month or so; America was still suffering from the economic recession of 1937. There were some old private houses along the broad, clean streets, and new apartment houses of six stories, none higher.

We had to stay in the Hotel Washington for about a fortnight, until our earthly possessions from Breslau arrived, transported, as I remember, by Schenker, a German firm that specialized in refugee removal. Then, in Queens, the big container disgorged our Breslau belongings: our Poelzig furniture, which now seemed outsized, for the living room; our beds, books, porcelain, glasses, and rugs; my bike; and even a newly bought German refrigerator, which was doubly useless since it had the wrong wattage and the apartment already had one. And so we moved into our cramped new home, which looked as German as we still sounded.

I remember both the thrill of freedom and its price—tremendous insecurity. We had been unimaginably fortunate in trading political terror for economic penury, but the latter was real. We were living off the money the Habers had loaned us to get our visas, but there were no clear prospects of income. My trajectory, in any case, was clear: to go to school, learn English, and adjust to a very different curriculum. My sister's was less clear: since her English was good, friends from abroad counseled that she should become an au pair, which would help out the family; but within several weeks something else turned up.

What kind of country these United States were seemed dramatically clear for a twelve-year-old refugee: a nation headed by the world's only effective democratic leader, a man of surpassing confidence and courage, Franklin D. Roosevelt; New York a state governed shrewdly and energetically by the wise, beneficent Herbert Lehmann, a wealthy Jew of German background; and New

York City run by a fiery, larger-than-life mayor, Fiorello La Guardia, half Italian, half Jew, and all American. How could I not be hopeful? On one of our first days in Jackson Heights, I took my bike to explore the local branch of the New York Public Library, another novelty, and lost my way. I asked a policeman for directions home. Only weeks before, a man in uniform had been a figure of dread to me, but this New York cop, grasping my linguistic disability, answered me helpfully in fragments of Yiddish and German.

By early November, I had started at the neighborhood school, Public School 152, Queens, where, because of my lack of English, I was put in a grade with kids younger than I. My first day at school was another, if minor, *Angstweg*. But I quickly discovered that my teachers and classmates were open, friendly, and helpful—blessedly different from my earlier school experiences in that other country.

Yet that other country remained with us as an ever-present, ever more dreadful horror. Nazi barbarism commanding German power dominated our consciousness, and it became ever harder to distinguish between the two. On the ship we had heard details of the surrender at Munich, the Western powers' abandonment of what had been the only free and democratic country in Central Europe, with the Sudetenland ripped from Czechoslovakia now turned into a Berlin-subservient and authoritarian state. The Western democracies were in retreat everywhere. In Spain, they clung to their policy of nonintervention, a cloak for passivity, which allowed Franco to gain steadily. My sympathies of course were on the Loyalist side, and in my little datebook for 1939, I recorded the Republican defeats, along with primitive maps I drew of the last bastion in Catalonia. (I still have this.) The drama continued to play out in Europe, where so many of our friends and relatives remained.

Within a week of our arrival in the United States, I was writing letters to these connections in the old world on my typewriter (and keeping the carbon copies). I had written letters on that typewriter from the moment I received it, and this served to keep us in contact with our scattered relatives—Habers in Paris, Kobraks in Berlin and others elsewhere in Germany, Uncle Ernst's family in England, and Uncle Peter in Toronto—as well as with friends. To say nothing of letters to our new acquaintances in New York, such as Mr. Heller. (This kindly man was, I discovered, a Roosevelt-hater.) Why did I do this? I probably realized that my parents had less time to attend to correspondence than I, but on my own I was eager to give and receive news, to write about politics to non-Germans. I suppose I didn't want to lose touch with Europe or my past. I was certainly worrying about all kind of matters—the daily trivia of life, school, what other kids might think of me (I was the only refugee in my class, perhaps in the school)—but the letter-writing came from an unconstrained, unexamined inner impulse. I was a stranger to myself and to introspection. I was assuming a double life: the German past, ever present, ever ominous, and the American present, immediate, uncertain but ever promising. By necessity and by psychological predisposition, I lived in both worlds.

Hitler was disappointed at Munich, angry at having been denied a war with Czechoslovakia, and his rage soon fastened on his oldest and most defenseless target, Jews. On November 9, taking advantage of the assassination of a German diplomat in Paris—shot by a crazed Polish Jewish youth whose parents were languishing in no-man's land, having been deported from Germany and refused entry into Poland—Goebbels and Hitler decided on the most radical, visible measure yet in their war against Jews: a carefully organized pogrom disguised as the expression of popular outrage, in which almost all Germany's synagogues were burned down and Jewish shops demolished. Some thirty thousand Jewish males over fifteen or sixteen were herded into concentration camps, suffering instant degradation and then the Nazis' well-practiced brutality. The shock of *Kristallnacht* was palpable. In New York we soon heard about the violence and contemptuous destructiveness of these Nazis who invaded private homes, the sadistic joy with which some of the SA carried out their tasks. This was a prelude to the organized bestiality to follow.

On November 11, the lead story in *The New York Times* opened: "A wave of destruction, looting and incendiarism unparalleled in Germany since the Thirty Years War and in Europe generally since the Bolshevist revolution, swept over Great Germany today as National Socialist cohorts took vengeance on Jewish shops, offices and synagogues for the murder by a young Polish Jew of Ernst vom Rath . . ." The press also reported correctly that this violence against property and individuals had evoked a mixed response from the German people, who could not avoid witnessing this meticulously planned explosion of their "spontaneous" outrage. Individuals may have demurred, and some were punished for their criticism of the Nazis' barbarity, but the silence of the Christian churches in the face of the destruction of sacred places, for example, and the general indifference or subservience expressed a total, almost unbelievable moral bankruptcy. Surely this radical flouting of even the most basic decency was connected with what had happened at Munich, with Hitler's sense that the democracies were succumbing to their own enfeeblement; they might protest his actions, but he knew his anti-Semitism was also gaining sympathy abroad, and that many countries were increasingly hostile to receiving Jewish refugees from Germany.*

This was the ruthless new phase in Nazi policy against Jews, the aim being to rid Germany of all of them and in the process steal their property. Jewish property, carefully registered months earlier, was now in one way or another being confiscated. Jewish prisoners in Buchenwald and Dachau were gradually released—but only after either renouncing their property or proving that they would leave Germany by a definite early date. Yet, by now, emigration, desperately desired, had become a nearly unobtainable goal.

We soon received airmail letters that told of friends or relatives who were "away," a circumlocution that meant that they were either safely in hiding or imprisoned in a concentration camp. My mother's cousin Heinz wrote from Berlin on November 13: "It will interest you to get a letter from me in these days . . . [ellipses in original] I am sitting with my friend Br., who demanded that I spend the night with him . . . Richard [Kobrak] came to see me day before yesterday, he too was on the road." In both instances, Aryans had sheltered these men until it became clear that "non-Aryans" who escaped arrest on November 10 would not be picked up. Perhaps an ambivalent popular response had contributed to this change in policy. In all the letters the main subject was emigration, accompanied by pleas for help and information. Yet our German relatives and friends sent us packages of sweets and other gifts for our first Spartan Christmas in America.

In early January 1939, Richard Willstätter, still in Munich, wrote to my mother. "I stuck it out here to the last possible moment and don't regret it. I escaped imprisonment by a hairsbreadth. I have had to give up my home and all other assets. I am patiently trying to get my passport in order to get to Switzerland, not to a university town but some remote corner, content with the many rich years and good memories." A veteran of the Great War, a Nobel laureate,

---

*The United States was uniquely forceful in its denunciation of Nazi violence. Days after the congressional elections had turned against his administration, President Roosevelt, sharpening a text prepared by the State Department, declared, "I myself could scarcely believe that such things could occur in a twentieth century civilization," and recalled the American ambassador from Berlin. Mayor La Guardia and other officials used far stronger language. On the other hand, the country was divided. Powerful groups supported the isolationism championed by the one-time hero Charles Lindbergh, anti-Semitism was rife and perhaps subterraneously growing, and a strong pro-Nazi group among German Americans, the so-called German American Bund, under the local Führer Fritz Kuhn, spread Nazi venom, including of course attacks on Roosevelt and his supporters. To say nothing of the upper-crust sympathy with so much of what National Socialism stood for. Joseph Kennedy, Roosevelt's ambassador to Britain, became a super-appeaser who claimed to "understand" the Nazis' problems with Jews. Businesspeople were impressed with Germany's economic dynamism, unfettered as the country was by troublesome labor unions.

sixty-seven years old, and this is what the Nazis had reduced him to! A few weeks later, he tried to cross the Swiss border illegally and was arrested, but finally his Swiss friend and former assistant Arthur Stoll somehow got him across the border.*

With *Kristallnacht* signaling the beginning of a far more radical and violent policy against Jews, the German government and individual citizens applied the process of further expropriating Jews and enriching themselves. Hermann Goering levied a special fine of a billion marks on the Jewish community. Jewish students were expelled from German schools and universities. Exclusionary provisions were continually added to the laws. And yet the pensions of retired or expelled civil servants were still being paid, and relatively prosperous Jews were only gradually pauperized.

The American press had been faithfully reporting all this, but an actual encounter with a victim brought the horror closer home. In early January 1939, a young neighbor from our old apartment house in Breslau called on us in New York: his head was shaven, a visible reminder of the ruthless induction of every new victim at a concentration camp, and his whole demeanor had changed; he was furtively disoriented, suddenly old. Herr Moses told us that he had been dragged from his home, thrown into a truck with countless other Breslau Jews, pushed into a train, and carried off to an unknown destination, which turned out to be the concentration camp of Buchenwald, recently enlarged in anticipation of an influx of new inmates. He told us that Nazi thugs had rushed upstairs into our empty apartment looking for my father, and in fact had searched for him in the homes of several of his Aryan patients. Herr Moses himself had been released from Buchenwald by guaranteeing that he would immediately emigrate: a delay in departure would have meant instant rearrest. He gave us news of other friends, some who had shared his fate while others, dragged from their beds, sometimes their sickbeds, had been insulted but left at home as too fragile.

Such a narrow escape! A mere six weeks more in Germany, and this could, this would, have happened to us. And if I had seen my father mistreated and then carried off, if I had lived through weeks or months of uncertainty and of

---

*Willstätter and his end exemplify some of the poignant paradoxes of German Jewish life. Ferdinand Sauerbruch wrote to a Munich physicist friend in May 1942, "As far as Willstätter is concerned . . . I have always visited him, only the last time I couldn't manage. But I shall keep an eye on him and a letter of some weeks ago informed me that he is much better and the danger not so great." Sauerbruch had made lamentable compromises with the Hitler regime but took minor risks to assist eminent Jewish friends: public accommodation, fleeting private decency. He also briefly protected other victims of Nazi persecution. Willstätter died in early August 1942, in his Swiss exile.

my mother's desperate efforts to obtain his release, if I had found him a changed person, physically abused and psychically humiliated—had I lived through that experience, it would have poisoned me forever against all things German, inured me against contacts with any subsequent Germany. As it was, reports of terror from afar confirmed and perhaps intensified my hatred—and my concern for the friends left behind.

Yet the Nazi pogrom of November 9, 1938, had an immediate, paradoxically beneficent effect on our family. Within a week of the Nazi outrage, the administration, faculty, and students of Bryn Mawr College decided to collect funds to support two or three refugee students from Germany. The American Friends Service Committee had long advocated and partially initiated similar programs, specially designed for Jewish and Christian non-Aryan students. Bryn Mawr instantly raised the money for two students, to have free tuition and free board. The AFSC and Bryn Mawr had a close link in the person of Hertha Kraus, a refugee scholar at the college who before Hitler had been in charge of public welfare in Cologne and in the early 1920s had cooperated with the AFSC in its efforts to feed German children. She knew my mother well, and that connection may have facilitated my sister's selection as one of those refugee students admitted to Bryn Mawr after Thanksgiving 1938.*

My sister left for Bryn Mawr at a time of maximum hardship for our family: my father was preparing for his English-language exam as the first step toward taking the medical boards that would eventually allow him to practice medicine in New York; he was worried about whether he might ever earn a living in America, and he studied relentlessly. My mother, somehow more robust and cheerful, sought and gradually found work tutoring children and introducing her method for teaching arithmetic at a few private schools in or near New York. While they were out of the house for most of the day, I was in charge of the daily shopping, and quite often of preparing our rather primitive evening meal. Money was so scarce that it was a major event when I got my first long pants, which cost a dollar on Fourteenth Street. At some point after my sister's departure, we took in a paying tenant, a friend's son, and the apartment became even more cramped. As my English improved, and in time surpassed my

---

*By March 1939, two hundred more such scholarships were available at other American colleges, yet remained unfilled. The hope was that eligible candidates, many still in Germany, others in England, could be given special visas. An Intercollegiate Committee to Aid Student Refugees had Mrs. Roosevelt as its honorary chairwoman. Some people today know of what *wasn't* done for the victims of European persecution—of the mean-spirited, anti-Semitic obstructionism of a Breckenridge Long in the State Department, for example—but they should know equally of the spontaneous efforts made by various individuals and organizations.

parents', I became somewhat less dependent on them and felt a still greater responsibility for them. At home, we continued to speak German, since to speak in flawed English would have seemed unnatural; I wrote my letters in German; and I read the occasional German book—even as I had the immigrant's experience of wishing to assimilate as quickly and as completely as possible. There was a brief interlude, in 1940 or so, when I tried reversing my first two names, signing an occasional letter as Richard. I abandoned that notion very quickly— partly out of pride in Haber's name, partly out of stubbornness. I had had enough trouble with who I was, with what we would now call my "identity" and didn't want to alter it. But that weighted term had not yet become fashionable! (My mother changed her name to Catherine and published under that name, but friends, even American friends, continued to call her Käthe.)

We read about the accelerating events in Europe in the press and in letters from relatives and friends: from Lotte Kobrak in Berlin, Marga Haber in Paris, and my father's aunt Grete in Breslau. Ernst Hamburger in Paris reported just before *Kristallnacht* on the declining morale and increasing chauvinism in France, where the mood was turning ugly and life for German exiles was becoming harder, even though France had once been so hospitable. (In 1937, Hermann Haber had been turned down in his efforts to be naturalized in France—after a two-year waiting period.) I wrote to all of them—to those in Germany out of deep concern, to those in free countries out of curiosity. Meanwhile, I still felt somewhat shy with my American classmates and in a world in which I was a stranger. I devoured so much news from Europe that Ernst Hamburger admonished me to spend less time on day-by-day events and to read Thucydides instead. (How right he was, as I discovered for myself some years later, and as I keep rediscovering at regular intervals.)

In early February 1939, I wrote to my sister at Bryn Mawr that Hitler in his Reichstag speech of January 30 had threatened that if international Jewry were to succeed in unleashing another war, then the Jews of Europe would face annihilation. It was the only news I sent her. I took Hitler seriously. A few weeks later, I noted in my intermittent diary that Pope Pius XI had died and was succeeded by the former nuncio in Berlin, Cardinal Pacelli, who was generally greeted as someone who had a special knowledge of things German, which was true. (Hamburger reported an amusing rumor in Paris: that the new Pope, when asked whether reports of his pro-French sentiments were correct, answered, "I spent ten years in Germany and you think I didn't become a friend of France?") The disappointment was all the greater when he, too, embraced appeasement—and worse.

The pace of disaster intensified. In mid-March, the Nazis completed the destruction of Czechoslovakia, declaring Bohemia and Moravia a German "protectorate" and recognizing Slovakia (under its own pseudo-fascist Catholic leader) as a puppet state. The news pictures of German troops entering Prague—one showed a weeping Czech boy on the sidewalk—had a huge impact, at a time when the public was not yet bombarded by such images.

Public and private events continued instantly to intersect. Correspondence with the Kubelkas ceased, and my worries about various non-Aryan friends in Europe grew more urgent. A month later, Franco completed his conquest of Spain, and tens of thousands of Republican soldiers ended up as unwelcome refugees in France. Would appeasement simply pave the way to fascist domination of Europe? Or was Neville Chamberlain's sudden stiffening after Hitler's absorption of Bohemia and Moravia a turning point? At last he had seemed to recognize Hitler's unappeasable aggressive intent. His government not only extended a military guarantee to Poland—Hitler's most likely next victim—but, for the first time in its history, introduced peacetime military conscription.

The guarantee to Poland was meant to warn Hitler that an attack on that country would precipitate another world war, but its military value to the Poles was close to nil. And when, at long last, Britain and France opened negotiations with the Soviet Union to explore the possibility of a common defense against Germany, they carried out the negotiations with exemplary dilatoriness. There remained a great deal of uncertainty about the "real" Chamberlain, deservedly an object of derision. I feared that he would discover new reasons for appeasing Hitler, who was already spouting venom about the Polish terror against the German minority living in Poland. In France, the plaintive question asking whether one was supposed "to die for Danzig" bespoke an understandable if ultimately suicidal reluctance to stop Hitler by force.

That spring, my Kobrak cousins in Berlin were finally able to leave for Britain, part of the *Kindertransport* that allowed thousands of Jewish and non-Aryan children to find refuge in British homes. Lotte's letters were full of the dearest solicitude for us, wondering how we were faring in the hard early phase of our life in America. Her husband, Richard, somehow always more "German" than my parents, was working with Pastor Heinrich Grüber in his office to help "non-Aryan" Protestants, and he had not realized the urgency of emigration until after the pogrom of November 9, 1938. Grüber belonged to the Confessing Church, that narrowly circumscribed opposition group to the Nazified Protestant Church, whose officials, Pilate-like, had washed their hands of Christians whom Nazi laws had redefined as non-Aryan and subject to the same discriminatory laws as Jews. Grüber was trying to help people who belonged nowhere; at first, the Nazi authorities recognized his organization because, in addition to giving material help to these people and setting up a school for their children, Grüber assisted them in finding ways to emigrate. Extrusion was still Nazi policy.

By January 1939, my parents had persuaded Hans Neisser to make out an affidavit for the Kobraks. By then, American visas were notoriously hard to come by: the U.S. immigration quota for Germans was oversubscribed, and requirements even for visa *applications* became stiffer. In May, Richard wrote to say that he now understood the need for "a changeover" [*Umschichtung*], "even though I already consider the profession of beggar as a divinely ordained one." So it was emigration—but where to go? My father urged speed, and in late July, Richard wrote again: "I will disregard the likelihood that the decline of the West, so fast approaching, renders all such reflections useless."

In late August came the bombshell: I brought home the newspaper with its banner headline that Germany and the Soviet Union had signed a nonaggression pact. Our whole mistaken worldview collapsed: we had believed, as both Nazis and Communists had preached for more than a decade, that the National Socialists' principal enemy was (Jewish) Bolshevism, and that the Soviet Union's principal enemy was fascism and especially Nazism, which Communists defined as the most terroristic, militaristic form of monopoly capitalism. In 1935, the Soviets had seemed to confirm their antifascist commitment when they had abandoned their vile campaign against social democracy and proclaimed their support of Popular Front regimes that joined Socialists, Communists, and other opponents of fascism; they had done this both in Spain and in Léon Blum's effort at a New Deal in France.

Our ideology had been very simple, then, and like all ideologies self-serving. The litmus test was whether one was for or against Nazism. Did one recognize Nazism as the single greatest, most monstrous threat? If the Soviet Union was antifascist, as it claimed it was and as seemed consistent with the original promise of its proletarian revolution, then one needed it as an ally, and the argument that there were "no enemies to the left" seemed credible. But we hadn't wanted to see the full extent of Soviet terror. Shocked by reports of Soviet purges and other atrocities, we took refuge in the idea that perhaps these reports were fascist-inspired or reactionary exaggerations. And earlier in 1939, we had continued to believe that somehow the Soviet Union was inescapably antifascist, whatever their internal misdeeds or crimes. There were ominous signs, and I had noted them: Stalin's removal in May of Maxim Litvinov, his Jewish foreign minister and preacher of collective security, and his warning that the Soviet Union would not pull other peoples' chestnuts out of the fire. Still, wouldn't the Soviets understand that a Europe dominated by Nazi Germany would be a terrifying threat? It was in their own interests as defined by realpolitik to oppose such an outcome. But this August news undermined all such speculations, as did the picture of a grinning Foreign Minister Ribbentrop watching Stalin sign the pact. And we didn't yet know of its secret annexes! For me (as for many others) this end of an illusion turned out to be something of a safeguard against later temptations to indulge in pro-Soviet fantasies.

On the day of the German-Soviet Pact, Richard Kobrak wrote again: "I fear that in a few days the fate of Europe will be fulfilled." His ever more desperate letters continued, while we learned from the press that Jews in Germany were subject to ever-greater deprivation and humiliation. As long as the United States was a neutral power, postal exchange was permitted. But Jews in Germany were required to post letters to foreign countries in person at the post office, and to put their names on the envelopes; by then, they were also required to add "Israel" or "Sara" as their middle name. By September 1941, they also had to wear the yellow star. We used mostly surface mail, indicating on the envelope what boat the letter was destined for; in that way, transatlantic mail took about a week or ten days. But soon our friends pleaded for airmail, which my father had been reluctant to use because of the added expense; letters from America that came by sea took forever to arrive and sometimes never did—the British blockade!—while letters from Germany to the United States went via Siberia and Japan.

A fortnight later, on September 1, 1939, the German army invaded Poland, after having staged a farcical mock attack by Poles on a radio station near Breslau. Forty-eight hours after that, Great Britain declared war on Germany, and France followed within five hours. We felt relief: only force could bring an end to the monstrous evil of Hitler's regime, and of course the Allies would prevail. Surely the French with their "impregnable" Maginot Line and the British with their invincible navy were much stronger than the Germans; so the military experts informed us, and faith allowed no other thought.

Meanwhile, Germany's rapid conquest of Poland proceeded in all its brutality, together with the ultimate, unexpected perfidy: Russia's occupation of eastern Poland. In the eighteenth century, Poland's neighbors had thrice partitioned the country, the last time extinguishing it altogether. This, then, was the fourth partition of Poland. The great British cartoonist David Low encapsulated this terrible moment in his witty and infallible record of British folly and Axis crime: a sketch shows Hitler and Stalin greeting each other like Livingstone and Stanley across a prostrate Poland. Hitler to Stalin: "The scum of the earth, I believe?" Stalin's reply: "The bloody assassin of the workers, I presume?"

The outbreak of war endangered our family and friends in France, where the French authorities feared "fifth columnists" (a term that had been coined by Spain's fascists a few years earlier, when they wrongly predicted their imminent capture of Madrid, with four columns outside and a "fifth column" inside) and immediately interned most German refugees, even though these people were in fact the very essence of anti-Nazism. Desperate letters arrived from Lotte Hamburger and Marga Haber; Ernst Hamburger was released within weeks, and Hermann Haber, faced with a choice between continued internment and enlisting in the Foreign Legion, chose the latter. But all of them now contemplated emigration to the United States. At the same time, our correspondents still in Germany wrote with enforced equanimity, since every word was composed with Gestapo censorship in mind. (I still have a postcard from Aunt Lotte stamped with a swastika by the *Oberkommando* of the Wehrmacht.)

After Germany's brutal conquest of Poland, the belligerents in Europe settled down to "the phony war," and months went by without significant military action. Meanwhile the Germans began their terror regime in Poland, but of that atrocity we knew little in the beginning, though we wondered if France and Britain realized the immense danger they were facing. (We now know that ever since the Munich conference, President Roosevelt—unlike most of his countrymen—had considered Nazi Germany an actual threat to the United States.) Immigration to the United States remained immensely difficult, though in that winter of 1939–1940, German Jews with the necessary papers could still escape the ever-tightening noose. As Chaim Weizmann of the World Zionist Organization had declared already, in 1936, for the six million Jews in East Central Europe, "The world is divided into places where they cannot live and places where they may not enter." But efforts to save individuals continued—and were sometimes successful.

The pace of disaster continued to intensify. In November, the Red Army attacked Finland, and the brave Finns briefly defied what turned out to be a surprisingly enfeebled juggernaut. Then, in April 1940, the Germans resumed their march to European hegemony: in a matter of days the Wehrmacht occupied Denmark and attacked Norway, where it encountered far greater resistance, but even Allied help could not prevent a final defeat: Norway came under the German heel, with the much-publicized help of fifth columnists and native fascist collaborators, who formed a puppet government under Vidkun Quisling—his name adding a key word to our political language and ideological orientation.

On May 10, the Germans launched their triple attack on Holland, Belgium, and France. Holland surrendered quickly—after the Germans' barbaric bombing of Rotterdam, intended to demonstrate their power and invincibility and sow defeatism among Belgian and French civilians. Day after day, news of Allied reverses poured in, and German troops, outflanking the Maginot Line, reached the Channel by early June. The Allied, mostly British, troops who had moved into Belgium were now caught in the German trap—and only "the miracle of Dunkirk," the successful evacuation of some 250,000 Allied troops from that famous beach, saved them. Our hope focused on Winston Churchill, who became prime minister at last, just as the German offensive in the west began. He tried to rally the French, even proposing a political union of Great Britain and France, and then, when the French prepared for a separate armistice, he vowed that Great Britain would carry on the war alone—against all odds. His broadcasts in May and June were electrifying: his resolve cast in historic eloquence, his defiance commanding faith and admiration: "We shall never surrender." I listened to all his speeches, even if it meant briefly neglecting my weekend job of delivering groceries from our nearby local market.

A world had been broken, and all in a matter of weeks. The Germans had become the virtual masters of continental Europe, having established a larger imperium than Napoleon's at the height of his power. On the day in mid-June that German troops marched down the Champs Elysées, I wept—and stayed home from school. Only Churchill's Britain defied the seemingly invincible Hitler, and in an unconscious suspension of disbelief, we believed Churchill. Somehow the thought of a final German victory was unimaginable, and so we persuaded ourselves that however desperate the situation, the cause was not hopeless, that in the long run Britain, supported by its empire, would prevail—provided, of course, that the United States helped. America was the last great hope—divided as it was within itself, but hope nonetheless.

At the beginning of the German onslaught, most German political refugees in France were interned in French camps under appalling conditions; veterans of Dachau thought them worse than that notorious hell. Some refugees were drafted into nonfighting units of the French army. Ernst Hamburger wrote to us on May 14 that he expected to be interned the next day. Desperate notes arrived in the daily mail as chaos enveloped a country, and a world, in shock. Like my parents, if independently, I again threw myself into epistolary work on behalf of the family. On May 18, I wrote to the French Information Center in New York, expressing in embarrassingly sentimental (Germanic?) fashion my great love of France. I said that a German refugee who had been a democratic parliamentarian in Weimar had been imprisoned in France at the beginning of the war; "only after an acute heart-illness, the fifty-year-old man was released." Press reports indicated that such people had been rearrested: was there a way to get him out? "I know that France is on the brink of being conquered but you will understand that I am worried about my best friend, who loves France just as much as I do." A certain M. Le Branchu, director of the center, replied on June 4 that "a few weeks ago the French government found it necessary to take new and stricter protective measures against men and women of German nationality."

Meanwhile, France's Third Republic signed its own death warrant, and a new authoritarian government under Marshal Pétain was established, its first act being to sign an armistice with Germany that divided France into zones occupied by either German or Italian troops, and zones (the southern third of the country) unoccupied and directly subject to Pétain's Vichy government. (The signing of the armistice continued the long history of symbolic injuries that France and Germany inflicted on each other: just as the French had forced the Germans to accept the punitive peace of Versailles in the same Hall of Mirrors where Germany had proclaimed the founding of its empire in 1871, so now Hitler commandeered the same railroad car in the same place, Compiègne, where Germany had been made to sign the armistice in November 1918.)

The armistice contained an ominous clause, obliging "the French government . . . to surrender upon demand" all Germans [or non-French] whom the German government named, the immediate target obviously being German political refugees. Five days later, Lotte Hamburger wrote to us from unoccupied France that she had last seen her husband on May 14; perhaps, she added, she would never see him again. On July 1, I wrote again to M. Le Branchu at the French Information Center, asking if there was a way of getting an endangered political refugee out of France. If this man is delivered to the Germans, I wrote, "he faces certain death by the brutal Gestapo." We knew that prominent Weimar politicians turned over to the Germans were murdered, the best-known instance being that of Hamburger's Social Democratic friend, the former finance minister Rudolf Hilferding.

Marga Haber fled with her three daughters to Domme, in the Dordogne, uncertain whether her husband was still with the Foreign Legion in Algeria.

On July 9, I inquired of the French Information Center whether Domme was in the unoccupied zone. It was. All was chaos—and fear, lest these people should fall into German hands. We now know that the Germans were remarkably slow in requesting their surrender; on the other hand, the Vichy government almost at once, and without German prompting, began to enact an anti-Semitic program on its own.

On the very day of the German-French armistice, an Emergency Rescue Committee was established in New York, with Reinhold Niebuhr, George Shuster, and others who had a fervent interest in German democrats, as sponsors. German political exiles in New York—some of them Social Democrats, some of whom my father knew—mobilized American labor unions and the Jewish Labor Committee to rescue their compatriots in France. These groups compiled lists of those especially endangered—including writers and artists with well-known anti-Nazi views. By August, the Emergency Rescue Committee had dispatched a gallant young American, Varian Fry, fresh out of Harvard, to Marseilles to organize a rescue mission, which entailed among other things obtaining a special supply of American visas; Eleanor Roosevelt was a major supporter of these efforts.

In early August we heard from Hamburger, who had rejoined his family after nearly three months "*de la vie militaire,*" presumably in some support unit. The American consul in Marseilles, having obtained his address, issued him a visa, but he needed a French exit visa, too, and French bureaucracy moved cautiously. Like other prominent refugees, the Hamburgers decided to leave illegally, crossing into Spain across the Pyrenees along a perilous path—mapped out by Varian Fry and his young associate Albert Hirschman—with whatever belongings they could carry on their backs. The philosopher Walter Benjamin took the same route at nearly the same time, but at the first stop in Spanish territory, Port Bou, fearing he might be forced back to France, he committed suicide on September 27.

In Spain, Franco's surprisingly accommodating authorities allowed the Hamburgers' passage to Lisbon. (An American historian of Spain recently told me that Franco's benevolence reflected his wish to have prosperous Sephardic Jews return to Spain from France and Holland, together with their bank accounts. Franco also liked "thumbing his nose at Hitler in minor matters." An amazing idea, that in these months before Hitler's extermination of the Jews had begun, Franco took such measures in the interest of greed!) From there, Hamburger let us know that the family had booked passage on a Greek ship leaving Lisbon for New York on September 28: "When I recall that I rejoined my family on July 30 after my demobilization and two months later hope to arrive in New York, that seems like a miracle, of which you are one of the key artisans."

I was deputized to meet the Hamburgers when the *Nea Hellas* arrived in Hoboken at 9:00 a.m. on October 13. The pier was crowded with tensely anxious people—after all, this was one of the very first ships bringing refugees from occupied Europe—waiting for the gangplank to be lowered. I spotted Thomas Mann, whom it was easy to recognize. After a while, I saw a corpulent man disembark with his wife, and Thomas Mann moved forward to greet him; the two embraced in a most delicate and hesitant manner. It was his brother Heinrich, coming from exile in France, a fellow writer and activist anti-Nazi with whom Thomas had the most complicated, competitive relationship. (I didn't know then that Thomas Mann's son Golo was on the same ship.) Other notables emerged, among them Franz Werfel, the well-known novelist, and his wife, Alma. Werfel had written an account of the Armenian massacre, *The Forty Days of Musa Dagh*, which I had read with passion. *The New York Times* reported the next day that Werfel had refused to explain how he had made his way from southern France to Lisbon: "It would be very dangerous to speak of it. Many of my friends are still in [French] concentration camps." I brought the Hamburgers to their temporary quarters on West Seventy-ninth Street, feeling grateful that our two families could thus help each other, with America as the common haven.

It was harder to get the Habers out of France. My father managed to get their name on the Emergency List, and by mid-July 1940 the American consul in Marseilles had been instructed to issue visas for them. But it was only in late September that Hermann was demobilized and could rejoin his family; shortly thereafter, Marga wrote that a trip to Marseilles required a *sauf-conduit* from the French authorities, which was not easy to obtain, and that the American consulate wouldn't issue a visa until the family had a French exit visa—which in turn depended, in Kafkaesque fashion, on their having received an American visa! Marga needed an introduction to "Mr. Fray [sic] who according to everyone is the key person for all difficulties." A few days later: "Who is Mr. Fray? He is called the 'almighty' in Marseilles." On four different occasions, Albert Einstein sent letters from Princeton, where he had come to the Institute for Advanced Study long before the war, either to the American consul or to my father on behalf of the Habers. Funds had to be raised to pay for their ship passage; Richard Willstätter, safe but hardly wealthy, helped. The Habers were finally able to leave France "legally" in April 1941, on a ship from Lisbon that was intercepted by the British, who briefly interned its passengers in Trinidad; they landed in New York in June.

In 1940, Yvonne Mercier and her three children, whom we had first met in Paris as friends of the Habers in 1933, arrived on a Pan-Am clipper, where I had spotted their names on the published list of arrivals. On first seeing us again, Yvonne Mercier, a vivacious, flirtatious, and sophisticated Anglo-French woman, said to my father, "Ah, now one can be sick again!" I spent part of a summer with the Mercier family, whose oldest son, Jacques, was roughly my age. Soon more Haber friends came over, including Joseph Blumenfeld and his wife, both Russian-born French citizens. I frequented this new European group, the admission ticket being my skill at playing bridge. I even earned some money at cards, but the real reward was the intense political talk—and Blumenfeld's friendship. I treasured Ossinka, as he was called, for his melancholy wisdom, more Russian than French. These new arrivals joined the mostly German refugee enclave in New York, which provided an element of cohesion, a haven of friendships, and a place for bickering. Émigré life— whether in Paris in the 1840s or in New York a century later—is always rich in harmony and hostility.

By dint of unremitting study, my father had passed the English examination for foreigners in December 1938, after a mere two months in America. For the medical boards that came next he had had to struggle to relearn all manner of details (he complained about having to memorize the foot's bone structure after almost twenty years of practicing internal medicine), but he passed the exam on the first try, and in the summer of 1940 had opened an office in Manhattan. Patients, in the beginning mostly fellow refugees, gradually came, and fellow doctors referred their patients and friends. At the same time, my father tutored other German physicians for their medical boards. American patients eventually came as well, but my father was having a difficult time—and all along no financial security. The unremitting strain of nearly a decade now was taking its toll on his health: he suffered from gastritis and other minor afflictions. Since I did the shopping and prepared the occasional evening meal, I took his stomach upsets as a kind of rebuke.

Jackson Heights and Forest Hills (socially a notch higher) had their share of refugees who became patients of my father, and by the mid-1940s, I encouraged some of my own friends and colleagues to consult him; one of them referred to the "Breslau circuit," and it was true that just about every medical specialty had its distinguished Breslau practitioner in New York. The Breslau circuit came to include the surgeon Rudolf Nissen, who in 1939 had left his post in Istanbul and come to New York via Boston. Nissen, who had been Sauerbruch's chief assistant, was himself perhaps the greater doctor. But even he did not get the kind of clinical appointment he deserved, though he established a superb private practice and had a position at the Brooklyn Jewish Hospital. For my father, who had had him as a friend from adolescence, Nissen's arrival in New York together with his wife, Ruth—a charming and beautiful "Aryan" Christian who had unhesitatingly joined him in his trek to Istanbul—was a joy.

Nissen (like my father and many of his colleagues) deplored the then still frequent practice of fee-splitting among doctors—and did so publicly. (The system was simple: the specialist to whom a general practitioner had referred a patient transmitted somehow a part of the latter's fee to the referring doctor.) He was also a passionate horseman, and I remember seeing him, dashing and stylish, on his black horse in Central Park. For me, too, Nissen was very special, though from time to time I would tease him. In his memoirs, he wrote that he and his wife thought of me as an adopted son, and we remained good friends even after he left New York for a professorship in Basel in 1952, where he spent his first happy years after Berlin; when I saw him there in his modern, quiet home, he was quite outspoken in his contempt for many things German, past and present.

So in those first years in New York we lived primarily in a German-European world, though we were developing contacts and new friendships with Americans. Given the nature of my parents' work, we had an easier time assimilating than many, I imagine. We certainly tried to keep up to date with both worlds we were living in. German-speaking New Yorkers had their own weekly paper, *Aufbau*, which conveyed essential news about the difficult lives of refugees and the far worse lives of those still in German clutches. And one had to keep one's sense of humor; my father's wonderful repertory of jokes, often self-critical, told their own story. One example: Hitler has been overthrown, decency has been restored, and Mueller and Schmidt, two good German *Bürger*, meet on a street corner in Berlin. Each is delighted to report that he now has his Jewish physician back, and his Jewish lawyer, and it's splendid to feel again that one is in good hands. Mueller adds ruefully, "If only they didn't speak the English so loudly on the street."

Life at home was difficult for me: both parents were working hard, and I had to combine schoolwork—which was unfamiliar but not too difficult—with managing most of the household: when Uncle Peter from Toronto sent a modest check for Christmas so that we could have something special, he sent it to me, seeing as how I was "the head of the family budget," as he put it. In July 1939, my Brieger grandmother, Oma, had moved in with us; she had gone from England to Toronto, but now Uncle Peter was repairing to Caldecote, so she came to New York. I had to sleep in the living room; she helped me in doing the daily chores. We had our only bitter argument in September 1939, with the outbreak of the war: her wish, dictated by the horrors of the Great War, was that peace should be preserved, mine was that Hitler's expansionist terrors be stopped, and that meant by force, the only possible way.

My mother was by then both tutoring and working with Max Wertheimer, the founder of Gestalt psychology, who had been intrigued by her material for teaching arithmetic (for which she was to receive an American patent in 1940). To his astonishment he thought the material was based on Gestalt theory, of which my mother, who had developed the material intuitively and pragmatically, knew next to nothing! Wertheimer was now one of the stars at The New School for Social Research, and he wanted her as an assistant so that she could learn the theory behind her practice. Then, in November 1939, she fell ill with a gallbladder attack and could attend to only the most essential obligations at the New School, spending a lot of time in bed.

A few weeks later I came home from school to find Oma, too, feeling unwell; for years she had suffered from hypertension, and that afternoon she was having difficulty breathing. We were alone together until my father came home in the early evening; then my mother arrived, too—in great pain—and my father sent her to bed. He tried to do what he could to help Oma, but a few hours later she was dead, and my mother had to be told of her mother's death. She and Oma had been inseparable, and her grief was the more touching for being so quiet and stoic, as she tried to conduct herself as her mother would have expected. A few days later, my father and I sat alone for a Jewish funeral service at the Riverside Memorial Chapel, with the characteristically Jewish plain pine coffin, without flowers, in front of us. Thus we said farewell to the most genuinely "Christian" of my forebears. My father wept—I think it was the last time I saw him cry. My mother, too ill to be with us, was at home, characteristically busy, changing the bedsheets, rearranging the living quarters, silently doing what her mother would have wanted her to do. Christmas was sad and subdued.

On the afternoon of New Year's Eve, I went for a bike ride, and when I came home I mentioned to my father that I had a slight stomachache. He asked me a few questions about it, examined me, but as was typical of him kept the possibly bad news from my mother, still in bed with her inflamed gall bladder, telling her instead that he had to go into the city and that I would accompany him to Manhattan. A quick blood test at the hospital promptly confirmed

his suspicion of acute appendicitis. A "Breslau" doctor performed the operation, and from the hospital I called my mother to tell her that I was fine and
appendix-less. (At my request, the appendix, immersed in formaldehyde, was
returned to me in a small bottle. As a trophy, I took it to school.)

The rewards of this last crisis were for me immeasurable: for ten days and for
the first time since I had come to the United States, I was in an all-American
surrounding, hearing almost nothing but English spoken twenty-four hours a
day, cared for by kind nurses—and supervised, I recall, by a beautiful head
nurse who wore an unforgettable red sweater over her uniform. Just as memorable was that the patient in the next bed had a radio, and he happened to be
listening to President Roosevelt giving his Jackson Day speech in Washington,
on January 8. I was enthralled by that amazing voice and by the president's
ebullience; I never forgot the opening, in which he mocked the absence of Republicans from "this great banquet," and wondered why they weren't there. It
reminded him, he said, of the story of a teacher asking her class "how many of
them wanted to go to heaven. With eyes that sparkled at the thought every
small boy in the class held up his hand—except one. 'Teacher,' he said, 'sure I
want to go to heaven, but,' pointing to the rest of the boys in the room, 'not with
that bunch.'" I had never heard such political high-spiritedness before, and it
enthralled me.

I had my new American heroes and heroines. One of them was New York's
great mayor Fiorello La Guardia, who always spoke of Hitler with fervor and
contempt. In regard to plans for the 1939 World's Fair, he had said that of
course it should include a German exhibit, to wit, a "Chamber of Horrors" for
"that brown-shirted fanatic who is now menacing the peace of the world." In
April 1939, I had heard a broadcast report that La Guardia was thinking of not
running again for office, so I wrote him an impassioned letter pleading that he
run again and apologizing for my bad English. His response: "Thank you for
your letter of April 11. I am glad you are in New York, and I think your English
is fine."

The letter-writing continued. In August 1940, I wrote to Erika Mann,
whose *School for Barbarians* (1938), a book on German education, I had just
read, thanking her for what she had done for "us refugees" and recalling my
days in German schools: "I remember especially well the fact that the teacher
in Protestant religion not once in over two years mentioned the existence of
the Old Testament." In my school experience, I had "felt only two things, a
strong contempt and hatred for the Nazis and how proud I was to be a Non-
Aryan!" Her response characterized much of the mood of the time: "Our im-

pressions are quite the same. You may be sure that everything will take a turn for the better, that is the wish and hope we must cling to."*

In the summer of 1940, as the Battle of Britain raged, we needed more than hope. The United States continued to be deeply split between interventionists and isolationists, between those who understood that as a matter of self-defense the United States should back Great Britain, short of going to war, and those who opposed all such efforts, believing the United States should never get entangled in this European conflict. For some isolationists other motives were at work as well: some of them saw in Hitler and in fascism "the wave of the future"; some sympathized with his anti-Semitism even if they found it a bit excessive. Roosevelt understood the German danger, but he also knew it was an election year and he would have to temper his wish to aid Britain with political prudence.

In mid-August, William C. Bullitt, who had been America's first ambassador to the Soviet Union and then ambassador in France and had just returned from Paris, gave a radio address sponsored by the American Philosophical Society. His was an authoritative firsthand report on the fall of France, which he blamed on French unpreparedness, on French unwillingness to see the German danger in time; he described the terror of German tactics, but above all he emphasized the cunning work of German spies and agents. The speech was meant as a clarion call to the United States, a warning that it, too, was threatened, that it was protected by the British navy, the destruction of which "would be the turning of our Atlantic Maginot Line . . . The soothing words, 'Maginot Line,' were the refrain of a lullaby of death for France." He warned against Nazi and communist agents and spies in the United States and, more immediately, demanded that as a first step in preparing for danger, America introduce conscription—an unheard-of peacetime measure. He asked for sacrifices and volunteers in the fight "against the enemies who are already within our country" and ended with the call to "Write to me and I shall try personally to put you in touch with the men and women" who know how you can help in your own neighborhood.†

---

*Some months later, my father wrote to her father, Thomas Mann, full of admiration for *Lotte in Weimar* but pointing out two possible mistakes in it. In Mann's handwritten response he wondered whether there would ever be a second German edition that would allow for correcting possible slips: "that depends, as so many greater things, on the outcome of the war. Odd to think that the English in addition to other matters are also fighting for *Lotte*."

†The speech contained a remarkable, if clumsy, precedent for a much more famous appeal: "When are we going to say to them [our legislators] that we don't want to hear any longer about what we can get from our country, but we do want to hear what we can give to our country?" Did Theodore Sorenson or John F. Kennedy hear or read that speech? And he also asked, "Why are we sleeping, Americans?"

Of course I wrote at once, and within a week Bullitt replied that he had told the Council for Democracy to get in touch with me. This council in New York, headed by the popular radio commentator Raymond Gram Swing, had as its goal to "instill in the minds of Americans the meaning, value and workability of Democracy . . . [while] the whole world is threatened by the menace of totalitarianism." One Mary Vreeland of the council wrote to me, and for a year or so I kept in touch with her. The first "assignment" she proposed to me was to "listen in on the foreign-language [German] stations and report on any subversive broadcasts." In February 1941, I duly reported that I hadn't heard anything "objectionable," though I noted that some broadcasts recommended "very strongly that all Germans should on a given day come to this or that tavern—what happens there is a wide field of speculation." Subsequently, I was asked to send the names of the taverns and the dates of meetings. In retrospect, I feel a bit queasy about these efforts, but it was a time when the German-American Bund was still poisonously active.

In November 1940, Roosevelt was reelected to an unprecedented third term. (In October, at a school election debate, I had been chosen to speak for Roosevelt, while a senior debated for his opponent, Wendell Willkie, "the barefoot boy from Wall Street," as Harold Ickes called him. That senior was a girl I admired hugely—from a distance, since I was distressingly shy with girls. But at least I won the debate—and FDR the election.) At Christmas time, Churchill visited Washington and gave a rousing speech before both houses of Congress, and once again I skipped my delivery assignments at the local market and stayed at home, glued to the radio. In the next few months Roosevelt demonstrated the true power of democratic leadership properly deployed: he and Churchill were the most effective democratic leaders during a century that witnessed so much enfeeblement of democracy.

Roosevelt's delicate, determined push to help Great Britain against Germany—beginning with declaring that the United States was "an arsenal for democracy" and winning Senate approval for the Lend-Lease Bill in March 1941, despite the deep split between interventionists and isolationists—was a great feat. A powerful group called the Committee to Defend America by Aiding the Allies, begun in May 1940, supported these efforts; it has remained for me a model of what well-organized individual citizens can accomplish. In July 1941 came the dramatic meeting of Churchill and Roosevelt on the warship *Prince of Wales* and the proclamation of the Atlantic Charter. That fall, as British losses at sea mounted and an American destroyer was sunk, Roosevelt ordered American ships "to shoot at sight." Hitler was surprisingly passive in the face of these ever more open American involvements.

Throughout 1940 and 1941 we were able to keep up our correspondence with the Kobraks in Berlin, who were now desperate to emigrate, their principal hope being pinned on the United States. But ever since 1938, demand far outstripped the supply of places on the national quota for German immigrants to the United States, and there was the difficulty of finding the dollars that could pay for their passage. Every guarantee was made to the American consulate in Berlin attesting that the Kobraks would find adequate support in the United States and would not be a burden on public assistance; my father, who assumed responsibility for these various tasks, turned to Richard Kobrak's brother Fritz, who, while a prosperous businessman in Danzig, had recognized the danger signals in time and was now in Argentina. He was what I suppose one calls "apolitical" in the German style, willingly remote from distressing news. In April 1940, answering an early inquiry from my father, he had observed that if the Allies were to win, they would impose another Versailles Treaty on Germany and another thirty years' war would ensue. (How often and in such different contexts this analogy was made!) In late May of that year he reported that refugees arriving in Argentina claimed that "life in Germany while not exactly a pleasure was still far from hell." By February 1941 my father pointed out that "deportation of Jews from Germany . . . was not limited to Baden . . . and is almost tantamount to a death sentence."

Richard Kobrak was continuing his work in Pastor Grüber's office, but by then, as my father reported to Fritz Kobrak, Grüber had been arrested; his office had been closed in January.* Then, in April, the Kobraks finally received a registration number from the American consulate, with the help of Hertha Kraus and the promise of support from the American Friends Service Committee. There was still the difficult question of the money for the passage: six to eight hundred dollars. In September, Lotte Kobrak wrote to say that they had heard that someone in New York could get Cuban visas for $400, with another $1,300 needed as a guarantee sum; in late October, the Kobraks telegraphed my father and the Habers to say they had the Cuban visas but now needed one thousand dollars for passage. Did the families in New York and Argentina squabble over how to get the money? There is no record, but every day mattered.

Meanwhile, I continued my correspondence with my father's Tante Grete (always called Auntie), who remained in Breslau in increasingly desperate con-

---

*Imprisoned and manhandled in the concentration camps in Dachau and Sachsenhausen, Grüber was released in 1943. After the war, he briefly held an official Protestant position with the East German regime. In recent years, conflicting stories about Grüber have appeared, none, however, casting doubt on his work in the late 1930s.

ditions. In September 1941, Lotte told us that Auntie, who had earlier been moved to a rooming house, had been ordered to move again, this time to a single room. (Beginning in September of that year, the Nazis had decided to herd all Jews together into ever more cramped quarters, require them to shop in certain stores and only at certain hours, and force them to wear the yellow star.) The night before the move, Auntie allowed a friend to help her pack her things, wrote various farewell letters (which we never saw), and then took her life.

In Lotte's last letter—or at least I have found no other—in early November, in the same soft, precise handwriting that was unchanged since the letters she had written to her brother during the Great War, she mentioned that she and Richard, too, had had to move to a single room, that they had been able to take some of their own furniture with them, that shopping was easier, that their unheated terrace, filled with sun, could serve as an extra room. There wasn't a single complaining note in Lotte's letter. To the contrary, she was reassuring, once more expressing her gratitude for my parents' help and her concern for our well-being. She was a woman of unfailing love and generosity, and by character and nature strong and beautiful.

The rest was heartbreak. After Pearl Harbor, all contacts with our German world ceased. We no longer knew what was happening to the Kobraks, who seemed so close to rescue. We stayed in touch with their children in England. After the war—I seem to have repressed the when and the how of this—we learned that the Kobraks had been deported to Theresienstadt, the ghetto camp in Bohemia where Jews and non-Aryans, many of them veterans of the Great War or in some other "special" category, were condemned to prison life in the shadow of hunger, disease, and death. My aunt Lotte, we somehow learned, was a source of unending comfort in Theresienstadt, tending to those worse off than she and my uncle, and to the end dignified. When shoelaces had to be replaced by plain string, she dipped hers in ink. Many thousands of people died in Theresienstadt, and many more were sent from there "east" to the death camps, and this is what happened to my aunt and uncle. (Decades later, I received confirmation from Yad Vashem, the Holocaust Martyrs' and Heroes' Remembrance Authority in Israel, that they had been murdered in Auschwitz.) Our family often talked of Lotte, of her young days, and of her bravery. I often think of her, and at predictable and unpredictable moments my mind suddenly fills with the horror of her and Uncle Richard's end. The sight of a German cattle car will do it. The rest are private thoughts.

In Auntie Grete's last letter to me she spoke of her pleasure at seeing that my sister and I had become friends. And it was true that Toni and I—though physically separated now that she was at Bryn Mawr—did draw closer out of mutual concern for our parents. I still thought of her as very privileged in her all-American milieu, so unfamiliar to me, and I didn't sufficiently understand her difficulties. She was studying psychology and philosophy and didn't share my all-consuming interest in what was going on in the world. When she brought a German boyfriend home, I bristled—unkindly. But we came to depend on one another—over the years, more and more.

The tensions that remained were of course intertwined with family dynamics. Toni had inherited some of my father's quick temper, so there was often tension between him and her, and my mother, with her mostly unobtrusive authority, would be (excessively?) protective of her. I tried, on my part, to steer clear of conflicts with either parent, being a cheering confidant to my father while cherishing an unspoken bond to my mother. For myriad public and private reasons I was especially close to them both, at once protected and protecting.

In the spring of 1941, the entire class of my school—the previous fall I had entered Bentley, a private high school in Manhattan, on a full scholarship—went for a field trip to Northfield, Massachusetts, where we stayed at the local youth hostel. On our return, which came right after Germany's invasion of Yugoslavia and Greece, I wrote to Mrs. Vreeland at the Council for Democracy that on our trip one of our teachers had given vent to openly avowed communist views: "She denied that we had any resemblance in this country to democracy and that only Communism can save us." I had argued passionately with this young student teacher over the issue of American aid to Britain: to her, it was an "imperialist war" that America should stay out of. I was angry at these new enemies on the left, with their insidious message. This was only one of many arguments with sanctimonious fellow travelers who saw no difference between "imperialist" Britain and fascist Germany and implied a moral equivalency between them, while they thought of us, of "interventionists," as tools of capitalism and fascism. Our teacher had kept silent on this point, so I appealed to Mrs. Vreeland, asking what could be done.

A few weeks later, Bentley's principal summoned me to her office and confronted me with the substance of my letter, bluntly reminding me that I was on a full year-by-year scholarship. And by July, I reported to Mrs. Vreeland that the school year had ended splendidly and the school itself was almost "a perfect miniature democracy." I was mortified at the time—and am embarrassed now, both by my initial reporting on a teacher and by my subsequent all-too-effusive effort to correct my indiscretion. But at least the incident taught me a lesson.

Of course things changed mightily in June 1941, with the German invasion of the Soviet Union. It was perfectly wondrous to see how within hours a war that had been an imperialist atrocity turned into a sacred democratic cause. But, then, a German victory over Russia would have been an unimaginable catastrophe, and the fiercely anticommunist Churchill instantly recognized the need to send all possible aid to the Soviet Union. Yet the German armies were breaking through the Russian defenses, and by September were advancing on Moscow. We thrilled to the defense of the capital that fall and the successful Soviet counteroffensive launched in early December, which drove the Germans back from the city (they had in fact advanced to a point only miles from the Kremlin). We speculated at the time that if Yugoslavia's sudden defiance of Hitler in April had not occurred—that defiance had forced the Germans to fight their way through the Balkans and on to Greece—the attack on Russia might have begun earlier, and the Germans might have conquered Moscow before winter, as they had planned. It was an exceptionally cold winter that year, for which the Germans in Russia were in any case totally unprepared. All through the summer and fall of 1941 the news from the battlefields in Russia and North Africa overshadowed all else.

At my school's outing to Northfield, I met a boy somewhat older than I named Goddard Winterbottom, who edited a weekly mimeographed "newspaper" with eighty-five subscribers. He asked me to send him articles on foreign affairs. (At that point, I was editor of Bentley's school paper.) He paid me a quarter for each piece supplied, but more important, he gave me the chance to vent my views. My pieces were embarrassingly pious and of course bitterly anti-German. In the school newspaper in the fall of 1940, I had tried to alert fellow students to the virtues of our endangered democracy: "The totalitarian state . . . wants to dominate the world, and should anyone not be satisfied . . . it offers them concentration camps." I also wrote short stories about imaginary heroes of the European resistance. I had little interest in the cloak-and-dagger stuff, but I was dazzled by what I imagined about their courage in fighting the loathsome Germans and their collaborators, the Quislings and the Vichyites—in the face of certain torture if they were caught. Intensely fearing torture myself, I had an unbounded admiration for the resisters—and it has stayed with me: I still judge people by whether I think they would have answered a resister's nighttime knock at the door asking for assistance or protection; I still plead that the many people who in the dark night of terror proved their decency in those years should be remembered and honored.

I fiercely argued with our friend Mme. Mercier about this and also with André Maurois, the well-known French (and Jewish) author who was living in exile in New York and whom I interviewed for my school paper. Both of them propounded "the truth" that Charles de Gaulle's Free French forces in London—where he had gone immediately after the French signed their armistice with Hitler—and the Vichy regime were *au fond* complementary, sword and shield! Maurois wanted me to believe that Marshal Pétain (who had sponsored or favored Maurois's election to the Académie Française) was a freedom-loving man. Their super-clever arguments offended my primitive view: you were either for or against Hitler. The world, at that time, seemed black and white. Of course, the situation in France was actually extremely complex, and the line between collaboration and resistance most fluid. (Louis Malle's film *Lacombe, Lucien* brilliantly portrays the contingency of choice between the two, as does Marcel Ophuls's *Le Chagrin et la Pitié*.)

On Sunday afternoon, December 7, 1941, listening to the New York Philharmonic on the radio, I heard the bulletin that interrupted the concert to announce the Japanese attack on Pearl Harbor. The next day the president spoke before Congress. The "day that shall live in infamy" had finally brought the United States into a war—with Japan, at the same time that it was already tacitly in an undeclared war with Germany. "Interventionists" felt relief—and apprehension lest public outrage dictate that war be waged solely against Japan; officials from the president on down were certain that evil and power were concentrated in Germany. But Hitler preempted this issue: in a move that historians still find puzzling, he quickly declared war on the United States. Now Roosevelt could fight on both fronts, and he quietly adopted a "Europe First" strategy. Churchill visited the United States again that Christmas, and together he and Roosevelt, akin in greatness, projected confidence in an Allied victory, instilling faith and hope among the "United Nations," the term Roosevelt used for the Allies fighting the Berlin-Tokyo Axis.

Overnight we Sterns became "enemy aliens" and faced a host of newly imposed restrictions, the worst being that on movement. (For every visit I made to the Merciers in Great Neck, Long Island, I needed official permission.) Alvin Johnson, president of the New School, and Max Wertheimer signed a form specifying that my mother "was appointed to his [*sic*] present post only after a thorough investigation which convinced us that nothing in her past allows any doubt as to her devotion to democratic principles, and that she is law-abiding, and loyal to the American Constitution." But the very term "enemy alien" hurt the most. Once more we were outcasts and, again, for no reason: were we not the most fervent supporters of the war against Hitler? Of course by comparison with what happened to enemy aliens in France and England, or to Japanese

Americans, we were treated most generously. (Eighteen months earlier, in Britain, male refugees of German nationality had been rounded up, interned, and some shipped to Canada. Among these was my favorite cousin, Ernest Brieger [he had anglicized his name], who was snatched from the Leys School in Cambridge and sent off to a camp in Canada. By Christmas 1940, I was in touch with him and allowed to send him a small parcel.)

The worst hurt was beyond our power to alter: being completely cut off from friends and relatives in Europe. (Occasional letters from Richard Will-stätter in Switzerland mentioned friends, but he died in August 1942.) Power-less, we fastened on the public news of the war, and in the spring of 1942 it was grim: the Germans had laid siege to Leningrad, were still close to Moscow, and were approaching Stalingrad; in mid-June in North Africa, where General Er-win Rommel had arrived in 1941 to rescue the bedraggled Italian forces that had been beaten by the British, the Germans recaptured Tobruk, and only the defeated British eighth army stood between General Rommel and Alexandria. If the Germans succeeded in Egypt, then would they in a giant pincer sweep south through the Caucasus and north from Egypt to join up in Palestine and the oil-rich Middle East?

In May 1943 my father was called to Grossinger's Hotel, in the Catskills, to examine an ailing Vera Weizmann, wife of Chaim Weizmann. (Joseph Blu-menfeld was the person who, remembering my father as Haber's friend and doctor, had recommended him to Weizmann; I called Blumenfeld to get per-mission to serve as my father's chauffeur on this trip.) When we got to Gros-singer's, I was put in the Weizmanns' sitting room to wait while my father examined Mrs. Weizmann; there I found the young philosopher and historian Isaiah Berlin, then recently come to America to work at the British embassy in Washington, talking with Meyer Weisgal, Weizmann's irrepressible aide. The next day, Dr. Weizmann, a gentle person radiating moral and intellectual au-thority, took me on a walk in the garden and talked to me of his vision for Pales-tine. With a sweep of the hand he pointed to the flowers along our path and said, "And the Negev desert will bloom!" To have Weizmann speak of his life's dream for his people was heady stuff for a seventeen-year-old. I was awed by Weizmann, who at the time was fighting his hardest political battles both with more radical Jews and with recalcitrant Englishmen.

We knew of German atrocities. The annihilation of the Czech village of Lidice in June 1942 as a reprisal for the assassination in Czechoslovakia of Reinhard Heydrich, deputy chief of the Gestapo and one of Hitler's favorite henchmen, became a lasting symbol of German brutality (as did the massacre in the French town of Oradour-sur-Glane in June 1944). And we knew of the heroic uprising of the Warsaw ghetto in 1943 and of the Germans' unspeakable liquidation of it. These public acts of barbaric terrorism were intended to elim-inate European resistance to Nazi occupation. The greatest crime—the exter-mination of the Jews—was committed more secretly, in "night and fog." Of course, news of it leaked out, beginning with an August 1942 report from Ger-hart Riegner to the World Jewish Council on Nazi plans for the extermination of all European Jewry, sufficient information for the Allies to have issued a statement in December 1942 that "from all occupied countries Jews are being transported, in conditions of appalling horror and brutality, to Eastern Europe. None of those taken away are ever heard of again." Yet most peoples' imagina-tions didn't or couldn't do more than extrapolate from what had happened be-fore—deportations and ghettos. We could imagine the ferocious cruelty of the concentration camps but not the satanic gas chambers. To use the phrase so of-ten intoned by Germans after the war, we in New York "didn't know about" Auschwitz or the mass exterminations, and perhaps somehow we didn't want to believe the rumors; perhaps we didn't want to know. We may have had a pre-disposition to shield ourselves from the worst, since what we did know, what was knowable, was sufficiently bitter and portentous.

The question of which governments and organizations knew, and when they knew, about the atrocities has justly become a fiercely controversial sub-ject. And what did the public in the Allied nations know? What penetrated people's awareness? Our greatest fear was a German victory, and hence we fas-tened on the war itself, since only Hitler's defeat could bring delivery. We cer-tainly feared for the lives of West European Jews, whom to a minuscule extent we could try to help. We could imagine the horrible suffering that was being imposed on them. But were we equally sensitive to the millions more in the east, caught in the midst of the war and almost entirely beyond all help? Did we recognize that they were the innocent, trapped victims of an anti-Semitic madness that had been born in the west, in Germany? These are the deepest questions that will never go away; they stay in my memory, painful thoughts.

In desperate wartime conditions and with passionate ideological conflicts, the temptation to escape to simplicity or to find excuses for the inexcusable is pervasive. In March 1943, Stalin ordered the killing of two Polish Jewish labor leaders, Henryk Erlich and Victor Alter, to whom the Soviet government had earlier given safe-conducts to travel to the United States via the Soviet Union. This crime became known, and American labor leaders, notably the Russian-Jewish David Dubinsky, head of the International Ladies Garment Workers, organized a memorial protest meeting at New York's City Center. My fervently anticommunist friend Ernest Hamburger gave me a ticket so that I could attend the rally. (Hamburger had also anglicized his first name.)

This was going on at the same time that American public opinion was being encouraged to think of Soviet Russia only in the most benign terms, as an essential ally. *Life* magazine published a special issue on the USSR in March 1943, with a cover picture of Stalin and a picture of a benign Lenin accompanying the main editorial, entitled "The Father of Modern Russia," which began: "Perhaps the greatest man of modern times was Vladimir Ilyich Ulyanov . . . He was a normal, well-balanced man who was dedicated to rescuing 140,000,000 people from a brutal and incompetent tyranny. He did what he set out to do . . . He made the Revolution make sense and saved it from much of the folly of the French Revolution." The editorial also addressed the question of free speech: "The Russians . . . live under a system of tight state-controlled information. But probably the attitude to take toward this is not to get too excited about it. When we take account of what the U.S.S.R. has accomplished in the 20 years of its existence we can make allowances for certain shortcomings, however deplorable." I absconded with the school library copy of that issue, for I thought it an extraordinary, unlikely apologia and couldn't part with it; I still have it.

The Erlich-Alter rally was an impressive event, with a huge picture of each of the assassinated men hanging as a kind of backdrop on either side of the podium. The union leaders denounced the murder, and then (this was an election year) our irrepressible Mayor La Guardia appeared, bounced up to the stage, mourned the dead, and concluded, "And I say to Uncle Joe, 'Don't do it again!'" Even then I was struck by his cheerful, paradoxical naïveté.

But I was vulnerable to the same arguments that had tempted *Life*. A month later, in April, the Germans announced the discovery of the graves of thousands of Polish officers—"murdered," they said, by the Soviets in Katyn Forest, near Smolensk. Since at the time we knew that the Red Army was carrying the heaviest burden of the war against the Nazis and would continue to do so at least until the day when a "second front" was opened in the west, I was among those many who wanted to believe the Soviet countercharge to the German accusation, which was that the Polish officers had been murdered by Germans. After all, for me murder bore a German signature, and I didn't want to give credence to the professional anti-Soviets who were clamoring for an independent investigation. It was only after the war that I accepted the truth about the Soviet crimes at Katyn—and then with great passion.

That June, I graduated from high school (I had skipped my sophomore year, so was a bit younger than the other seniors), and in July entered Columbia College, the small, male undergraduate division of Columbia University, then still presided over by the extraordinary Nicholas Murray Butler, an ambitious internationalist and closet anti-Semite. I was admitted on a scholarship, and throughout my college years lived at home in Queens and commuted to Columbia—a matter of financial necessity for certain, but perhaps also because of a psychic predisposition on my part to stay close to home, and because my mother's maternal instinct to push the young out of the nest was stunted.

Columbia then had many Jewish students—it had always been more open to them than the other Ivy League schools—but there were hardly any Jewish teachers. On the first day, a boy ahead of me standing in the registration line was clutching *PM*, New York's left-liberal afternoon newspaper, and we fell to talking. His name was Allen Ginsberg, and we became very close friends in our freshman year, spending a great deal of time together. He came to Queens to visit my parents, pronounced my mother more original than my father, and generally was refreshingly open, unconventional, outrageous—and sweet, spouting literary and poetic references; he was a serious poet already, and I learned much from him. Together we co-chaired a Roosevelt for President club in 1944.

My friendship with Ginsberg was precious to me, and when he had his first serious scrape with the college, inter alia, for writing obscene messages on the dirty windowpane of his dormitory room, I tried to persuade the associate dean of his "innocence," urging him to drop sanctions. Allen's several clashes with the college became celebrated; he was suspended for a year or so, but we stayed in contact, and I saw him with the leading figures of the Beat Generation—in all their free, alcoholic, and addicted ways. (He passed out at a party of ours, and I took him home.) In 1947, when Allen was in the Merchant Marine, he wrote to me regularly—hilarious, outrageous letters, including one with a brilliant full-page definition of the bourgeois (which I must have asked for): "a constipated, unimaginative member of the community . . . He believes especially . . . in absolutes in politics, art, morality, and religion and cannot accept a human being who deviates from his image. He believes in the evil of happiness, that is, that generally pleasure is sin. So he disapproves of impulsive (Rousseauean) living, of sex, drink, conflict and violence, dope, gambling, talking back to parents and authorities, love (except in a bastardized U.S. form), art . . ." We were scarcely out of our teens, and here was this latter-day Flaubert!

But when still in college we had wondrous times together. I was president of the College Debate Council when Columbia was challenged to a debate with the U. S. Military Academy at West Point, and I chose Allen as my companion; it was Ginsberg and Stern in May 1944 on the topic "Resolved: That an International Police Force Would Best Serve World Peace." I can't remember which side won the debate, but I do remember that we made an excellent, if perhaps in West Point eyes somewhat exotic, team, and I can't forget Allen standing on a bluff overlooking the Hudson River below and reciting Wordsworth's "Lines Written a Few Miles above Tintern Abbey, On Revisiting the Banks of the Wye."

At Columbia, I started on a premedical program, true to my German forebears, but from the very beginning I was captivated by Columbia's required courses in history and literature, still then Eurocentric to the core. We were studying the history and classics of the very civilization that was being threatened by a Germany that spiritually repudiated all that the West stood for, though Germans had materially mastered the West's scientific and technological advances. I had the inestimable good fortune of finding and then fastening onto two great teachers and master stylists: Jacques Barzun, the product of a classical French education, and Lionel Trilling, more knowing of European literature than anyone I had met before (or perhaps since). It was Ginsberg who gave me the tip to take Trilling's course on English Romanticism; at the time, Trilling was not yet the famous figure he was to become, and in fact was overshadowed by others in a great department. The experience of that and other Trilling courses was humbling and life-transforming. Barzun and Trilling taught us not only the assigned subjects but writing as well, making close, devastating, often ironic comments on our efforts. My premed interests faded, for I lacked the aptitude and passion for the natural sciences and felt the immediate enticements of history and literature.

In April 1944, when I was in my third term (wartime Columbia was on a relentless three-term-per-year schedule), I had to decide on a major—and for a while I floundered. One way I framed my dilemma at the time was like this: my interest in becoming a physician was genuine, but was I ready to give up Trilling, with whom I was discovering the stupendous questions of the great books and the complexities of the European past, for organic chemistry? Fascination with literature, which I suppose was reinforced by my passionate concern for the unfolding world crisis, made me wish to turn to a study of history, with the eventual prospect of teaching. I had several conversations with Barzun about this. At first he urged me to stay with medicine and keep history as a lifelong mistress, but at our second meeting, when I confessed my continuing wish to major in history, he asked further as to what I really intended to do. To teach, I replied. Would I, then, want to teach at the Lawrenceville School, he inquired; he had friends there. When I said yes, he said something distinctly encouraging. I have always admired the subtle test he gave me: is your interest genuine, or do you have delusions of a university career?

Just at that critical moment of indecision, I received the most authoritative advice. In April 1944, I accompanied my mother when she went to see Albert Einstein in his home on Mercer Street, in Princeton, to show him her material for teaching arithmetic. I waited in his (very German) living room, awed to be in his house and even more awed when he came down from his study. He reassured my mother that her approach was sound and important. Then he asked me in the simplest, caring way what I was doing—in such a kindly tone that I don't think I was the least tongue-tied, which lesser figures could make me. I confessed my career uncertainty and he responded, "That's simple: medicine is a science, and history is not. Hence medicine." But I followed my instinct and chose history, which after all has an element of science to it, and retained my lifelong awe of the white coat, trusting it stood for much more than science. My father was disappointed—and probably worried as to whether I could make a go of it.

In college, I continued writing or speaking about current affairs; I even won second prize in the competition for the Curtis Oratorical medal for some evocation of a future Europe. (No first prize was awarded!) I gave regular political comments on the campus radio; I suppose I somehow wanted to pass on the lessons of failed democracies to my American contemporaries, many of whom, I feared, either took freedom for granted or found it tainted in its American form. In hortatory terms, I expounded on the unique value of democracy, knowing that postwar America would have to reform its deficiencies, above all its discrimination against Negroes and the crimes of Jim Crow. I don't think I realized then that the passion of my political engagement had its inner source in my German experience. It *felt* American.

That German experience could also distort judgment and deepen prejudice. In those days, being a "left-liberal" included almost automatically being skeptical about capitalism: I had read about the "robber barons" of old and was sure that the rich tended to favor authoritarianism, perhaps even fascism; they certainly were anti-Roosevelt. But to me the Nazi regime, in all its generalized criminality, remained the greatest threat and vilest enemy, while the heroism of the Red Army softened my suspicions of the Soviet regime. Intellectually, I tried to make distinctions between German and Nazi, but emotionally I doubt that I could. And like many people, including Churchill, I thought that the perpetrators of the failed attempt on Hitler's life, made on July 20, 1944, were merely old-style Junkers or Prussian officers following their own nationalist interests.

By now, enemy alien though I was, I felt entirely American; I even laid claim to the American past, writing about "our" forebears and their suffering at Valley Forge. I believed in my being American and never felt any presumption or transgression in this belief, though deep down I knew it wasn't my birthright. And I applied for citizenship at the first legal moment I could, in 1947, at age twenty-one. My citizenship hearings were held up because of my membership in the Council for Democracy—perhaps an organization with a similar name was on some Justice Department list of pro-communist organizations. A first taste of McCarthyism *avant la lettre*! Bullitt assured me of his help, if needed, adding, "In 1940 when I recommended the Council to you it was certainly a thoroughly non-communist organization, the prime mover in which was Mr. Henry R. Luce." In the end, I didn't need help from Bullitt, who shortly after his 1940 speech had become a fierce critic of Roosevelt's policies.

Studying European history and literature, I learned to see Europe's past not in purely national terms but as a constituent part of Europe's unity; this shook me out of some facile prejudices. Reading Nietzsche was revelatory in a different way: I thought him a supreme psychologist and a troubling critic of philistine mediocrity and of democracy. Nietzsche was a much sharper, unforgiving critic of the tyranny of the majority than John Stuart Mill—hence a critic that made one deepen one's political assumptions. (I began then to construct my notion of "the gentle Nietzsche," interpreting the bombast about superman, for example, as being a plea for self-overcoming.) The current view of Nietzsche as a precursor of Nazism made no sense to me, and in fact it made me realize how complicated the question of Nazi roots really was; all the tomes and slogans about Germany's inevitable path "from Luther to Hitler" seemed puerile and wrongheaded.

Outside of college, I still moved in my parents' European and German circles. Within them as beyond them, people held sharply divergent views on what should happen to a defeated Reich. Émigré social democrats believed in the possibility of a democratic Germany and were ready to work for it. In 1943 my father's old friend the philosophy professor Siegfried Marck, now teaching in Chicago, co-authored a book entitled *Germany: To Be or Not to Be*, insisting that the country had the potential for democratic regeneration, that Nazism had been hardest on German democrats, and that the persecution of Jews was but one part of the Nazis' massive criminality. Weimar had been destroyed by many forces, Marck said, including the Communists; therefore, to allow the Soviet Union to establish a "totalitarian" system in postwar Germany would be disastrous. Postwar occupation forces would find that Germany's municipal administrations had a longer democratic tradition than any other political bodies in the country; this was a useful reminder. His book echoed the thoughts and hopes of the American Friends of German Freedom, the organization that had helped to establish the Emergency Rescue Committee and that included Reinhold Niebuhr and Thomas Mann.

On the other side were supporters of the Morgenthau Plan, certain of their "realism," who believed that only a deindustrialized and pastoral Germany could be disarmed in spirit and in fact. There were many ideological counterparts to Roosevelt's Secretary of the Treasury Henry Morgenthau, who—like the British diplomat Robert Vansittart—thought that Germans were incurably and genetically aggressive, militaristic, and prone to criminality. A particular version of Vansittartism cropped up in the Committee to Prevent World War III, headed by Rex Stout, the well-known writer of detective fiction, and joined by Mark Van Doren, Allan Nevins, and William Shirer. Under the group's auspices appeared a book in 1944 by T. H. Tetens (a German émigré), *Know Your Enemy!*, with a preface by the biographer and popular historian Emil Ludwig—whose book *July '14* I had read as a child. Tetens argued that the German character was fixed: "The German people have proven that they are always ready to support the criminal policies of their governments and to fight to the limit for the realization of their Pan-German plans for world conquest." Hence the country should be dismembered altogether, treated as a permanent pariah among the nations of Europe. I wrote a sharp critique of that book, mocking Tetens's notion that all German democrats were mere tools in the hands of the General Staff. The book was guilty of "falsification of history," an "example of how not to write historical essays." Hate, I argued, was not a basis for building peace, and I recalled that Emil Ludwig had written a highly favorable biography of Mussolini.

It has become a postwar myth in some German circles that German exiles in the United States all favored and successfully peddled a punitive policy for a defeated Germany. There were some, no doubt, the vociferous Ludwig among them. Perhaps Einstein sympathized with such harsh views, though he remained largely silent. But among those in responsible positions, a far more nuanced view prevailed.

And still, as we in New York finally watched the end of Nazi tyranny in

1945—a tyranny that in a mere twelve years had destroyed a world—the feeling of infinite relief was mixed with hatred. When the concentration camps and death camps were liberated by Allied troops, we saw the stark, unambiguous evidence of the Nazis' mass murders, of a hellish bestiality that far exceeded our worst imagining and brought tears to hardened warriors. From Auschwitz, liberated by the Red Army on January 27; from Bergen-Belsen, liberated by British troops on April 15; from Dachau, liberated by American troops on April 29, came pictures and reports that surpassed our grimmest apprehensions. Those starving remnants of humanity, inhabiting the harrowing margin between life and death, they who were made to bury their fellow sufferers—each and every one of these constituted a searing indictment of the German people. But in truth, even before that, not many among us had mustered much compassion for the German victims of the firestorm bombing of Hamburg in 1943 or of the bombing of Dresden in February 1945. That inhuman German violence had infected Germany's enemies as well was another aspect of what we came to think of as uniquely evil.

CHAPTER 5

★

WHEN THERE WAS
NO GERMANY

ON MAY 8, 1945, THE DAY of Germany's unconditional surrender, the German state ceased to exist. The German threat, defeated at last, turned into the German Question: What would become of this nation, now a ward of the Allied victors? How would its people come to understand its past and prepare for its future? The Anglo-American insistence on Germany's unconditional surrender, which remains controversial to this day, at the time seemed an appropriate lesson to have drawn from the Great War, after which Germans indulged in the poisonous myth that "leftist traitors" and Jews had stabbed an undefeated German army in the back. This time, it was resolved, the German state and army must bear responsibility. The Western Allies' demand was also meant to reassure the Soviet Union that the former's making a separate peace with Germany would be categorically ruled out. These arguments seem valid to me, more valid than the claim that the demand of unconditional surrender encouraged Germans to fight on and hence prolonged the war. In any case, May 8 was a day of grateful deliverance: the Nazis' horrendous tyranny, supported to the last by most Germans, was crushed by a coalition that only Hitler's mad ambition could have forged. Only Hitler's hubris and German aggression could have brought American and Soviet troops to the heart of Europe—where, unexpectedly, they remained for half a century.

The German state had disappeared, but the German people remained, in rubble, hunger, grief, and desolation. Some seven million Germans had lost their lives or were somewhere still in foreign lands; transportation and communication were in chaos. Families were torn apart, and millions of men, women, and children straggled along through forsaken countrysides; soon millions more came pouring back from the east into a truncated country, divided among its Allied occupiers. The Germans were shell-shocked, and as they began to clear away the physical rubble, they seemed only dimly aware of the moral ruin that had befallen them. In a mere twelve years, they and their Nazi leaders had wrecked a world and left for themselves an inescapable burden of guilt and responsibility. In 1940 they and their European minions had been masters and exploiters of the continent; five years later, they were degraded, confused, and uncertain pariahs. To the end, most of them had believed that the providential Führer could work yet another miracle. Never before had they known such total defeat and disgrace.

Most of us on the outside had always believed in an ultimate Allied victory—an irrational hope, gloriously fortified by Churchill's rhetoric and British stamina, its origin in our disbelief that such evil could triumph in Europe. The hope had gradually acquired a certain realistic basis after the German surrender at Stalingrad in February 1943 and after the Allied invasion of France in June 1944, though even then the Germans had the capacity to launch new weapons and offensives. But by the winter of 1944–1945, the Red Army advanced relentlessly from the east while Anglo-American troops, backed by awesome air power, reached German lands from the west, and finally the enemy was crushed.* But at what cost, so unevenly divided among the Allies!

Well before the end of the fighting, the Allies had begun to plan for the eventual disposition of a defeated Germany. They agreed on the demarcation of first three occupation zones and then later, at Churchill's urging, four, with a French zone added. The Soviet zone would embrace Berlin, the Nazi capital, but the city would have a special status of its own; divided into four sectors, with each sector occupied by one of the victorious powers, it would be the seat of an Allied Control Council of the four military commanders, who would design and execute common economic policies for all four zones.

At the Potsdam Conference of the Big Three in July 1945, the Allies made further decisions, including the establishment of "temporary" Polish and Soviet administrations of German territories east of the Oder and Neisse rivers: Kant's

---

*A German joke of the time from just before the surrender: Two soldiers dream of what they will do after the war is over. One simply wants to go home to a clean bed and his mother's cooking. The other says he needs to recover from the unrelenting pressures of military life—he wants to go off and bicycle all the way around the borders of Germany. The first asks him, "And what will you do in the afternoon?"

Königsberg went to Russia, but most of East Prussia and all of Silesia, including Breslau, went to Poland. Millions of Germans were expelled from ancient German lands; Czechoslovakia expelled three million from the Sudetenland.

Germany's defeat also brought to light the full extent of the Germans' barbarism, and the pictures we saw of the liberated camps filled even the eyes of the soldiers who took the photos with tears and all of us with revulsion. We didn't yet know about the systematic extermination of the Jews, but what we knew was enough for most of us—for me—to become indifferent to the sufferings of Germans during and after the war. True, the country was in ruins and despair, physically devastated and morally bankrupt; that much we knew. We assumed that many Germans still clung to the Nazi faith, and we soon came to realize that many of them, certain of their own innocence, were consumed with self-pity. Outside of Germany, abomination and mistrust prevailed. The punitive decisions taken at the Potsdam Conference, and the ensuing expulsion of some ten million Germans from the east, aroused little or no compassion. It was the Germans themselves who had begun a program of "ethnic cleansing" in Eastern Europe, to use today's parlance; the Czech and Soviet moves seemed responses to it. That Germans, too, were often innocent victims of the sadism that Hitler had unleashed we acknowledged only later.

In the horror of the time, I had little or no emotional response to Breslau's becoming Wrocław—after all, my family and I had been expelled from it. I had been indifferent to the city's fate during the war itself: its physical existence had been sacrificed by Hitler's order that Breslau—fully garrisoned by 1944 and then encircled by the Red Army—had to hold out to the last. Now its future lay in Polish hands, as part of the territory allotted to Poland as compensation for Ukrainian territories in eastern Poland annexed to the Soviet Union. I didn't then think of Breslau as an inextinguishable part of my being; my recovery of a sense of belonging to it was a later part of my life's journey. And when my apolitical mother talked of her native city, which she often did—calling it invariably Breslau, Germany—she was simply referring to a fact of the buried past, certainly not expressing any hope of future change.

Things German suddenly became remote to us in New York. Just as for me the death of Franklin Roosevelt, in April 1945, overshadowed Hitler's suicide a fortnight later, so the dropping of the first atomic bomb on Hiroshima overshadowed VE-Day and left a more compelling memory. I knew that a whole new, frightful era had begun. Sometime before that, my uncle Otto Stern, who I learned later had been a participant in the Manhattan Project, had told me that awesome new weapons were being forged, that future wars would be far more calamitous than the present one. (In December 1944 he may have been the first to alert Einstein to the development of atomic weapons.) When I heard the news of Hiroshima, I at once recalled Uncle Otto's unspecific warning. At the time, I thought that the use of the first bomb was a necessary and justified means to prevent untold American casualties in a prolonged struggle; I wondered about the second bomb, dropped on Nagasaki—and not much later fell in with those who questioned whether a trial demonstration of the bomb might not have sufficed to persuade Japan to surrender.

In what was quickly dubbed the atomic age, the need to preserve the wartime coalition seemed critical, and its feasibility became the subject of passionate controversy. I had no doubt about the desirability of continued alliance with the Soviet Union, though I was aware of conflicting interests and of the Russians' ominous provocations, and I was not uncritical of American policies. During the war, the United States and the USSR had tried to submerge their ideological conflicts in the desperate struggle against a common enemy. With the demise of that enemy, their respective ideological fear and loathing of the opposing system found aggressive political expression: West and East fell into all manner of rivalries, driven by ambition and fear.

By the winter of 1944–1945, the future of Poland had already become the principal divisive issue. The Polish home army's uprising against the Germans in the summer of 1944 had been crushed by the Nazis while the Red Army watched from its positions nearby, on the other side of the Vistula River; now the Soviets were determined to install a pro-Soviet government in that old anti-Russian country. I kept daily diary entries about political events at that time, and many of them recorded the Soviet hostility to the democratic Poles, the verbal promises of democracy that were then abandoned. On December 30, 1944, for example, I wrote, "There will be trouble between USSR & Western Allies" on this issue. And in April 1945, in a radio program broadcast on the American Forum on the Air, a regular feature with students debating issues of the day, I pleaded for the preservation of Allied unity, but noted Soviet violations of their commitments with regard to Poland. We now know that as early as May 1945, Churchill had penned the phrase "iron curtain" to depict the effect of the Red Army's isolating Eastern Europe from the rest of the continent. Did his premonition both stiffen and weaken his resistance to Soviet expansionism?

The trials at Nürnberg, beginning in November 1945, of German army and party leaders charged with exactly documented plots in pursuance of war crimes and crimes against humanity, seemed to demonstrate the cohesion of the Allies who organized the prosecutions. At the time, I didn't see any dilemma in having British and American judges work side by side with Andrei Vishinsky and other well-known figures who had been participants in the Soviet purges of the prewar years, nor did I foresee that some Germans would come to dismiss this meticulously prepared trial as "victors' justice"—as if a court composed of Germans could have been formed fairly or expeditiously. The Soviet Union had, unquestionably, borne the greatest burden of the war, and the heroic, improbable recovery of the Red Army and its march to Berlin gave it a kind of moral capital; we were ready to disbelieve the stories that cropped up about Russian atrocities in that push into Germany. We didn't want to know.

Nor did I notice the coincidence that the time of Germany's disappearance, its temporary and blessed demise as a threatening subject, was the time in which I began my American career. It was between 1945 and 1949 that I became an American citizen, teacher, husband, and father, and formed my closest American friendships, while at the same time I became ever more conscious, both professionally and in my inner self, of my European, though not specifically German, heritage. For very different reasons, but at roughly the same time, many Germans began to discover their European identity and become supporters of a common Europe.

By 1945 my parents had gained a somewhat more secure existence in New York. My father's practice, which now included ever more American patients, had grown. And my mother's life took a remarkable turn: For the preceding years, she had been introducing her method of teaching arithmetic in various schools; with Max Wertheimer's encouragement, she was preparing a book on that method. In 1943 my sister, having completed a year at the Bank Street College of Education, introduced to my mother a fellow student there, Margaret Bassett, who with her own pedagogic gifts found this whole approach to teaching immediately appealing. She became my mother's helper and in 1944, with a loan from her father, was able to found a nursery school in Manhattan where my mother's educational principles and games could be put to practice. Out of that school—and a collaboration among my mother, sister, and Peggy that lasted until my mother's death—grew various books. The first, *Children Discover Arithmetic*, was published in 1949, with an endorsement from Einstein attesting that her approach "would be of real value to the teaching . . . of arithmetic." The books and my mother's arithmetic material had a considerable effect on American education. I can see in retrospect that Structural Arithmetic was yet another example of how German ideas developed and flourished in the United States: another instance of a transplant that combined insights and virtues from both countries. The nursery school, run on a shoestring, attracted a group of enthusiastic parents who recruited some extraordinary children: I remember Johnny LaFarge and the daughter of the photographer Diane Arbus, Doon, among them. My mother was launched on a new American career.

Meanwhile, I graduated from Columbia College, having majored in history and political theory; my parents thought of my Phi Beta Kappa key as some special token of my Americanization. A month after graduating in June 1946, having been a teaching assistant in my senior year, I was appointed lecturer in contemporary civilization and deputized to teach Columbia's famous core course in that subject in the university's College of Pharmacy. Perhaps the department head, suddenly needing a teacher, calculated that the possible harm I might wreak would be less serious if inflicted on future apothecaries than on regular students. And thus at the age of twenty, I became financially independent, if at a risible level. It was my special luck that the work indispensable to academic survival and economic self-sufficiency also engaged my inner self. I was lucky to start when I did, but even then an inner appetite transcended academic boundaries. After Hitler, civic passivity wasn't a psychic possibility.

Teaching at Columbia was yet another form of an ambiguous life, since I was attached to a department in which I was also about to begin graduate studies, hence at once independent and dependent. No matter: I loved teaching Columbia's fabled "core" course in Western civilization, and for me it was a continuous process of learning, albeit learning on the run. To me the history I taught was a drama, a drama of ideas and people caught in great historic processes, and I was teaching it at a time when Western civilization had just triumphed over the danger of its extinction. I was unsure of myself, but not of the subject: I don't think it ever occurred to me that it could be dull.

Peggy Bassett was a remarkably attractive and independent woman, some years older than I; in many ways she was enticingly different, bonded to nature, artistically inclined, generous, and, at first, indifferent to politics—a quiet person, at once practical and cheerfully naïve. She had enjoyed a sheltered life in, on the paternal side, a very old American family, with the Puritan ethic running strong in her father. We began to take note of each other, we fell in love, and despite or because of huge differences between us, in 1947, early love led to marriage.

The Bassett family extended trust and friendship to my parents. Mr. Bassett, a distinguished inventor-engineer and in wartime a corporate executive, showed immense interest in my mother's work. He was that vanishing type in America, an "inner-directed man" (or so David Riesman, who had worked for him during the war, depicted him), a specialist in fact on gyroscopes—who ran by his own gyroscope. He shunned the social life of his class, spending his spare time as an amateur artist, craftsman, and a gifted collector of American antiques that were illustrative of artisanship over the span of the country's history. I fondly respected this extraordinary person. At our initial formal meeting, he wondered how this twenty-one-year-old would earn a living: "By teaching and writing," I replied—and for the rest of my life, that is what I tried to do.

We disagreed on most political issues, and we discussed our differences; in some ways, he was a democratic education for me: honest disagreements, candidly discussed, help to clarify and strengthen one's own position. I suppose I tried at times to convince him of my apprehensions; I doubt that I much succeeded. He didn't attempt to convert me, and I relished the many values we shared—without much speech.

In 1948, a year after Peggy and I were married, our son, Fred, was born; three years later, Katherine. At the time, the bourgeois world and our immediate milieu were full of ideas and prescriptions for bringing up children. Peggy and I had our own ideas, my notions being simple, owing something to Rousseau's *Émile*, a book I treasured. My mother had her own methods, some of which I thought manipulative, and at one decisive moment with her I declared that we would bring up our own children; she respected that—with regret, I suppose. No doubt we made our own mistakes, and perhaps in ordering my priorities between family and work I may have favored the latter, but then I had to make my way with the unspoken, habitual justification, I suppose, that "in the end" the family would benefit from my efforts. I was in any case a rather "European" husband inasmuch as I left most household work to my wife. (I contended, only half-jokingly, that I had done my cooking during my pre-adolescent stage). But my attachment to my children, at every stage of my life, was joyfully central and vital.

And even here in the life of my new American family the question of my German past entered. Peggy's closeness to my parents facilitated my children's attachment to them, so they grew up with a strong affinity for all four grandparents and certainly for the Europeanness of my parents' home. I took them to Europe in their youngest childhood, wishing them to feel at home there. Much later, people would ask me whether my children spoke German. In the early 1950s, I felt no urge to have them learn the language of a country that had expelled me, a language they were unlikely to find as easy or natural as I did. I wanted them to master French, though, and to speak it better than I, to have their own untroubled ties to Europe. Their French *is* better than mine and they have their own close relations to Europe. (Katherine in fact became a historian of France—to my immense pleasure.)

My parents' and my attitude toward Germany remained unchanged in those early postwar years, hardened if anything by the revelations at Nürnberg: suspicion and hatred tinged with regret of a country that had embraced National Socialism, indifference to its suffering, concern for former friends who in one way or another had also been victims. But the unarticulated distinction between a people's conduct and a people's heritage remained: we spoke German at home, and I continued to read my favorites—Heine and Nietzsche—in German.

The first European friend with whom I began corresponding was Werner Kubelka, the son of our Prague friends, who along with his sister had been expelled from Czechoslovakia. His mother had died in the trek, and his father, certified by Czech authorities as loyal, remained in Prague. Werner, now nineteen years old, wrote to tell me he had been drafted into the Wehrmacht, then expelled, and had fetched up in Göttingen. Our intensive exchange of letters was supplemented on my part by packages of coffee, cigarettes, and tinned goods. In one of his earliest letters he wrote, "You were hounded out of Germany even though you were born there, and we are driven into Germany though we never lived there." This was the madness of Central Europe in a nutshell—how could I not feel a kind of closeness with him?

Every letter bespoke his yearning for a new *Heimat*, that loaded, lofty word that strikes far greater chords of memory than *home*, its literal equivalent. He wanted a new beginning, a life with money, a life in the United States. At the end of 1946, his father fled Czechoslovakia, fearing that at any moment the authorities might restore his Czech citizenship and then prevent him from leaving. Now father and son were planning to leave Europe together—the archetypical experience of the time. In August 1948 they managed to get to Geneva: "Awakened from a decade-long bad dream, now again in the beautiful world." By the end of the year, they made their way to Rio de Janeiro, where friends helped them to start a new life. Werner soon decamped to Vancouver, with a Brazilian wife.

My parents resumed their contacts with those of our German friends, colleagues, and former patients, who amid their own suffering had retained a steadfast decency. In August 1946 Major von Zerboni sent my father a long report detailing Breslau's destruction, much of it ordered by the SS determined to leave nothing to the Russians. "Our Vaterstadt," Zerboni wrote, was 80 to 90 percent destroyed. My father had shed his tears earlier—but he saved the letter. My mother dispatched many a CARE package to the women friends who had helped our relatives; my father sent packages to Karl Bonhoeffer, the psychiatrist in Berlin whose two sons and two sons-in-law the Nazis had executed. (Another son, Karl-Friedrich Bonhoeffer, a faithful student of Fritz Haber, was one of the first Germans to visit us after the war.) He also sent packages to a former fellow student and colleague, Mortimer von Falkenhausen, a conservative German patriot whose family included the German commander of occupied Belgium and Nazis and anti-Nazis. In February 1948, Falkenhausen wrote to him: "What I will never be able to understand is that countless Germans allowed themselves without protest to be demeaned into gruesome criminality, and to become bestial murderers and despoilers, and found it all perfectly normal. That will cling to Germans like a mark of Cain, and hence you will understand that I feel shame, all the more so as there has been no progress." But we wondered whether many Germans felt that shame, and I know of no evidence that Falkenhausen supported the efforts made by some Germans to disturb the prevailing self-pitying.

Published and private reports left no doubt that most Germans sullenly or defiantly retained their sense of innocence and hurt. They claimed they hadn't known of the crimes that the "few villains at the top had committed"; they knew only of their own wretchedness and of the hardships now imposed by the occupying powers. Some of Germany's most eminent citizens, such as Otto Hahn, who had combined personal decency with public conformity during the Nazi period, wrote to friends who had had to flee the Third Reich saying that the Allied occupation was barely better than German occupation policies in the east! I remember that Uncle Otto (whose Nobel Prize in Physics for 1943 was in fact bestowed on him a year later, at the same ceremony where Hahn received his Nobel in Chemistry) was appalled by this complicity with postwar German assertions of innocence; he derided what he called the legend that for "moral reasons" German scientists had not wanted to build the bomb. He never touched German soil again. Later, it became common for German scientists to lament Germany's losses of great scientists and artists because of Nazi rule, but at the time, German faculties made negligible efforts to have their émigré professors return, and the latter were themselves divided. Some very few were ready to accept posts in Germany, a few more paid visits to German territory or accepted honors there—but many stayed away altogether, perhaps a sign of deepest hurt. One of the greatest of émigrés, Thomas Mann, returned to Europe after his American interlude, and settled in Switzerland.

While in 1945–1949 things German perhaps faded for me for a time, my attachment to Europe grew. Our French friends left New York to go home, leaving in their wake the most urgent invitations for us to visit them. We developed minor but psychologically important ties: I saved pennies to support Spanish Refugee Aid, that is, to help exiled Spanish Republicans, and Peggy and I became "foster parents" to a Sicilian child, and later a Greek one: we contributed to their subsistence and regularly exchanged primitive letters. Europe, I suppose, was some kind of nostalgic romance; America was absolute and compelling reality.

Between 1945 and 1950, amid the great reversal of alliances and the threat of increasing discord, a new Western order emerged, a period signaling the transformation of world politics. The Soviets—gradually—imposed their social and political system on the countries of Eastern Europe, where the Red Army remained ultimate arbiter. The United States, on the other hand, by late 1945 had begun the demobilization of its conventional forces, withdrawing most of its troops from Europe. The Western democracies in Europe were trying to rebuild their countries; in France and Italy powerful communist parties, living off their record of anti-German resistance during the war, came close to winning power. They represented the "peaceful" arm of Soviet policy. The cold war was, slowly but indubitably, beginning. In my emotional-political life, Britain had a special place, since at first it alone had resisted Nazi aggression, and resisted the blandishments of peace after the fall of France and after the onslaught of the blitz on its cities. All the more electrifying was the British election of July 1945, when the great wartime hero, Churchill, was sent to pasture, as he himself put it, and Labour gained a spectacular victory. Clement Attlee's government, composed of exceptional persons, had to deal with successive economic crises and with Britain's slow retreat from empire, but it also went far to create a welfare state, as did the Scandinavian countries.

In retrospect, I think that three great plans had a decisive part in shaping postwar Europe—and, incidentally, did so when statesmen were making efforts consciously to learn from the past, though this was scarcely noticed at the time. In Britain, the Beveridge Report of 1942 aimed to create a welfare state that would lessen the class conflicts that had weakened the nation before the war. The Marshall Plan of 1947, initially open to the USSR and Czechoslovakia as well as to the nations of Western Europe and including the three western zones of occupied Germany, made clear that the United States recognized European recovery as a political necessity and a step toward European integration. (The Soviet Union, after showing initial interest, refused to participate in the plan, and forced Czechoslovakia to follow suit.) This unprecedented act of self-interested generosity did much to cement American-European ties, which were further strengthened in 1949 by the creation of the North Atlantic Treaty

Organization, a western alliance aiming at coordinating the military and political strategies of its members. And, third, the Schuman Plan of 1950 created an iron, steel, and coal community between France and West Germany, a collaboration that was meant to resolve age-old economic and political rivalries. These three plans expressed the great hopes of the early postwar years, and by and large they proved successful.

The cold war between the West and the Soviet Union from the start had its focus in Germany, where Allied responsibilities were supposed to converge but increasingly diverged. The outward sign of the breakdown was the effective end in 1946 of the Allied Control Council in Berlin. The Western and Soviet zones became ever more separate, and Germans were torn between identifying with the Western powers (itself a great intellectual reversal of German opinion) and clinging to their hopes for national unity.

One of the last joint Allied decisions was Allied Control Council Law 46, on February 27, 1947, which declared that "the Prussian state . . . is abolished . . . from early days . . . the bearer of militarism and reaction in Germany." Of course, by then Prussia had long since ceased to exist and much of it was now Polish territory, but here was its formal abolition. Historians have had their sport with the question, When did Prussia die? Some have argued that it died with the founding of the Second Reich in 1871, when Germans (in Nietzsche's phrase) became *reichsdeutsch,* when old Prussian virtues such as austerity and rectitude seemed to lose their grip and industrial capitalism ushered in different mores. Some of the Prussian presumptions lived on in the German empire—but, ironically, in the Weimar Republic, Prussia proved to be the bulwark of democracy.

American policies in Germany now also changed: as early as September 1946, Secretary of State James Byrnes had indicated American sympathy for Germany's suffering and a willingness to promote its recovery. In fact, American statesmen rightly tired of the repeated fruitless meetings of the Allied foreign ministers concerning German questions, and they began pushing their own initiatives. One major issue concerned Russia's demands for reparations from all the zones of occupied Germany, which seemed reasonable, given the devastation that Germans had wrought in the USSR. But these extravagant extractions contributed to Germany's impoverishment, which in turn made greater demands on the three Western powers, which feared that Germans without food or hope might succumb to communist temptations.

The original Allied aim had been to create a demilitarized, decartelized, de-

Nazified Germany; actual policies directed to this goal were initially handled separately in each zone. The U.S. zone, under the direction of General Lucius Clay, had at first followed a harsh course, symbolically represented by a ban on fraternization (which was soon breached). U.S. efforts at de-Nazification, however, were ill-starred. Some Nazi officials were prosecuted or removed from office, but justice moved slowly, and was mocked and maligned by many Germans. Millions of citizens were required to fill out lengthy questionnaires about their pasts, and truly blameless Germans tried to shield compromised friends faced with Allied investigations by issuing what came to be known as *Persilscheine*, affidavits of clean political health. Others denounced their fellow citizens to the Allied authorities: mendacity and mean-spiritedness, well practiced in the Third Reich, didn't die with it.

Americans also had admirable though naïve notions of "reeducation." They wanted to give German education a democratic substance, and the Amerika-Häuser established in various German cities had ambitious programs to acquaint people with American life and culture. Our most effective effort may have been the many visitors' programs that allowed individual Germans to live for a while in the United States, which at this point was in intellectual-scientific matters a country without peers. Many of West Germany's subsequent leaders studied in the United States during the 1940s, imbibing something of a vibrant and dynamic country that readily acknowledged its own need for improvement. American power and American bonhomie—as expressed in the many gift cartons of cigarettes—may have been more persuasive than lessons in civics, but America's unquestioned commitment to the creation of a democratic Germany was also a dictate of political interest consonant with the former's support for democratic (hence presumably pro-American) governments in Europe.

The military commanders in the four zones allowed for the revival of political life in their territories, and in the western zones a free, if licensed, press allowed for political expression. The different interests and styles of the United States, Britain, and France made for varying policies, while the Soviet Union's "land reform" in its zone, with the expropriation of large landowners, began the introduction of Soviet-style socialism in the German countryside. The most radical Soviet political innovation was a forced merger of the Social Democrats and the Communists into one party, intended, its advocates claimed, to overcome splits within the working class; but the new party soon fell into a Stalinist pattern. In the western zones, Social Democrats vehemently opposed this effort, while local free elections eventually constituted parliaments in the old

German entities. The fact that Germany had a democratic past and a legal tradition, even though this had been suppressed by the Nazis, eased the task of restoring local German rule.

Two major parties emerged in the western zones, first the Social Democrats, led by the fiery, charismatic Kurt Schumacher, whom the Nazis had incarcerated in concentration camps for ten years. His overriding aim was to achieve Germany's unity, and he opposed every deepening of Germany's division. His party's aims were traditional: a democratic polity, a socialist economy, and the nationalization of basic industries. Schumacher's strident insistence on the primacy of national unity (as against integration with the democracies of the West) had many motives, not least his wish to be second to none in German patriotism: he well remembered that right-wing parties in Weimar and before had cloaked their material interests in a truculent nationalist rhetoric that vilified the "Reds" as being insufficiently patriotic. It has always seemed to me that the Social Democrats, however timid and uninspired they were at times, had all along been the true patriots, defending a country in which for decades they were treated as second-class citizens. They had been the consistent defenders of Weimar's democracy, and consistently anti-Nazi—a legacy that after 1945 they seemed reluctant to extol. Did they think it would be an electoral liability?

A new party emerged as well, the Christian Democratic Union, with programs similar to the newly founded Christian Democratic parties in postwar France and Italy. The CDU was a non-denominational party, in that sense different from the old Catholic Center, so it now comprised both Catholics and Protestants, the Catholics no longer being a minority in the western zones. The party represented what was left of the German *Bürgertum* but also sought to attract the younger middle class and the still homeless expellees from the lost territories. The CDU was led by Konrad Adenauer, who in the Weimar Republic had been a leading Center politician and the mayor of Cologne. After the Nazis deposed him in 1933, he went into what Germans call "inner emigration," a complete withdrawal from public life, inwardly opposing the regime; he was repeatedly, if briefly, imprisoned, and at times hid in a monastery. He assumed his new role in his mid-seventies; his retirement, as he put it, was behind him. An authoritarian figure by temperament and conviction, this ramrod, somewhat inscrutable person appealed to many Germans as a kind of father figure. Adenauer, a "Westerner" by his Rhenish birth and by orientation, had never been a nationalist, and early on in his postwar career called for a "United States of Europe." He tried to control the divergent wings of his party, some very much to the right and tainted by a Nazi past, others with a more progressive agenda, and for practical economic strategy he relied on Ludwig Erhard, a truly innovative, independent economist and designer of Germany's "social-market economy," somehow balancing maximum economic freedom with an equitable base of social responsibility. In retrospect, I would call it capitalism with a conscience.

The semblance of Allied unity remained, and negotiations persisted concerning final peace treaties, as did the Germans' hopes for reunification. But there were ominous problems, especially due to Soviet violations of prior agreements and suppression of democratic expectations in Eastern Europe. Apprehension about these problems was given dramatic expression in Churchill's speech in March 1946, in Fulton, Missouri, when the very person who had so correctly warned against the threat of Hitler proclaimed a new and dire threat from the Soviet Union, with its newly acquired empire hidden behind an "iron curtain," determined to expand its power. It was a threat that called for greater Anglo-American cooperation. At that time, I wrote in my makeshift diary: "During Churchill's speech I felt as if a ghost had come forth from his grave and warned us of the world below. Oh, but that ghost has such power and so little vision." How wrong I was! For Churchill supplied both the diagnosis and the prescription: in a speech in Zurich that September, he stunned the world by calling for a united Europe: "The first step in the re-creation of the European family must be the partnership between France and Germany." This was a most daring vision of someone who knew about the historic enmity between those two nations. The two speeches were complementary, even if that was not quite clear at the time: on the one hand "a special relationship" between the United States and a Britain that Churchill still thought of as Great, and on the other a continental union that could give Western Europe at least a chance for recovery, perhaps for greatness.

As Allied unity turned ever more clearly into Allied rivalry and confrontation, each side began to woo the German people ever more intensely. The Western Allies softened their policies, somehow assuming that their three zones might eventually form a political unit. The price they wanted paid for a unified Germany was free elections throughout the entire country, a procedure that would show up the Germans' rejection of a Soviet system. The Soviet Union, in turn, preached German unity according to their original vision of a unified, demilitarized Germany that, they hoped, they could ultimately control—or whose richest parts, such as the Ruhr, they could at least wrest from Western control.

The Germans were at once victims and profiteers of the cold war. The restoration of their nation's unity became ever more remote, while the prospect of a new German polity tied closely to the West became ever more likely—and welcome. After all, the West was alluring in many ways, and many Germans had overcome their long-cherished anti-Western sentiments. At the time, I encountered some Germans who went further, propounding a preposterous earlier affinity between Germany and the United States, saying that Germany's attack on the USSR in 1941 had anticipated American interests and that the two were now ready to join in a new anticommunist crusade. Meanwhile responsible Germans in the western zones warned against taking any militaristic steps and above all demanded that Germans make a clear renunciation of all nuclear weapons forever.

The conflicts in world and German politics were real—and rife with irony. The American insistence on German demilitarization worked so well that some Germans became critics of *American* militarism. In all this uncertainty, American foreign policy offered a constructive response to the breakdown of unity among the former Allies: President Truman, unwilling to wait indefinitely for Stalin to change his stance, was also intent on building a Western order—without closing the door to compromise with the USSR. Not that America's task was easy. Even from its allies there was dissent: while America was at the zenith of its power, the French were battling the many consequences of their defeat in 1940, wanting to be a great power and yet fearful of the least whiff of Germany's revival. In early 1947, after a winter of calamitous cold, the British, in austerity and hardship, began to help out the Germans in the British zone: "Our reparations to the Germans," they quipped.

Americans had welcomed demobilization after 1945, but two years later, they were asked to undertake new commitments. In 1947 the Truman Doctrine promised aid to Greece and Turkey, countries that Britain could no longer afford to defend and that were, it was thought, threatened by Soviet expansionism. The U.S. Congress and the country at large still had a strong isolationist strain: to win domestic support for this new and expensive American resolve to resist communism everywhere, the danger of communism was driven home in ever more alarmist tones. The administration justified the new commitments in strident rhetoric; demagogues began to hunt people who they claimed were domestic foes as well—people suspected of communist links, people who could be charged with having been "premature anti-fascists" (supporters, for example, of the Loyalists during the Spanish Civil War). That there were American Communists and fellow travelers was acknowledged fact, but what constituted "un-American" activities? Sweeping investigations of fellow

travelers and Communist Party members present or past became routine; textbooks were censored and suspicion spread, as I discovered personally at the
time of my naturalization hearing in 1947. Was this excessive zeal perhaps itself un-American? It was not an easy time for liberals, often critical of American policies at home and abroad, for they were targets of suspicion from the
right and subject to shameless abuse from Communists or their sympathizers.

I had my own experience of this passionate ideological struggle. I was appalled by the hysterical fallout in America of a foreign policy I basically agreed
with. At some point in 1947–1948, for example, I visited a somewhat older and
exceptionally clever British historian with whom I had been in graduate
school; he now had a good teaching post at a distinguished New England college. Late at night at his home, we fell once again into an acrimonious political discussion, during which I defended America's foreign policy, which he
maligned as being a provocative anti-Soviet policy. Suddenly he left the room,
then returned with horrifying photographs he had taken at Bergen-Belsen:
"That is where your views lead to!" he pronounced angrily. By this time I was
used to polemical attacks from the so-called left, but this absurd and cruel remark epitomized for me the ideological ruthlessness and confusions of
the time.

For me, any lingering, wavering hope that the Soviet Union, itself insecure,
might abandon its aggressive course and try for compromises ended in February 1948, with the communist takeover of Czechoslovakia, a nation that until
then had tried to preserve its own democracy while supporting the Soviet
Union in foreign policy. Jan Masaryk, who had been foreign minister in the
now toppled noncommunist government, and son of the much-admired father
of the Czech Republic, died when he either jumped or was pushed out of his
office window—a mystery still, and a lasting source of liberal outrage. The
communist coup in Prague sealed my view, even aside from my emotional
attachment to Czechoslovakia, that the Soviets were bent on imperialist
aggrandizement.

A few months later, the Western powers introduced a desperately needed
currency reform in their German zones, replacing old and nearly worthless
money with a new currency, the deutsche mark. The new currency, simultaneous with the end of rationing, eliminated the black market and sparked an
economic recovery that astounded the Germans themselves—and later the
world. But the introduction of the new currency into the three western sectors
of Berlin, which were defiantly free while the eastern sector of the city was kept
under strict Soviet control, provoked a dramatic Soviet riposte; days later, the

Russians imposed a blockade of the entire city, cutting off all surface routes to the capital from the western zones, and demonstrating to all the world that Berlin was an enclave in a red sea, seemingly at the mercy of Soviet power. The Soviet hope was at best to block the creation of a West German state or at least to force Western troops out of "their" Berlin.

At stake in 1948, in this first Berlin crisis, was the freedom of West Berliners and the credibility of Western resolve, and the crisis threatened war. General Clay urged the dispatch of an armed train to Berlin, testing the Soviets by leaving them with the choice of a military showdown or a diplomatic defeat. Cooler heads prevailed, and a quickly improvised U.S. airlift supported by Britain's Royal Air Force supplied three million West Berliners with the bare necessities of life for the next ten months. At the receiving end, Ernst Reuter, lord mayor of (West) Berlin, a patriot and fervent democrat, rallied his people to accept the temporary privations and thus preserve their freedom. Reuter became the first postwar German politician to be widely celebrated in the United States. A young Social Democratic star in the last years of the Weimar Republic, he had been imprisoned by the Nazis in 1933 and when released had emigrated to Ankara, then had patriotically returned to Germany as soon as postwar conditions allowed. The Soviets ended their blockade in May 1949: the airlift had been a triumphant success, a dramatic display of American (and British) ingenuity and prudence; thanks to it, the city that had once been famous as the seat of Nazi power became a cherished if embattled symbol of democratic resolve.

In the summer of 1948, the Western Allies authorized the creation of a German Parliamentary Council made up of representatives from state parliaments in the western zones, and charged with drawing up a constitution for a new West German state. Many of the council's members had been politically active in the Weimar years, and all remembered the shortcomings of that first democracy. The two main parties, with equal representation, predominated, though splinter parties existed as well: Communists on the left, others mostly on the right, with a powerful group representing embittered nationalist expellees. The council's drawn-out deliberations, with Adenauer as chairman, were impressive evidence of the capability of the emerging politicians. In this enterprise, too, the recollection of Weimar's failed past successfully instructed the present.

The Parliamentary Council reflected West German opposition to anything that might prolong or deepen the division of Germany. Did they feel this because of an understandable sense of national cohesion or out of a particular concern for the Germans in the Soviet zone? I suspected the former, along with an early disregard for the Germans in the eastern zone. Since most council members feared that the result of their work might seal the division of their country, they insisted that the final draft be labeled "Basic Law" and not "Constitution," so as to stress the provisional framework of the new polity. (They forgot the truth of that fine French saying: *"Il n'y a que le provisoire qui dure."*) In fact the Basic Law lasted longer and commanded greater respect than any previous German constitution, and it was flexible enough to serve as the principal instrument for the eventual reunification of Germany in 1990.

The Basic Law provided for a parliamentary democracy incorporating elements of previous German and American constitutional arrangements. The old German tradition of a federal system was retained, giving considerable powers to the individual states, or *Länder*. The United States supported the federal structure, which the CDU favored, while the Social Democrats would have preferred a more unitary form. Given the horrors of Nazism, the document had to begin with an extensive catalogue of inviolable civil and political rights for German citizens. And the lessons of the Weimar failure were heeded: for the first time a constitutional court was created, borrowing from the American arrangement to allow not only for judicial review but for an authority that could (and did) outlaw political parties or actions adjudged to be subversive of democracy. Unlike Weimar's practice, the president of the new republic would be elected indirectly, hence could not claim a popular mandate, and was shorn of emergency powers. The president would be more of a nonpartisan figurehead, more like a modern British monarch than a national executive, a person, it was hoped, of moral authority. The chancellor's powers were strengthened, on the other hand, and various provisions were included to shield the new republic from the political instability that had weakened Weimar.

The United States was a most active promoter of this step toward semi-sovereignty for a semi-Germany. In April 1949, the three Western Allies agreed on an Occupation Statute that would be presented to any new West German government, according to which Allied troops would remain on German soil but Allied military government there would end; three Allied high commissioners would supplant the military commanders and would supervise the new state's foreign policy; they would retain the right, under specified, unlikely conditions, to resume control over their former zones. By May 8, 1949— exactly four years after Germany's unconditional surrender—an eminently workable instrument had been devised and was ratified by the Western Allies. In itself this was no guarantee for success. Would Germans accept this new instrument? Would they play by its rules and learn to practice democracy? Would a political culture emerge that would sustain a liberal state?

But the Western Allies (France being the most skeptical) and West Germans had good reasons to be satisfied: within four short years, and despite economic hardship and massive uncertainties, the groundwork for a new Germany had been laid. There was no triumphalism; for that the wounds of division were too raw.

In the aftermath of Europe's liberation from Nazism and amid the huge movements of people during the first years after the war, there emerged another category of people in anguish. Displaced persons, they were called— among them many Polish and other non-German Jews who had survived the various horrors of the war and were now housed in wretched refugee camps in Germany, of all places.

Many of these yearned to go to Palestine, where a Jewish homeland, promised by Great Britain in 1917 in the Balfour Declaration, had yet to be established. Britain, being the League of Nations' mandate power in Palestine, had put severe restrictions on Jewish immigration there before and during the war, even when Nazi murder had made such a homeland a moral and practical imperative. Now the terrible fate of these stateless survivors brought vast new support to the Zionists' long-cherished, often deceived hopes. Liberal opinion favored these hopes, which had become a powerful secular cause of establishing historic justice, but Attlee's Labour government continued Britain's pro-Arab policy. The Jews already in Palestine were enraged, and some resorted to ever-increasing acts of violence. (Perhaps the worst of these occurred in July 1946, when Jewish terrorists destroyed the British headquarters in the King David Hotel in Jerusalem, killing one hundred British, Arab, and Jewish personnel. My cousin Ernest Blake, alias Brieger, by then a captain in the Queen's Royal Regiment in Palestine, escaped the explosion by only a few minutes. His views on Zionism and mine rather sharply diverged.) So the question of Israel and Palestine became a key, divisive issue in most parts of the world, certainly in the United States. The British were ready to relinquish their mandate charge in the Middle East, once a pleasantly exotic scene for them but now ever more violent; the issue bedeviled the emergent United Nations.

My having met Chaim Weizmann may have bolstered my interest in the Zionist cause; his Western, liberal outlook made me think that he, and not extremists of various stripes, represented the heart of Zionism. I allowed my life to be unduly simplified by identifying what was to become Israel with him and by disregarding the power of bellicose Jews. Weizmann deplored Jewish terrorism, which he thought negated his work. In April 1947, he wrote to a defender of the Jewish terrorists: "They have chosen the revolver and the bomb as salvation in the present . . . I confess I doubt whether the Messiah will arrive at the sound of high explosives." In January of that same year, Einstein wrote to friends in Palestine: "Our powerlessness is bad; if we had power, it might be worse."

My father and I continued to be connected with the Weizmanns by fortuitous events: on May 14, 1948, the very day of the proclamation of the state of Israel, instantly recognized by the United States, I carried my father's electrocardiograph to Dr. Weizmann's apartment at the Waldorf-Astoria, and my father was in attendance with Weizmann when the call came from Tel Aviv that the latter had been chosen president of the new state. A month later, when President Truman invited Weizmann, then in very poor health, for a state visit to Washington, my father traveled with him.

Like many people, I was a totally secular pro-Zionist, though the term didn't occur to me. Already as a child I had felt that if one was persecuted as a Jew, one became a Jew, one identified with Jews, and the fate of Jews commanded instant loyalty—though even in those days, criticism of Jewish action or leaders didn't constitute disloyalty. I thought of Palestine, then of Israel, as a haven for victims; the socialist dream of the kibbutz had its own appeal, while the Orthodox Jewish minority seemed marginal. Did I at times feel embarrassed, even uncomfortable, about belonging to the minority of Jews whose families had converted? Yes. Did I mind being ignorant of Jewish rituals and holidays? Yes. But I was not attuned to organized religion of any kind, so I never thought of "unconverting." I was reassured by Weizmann's choice of my father as his doctor, and by the way he ignored what in his autobiography he called the "apostasy" that Fritz Haber had introduced into the family. In any case, most people assumed I was Jewish: why else would my family have fled Germany? Oddly, in both postwar Germany and the United States, people didn't realize there was a category of "Jewish" Christians. Certainly I encountered subterranean anti-Semitism in America, but the occasional taunt made by American Jews about my having been born into a converted family hurt more.

I felt a rough and never easy equivalence between inner and outer identity. The thought that Hitler had made me a Jew, annulling the commitments my grandparents had made to Christianity, seemed intolerable, even as I realized that it had been National Socialism that had made me feel my Jewish kinship. In much later years and in a second marriage, my sense of being a Jew became still stronger, even as the dream of Israel faded, as the last of the great twentieth-century utopias was threatened by self-betrayal. Isaiah Berlin once said to me that one knew one's loyalty if one could feel ashamed of the action of a nation's government. As I write this, and with his thought in mind, I have not a scintilla of doubt that I am an American and a Jew.

The 1948 election was the first time I could vote: sixteen years of Democratic rule had been an unparalleled success, and, despite my occasional misgivings, I thought Truman's foreign policy, brilliantly executed by his secretary of state, George Marshall, a triumph of creative, responsible leadership, always aiming at bipartisan support. And yet I was troubled by Truman's campaign, which struck me as excessively demagogic in its attack on an—admittedly—"do-nothing" Congress. His chief opponent was Thomas Dewey, a rigid, unappealing Republican surrounded by still less attractive advisers and some self-righteous proponents of a policy to force a "rollback" of Soviet power. For many of my friends, the great temptation was Henry Wallace, Roosevelt's earlier vice president, by 1948 a relentless critic of administration policy and implicitly a Soviet apologist, for which he received support from fellow travelers and left-leaning individuals who thought the cold war was largely an American invention. I thought Wallace a dangerous servant of delusion. But Dewey was frighteningly unappealing, though his victory, according to polls and pundits, was inevitable. Hence if Truman was going to lose anyway, I felt free to cast my vote for a noble, hopeless cause: Norman Thomas, habitual presidential candidate of the American Socialist Party. I had met Thomas at a friend's house and been impressed by his personal decency; I knew him to be both an outspoken anticommunist and also a critic of American nuclear policy. Yet on election night, I rejoiced that a plurality of voters had shown better judgment than I, and I reveled in Truman's upset victory. Perhaps it is just as well to make a mistake like this at the very beginning of one's formal civic life.

In retrospect, I believe those years saw American statesmanship at its most constructive and visionary. At the time, I regretted the gradual breakup of the wartime alliance, but the designs of Soviet expansionism, driven by fear and ambition, made a collective Western defense an imperative. In Dean Acheson's famous phrase, we were "present at the creation," but we couldn't know we were at the beginning of what much later was called *les trentes glorieuses*, three glorious postwar decades in which Western Europe, ever closer to some form of integration, also managed to create a more prosperous, less inegalitarian society.

I caught an early glimpse of yet another ideal in the process of realization: the United Nations Universal Declaration of Human Rights. The Nazi genocide and the Nürnberg trials made clear the need for such a binding commitment, and a UN commission was preparing such a document in 1947–1948. A key figure in the drafting of the document was Boris Mirkine-Guetzevich, a French lawyer who during the war had found refuge at the New School in New York. Our friend Hamburger was his collaborator, and he tutored me in the importance of the UN—I think he hoped I would eventually work there—and he also explained the conflicts within the commission.

Meanwhile, I also had a distant glimpse of the American occupation policies described as the three Ds—de-Nazification, demilitarization, and decartelization, bolstered by self-confident efforts at German reeducation—my own experience insignificant in substance but useful for my education. In 1948, Kurt Hahn came to the United States to solicit American foundations' support in reeducating Germans. Hahn had had a distinguished career in the Weimar Republic, at its very beginning as an adviser to Prince Max von Baden, later as director of an elite boarding school in Salem, a school much frequented by aristocrats and well-to-do Jews. Hahn had warned conservatives against trusting Hitler. The Nazis, according to whose laws he was a Jew, briefly imprisoned him; he immigrated to Britain, where he established a famous school at Gordonstoun, in Scotland, at which the prize pupil had been Philip Mountbatten, who had that year become Prince Philip, Duke of Edinburgh. Hahn, an imposing presence, had reopened Salem in 1946. Now he wanted American support for the creation of many Salems, thus furthering the cause of German reeducation. Paul Ehrlich's grandson Günter Schwerin, a graduate of Salem, told Hahn that I would be a good person to draft the necessary memorandum for him.

We met: Hahn outlined his basic pedagogical ideas and practices, which seemed to call for a democratically chosen elite; the task of education was to train cadres of leaders. The first requirement, the free development of character, was best achieved by the most austere regimen, with a heavy emphasis on physical endurance and with a tough inculcation of self-reliance (such as the later programs of Outward Bound). I was less impressed by his insistence that cold showers (and other tribulations) could subdue or perhaps sublimate the more sensual desires of male youth.* As I took my leave of Hahn, promising to draft a proposal by the next day, I asked if I should mention Prince Philip's presence at Gordonstoun. Hahn commanded me to sit down again and re-

---

*In his 1986 autobiography, Golo Mann, an alumnus of Salem and a lifelong admirer of Hahn, wrote about the worst error of Hahn's pedagogy: "Kurt Hahn knew next to nothing about sexuality and sexual education. The cause: the inclination which was in him, the homo-erotic he disapproved of morally and with an incredible effort of will he suppressed it in himself."

buked me for so egregiously vulgar, so "American," a question. He thought I had understood him; of course, the answer was no.

I wrote the report overnight (for which I was paid, I believe, one hundred dollars—with which I bought my first skis), delivered it the next morning, and some hours later discovered that in my typed report I had skipped a line. I rushed back, asked to have a chance to correct the mistake, and was told that it was too late. I insisted. Finally Hahn's secretary produced the handsome leather-bound album with my report as its principal text—and there I saw the frontispiece photograph of Philip Mountbatten playing polo at Gordonstoun. For me, this was an enriching lesson, an insight into German idealism. Some years later, in one of my first essays, when I coined the term *Vulgäridealismus* (a variant of the Leninist epithet *Vulgärmarxismus*) it was very much with Hahn in mind. I found his high-minded hypocrisy, which took itself so very seriously, repellent. Despite celebrity alumni and my report, the foundation declined to support new Salems as the salvation for Germany. Perhaps I did, and do, Hahn an injustice, and perhaps the album was not his idea; we were to have many friends in common, and they all thought him a moral paragon. But the noble stance covering crafty self-interest—that was a mixture that I came to recognize well, and not in Germany alone.

Those years when there was no Germany coincided with my still more intense study of European history. In my senior year at college, I had taken a colloquium that Barzun and Trilling taught together: we met every Wednesday night, discussed an assigned book, and we dozen or so students—including such intimidating fellow students as Joseph Kraft and Byron Dobell—had to write three essays per term, memorably and separately edited by Barzun and Trilling according to the unassailable tenet that style and substance were inseparable. The syllabus began with William Blake, Rousseau, and *Faust*, and ended with Freud: Here were the great masterpieces of modern European thought, taught by two men who were very different yet brilliantly well attuned to each other, both of them convinced that great literature illuminated the moral life. It was hard to read Burke, Tocqueville, Dostoevsky, and Nietzsche and not understand the need to rethink some of the simplistic verities of democratic optimists such as John Dewey. Reading *The Brothers Karamazov* and the parable of the Grand Inquisitor had, I believe, an immediate, unsettling effect on me: it deepened my brooding about totalitarianism. "There are three powers, three powers alone, able to conquer and to hold captive for ever the conscience of these impotent rebels for their happiness—those forces are miracle, mystery and authority." Dostoevsky and Nietzsche taught me to better understand the complexities and fragility of democracy—and the place of the irrational in politics. For Barzun and Trilling, literature and history were so obviously inseparable as to make explication, let alone theory, a supererogatory extravagance. I hope I have heeded their lesson.

This was all very much in my mind when I began my graduate work in European history and political theory. The principal requirement was to write a master's thesis, and my choice of topic proved a lucky one. I picked a German writer as subject: Arthur Moeller van den Bruck, of whom I knew little more than that in the early 1920s he had written the influential *The Third Reich*, a book with an evident connection to the rise of National Socialism. I studied his life and work, which reached back to the end of the nineteenth century, to his intellectual forebears and their violently "anti-Western" sentiments, their rejection of the ideas of 1789 and the Enlightenment. His fierce antiliberal stance was mixed with ideas of a great Germanic destiny. He belonged to what some critics called "the conservative revolution," which demanded a new, stricter authoritarianism, different, however, from the old prewar bourgeois regimes. I discovered how far back this kind of thought went and how it was a German variant of a European phenomenon. I learned to concentrate on ideas in context and in relation to an individual's private and public experiences. I had stumbled on a potentially rich subject, of intrinsic historic importance but topical because it contributed to an understanding of the ideological roots of National Socialism.

My good fortune in turning to European and German history deepened when, in the fall of 1948, I met Henry Roberts, newly appointed at Columbia, who had just returned from a two-year stint as a Rhodes scholar in Oxford, which had followed his wartime service in the research and analysis section of the Office of Strategic Services, the wartime predecessor to the CIA. He had been dispatched to Rumania after its armistice with the Allies in September 1944; the next March, he witnessed the ruthless communist coup in Bucharest, executed under the personal direction of Andrei Vishinsky. Henry had studied German history at Yale, with Hajo Holborn as his mentor.

Henry was ten years my senior, and we became friends, as did our families; we even shared an office for a while. His was one of the keenest historical-philosophical minds I had ever encountered or was ever to encounter, one in which moral rectitude, astounding intellect, and sparkling wit were marvelously blended. His wartime experiences and postwar work with Hugh Seton-Watson, a pioneering British historian of Eastern Europe, that neglected area, was exciting for me to learn about; and his study of Rumania, published in 1951, remains a model of analytic narrative.

Soon I met some of Henry's associates from the OSS, men and women of his generation and an earlier one who were becoming the leading postwar Europeanists in our universities: Leonard Krieger, H. Stuart Hughes, Carl Schorske, Franz Neumann, Felix Gilbert, and Hajo Holborn, men of extraordinary erudition and a deep, analytical concern with politics; these three last were German émigrés with an intense interest in the German past and the uncertain German future. They had conflicting interpretations—Marxist and liberal—but a shared sense that the study of the German past, and hence of the path to National Socialism, was an imperative of historical investigation and moral understanding. To encounter at a formative moment in my life this group of outstanding scholars, hardened by their experiences as wartime intelligence officers, steeped in the actuality of politics, and wiser for having had to analyze instantly the complexities of given events—this was an intellectual gift. Sometimes I say that I wished for "A Peacetime Equivalent of the OSS"—the formulation referring to one of my favorite essays, William James's "The Moral Equivalent of War," that quintessential American text of 1906, arguing that modern war is suicidal but that the civic and human virtues mobilized by war needed to be enlisted in collective peacetime pursuits.

In 1948, I also met Richard Hofstadter at Columbia; at the age of thirty-two he had just completed *The American Political Tradition*, a critical, rigorously analytical reinterpretation of American history, a classic to this day. He became a close friend, a mentor, and a model. He had an instinctive sense that the historian must also be a writer, a guide or interpreter to a large audience, and mustn't be insulated from the intellectual world around him. For Hofstadter, as for almost all scholars at the time, the memory of Weimar's fall and of National Socialism's ruthlessly functioning terror was a moral background to much of his work. Our interests intersected even more closely when in the early 1950s, Hofstadter organized a major study of the radical right in America, a project supported by the Fund for the Republic, that admirable offshoot of the Ford Foundation. Dick and I regularly exchanged draft manuscripts for each other's criticism, a common practice at the time, and I profited hugely from reading drafts of the books he wrote with such profundity and speed. The friendships with Henry and Dick extended to our families, in fact to three generations, for the Robertses and Hofstadters became my father's patients and my parents' friends, and when our children arrived, they, too, became close. We were lucky in the extreme.

At the time, I thought I wanted to become a European cultural historian, with a particular focus on Germany and a particular concern for what we then called "cultural history," blending Europe's intellectual and political history. I had lived through a small part of the German horror, but enough to feel and recognize its centrality; now I lived among and studied with humanistic American scholars, themselves committed defenders of a liberal society. My private and professional lives began to intersect in many ways, and Europe had a priority over Germany in both. My politics were those of a critical liberal, convinced by life and literature that freedom was the greatest good and that civic participation was both a duty and a privilege. My life was wholly in the United States, but my attachment to Europe and my curiosity about it remained a strong inner force. Only in retrospect do I see that the years when there was no Germany prepared me for a different life with Germany in the years to come.

★

CHAPTER 6

THE FEDERAL REPUBLIC: NEW BEGINNINGS

WHEN A NEW GERMAN STATE emerged in October 1949, the Federal Republic of Germany, it had only limited sovereignty and was considered provisional, operating under a strict Occupation Statute (benevolently interpreted) and the Basic Law drawn up by West Germans (as we called "our" Germans). To emphasize the modest, pro-Western character of this new state, the small river town of Bonn, on the Rhine, became its capital. Unlike the brilliant *Todestanz* of Weimar and the hysterical malignancy of the Third Reich, the Bonn Republic, as it came to be known, was a quiet place for some years, provincial and reassuringly boring. It was meant to endure until such time as a peaceful "reunification" of the German nation could somehow be achieved.

The Federal Republic was a creature of the cold war, conceived as the only possible answer to the breakdown of Allied unity, markedly evident since 1946–1947. Its creation was a tribute to American statesmanship, to constructive (West) German responses, and to Stalin's intransigence. And its establishment was quickly followed by the creation of the "other" German state, with the transformation of the Soviet zone into the German Democratic Republic, a nearly subservient satellite of the USSR. Neither of these two German states recognized the legitimacy of the other, and by their existence and in their rival social and political systems, they duplicated the larger divisions between West and East. The two states, of unequal size and power, were quickly integrated into the two rival blocs, and though there was socialist opposition to Bonn's integration in the West, there were countervailing forces as well: a socially responsible free-market system that produced an ever higher standard of living, along with the immense appeal of the United States—the country that had dramatically withdrawn from Europe after its victory and then had returned, assumed unprecedented responsibilities, and shown its will and power in the Berlin airlift. The Germans in the Soviet zone had little liking for and less choice about their "protector," which was still depleting what was left of the East German economy, even as it was bestowing on it all the hallmarks of the Soviet system: a dictatorship with a "socialist" economy that excelled in demanding sacrifices of its people. Bonn had one other trump, the legitimacy that comes from a free election, while the GDR could boast that it was the first socialist state in German history, purged of the Junkers and capitalists who had allegedly driven the country into catastrophe.

At the time I saw the Federal Republic as a daring American construction, and I remained deeply distrustful of German political maturity and reliability; perhaps I was no more skeptical than Adenauer himself. And not for one moment did I think or dream that this new provisional state would have a permanent impact on my life, which was still marked by deep repugnance for almost all things German. I expressed this distrust and repugnance in simple ways: for example, it was inconceivable that one might buy a German car. When I bought my first car, in 1948, it was an English Austin, small and cheap to run. And as I have said, the thought of returning to Germany never even occurred to my parents and most of their friends: we weren't exiles, we were immigrants, and we had put down new roots in congenial soil. I was focused on my life and career in the United States, even though I had a deep longing just to go back to Europe, which perhaps I idealized, even as I somehow demonized the country that had expelled me.

The tasks facing the Federal Republic were immense: to develop a viable democratic polity, to clear away the physical and mental rubble left from the war, to regain some rank among the nations of the world, and to protect and promote German interests while preserving the protective shield of the West. Some half million German soldiers remained prisoners of war in the Soviet Union, with which the FRG had no diplomatic relations. How deeply could it integrate with the West without jeopardizing all hope of Germany's becoming one nation again? How would it deal with the problems of de-Nazification, when so many Germans were indulging in one form or another of collective amnesia? How would it overcome the deep suspicion and revulsion that things German aroused in so many people?

But West Germany had major assets as well. With its population of some fifty million, and its huge industrial potential balanced by rich agrarian lands, it was by

1950—despite the ruins of its cities and the remaining restrictions on the exploitation of its resources—on the cusp of recovery: the deutsche mark and a free market spurred capitalist innovation; a disciplined work force spurred production. Ludwig Erhard, Adenauer's minister of economics, enforced a policy of liberalizing the economy and instituting a program of socially responsible capitalism, sometimes even dubbed welfare-state capitalism. People began to marvel at West Germany's economic progress, which was helped of course by the Marshall Plan and further promoted by the influx of millions of refugees from the east; in rebuilding their own lives, they were helping to rebuild West Germany. Soon people began to speak of an economic miracle, a *Wirtschaftswunder*—the more remarkable as conventional wisdom had assumed that the postwar era would be marred by a worldwide slump, if not collapse. And democracy of course thrives on economic hope and satisfaction, a coupling largely denied to Weimar.

I was even more impressed by what I saw as a political miracle. The new Bonn Republic had extraordinary luck in its new leaders, for at all levels of government, citizens of decency and competence assumed political responsibility. To be sure, they often served alongside citizens tainted by Nazism or the inevitable timeservers, but they set a tone that inspired some confidence abroad.

Bonn's first president was Theodor Heuss, an amiable, unpompous Swabian with a fine touch of irony, an exceptional virtue in German politics. I came to think of him as a rare *Glücksfall*, a stroke of good fortune, in German history. He had been a liberal member of the Reichstag in Weimar, belonging to the hapless Democratic Party, whose vote shrank in every election after 1919. In 1933 the party, consisting of five (!) members, voted for the Enabling Law that established Hitler's dictatorship. (The five had been split among themselves but voted in unison.) Thereafter he faded into the unpolitical realm, publishing the occasional nonconformist piece, innocuous enough to pass the censor but cheering to the like-minded who could read between the lines. He also wrote a biography of Hans Poelzig.

Parliament elected Konrad Adenauer as first chancellor by one vote, his own. He assumed office as a septuagenarian, a figure of seeming integrity, authoritarian by character and conviction, untroubled by even a trace of self-doubt. He had little faith in his own people and great and justified fear of ultranationalists, especially among the expellees, many of whom peopled the right wing of his party. Given the rhetorical barrage that had marked the Nazi empire, Adenauer's reticence proved an asset. Critics complained that he knew but two hundred words, to which a wit replied that if he knew more, he would be clever enough not to use them.

Kurt Schumacher, leader of the opposition Social Democrats and an arch foe of the Communists, had been one of the few rising stars of his party during the late Weimar years and had suffered in concentration camps in the Nazi period. Ernst Reuter was another such star within Social Democracy, but his death in 1953 removed one of the FRG's most attractive public figures. He was then grooming another one-time exile, Willy Brandt. Not surprisingly, beyond these impressive leaders of Social Democracy one saw other unattractive, vengeful figures in West Germany's public life; they had always been in plentiful supply.

Perhaps more important than the clauses of the Basic Law or the qualities of leadership, the new polity had what most of its antecedents had lacked—what the ancients called *fortuna*, luck in its historic setting, luck in the wisdom of its suzerains. Fear of Soviet aggression had hastened the process of Western integration and made West Germany's tie to the Western alliance an imperative. The United States, the most powerful Western nation, and one cheerfully distant from Germany, pursued a policy of benign encouragement, while Germany's neighbors, ever mindful of the German past, were far more skeptical. Put hyperbolically, some fifty million Germans benefited from the (very real) Bolshevik threat while eighteen million were condemned to suffer it.

Inescapably, Bonn was saddled with issues arising from the Nazi past, its full horror only gradually being disclosed. One issue was relentlessly practical: How would it deal with the millions of ex-Nazis? How far would it go in punishing Nazi criminals or in offering amends to their victims? Lurking behind the practical-political issues was the deeper moral issue of German guilt. The Federal Republic certainly marked a new beginning, but it was very far from a total break with that guilty past. There was no *Stunde Null*, no point zero. Citizens of the early Federal Republic were still traumatized; they lived with distorted and disturbed memories, combining personal grief with historic losses. They had lived through a succession of upheavals marked by intensity and suffering, all bound up with a whirligig of triumph and defeat. And there were continuities outside—among Germany's former enemies and among the refugees—continuities of outrage, of revulsion and mistrust, if also of hopes that the defeated decencies of German life might yet reassert themselves, that the self-righteous, murderous aggression had finally burned itself out.

The moral-intellectual questions could be repressed, but not the practical-political ones. To begin with there was the Germans' collective amnesia, which has also been called "a negative memory." A few leaders, such as Mayor Reuter and on rare occasions Adenauer himself, recalled the Germans' crimes, but there seemed little psychic openness to confronting the past. Yet it was clear that the manner in which Germans understood that past and dealt with its legal consequences would shape the future of the new state. The Allies had turned the job of de-Nazification over to the Germans themselves, and the Bonn Republic bungled the task: for reasons unhappily connected to U.S. policy, most ex-Nazis—including government bureaucrats, judges, teachers, and professors—escaped unscathed and continued in their old jobs. The full extent of these distressing continuities has been revealed only in recent years.*

It has been plausibly argued that a genuine cleansing, a real purge, would have turned millions of Germans into pariahs and enemies of the new democratic regime. But instead, American interests dictated strong support for Adenauer's policy of clemency. This seemed to be a success: as one of the shrewdest observers of the German scene, Franz Neumann, an émigré with strong Social Democratic leanings, wrote in 1950, "Despite the Cassandras of United States foreign policy, it cannot be overstressed that the West has so far won the battle for Germany." But the victory was bought at a price.

As it happened, these early years of the Bonn regime were also the years when I began teaching German history and began working on a doctoral dissertation that explored aspects of the cultural-intellectual milieu of Wilhelmine and Weimar Germany that favored the rise of National Socialism. This German past—meaning in the first instance the haunting question of how a democratic state, bolstered by its guarantees of traditional civic rights, could turn within weeks into a savage and successful tyranny backed by the enthusiasm of millions—served as a warning to citizens of endangered democracies. The end of Weimar was very much a live memory then, and German became the language of political fatality, as perhaps it still is.

The German past was to shape my life in the American present, not only in the classroom and in research but also in informing my responsibilities as a citizen of country and university. At decisive and dangerous moments in cold-war America, the memory of German civic passivity sliding into complicity prodded me into action. How much that German past affected me, how civism became a personal imperative—all this has become clearer to me now. And I now see, too, that this was a generational matter as well. In 1996, the (younger) German historian Jürgen Kocka, speaking of a Berlin publisher, said, "[Wolf Jobst]

---

*A piquant example: Hannah Arendt's postwar German editor was Hans Roessner, a former SS *Obersturmbannführer* now employed in a distinguished German publishing house. The Nürnberg judgment had declared the SS a criminal organization. Arendt, a German Jewish philosopher living in the United States, had no inkling with whom she was dealing. (Nor did I, when, in the most flattering fashion, Roessner turned down an early, incomplete version of my book on Bismarck and his Jewish banker, claiming it was not a financially viable proposition.)

Siedler belongs to the generation of [Jürgen] Habermas, [Joachim] Fest, [Ralf] Dahrendorf and Fritz Stern who in their youth, but very consciously, experienced the German catastrophe in very different ways, and whose life thereafter as intellectuals, as public scholars was marked by the attempt to explain this experience, again in very different ways."

I FIRST VISITED the Federal Republic in the summer of 1950, realizing a five-year-old aspiration to return to Europe. Doing research for my dissertation was the excuse, but Western Europe was the passion. We made the crossing on the *DeGrasse,* a wonderfully slow French ship, with all the free wine and cheese I could dream of—and memorable fellow passengers. Dean Dixon, the black conductor, was en route to his adopted home in Paris, where, he explained, he could walk about with his white wife without having to endure malevolent stares; Peggy and I often ate with them, and we found his quiet reflections on American prejudice very poignant. I became friends with Jean Bruneau, a professor of French literature, and a devilish flirt with all the women on board, who on the night of the captain's dinner appeared with the rosette of the Resistance in his lapel; it was the highest honor of the Resistance, he explained to his frivolously ignorant friend. (Bruneau had been in Dachau for a year.) I talked with Werner Jaeger, the renowned German classicist who was now at Harvard, and traveling in first class.

To rediscover Europe with my American wife and two-year-old son was thrilling. Europe had a feel of home. We spent the first week in England, visiting the family homestead, the ancient rectory in Caldecote, and found it appealingly austere (rationing still prevailed). France was freer, despite the strict currency controls. I reveled in being back in Paris, the more so as I had a professional errand: Edmond Vermeil, a French Germanist, was preparing a volume on the origins of National Socialism for UNESCO and had asked me for an essay on Moeller van den Bruck, on whom I had written my master's thesis. Vermeil didn't use the thesis, but our time in Paris was bliss, and seeing old friends was a further wonderful bonus.

Peggy and our son, Fred, returned to Caldecote while I went on alone to Germany, and with that first crossing into German territory my contempt for uniformed Germans instantly surged up, but perhaps I was superimposing Nazi faces on what might have been innocent people. With the visa I had for the three Allied zones came the warning that it was "not valid for travel to Berlin by surface routes . . . The Allied High Commission and the Occupation

Powers cannot accept any responsibility for any documentation which may be necessary to transit the Soviet zone of Occupation." Of course I carried plenty of coffee and cigarettes as prospective gifts, and felt that going beyond their legal limits was a petty, pleasing triumph.

I had chosen Munich, a city I didn't know, as the best place to do my research, and I thought that my stay there would be endurable because of the presence of friends. Kubelka cousins, whom I had not seen since my memorable vacation in the Czech mountains in February 1938, lived nearby. And in Dachau, a name so horribly familiar, lived "Aryan" friends of my parents, Karl and Elli Hacks, he a lawyer and at the end of Weimar a member of the radical SAP; she an assistant in my mother's kindergarten in Breslau. The family had behaved impeccably in the Nazi era. I struck up a correspondence with one of their sons, Peter, a little younger than I.

I lived in a cheap rooming house and spent most of my time in the university library, but despite my work and these friends, I felt lonely and displaced. Was I a hostile alien in what had been my native country? The city was still full of rubble and half-destroyed buildings, and American troops were omnipresent. But I felt no sympathy, perhaps even pangs of satisfaction. After all, the Germans had brought this on themselves! Perhaps this was callous, a symptom of my still-strong hatred. Casual conversations with strangers, who were full of self-pity and often volubly anti-American, didn't help.

My brief stay in Munich afforded me a lasting gain: I met Franz Schnabel, the principal professor of modern history at the university. In the Weimar years, Schnabel, a Catholic, liberal by temperament but not ideology, had written a masterly four-volume history of pre-1848 Germany, unorthodox in both scope and outlook, that I greatly admired. It was a Catholic, South German response to the works by the late-nineteenth-century historian Heinrich von Treitschke, who was fervently Prussian, militaristic, and anti-Semitic. Schnabel had been a reserved supporter of Weimar, aware that democratic citizenship placed great responsibilities on the historian, the more so given the weaknesses of the German *Bürgertum*, with its acceptance of material success and political passivity. In the last great crisis of Weimar, when in 1932 Chancellor Papen ousted Prussia's democratic government, Schnabel had denounced the step: "Even if discussion should be closed and in the future everything should be dictated [from the top] in the German fatherland, it still remains the duty of the intellectually leading group to raise its voice for as long as was possible. Even if every word was powerless as against previously decreed decisions," one still had to speak out. That of course was precisely what the great majority of German intellectuals did not do.

I went to hear him lecture—a small man with a stern, melancholy face addressing hundreds of students in a dispassionate tone on the religious wars of the sixteenth century. I introduced myself; he invited me to his small apartment—in its relaxed formality, a first for me—where his sister served us coffee and cake. He encouraged me in my work and reminisced about his life. Thought too liberal by Catholic faculties and too Catholic by Protestant ones, he had begun his career in his native, liberal Baden as a *Gymnasium* teacher, later promoted to the Technical University of Karlsruhe, until the Nazis, in 1936, forbade his teaching altogether, banned his books, and didn't allow the completion of his projected fifth volume. He told me with a touch of ironic pride that it had taken two wars and two revolutions for him to get a professorship at a regular university.*

Most German historians at the time were narrowly conservative or reactionary; hence Schnabel, a clear force for the good, was controversial or marginalized. He was open-minded, with only a whiff of the traditional German professor, regretful of the Germans' loss of faith in the nineteenth century, skeptical of Enlightenment thought and its "mechanistic" legacy, and conventionally troubled by American ascendancy, the United States being at the time the nation that seemed best to embody the Enlightenment in its public ideals. He teased me with the analogy then popular in Europe that the United States was Rome to Europe's Athens—a complacent conceit I found offensive, quite aside from the fact that this Athens was morally and materially bankrupt.

At our last meeting, Schnabel complained to me about the cramped quarters assigned to him and his sister, housing being still desperately scarce in Munich. Couldn't I urge the American authorities to get him a larger abode? The Bavarian minister of education, Alois Hundhammer, once a Nazi prisoner and now a person of reactionary-clerical views, thought of Schnabel as an enemy. Schnabel's risible overestimation of my capabilities—a frequent but not always happy experience—was significant in revealing the ongoing fierce conflicts in Germany. I could not help him with his living quarters, but we continued to correspond.

Chance led me to another historian and a lifelong enthusiasm. After Munich, I traveled to Switzerland, hoping to spend three days in Silvaplana, so clear in my mind from our vacation there in 1930. I didn't get there, but in Zurich, I happened to find a copy of *My Path to History*, a slim volume by the splendid Dutch historian Johan Huizinga. On a sunny alpine meadow be-

*I have since learned that he, too, had made his ideological gestures of accommodation toward the National Socialist regime, at the same time as he was trying to find a position outside Germany, looking even to the—uncongenial—United States. He was made an honorary foreign member of the American Historical Association.

neath the Jungfrau, I read his essays, which were aglow with literary and aesthetic insights. I was delighted by his impressionistic yet scholarly approach to the past, by his wish above all to furnish "a bright and lively narrative." I did not yet know about Huizinga's courageous opposition to the occupying German authorities who, in 1940, insisted that the University of Leiden expel its Jewish members. This admirable man and historian became another distant model. Such ideal or idealized figures have always been a spur and a reproach to me; above all, I believe in their sustaining power.

On that same trip, I bought a copy of Freud's *Civilization and Its Discontents*, tattered by now, and have often thought about what he called the imminent threat in *"la misère psychologique"* of groups, "most menacing where the social forces of cohesion consist predominantly of identifications of the individuals in the group with one another, whilst leading personalities fail to acquire the significance that should fall to them in the process of group-formation."

Peggy, Fred, and I left Europe in mid-August, at almost exactly the time of North Korea's invasion of South Korea. Failing to recognize the immense significance of this attack, and troubled by what I thought was Truman's overreaction to it, back in New York I mentioned my worries to gentle Lionel Trilling, and earned his fierce rebuke. I quickly realized that my ignorant response to the invasion was a symptom of Eurocentrism at its most lamentable, that Korea affected the whole world and would have a major effect on all of us. I think I learned from this capital misjudgment.

North Korea's aggression vastly intensified the American leaders' fears of Soviet expansionism, already heightened by the detonation of Russia's first atomic bomb the year before. Korea was, perhaps, a signal for an imminent Soviet move on the most vulnerable target in Europe: West Berlin, or the Federal Republic itself. An open discussion about the possibility of German rearmament began at once—I say open because we now know that thoughts of it had been bruited about earlier, in the mind of Adenauer and among some Americans.*

Permanent German disarmament had been an article of faith for the Allies, and obviously Germany's neighbors, whose memories of German aggression were fresh and bitter, were desperately opposed to any revival of German militarism. And how would Germans themselves respond to a reversal of this Allied

---

*Many decades later, in an oral history session with General Lucius Clay, my colleagues and I asked him about the precise intent or circumstance of messages dealing with West German rearmament that he sent to Washington on specific days in 1950. Mostly he couldn't remember, but when I asked him where and when he first *thought* of German rearmament, he replied that already in the late 1940s, inspecting a troop of German border guards (*Grenzpolizei*), he had said to himself, "My, they would make good soldiers!"

policy? For five years they had been told they could never again be trusted with any kind of army or weapons, with the symbols of power that once had meant so much to them, and now they should rush to the colors? Might a restored army once again threaten democracy, once again become a state within a state? Would not a West German army also be a barrier to the cherished dream of Germany's reunification? But Korea fired America's resolve to find a way of creating a trustworthy, safe West German army. It was a hard sell everywhere, but especially among liberals, to say nothing of the French. The debate about whether to build up a West German army and how to integrate it into a western alliance lurched between the pragmatic and the emotional-moral. Once more the question: What kind of people were these Germans, anyway?

In the winter of 1950–1951, I was told that my instructorship at Columbia would end in June. This was a serious blow, as our second child was due that summer, and I worried that now my incompetence was contributing to what felt like another expulsion. Columbia had become a home, a place of life-enhancing friendships. Then the unexpected: though my dissertation was unfinished, Cornell offered me a one-year "acting assistant professorship." I was to introduce my own version of a Western civilization course to some three hundred undergraduates there, and—as a life-changing bonus—I was also assigned to teach a graduate course on modern German history.

That was the more or less accidental start of my work as a German historian—and two things stood out at once: my own unpreparedness, having never studied German history as such; and, second, the paucity of historical works on Germany, especially in English. There were a few conventional texts and some narrow monographs, but the field was largely unexplored—an inconvenience then, but what a remarkable opportunity for my generation!

The most popular survey at the time was A.J.P. Taylor's *The Course of German History* (1951), a winningly written tale of German successes in aggression and failures in politics. Taylor, ever mischievous, excelled in apodictic epigrams; everything was explicable, everything led to the eventual catastrophe. To argue with his work was a bracing exercise, and I certainly did, objecting to what might be called his inevitability view of history. Taylor's brilliant mentor, Sir Lewis Namier, had also written on Germany, stressing the pernicious anti-Slav sentiment of German bourgeois liberals in 1848. Thorsten Veblen's much older *Imperial Germany and the Industrial Revolution*, a masterpiece of quirky analysis, emphasized the discrepancy between a modernizing economy and a feudal, militaristic ruling class. Many lesser works were variations on the theme "from Luther to Hitler," suggesting that Hitler was the culmination of old Germanic traditions of authoritarianism and militarism. (This, I always thought, was the negative version of the National Socialist creed that proclaimed Hitler as the savior of old German virtues, the crowning of German history.)

Franz Neumann's difficult account of the structure of the Third Reich, *Behemoth*, written in 1942, was a Marxist tour de force, but it paid little attention to the cultural or psychological elements in German life. In late 1951, Hajo Holborn's *The Political Collapse of Europe* appeared just in time for me to digest it for my lectures. His harsh judgment of imperial Germany's policies was important to me, and his sense of the duties and limits of modern statesmanship remains relevant today. A year later his essay on the divergence of German political thought and practice from Western processes argued that it began at the very height of Germany's cultural development in the late eighteenth century. This key question in interpreting German history had contemporary overtones: how "Western" was the Federal Republic in political alignment and in spirit?

The Cornell years were hard: I was expected to teach four graduate and undergraduate courses; and for academic survival I had to finish my dissertation, which dealt with three German writers whose nationalist jeremiads, composed over the years from the 1850s to the 1920s, had found powerful echoes in the German public and among the educated elite. Such laments against modernity were common enough in other European countries, but they carried far greater political weight in Germany than elsewhere. I was studying what I came to call a "Germanic ideology," fiercely anti-Western, antiliberal, antimodern, and, mostly, anti-Semitic, with yearnings for Germany's national rebirth, for a new faith, community—and leader.

A couple of weeks before I defended my dissertation in May 1953, Columbia told me they were looking for a German historian, that if my defense went well I might be offered the job. When Columbia made me the offer—at a lower salary than Cornell had proposed and without Cornell's assurance of future promotion to tenure—I took the job.

My salutary two years at Cornell left me with instructive memories. I had been appointed in order to replace a colleague on leave, and the History Department had wanted me to introduce a radical alternative to that professor's carefully mapped "Western Civilization" course. Naturally, he resented me from afar. Toward the end of my first year, a colleague remarked to me at a social gathering, "But you don't sound like a Nazi." I was stunned, but evidently the absent professor, a Germanophobe of the first hour, had said that the way I described my dissertation made me sound like a Nazi apologist! A defining lesson in collegiality!

In the fall of 1952, during my second year at Cornell, I was an enthusiast for Adlai Stevenson, the Democratic candidate against Eisenhower, but thought that my dissertation cum teaching demanded political abstinence. The appalling demagoguery of Nixon's "Checkers" speech so alarmed me that I organized a local Volunteers for Stevenson chapter at Cornell. As a complete unknown on campus, I needed reputable colleagues as heads of the chapter, while I promised to do all the work—and we managed to publish an endorsement for Stevenson signed by 132 Cornell faculty members, including Hans A. Bethe, Max Black, and Mario Einaudi. I collected more than a thousand dollars, enough to have the local Democratic Party demand a hefty share of it; I demurred, we compromised, and I have often thought that this brush with party maneuvers ended a political career before it had begun.

I never regretted my decision to return to Columbia, where I continued to teach German history. Major new works were appearing: in 1952, Alan Bullock's masterly *Hitler*, and a few years later Karl-Dietrich Bracher's book on the dissolution of Weimar, a model in substance and method, though some German historians criticized it, since it didn't fit the prevailing superficialities. In 1959 appeared an astounding study of Max Weber and German politics by Wolfgang Mommsen, a German historian then only twenty-nine years old—and destined to become a leading figure of a new and superb generation of scholars.

And in this trying time in America, with McCarthyism still gathering strength, there was much talk about Weimar. Many a left-winger talked of Gleichschaltung, and compared Eisenhower to Hindenburg and McCarthy to Hitler. This was dangerous nonsense, I thought: false analogies between past and present. What was happening was bad enough in American terms: an irresponsible political witch hunt was punishing culpable and non-culpable partisans of left-wing causes and creating an atmosphere of fear and intimidation. Many people, especially in the academic world, behaved cravenly. But it was also a time when conservative Republicans, such as Senator Ralph Flanders of Vermont, defended basic decency, and when an influential broadcaster, Edward R. Murrow, made a television documentary about McCarthy that hastened the senator's self-destruction. (For its repeated showing I collected funds.) We now know that Soviet espionage was in fact quite pervasive, but American anticommunist efforts at thought control, the imposition of government loyalty oaths, and other tactics for eliminating "subversives" or "premature antifascists" struck me as deserving the very name that McCarthyites used for their opponents—un-American.

The homecoming to Columbia proved to be especially stimulating because the university had become ever more internationalist—a reflection of America's new position in the world. An influx of federal and foundation grants allowed for the creation of a School of International Affairs and various regional institutes, and also for a special seminar on European politics involving scholars from Columbia and outside: Franz Neumann and Henry Roberts belonged to the seminar's Columbia contingent; Hajo Holborn, Felix Gilbert, Herbert Marcuse, Leonard Krieger, H. Stuart Hughes, and Carl Schorske came from the outside; and I was lucky enough to be appointed its rapporteur. I was struck by the style and manner in which these men who had served in the wartime OSS analyzed contemporary politics. I also attended a history seminar marked by sparkling arguments among Neumann, the Hegelian-trained Marxist political scientist; Holborn, the German-trained historian who combined deep liberal principles with political realism and philosophic circumspection; and Roberts, ever the sane, skeptical, pragmatic American voice. These two seminars, filled with human drama and political enlightenment, were good examples of "cloistered" academics coming to grips with the outside world. That Germany was often the focus of discussion did not seem surprising to any of us. After all, while the cold war was being fought on many fronts and in many guises, Germany remained the existential battleground.

When Stalin's death in March 1953 was followed in June by a revolt of workers in East Berlin, who took to the streets to protest new labor "norms," and when, within hours, the demonstrations spread to other cities in East Germany, with demands for better conditions mingling with pleas for free elections, the basic issues of the cold war—being played out in the heart of Europe—could not have been clearer. Soviet tanks soon crushed the protests, ending what had been the first defiance of Soviet rule in its satellite states, but it wasn't lost on us that *workers* had taken the initiative to rebel against what Communists celebrated as a workers' state, perhaps even a workers' paradise.

America's successive high commissioners in Bonn, John J. McCloy and James Conant, had always been intent on strengthening democratic developments in West Germany, and slowly West Germans began to change their views of the United States, relinquishing older stereotypes of Americans as naïve cowboy occupiers and seeing them rather as representatives of a model society to which a new generation of Germans could flock for instruction. Education would be central to the building of democracy. A signal event, then, was the founding of the Free University of Berlin, in 1947–1948, a direct response of some scholars having been expelled from Berlin University, now in the Soviet sector. Other students and a few teachers from the East rebelled against communist conformity, migrated to West Berlin, and, with American help, created the Free University. The grand old man of German history, Friedrich Meinecke, now an octogenarian, was persuaded to become the school's first rector, and almost at once Columbia's then president, Dwight D. Eisenhower, agreed that Columbia should "adopt" the new institution.

Neumann became the chief architect of American aid to the FU, and of the special relations between the two universities. The Free University received support from the city of (West) Berlin and from the High Commissioner's Office, but Neumann also pressed the Ford Foundation to support it; Ford gave more than a million dollars for a library, a large lecture hall, and a student cafeteria to accommodate the students—especially the roughly 40 percent of the total—who, at considerable personal risk, were commuting from East Berlin. Neumann also persuaded Ford to establish a faculty-exchange program, allowing Columbia professors to teach in Berlin and Berlin professors to come to Columbia. Ford's considerable investment reflected an American awareness that the cold war had to be waged on the cultural level as well.

By 1954 the Federal Republic was economically and politically quite strong. Adenauer's reign, dubbed "chancellor democracy," was giving Bonn a stability that Weimar had never had. He drove hard for Western integration and shrewdly sought moral rehabilitation for his country as well: in 1952 he concluded an agreement with Israel's prime minister, David Ben-Gurion, pledging three billion deutsche marks as reparations for the Jewish people, to be paid over the next twelve years; the funds financed Israel's most immediate military needs. Throughout this time, the United States and Adenauer tried to devise means by which German manpower could in some form be added to West Europe's defense. Various plans for a European Defence Community that included West Germany were debated—indeed they dominated the international agenda.

The threat of such a development prompted Stalin in 1952 to make a dramatic proposal for a unified Germany that would remain neutral and free of all occupation troops, a kind of vacuum in central Europe. After intense if brief discussion, the Western powers, backed vigorously by Adenauer, rejected this last-minute Soviet effort to block West Germany's further integration with the West. And thus was the de facto division of the country reaffirmed. The West German elections of 1953 demonstrated that Adenauer was solidly supported, but the Social Democrats also gained slightly.

The United States, needing Adenauer, made concessions to him—most notably in allowing the early release of industrialists whom the Nürnberg courts had sentenced to jail for war crimes. West Germany was converting the Allies' (already deeply flawed) policy of de-Nazification to one of official leniency. Under Allied rule, for example, 53,000 civil servants had been stripped of their positions as Nazis, and by now all but 1,071 had been reinstated. Judges and professors returned to their posts, and Adenauer even allowed prominent ex-Nazis in his ministerial entourage. Critics spoke contemptuously of a "restoration." The East German regime especially delighted in picturing Bonn as a nest of Nazis and "revanchists." In retrospect, I would say that Adenauer allowed for an impermissible continuity of personnel in order to advance a radically new and Western orientation in West German politics. He had his own narrow political interests, too, of course, but his stance also expressed his distrust of his own people's maturity, purged or not.

Neumann asked me to join him teaching in the summer semester of 1954 at the Free University, and I leapt at the opportunity for another trip to Europe. The crossing was again on a French ship, the *Liberté*. (In its first incarnation it had been a great German boat, the *Bremen*, which the French took over as reparation and rebaptized, removing every sign of its German origin.) I corrected blue books during the voyage, throwing them overboard as I finished grading each one: somehow that gesture fit my joy at being on the boat; my son remarked years later that he never saw me so happy as on a transatlantic crossing. On shipboard, we heard of the Supreme Court's unanimous decision in *Brown v. Board of Education* that school segregation was unconstitutional. To someone who was about to teach the Germans about the virtues of American democracy, this was a glorious gift!

After a brief, joyous stop in Paris, we took the train to Frankfurt, American army headquarters. Since I was a guest professor at the Free University, we had been provided with the High Commissioner for Germany's (HICOG) official travel orders, issued in English and Russian, for the daily military train from Frankfurt to Berlin. We had arrived a day ahead of schedule, so these were not valid until the next evening. I rushed to headquarters—the former IG Farben Building, designed by Hans Poelzig and spared from Allied bombing for eventual Allied use—where a kind Captain Brown assigned us to an army billet and exchanged greenbacks for occupation script, transactions done with more benevolence than legality.* He exchanged more than I needed and briefed me on the Soviet threat, against which the United States had large arms depots

---

*While I was chasing down the new orders, I left my family at the railroad station, expecting to return quickly. The children had some ice cream, and Peggy no money; the waiter loudly insisted on what was due. Fred, now six, jumped up on the table and uttered the only two sentences in German I had taught him: "Ich bin Amerikaner! Wo ist die Polizei?" (I am an American. Where is the police?)

with which to arm Germans, if need be; as for the case of an actual Soviet move, we would have a seventy-two-hour warning ahead of time!

The night train ride to Berlin was memorable. Soviet regulations demanded that once on East German territory, still "protected" by Soviet troops, the shades had to be pulled down. At dawn, through a crack, I spied a Soviet soldier, gun slung on his shoulder, standing there in the middle of Europe: what a strange apparition! The train stopped for a longish, unscheduled period at one point early in the morning; curious, we cautiously opened the shades: we were on a siding at the Magdeburg Station, about fifty miles from Berlin. Across from us, a large crowd of commuters were waiting for their train; they waved at my three-year-old daughter, and when our train began to move again, she yelled, "Bye, bye!" The East Germans responded in unison. An innocent version of spreading American influence (of mocking Soviet-type rule?). An irresistible sport.

The Free University had found us quarters in a Dahlem villa, close to all the scattered buildings that made up the university. The leafy suburb of Dahlem was also the center of the American presence in West Berlin, a kind of Little America, including barracks, soldiers' quarters, and the centerpiece, Truman Hall, with its cinema and shops. Captain Brown had already alerted the cultural sector of HICOG to our arrival, and from the beginning I enjoyed a close rapport with them. To have a shelter of American identity in a country that had once been, but now no longer was, my own was psychologically important.

I came to Berlin with all manner of mixed emotions. There was simple strangeness: I had never lived in Berlin, for even in childhood I knew London and Paris better. I had to orient myself in many new ways, especially with the people I met—whether our landlady with her upper-class snobbery or local people of one sort or another. Suspicion and preemptive hostility on my part prevailed: what had the person I was meeting done ten years earlier? Had he, or she, been a Nazi, or worse? On the way to Berlin, I had met Paul Roubiczek, a Czech philosopher in Cambridge, also now teaching at the Free University, and he presented me with a marvelous anecdote on this theme. In 1946, when the trains had begun to run again in the British occupation zone, a British officer came into a compartment with three Germans already seated there. After a while, he saluted the first German, and asked, "Were you a member of the National Socialist Party?" The German replied angrily that of course he hadn't been a member; in fact hardly anyone had been—just a few people at the top had been responsible for all that had happened. After a while, the officer posed the same question to the second German, who replied in even angrier terms that he was offended by the very question. "Here you British are trying to teach democracy, and then you come snooping around asking about political opinions." In any case, no, he hadn't been a member. On being asked the same question, the third German replied, "In 1937, I had a wife and three children. My job depended on my joining the party, and I did." The British officer saluted him and responded, "Thank you. I'd like to go to the dining car and was looking for someone who could keep an eye on my luggage. Would you?" Innocently, I told that story at the first dinner party I attended in Berlin and discovered that it was a perfect litmus test: a few Germans could laugh at it, but most of them responded with sullen silence.

Over and over again, I would hear stories about the first years of occupation, about Germans denouncing other Germans to the Allied authorities or, less often mentioned but perhaps more common, the reverse: Germans falsely attesting to each other's political purity, thus allowing for this massive continuity. How much rank opportunism, a characteristic of life in the Third Reich, seemed still to prevail among the Germans I talked to!

Early on, I began to wonder whether to talk of "the Germans" wasn't a dangerous simplification. They were such a divided people. Was their national identity in fact feebler than that of an older people? Was that why they were subject to these alterations between radical chauvinism and deep self-doubt? Was this connected to Germany's late unification and the divisions and traumas that followed? Inevitably and unconsciously, I connected my immediate impressions to historical speculation, shuttling back and forth between what I perceived in the present and remembered about the past. There remained the hope that with American help, West Germany, at least, would yet redeem itself. For that to happen, people would have to unlearn the mendacious and self-serving simplicities instilled in them in the past and learn something about the complexity of history and their own culpability.

My lecture course at the Free University was "The European Crisis, 1890–1950, with particular attention to America's role." The interplay between domestic and foreign conflicts at work in the outbreak of the Great War and its aftermath seemed unfamiliar to the students, as did my asides—such as that anti-Americanism, particularly in Germany, went back to the 1870s, a time of economic boom-and-bust, but that the antipathy had little to do with the actual America of that period. I emphasized the fear of modernity that Germans projected on America—and, often enough, on Jews as well. The students treated these unusual interpretations of German history with sympathetic seriousness; perhaps they were the first student generation in Germany not poisoned by chauvinism or militarism.

The students' willingness to confront the complexities of their past and to explore Germany's troubled relationship with the West was in contrast to the then prevailing silences of much public discourse. Many older Germans I talked to had a distorted, mostly self-exculpatory and self-deluding, picture of their past. They blamed German failures after 1918 on Versailles, or on the Great Depression, or on some other external agency; after 1945, everything was America's fault, including the "sellout" at Yalta, by which they meant the "surprising" failure of the Western Allies to make common cause with Germany against the Soviet Union. These people, still living among devastated ruins, said little overtly about the horrors of the wartime bombing of their own country: were their memories repressed because of the pervasive evidence and some sense of what Germans had inflicted on Warsaw and Rotterdam? It wasn't until the 1990s that German writers began to address the terrible destruction wrought by Allied air raids, the death and mutilations of more than a million people. It is hard to explain the earlier silence, but easy to speculate that the sudden later eruption of feeling may have fortified present-day pacifist inclinations in Germany.

Self-pity, as I had noticed on my first return to Germany, was the undertone of many conversations. And so was the suspicion Germans expressed about one another. West Berliners lamented the materialism of their compatriots in West Germany. I was reminded that Germans often complained of German divisiveness—a common theme. At a public playground that Fred visited, I noticed unchecked aggression in the sandbox, taunting hostility among the children, uncomprehending harshness between parents and children. Was I looking for signs of dissonance, or was it that prior experience and historical interest alerted me to what in other circumstances I might have ignored?

Berlin was the place and symbol of the deepest division in German life, with its as yet porous, though strictly policed border between the two German states. Citizens of the former occupying powers could go into East Berlin at a few specified crossings, and I looked forward to visiting the Soviet sector as a kind of forbidden experience. The first time, I stayed for only ten minutes, long enough to feel its utter foreignness and an uneasy fear of its arbitrariness. Walls were plastered with party slogans, and my first sight of a *Volkspolizist*, that dreadful combination of Nazi face and Soviet uniform, made me shudder. I was unwittingly reliving a part of my youth, mistaking a policeman's grimness for a Nazi face. The unease was genuine.

As it happened, on the next day came the festive opening of the university's Henry Ford Building. There were many speeches, but none more impressive than that given by the marvelously austere James Conant, ex-president of Harvard and now the high commissioner in Bonn. When I was introduced to him, I mentioned that I had been over to the eastern sector very briefly but had no desire to go back. He instantly rebuked me: "I thought you were a historian! You have an obligation to bear witness, to observe what is there to be seen!" I took his rebuke to heart, as at once a reassurance and an injunction—a historian's job is to be awake to the present as well.

The highlight for me that summer was attending the ceremonies commemorating the tenth anniversary of the attempt on Hitler's life, made on July 20, 1944, about which Germans had been largely silent, being uncomfortable with the memory of this most spectacular effort to overthrow the Nazi regime. Many still regarded as traitors the army officers who had joined in the conspiracy, and extremist papers such as the *Soldatenzeitung* vilified all efforts at honoring them. The public ceremony was in the Free University's newly opened Auditorium Maximum. At the time, I wrote, "The audience sat in silence, as at a funeral, no one applauding as Heuss and Adenauer walked down the aisle . . . or as the last notes of the second movement of the Eroica died. Heuss . . . spoke quietly and quickly, without pathos, recalling the anguish of the men who had chosen themselves murderers of murderers and had paid for their courage in torture and death . . . He concluded 'Our debt to them has yet to be fulfilled.'"

On the afternoon of July 20, another memorial was scheduled in the courtyard of the Ministry of War, a building known as the Bendlerstrasse Block, where some of the leading conspirators had been found and then murdered. The principal speaker was to be Hermann Lüdemann, our family friend in Breslau. After his release from a concentration camp, he had run a movie house in Berlin, and had joined a socialist subgroup linked to the chief plotters of the 20th of July, army officers who had access to Hitler; the co-conspirators and projected leaders in a post-coup government included Socialists and Communists. After the coup's failure, Lüdemann had been thrown into a concentration camp once again. He survived, and in 1946 became the first minister-president of Schleswig Holstein, in the British zone. I wanted to meet him, and went to the Bendlerstrasse, unaware that one needed an invitation to the event. Supplication at the gate was of no avail; the police sent me away. Impulsively, I repaired to a stationery store, bought a piece of paper and an envelope, and scrawled a note to Lüdemann; thus armed, I ran back and breathlessly asked a policeman to deliver this urgent message to the (former) minister-president, then volunteered to do it myself—and thus was allowed into the small courtyard, filled with the widows and children of the slain heroes and many members of the current West German government.

Lüdemann's eloquent remarks ended with the admonition that "the goals for which the victims gave their lives, a unified German Reich in which the German people can live in peace and freedom and enjoy happiness," must still be realized. Then Adenauer, irritated that a Social Democrat had been given pride of place, unexpectedly rose to speak, asserting simply that we were there to honor those who had given their lives "trying to save the honor of the German people." I was instantly impressed by that *trying*. (The local press made no mention of Adenauer's having said this, a token, it seemed to me, of the continued indifference cum embarrassment about the regicides of 1944.)

As I looked at the people in the courtyard—old, distinguished, and sadly proud, dressed in mourning, faces hardened and humbled by suffering—I felt a sense of shame for my indiscriminate hatred of Germans. To Lionel Trilling, I wrote right afterward that for me this had been a "moving, even purging experience . . . [W]hat saddens me: the 20th of July could have become a great saving and unifying symbol, except for today and for a few, it is forgotten and even maligned. Heuss himself felt constrained to justify what should have been celebrated. Unlike any other German historical event, this act of desperation . . . involved what might be called the 'good Germans' from every element in society—clergy, soldiers, civil servants, students—all risking everything for what after all were commands of conscience alone—a little belated, to be sure."

And here they were at the Bendlerstrasse, diverse representatives of what had been Germany's elite, many of them liberated from its callous provincialism only by a catastrophe, but an elite nevertheless. They and their murdered colleagues had risen above political passivity or even complicity and had united in resistance to Hitler, however belatedly. How different the postwar German spirit would have been if their memory had been cherished! Or, indeed, how different the world would have been if the 20th of July coup had succeeded! This remained for me a telling example of the openness of history, of the role of accident in it.

At the ceremony, I gave Lüdemann my message and phone number; he called and we met: a memorable figure then in his sixties, tall, haggard, with a shock of white hair. After making various private inquiries, we talked about the current scene; he said that Adenauer was a scoundrel (*Schuft*), who appealed to the meanness of the German people, which put the Social Democrats at a disadvantage; American support of him added to the SPD's plight. I supposed I expected some special aura or nobility about Lüdemann, which he lacked, but it was good to have seen this embattled, historic figure from my childhood.*

The one discordant note in the 20th of July commemoration was struck by Otto Dibelius, Evangelical bishop of Berlin, who delivered the principal sermon at the first ceremony. He praised God's mercy, manifest even in the days of most horrible German suffering, and he explicitly referred to the Germans expelled from the eastern territories. That very day, I wrote him to say that "I was astonished, even wounded, that your sermon . . . highlighted only the bitter experiences of the German people [who] are already and greatly aware of them. Would not this historic hour have been appropriate and would your authority not have prescribed that you speak for once also of the bitter experience of the completely innocent people, the millions from all over the world who by German hands lost everything, including their lives?" His answer came, swift and untroubled, insisting that he had spoken "of the millions who did not survive and whom we don't forget. In that connection I also thought of those who through German guilt lost their lives." I wondered at his obtuseness: he "thought" of the others but did not speak of them—a lamentable silence. (He had given early, voluble support to National Socialism, I learned later, made easier by his avowed anti-Semitism.)

Days later, I called on a venerable historian, Siegfried Kaehler. True to his conservative-elitist views, he had kept a certain distance from the Nazis, no doubt regretting their plebeian character. I mentioned to him how moved I had been by the commemorations and by Lüdemann in particular. "That scoundrel!" (*Schuft* again) he said. How so? I asked. He referred to Lüdemann's womanizing. I objected: a man who had been once imprisoned and had then volunteered to join the conspiracy against Hitler, thereby risking his life and ending up for a second time in a concentration camp, didn't seem to warrant the negative term. Kaehler responded, unfazed: "We couldn't all get entrance tickets to the concentration camps." I was stunned and speechless by this amazing comment, and left quickly. (Again I learned later that immediately after Germany's unconditional surrender, Kaehler had written to his son: "If universities continue to exist, then it will be our duty to preserve and defend the transmission of the true and real Germany against the defamation already set in motion by democratic Jewish propaganda and Anglo-Saxon self-righteousness.")

---

*In 2001, in response to my inquiry about some Lüdemann papers, the Friedrich Ebert Foundation sent me just one letter of his—his first postwar letter to our friend Ernst Hamburger, telling of his terrible experience in the Nazi camps and asking about various friends now in New York. "Does Stern tell jokes as well in English as he used to in German?"

Yet I met many quietly sympathetic, admirable Germans. An old colleague of my father's, Hans Freiherr von Kress, a doctor of serene humanity, who at the beginning of what he later called "our time of guilt" had foresworn the possibilities of an academic career and withdrawn to private practice, quietly helping Hitler's victims. We were to meet again when he became rector of the Free University. And there was Werner Philipp, a specialist in Eastern Europe, with whom I had an instant sense of unobtrusive moral earnestness and decency; a deep friendship across generations bound us together. On one of my last days in Berlin, I met the young political scientist and historian Karl-Dietrich Bracher, who was just finishing his book on the end of Weimar. (He was married to Dorothee Schleicher, whose father, a son-in-law of Karl Bonhoeffer, had been in the anti-Hitler conspiracy and been killed by the Nazis.) These human contacts with untainted Germans were an essential bridge to my continued involvement. I knew they had endured a test that others, myself included, had been spared. (That didn't inure me to the occasional remark congratulating me on my good fortune at having left Germany "in time," whereas the speaker and others had had to suffer war, hunger, and defeat.)

At the Free University, I also participated in a doctoral seminar taught jointly by Franz Neumann; Ernst Fraenkel, a political scientist who had left Germany in the 1930s and returned; and Otto Suhr, a Social Democratic politician and later lord mayor of West Berlin. I saw a good deal of Neumann that summer; he could be politically outrageous in his utterly ruthless and uncompromising way, but he could be lovable as well—or at least he was that summer.

Neumann dominated the seminar—doctrinaire, incisive, brusque. In many ways he was a forbidding person, all intellect, contemptuous of many of the students, only occasionally revealing his deep melancholy and unease. He wasn't happy in his skin, as the French would say. But in response to receiving an honorary doctorate from the Free University, he gave a formal lecture on "Anxiety and Politics" that was electrifying: the Marxist relying on Freud's theoretical insights about the relationships among alienation, guilt, and aggression. The emphasis was not on monopoly capitalism but on the power of the irrational; on the psychological link between anxiety and Caesarist movements in history, with their conspiratorial views. To me, this lecture, deeply grounded in the great texts of the past, was an astounding and utterly congenial revision of Neumann's previously held views.

The lecture also had a hidden private origin. Neumann had come to Berlin with a German lover, a young and very attractive scholar named Helge Pross.

It was rumored that he might return to Germany altogether—and his view that National Socialism represented a particularly malignant form of a common political deformation, not a uniquely German phenomenon, would have made such a transition easier, as would his evident happiness with his companion. A return would have given him a political forum, and a way to help build German democracy. But on September 2, driving in Switzerland with a friend at the wheel, Neumann, still so young at fifty-five, was killed in a head-on collision. It was a huge loss.*

In the immediate aftermath of my summer in Berlin, I had an instructive experience of anticommunist willfulness. I had been so stirred by my experiences in the divided capital that I quickly accepted an invitation from *Commentary*, then a distinguished liberal journal, to write an account of them. I delivered it to the managing editor, Robert Warshow, an admirably gifted, morally compelling person with whom I enjoyed working. A few months later, he commissioned from me a review of Ernst von Salomon's tendentious and meretricious book *Fragebogen*, which mocked the then-famous American questionnaire that millions of Germans had had to fill out as a prerequisite for postwar civic employment. I wrote the review, but Warshow suddenly died, and the piece was returned to me by someone else—in galley proofs, and too late to be altered. All manner of political editing had gratuitously added anticommunist comments to my discussions of Nazism. When I refused to allow the altered piece to appear under my name, Elliot Cohen, *Commentary*'s legendary editor, yelled at me over the phone. I was a mere refugee, I was acting "un-American," and he had the power to "make me" in public life if only I would be reasonable. This intimidation mixed with promised reward didn't appeal to me, and I stuck to my guns. He later apologized, but the ill-tempered attack gave me a whiff of what illiberal anticommunism was like.

At roughly the same time, I had a different kind of encounter with "liberal" anticommunism. In May 1954, I was informed that I had been made a member of the American Committee for Cultural Freedom, the American branch of a formidably impressive international organization, the U.S. membership of which being a virtual Who's Who of American intellectuals and writers and the non-U.S. members including Raymond Aron, Denis de Rougemont, Ignazio Silone, and W. H. Auden; the honorary chairmen included Karl Jaspers and

*The Venona files of NKVD agents reporting from the United States to Moscow during the war point to Neumann as someone who passed OSS reports to the Soviets. I agree with Arthur Schlesinger, who worked with Neumann in the OSS and found "this almost inconceivable." Neumann was always violently critical of Stalin and Soviet communism.

Reinhold Niebuhr. (I learned later that Diana Trilling had nominated me.) I solicited funds from colleagues for the committee's efforts to rally "intellectuals . . . in a responsible and serious struggle against communist totalitarianism." Then the executive director asked for my help in a projected book, *The Party Line*, about the Communists' efforts to "manipulate public opinion" in the United States, focusing on six "key illustrations of Communist campaigns," beginning with the war in Spain, the campaign to transpose "the roles of Mihailovitch [*sic*] and Tito," and ending with the defense of the atomic spies Ethel and Julius Rosenberg. The outline began with a claim that it was necessary to investigate the susceptibility "of politically unsophisticated humanitarians and civil libertarians." I wrote back that I recognized the potential of such a study but had "serious misgivings" about the outline, which proposed an "unhistorical and unscholarly procedure" by taking for granted what it set out to study. I ended my detailed criticism by noting that if the project, of which I had not heard before, had actually commanded "the most prolonged enthusiasm of the membership [as claimed], then it might perhaps be better if I were to leave the Committee." My letter was acknowledged with nothing but an invitation to come to the next membership meeting. I resigned instead.

The demands of containing the Soviet Union were real enough—and West German rearmament remained an American desideratum, continuing to be the subject of difficult negotiations among the Western Allies and within the Federal Republic. Still, by early 1955, agreements were in place that provided for the Federal Republic's inclusion in the North Atlantic Treaty Organization, the establishment of an army (subject to some restrictions) within NATO, and the end of the Occupation Statute. Precisely a decade after Germany's total defeat, Adenauer's goal had been achieved: the Federal Republic was a fully sovereign state and firmly integrated in the West. But he never renounced the ultimate goal of reunification—indeed he promised that the Federal Republic would reach "a position of strength" that would at some point force the Soviet Union to relinquish its satellite. Many Germans thought this was a false promise; some even thought of it as Bonn's *Lebenslüge*, the lie on which a life is based. But for the moment Adenauer's policies and American plans had triumphed.

The new army had been carefully prepared to be different from all previous forms of German militarism. It was to be under strict civilian control, never again a state within a state, and based on universal military conscription. In the felicitous phrase of the time, the soldier was to be "a citizen in uniform," aware of the dangers of blind obedience (*Kadavergehorsam*). When inspecting one of the first battalions, President Heuss, a civilian to the core and a perfect symbol of a new era, urged the soldiers, with gentle irony, "Now run along and be victorious." [*Nun siegt mal schön.*] Unimaginable lightness of military being.

Adenauer built on his new strength; in 1955, he traveled to Moscow, won the release of the remaining German POWs in Russian camps, and established diplomatic relations with the Soviet Union. But his heart and mind were in the west, and in 1957, together with his fellow Catholic and Christian Democratic leaders Robert Schuman in France and Alcide De Gasperi in Italy, he negotiated the Treaty of Rome, which created a common economic market of the three countries plus Belgium, the Netherlands, and Luxembourg. This was a momentous step in the integration of Europe and the rehabilitation of West Germany—and a triumph for the apostles of European unification, among them the foremost proponent of this vision, Jean Monnet, aided inter alia by Robert Marjolin, another French visionary. Ever since the Marshall Plan, the United States had been pushing for this kind of European integration, which generated genuine enthusiasm. The older generation drew the correct lessons from the disasters of two civil wars in Europe, and many of the younger generation welcomed the idea of a super-national identity, of a new home. From now on Bonn would have to balance its European policy with its dependence on the United States—and by and large it succeeded. I had my private enthusiasm for this new Europe as a world-historical beginning.

The achievement was all the more welcome given the disasters of the fall of 1956, when Poland and Hungary, the Soviet Union's key satellites in Eastern Europe, both tried to throw off the Soviet yoke, while at the same time an ill-advised Anglo-French-Israeli conspiracy sought to overthrow Egypt's president Gamal Nasser after he nationalized the Suez Canal. (British prime minister Anthony Eden, a celebrated anti-appeaser of the 1930s, was obsessed by the thought that Nasser was a lesser Hitler and that only force could stop him.) Soviet tanks rolling into Budapest to crush the armed resistance of the freedom fighters was a heartbreaking demonstration of Russian ruthlessness and Western impotence. Meanwhile the Anglo-French expedition failed miserably, having also aroused Americans' ire; we saw it as the last gasp of armed European imperialism.

My friends were much involved in what was happening in Eastern Europe, and they pulled me into some of their efforts. Shepard Stone, director of international affairs at the Ford Foundation, instantly recognized that the thousands of Hungarians who fled to Austria not only needed help but also constituted unique sources of intelligence about the Soviet imperium. He repeatedly traveled to Austria—according to legend with suitcases of greenbacks from the foundation. (Ford even contributed a bulldozer to help refugees cross snow-covered mountains into Austria.) Then, when he had to write a paper on German unification—the subject that wouldn't go away—for a big international conference in early 1957, he asked me to prepare a draft for him, which I did, and it was a useful way for me to clarify my own thoughts on the subject.

One had to begin by acknowledging that Germany divided was a source of conflict and instability, and yet it could hardly be imagined that a united Germany, which would have the third most powerful economy in the world, would be a stable minor nation, like a satisfied Switzerland. And a neutralized Germany, politically adrift, might at some point yield to Soviet blandishments (such as accepting territorial "adjustments" at the expense of obdurate Poland). I thought the Federal Republic must remain integrated in the West, but that an Allied study of the huge inner-German issues attendant on reunification should be undertaken. "Gladstone's reflection," I concluded, "that we have no right to expect political problems to be solved in less time than it took to create them may jar and discomfit us. But the West may take heart . . . from the unpredictable power of man's spontaneous will to freedom, which has brought glory and misery to Hungary."

For the moment, though, Bonn had *fortuna*, most evident in its startling economic recovery. (In fact, Germany's destruction had not been as great as the surface damage at first suggested; her industrial capacity in 1945 was greater than it had been in 1939; her reconstruction was immensely aided and accelerated by the economic consequences of the cold war; and her very partition favored an economic boon in the West.) The standard of living improved, with American-type consumerism replacing earlier class divisions: consensus, not class conflict, seemed to be the prevailing mode. Yet Erhard's liberalized economy brought with it a rapidly increasing inequality in the distribution of wealth, though in some large industries a measure of workers' co-determination had been installed, a minor gesture in the direction of industrial democracy. And the new pleasures of relative prosperity may also have favored a kind of moral amnesia: some of West Germany's best writers, such as the novelist Heinrich Böll, depicted a smug society that excelled in collective denial.

In dealing with the practical legacies of the Nazi past, inevitably linked to the deepest moral issues, Adenauer devised a shrewd implicit compromise. On the one hand he insisted on legislation to establish the rights of ex-Nazis for continued positions and pensions—at best a barely defensible pragmatic arrangement—and on the other hand, having already concluded the agreement with Israel, he insisted equally on restitution of some kind for the victims of Nazism. A professional career, for example, that had been interrupted or ended by Nazi fiat qualified for retroactive compensation. This seemed to me a minimal demand of political decency.

It was in this way that Adenauer's policies directly affected the lives of my parents. Several colleagues of my father's testified that considering his record as clinician, teacher, and scientist, he would eventually have been appointed a full professor. In 1957, Bonn's Ministry of the Interior appointed him retroactively to that rank as of 1939, and thus entitled him to various benefits according to civil-service provisions. (The New York lawyer who represented my father's claim to restitution also, unbeknownst to me, requested compensation for me for my interrupted education. In 1960 he surprised me with the news that he had secured the promise of one thousand dollars for me. I was upset and wanted to refuse, but so as not to offend my father's friend, I accepted the money and turned it over to my father. I didn't want to have my experiences in the Third Reich assessed in material terms, nor my relations to the Federal Republic burdened by this gratuitous gesture, quite aside from the fact that I was certain that in educational terms the eventual benefits of my transplantation far outweighed the deprivations.)

At the same time, my father successfully testified on behalf of ex-prisoners of the Nazis whose claims for medical compensation had been rejected. German doctors almost routinely denied any link between a person's concentration camp incarceration and subsequent physical disease. But the traumatic origins of internal disease was my father's subject, and insofar as his and others' judgments had, if reluctantly, been accepted by the authorities on behalf of World War I veterans who showed that the psychic shock of battle and the constant fear of trench warfare could induce physical disease, it would be morally and legally indefensible to deny Nazi victims the same protection. In cogent arguments, my father battled the medical obscurantism and moral indifference of German court physicians who may have been proud of their fidelity to principles of public parsimony and perhaps less aware of the power of their continued prejudices.

ON MY RETURN from Europe in 1954, my hands full with teaching and professional chores, I cheerfully postponed what should have been my next assignment, turning my dissertation into a book, a necessary career move. Instead, I pursued an old dream. During a chance talk with a new paperback publisher I suggested to him an anthology of essays showing how representative modern historians thought of their craft, a book that illustrated the development of modern historiography. Was I unconsciously taking a break from the Nazi past, returning to my old love of Europe itself?

I had taught a seminar about some of the great historians from Herodotus and Thucydides to Machiavelli, but what about the historians who were our immediate predecessors, even our contemporaries, men and women who wrote while history was becoming central in the national cultures of the West and given primacy in compulsory education? In the early nineteenth century, history had also become an academic discipline; some called it a science or, as the Germans put it, a *Wissenschaft*, a body of documented knowledge.

That history was a political and professional battleground I knew: history had ever been a political weapon; all great causes try to claim that the past legitimizes their current positions, as in the rival interpretations of the Reformation and Counter-Reformation or in the never-ending arguments about the French Revolution. In our own time, as I wrote in the introduction to what became *The Varieties of History*, "Soviet and German totalitarian regimes destroyed the freedom of historical inquiry . . . History became a political weapon, the historian a warrior at 'the historical front.'" I wanted to include in the book examples of German and Soviet orthodoxy, and I chose an epigraph from the great English legal historian F. W. Maitland: "an orthodox history seems to me a contradiction in terms."

Many voices had testified to the power of history, but none more starkly than Nietzsche:

> But the man who has once learned to crook the knee and bow the head before the power of history nods "yes" at last, like a Chinese doll, to every power, whether it be a government or a public opinion or a numerical majority; and his limbs move correctly as the power pulls the string. If each success has come by a "rational necessity," and every event shows the victory of logic or the "Idea," then—down on your knees quickly, and let every step in the ladder of success have its reverence. There are no more living mythologies, you say? Religions are at their last gasp? Look at the religion of the power of history, and the priests of the mythology of Ideas, with their scarred knees.

Yet many historians simply did what they did and considered their work as self-justifying. Only a few acknowledged their premises, didactic intent, or philosophic concern.

I read voraciously, until a sturdy table broke under the pile of books I was combing, but gradually I was able to put together selections from historical practitioners beginning with Voltaire, all who, while they may have disagreed on many things, knew that in the new, largely secular world, people expected history to offer guidance to the deepest existential questions. I started the anthology as a labor of love, as a work of self-instruction and edification, but I nearly lost myself in all the contradictory but often exhilarated confessions of practicing historians—whether the austere Fustel de Coulanges, demanding the extinction of the self in the pursuit of what he thought of as the new science, or the ebullient Thomas Babington Macaulay, certain that literary mastery could re-create the drama of a broadly reconstructed past, or the astounding statement of one of my political heroes, Jean Jaurès, who in his *Socialist History of the French Revolution* wrote, "I will not forget, just as Marx himself never forgot . . . that economic forces act on men. Men have a prodigious variety of passions and ideas; the almost infinite complexity of human life cannot be brutally and mechanically reduced to an economic formula." Or any other formula, I might add.

The greatest thrill came when I discovered a virtually unnoticed fragment in volume fifty-four of Leopold von Ranke's collected works, written in the 1860s: "We see before us a series of events which follow one another and are conditioned by one another. If I say 'conditioned' I certainly do not mean conditioned through absolute necessity. The important point is rather that human freedom makes its appearance everywhere, and the greatest attraction of history lies in the fact that it deals with the scenes of that freedom." Ranke, who when he was twenty-nine years old had coined what may well be the best-known definition of the historian's purpose—that he must show *"wie es eigentlich gewesen"* (how it actually was)—was certainly not a narrow-minded positivist, as later historians pigeonholed him. He taught that the past must be reconstructed from authentic original sources, that historians should aim to connect the particular to the universal, the individual event to its broadest context. If only the Germans, master practitioners of the new discipline of history, had remembered Ranke's injunction about freedom and universal history! Complexity and context remain our prerequisites.

I spent two years finding and choosing representative selections, translating some of them, writing introductions to each and a comprehensive introduction to the whole anthology. This was daunting work, but it allowed me to set the historians in their proper European-American context and define my devotion to Clio and her disciples. It also allowed me to indulge my pleasure in admiration: fervent admiration of one's forebears is alternately inspiriting and inhibiting, inducing chronic dissatisfaction with self and occasionally acting as a spur. When my manuscript was finished, my friend Henry Roberts remarked, "I would have thought one would do this at the end of one's career, not the beginning." The comment was devastating at first, but fifty years later, I want to record that I would have neither the energy nor the nerve to undertake such a project now.

The Varieties of History from Voltaire to the Present appeared in 1956, an enlarged edition in 1972. American and European scholars commended it—and it has remained in use and in print! In a certain sense it became an urtext for me: inspiration and instruction all at once. My work on it left me with a strong sense of what I think of as the openness of history: of there being no inevitability in the historic process, no predetermined course; contingency—or, in Ranke's word, freedom—is always present. Put prosaically, the past contains the seeds for many futures. The past is also open to ever-changing interpretations; by its very value, it is ever vulnerable to theft and distortion. It is open to the most violent distortions; we know, as Ranke did, that his ideal of an "objective" past is unattainable, since our accounts are ever filtered through subjective experience. But the effort to reconstruct the past with the greatest possible exactitude, hearing as many of its diverse voices as possible, remains the aim.

In some ways *The Varieties of History* remained a silent partner in all my future work. The book sharpened my sense of the historian's task. If the past is open, then so is the present. The study of the past should encourage the historian's activism in the present, encourage civic engagement, which for many of our predecessors enriched their understanding of the past. The book validated my own private, unarticulated predisposition to live in several worlds, to be an engaged citizen.

My next two efforts in German history were studies in very different genres: one emphasized contingency in history, the other was a speculative effort about continuities. Both were essays, a form for which I have a special fondness: they allow for a tentative tone; they might even add to what Richard Hofstadter called "the speculative richness of history."

The first was a study in miniature, an effort to catch something bigger in the proverbial grain of sand. In reviewing an authorized biography of Konrad Adenauer, I came across a brief mention that in 1926 he had been a serious candidate for the chancellorship of the Reich. I was intrigued: What did this say about Adenauer, the key figure in the current German drama? What might have happened if this Rhenish, Catholic, and conservative democrat had become chancellor under President Hindenburg, that Prussian Protestant? I studied the cabinet crisis that had brought down the previous government, a frequent occurrence in Weimar. Its immediate cause concerned symbolic politics—the question of the republican versus the imperial flag—but other afflictions of Weimar, such as the danger of right-wing plots, also appeared. Adenauer proposed a broad-based coalition that would offer some promise of stability; he favored an unambiguously "Western" foreign policy as against Stresemann's effort to balance Western reconciliation with ties to the Soviet Union. Stresemann, indispensable foreign minister and the one towering political figure in Weimar, was skeptical about Adenauer's candidacy, as I discovered in his papers, now in the National Archives in Washington (American booty of the war). Adenauer grasped the difficulties and quickly returned to his magisterial position as lord mayor of Cologne.

My essay on Adenauer's candidacy combined close archival research, in itself always an adventure, with speculative comments about Weimar in general, about the need to consider politics in the wider context of sociocultural conditions. And then the question of contingency: Might Adenauer have overcome the obstacles of the Weimar system and given it enough stability to weather the Depression and survive right-wing radical fury? "Can one suppose that Adenauer was the right man? Can one read back into those earlier years the maturity, the active, even belligerent, political intelligence of the present-day Adenauer?" Perhaps I was carried away, but I thought Adenauer's 1926 candidacy had been a major possibility, and I posed the question of whether the German catastrophe might have been averted. I thought it might have been—indeed not only then but at other historic points—and I still do.

As if to balance this foray into contingency and micro-history, I next turned to reflection about some long-term continuities in German society that might have helped to pave the way for the ultimate catastrophe. (The occasion was a keynote speech to the Pacific Coast Branch of the American Historical Association in 1957.) I wondered about "The Political Consequences of the Unpolitical German," arguing against the then still popular notion that there had always been two Germanys: the good, embodied in the self-definition of "a nation of poets and thinkers," versus the bad, militaristic, authoritarian Germany that brought us Hitler. Instead, I suggested, the great exaltation of *Bildung* in nineteenth-century German society, productive as it was, facilitated a neglect of, even a contemptuous retreat from, politics, which allowed for the gradual, often half-conscious acceptance of political nonage, as became clear in the ponderous anti-Western rhetoric of German intellectuals during the Great War and in the violently antidemocratic agitation of the last years of Weimar.

How could so many people of such intellectual eminence and moral intent endure the blundering authoritarianism of the empire, the divisiveness of Weimar, the tyranny of Hitler?

The Germans' near sacralization of culture (seemingly close but categorically different from Matthew Arnold's definition of culture) cloaked German Protestantism's pervasive secularization. The worship of art plus the cult of the nation served, perhaps subconsciously, as surrogates for religious faith. I spoke of the high-minded *Bürger's* disdain for the merely practical and material as *Vulgäridealismus* (as opposed to the common German terms *Vulgärmarxismus* or *Vulgärliberalismus*). With its class disdain for the culturally unpropertied and untitled, it only deepened the country's political divisions, offering a metaphysics of snobbery. And it allowed Germans to use their greatest achievement, their culture, to augment and excuse their greatest failure, their politics. But now, in the present, a more pragmatic, realistic attitude was gaining hold: "What so many Germans for so long dreaded and denounced—the Americanization of German culture—seems now to be taking place, quietly and fitfully, but to the apparent pleasure of the Germans and to the likely benefit of their still untested democratic regime." Recent scholarship suggests that German *Bürger* of the nineteenth century were more active and more liberal in local politics than I had assumed, but Thomas Mann's celebration of the "unpolitical German" during the Great War as the authentic German exemplified a German tradition, which he himself later recognized as dangerous.

I wrote that article under idyllic conditions: at the Center for Advanced Study in the Behavioral Sciences at Stanford, established by the Ford Foundation as a haven for scholars in the humanities and social sciences, and designed to enrich individual work by a kind of spontaneous and lightly organized collaboration across disciplines, age, rank, and nationality. It was my first free year ever—and I was in the company of brilliant colleagues of all ages and amid the wonders of the Bay area. In 1957–1958 economists predominated at the center: George Stigler and Milton Friedman, Kenneth Arrow and the wonderful Robert Solow, all future Nobel laureates, all inspiring and all collegial. (In fact, to have Friedman comment on that essay of mine was an exacting, exhilarating experience.) The economic historian David Landes was there, as was John Bowlby, the English psychoanalyst, working on his trilogy about attachment and loss, a man of humane wisdom, whose voice I hear as I write this.

I made many friends that year, but none was as life-changing for me as a young German named Ralf Dahrendorf. At twenty-seven he may have been the youngest at the Center. At our very first encounter he quickly told me he had been enrolled in the youngest branch of the Hitler Youth (he didn't yet tell me about his time in a concentration camp), and I told him with equal candor that I had been born in Breslau and didn't mind that my native city was now in Polish hands. The preliminaries were now concluded.

Dahrendorf was a prodigy: his mastery of German *Bildung*, lightly borne, had already been certified by a doctorate in classics; subsequently a doctorate from the London School of Economics attested to his mastery of Anglo-American empirical and analytical social thought. To boot he was passionately interested in German politics; he was the son of a leading Social Democrat whom the Nazis had twice incarcerated. He took life at a gallop, crossing fields and boundaries, but lingering long enough to engage in important controversies. He was restless and dynamic, questing and critical.

A week after we met, I invited him home for lunch to listen to the broadcast results of West Germany's third parliamentary election. An Adenauer victory was likely, but that the Christian Democrats won by a 50.2 percent margin, a greater victory than any party had ever before scored in German history in a free election, was dismaying. The people had voted for ever-growing prosperity, embodied in the much-vaunted economic miracle, and for a foreign policy of "no experiments." But above all, I think, they voted for an authoritative leader, which troubled Ralf and me. "The German Question" haunted us. Some years later, Ralf wrote his influential *Society and Democracy in Germany*, acknowledging "this is a book of passion, much as I have tried to filter emotion by information and reason."

Friendships with Germans had already been a bridge to a deeper reinvolvement with German life. Ralf was a friend with whom I would share unending conversations in many places and on two continents. I already knew in Stanford that this gifted person, focused, driven, open to adventure and travel in beauty, would have an astonishing life.

At the Center, I finally began a massive revision of my dissertation, and it appeared in 1961 as *The Politics of Cultural Despair: A Study in the Rise of the Germanic Ideology*. At the core was a detailed study of the lives and works of three influential German critics, spanning three generations: Paul de Lagarde, 1827–1891; Julius Langbehn, 1851–1907; and Arthur Moeller van den Bruck, 1876–1924. Lagarde had believed that the extrusion of Jews was a precondition for a German national renewal, and Moeller van den Bruck's book *The Third Reich*, published in 1923, popularized the term that Hitler was to give to his new regime. The three men detested the Germany of their times. They described "a new type of cultural malcontent . . . They wrote directly out of their own sufferings and experiences, and hence the psychic dimensions of their biographies were singularly relevant to their work."

All three, writing under different historic conditions, fastened on one root evil: liberalism. They attacked it because it seemed to them the premise of modern society from which everything they dreaded sprang: the bourgeois life, Manchesterism, materialism, Parliament and political parties, the lack of political leadership. Moreover, they thought liberalism was the source of their inner suffering. "Theirs was a resentment of loneliness; their one desire was for a new faith, a new community of believers, a world with fixed standards and no doubts, a new national religion that would bind all Germans together." Their thought touched on—and reflected—the era's loss of religious faith, which wasn't marked, as it was in France, by a struggle between believers and nonbelievers: "The educated German," I wrote, tended rather "to glide into unbelief." My three critics, whom great and gentle Germans praised because of their "idealist" attacks on modernity, fostered the mood of discontent that foreshadowed the National Socialist synthesis: its attack on the "rottenness" of modern German culture and the exultant promise of a great *völkisch* future. In a conclusion entitled "From Idealism to Nihilism," I wrote, "A thousand teachers in republican Germany who in their youth had read and worshiped Lagarde or Langbehn were just as important to the triumph of National Socialism as all the putative millions of marks that Hitler collected from German tycoons."

I tried to put the three thinkers in the context of German intellectual and political history, but I also emphasized that at every point this particular hatred of modernity and liberalism was a European phenomenon, that this cast of thought and longing could be found in other writers such as Dostoevsky (whose slanted dissemination in Germany Moeller organized). I was dealing with a variant of European *idées-forces*, which only in Germany informed a political mass movement. I was hostile to these thinkers because I found their ideas repellent and a prelude to National Socialist success, but perhaps also because I sympathized with their unease about modern culture and was therefore the more angered by their facile, dangerous prescriptions for reform. I suppose I found the three men passionately uncongenial.

But I didn't think I was describing something that was safely in the past: "Rather we must accept the fact that this kind of rebellion against modernity lies latent in Western society and that its confused, fantastic program, its irrational and unpolitical rhetoric, embodies aspirations just as genuine, though not as generous or tangible, as the aspirations embodied in other and more familiar movements of reform. Cultural pessimism has a strong appeal in America today."

From writing that book I learned something about the power of unreason, about the many forms of distress that modernity evokes, about the psychic consequences of secularization and the temptation of political pseudoreligions, about the European component of fascist and National Socialist ideology. As a scholar, I was fortunate because I was treading new ground: the ideological origins and cultural background of National Socialism were still largely terra incognita. Dealing with the enemies of liberalism steeled my own deepest loyalty to it. The power of antiliberalism was all the more reason to defend liberalism's basic tenets.

It is gratifying that the book was well received and has remained in print. It is less gratifying that it is still relevant. The revolt against "the West," with its putative materialism and spiritual emptiness combined with hegemonic arrogance, has grown, and has emboldened fundamentalist rhetoric and terror everywhere.

THE 1950S ENDED with a historic change within the Federal Republic: in 1959 the Social Democratic party formally abandoned its Marxist platform and prepared for new leaders. Since the 1890s, it had been riven between Marxist orthodoxy and a "revisionist" commitment to gradualist political democracy; in the early years of the Federal Republic, the party persisted in the course set by Kurt Schumacher, insisting on the nationalization of basic industries. But while it had won important local and state elections, it had lost every national election. Seven years after Schumacher's death in 1952, a new platform, called the Godesberg Program, was adopted. The party finally scuttled the old Marxist orthodoxies, including the notion of an inherent class conflict, and proclaimed itself a people's party, no longer an exclusively working-class party. It also now accepted NATO and Western integration. The man being groomed as leader of the SPD was Willy Brandt, who at the age of forty-six entered national politics exuding youth, hope, and energy.

At just this point, chance steered me to a study of the time of Bismarck, who in the 1860s recognized the importance of a socialist movement and who, a decade later, as first chancellor of the unified Germany, assailed the Socialists as unpatriotic "enemies" of the Reich, a false curse under which they were to suffer for a century or more. Bismarck ruled Prussia and later Germany from 1862 to 1890, gradually emerging as Europe's master statesman. My friend and colleague

David Landes, an expert on nineteenth-century international finance, had been asked to write a history of a Berlin bank, whose owner, Gerson Bleichröder, a Jew, had often been called "the German Rothschild." For more than three decades Bleichröder was Bismarck's private banker. Landes had been given thirty-three cartons containing some of his correspondence with German and European notables during the long Bismarckian era; a partner of the Bleichröder Bank had taken these files to New York after the Nazi seizure of power. Landes suggested that together we write a short book about Bleichröder.

I glanced at the material, fishing for quick clues, and chanced on a letter written in 1888 by a confidant of Bismarck, warning Bleichröder that Russian troops were moving toward the Austrian border, hence that any financial help given to Russia at that time would be in the nature of a war loan. I knew that Bismarck at the same time was telling the young emperor William II the very opposite about Russia's intentions. I was intrigued. Although there were some ten thousand studies about Bismarck, none dealt with him and his Jewish banker and confidant. I accepted Landes's offer of collaboration, and tried to complete other obligations. (I was also teaching a doctoral seminar then, and in its first year I had some prize students: István Deák, Peter Novick, and Harold Poor. The dissertations they were working on were the first of some thirty published by my students, and I particularly cherished this part of teaching.)

We knew that Bleichröder had close ties to Baron James de Rothschild, himself a legendary figure. David had secured access to the Rothschild Archives in Paris, so we decided to spend a sabbatical year together working there in 1960–1961. A grant from the Social Science Research Council helped to get Peggy, Fred, Katherine, and me to Paris—once more by ship—and I was thrilled by the prospect of spending a year in France, even if the actual stay had its inevitable rough spots. (On one of our first days in Paris, Seymour Martin Lipset, friend and colleague, took me to the Jean Moulin Club at which Pierre Mendès-France, a political hero of mine, spoke. I understood his speech perfectly, which allayed my fears about linguistic incompetence. But the next morning I had to take our car to a repair shop—and understood nothing.)

David and I began our work in the dust-covered attic of the Rothschild Bank in its original mansion on rue Laffitte, where the heavy entrance door was, presumably, protection against revolutionary crowds of earlier times. We went through decades of correspondence, the letters interspersed with countless bills of exchange (forerunners of modern checks). I must have looked at thousands of these slips of paper. Early on, I saw one drawn on the bank of Rothschild Frères and made out to the Bleichröder Bank in favor of and signed by Cosima von Bülow, née Liszt. Now, Cosima, mother of Richard Wagner's children, later even his wife, promoter of virulent anti-Semitism, was one of my most unfavorite women of the nineteenth century—and to discover that she was banking with Jews! No bill of exchange compared to this one, and now it hangs, framed, in our hall—my only theft!

The banking world was new territory for me, but Landes was the perfect mentor, with his unclouded view of human nature and a novelist's eye for people's quirks and motives. He was amused when I registered surprise that the Rothschilds had made a great deal of money on the reparations France had to pay the victorious Germans after the Franco-Prussian War in 1870. Profit from your nation's misery? Landes rebuked me: I was a naïve novice. The reward of writing is learning.

The vast, virtually untapped Rothschild Archive was but a beginning. The Bleichröder-Rothschild-Bismarck triangle, touching so many points of European politics—led us to ever more sources, again most of them unused. On an impulse, I went to the Archives of the French Foreign Office. The hushed, formal atmosphere at the Quai d'Orsay was special. Like other European nations after the Great War, France had published its pre-1914 diplomatic reports, but I wanted to double-check the handwritten reports of the comte de St. Vallier, French ambassador in Berlin and confidant of Bismarck and Bleichröder, and discovered that his reports on the German domestic scene, on his intimate conversations with Bismarck, had not been published. I had found a priceless source for the critical years 1878–1882; Bismarck had clearly reveled in unburdening himself to a clever interlocutor on whose discretion and understanding he could count. He flattered him with indiscretions!

Bleichröder's papers contained a rich trove of private letters *to* him; but his answers were mostly missing—his voice had to be recovered. A key depository was the Bismarck archive itself, housed in Bismarck's estate in Friedrichsruh, near Hamburg, and under the control of the chancellor's grandson, also named Otto, a CDU member of the Bundestag. (I found later the record of Prince Bismarck having joined the Nazi Party in May 1933.) How did one get access? I asked a German colleague, Peter Rassow, at one time a historian in Breslau, a man of flawless conservatism, for a letter of introduction to Prince Bismarck. Thus armed, I asked the prince for an appointment; he arranged and broke quite a few. Finally, I went to his office in Bonn and pleaded with his secretary. "Don't you understand?" she exclaimed. "The prince has no intention of seeing you. He hates historians." She offered to telephone me in Paris on the next (rare) visit the prince made to Bonn so that I could appear unannounced in his office there. In short, she conspired against her boss, and I thought that her cheerful disloyalty was a happy sign of a new Germany.

And the plan worked. I planted myself in his office where he could not avoid seeing me. I had been coached to address him as *"Durchlaucht"* (Serene Highness), which I did, and quickly explained about the book; I remarked that it would be awkward to have to write that the only archive closed to its authors had been Bismarck's. (I was living on borrowed chutzpah: Landes had suggested this formula.) Instantly, he denied any difficulty; he said that, yes, there was a packet of Bleichröder letters, and we negotiated a deal by which he would entrust the file to the U.S. Embassy in Bonn, which would then send it via diplomatic pouch to the U.S. Embassy in Paris. It worked.

It was a glorious year for me in Paris, immersed as I was in these exciting efforts to resurrect the past and also witnessing the present—and not just the European present. John Kennedy's election in November 1960 was cause for celebration. It was the first time I had cast my vote for a winning ticket, and I was thrilled by his inaugural speech, which I read aloud to my family; his phrase "civility is not a sign of weakness" became an oft-invoked saying among us.

The drama of French politics was intense at that time: President de Gaulle's efforts at ending the brutal Algerian War encountered ferocious opposition from the proponents of Algérie Française, and France was in turmoil. The appalling use of torture by the French troops in Algeria was becoming known, and by the spring of 1961, the war was spreading to France itself, with terrorist attacks using *plastiques* (explosives) in Paris and elsewhere set by *le musulman*, as the French nastily referred to Arabs. My sympathies were with de Gaulle, as they had been since 1940 (even if the manner of his return to power in May 1958 had dismayed me). He was pursuing a cautious but committed course, and at great risk, hoping to end the conflict gradually, winning support in France itself by the same ambiguity that had inspired him to say to the *colons* in Algeria, *"Je vous ai compris"*—"I have understood you."

Paris also allowed for moments of what I called political tourism, but they were also important to me as experiences of lived political history. A group associated with the Congress for Cultural Freedom, for example, headed by Pierre Emmanuel, a French poet who had been in the Resistance, organized an international meeting in Spain, "The Idea of Europe"—the first such event in Franco's Spain—and even to be a mostly silent member of a group connecting with Spanish intellectuals who might be important in the anticipated transition to a post-Franco regime was heady stuff—and in Madrid at that! I

asked about the relative freedom of our discussions (which were in French)—
was there no informant present?—and a Spaniard smiled, pointed to an elderly
man in the front row, and said, "He is from the police. He doesn't understand
French." I took that to be an excellent sign of a dictatorship in decline—and at
a time of great promise, for the formation of a common European market suggested that "the idea of Europe" was becoming (partial) reality.

Ralf Dahrendorf and I met repeatedly that year—by then my friend from
Stanford was a professor at Tübingen. For him and for colleagues of our generation, the quest for what had gone wrong in the German past was all the
greater a challenge given that the prevailing milieu was still so conservative
and silent. Through Dahrendorf and through my own efforts, my contacts with
Germans were increasing: Bismarck and Bleichröder became a bridge to historians, bankers, even politicians. Gradually I realized that the Bleichröder
story was but an opening chapter in what was the biggest subject I could imagine: the relations between Germans and Jews, the whole history of a relationship that began in hope and ended in all-embracing horror.

The German Question erupted again on the world stage that summer,
when the status quo was threatened from above by Nikita Khrushchev's repeated bellicose insistence that in the absence of a four-power settlement the
Soviet Union would conclude a separate peace treaty with East Germany, thus
threatening Allied rights in Berlin. East German citizens had been fleeing their
country for the West for some time, but now there were floods of them—some
two hundred thousand in 1961 alone crossed the border in Berlin—marking a
spontaneous threat from below. This was indeed a genuine crisis, and the East
German–Soviet response was brutal: on August 13, in the early hours of the
morning, East German police and soldiers began to build a high concrete wall
sealing off East from West Berlin; Soviet tanks protected this German operation.

The West Germans, especially West Berliners, were disappointed in the
careful Allied response to this illegal provocation, which consisted mainly of
diplomatic denunciations and an increase in the Allied military presence in
the city, for the Wall had instantly created cruel difficulties for many German
families—and not only Berliners. But President Kennedy's triumphant visit
there two years later, and his rousing "Ich bin ein Berliner" speech, rekindled
West Berlin's fealty to the United States.

BY THEN I had resumed my full-time life in the United States, and if I were to
define my responsibilities, I would appropriate the abominable slogan *travail,
famille, patrie* (which for the Vichy regime replaced France's revolutionary

trinity of liberty, equality, fraternity). I returned to teaching undergraduates and graduates—the former eager and playful, the latter confronting the graded rigors of a professional career—both of which I enjoyed. I once said that a culture must know how to "coax talent into achievement." Without knowing it, I was defining what was my chief pleasure and ambition in teaching—an ideal that made drudgery worthwhile.

Though teaching was my principal responsibility, I was increasingly involved in writing and speaking about European affairs. On various occasions I celebrated the Treaty of Rome at the dawn of a new Europe. And Arthur M. Schlesinger, Jr., invited me to his White House office in Washington to report on my impressions of Germany. I also became more and more active at the Council on Foreign Relations, where European affairs was my principal focus and where, in 1962, I began what turned out to be a thirty-year stint as its reviewer of books on Western Europe for *Foreign Affairs*. To read, even merely to peruse, some thirty or forty books a year and write short but, ideally, incisive comments about each, was marvelously instructive.

On my return from another trip to Europe in 1962, I found my father in precarious health, with a self-diagnosed case of extreme hypertension. He continued his practice, however, which by then included some of my best friends and colleagues. In the first week of November, after he himself had suffered several minor heart attacks, he responded to a nighttime call from a very young colleague of mine who told him his wife was apparently having a heart attack. My father took his portable ECG, climbed up four flights of stairs to the couple's apartment—and found the young lady with a severe stomach upset. Days later—it was November 9—he himself was taken to the hospital, and I rushed over after classes: at first he said he felt better, but a short while later, I heard him say softly, "I hear the death rattle [*es röchelt*]." It was his last diagnosis. I was with him at the end.

My grief was immense, and the support of family and friends essential. And though I know that my father's death's occurring on what was a historic date in the history of his country (the abdication of the Kaiser in 1918, Hitler's failed coup in 1923, *Kristallnacht* in 1938) was an accident, it still felt eerie. (Eerie, too, that Chaim Weizmann also died on that day.) My uncle Otto, the physicist, wrote my mother that when he heard the news, "I couldn't think for an hour." It was an obliterating loss—and not merely a personal one. My father's generation, in its transition from a relatively repressed and pre-democratic age to a relatively open and democratic one, marked a very important and special moment in German culture, and the character of that generation had all but disappeared.

Fred and Katherine—quietly compassionate and wonderfully companion-able—sustained me, as did Peggy, who continued to work with my mother, who gradually and with our and Toni's help constructed a new life. But it was hard for all of us.

My father was spared the tragedy that followed a year later. In November 1963, I was on jury duty in New York when, returning after lunch to the big jury room, I saw small groups of people huddling around the few transistor ra-dios, riveted by the news that President Kennedy had been shot and, a short while later, that he had died. People began to cry, others were hushed in hor-ror, and my own feeling was one of stunned, disbelieving grief—and fear. What did it mean? I had been beguiled by Kennedy's style and wit, by his team at the New Frontier, awed by his (and his brother's) handling of the Cuban missile crisis, and above all I had cheered his American University speech the previous April, when avoiding all American triumphalism he called for improved rela-tions with the Soviet Union. I felt the loss as incalculable. The world was in mourning. The murder of Kennedy evoked a universal identification with America—especially among Germans, most fervently among Berliners. Such a spontaneous outpouring was not to be seen again until September 11, 2001.

The 1960s were tumultuous in many countries, but I was especially aware of sharpening tensions and conflicts in West Germany and in America—and some of these had the potential of pulling our countries apart. In the Federal Republic, the Nazi past was finally emerging as the inescapable moral drama of the present time, and in the United States the murder of Kennedy ushered in a world of violence yet also of hope, as the civil rights movement gathered strength, and as opposition grew to American involvement in the Vietnam War. By the mid-1960s, in most Western countries, university students, angry at bland conformity and a seemingly senseless way of life, rallied to voice their grievances: ideology, which had been pronounced as ended, suddenly became trump, the common coin of a generation in righteous indignation.

The West German public was jolted out of its pervasive, cultivated amne-sia, for the time of internal reconciliation and of the quiet reintegration of ex-Nazis was passing, and the hour of facing up to German crimes had struck. People were awakened from their undogmatic slumber. The Nürnberg trials had often been dismissed as "victors' justice" or as a final judgment that was sufficient unto the day: the top criminals had been dealt with, and there was nothing left to do. But then the gripping Israeli trial of Adolf Eichmann in 1961 made the Holocaust an indelible part of the world's collective memory. In Germany, a succession of further war crime trials altered the public mood even more—most notably a lengthy trial meticulously prepared by Fritz Bauer, Hesse's state prosecutor (an exile during the Nazi period), who was determined to bring perpetrators to justice and demonstrate the complicity that had enabled Nazi criminality. Begun in Frankfurt's largest hall in 1963 before crowds of spectators, this trial documented the full horrors of Auschwitz.

In 1963 a play by Rolf Hochhuth, a then unknown Swiss writer, caused a huge uproar. *The Deputy* portrayed and indicted the Pope's silence in the face of the extermination of the Jews, of which he had been one of the first to be informed. The play, produced all over the West, aroused instant and intemperate protest, but it nonetheless successfully opened a debate about the "bystander," even one at the very pinnacle of moral power and responsibility. (At a stormy meeting in New York, I defended the dramatist's intent but remained critical of his all-too-one-sided negative depiction of the Pope.) Germans, thus bombarded by dramatic historical revelations, began to realize the political-moral dangers of an insufficiently examined past, meaning not National Socialism alone but the course of German history in the modern era generally. And the propaganda emanating from the rival East German state, which boasted of its own purity while pointing to the West German whitewashing of the fascist past, may have contributed in a minor way to the West German "awakening."

Unexpectedly, I became involved in some of the efforts by Germans to rethink their history. In 1963, Georg Eckert, head of the International Institute for Textbook Research, in Braunschweig, asked me to a West German–U.S. conference on history textbooks that dealt with the first half of the twentieth century. (James Conant participated in our meeting: he had returned to West Germany in August 1961 to advise on educational reforms.) We examined existing German and American texts and drafted revisions of them that might be acceptable to both sides. I concentrated on accounts of the Great War, questioning the then still prevailing view that the European powers had "slithered" into the conflict (a phrase used by Britain's wartime leader David Lloyd George) and therefore were not burdened with exceptional responsibility for it. German historians took this view too, since it gave the lie to the "war guilt clause" of the Treaty of Versailles that had singled out German aggression. I pushed for a more critical assessment of German foreign policy, also calling for greater attention to the connections between domestic and foreign policies. National histories, I said, should be written in a European context, as Ranke had done in his work. In time, German textbooks and the historical world generally began to adapt to an emergent international consensus on key issues. (On my return from Braunschweig, a chance remark made by Henry Roberts

that I could be of great help to the Germans in their debates about the past genuinely jolted me. This thought simply had not occurred to me: I was stumbling
into that role.)

But it was certainly true that for reasons both private and professional, the
Great War has always been a subject of the most intense interest to me, for its
own singular horror and as the precondition for the later totalitarian criminality.
Even as a boy, I had thought about the war, read about it, and, on my walks with
my father in Breslau, talked about it. And now in the 1960s, the German historical guild was plunging into its fiercest and most divisive debate on the very
issue of Germany's responsibilities for the outbreak of the war and the war's du-
ration. In 1961 a book had appeared with the provocative title *Griff nach der
Weltmacht* (Bid for World Power; the English-language edition was published
with the innocuous title *Germany's Aims in the First World War*), by Fritz
Fischer, a Hamburg historian previously known for his work on nineteenth-
century Protestantism. (Fischer had visited me at Cornell in the winter of 1951;
I remembered him as a somewhat unworldly person, high-strung, secretive,
with a conspiratorial view of the world, rather protective of Germans under the
Third Reich; I knew nothing then of his past, and only fifty years later, when
participating in a memorial meeting for him, learned that he had briefly been
a member of the most Nazified Institute of German history.) Fischer insisted,
on the basis of new material he had found in old archives then located in East
Germany, that Germany's imperial leaders had planned a war from 1912 on,
fearing that time was working against them and that Russia's growing industrial
might was an ever-increasing threat; that in July 1914 they had opted for an aggressive course—either to inflict a diplomatic defeat on the "encircling" entente of Britain, France, and Russia and thus disrupt it, or to risk war; and if the
latter, the war aims from the beginning would be to establish German hegemony over the continent once and for all. Fischer also intimated that a line of
continuity linked this wildly expansionist ambition to Hitler.

German historians were then still dominated by conservative nationalists—
many of whom had fought in the Great War and all of whom had grown up defending Germany against the "war guilt" charge, and none of whom wanted to
portray the Nazi past as anything but a terrible aberration. They were outraged,
both genuine conservatives who had resisted Nazism, such as Gerhard Ritter,
and younger, less principled men who had forgotten their own involvement in
the "aberration" and hoped others would not discover it. Something of a generational conflict was shaping up, with the elders wanting to protect and per-

petuate an untarnished view of German history minus Nazism, and the younger ones cautiously critical of the old guard.

The German fight over Fischer spilled over to the United States. A group of us, including Hajo Holborn at Yale, Hans Rosenberg at Berkeley, and Klaus Epstein at Brown, had prepared a lecture tour for him in March 1964, financed, as such trips often were, by a cultural section of the West German Foreign Office. But in February the Foreign Office cancelled the trip without explanation. Now it was our turn to be outraged. We would have been even more outraged if we had known then what we know now—that Ritter had written to Foreign Minister Gerhard Schröder (a different man from the later chancellor) warning him against the projected trip. "We German historians are most deeply troubled at the notion that Herr Fischer might propagate his completely half-baked theses in America under the indirect auspices of the Foreign Office. I don't hesitate to consider this as a national misfortune."

We quickly sprang into action. I obtained alternate travel funds for Fischer and we sent a collective letter to Die Zeit protesting the Foreign Office maneuver, which "shows an unfortunate mixture of bureaucratic arrogance, misconstrued raison d'état and autism [Instinktlosigkeit] in regard to reaction abroad." German efforts to silence Fischer made us listen the more sympathetically to him when he came. In Germany, meanwhile, he was being publicly accused of being a "Nestbeschmutzer," someone who fouled the nest. Germans often confound fouling and cleaning one's own nest. Intrigue and innuendo quickly outpaced argument, and soon we would have a close look at illiberalism in practice. Fischer later wrote me what it was like to live amid the "hostile coldness of my colleagues . . . I have rarely experienced a more contemptible society than this collection of my closest colleagues." I doubt that he tried to hide his contempt; I think he relished and exaggerated his victimhood.

That summer, the president of the Association of German Historians, Karl-Dietrich Erdmann, invited me to attend the association's triennial convention in October in Berlin, and then I was asked to participate in a panel discussion about war aims (a code phrase for the Fischer controversy), scheduled to take place on the fiftieth anniversary of the outbreak of the Great War. Quickly I prepared for what I assumed would be an academic discussion; instead, as I wrote immediately after the occasion, the session took place in the Auditorium Maximum of the Free University before an impassioned audience of more than one thousand listeners, whose boos and catcalls lent drama to the occasion.

Fischer's most vigorous and most eminent foes, including Ritter, scored powerful points concerning his modus operandi, including misleading use of evidence. Fischer and his two assistants seemed on the defensive, mixing minutiae with invectives. Toward the end, the two foreigners present spoke: Jacques Droz of the Sorbonne, and I. Droz, a superb historian and a distinguished member of the French Resistance, gave a judicious and on the whole pro-Fischer account of the controversy. I emphasized the novelty of Fischer's work and suggested that every new historiographical thesis is formulated too sharply and too one-sidedly when first advanced. I quoted Ritter, who had written of "a [German] miscalculation that borders on blindness" in July 1914. I added,

> This chronic blindness, this false estimation of oneself and others, demands an historical explanation . . . The style of German imperialism shows a rare combination of *Angst*, arrogance, and—in assessing the non-German world—political ignorance and insecurity . . . Perhaps Professor Fischer has strained the continuity thesis, but the counterthesis which posits that all the miscalculations and derailments of German policy in the twentieth century were but occupational accidents [*Betriebsunfälle*] is even less satisfactory. Is it in fact possible to have a series of accidents without surmising that there may be something wrong in the whole enterprise?

I knew this was a polemical formulation, yes—but I didn't expect the thunderous applause from the students that greeted it. The pandemonium changed the entire atmosphere, so much so that Fischer's antagonists ostentatiously avoided speaking to me after the session.

I had caused an éclat, and *Der Spiegel* (without authorization) published my speech. I suddenly became known in Germany and acquired new friends and new opponents—it was a heady experience. Shortly after, I visited Lionel Trilling in Oxford and told him about what had happened. He sighed. "And nobody in New York will know about it!" That was largely true, but in 1999, when asked about the decisive moments in the 1960s, the liberal historian Heinrich August Winkler mentioned his "vivid memory of the historians' meeting in 1964 . . . when the liberating battle [*Befreiungsschlacht*] in the 'war guilt question' occurred. Fritz Fischer and Gerhard Ritter were the opponents, and Fritz Stern was the person who insured Fritz Fischer's victory."

The Fischer controversy turned very heavily on the person of imperial Germany's last effective chancellor, Bethmann Hollweg, and he and his policies were seen in a new light when Erdmann first published nuggets from the diary of Bethmann's closest confidant, Kurt Riezler. Bethmann and Riezler had been a strange, intimate tandem: the German chancellor from 1908 to 1917 and a brilliant young scholar, a classicist by training, by cast of mind a philosopher and moralist, married to the daughter of the great German Jewish painter Max Liebermann. The realization that a Riezler diary existed made historians, myself included, lust for it, but Erdmann claimed sole rights and refused access to the full text. Riezler had left Nazi Germany for New York and took his diary along; I finally asked Riezler's daughter Maria White for a copy of it, which she gave me, together with permission to quote from it. (Erdmann objected to my procedure, and we had a brief public dispute. Only after his death in 1990 did we learn that as a young man he had marginally served the Nazi cause.) I used this material in an essay I was writing on Bethmann Hollweg and the war—my contribution for a Festschrift for Hajo Holborn.

The melancholy Bethmann was a proponent of German expansionism, but during the war he had become ever-more embattled with Germany's military leaders, and Riezler's diary bristled with anger at "these powerful incompetents in uniform and their blind, brutish faith in force . . ." Unwittingly, Bethmann became a front for the very forces he detested. After Germany's defeat, he wrote self-censored memoirs, sparing his unappeasable enemies among the military, especially Tirpitz, and the wild annexationists. His semisilence, though understandable, facilitated the second and worse triumph of the very passions he deplored.

In one way or another, I kept working on the Great War. Impulsive and passionate interest made me volunteer an introductory note to a new translation of Élie Halévy's *The Era of Tyrannies*, which included that superb historian's Rhodes lectures of 1929 on the war. Ever since I read these lectures as a student, I had thought them a model of interpretation, more promising than the earlier, sterile efforts to explain the war's complexities by building on mostly diplomatic documents. Halévy did it differently; he set out to study "the earthquake itself. I shall attempt to define the collective forces, the collective feelings and movements of public opinion, which, in the early years of the twentieth century, made for strife." He analyzed the deep stresses and strains in Europe that culminated in war and revolution, seeing importantly that foreign and domestic policy are inextricably linked. I underscored what I thought was Halévy's pedagogic intent: to fortify civic virtue. And I concluded, "The wars and revolutions of our time have been made possible not so much by a few leaders or sects as by the multitude of passive citizens who smugly thought that politics was the responsibility of statesmen." (I enjoyed writing about Halévy himself, too, author of the superb multivolume *History of the English People*, for I esteemed the man as much as his works: he was a *moraliste*, a writer who recalled Tocqueville's virtues, and a mentor of Raymond Aron.)

In all this work, I wrote from heart and mind, convinced that the Great War was the catastrophe that begat the subsequent catastrophes, and the times we lived in suggested frightening parallels. I was struck by the pertinence of some of the themes to the tragedy in Vietnam: "The military delusions, the escalation of propaganda, the impact of the war at home . . ." And yet I don't think I ever quite realized how my life was pouring into my work, how much my work informed my life. I suppose I simply couldn't subordinate passion to duty (that is, stick exclusively to Bismarck and Bleichröder). I thought about writing a short history of the Great War, and even talked about it several times with Michael Howard, that military historian par excellence: we encouraged each other to write such a book. He did, and I didn't, but instead, in 1965, I taught an undergraduate seminar on the war. A splendid student in that class, Jay Winter, devoted his scholarly life to the subject. The war and the many questions of contingency stayed in my imagination: what if two trains had not left their stations? What if in June 1914 Archduke Franz Ferdinand had stayed put? And what if, in March 1917, Lenin had not boarded that sealed car on a German train to St. Petersburg? Much later I once or twice lectured to Germans on my variant of Ranke's great dictum, "how unfortunately it didn't happen" [*wie es leider nicht gewesen*].

It may have been the Fischer brouhaha that encouraged other Germans to promote the public airing of historic-political issues. In 1965, Hermann Glaser, Nürnberg's Social Democratic commissioner for culture, organized the first of a series of open conversations (*Nürnberger Gespräche*). Himself a historian, he was convinced that Germans had not yet confronted the pernicious elements of their past, the pious myths, the sentimental Germanism, that helped pave the way for Hitler, and he thought that his city, given *its* past, was the appropriate place for such gatherings. For four days, we read and discussed prepared papers, got together for meals, and talked well into the night.

Glaser's group represented a wide spectrum of informed people, and we all had a sense that we were assembled to tackle issues hitherto slighted or evaded. It was there that I first met a young CDU political scientist and soon-to-become Bundestag deputy, Bernhard Vogel, and Waldemar Besson, a dedicated political scientist and educational reformer, who with Dahrendorf was in the process of founding a new reform university at Konstanz. Fritz Bauer, the prosecutor of the Auschwitz trial, spoke scathingly on the question "What has Auschwitz to do with 'the German *Mensch*'?" Writers, journalists, and politicians from the major parties participated. We differed among ourselves, but a reformist, liberal impulse dominated. One particularly keen analyst of past misdeeds among German writers was Hans Schwerte, a well-known professor at the University of Aachen, and later its head. A few years ago a journalist discovered his true identity: Hans Schneider, Heinrich Himmler's close collaborator! In retrospect, I would say that he, too, belonged to a cross-section of German intellectuals in the Federal Republic.

Meanwhile the Federal Republic was discovering that there was life after Adenauer; after much dithering, he resigned in 1963, and Ludwig Erhard, affable proponent of the republic's free market economy and putative architect of its economic miracle, became chancellor. The president was Heinrich Lübke, a weak, colorless man whose links to the Nazi past made him especially vulnerable. For a couple of years, I would attend the *Nürnberger Gespräche* and could catch up on German politics, which under Erhard became less stable and marked by growing opposition to American policies in Vietnam. There was always a residue of anti-Americanism — on the left in opposition to unfettered capitalism, the militant cold war, and our race problem, and on the right skepticism about America's "materialism," lack of culture, and habit of lecturing Germans about their country's brown past.

My connections to Europe intensified in the 1960s. For my second sabbatical, in 1966–1967, I accepted an invitation from Nuffield College and St. Antony's College in Oxford to spend the year there. How could I refuse such a temptation, with so many friends and so many significant scholars to talk with? I looked forward to seeing James Joll, sub-warden at St. Antony's and a distinguished historian, who combined a most generous temperament with stringent judgment. In European terms, he was a Social Democrat of liberal principles and progressive social policies. We remained close until his all-too-early death.

My intentions were honorable: to get on with Bleichröder. But, as so often, I allowed myself to be distracted, less by the prescribed pleasures of Oxford than by unexpected challenges. Alan Bullock, founder and master of St. Catherine's College, was celebrating the opening of a new college auditorium with a lecture series, "Writers and Artists of the Nineteenth Century," and asked me to give one of them, alongside Isaiah Berlin on Tolstoy and Bullock on Wagner — an intimidating honor that had me *"freudeschlotternd,"* shivering with joy, to use a Karl Kraus formulation. I suggested as subject Theodor Fontane, whose novels I was devouring for my work on Bleichröder. Bullock objected that no one at Oxford had heard of Fontane. So I chose Nietzsche instead, and at the very least it was a quixotic pleasure to present my notion of "gentle" Nietzsche, the so un-German critic of German culture and the unsurpassed European psychologist, as against the then prevalent view of him as the prophet of "superman" and the "blond beast."

Another disruption came my way: a Columbia colleague, the social philosopher Charles Frankel, then serving as assistant secretary of state for cultural affairs, wanted to have three scholars "survey informally the attitude of the rising generation of elites in Western Europe and the . . . relationships between them and Americans." He asked me to go to West Germany for two weeks of intensive interviews, and then submit a report on German youth and the efficacy of U.S. cultural programs in the Federal Republic. I agreed, receiving my instructions from Frankel himself in Paris, where he was head of the American delegation to UNESCO, and off I went on a whirlwind tour of Germany, then in a season of exceptional turmoil.

In November 1966, after the breakup of Ludwig Erhard's government, the CDU and the SPD formed a joint government, a "grand coalition" — an end to seventeen years of CDU-CSU predominance and the first time that Socialists joined a Bonn government. Kurt Georg Kiesinger became chancellor, Willy Brandt vice-chancellor. But whatever Kiesinger's merits, his past carried a blemish: in 1933, at the age of twenty-nine, he had joined the Nazi Party. During the negotiations leading up to the new government, Günter Grass wrote two public letters. One was to Willy Brandt, warning him against this alliance: "The youth of our country will surely turn its back on the state and its constitution: it will stray misguided to the left and the right as soon as this wretched marriage is decided." If there had to be a grand coalition, then at least not under Kiesinger, whom Grass addressed directly in a second letter: "How can we honor the memory of the tortured and murdered resistance fighters, the dead of Auschwitz and Treblinka, if you, then a follower [*Mitläufer*], dare to determine the political guidelines of today?" Grass was a self-designated and fearless conscience of the nation — as we need to remember when judging his later politics, which bordered on the irresponsible. And in one regard he was right. West German youth did move further right and further left, most especially the latter, while the neo-Nazi party, the National Democratic Party (NPD), continued to gain in state and local elections. It was true that for the first time there was no effective opposition in Parliament, but the grand coalition gave the Social Democrats "respectability" on the federal level, and Willy Brandt, as foreign minister, took the first steps toward a West German version of détente, *Ostpolitik*.

I found that West Germans' spontaneous identification with the United States, so clear at the time of Kennedy's assassination, had paled by now. Meanwhile, many intra-European exchange programs—especially the generous Franco-German youth exchange program—became still more important, even though the great passion for Europe that had marked the Adenauer era was also over. Young West Germans quickly fastened on the discrepancies between American ideals and American reality, pointing to our race problems and persistent poverty. The war in Vietnam was the most general target of attack. The left condemned it as an extreme example of American neocolonialism, and the right as an example of America's irresolute pursuit of its own ends. To Frankel I reported that programs administered by the British Council and The French Institute were given higher marks than the American ones because of their greater independence and objectivity. A British official said to me, "You do seem to ram propaganda down their throats." We needed greater candor and self-criticism, I said. We should discuss the war frankly, acknowledging the powerful opposition to it at home. I made various suggestions, recommending professorships for American scholars at German universities, hoping they would help to correct Germans' massive ignorance about the United States.

I made private, critical comments to Frankel, too, who appreciated "perspective and practical bite" and hoped to implement some of my recommendations right away, but, he added, "Santayana once defined a fanatic as a man who redoubles his efforts after he has forgotten his aims. I fear he didn't know. He was also describing our earnest bureaucracy at its most efficient." I doubt that my efforts improved things, but I learned a lot.

One day at Oxford a tantalizing postcard from a German colleague, Hans-Ulrich Wehler, sent me scurrying to Cologne; he had important Bleichröder information, he wrote. Wehler, a fiercely liberal historian in a still-authoritarian milieu, was to become the most prodigiously productive historian of his generation. He told me that at the Bismarck estate in Friedrichsruh, packets of Bleichröder letters and accounts were stored in the attic above the stables. The prince, he added, would never permit me to see this all-important treasure, so there were only two ways to get it: either seduce the secretary or, under cover of night, use a ladder to climb over the fence and into the attic, following the map he drew for me. I trusted myself with neither of these methods—unusual trials in the service of Clio—and asked Bernhard Vogel, a party colleague of Bismarck's in the Bundestag, to intervene on my behalf.

Prince Otto received me in Friedrichsruh, puzzled why I had gone through an intermediary—after all, I was always welcome. I replied that I hadn't known that. Alas, he added, I would find nothing in the archive, but I was free to look. I asked whether if "the nothing" were to yield something, I could take it back to my hotel to read. He grudgingly assented and directed his most amiable secretary to take me to the stable. To her astonishment, I instantly found the packets, and she ordered the prince's car to drive me back to the hotel. I spent the night dictating into my recorder. The next morning the prince called, demanding to know what I had found. Thinking that the last thing he would want to hear was that I had found the entire financial record of Bleichröder's transactions for the Iron Chancellor, I said, truthfully, that I was particularly interested in Bleichröder's personal letters, which often dealt with political matters. "You mean Bleichröder *advised* my grandfather?" he exclaimed incredulously. I must immediately come back to see him. I demurred, speaking of not wanting to intrude on his time and mumbling about my own time constraints; ultimately he yielded, for he was himself leaving for Spain the next day. I then asked him if I could microfilm some of the material. He didn't refuse—and so I got possession of the indispensable substructure of what became the book on Bismarck and Bleichröder. How much one owes to chance meetings, to friends.*

The late spring in Oxford was dominated by news from the Middle East, and I remember the excited, occasionally rancorous discussions in college about Israel, whose security seemed increasingly threatened by the possibility of war. In May, Egypt's President Nasser demanded that the UN peacekeeping forces be removed from the Sinai Peninsula (they were) and he threatened to close the straits of Tiran to Israeli shipping. Egypt was allied to Syria and hoped to win over hapless Jordan as well. The crisis escalated with reports of Egyptian troop concentrations in Sinai while American, Russian, and European governments worked openly and secretly to prevent war. Israeli hawks saw the danger—and the opportunity. On June 5, Israel struck its preemptive blow, which in a matter of hours wiped out Egypt's air force. Sympathy for Israel, perceived as the underdog, was manifest all over Europe. For the next several days, there

---

*A brief memorable vacation also had its historic moment: In March 1967 I decided to take the family on a trip to Greece, beginning in Athens and ending on the island of Spetsai (where I finished an essay on the Great War). It was a splendid trip, a much too abbreviated grand tour, and we happened to be in Athens on Independence Day, March 25. I noted tanks ringing principal squares in preparation for the celebrations, and remarked to the family that it seemed to me that the military was staging an exercise for a coup. A month later, "the Greek colonels" did overthrow the Papandreou government and established their brutal rule. And I found out later that they had used Independence Day for a rehearsal.

was nothing but anxious uncertainty and then the astounding denouement, first heard when a BBC reporter spoke of an unprecedented "instant victory" for Israel (with, as an added human touch, a report that Winston Churchill, grandson of the prime minister, had flown over Israeli positions, dipping his wings in salute). For most, there was a kind of euphoria in learning that David had beaten the Goliath of the Arab armies, and a surprised awe of the Israeli mastery of strategy and tactics. At that moment, the American saying that nothing succeeds like success seemed apt, as Israel bloomed, a Western triumph on biblical soil—even though true peace remained remote and there was unease about the disposition of Israel's captured positions in the West Bank and Sinai.

The West seemed thrilled by Israel's triumph; I think the victory was the last thing Germans thought Jews capable of. Their government's support of Israel was second only to that of the United States, while the East German regime pilloried Bonn's alleged collusion in what they called Israeli-American imperial conduct. The German right turned out to be far more pro-Israel than the extreme left, among whom sympathy for the Palestinians and the dismay about Israel as a colonial power intensified.

ON MY RETURN to the United States in mid-summer 1967, I was shaken by my apprehension that two processes, seemingly distinct and yet inextricably linked—the escalation of the war in Vietnam and growing student unrest throughout the Western world—presaged danger. I became even more involved in America's political life in general and Columbia's in particular, acting on impulses born in earlier times. Put differently, I responded to certain crises with unaccustomed sure-footedness. Probably in the back of my mind were thoughts about the Great War and movements driven by fanatical unreason; I doubt that I actually recalled that I had already written about the descent "from idealism to nihilism." But Europe's disasters were more deeply embedded in my conscious and unconscious than I realized. And not always for the best. Henry Roberts once said to me, "Your alarm bells go off very early." Perhaps I did have something akin to "the imagination of disaster," alternately a short-term advantage and a long-term affliction.

Homecoming also meant renewed close ties with the Roberts and Hofstadter families. These friendships involved every member of my family and theirs. Henry had become the overburdened head of Columbia's Russian Institute, our jewel among regional institutes, and he continued to combine scholarship, public affairs, and a private life filled with family, friends, and poetic musings. At the very time of my return, Hofstadter's new book appeared, *The Paranoid Style in American Politics*, in which he warned against assuming that "the paranoid style" was an American peculiarity: "the single case in modern history in which one might say that the paranoid style had a consumatory triumph occurred not in the United States but in Germany." Dick and I shared a historic-political interest in the irrational outbreaks that marked the 1960s.

At the end of the academic year 1967, Henry left Columbia and his huge burdens there in order to move his family to their house in Vermont, and to teach at Dartmouth. This was a loss—in which we were not altogether innocent: Peggy and I had inherited an old Bassett family homestead in Vermont, and sometime in the 1950s, the Robertses had bought the house next door. My parents had come to Rochester every summer, too, and felt it was "home," as I had recalled at the time of my father's death. The place had a great view of the Green Mountains, which Henry, characteristically, dubbed "the Ur-mountains," because every foreign visitor insisted that the view reminded them of some pastoral beauty in their own past. At least if I lost Henry's colleagueship at Columbia, I knew that I would have the continued pleasure of the Robertses' company in Vermont.

In 1965, before Oxford, I had been shaken by the radicalization of American politics and had searched for ways to enter the debate about the Vietnam War and effectively voice my concern that student unrest, if ignored, might escalate into grave trouble. Lyndon Johnson's landslide victory over the hawkish Barry Goldwater in 1964 had been reassuring, but soon it became clear that because of the Vietnam War, Johnson's Great Society program would end in malign neglect. After the Tonkin Gulf Resolution of August 1964, as American involvement in the war steadily grew, so did skepticism about Johnson's candor and policy. To some, the war was an absolute necessity to continue the containment of communism, which, if unchecked, would spread all over Southeast Asia— the fabled domino theory. To others, American participation was a dangerous commitment to a corrupt South Vietnamese government, entailing vast risks, perhaps even a war with China. To me American policy seemed a nightmare of mindless escalation: it recalled, on a lesser scale, the slaughter in World War I, when soldiers were sent to their deaths because "one more push" would prove decisive. And the war's human and political cost was dividing us at home and estranging us from our allies abroad. It was not a time for passivity or private lament; I thought "moderates" needed to act. (Decades later, I became interested in a group of German patriots who in 1916 were quietly concerned about militaristic pan-Germanism, finding themselves estranged from both super-patriots and pacifists. Among them was the remarkable theologian-philosopher Ernst Troeltsch, who brooded over the fate of "moderates.")

In February 1966, I went to see Senator J. William Fulbright, the most responsible critic of American involvement in Vietnam, who had just conducted Senate hearings on the war; he encouraged my idea of organizing an academic group to make a public appeal against the war. On the same day—and in quest of another opinion—I visited John Palfrey, ex-dean of Columbia College and now in Washington on the Atomic Energy Commission. Palfrey was an informal man of formidable intellect and original mind, a citizen-patriot *sans phrase*. I told him what I had in mind; did he not think that the war was our paramount danger? "Hell, yes," he answered. "We can lose a hydrogen bomb in Spain, but because of the war we can't get anyone at the White House interested." (A few weeks earlier, a B-52 carrying four hydrogen bombs had crashed in Spain; of the four bombs, three crashed near the village of Palomar, but the fourth sank off the coast—and was not found until early April.) Doubly encouraged, I left for home. But at the airport I bumped into Ithiel de Sola Pool, the well-known political scientist at MIT whom I knew from my days at Stanford. He asked what I was doing in Washington, and I told him of my misgivings about the war. He burst out, "But Vietnam is the greatest social-science laboratory we have ever had!" He wanted me to go there and see for myself what great projects of social engineering his colleagues were embarked on. I was aware that social scientists were indeed enthusiastic about various "land reform" ideas in Vietnam, but I was appalled at what struck me as callous indifference to a mounting horror. I returned to Columbia certain that something should be done.

I wrote to twelve colleagues whom I presumed shared my "uneasiness about the war" and asked them to an organizational meeting. I thought a collective effort would be more efficacious, and, we discovered, the very fact of working together raised our spirits. As citizens who so far had said little or nothing about the war, we should now consider contributing to the debate. I lacked expertise, but "as a European historian, I know that the passivity of moderates can be pernicious," I explained. The group—including Hofstadter, William Leuchtenburg, Henry Roberts, David Truman, Alexander Dallin, and Daniel Bell—met later that month. (I. I. Rabi sent a handwritten note: "I would like to come to future meetings, if any, if possible. Your concerns are shared by myself and most people I know in and out of government.")

First we planned a public statement, but then we decided on a private letter to President Johnson, knowing of his angry indifference to public questioning. We labored hard on the letter's substance and stylistic precision. Hofstadter wrote me: ". . . the whole thing should be within an ecumenical framework, emphasizing a certain amount of understanding of the difficulties of the administration . . . and in a phrase dissociate the signers . . . from those who have identified themselves with the Vietcong." In May, we sent off our letter, joined by Robert Merton and Wolfgang Friedmann, a German refugee and professor of international law. Our five-page letter asked for what is hardest in wartime: "to reexamine one's course of action." The United States had begun with a strictly limited goal, but "we have moved toward a new and dangerous set of policies in which our commitment seems limitless, our position isolated, our motives impugned throughout the world." We worried about the "effects of this war on the American mind" and suggested that a prolonged commitment in Vietnam was almost certain to make for frustration, "which will both jeopardize our liberties and encourage those forces opposed to social progress." We opposed a commitment "to an unrelenting crusade to wipe out a hostile ideology in every corner of the world . . ." and made nine specific recommendations— not to mine the port of Hai Phong; not to continue a buildup of American combat troops in Asia; not to intensify the air war but to indicate willingness to negotiate with the Viet Cong; to give asylum for Vietnamese loyal to us; to make plans for economic aid in Asia, and so on. We hoped that our letter might be a first step in establishing ties between scholars and the administration.

But the military escalation went on, and brought with it inflated rhetoric. Defenders of our ever-deeper involvement regularly invoked "Munich" and labeled opponents of the war as appeasers. In June, I wrote to *The New York Times*, arguing that "the analogy . . . is grossly inappropriate, and it is alarming to think that our leaders have given credence to it." In 1938, Hitler's Germany, already the most powerful nation in Europe, with a record of expansionism and ruthless violations of international law and human decency, had laid claims to the Sudetenland, the strategically important part of a free and democratic Czechoslovakia; to accede to Hitler's demands, as was done in Munich, was morally and politically wrong. But nothing in Vietnam bore any relation to that earlier situation. Alas, American "hawks" still like to invoke ill-remembered moments of Europe's travails in order to justify dangerous or reckless policies.

In mid-June we received an answer—of equal length!—from President Johnson. Essentially he restated his position: that the United States must support the South Vietnamese effort to build up their nation free of North Vietnamese aggressive interference. He had done some of the things we had urged, he said, and he counseled "patience and forbearance." He appreciated the privacy of our effort: "It is always good to hear from gentlemen." But he held out no hope for an early end: "If you think there have been problems so far, I can only suggest you hold on for the next round."

That is precisely what most of us were unwilling to do. In early August, seven of us signed another letter to Johnson saying that his reply, like the subsequent bombing of the oil depots of Hanoi and Hai Phong, pointed to a dangerous policy of escalation. "We deplore the predictable results such a policy has already had: our commitments remain limitless, our position has become far more isolated, and our motives are even more widely impugned than before." At least we were on record, but we knew we would have to find another form of protest.

All the while I had been watching the student movement both in the United States and in the Federal Republic, where a new mood was surfacing: the quiet or skeptical generation had had its day, and a new generation of students was showing signs of impatience, which some of them expressed as an ideological attack on all authority. West German students were discovering how Nazified their universities had been, how the older generation had preferred denial to truth, and the distorted past fed their anger and suspicion. And in America the ideology of the New Left mixed a not very original critique of "late capitalism" with a simplistic formula subsuming all political evil under the term *fascism*. The war in Vietnam—proof of capitalist-imperialist aggression—fired student protests, which broke out all over the world with immediate targets as well: in Berlin, for example, Axel Springer, right-wing press magnate, was the chosen foe; in Berkeley the Free Speech Movement demanded "to hear any person speak in any open area on campus at any time on any subject."

The two cities became major battlegrounds where radical students fought what they took to be the corrupt establishment. For all the local differences, there were striking similarities, although initially the scene in Berlin was much more violent. In June 1967, at a demonstration in Berlin, police shot and killed a theology student, Benno Ohnesorg. The conflicts moved from street to campus and back again: students used forcible tactics on campus; police mustered a different force on the streets. "Gurus" of the rebellious students at the Free University (including my ex-Columbia colleagues Jacob Taubes and Herbert Marcuse) addressed mass meetings, encouraging resistance to a morally bankrupt capitalist-imperialist system. The embodiment of all that was wrong with the modern world was the United States. Marcuse, fabled exposer of "repressive tolerance," seemed undisturbed by aggressive intolerance in the very nation that had offered him a safe haven.

In 1965, David Truman, a fine political scientist who was then dean of Columbia College, asked me to give the traditional opening talk to incoming students. I talked to them about the background of the current unrest, and summarized the various disasters that had preceded their birth—that chain of horrors that I called the Second Thirty Years' War, 1914–1945, more frightful even than the first, and culminating in the murder of six million Jews. I told them that the past should give them "a firmer sense of the permanence as well as the precariousness of our civilization, a better perspective on your own dissatisfactions and discontents, a better realization of your own historic role and responsibility." I understood that this first post–World War II student generation had new questions and above all a new and explosive impatience, since preceding generations had failed "to ask the fundamental questions about the dignity of man, the possibilities of beauty in modern life, the translation of modern life into the good life." So they should ask such questions and challenge convention—but with tolerance. I very deliberately ended by recalling "that so radical a Marxist as Rosa Luxemburg cried out weeks before her death, 'Freedom is always freedom for the man who disagrees with you.'" I tried to appeal both to the potential radicals among them and also to prepare their elders for what I expected would be a serious confrontation in which the principles and practices of civility and liberality would be tested.

After my return from Oxford, I reassembled our earlier Vietnam group. Since a private approach to the president would now be futile, I suggested that we prepare a pamphlet about the human and political costs of the war in Vietnam—on the model of George Bernard Shaw's *The Intelligent Woman's Guide to Socialism and Capitalism* (I was thinking of the effectiveness of the Fabian Society in pre-1914 England), a document that would briefly state why the war injured our national interest and why the administration should seek a negotiated peace, beginning with an immediate pause in the bombing. The hope was that such a reasoned statement could reach and further inform people already weary of the war. By early 1968, I had persuaded a major publisher to take our pamphlet, and they anticipated an initial printing of one hundred thousand copies.

Meanwhile our campus, like that of other universities, was becoming more and more agitated. In the spring of 1967, Grayson Kirk asked me to become dean of the college, succeeding David Truman, who in a general reshuffle had been named provost. I was tempted, for I felt a sense of responsibility to Columbia, but my unfinished book made me hesitate, and I declined. However, I warned Kirk that escalating student protests were a key issue. Kirk was nonplussed; perhaps he was even relieved that someone with such distorted interests would not be joining the inner councils of what he thought of as a tranquil university.

I made a similar remark to Gerald Freund of the Rockefeller Foundation, who wanted advice for a weekend conference at the foundation's idyllic center at the Villa Serbelloni, Pliny's old retreat on Lake Como, about the crisis in Western historical writing. I didn't quite see the crisis, I told him, but the international student unrest was "a serious, pervasive, and hitherto much too narrowly construed phenomenon" that merited urgent attention. His response, like Kirk's, was disbelief. The complacency of the powerful is repugnant under all circumstances, but at the onset of a storm it presages disaster. What was needed at the time was awareness and reform; instead, most administrators clung to the old routine and haughty remoteness.

Some students and teachers were becoming angrier about the university's complicity with the "military-industrial complex," hence with the Vietnam War itself. In February 1968, a group of Columbia professors, myself included, signed a letter to Kirk pointing to the long-standing link between the CIA and Columbia concerning classified research, which had only recently been revealed and which "aroused the deepest concern . . . among colleagues . . . in other countries." As this impaired our own work and effectiveness, "we respectfully request that you sever the current relationship with the CIA." It didn't take great diagnostic powers to realize that American campuses were increasingly impatient with "business as usual."

On March 29, after much work, I distributed the second draft of our pamphlet on Vietnam; two days later, Johnson withdrew from the presidential race. We were jubilant, and I congratulated our group on "our instantaneous obsolescence." We decided to amend, not abandon, the text, since we were within days of the publisher's deadline.

But then Columbia plunged into a crisis. The murder, on April 4, of Martin Luther King, Jr., left most of the nation in shock and grief. Chaplain John Cannon organized a memorial service in the chapel on April 9, which Kirk and Truman attended and at which the rector of Harlem's St. Philip's Church gave the main speech. As Truman spoke, Mark Rudd, leader of the local chapter of Students for a Democratic Society (SDS), marched to the podium, grabbed the microphone, and denounced the dignified service as an "obscenity, given the university's racism." At the end of the service, Cannon insisted that whatever one might think of what had just happened, in his chapel anyone wishing to speak "in the spirit of truth" would always and at any time be welcome. He said not one word of criticism of Rudd; in fact, his remarks seemed to condone Rudd's action and invite repetitions of it. I was appalled. The semi-official history of the university recalls that I caught up with the departing Rudd and told him that his actions in the chapel were akin to the takeover of socialist meetings by Nazis in Weimar Germany. Cannon's conduct troubled me even more, and I wrote him at once, warning that most demagogues, Hitler included, always claimed and perhaps believed that they "talked in the spirit of truth." I received no answer. Such preemptive indulgence, I thought, could only serve to embolden students: a minority of radical students already thought that the university was infinitely "pushable," and they were determined to bring it to its knees.

I knew Columbia had special flaws and vulnerabilities, dictated in part by our location at the edge of Harlem. In the one representative, half-elected body we had at the time, the University Council, I warned the university not to pursue its plan to build a gym in Morningside Park, which seemed like a private intrusion on public space, and its construction an affront to our Harlem neighbors. But the trustees persisted, and I came to fear that they and some of the school's administrators, living in a world of insulated privilege, were half blind to the changes going on around them. The announced plans for the gym enraged black students particularly and gave radical white students, egged on by Rudd, a focus for protest.

I was in Europe at a Nürnberg Colloquium when Columbia erupted. Fred, then a Columbia College student, called to tell me that students had occupied the chief college building. I flew back immediately. The campus had become part carnival, part battleground—with violent and obscene language emanating from defiantly dressed students busy occupying additional buildings, while counterprotesters rallied as well. The radicals were well organized—"dizzy with success," to use the Leninist phrase, appropriate to a moment when many of them really thought they, together with their brethren in other parts of the world, were the vanguard of revolution. After all, violent student protests were occurring in Mexico, California, Paris, and Berlin. Columbia became a magnet for young radicals, and as their numbers grew, new buildings were occupied, as was the president's office. Some of the leaders hoped to rally the Harlem community to join their protest. The enthusiasm aroused by the students' violence and joyful destructiveness appalled me. I was dumbfounded by colleagues who seemed to pardon violent tactics by virtue of "idealistic" intentions.

The university was in chaos, and its normal life totally disrupted. Instead of classes, endless meetings were held and ever more dire rumors about the prospects of still-greater violence circulated. People huddled with friends at all hours of the day and night; I stayed in closest touch with Dick Hofstadter, for our concerns were identical: we feared that our university was bent on a course of collision and self-destruction. The administration, itself divided, had to end the occupations, peacefully if possible, and by police action as a last resort. A faculty committee tried to mediate; a few of its ambitious leaders assumed that there was a kind of moral equivalence between the guardians of the university, however misguided, and the students occupying the buildings. I was asked to join that group, but after a couple of days was excluded as being insufficiently pro-student. The student leaders clung to their demands, with a general amnesty as their (self-indulgent) prerequisite, and an end to the ban on demonstrations inside university buildings. I believe many of them actually wished for an ultimate confrontation with the police that would inflame the campus.

After days of pandemonium and the failure of faculty mediation, the administration, pushed by the trustees and pressured by other universities that feared the consequences if Columbia folded—but also aware of the huge negative publicity—requested the New York City Police to clear the campus. (It had prepared for such an eventuality.) The very notion of setting the police against our students was a terrifying violation of tradition, even though by then we were unwilling hosts to "revolutionaries" from outside who had joined the students. In the early morning of April 30, the police cleared all five buildings and arrested the occupiers; in the immediate aftermath, the police lost control of a crowd of bystanders and more violence ensued, more blood was spilled. Some 700 people were arrested and 140 students and faculty injured (the most seriously a policeman). Radical student leaders of course wanted to be "busted"; in such a melee, they thought, the police would tear "the mask of liberalism" from the face of their reactionary enemies. The revolution had its "martyrs." "Police brutality" gave the radicals a huge boost and won them new supporters.

Some professors now openly sided with the students, dreaming that this was the dawn of a new age, perhaps feeling a rush of youth as "very heaven." I found the "revolutionaries on fellowship," as I called the graduate student rebels, unappealing, and their faculty supporters even less comprehensible. I wondered what kind of emptiness must have afflicted these tenured teachers, what kind of discontent and anger must have been seething in their psyches.

By morning, on a devastated campus, the SDS called for a strike, vowing to bring the university to a standstill. A faculty meeting was called, the sole business at hand being a motion from the earlier faculty group calling on all teachers to join the strike. More than a thousand teachers crowded into McMillan Theatre to give or hear eyewitness reports on police violence. Most professors, enraged at the administration, favored the idea of the strike. A few dissented. I spoke against the motion, saying that I deplored the violence on campus but had seen "idealistic" students successfully disrupt universities before. Nazi students had done this in German universities even before Hitler's assumption of power. (Other professors at other universities who, like me, had European pasts made the same point, such as Alexander Gerschenkron at Harvard and Martin Schwarzschild at Princeton.) The faculty should not side with a minority of students who had brought coercion to the campus and acted as if their revolutionary ends justified their means. After I finished, the meeting was briefly adjourned, and upon resumption, the motion in favor of the strike was withdrawn.*

At the time, I was teaching an undergraduate course in twentieth-century European history that had more than a hundred students. On the first day, I had spoken about the potential risks and advantages of studying near-contemporary history. Advantages included the availability of pictures—as, for example, the picture of Sergei Eisenstein sitting on Russia's actual imperial throne, smoking a cigarette as he directed *Alexander Nevsky*; the picture caught the giddiness of revolutionary liberation. In May, *Life* magazine published a picture of one of my students from that course, David Shapiro, sitting in Kirk's chair in the same defiant posture as Eisenstein, smoking Kirk's cigar. Symbolic politics! My rapport with most of the students was good in any case, and I could understand the anger or confusion of the politically and morally engaged ones, as well as the distress of those who objected to having a minority disrupt their studies. My scorn was reserved for colleagues who, I feared, came close to pandering to students.

When the strike organizers proscribed attendance in the classrooms, asking

---

*The earliest and best account of Columbia in 1968, *Up Against the Ivy Wall* (New York: Scribner's, 1968), by Jerry Avorn, Paul Starr, and other campus journalists, gave an account that has the advantage of "objective" immediacy: "Fritz Stern, a respected historian, rose from the balcony and delivered what was to be the resolution's *coup de grace*. Stern had been in Germany . . . and had written on April 23 to a colleague at Columbia that, after seeing the German radicals, he far preferred Columbia's SDS. In the few days since his returning he had been asked to serve on the Ad Hoc Faculty steering committee and then, when Westin [co-chairman of the group] sensed he was too conservative for the group, had been asked to leave. As Stern began to speak the faculty members turned in their seats to look up at him. Seated next to him was Lionel Trilling, nodding approvingly at each point his colleague made. In a level but forceful tone, Stern said: 'I am utterly removed from your thoughts and sentiments and I am opposed to both the aims and the contents of your resolution . . . I remember that it was only twelve hours ago that Professor Bell [made] it clear that the administration had moved very much closer to the points of our resolution than had the SDS. You now come out condemning it, but I miss any similar statement condemning the other side.'"

teachers to meet students off campus, I continued this class at the usual lecture hall, and perhaps half of my students showed up. A group of them waiting outside told me they wanted to attend but please couldn't I move off campus? I offered to *repeat* the lectures off campus, but the students wanted neither to impose double work on me nor to break the strike. I offered to announce at each class that attendance at it did not constitute breaking the strike—that sham worked for a while, to the annoyance of my more "progressive" colleagues.

These were excruciatingly difficult days. Gratefully, I remember a chance encounter with the philosopher Sidney Morgenbesser, who was on the side "opposite" to mine and who asked me, "Fritz, why do you look so angry?" (The colleagues who seemed frozen in psychological solidarity with the radical students did annoy me.) I took Morgenbesser's remark to heart as a friendly plea for reason—and by and large, though collegiality had momentarily snapped, civility returned before long. I saw that some people straddled, wishing neither to endanger the university nor to desert their students. Trilling said to me at the end of the semester, "I agreed with you every other day."

The campus went on resembling an armed carnival, and the uproar didn't die down. On May 2, I spotted Allen Ginsberg, coming back to his alma mater in its time of crisis to address a student rally; he ended with "Kirk must probably go." The word *probably* suggested Ginsberg's humane uncertainty, which was alien to the prevailing dogmatists. Later he came to my office, chanted his Hindu chants, and walked back with me to my apartment nearby, his arm companionably on my shoulder. This sight may have confounded students and colleagues who had thought me hopelessly reactionary or anachronistic.

Our Vietnam project became a symptomatic victim of the campus revolution. The scholars who had worked so harmoniously together now refused to sign off on a common text. Passionately agreed on Vietnam, equally passionately at odds over campus issues, the group fell apart. It was another sign of the precariousness of the liberal position, an easy common target of radicals and reactionaries, caught between unresponsive authority and irresponsible rebellion.

I quickly brought together another faculty group, similar to the Vietnam one, if more conservative in spirit. The university was going to be "restructured," and trustees and conservative alumni had to be persuaded of the urgent need for reform; on the other hand the faculty had to be warned against submitting to extravagant demands for student power. The slogan favoring the involvement of students in university decision-making was "participatory democracy," which I anticipated would end in "participatory boredom." (I wasn't altogether wrong.) Basically our group demanded accountability and peace, and hence it was wonderfully ironic when a friend labeled us the "Stern gang," as if we were the Jewish terrorist group in Mandate Palestine just before the birth of the state of Israel.

The university hobbled to the end of the semester, with occasional disruptions. On May 21, SDS students occupied Hamilton Hall for the second time, and that night the police were again called on campus. I spent the night with David Truman in his Low Library provost's office, not wishing him to be alone; at some point, we both crouched beneath his desk as bricks came sailing through the window; the sound of shattering glass was frightening. At that second "bust," the police behaved with great caution, and most students anyway opposed what they regarded as a self-indulgent, all-white effort. Wise counsel prevailed on Hofstadter to give the commencement speech that year, traditionally the prerogative of the university president. (Diana Trilling, expressing the fears that beset some people at the time, warned me that by encouraging Hofstadter to speak, I was putting my friend in mortal danger, that his life would be at stake.) He delivered a magisterial speech, his very presence symbolizing the substance of his quiet eloquence: that the faculty *was* the university, an essential, liberal institution of our civilization.

By now the salience of student discontent being obvious even to the Rockefeller Foundation, they solicited my views before charging me with arranging an assembly of the best people on the subject for a meeting at the Villa Serbelloni the following autumn. I said that the student agitation fed on legitimate grievances in university governance and was responding to a new radical ideology; the university had become a surrogate for society, and its very openness and fragility made it an ideal target. I accepted Rockefeller's charge, enlisting as co-sponsor Franklin Ford, fellow historian and dean of arts and sciences at Harvard, and Alan Bullock and Ralf Dahrendorf as European advisers. The gathering could help us to learn from one another.* The group met over Thanksgiving 1968, including Kingman Brewster from Yale and Hanna Gray from Chicago (a few years later Brewster wrote me, thanking me for "the Serbelloni introduction to H.H.G.!"; by that time, she had become his provost at Yale), the psychologists Erik Erikson and Kenneth Keniston, and Roger Heyns,

---

*I was hoping that the Columbia experiences could be a lesson to other institutions. That summer, Archibald Cox of the Harvard Law School headed a commission to investigate the Columbia disorders. I begged him to understand that there was more wrong at Columbia than he and his commission would be able to discover—more than the infamous naked lightbulbs in the dormitories—and that what had happened at Columbia could happen elsewhere. His report should see to it that Columbia at least serve as a negative lesson. He kept saying that it could never happen at Harvard. But it did, and only a year later.

chancellor of the University of California at Berkeley, among others. I emphasized the diffuse context of student unrest and the fact that only a convergence of many causes could have brought about so forceful and pervasive an eruption. For three days we argued from many different positions; the temper of our discussions reflected, I suppose, the Burkean dictum: preserve and reform.

But preservation and reform were almost impossible in the catastrophic summer of 1968. The murder of Senator Robert Kennedy in the midst of his promising campaign for the presidency, race riots in the South and North, ever-growing violence, bloody confrontations in Chicago during the Democratic Party Convention—all this was heartrending. And the news from Europe was even worse: the "Prague Spring," launched when Czechoslovakia's communist leader, Alexander Dubcek, embarked on a program of reform that allowed for a measure of freedom and promised "Communism with a human face"—a new and a more prudent version of the Hungarian lunge for freedom in 1956—was brutally killed when, in August, Soviet troops, supported by troops from most of the satellites (including East Germany), invaded Czechoslovakia, smashed the reform movement, and imposed a new regime of terror. Brezhnev elevated repressive force into principle; his doctrine asserted that the USSR had the right to intervene in states whose socialist principles were threatened. I was close to tears when I heard the news. The liberal spirit was everywhere under attack and in retreat. (At least there was dissent within the communist world. The Italian Party denounced the invasion.) But W. H. Auden said it perfectly in "August 1968":

The Ogre does what ogres can,
Deeds quite impossible for Man,
But one prize is beyond his reach,
The Ogre cannot master Speech.
About a subjugated plain,
Among its desperate and slain,
The Ogre stalks with hands on hips,
While drivel gushes from his lips.

For me the public gloom was deepened by private grief. It was a time when I lost close friends: Hajo Holborn and Rudolf Nissen, both paternal mentors, who had treated me, in their different ways, like an adopted son. And Dick Hofstadter—with whom, in the face of the mounting trouble at Columbia, I became ever more closely linked—was in declining health, even before he was given a fatal diagnosis of leukemia. In his last fortnight in the hospital, I was with him every day; he died in 1970. Every loss diminishes one's own life—and somehow redoubles one's responsibility. At the end of his life, Hofstadter had been working on a history of American violence. The last sentence of his study has remained in my mind: "The nation seems to slouch onward into its uncertain future like some huge inarticulate beast, too much attainted by wounds and ailments to be robust, but too strong and resourceful to succumb."

In March 1969, given the continuing troubles at Columbia and other universities, our "Stern gang" drafted a statement, "The University as a Sanctuary of Academic Freedom," insisting that while reforms were necessary, force was inimical to achieving them. We collected eight hundred signatures on campus, from people who represented a wide spectrum of opinion; the statement was published as a full-page ad in *The New York Times*. Days after it appeared, a student warned me that I had been singled out as a target, and pleaded with me to clear my office of valuable papers. Others received grimmer threats. So our campuses were now experiencing European levels of violence. Radical students around the globe were learning from one another, not by some secret conspiracy but by simple contagion or emulation. I wrote to Bernhard Vogel: "Columbia students must hurl bricks at windows and policemen in order to show that they are no less revolutionary than their comrades in Paris and Berlin."

In the circumstances, I was reluctant to leave the campus even for a bit, but that spring, Columbia dispatched me to various alumni groups in the United States and, as a reward for domestic service, to Europe and even to Istanbul to explain what had happened the previous spring, and to reassure the less than faithful that their alma mater needed and deserved help now more than ever. Also, outraged conservatives had to be persuaded that the student movement was more than a minor left-wing conspiracy. I learned something on every one of these trips. My friend Jacques Droz, who had initially sided with protesting students, had been chased off the Vincennes campus of the University of Paris by *gauchistes*; he thought the revolution, if that is what it was, was devouring its own protectors. Alan Bullock, a model of reasoned toughness, remarked that this was the third battle in his life: the first against the Nazis, the second against the Communists in the cold war; the third, within the academy, was "the most insidious because it is a civil war."

In the Federal Republic, horror stories abounded: in most universities, intimidation had become routine. In their disciplined campaigns against academic opponents, militants brandished the old fascist threat: "we shall break you." Terror escalated in regular steps: disruptions and occupations were followed by obscene personal attacks, and, finally and most revoltingly, direct threats were made against faculty children. Günter Grass, hardly an establishment figure, viewed the SDS and the student movement cynically; radical students, he thought, were corrupt and could easily be co-opted. But of course, liberals were everybody's favorite targets, caught as they were between left-wing, coercive utopianism and right-wing paranoia. When German students attacked reformist opponents as *Scheissliberale*, "shitty liberals," I thought of them in the long line of Germanic vilifiers of liberalism; I had as little empathy for them as they had with the likes of me.

In an essay titled "International Student Movement," I suggested some of the common sources of what I saw as an international rebellion, though I recognized the national issues and traditions that had formed the individual outbreaks. And distinctions had to be made: I recalled the humane ideals set forth in the founding statement of Students for a Democratic Society at Port Huron in 1962, calling for a new form of radical democracy. I noted the barely articulated rage against bourgeois life, against boredom, against convention, against "the hundred varieties of suburban life, with two cars and no meaning, and with moral hypocrisy as an additional burden." These criticisms deserved sympathetic attention, even if the answers the young proposed were naïve and their tactics self-destructive. It was regrettable that their ideals and hopes were often buried by the brutalities of militant rhetoric and the steady escalation of coercive tactics. But their elders who neither understood their grievances nor warned against their remedies were also blameworthy. The slogan "Don't trust anyone over thirty" signified an intergenerational conflict, an old theme in German life. "In Greece and Spain and Czechoslovakia . . . the heroic resistance of students is essentially different from the movements in the West: there, students are battling for the traditional freedoms that our students take so much for granted that they heedlessly put them in jeopardy." I should have added Mexican students as well.

The haughtiness of the older generation in power was matched, I thought, by the arrogance of the "gurus" who eagerly inspired the students, men who prided themselves on their superior insight into the historic process, who encouraged and incited the young to make instantaneous demands, who insisted that we were already "objectively" in a fascist state and that tolerance, that precious and precarious achievement of centuries, was "repressive." (I was thinking especially of Herbert Marcuse, who in 1967 had delighted in being the idol of Berlin student radicals, "idealists" with storm trooper tactics.) But there were important other models, too: in June 1968, the philosopher Jürgen Habermas, an early supporter of student protests, warned against "left-wing fascism."

Some teachers, I thought, were driven by pangs of guilt—guilt about their earlier passivity, perhaps guilt about their privileged, bourgeois lives, guilt at having grown old without having had a revolutionary experience. I cited the Paris slogan "We are all German Jews." Was the putative passivity of the Nazis' victims being used, by some twisted logic, as a reason to attack universities? Radical students in America (many of them from affluent, often Jewish families) were embarking on careers of material promise, but they were affecting immiseration and victimhood, influenced by fatuous professors who encouraged them to see in the poor (and in women) the Ersatz for the co-opted proletariat.

I was angry at the jubilant desecration of the university, and afraid that we were betraying our patrimony.* We teachers had been entrusted with something ancient and precious and were allowing it to be violated. I was afraid of the radical youths who were intoxicated by their own rhetoric, enthralled by the initial successes of violence, and convinced of their historic role as iconoclasts. I resented the crude anti-Americanism that they often spouted, the false analogies they made between an errant America and Nazi totalitarianism. I thought of them as unwitting wreckers of reforms that many of us had not only envisioned but were trying to enact. Their disruptions were not cost-free: I feared a massive backlash, a reaction by conservative yahoos who would feel justified in their paranoid hatred of liberal (and expensive) institutions.

Perhaps I overreacted, as some of my colleagues charged; perhaps with the European past in mind, I saw things too starkly. When colleagues heard murmurs of dissent, I may have heard the distant sound of marching thugs. In the end, there weren't marching thugs but, in the United States anyway, the triumph of a well-financed "silent majority" who voted Richard Nixon into office with his familiar theme of "law and order." In time, Nixon and radicals of all ages confirmed each other in their dreadful mixture of cynicism and paranoia. As the fine American historian Alan Brinkley recently wrote, "However much radical politics seemed to dominate the public face of 1968, the most important political legacy of that critical year was the rise of the Right . . . American liberalism has been wandering in the political wilderness ever since."

It is impossible to draw up a balance sheet of the student movement. After all the dislocations and disturbances, the governance of universities in the United States probably improved; accountability and social responsibility be-

---

*I was also angry at young people who wanted to opt out altogether. I once ended a stormy discussion with a self-indulgent hippie-relative with an ultimate insult: "You are not even a citizen."

came recognized goals. Our institutions proved more resilient than those in Europe, yet still we paid a heavy price.

In continental Europe, 1968 had paradoxical consequences: many a progressive, reformist scholar moved to the right, forever wounded by the students' mindless attacks. Even now, conservatives blame much of what has gone wrong in the academy and in society on what Germans call the "sixty-eighters." On the other hand, many of my European friends and colleagues, especially in Germany, attribute a great moral awakening to that year, believing that the student revolt brought about the long-overdue confrontation with Germany's past. The mythic year 1968 is remembered by some as a year of unpardonable violence, by others as the year when encrusted institutions were finally defied, and hypocrisy and unpardonable silence were exposed. There is a measure of truth in both judgments.

LUCK IS ALL —accidental encounters transformed by often unconscious predispositions into something life-changing and life-enhancing. I was in Bonn in January 1970, at a German-American Conference, the sixth annual affair at which "leading" personalities from government, business, press, and academia, old hands in international politics and the German-American relationship, took stock of transatlantic politics. On the second morning, the principal topic was the international student movement, and my essay served as an introductory text.

I forget what was said, but I still have the penciled note slipped to me in the course of that morning: "Shall we have lunch together or do you have other plans?" It was signed Marion Dönhoff. We had lunch together—and we talked about many things, including my article, which she found much too conservative. Could I have sensed then that this meeting would lead to a friendship that would change my life and my relations to my native country?

At the time, Marion Countess Dönhoff was publisher of *Die Zeit*, West Germany's foremost weekly newspaper, defined by its clear left-liberal voice— *her* voice, in fact. I had read her articles, and knew that hers was a passionately reasoned plea for a new policy toward the East (*Ostpolitik*), above all for reconciliation with Poland. A friend of the United States and of many Americans, she had little use for cold-war rigidity.

She was a woman of a discreet, unconventional beauty, with a most expressive face reflecting an inner radiance, and a great smile. She was short, attired in understated chic, a perfection of modesty. *Schlicht* is the German word that

comes to mind: simple, classic elegance, the very opposite of demanding ostentation or German self-importance. She had great charm, and yet her bearing
suggested distance and inspired respect, if not awe. At the paper she was always
called *Gräfin* (Countess). So young in spirit, so mature in judgment! (She was
sixty, I forty-five.) I admired who she was and what she stood for; deep affection
was to follow. She combined Prussian austerity with human warmth, a phrase of
mine that Helmut Schmidt quoted in his eulogy to her in March 2002.

Our first conversation made clear that the Countess's interests were intense
and universal, political and personal. Unfailingly she went to the heart of
things; she had a journalist's questing appetite for facts and a moralist's depth —
and an astounding knowledge of the world. I didn't then know the full story of
her early life: only that she had been born into an East Prussian family of old
nobility, brought up in Spartan luxury in an old world where privilege prescribed responsibility. The rest I learned in time.

Shortly after that first meeting, she sent me a copy of a brochure privately
printed in 1945 (!), *In Memoriam. 20. Juli 1944. Den Freunden zum Gedächtnis*,
a brief memoir of the July 20 conspirators who had been her friends, and who
after the failed coup had been murdered by the Nazis. She had known of the
planned conspiracy, and she knew some of the men who were designated to
serve in a post-Hitler regime. The Dönhoff estate in East Prussia had been a
convenient meeting place for some of these men, but the Gestapo, questioning
her, could not penetrate her involvement. Not long after our lunch, on one of
the first walks we took together in what turned out to be a favorite vacation spot
for both of us—wonderful Sils Maria, in the Engadine, and very near the Silvaplana of my youth—we talked again of the attempted coup. I told her I
thought it odd that no great play had been written about it, that there was no
Schiller equal to the task, and we decided to write such a play together—time
(and talent) permitting! Given my passionate regard for these heroes and their
families, the Countess and I had an immediate bond, but it wasn't always an
easy harmony: she was unforgiving of the English who, before and during the
war, had repeatedly rebuffed these German patriot-resisters, while I argued
that they had historic reasons for their distrust. Details we disagreed on, funda-
mentals we shared.

When we first met, I think I also knew about her fabled solitary trek, in January 1945, on her favorite horse, from Friedrichstein, the Dönhoffs' ancestral
home in East Prussia, all the way to the Metternich family in Westphalia. The
journey, of seven hundred miles, took her seven weeks. She left just ahead of
the Red Army, which burned down her family's great manor house; the ruins

are now in Polish hands. I can't remember if we ever talked of our shared experience of being uprooted from our homes, though we certainly spoke of our utterly different pasts, but the unspoken, the unconscious may spin its own special tie. Only in Berlin in 1992 did we discuss together "Lost Homes" at a public meeting of Poles and Germans.

About the student movement, she had a more hopeful view than I. She had more sympathy for radical students than for antiquated professors in encrusted institutions. The universities needed shaking up, greater openness, and some degree of democratization, she believed. When I said good-bye to her, I had no inkling that our meeting was to mark a "new beginning" for me, too.

That German-American Conference occurred just after Bonn had experienced a dramatic transformation, in truth a "new beginning." Willy Brandt had just become chancellor as head of a Social-Democratic-liberal coalition. In the fall elections of 1969, the Social Democrats, with almost 43 percent of the vote, had scored their best results ever, while the Free Democrats, an internally split swing party, had lost votes and yet they were now firmly in liberal hands. The two parties, with a slim majority in Parliament, decided to form a government. Walter Scheel, head of the FDP and an equally determined champion of a new policy toward the East, became foreign minister. The change was hailed as a "second founding" of the Federal Republic.

Brandt's ascension signified a radical turn in German history: It marked the first transition of party power in twenty years of the Federal Republic. Not only was he the first Social Democratic chancellor in nearly forty years, but his entire life had been shaped by his fight against Nazism. He was right in thinking that his rise to power signaled Hitler's final defeat, as he said to a group of foreign journalists. The highlight of the German-American Conference had been a dinner where I had a chance to meet Brandt, whom I found appealing in his simple, thoughtful, even brooding manner. He spoke of his plans and hopes, an impressive agenda without even a tinge of triumphalism or partisan narrowness. I had admired him from afar, and now I was much taken by him.

Born in 1913, Brandt, an illegitimate child (a fact that Adenauer had shamelessly exploited against him), had in his late teens joined the SAP, Weimar's radical left-wing party opposed to the moderate and, in its view, supine Social Democratic Party. (Later when we came to know each other, I asked Brandt about Ernst Eckstein, the SAP leader in Breslau. His eyes lit up, and he recalled, "We had a special fund in his memory—and I helped to collect for it.") When the Nazis came to power, the twenty-year-old Brandt fled to Norway and became active in an international radical offshoot of the SAP called "New

Beginnings." He briefly served as a courier for the anti-Nazi underground in Germany and until 1945 remained in exile, first in Norway, then in Sweden. He was a respected figure in German exile politics, particularly among a younger generation that not only fought Hitler but acknowledged that failures on the German and European left had eased the path of Nazism. His experience of Scandinavian socialism, successful and gradualist, purged him of his more radical-revolutionary views.

After the war, Brandt returned to his devastated homeland, first as a journalist in Norwegian uniform. Then, having reclaimed his German citizenship, he joined the SPD and was elected to the Bundestag. He entered Berlin politics, in which the unforgettable Ernst Reuter, also a one-time exile, was his great mentor. In 1957, Brandt succeeded Reuter as lord mayor of (West) Berlin and, as Reuter had been tested by the Berlin blockade of 1948–1949, so Brandt was tested by the next great crisis, the building of the Berlin Wall in 1961. Though at first enraged by President Kennedy's cautious response to this Soviet provocation, Brandt came to see Kennedy as a model, and soon Brandt himself was an international presence. He may have been one of the few European statesmen who had particularly high regard for both Kennedy and de Gaulle — feelings that were reciprocated.

While Brandt had been an unsuccessful candidate for chancellor twice before, his third campaign had an American touch and a German core. Despite his mystifying alternation between exuberant energy and melancholic lassitude, he was a vigorous campaigner, exuding youth and confidence. Günter Grass and other prominent writers and artists organized massive support. Brandt's inaugural speech reiterated his campaign promise: to "dare more democracy," including social reforms at home and reconciliation abroad.

Brandt had for years belonged to the pro-Western wing of the SPD, accepting Adenauer's policy of Western integration, and he knew better than most that the Federal Republic depended upon Allied protection — as most evident in Berlin; he never wavered in his commitment to the Atlantic alliance. But he was also determined to intensify the policy he had begun as foreign minister under Kiesinger, an *Ostpolitik* aimed at reducing tensions between Bonn and the Soviet bloc and thus promoting a German variant of détente. He was ready to strike out on new paths, knowing that in the process he would have to force his own people to shed treasured illusions: about lost territories and the prospects of reunification. It was time for West Germans to deal differently with East Germany and to accept the existing borders, thus reassuring Czechoslovakia and

Poland that they had nothing to fear from Bonn, that East bloc tirades against "West German revanchism" were nothing but Soviet propaganda salvos.

The Brandt government embarked at once on its pursuit of *Ostpolitik*, inaugurating a new, dynamic phase in West German foreign policy. *Ostpolitik* meant above all the renunciation of force and the recognition of existing borders—in themselves two momentous steps toward pacification. A time of daring actions began, involving multiple goals, changing tactics, and combining dramatic visibility with all the nuances of back-channel diplomacy. I can do no more than offer a brief summary of the unfolding drama.

Brandt's closest adviser, the nimble tactician Egon Bahr, was at his side, but the goals were Brandt's, as were the style and the moral courage. He wanted to improve the lives of Germans on both sides of the Wall through a policy of effecting "change through rapprochement." A complementary prerequisite was the forging of better relations with the Soviet Union and Poland.

The government's determination to find a better modus vivendi with East Germany already required a break with Brandt's CDU predecessors. For twenty years, the CDU and its allies had insisted that West Germany would have no dealings with East Germany, indeed would have no diplomatic relations with any state that recognized it (the Soviet Union excepted). The very name of the German Democratic Republic caused trouble: conservative papers and politicians insisted on calling it "the zone" or referred to it as the "so-called GDR."

In March 1970, Brandt undertook a historic first; he arranged to meet the East German head of government, Willi Stoph, and for that purpose traveled to Erfurt, deep inside the GDR, the capital of what had been (and is again) Thuringia. His trip took him through the heart of Reformation country and to cities such as Gotha and Eisenach, which were landmarks in the history of German socialism. The citizens of Erfurt gave him a hero's welcome, breaking through police lines and shouting, "Willy, Willy!" Brandt beguiled people by his simple presence, his utter lack of bombast. His hosts were not pleased with his reception, and Stoph was all the more insistent that his government's irreducible demand was for West Germany's full diplomatic recognition of his state, though this would have amounted to an implicit renunciation of any ultimate hope of German reunification. Brandt's definition of Germany's situation was that it was two states in one nation, while the East Germans spoke of two nations on German soil. For Brandt, the Erfurt trip was emotionally thrilling but politically chilling. Two months later, in return, Stoph paid a visit to Kassel, where there was no popular welcome for him. He merely reiterated the East German position.

Brandt was undeterred; in Moscow he negotiated a nonaggression treaty with the Soviet Union, also specifying that all existing frontiers were inviolable—a radical new West German acceptance of reality. The Russians accepted an epistolary supplement that reiterated that Germans could achieve reunification through the rights of self-determination. The treaty signified a reciprocal gain; the Soviet Union had to abandon its choice propaganda charge, that is, that the Federal Republic was revanchiste, intent on winning back the territories lost at Yalta and Potsdam; Brandt established a special relationship with Brezhnev, who in turn welcomed better relations with Bonn at the very time when Soviet relations with China were worsening. (There were even military clashes.)

A still greater challenge came vis-à-vis Poland: the Federal Republic had never recognized the finality of the Oder-Neisse border, thus leaving Poland fearing—quite aside from the mutual animosities that history had bred in both peoples—that Germany might want to reclaim its territories in Silesia and East Prussia. Brandt now extended the same guarantee of inviolability of borders to Poland, and this became the heart of a German-Polish treaty.

Brandt invited Marion Dönhoff to join the official delegation that would go to Warsaw to sign the treaty in December 1970. She accepted and then at the last minute withdrew; even for her it was simply too hard to imagine drinking to the formal cession of her ancestral home. In a handwritten letter, Brandt told her that he understood, that he had done his own "weeping" as he prepared the treaty's final documents. He went to Warsaw: his spontaneously kneeling, head bowed, in front of the memorial to the Jewish uprising in the Warsaw ghetto in 1943 remains perhaps the most poignant gesture we have of true political contrition—of apology as an act of courage, not convention or political opportunism. As he put it himself, "I did what human beings do when speech fails them. I thought of the millions who had been murdered." A reporter at the time wrote, "He who does not need to kneel knelt, on behalf of all who do need to kneel but do not—because they dare not, or cannot, or cannot dare to kneel."

Brandt's symbolic gesture—and his policies—aroused violent opposition in West Germany. In a public opinion poll at the time, 48 percent of West Germans considered Brandt's kneeling excessive, and only 41 percent approved of it. And the opposition to these treaties, which required parliamentary ratification, was ferocious. There was skepticism abroad as well; U.S. secretary of state Henry Kissinger was a wary observer, and his boss, Richard Nixon, had paranoid fears about Brandt and his policies. Kissinger thought that *Ostpolitik* could end in the reassertion of German nationalism—odd, given that its beginning was renunciation. Other American statesmen, including Dean Acheson, were suspicious and hostile as well. They feared that the Federal Republic might deviate from America's side—but at the time I thought America was in danger of deviating from itself.

Brandt then had both formidable opponents and supporters. Among the latter, perhaps none was more authoritative than Marion Dönhoff, who in articles and speeches hailed his new policy. Having early on insisted that reconciliation with Poland was a primary goal as part of a policy of détente and that it required German renunciation of the eastern territories, she had put her feelings about this in a serene, magnanimous formulation years before: "I do not believe that hating those who have taken over one's homeland necessarily demonstrates love for the homeland. When I remember the woods and lakes of East Prussia, its wide meadows and old shaded avenues, I am convinced that they are still as incomparably lovely as they were when they were my home. Perhaps the highest form of love is loving without possessing."

In October 1971, Marion Dönhoff received the Peace Prize of the German Book Trade and used this highly public affair to hail what had been accomplished in the recent treaties. She didn't think it was the beginning of a new era, but rather the end of an old sterile period when both sides had clung to the maxim "all or nothing." She was a vociferous supporter of détente, accepting only in part the view expressed by Kissinger, her friend, that "détente is the mitigation of conflict between adversaries, not the cultivation of friendship." She went further, hoping for a gradual amelioration of the adversarial atmosphere; she reached out for understanding and friendship across borders and despite ideological enmity.

The most painstaking negotiations among the four ex-Allies, prodded by Brandt's team, led finally, in June 1972, to a four-power agreement about Berlin, with both sides registering some gain. West Berlin was recognized as not being part of the Federal Republic, but West Berliners could carry West German passports. All parties understood that this new agreement eliminated Berlin as a constant flashpoint of violent crisis.

In November 1972, Brandt's coalition scored a resounding electoral victory, and in December, the two Germanys signed a basic treaty by which each renounced the use of force in their relations, recognized the borders as inviolable, and recognized the other's independence. This freed the way for both countries to become members of the United Nations and committed East Germany to respect human rights as defined by the UN Charter. But it fell short of granting East Germany full diplomatic recognition: from now on, there would be "permanent missions" in East Berlin and Bonn, not regular embassies. Travel restrictions between the two Germanys were eased, and life generally became better for Germans on both sides of the wall. That had been Brandt's central goal.

The CDU and its allies kept up their polemical resistance, however. They charged Brandt with betraying national interests, with having slighted the hope for reunification. Still, the several treaties were ratified, with the CDU abstaining from the votes. But the anti-Brandt campaign had its impact. In January 1972 he agreed to a decree [*Radikalenerlass*] that banned radicals (or members of groups defined as subversive) from civil service jobs. By long tradition, many different types of jobs qualified as being within the civil service, so the measure affected millions of people. Brandt thought he was reassuring his critics, who often spoke of the way the enemies of Weimar had abused democratic rights, but there were well-meaning, also tendentious protests all over the world against this new German "authoritarianism." That decree was an invitation to deliberate misunderstanding, and for some people it overshadowed Brandt's successes and revived anti-German feelings on the left. Brandt himself came to think it had been a cardinal mistake.

Much of the outside world had a very different view when, in December 1970, Brandt received the highest accolade, the Nobel Peace Prize. The former exile returned to Oslo as European statesman, where he spoke eloquently, branding war not as the "ultima ratio" but as the "ultima irratio," and peace as the realpolitik of our time.

Brandt was the third German to receive the Nobel Peace Prize. Gustav Stresemann, Weimar's bridge-builder to France, had been the first (together with Aristide Briand); the pacifist publicist Carl von Ossietzky the second, selected in 1935 while incarcerated in a Nazi concentration camp (Brandt had campaigned for him to get the prize); and now Brandt. For all three, it can be said that they received honors abroad and venom at home: an unhappy comment on the blind vileness of self-proclaimed patriots.

Ostpolitik and the effects of détente were and are much debated. A decade later, as we shall see, I violently objected to subordinating the defense of human rights to the presumed defense of détente, but I doubt that *Ostpolitik* foreordained that later position. In any case, in the spring of 1971, I wrote, "the Brandt government—measured by its collective intelligence and political good will—may be the best government Germany has ever had," and I would let that early judgment stand.

AT HOME there was no peace. President Nixon had promised a gradual "Vietnamization" of the war and an attendant withdrawal of American troops, but the country remained in a state of attenuated anxiety. The president was driven by paranoia, suspicious of all critics, thinking of them as pseudo-Communists or liberal weaklings, perhaps even as potential traitors who should be under surveillance. Paranoia in power puts everyone on edge. And whatever momentary calm had set in Nixon shattered on April 30, 1971, when in a particularly mawkish speech, he announced that American forces had invaded Cambodia, a country hitherto spared American troops. For many citizens, this seemed a devastating violation of his promises, and rekindled an antiwar fury that swept much of the country and almost all campuses. On that day, I noted in my diary, "this is the beginning of a real constitutional crisis." The nation was divided as it hadn't been since the battles between isolationists and interventionists before Pearl Harbor.

I appealed to friends to register our protest: on May 6, a group of historians, including Felix Gilbert, C. Vann Woodward, Gordon Wright, Hofstadter, Leuchtenburg, and I, sent a long letter to *The New York Times* (in those days the paper published a few long, substantive letters every day instead of today's custom of snippets by many). We referred to the president's action as "a disastrous and indefensible re-escalation of the war . . . a catastrophic reversal of American policy since 1968, and we condemn his reckless disregard of the effects of his futile policies abroad on the fabric of our life at home." We appealed to like-minded citizens to express their condemnation: "The hour is late and the country's danger great." Our efforts may have had no or only minimal effects, but that they were appeals to public opinion does matter in a democracy. At the time, I was hoping for the establishment of a bipartisan committee of moderates, led ideally by former NATO commander General Lauris Norstad, that could present a strong case for the United States' withdrawal from Indochina.

I made my private protest to Kissinger. He and I had met in the 1960s and he had repeatedly asked me to talk at his international seminar at Harvard. We were cordial colleagues. I suspected that a very favorable review I had written in 1958 of his book on Metternich, Castlereagh, and the Congress of Vienna had left a pleasant taste. I admired his intellect, insight, and wit and found his achievement impressive. His relations to Nixon I thought uniquely bizarre and complicated.

I began our conversation about the Cambodian invasion by saying that neither Bismarck nor de Gaulle would have done this, knowing that these statesmen, not Metternich, were Kissinger's real heroes. He alluded to the immense pressure Nixon was under, and spoke of professors from Harvard who had descended on him to protest publicly though many privately assured him of support; this only strengthened his contempt for liberal academics. He said he appreciated my private visit and had heard of my fears about the domestic consequences of Nixon's policies. As I left, still criticizing Nixon, he said something amazing. "Don't forget," he said, "he is not my president." I suppose this was a reference to his earlier allegiance to Nixon's foe, Governor Nelson Rockefeller. What sublime disloyalty!

Few universities were spared upheavals and disruptions in these years, and I joined some of the international groups that tried to bring order to the campuses, but I was dismayed to find that many a liberal scholar or critic had turned authoritarian. Even the most remote places felt the tremors of passionate conflict—including the newly founded university at Konstanz, on Lake Konstanz. Established in the early 1960s by Kurt Kiesinger, then CDU minister-president of Baden-Württemberg, with Dahrendorf and his colleague Waldemar Besson as its intellectual fathers, the school was originally intended to be a small reform university (without the traditional faculties of law and medicine) that would emphasize interdisciplinary work. In the slogan of the day, small was beautiful, and the university's size, location, and character gave Konstanz a good chance at excellence. One innovation was the recruitment of "permanent visiting professors" from abroad, who would teach there for at least one semester every three years. In 1966, I had received such an appointment and accepted this wonderfully oxymoronic position: permanently temporary. Columbia had reluctantly agreed, knowing that I would put it first, and indeed I did not take up the Konstanz arrangements for years. Still, the prospect of working with two much-admired colleagues pleased me, as did having a potential base in Europe, only a stone's throw from Switzerland.

In May 1971, I went to Konstanz for the first time and then only for a little more than a month. Peggy and I were put up in cramped quarters in a fake castle on the shores of the lake that was owned and occupied by the bizarre widow of Wilhelm von Scholz, a Germanic poet whose memory she fiercely promoted. In the garden was a bench marked THE POET'S BENCH, and once, by design or accident, I sat on it, to her dismay, for doing so seemed sacrilege.

By now Dahrendorf was Walter Scheel's state secretary in the Foreign Ministry, so my closest associate at the university was Waldemar Besson, a political scientist trained as a historian. A dynamic, massive figure, Besson was energetic, quick-witted, brilliant, wonderfully provocative, and unintimidable. He belonged to that generation of German scholars, born in the 1920s, who by prodigious productivity seemed determined to make up for the flawed or missing work of the preceding generation. Besson impressed me as a Burkean liberal, an all-too-rare synthesis of liberal temperament and conservative principles. He was a vigorous opponent of intolerant student radicalism, of which even in Konstanz there was a noisy representation. (One day Besson received a large package addressed to "the fat reactionary pig"; he didn't open it.) Fiercely dedicated to German freedom at home, he stood for prudent realpolitik abroad.

On an early June day, he and I wandered along the lakeshore ruminating about prospects for the country, the world—and ourselves. With characteristic gusto he urged me to buy a house by the lake—still affordable at the time—and to think of Konstanz as a semipermanent base. It was an enticing prospect. Two days later, he suffered a kidney stone attack; writhing in pain, he was asked if he was allergic to penicillin and he mumbled an uncertain answer. He was given a penicillin shot as a routine precaution, and within hours he was dead. It was a private loss to me and a great loss to public life in the Federal Republic.

The rector of Konstanz asked me to give the first Besson memorial lecture, which I called "Toward a New German Past," an allusion to Besson's planned history of modern Germany. (This was, oddly, my first extended piece written in German, and I didn't find it easy to compose. Still it was somehow appealing to do so; my German had an American, slightly freer, perhaps mischievous tone.) I argued that German history could not forever be seen exclusively from the perspective of 1933 or 1945, and warned that to think of National Socialism as the culmination of German history would be wrong and would be to accept Nazism's triumphalism. What was needed was a European or comparative approach to the German past: the National Socialist period should be studied in the context of Europe's Second Thirty Years' War. The question "Why Hitler in Germany?" should be supplemented by "Why Hitler in the Western world?" The ambiguities of people's accommodation to totalitarianism should be studied, for temptations existed everywhere, as did political vulnerability, human cowardice, insecurity, treason, and inhumanity. I pleaded that attention be paid to the symbols and rhetoric of the past, that we examine rationally the place of the irrational in political life.

The lecture was well received—I noted in my diary that Dahrendorf called it "magnificent" (grossartig), an encouragement that meant much at the time. When it was published in pamphlet form in 1972, I sent a copy to the Countess, as I sent her all my subsequent writings; she became one of a handful of people I wrote for, and her response mattered. Writers need a few master readers. I suppose she offered further incentive for me to write for a general audience.

My stay in Konstanz was a peaceful prelude to an intense involvement with the West German educational system. The Organisation for Economic Co-operation and Development (OECD)—a very effective body and a legacy of the Marshall Plan, composed of twenty-three "advanced" industrial countries and designed to promote policies for economic growth and rising living standards—asked me to join four other "experts" to review German educational practices, covering everything from preschool to university. The commissioning of such reports—which included recommendations for reforms—in member countries was one of the OECD's principal and most highly valued tasks. To select the Federal Republic at that moment may have been an administrative coinci-dence, but it came at a time when education was a burning issue there, in the context of university disturbances but also in light of Brandt's initiatives for more democracy.

I was intrigued; abstract debates about education always bored me, but the fate of universities amid an unprecedented onslaught had become an absorb-ing interest. I accepted the OECD invitation, yielding again to a reasonable temptation at the expense of exclusive concentration on my scholarly work. Writing a big book is one long exercise in delayed gratification, and I may of-ten have made a wrong choice—or, more likely, have assumed that I could do all sorts of things simultaneously, thus unconsciously opting for a life on the run, at the cost of reflection and learning. Nietzsche's warning has always been an uneasy companion: "All of you to whom furious work is dear, and whatever is fast, new, and strange—you find it hard to bear yourselves; your industry is es-cape and the will to forget yourselves. If you believed more in life you would fling yourselves less to the moment. But you do not have content enough in yourselves for waiting—and not even for idleness."

It was a motley group, our team of examiners: Our chairman was Alain Peyrefitte, an austere and remote person. A prominent Gaullist and former min-ister of education, he was a prolific author, our most distinguished and—in mat-ters German—our least knowledgeable member. Jack Embling was deputy secretary in England's Department of Education and Science, a quintessential civil servant, unflappable, skeptical, wisely inquisitive. The Swede Torsten Husén, a veteran of OECD reports, and Harold Noah, from Columbia's Teach-ers College, were professional "educationists." I was to concentrate on university conditions. We were sent massive amounts of background material, heaps of recent reports that various bodies had prepared, and then, in the summer of 1971, began a minutely planned tour of six West German cities where we discussed education with all sorts of people, from ministers to teachers and students. I would sometimes escape from the official meetings to have my own informal interviews—fugitive moments that were often the most enlightening for me.

By tradition and according to Bonn's Basic Law, education was the responsibility of each individual *Land,* though the government was then sponsoring plans for greater federal coordination. Dahrendorf, in his influential 1965 book on educational deficiencies in the Federal Republic, had been provocatively right: lamentably little "modernization" had occurred in Germany's educational system, no realization of Allied hopes for "democratization." German professionals hunkered down in "pedagogical defeatism" and resisted reforms.

As we flew into West Berlin, I remarked to Peyrefitte that our primary focus here should be on the Free University; he agreed, assuming the name meant that students paid no tuition, though that was (and to a large extent still is) true of all German universities. On our arrival, a university administrator I knew well gave me a confidential letter telling me that our appointments with independent people, including the ex-rector Hans von Kress, had been sabotaged. Instead, a meeting had been arranged with the Free University's vice president, Uwe Wesel, a law professor with strong left-wing sympathies who tried to reassure us that the university was in good order. He was standing in for the thirty-year-old rector Rolf Kreibich, a left-wing Social Democrat who was sympathetic to the students. According to a new university law, the rector had to be elected by all members of the university, and Kreibich had won against a former rector and senior law professor, so he was a first in German university administration. The older senior faculty and most Berlin politicians had been dismayed.

An OECD adviser who was with us, Barry Hayward, and I sneaked out of a meeting with Helmuth Becker, head of the Max Planck Institute for Education and Human Development, who was giving a complacent account of life at the Free University, and set off for a prearranged visit with Günter Grass, at his wonderfully uncluttered, spacious home in an old Berlin house, where the talk was free and healthily critical of all protagonists. Hayward was thrilled with Grass's friendly iconoclasm. I had met Grass, my contemporary, on previous occasions (once at a family dinner at which he prepared wild boar); I admired him greatly, both for his two masterpieces, *The Tin Drum* and *Dog Years*— novels that restored the beauty and power of German prose after the Nazi corruption of the language—and for his political involvement, including his work for Brandt's election campaign in 1969. (We saw each other later as well, but our contact waned in the 1980s, as his strident and unoriginal anti-Americanism waxed.)

My confidant at the Free University, who warned that our group was being fed official pap, organized a secret meeting at a private home. I took Embling along to that meeting, which had the atmosphere of an underground session of resisters. Some of the university's best-known professors, many of them with impeccable liberal credentials, including Otto von Simson, art historian and a one-time refugee from Nazism, drew a despairing picture of pervasive ideological terror and hatred all but destroying the possibility of regular instruction. Each had his own episode of outrage to recount. I'll never forget Embling's comment going home in the cab: he hadn't believed my earlier accounts of turmoil, but now he understood. He mumbled, "I say, *hatred*! What an extraordinary word to use in a university!"

In Frankfurt I talked with Jürgen Habermas, followed by dinner at his home with his wife, a remarkable woman of great warmth. I thought him a model for reformers: he had been sympathetic to the students' early demands, understood the need for thoroughgoing reform, but rejected all forms of violence. However radical his ideas about reforming the universities, his parting words were all the more moving: "In some way our heart still belongs to the old university." Our hope was to salvage as much of it as we could and make it viable in a changed society.

By fall our report was done, communicated to OECD and to two appointed German "respondents," with whom we were to have the customary "confrontation meeting" in Paris in November. The two were my friend Bernhard Vogel, by then CDU minister of education in the Rhineland-Palatinate, and Hildegard Hamm-Brücher, state secretary in the Federal Ministry of Education and Science, a leading and truly liberal member of the Free Democratic Party.

Our report emphasized the imbalance between West Germany's startling economic progress, the much-touted *Wirtschaftswunder*, and its educational backwardness. Inequalities in the old German system persisted: discrimination against working-class children, women, Catholics. Some 90 percent of children had no hope of getting near any university, matriculation to which was appallingly slanted in favor of the propertied and educated classes. In this we were supporting what Dahrendorf and others had already established, and we could add comparative material: other OECD countries were far less discriminatory.

The report's short section on universities, which I helped to write, stressed that the old system, in which full professors had almost complete power over

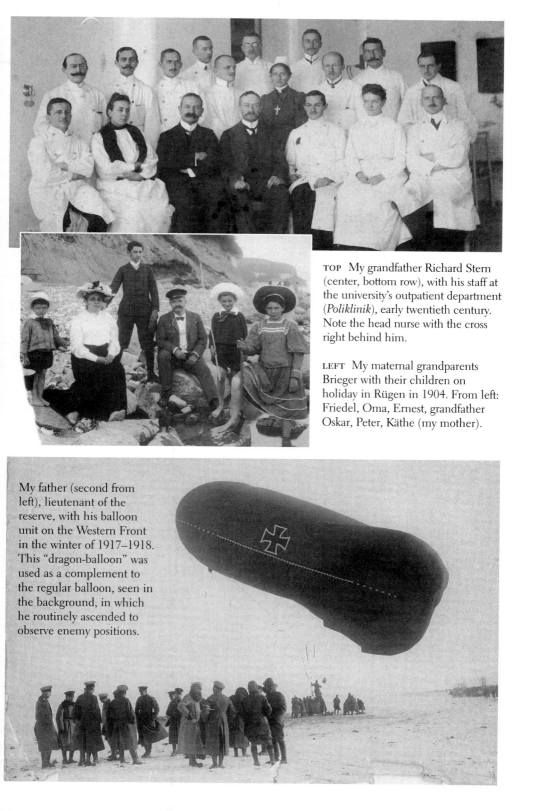

TOP My grandfather Richard Stern (center, bottom row), with his staff at the university's outpatient department (*Poliklinik*), early twentieth century. Note the head nurse with the cross right behind him.

LEFT My maternal grandparents Brieger with their children on holiday in Rügen in 1904. From left: Friedel, Oma, Ernest, grandfather Oskar, Peter, Käthe (my mother).

My father (second from left), lieutenant of the reserve, with his balloon unit on the Western Front in the winter of 1917–1918. This "dragon-balloon" was used as a complement to the regular balloon, seen in the background, in which he routinely ascended to observe enemy positions.

RIGHT The wedding party, in 1917, of my father's older sister, Lotte, and Richard Kobrak. On the staircase of my grandfather's villa, Richard (with a cape over his uniform) and Lotte at center; immediately behind Richard, Käthe Brieger and, on her left, Rudolf Stern; on the extreme left, Hans and Gustav Neisser.

ABOVE LEFT A portrait of Fritz Haber by Emil Orlik, with Haber's inscription to my father in 1926. His dedicatory verse: "If you want to give every day / Its proper meaning / You must strive contentedly / And, in striving, find contentment."

ABOVE RIGHT My parents, my sister, Toni, and me at Fritz Haber's country estate in Witzmanns (Württemberg), near the Lake of Constance, in July 1928.

HOLLAND-AMERICA LINE

T.S.S. STATENDAM. 28291 Tons Register — 38950 Tons Displacement.

RIGHT My postcard of the SS *Statendam* where I marked the location of our deckchairs with an X. I wrote on the back, "The boat which as emigrants brought us from Rotterdam to the USA! (9X 1938) Arrived in Hoboken."

ABOVE Allen Ginsberg (standing) and Columbia classmates. From left to right: FS, Arthur Lazarus, Victor Tejera, and a friend.
(Courtesy of the Allen Ginsberg Trust)

LEFT Leaving Berlin in 1954 on the military train: my first wife, Peggy, and Herr Hartwich from the Free University, with my children, Fred and Katherine.

The great controversy about Fritz Fischer's book on German war aims, 1914–1918. *Der Spiegel* published the speech I gave at the meeting of the German Historical Association in October 1964. "U.S. Historian" is second from left, Fritz Fischer on the right.

ABOVE During the crisis at Columbia, the "Stern gang" goes public at a press conference in March 1969. From left: Lionel Trilling, Charles Frankel, FS, Richard Hofstadter, Jack Beeson.

RIGHT Friends in Aspen, Colorado, in the late 1970s: FS, Nibby Bullock and her husband, Alan Bullock, with Marion Dönhoff.

RIGHT FS with Czesław Ostańkowicz, a former officer living in what had been my grandmother's villa. Wrocław, 1979.

LEFT Lev Kopelev at Anna Akhmatova's grave, 1979.

BELOW Addressing the German Bundestag, June 17, 1987. Note on the upper left, on the government bench, Foreign Minister Hans-Dietrich Genscher and next to him Chancellor Helmut Kohl. (Courtesy of the German government press office)

August 1987, with Pope John Paul II and Cardinal König, a key champion of the Pope's election.

ABOVE Willy Brandt at Columbia, 1987.

RIGHT Liberalism defended: our *New York Times* ad, October 26, 1988.

ABOVE At the U.S. embassy in Bonn in 1993, with Henry Kissinger and Ambassador Richard Holbrooke.

LEFT My wife, Elisabeth Sifton, and Marion Dönhoff at the German Historical Institute in Washington, D.C., 1996.

RIGHT Bronisław Geremek and me after I was awarded the Peace Prize of the German Book Trade, June 1999.

BELOW With Ralf Dahrendorf on the same occasion. (Courtesy of Martin Joppen Photographie)

LEFT My children, with their spouses and children, at home in Europe (Burgundy), 1998.

RIGHT Introducing my grandchildren (Laura and Philip Brennan, and Michael Stern) to Sils in 1996.

BELOW Receiving an honorary degree at Wrocław University, 2002, in its resplendent baroque auditorium, the Leopoldina, where my parents had received their doctoral degrees some ninety years before!

university policy and, worse, control over the lives of junior colleagues, assistants, and students, was anachronistic and unacceptable. As a government official said to me, this was *"unser grösstes Sorgenkind"* (our biggest problemchild). Reform of admission policies and of governance were imperative. We listed specific reforms, but warned against "pedagogic utopianism," and we noted that in some places "university life has come close to complete disruption," since radical groups, ironically authoritarian, were trying to "transform universities into training grounds for a . . . revolutionary type of society." The students' justified demands for better instruction should not lead to neglect of research; moving the latter to nonuniversity institutes—such as the steadily increasing number of Max Planck Institutes—was injurious. We recommended that an independent commission "composed of men and women from all walks of life *except* from the universities themselves" prepare a report that could be the basis for actual reform.

At "the confrontation meeting" in the handsome Palais Chaillot, in Paris, all very formal, our two German respondents were joined by some thirty experts from other OECD countries. I am not sure what benefits the Federal Republic derived from our report in the end, which was attacked and defended in the Bundestag, then probably lost in a sea of pedagogic memoranda. But education remained a persistent problem in Germany, often a political football as well. When in 2002, the OECD published the results of a PISA (Program for International Student Assessment) study, based on tests involving 265,000 high school students in thirty-two countries, Finland did best in reading literacy, Japan and Korea in mathematics and science—and Germany ranked *below* the OECD average. This caused much public soul-searching; *Bildung* was a major issue in the election campaign of 2002; recently, SPD ministers—of all people!—called for the creation of "elite universities," and private universities have made their first appearance. As so often in Germany, recriminations rather than reforms ruled the day.

The benefits of our efforts may have been modest, but I learned a great deal, I met some impressive officials, Peyrefitte and I continued to see each other and to exchange books, and Vogel and Hamm-Brücher became friends and remain so to this day: two champions of the liberal spirit, two politicians with the strongest moral concern for not forgetting the horrors of the past.

In my dismay at the violent strain among West German students at that time, I may have thought too little about what provoked them: the rigidity of academic structures and the entrenched self-interest of the privileged, authoritarian professoriate. And what we didn't yet know was the appalling continuity with Nazi times: the universities were full of men old enough to have been teaching in the Nazi period, and younger ones who had served the regime in such egregious fields as racial "research" and population resettlement plans. Only in the late 1990s, for example, was the entanglement of various prominent historians with Nazism uncovered. The students of these professors, some of whom became liberal historians in the next generation, had not been asking their *Doktorväter*, "And what did you do in the Third Reich?" The elders didn't talk, and most of the young didn't dare ask—yet another instance of my contention that the mood of the twentieth century can be summed up in the phrase "They didn't want to know."

CAUGHT AS I MAY HAVE BEEN between present and past, teaching and the unfinished book on Bismarck and Bleichröder kept me moored to the past. Most summers, I worked away on the book at our house in Vermont, where I withdrew to a study built into the corner of an old cow barn. I remember at some point abruptly ending a letter to my son, explaining, "I have to go back to my cell and finish my sentence." As so often, the true or in this case the double meaning of a remark became clear to me only later. But an unfinished book does feel like a sentence—term undetermined.* It was usually a very busy time in Vermont, often with my mother in residence; Katherine mastering horses by day and minding her grandmother by night: the beginnings of an ideal pedadogue!

For years I had scoured archives and read the secondary literature, and I had drafted many chapters. I had lost my instigator-collaborator—David Landes had to abandon Bleichröder for other tasks—and I was working alone. Most of the pieces had been assembled, but the edifice had yet to be constructed. I needed uninterrupted time, preferably away from Columbia but with good library facilities and some clerical help—and once again chance and luck aided me. In 1972–1973 the newly established Netherlands Institute for Advanced Study (NIAS) offered me a fellowship.

Just getting to Holland was a joy: we could still indulge in the grand pleasures of a transatlantic voyage, preferably on a French ship, days of life on the sea, with the ever-changing color and motion of the ocean, an existence si-

---

*In July 1975, George Kennan, whose draft manuscript on the Franco-Russian alliance I had just read and commented on, thanked me, and he seemed to understand the mood I was in: "history is a lonely business . . . and such words give me heart to complete the work . . . I have worked, since I saw you, both in the Public Records Office and in the Slavonic Collection of the Helsinki University Library—low grade ore, in both cases, but not wholly devoid of metal."

multaneously dreamy and cosseted. Our age, with its ever-greater speed, has had to jettison many of the old comforts.

NIAS is housed in a converted police barracks in a prosperous northwestern suburb of The Hague, within walking distance of the dunes and beaches of the North Sea. It was a haven for scholars from many countries and disciplines: truly interdisciplinary by human sympathy and intellectual curiosity, not by prescription. That year, a British economist, several Dutch political scientists, and a Norwegian linguist, Ragnar Rommetveit—who introduced me to Kierkegaard's aphorism that "life is lived forward but understood backward"—were among my colleagues. For some of the time the witty, wise Shmuel Eisenstadt, a cosmopolitan sociologist with a base in Israel, and his generous wife were also there. I became very fond of the Netherlands, a truly tolerant country—so small, so rich in genius, with such an amazing history. I thought to myself, if I could do it over again, I would specialize in Dutch history.

There was hardly an evening discussion without some poignant story of the war years, still so close. The woman who in effect ran NIAS, Els Glastra van Loon, had been a major figure in the Dutch underground; I noticed that she, like many people who had behaved admirably and at great risk during the war, made very little of her engagement, saying that the initial step was an immediate impulse born of a sense that one couldn't do anything else. Subsequent commitment to the various forms of resistance required deliberate, secretive planning and plotting. There will never be a full count of the many unknown men and women like her who behaved with what I call "active decency," and yet their story is part of Europe's catastrophic decline during German dominance—and should be honored.

I met a Dutch psychoanalyst, David de Levita, who as a Jewish child had been hidden by a Dutch farming family whose son had joined the Waffen SS. These are the wartime complexities too often simplified and trivialized. He had written a book on identity, inspired by Erik Erikson—a theme then far from faddish, and suggestive for my understanding of Bleichröder—and later he specialized in treating children of survivors, "second-generation victims" traumatized by the experiences of their parents. He and his wife have remained good friends; we often talk about the most puzzling aspects of uprootedness, a common affliction of our times.

My stay at NIAS coincided with a collection of my essays being published by Alfred A. Knopf, for whom I had been scouting European books for about a decade, *The Failure of Illiberalism: Essays on the Political Culture of Modern Germany*. I acknowledged my preference for the tentative tone of the essay, and expounded on my view that "moods, feelings, and ideas do change the world. How they change the world, and in combination with what other circumstances and interests, is a central . . . subject for the historian." Illiberalism was a state of mind common to all peoples and individuals at moments of sudden danger, but, I wrote, "German society, far from keeping down the illiberal impulse, fostered and formed it into a habitual response . . . the upper classes, frozen in fear and cramped in their egoism, did not seize possibilities of reform and collaboration. Instead of building bridges, they built moats." The deepening internal conflicts helped to shape Germany's truculent, autistic foreign policy, and contributed decisively to the final descent into the Great War.

I also contended that the lessons of the German past had special relevance to the United States, engulfed in both war and domestic conflict and violence. I objected to the way supporters of the Vietnam War vilified its critics by referring to Munich and appeasers and, at the opposite end of the political spectrum, the equally facile, false analogies made to fascists or Gestapo in order to vilify governments and universities. America once thought itself the savior of the West; its detractors now thought it "the terror of that world . . . As [America] staggers onto a path of power and responsibility from which no nation has returned unharmed, and does so under conditions more precarious and more decisive than any other nation ever faced, her greatest asset may be her liberal tradition, however imperfectly embodied and however often challenged."

Two essays in the book were preliminary sketches for the work on Bismarck and Bleichröder. In my effort to capture the spirit of their times, I had been turning to novels and plays; I began one essay with Ibsen's *Pillars of Society*, published in 1877, a radical depiction of the moral pretensions and actual crimes of capitalist society, which I saw as a dramatic commentary on the *Communist Manifesto*, without the comforting hope that a social revolution would create a new man in a newly virtuous society. In a second essay I argued that the rapid triumph of industrial capitalism had wrought even greater changes in German society than national unification in 1871. I linked the sudden outburst of virulent anti-Semitism in the 1870s to the great depression of that decade, which had brought to light pervasive corruption in which individual Jews were implicated. Hence an attack on Jewish greed and power served as an alibi for German infractions—the attack could appear as an avowal of German idealism. I was trying to emphasize that anti-Semitism could suddenly become an alluring assertion of German or individual innocence. "All of this is hard to document and easy to exaggerate, but the paranoid underworld of politics in an age of affluence and cultural unease cannot be overlooked."

Four responses to my book were especially important to me. Geoffrey Barraclough, an English historian of medieval Europe, rightly saw me on the side of the younger German historians such as Wehler and Kocka, but wrongly and ironically pitted me against one of my mentors, Hajo Holborn, whom he incorrectly considered a prime representative of the complacently liberal older school. He was only half right, for my premise was defiantly liberal. Martin Jay, a distinguished American historian of German thought, noted that in fastening on illiberalism in Germany, I hadn't paid enough attention to the shortcomings of liberalism.

But the words that meant the most to me came in a letter from a master historian and close friend of Hofstadter, C. Vann Woodward. The tiresome nature of academic specialization being what it is, I met and worked with scholars of American history all too infrequently, so Woodward's letter was unexpected, embarrassingly kind, and reassuring: "So far I have read only the introduction, but it tells me that I have much to learn from you about the historian's personal involvement in the history he is writing, about the keenness of insight that involvement can inspire, and the profound understanding and sympathy it can awaken. It is a beautiful and moving statement." At a later time, Woodward and I came to collaborate in an effort to defend American liberalism against its high-placed, powerful enemies.

His generous remark didn't fully sink in: I don't think I was aware of my "personal involvement"—and yet, of course, there was a connection between my book in progress on the Jewish banker and the German chancellor—so painstakingly amassed from so many fragments—and my own life. The third part of my unfinished book was called "The Anguish of Assimilation." But the work was also a tutor to me, and it helped me understand my own world, and deepened concerns that had been there from the start. It was also teaching me something about the centrality of economic power, of material power generally.

NIAS gave me a chance to finish a first draft of the Bleichröder book— almost. But worries about American conditions intruded. True, Nixon was winding down the Vietnam War, even as the shadow of Watergate fell on his administration, for by that spring, suspicions that Nixon had been involved in a criminal conspiracy were mounting. My Dutch friends were amazed that the American public could be so moralistic, so persnickety as to think of attacking, let alone impeaching, a president who had had so many successes in foreign policy, as in his dramatic "opening" of China. Europeans thought us naïve moralists—didn't politics always have a blemished underside? Cynically, they misjudged Nixon's self-destructive paranoid streak and underestimated the respect that most Americans have for constitutional probity.

But the personal shocks were the deepest. The year at NIAS was overshadowed by private grief, for in the early fall, Henry Roberts died of pancreatic cancer. I flew back and spoke at his funeral in the village church in Vermont. A few months later, my mother had a stroke, and again I returned to America, days before her death. It felt as if the losses were coming all at once: first Hofstadter and then Roberts, my first two anchors to America, and now my mother, so fully adapted to her new country because so firmly rooted in the memory of the old one. To lose one's closest friends when they themselves were young was wrenching desolation. But how immensely fortunate I had been to have them! For my family these were terrible losses as well, and their support was life-sustaining.

Still in thrall to medical lore—I suppose an inheritance from my overly anxious father—I became worried about threats to my own health. From Holland, I went to see my friend the London psychoanalyst John Bowlby, seeking solace and wisdom. In his home in Hampstead, he took me into his somber study and tried to help me understand that the death of a parent or a friend caused more than psychological anguish. It represented a physical onslaught as well; it affected the body as if a leg or arm had been cut off. Like all great truths, this was a simple, profound one. In later life, I had occasion to pass on Bowlby's wisdom to mourning family and friends. After many months, my grief allowed for grateful memory.

My stay at NIAS allowed me to travel often to the Federal Republic; in March 1973, I first visited Marion Dönhoff's home in Blankenese, a prosperous suburb of Hamburg, a quiet place of villas and woods quite close to the mouth of the River Elbe, where ships passed to and from one of Europe's busiest ports.

On the ground floor of her small house was a single large room, at once study, living and dining room. On its walls hung a beautiful Gobelin tapestry, one of the few treasures from her past, and landscapes of Kirchner, Nolde, and Corinth together with a panoply of paintings by Hundertwasser. She had her books here—the classics and the contemporary works—her records, her somewhat disordered papers, and, centered in the middle of the room in front of a large window facing the garden, her desk, with photos of Friedrichstein and of Heinrich von Lehndorff, her favorite cousin, who had been killed in action on the eastern front. At that desk, pencil in hand, she wrote her columns and books in her limpid, well-argued prose. It seemed to me a perfect, timeless room, exuding her pleasure in unobtrusive beauty, her sense that work and life are one.

We talked and talked—we never finished talking—of politics and history, of friends and wrongheaded people, of public matters and, at times, of private ones. We talked of plans for the future and memories of the past. We would walk her dachshund, the one creature she allowed, perhaps even encouraged, to be naughty and ill-trained; perhaps he expressed a defiance that she suppressed in herself and disliked in others. She thought "accidents" had done much to shape her life, and she assumed this was a universal experience. She delighted in recalling the story of how she had once asked Kissinger and me what would have happened to us absent Hitler. Henry said he would have become a high school teacher in Fürth, his native town; I said I would have become a physician in Breslau. Yet none of us, the Countess included, asked what would have happened to her without Hitler. Would her brothers have taken charge of Friedrichstein? Would she have stayed there, or would she have gone to a city and become a great journalist, a moral authority, and an aristocratic champion of democracy? All our lives are full of accidental, unexpected turns.

She knew about accidents of the serious kind and thought that she had a *Schutzengel*, a guardian angel, who protected her. She certainly had an offhandedness in dealing with illness: once, when she was plagued by an unyielding cough, I asked if she had seen a doctor, and she replied, "Of course not, I don't believe in them." Well, did she have a fever? "I don't even have a thermometer . . . Illness is for hypochondriacs," she said.

Over the next three decades, I stayed countless times in her home, relishing her friends, who gradually became mine as well, relishing her unostentatious old culture, and her inquiring mind about the new and the young. After a very few years, she suggested that we move to a first-name basis. And then, I believe some twenty years after we met, she proposed the *du*, the intimate address, initiation of which, by German custom, involves a complicated gesture, interlocking arms, with each person holding a glass for a silent clinking before the celebratory drink. But then clinking of glasses with modest amounts of champagne or wine had become settled routine at our meetings—in Hamburg, in New York, in Sils Maria, at many meetings on both sides of the Atlantic. I met her extended family, beginning with her favorite nephew, Hermann Count Hatzfeldt, heir to a grand castle and wooded estate in Westphalia. But the best times were in the formal informality of her home. If there was one place in Germany that felt like home again for me, it was in her house and in her company, in everything she said and didn't say. My friendship with the Countess was also "a new beginning."

When I say I have great faith in friendship—a gift of life that I learned about as a child and that has immeasurably enriched my life—I don't mean I adhere to the effusive, specifically German cult of friendship. But I do cherish the quiet sense of trust and affective closeness with certain men and women, ties that spring from immediate delight at first encounters but that deepen over time and deserve special solicitude and celebration. Friendship makes one stronger—and also more vulnerable: a loss by death or, rarely, by rupture is hard.

My European friendships blossomed, not just in Europe but also in the United States. After my mother's death and a small inheritance, Peggy and I bought a house in Princeton to spend weekends in—it was reachable by public transport and close to the Institute for Advanced Study, where my friend and mentor Felix Gilbert was a permanent member. Felix—named after his ancestor Felix Mendelssohn Bartholdy—had been a student of Friedrich Meinecke's in Berlin; he had left Germany in 1933 and eventually come to the United States, where, after serving in the Central European section of the OSS during the war, he came to be recognized as a preeminent historian, a Renaissance scholar both literally and metaphorically, a man of the shrewdest psychological and political acuity. Felix was a talent scout par excellence, helping in the institute's selection of foreign scholars for year-long fellowships. So it was in Princeton that I came to know well some wonderful Europeans: Jürgen Kocka (whose wife came from Breslau), Karl-Dietrich Bracher and his wife, the Thomas Nipperdeys, and the remarkable historian twins Hans and Wolfgang Mommsen. I already knew the astoundingly prolific Hans-Ulrich Wehler and Rudolf von Albertini, a Swiss historian who lived in an ancient family castle near Chur and taught in Zurich. With all these ties and my native inclinations, Europe was gradually becoming a second home.

In retrospect, I see that I had a predisposition for being an "engaged observer" (a phrase that Raymond Aron used for himself), but that tendency did not fully develop until that year in Holland. I understand Woodward's response to my book of essays more clearly now than I did then. As Barthold Niebuhr, great scholar-diplomat, wrote in the late 1820s, "When a historian is reviving former times, his interest in them and sympathy with them will be the deeper, the greater the events he has witnessed with a bleeding or rejoicing heart." And Niebuhr acknowledged even deeper influences: "There is an enthusiasm which is engendered by the presence and the association of beloved friends; an immediate influence, whereby the muses appear to us, awakening joy and strength in us and brightening our vision: to this I have all my life owed what was best in me."

The interweaving of professional, political, and personal interests marked my historical work, but also, as I realized increasingly during my year in the Netherlands, my concern about Israel. I had followed the struggle for a Jewish homeland in Palestine for years—certainly since I had met Chaim Weizmann as a boy, and since Palestine had been a remote possibility for my family's emigration. And now, in 1972, my time at NIAS began with the murder by Palestinian terrorists of Israeli athletes at the Olympic games in Munich: a terrifying tragedy. Events in the Middle East continued to absorb me throughout my time there.

I hadn't gone to Israel until 1971, when my friend and one-time student Jay Winter, then teaching in Jerusalem, acted as guide to both the ancient glories and the recent past. He had begun by taking Peggy and me on a walk on our very first night in a moonlit Jerusalem, mysterious and moving. He had shown us the battle sites of the recent wars, and we had visited an early kibbutz; I had always thought that the dream of creating a "new man" and a "new woman" in a primitive, peaceful socialist community was one of the twentieth century's great and partly successful utopias. We learned from him of Israeli excesses and atrocities in 1948, of the mass expulsions of Palestinians (not common knowledge at the time). By what means this "unawareness" of the harsh truths attending the founding of the state of Israel had been achieved remains a pertinent question, especially for those of us concerned about "forgetting"—in some way, Israel's sense of legitimacy depended on the war of 1948 being seen as one exclusively of defense. A complicated sense of identification with Israel grew in me: certainly it wasn't my country; Hebrew wasn't my language; but I felt an affinity for this country of refuge and of hope, of defiance after devastation, feeling like a stranger who partly belonged. Jay took us through the Judean wilderness, awesome in its mysterious desolation, to Masada, a carefully cultivated symbol of Jewish resolve, not intransigence.

The years after Israel's 1967 victory had been marked by a massive revival of an old weapon: terrorism. This was not new in the Middle East or elsewhere: under the British Mandate for Palestine, Jewish underground organizations had resorted to it. But now, though the Israelis clung to a policy of no compromise, ever, with terrorist attacks by Palestinians—to meet terrorist demands was to encourage the effort and capitulate to its logic—terrorism grew anyway, out of fanaticism, out of a sense that only violence, and the deadlier the better, would bring political results. Perhaps not coincidentally, terrorism appeared in Western Europe at the same time.

After I left NIAS in July, work and worry took over. On October 6, 1973, on

Yom Kippur, we heard the radio bulletins: Egypt and Syria, armed by the Soviet Union, had launched a triumphant surprise attack on Israel. In the next few days, Israel was in mortal danger until—with the help of the United States—the threat of defeat turned into yet another, if very costly, Israeli victory. Israeli troops advanced to the gates of Cairo, having trapped a large part of the Egyptian army at the Suez Canal. At the same time, the Arab countries ordered an oil embargo on the United States (and the Netherlands, which had also helped Israel). Finally, the two superpowers forced a cease-fire on the combatants, though Israel was reluctant to give up its uniquely favorable position. The fighting ended on October 28, when General Tal—the Israeli Rommel, as he was called—sat down with his Egyptian counterpart to sign a cease-fire.

The costs of the Yom Kippur War had been tremendous. At the time we believed that the United States was the sole supplier of weapons to endangered Israel, and West Germany had resented the use of its ports—done without consultation and in full daylight—for the transport of this matériel. Kissinger made no bones about his contempt for these European cavils. But we now know that Willy Brandt, in a lone (and possibly unconstitutional) decision, arranged for the instant delivery of a high-tech electronic weapon that the Israeli air force desperately needed. And still the prevailing picture at the time was of a passive Europe denying the United States necessary bases, acquiescing to Arab demands. French foreign minister Michel Jobert said of the Arab attack, "Is it necessarily unforeseen aggression to try to go home?" And the New Left in Europe attacked Israel as being a criminal pawn of the United States. The paths of the United States and its European allies were already diverging when the price of oil quadrupled and "the oil shock" put Europe's recovery and the world economy in jeopardy.

This was clearly a deep, long-term crisis. I thought that the war and its side effects had ended a whole era and ushered in a period of immense danger, the more so since, simultaneously, the United States was being shaken by the ever-widening Watergate scandal: the very height of the Yom Kippur War was concurrent with the "Saturday Night Massacre," when Nixon fired his attorney general for daring to place his constitutional responsibilities above the president's deranged orders, and the country confronted the possibility of a presidential impeachment.

To be a passive observer at such a time of foreboding was painful: I needed to voice my concerns. After a couple of weeks, I drafted an essay, and when it was done, uncertain as always, I looked for a mentor's judgment. I asked Lionel Trilling to read it, and he pronounced it "smashing." Emboldened, I sent it to

Norman Podhoretz, *Commentary*'s editor—and not yet the hawkish neocon-servative he was to become. In April he published "The End of the Postwar Era" as the lead piece—again with unanticipated and, for me, life-changing consequences.

My epigraph for the article was Nietzsche's warning: "A great victory is a great danger. Human nature bears a triumph less easily than a defeat: indeed it might even be urged that it is simpler to gain a victory of this sort than to turn it to such account that it may not ultimately prove a serious rout." This had been his response to the German victory over France in 1870, afraid that Germans would swagger in hubris, as indeed they did. I was afraid that Israel's triumphs might spawn dangerous illusions. We needed to recognize that the era that had begun in 1948–1949, the years of the Marshall Plan and the establishment of Is-rael, NATO, and the Federal Republic—a period that "may well have marked one of the least expected and one of the most promising leaps forward that our civilization has had to record"—was now over. It was imperative that Europe re-alize it had been fighting a rearguard action against its own decline since the be-ginning of the century, certainly since the Great War. West Europeans had come to take for granted the permanence of their economic miracle, just as Is-raelis might mythologize their military miracle, but these presumptions were dangerous. Israel had come into existence after the near-extinction of European Jewry, when Zionist claims appeared morally irresistible.

But now many Europeans were becoming critical of Israel, so much so that it, in turn, was becoming solely dependent on the United States. Meanwhile, Palestinian grievance and belligerence wouldn't go away, for "the Palestinian Arabs who in 1948 became refugees from their country had been made to suf-fer for the crimes of omission and commission that the Europeans had commit-ted against their Jews." Israel was saddled with the burden of anti-Americanism and, in some quarters, a latent suspicion of Jewish power. Western Europe itself was in danger of losing its footing: at odds with the United States, threatened by Arab economic power, it might suffer such socioeconomic strains as to endan-ger political stability. In a phrase that had unexpected resonance, I wrote, "Cap-italism in contraction is as much of a social and political monster as capitalism in expansion tends to be a miracle." At the end of the Great War, Europe had been ready for social democracy as a corrective to the injustices of capitalism, but the Bolsheviks—unwittingly—saved European capitalism "by splitting Eu-ropean labor and by presenting conservatives with a challenge and a convenient and genuine *bête noire*. What Lenin, Trotsky, and Stalin worked and hoped for—the collapse of European capitalism—they in fact helped to prevent. King

Faisal may succeed where Lenin failed—though such a success is the last thing he desires," I concluded, with a touch of historical hyperbole. But as usual I was trying to emphasize the urgency and context of the danger in order to rally a collective defense. I hoped that West Europeans, "in the face of their newly discovered vulnerability," would not "succumb to a 'sulky neutralism,' to a collapse of will, to a 'European Buddhism,' that Nietzsche long ago foresaw as a particularly pernicious form of nihilism."

This cri de coeur voiced as historical-political analysis had an unexpected effect on my life. In April, days after the article had appeared, McGeorge Bundy's office called; he wanted to see me to discuss my piece. I thought of Bundy as a formidable, awesome presence in American life—former dean of arts and sciences at Harvard, President Kennedy's national security adviser, and now president of the Ford Foundation; he was a fiercely intelligent, astoundingly knowledgeable man of wit and self-assurance. He was intimidating in his questioning of me over lunch, which included other Ford Foundation people: David Bell, an economist in charge of development aid; Frank Sutton and Craufurd Goodwin, in charge of European and international affairs; and two program officers from Bell's division. My article sat at the center of the table, and Bundy would from time to time grab it, read a passage, and demand elucidation. Bell asked me, "Does Europe matter?" to which I probably replied with more passion than precision. The atmosphere was a cross between an intense conversation and an oral examination: perhaps that's what an oral examination should be, at once exhilarating and searching. At the end, Bundy called the piece "uncommonly good." Ivo Lederer, a fellow historian and program officer in the Ford Foundation's international affairs division, took me to the elevator, saying, "Mac is really excited by the piece" and if I ever wanted anything from Ford, I should let them know. An intriguing invitation, particularly coming at the moment when I was at last finishing my labors on Bismarck and Bleichröder and already thinking of the next big assignment. I would later follow up on that open-ended invitation, an act that would take me far beyond Germany and add new worlds to my political education.

TWO DECADES AFTER its birth, dramatic changes were shaking the Federal Republic: in May 1974, Brandt suddenly resigned, after one of his chief aides was uncovered as an East German agent who had had access to top-secret documents. The entire affair has remained murky: Why this failure of West German counterintelligence? Had members of Brandt's entourage worked against him?

Brandt stayed on as SPD chairman, but Helmut Schmidt instantly succeeded him as chancellor. Schmidt, a very different type of man, decisive and
energetic, had proven himself in his first political post in Hamburg. In 1953 he
became a Social Democratic deputy in the Bundestag. By virtue of his many
talents, he rose rapidly to the top of the parliamentary party, and under Brandt
held key cabinet posts; quick success did not dampen his supreme self-
confidence. He didn't suffer fools gladly, whether at home or abroad, and
didn't conceal his views when they were harsh. Perceived as a clever realist and
pragmatist, he was in fact a man of many gifts and broad interests—he was an
accomplished pianist—who embodied his faith in the possibility of effective
democratic leadership. A centrist who came to power at a time of a deep recession, with the country trying to cope with the effects of the oil shock, he had
to disappoint his own party by slowing the extension of the welfare state. (In
jest, but with some justification, he was often called the best chancellor the
Christian Democrats had ever had—the jibe was meant to refer to his economic prudence and authoritative style, but it was also an apt comment on the
quality of the two CDU chancellors after Adenauer.)

Schmidt continued Brandt's foreign policy, augmenting it by a special relationship with France and his personal closeness to President Valéry Giscard
d'Estaing; Schmidt has written that friendships among statesmen are a major
element in world politics—and friendship is based on trust. He had such relations also with Gerald Ford—a friendship that continues to this day. Such ties
eased Schmidt's decisive presence on the world stage, as demonstrated when,
in 1975, the Conference on Security and Cooperation in Europe (which included the United States and Canada) concluded its two-year deliberations
with the adoption of the Helsinki Final Act: this would have been unthinkable
without détente and West Germany's *Ostpolitik*. Its balanced recognition of
the principal interests of East and West were as close as Europe came to a final
peace settlement.

The Organization for Security and Co-operation in Europe that now took
the place of the conference (OSCE) adopted three basic agreements, or "bas-
kets": the first a guarantee of the inviolability of European borders, a tacit
recognition of Soviet-imposed changes after 1945; the second a promise of
greater trade facilities, a provision also favoring the Soviets; and the third
a commitment on the part of all signatories to "respect human rights and fundamental freedoms, including the freedom of thought, conscience, religion or
belief" and to promote "the effective exercise" of these rights, including wider
freedom of travel. This third "basket" established a principle without means

of enforcement, and at first its explosive importance was underrated in the West.

William Bundy, McGeorge's brother, and a senior diplomat, was right when he wrote that the Helsinki Accord was "perhaps the most idealistic document ever subscribed to by a coherent group of nations." The Soviet leaders, pleased about the first two provisions, were divided about the third, some rightly fearing that it might open the door to foreign influences in their carefully insulated world, others viewing it as little more than a scrap of paper, a concession to bourgeois hypocrisy. In fact, the acceptance was to haunt them. Dissidents in the Soviet Union and in the satellites quickly grasped the hidden promise of what in the West may have seemed like mere pieties. The provisions on human rights were life-giving arguments in tyrannical regimes, establishing some hope for those without a voice. As early as January 1977, three Czech intellectuals, including Václav Havel, announced the founding of Charter 77, which pledged to promote and protect "civic and human rights in our own country." Dissidents in Poland and the Soviet Union could appeal to those principles that their own leaders had cynically or carelessly accepted.

Suppression, after all, was the hallmark of the communist regimes; Alexander Solzhenitsyn, Czesław Miłosz, and many others had brought that message to the West for decades. I had read Nadezhda Mandelstam's *Hope Against Hope*—a book beyond praise, which leaves one with a kind of dedicated humility—and considered her insistence that "Silence is the real crime against humanity" a historic truth and moral command all at once. To those who speak out or to those who defend those who speak out, we owe everything. If more people had spoken out and demonstrated civic courage in the twentieth century, history would have been very different, crimes might have been avoided, lives spared. There have always been such individual voices, insufficiently heeded or protected, crying out for new beginnings.

Conditions within the Soviet orbit varied from country to country, of course; the East German regime felt especially vulnerable, given West Germany's power and proximity, and hence was especially adept at repression. The Polish and Hungarian governments, discreetly encouraged by Western contacts, pursued policies of indeterminate, intermittent leniency. But the full horror of the Soviet monolith had shown itself for what it was in the Warsaw Pact invasion of Czechoslovakia in August 1968 (the last occasion when German troops crossed a foreign border in hostile intent, as I often reminded German audiences in the eastern *Länder* after 1989).

That earlier assertion of Soviet power had some small bearing on my life in

1975. In 1960, I had attended my first International Congress of Historical Sciences, in Stockholm; had spoken at the next one, in Vienna in 1965; and had looked forward to the 1970 meeting scheduled for Moscow, an opportunity to meet friends and colleagues and, under presumably favorable conditions, to see Russia, where I had never been. But after the invasion of Czechoslovakia, I cancelled. The next congress was scheduled for San Francisco in 1975, when the Soviet delegation was assigned the opening panel on the first day, in a session titled "History and Society," in which I was to be the American commentator. My formal task was to engage the Russian historians in a serious professional argument; my informal one was to participate in a Western effort on behalf of persecuted colleagues. While I studied recent trends in Soviet historiography, my heart was in the other task.

The post-1968 Czech puppet government had organized new purges and with particular thoroughness had gone after historians who had done genuine research, with minimal adherence to Marxist-Leninist orthodoxy, and had cultivated contacts with Western colleagues. (For example, Eduard Goldstücker, a supporter of Alexander Dubcek in promoting intellectual freedom and a specialist in German literature, especially Kafka, whose works were banned in Soviet lands. As a known leader of the "Prague Spring," he had to flee the country after the Soviet invasion. When I met him in Prague in the 1990s he told me that he was proud that Brezhnev, at his showdown meeting with Dubcek, had singled out Goldstücker as a key enemy.) The new rulers removed some 70 to 80 percent of all historians in the academies and universities, sent some to prison, and forced others to menial posts in remote areas, depriving them of access to libraries and archives.

Western historians, led by Eberhard Jaeckel and H. A. Winkler, decided to distribute carefully orchestrated appeals at the San Francisco meeting on behalf of these Czechs. Jaeckel had already spoken up for them in Moscow, and in May 1973 he asked Chancellor Brandt, to whom he was close, to mention their plight to Brezhnev; perhaps Brandt could cite Louis Aragon's remark that Prague has become "this Biafra of the spirit." Jaeckel prepared a list of the expelled historians and persuaded a German publisher to print six thousand copies of a brochure, *Acta persecutionis*, which accused the Czechoslovak Communist Party of having removed 147 historians, names supplied, and of steadfastly continuing "its extermination campaign against all of Czechoslovak culture and against historians." Copies of this brochure, printed in several languages, were shipped to America, and we saw to it that they were distributed at the congress, attended by nearly 1,500 historians from all over the world except China. Jaeckel, Winkler, the Dutch historians Maarten Brands and Henk Wesseling, David Schoenbaum, an American colleague, and I collected signatures for a petition to the Czech government on behalf of our purged colleagues. On August 28, the seventh anniversary of the Soviet invasion, we held a press conference, where I announced that we had 160 signatures, including those of well-known Marxist historians such as Eric Hobsbawm and Albert Soboul. I don't think that any of us at the time reflected that what we were doing, after all at no risk to ourselves, was what a previous generation of historians had failed to do for victims of the Third Reich.

The fact that the association had a Soviet president at the time signified the prevailing spirit of détente. Mr. Zhukov's opening remarks were full of pieties about "peaceful coexistence"; the Soviet paper "History and Society" that I was to comment on was a ninety-six-page exposition of Soviet historical ideology, inflammatory in its wooden banality and cast in prescribed ideological turgidity. My manifest intent at the first morning session was to have a scholarly debate with these people, but quite soon we were replicating the old political conflict. I wanted to expose the fundamental difference between history in an admittedly imperfect world and history in the allegedly perfect Soviet world. N. V. Sivachev, one of the six authors of the Soviet paper, spoke briefly and beguilingly, and I responded by regretting the disparity between the tone of his greetings and the unusually "rigid political-ideological character" of the paper itself, with its typical assertions such as "At the highest stage of development of the social sciences which has found its embodiment in the theory of historical materialism, the Communist Party principles and scientific objectivity organically coincide." Even Marxist historians would boggle at this definition, I said, and challenged their conclusion that "it is a historical fact of today that modern bourgeois historiography has manifestly moved to the right in its interpretation of social progress." Were these terms even applicable? "If they retain any meaning, it is not our side that has moved to the right in the last thirty years." After all, Western historians were writing about hitherto neglected classes and themes: the history of the child, the deviant, the working class, women, victims of society. And in America we were witnessing the long-overdue reassessment of the history of blacks. History alive to social and intellectual transformations "is capable of progress; history as the handmaiden of church or state or nation or class is history imprisoned."

The Soviet paper had ended on a political note, calling for a curb of aggression against Arab states, so I closed by insisting that "the violation of intellectual freedom by *any* regime is a threat to all of us" and quoted *L'Unità*, the organ of the Italian Communist Party, which had vigorously defended freedom of culture "as a foundation of Socialist democracy." In Czechoslovakia, I reminded them, "dozens of intellectuals [have been] deprived of their teaching posts and placed in great material difficulties. To our colleagues who are victims of such persecution anywhere in the world, we owe a ringing affirmation of solidarity."

That afternoon, Sivachev (who had once studied under Hofstadter) answered some of our criticisms, and we argued about Dimitrov's old and dangerously inadequate definition of fascism, which the Russians clung to. But things got really heated when I pressed the point that there was controversy *within* the Soviet camp and cited the censuring of a Soviet historian, M. Ia. Gefter, on February 10, 1971.* Two members of the Soviet academy who had been present at that censure were in the audience, and the Soviet delegation became noisily agitated. Academician Mintz jumped up, and in great excitement wagged his finger at several of his fellow delegates—I suppose he was instructing them on who should lead the countercharge. I had touched a raw nerve. Was it then that I picked up the Soviet aphorism "In Soviet society, the future is certain, only the past is uncertain"?

At another panel, where the excellent English historian D. C. Watt was the principal speaker, I questioned a Soviet assertion that "peaceful coexistence" had always been Soviet doctrine, recalling that Lenin and Zinoviev had clearly expected a final showdown with capitalist countries. After it was over, Watt said to me, "I didn't mind you kicking them in the balls, but three times running?" In a summary report on the conference, I believe in the Soviet paper *Kommunist*, I was, amusingly, called "a NATO historian." I felt I had earned the sobriquet, though more pleasing was George Kennan's letter to me: "I have never seen a better statement addressed to the Soviet historical fraternity—brilliant and unanswerable . . . the ways in which such a challenge finds its effect in the Soviet Union are wild and wonderful," he wrote to me, "and often long delayed; but they do find it. There are many people there who are in this respect on our side, and among them will be some who will know how to make use of such a statement."

———

*Only in the postcommunist era did I learn of Gefter's extraordinary courage: in 1968, he had demonstratively walked out before a vote at the Institute of History endorsing the Soviet invasion of Czechoslovakia.

WRITING ABOUT HONORABLE FIGURES and expressing legitimate admiration of them, as we did at San Francisco in honor of our Czech colleagues, appealed to me. To record the brave exceptions, the supporters of decency, the ones who spoke out, to confront the world with historic alternatives or moments seemed important.

Weeks after San Francisco I was lucky to be invited to deal with a subject that would call for such an exercise. In the spring of 1976, the fourth and final volume of Ernst Reuter's Collected Papers was to appear, the culmination of a formidable publishing venture in honor of Berlin's mayor during the Soviet blockade of Berlin in 1948. The publisher was Wolf Jobst Siedler, one of the finest of German postwar publishers; he had strong liberal-conservative principles and was himself steeped in history, proud of his Prussian roots and of all that had been creative and decent in Prussia's past; he was also brilliantly attuned to the German realities of his own time. (As a youth he had been incarcerated by the Nazis for subversive activities.) Now he asked me to be principal speaker at the city government's festive celebration of the completion of the posthumous edition of Reuter's letters and speeches. Chancellor Schmidt was to be the final speaker. I had known little about Ernst Reuter beyond his heroic days as mayor. As happened to me so often, I faced a rewarding crash course in preparation.

Born in 1890, Ernst Reuter grew up in a Germany that was politically immature and socially divided, well administered but badly governed. In 1909, a German jurist remarked that on only one point was there "complete unanimity, and that is the staggering *lack of political leaders of great stature* in Germany." The young Reuter found the inequalities of German society appalling and as a twenty-three-year-old in 1913 wrote to his parents, steeped in rigid Lutheranism and conventional patriotism, "I cannot help being a socialist . . . It is a passionate and burning love for my comrades [*Volksgenossen*] and for what I have come to see as right." The parents could not condone the son's faith in democratic socialism as the road to social justice, but he repeated to them Luther's celebrated words: "I can do no other."

In his formative years Reuter encountered some of the political forces that his country would confront later, such as his parents' sense of socialism as an attack on their moral universe. He, in turn, was appalled by the imperialist lust of Germany's leaders. As a prisoner in a Russian camp during the Great War, Reuter learned Russian and briefly fell for the Bolshevik promise. But, he wrote later, "Every new wave of fellow-travelers had to fight its own way through to the realization that communism was an abhorrent negation of its promise." Reuter broke with communism in 1921.

In 1913, he had already said that "the fate of democracy rests on faith in history," a mantra for his commitment to workers' education, made in a spirit similar to that of socialist circles elsewhere, as in the efforts of R. H. Tawney in England and Jean Jaurès in France. He fought National Socialism with exemplary courage, and after its victory, the thugs in power tortured him; he eventually found refuge in Turkey, where he stayed through the war. After 1945, Reuter thirsted to go back to Germany, to help build a democratic society there, which he knew required a true explication of the roots of National Socialism deep in the imperial past. He excoriated the servility of the Germans that had made the triumph of the Nazis possible. The Social Democrats of Weimar had committed many sins of commission and, especially, omission, but after the war, they deserved more historic credit than the German bourgeoisie was willing to give them or than they themselves demanded. Reuter resented Adenauer's contemptuous treatment of Social Democrats, his tarring them with the old brush of "lack of patriotism," and his insinuating a commonality between Communists and Socialists because they had a common father, Karl Marx. At every stage of his career, Reuter had been a model of civic courage; Germans needed such models—and many, I think, were made uncomfortable by them. (Jean Jaurès is buried in the Pantheon in Paris; there is no German Pantheon and if there were, I doubt that Reuter would have been given a place in it.)

As the festivities in Berlin began and I launched into my talk, Helmut Schmidt was sitting in the front row, busily scribbling notes for his concluding remarks. When I got to Reuter's career in urban politics—as mayor of Magdeburg, he had made a formal visit to New York City in 1929—I suddenly improvised, remembering Schmidt's recent denunciation of President Ford's indifference to the then-imminent bankruptcy of New York City and his constructive counsels regarding the city, and added, "Herr Bundeskanzler, I bring you grateful greetings from the city of New York, America's last colony." When we walked out together, I said I hoped he hadn't minded my allusion, and his vociferous response was: "I love giving unsolicited advice." Schmidt told me of the grievous shock he had felt in September 1953 when, en route to Bonn to take his place as newly elected deputy to the Bundestag, he heard the news of Reuter's sudden death. Reuter had been a model for him. In the Bundestag elections that year the Social Democrats had been badly trounced, and Reuter had admonished party leaders to assess their own responsibility for the electoral failure. Schmidt was to be no less candid with the party.

But there was a lighter—and instructive—side to what for me was a demanding occasion. Siedler had invited Schmidt and his admirable wife, Loki, and me to lunch before the festivities and in the course of that lunch he told a joke: A Soviet cosmonaut returns to earth after having been in space longer than anyone else. He is fêted at the Kremlin, where Brezhnev takes him aside and asks him if during his long sojourn he saw God. The cosmonaut answers, yes. Brezhnev swears him to secrecy, saying if anything like this leaked out, he would have to do what one would expect of a socialist leader. The next stop on the cosmonaut's triumphal tour is a visit to the Pope, who asks the same question, and the cosmonaut, duly instructed, says, no. The Pontiff says he had been afraid of this but demands silence as well. Next stop: Bonn. Chancellor Brandt poses the same question. Confused, the cosmonaut says, yes, and Brandt asks, "And he looked like me?" Schmidt guffawed loudly at this, which said something about his view of Brandt then, though they had a genuine affirmation of friendship later on. In any case, they shared a genuine enthusiasm for Reuter.

On that occasion, I also met Reuter's son Edzard, roughly my contemporary, who had grown up in Turkey; I told him that if life had turned out somewhat differently and if my father had been offered that position in Ankara, we would have grown up as "Young Turks" together. Here, too, began a friendship with a remarkable figure in German public life, a Social Democrat who subsequently rose in the corporate world to be CEO of Daimler-Benz.

Weeks after my talk, Walter Scheel, now president of the Federal Republic, awarded me the Officer's Cross of West Germany's Order of Merit. At a reception in New York, the German consul general handed me the actual decoration, a special occasion, with old family friends, the Hamburgers, representing the past, together with my family and American friends and colleagues. In response to the consul's remarks about my "contributions toward a deeper understanding" between Germany and America, I spoke of my parents, who, despite their grievous disappointments, had helped me to maintain my ties to Germany, to its language and its culture.

My own personal connections may have been getting stronger, but in 1977 relations between the two countries became more difficult. At the top, personal dissidence: Helmut Schmidt had been close to Gerald Ford, but the personal chemistry between him and the newly elected Jimmy Carter was cool at best. Perhaps style was even more divisive than substance: the very self-confident

Schmidt made no secret of his low opinion of the newcomer on the international scene, and was even more open in his distrust of Carter's national security adviser, Zbigniew Brzezinski, holding him responsible for what he thought was Carter's volatility. Schmidt also had little use for Carter's efforts on behalf of human rights in the Soviet Union, which he thought would end up being counterproductive. They agreed on the desirability of détente but not on the means of its cultivation.

Schmidt's greatest challenge came with a wave of terrorist activity begun by cells such as the Baader-Meinhof gang and the Red Army Faction, whose members murdered industrialists and bankers, judges and police officials, and posed an immediate threat to the nation. His decisive moment came when terrorists captured a Lufthansa plane, diverted it to Mogadishu, threatening to kill all passengers unless the terrorists' imprisoned comrades were released. Schmidt sent special units of West German border guards to storm the plane: they were successful, and Schmidt's stock rose everywhere. The fact that the Federal Republic could suffer these attacks and yet preserve basic civil liberties was in no small measure due to Schmidt's leadership. Eventually the violence subsided and a mostly nonviolent protest movement gained wide support and soon metamorphosed in the Green Party.

IN THE SUMMER of 1976, I completed the manuscript of *Gold and Iron: Bismarck, Bleichröder, and the Building of the German Empire*—from start to finish, sixteen years of my life! And, the many bouts of doubt and worry notwithstanding, I can say it was a rewarding investment of time, certainly the single greatest learning experience in my scholarly life, as I tried to reconstruct the hitherto ignored thirty-year connection between Bismarck the Junker and Bleichröder the Jewish banker. Bit by bit, I had discovered that Bleichröder not only supervised Bismarck's growing fortune and investments but was deeply involved in politics and international finance. He was also intermittently Bismarck's secret agent—a major shadowy and vilified presence in the Europe of his time—though later historians had barely given him a footnote. Bismarck himself, in his three-volume memoirs, mentioned Bleichröder only once, as someone else's messenger, so why would German historians have looked for the—to them—disillusioning story that the Iron Chancellor not only was interested in "mere" money but had entrusted the cultivation of it to a Jew, whom he eventually referred to as my "friend" (a sparse category in Bismarck's life)? It was

Bismarck who persuaded the king to raise Bleichröder to the ranks of hereditary nobility, the first unconverted Prussian Jew to be so honored. How were the ties between these two men created, and how had Bleichröder—as a consequence of his tie to Bismarck—become so involved in European and Jewish life at a time when united Germany rose to the pinnacle of power and Jews gained a moment of precarious prominence? Toward the end of my work, I came to understand that the relationship I had so carefully reconstructed was a central drama in German Jewish history; I wrote, "it may be pardonable exaggeration to say that Bleichröder is everything that has been left out of German history."

Bleichröder both collected and dispensed intelligence. His work exemplified the ties between politics and high finance and facilitated Bismarck's dealings with the press, inter alia. He served as adviser, lobbyist, even kingmaker, and he was discreet banker and lender to Prussia's feudal elite in its harsh, usually concealed, struggle to survive economically in an increasingly capitalist world. As an international banker, close to the Rothschilds, Bleichröder participated in Europe's financial penetration of the rest of the world—from Mexico and the United States (whose bonds Bismarck bought and sold) to the Congo and Samoa. Bankers were diplomats in mufti. I had had to chase after all of these adventures, including the very complicated efforts in the late 1870s on the part of international Jewry (and I noted that something like this existed—or came into being at special occasions) to persuade the European powers to force the emergent Rumanian state to grant equal rights to Jews. Mine may have been the only book that used the private archives of Bismarck *and* the archives of the Alliance Israélite in Paris!

The spectacular rise of Bleichröder himself seemed to bear out my epigraph from Heine: "Money is the god of our time, and Rothschild is his prophet." Bleichröder epitomized what I called "the anguish of assimilation": the patriotic parvenu, the wealthiest man in Germany, the arriviste who never arrived, whose lamentable efforts at being accepted made him the object of backstage malice and whose putative power made him the ideal target for the rising anti-Semitism of the 1870s. He was quietly mocked by the elites and often noisily—and falsely—vilified by the rabble. He made his craven, proud ascent in a society that was peculiarly both hostile and hospitable to Jews. The story ended with two of his grandsons appealing to the Nazi minister of the interior for exemption from having to wear the yellow star, a supplication that was denied them by Adolf Eichmann.

None of this I knew or could have known at the outset. In the final stages of writing, I worried about the possible consequences of my presenting this damaging picture of Bleichröder and, by extension, German Jewish plutocrats. His very success, glaringly, garishly exhibited, made him an easy target. "Even the most imaginative anti-Semites could not have invented this figure, at once so powerful and so vulnerable," I wrote. He could have appeared in one of Thomas Mann's merciless, if disguised, portrayals of wealthy German Jews (not all that different from the "purse-proud" bourgeoisie of most European countries). Was I in danger of promoting or validating anti-Semitism? I remember talking to Salo Baron, Columbia's sage master of Jewish history, about this point; he understood that the book might harm the Jews, but "truth will help."

In retrospect, the rewards had been immense: archival work in many places in Europe, the drudgery and the exhilaration! To work in the archive of the Quai d'Orsay, to walk the corridors of that historic place—what a gift to a hungry imagination! To read Disraeli's letters in his country home, Hughenden Manor, to gain admission to the Bismarck archive on his estate, to discover that Bleichröder had been present at Versailles at the very time when Bismarck was dictating his harsh, portentous terms to the defeated French—a thousand details of surpassing interest! All this perhaps to compensate for the dreary drilling in often dry or disappointing holes. To say nothing of the archive that began it all: the thirty-three cardboard boxes of Bleichröder materials. I had taken some of the boxes with the thousands of key letters and documents with me—to Paris, Oxford, and Wassenaar. I knew that they had immense scholarly value, but I was retroactively taken aback when in 1971 the owner deeded them to Harvard as a gift valued at $52,250 (partly just for the autographs)—they had been with me three times across the ocean and spent many summers in my cow barn in Vermont!

The costs of all that work—the roads not traveled—are mostly forgotten: the rewards remain in my mind. Delving into that past led me to persons who lived in analogous worlds at present; men such as Gilbert de Botton (in the 1970s, head of the Rothschild Bank in Zurich) and George Soros, James Wolfensohn, Sir Sigmund Warburg, and Henry Arnhold of the New York bank of Arnhold and S. Bleichroeder. I was fortunate in encountering many men and women in realms beyond scholarship, who became friends and thus enhanced my life. Not to mention the many scholars in different countries from whose collegial help I benefited.

The reception of the book astounded me. Historians I admired were extremely kind, and both American and English reviewers were generous. Golo Mann, in a long review in the *Neue Zürcher Zeitung*, my favorite newspaper, began, "This is one of the most important historical works of the past few decades . . . The work of a writer in whose hands question, thought, perspective and narrative become one, who rarely theorizes, preferring the golden tree of life to concepts." He commended what many others criticized: my judgment that political considerations outweighed the economic ones in many of the decisions of the time. I was pleased when *The Economist* said that "the book resembles the great nineteenth-century novels," and *The Listener*, comparing the book to *Buddenbrooks*, saw greater lessons in this "non-fictionalized form . . . a terrifying masterpiece."

And the personal letters!—from William Langer and Alan Bullock, for example. And out of the blue came a missive from John Kenneth Galbraith: "a sublime book—with a sublimely ghastly ending. I would rather have written it than anything I've read in years. But there is some racial aspect here too. No Scotchman could possibly have done it." Yet disappointments came, too: A.J.P. Taylor, many of whose works I had reviewed with meticulous appreciation, wrote a long article in *The New York Review of Books* that excellently retold the substance of the book, making it sound as if the facts in it had always been known. And an American colleague I met by chance at an airport said to me quite seriously that so far he had read only the introduction but that was enough for him to think, "It is too well written for me to trust it." *The Journal of Modern History* carried a four-page denunciatory review that complained, "First, this is an extremely old-fashioned book. Written in a heavily literary mode . . . Stern resolutely abstains from any systematic contextual discussion . . . he fails to realize the potential of his subject . . . rarely extracts the fullest significance of his descriptions." By depicting the political accommodationism of the German bourgeoisie I wished "to enshrine liberal democracy as an immanent purpose of the historical process, the manifest destiny of the bourgeoisie, which in the German case is somehow alienated." To be so caricatured was troublesome; in retrospect, it seems comical.

Wolf Jobst Siedler commissioned a German translation (later the book appeared in French, Dutch, and Italian as well): an arduous task, even for the author, since I had to go back and provide the German originals of the innumerable archival citations I had painstakingly translated into English. The reviews were plentiful and gratifying on the whole; that German historians had followed Bismarck's lead in suppressing Bleichröder was much commented on. Many reviewers noted my critical stance toward the then almost faddish insistence on theoretical and structural analysis and the attendant downgrading of narrative history. I was pleased to have a review from an East German, Ernst Engelberg, among orthodox Marxist-Leninist historians a relatively free spirit. He had various objective and ideological criticisms, but acknowledged that I had fully presented the ugly underside of the new capitalist age. He regretted that I had paid insufficient attention to changes in class relations and "to the workers' movement, which with many sacrifices led a victorious campaign against the Bismarckian regime . . . Such a disregard of the organized and struggling workers' class is scientifically inadmissible and morally insulting." And yet, he said, for all the shortcomings, the book was "meritorious, indeed indispensable."

The German edition soon made the bestseller list; and it seemed to get the attention of the political class, absorbed as it was and is by the ever problematical connection between politics and finance. Newspapers carried a picture of Walter Scheel reading the book on vacation; Helmut Schmidt, responding to complaints from parliamentarians about being insufficiently recompensed, said he knew they all wanted "a Bleichröder." Helmut Kohl read it. The press reported that his successor, Gerhard Schröder, read it during his holiday, subsequently lending his copy to a Dutch writer as the best introduction to understanding the German past.

After the book appeared in France, four heads of the Rothschild Bank in Paris invited me to lunch at the bank's headquarters, on the rue Laffitte. By then, the mansion had been modernized, and Baron Alain asked me how I liked the new structure. I confessed that I had preferred the authentic old nineteenth-century building, and he sighed. "Ah, the nineteenth century! That's when you could still make money!"

CHANCE MADE ME TURN to a later, loftier—and no less complicated— exemplar of German Jewish life. In 1978, Gail Potter, Aspen Institute administrator and energetic activist, telephoned me: Aspen was co-sponsoring a centennial symposium to take place in Jerusalem in March 1979, in honor of Einstein's birth. The program called for scientists to analyze Einstein's unique place in modern science and for humanists—including Erik Erikson and Isaiah Berlin—to consider Einstein the private and public person. Potter wanted me as a speaker as well, and my instant response was resolute dubiety: I knew almost nothing about Einstein's physics or even of the older science he had overthrown; how could I speak about him, in that company, and on what subject?

But justified reticence contended with an appetite for something new, with what in retrospect I would call intellectual-political wanderlust, coupled with the lure of working in new archives. What compelled me finally to accept was the recollection that a decade earlier I had looked at the Einstein archive at the

Institute for Advanced Study in Princeton and found some fascinating letters, including a few touching on my family. And in 1976 as speaker at the opening of a new library at the University of Chicago, I had literally stumbled into an adjacent, unrelated exhibition of the papers of the German physicist James Franck, Nobel laureate and exile, discovering there an exchange between him and Einstein in 1945: old friends fighting, in Germanic seriousness, about the nature of the German character. So I accepted Potter's invitation, thinking that Einstein's deep, ambivalent relations to Germany might offer a possible focus. I was a stranger in a new world, stumbling but eager. And it never occurred to me that Einstein would be an astounding, in a way redeeming, complement to Bleichröder in the history of German Jewry. Both men scaled pinnacles of achievement, but Einstein had an almost visceral dislike for wealthy Jewish superpatriots.

The pleasant part was a return to archives, to that necessary but never sufficient search for unknown nuggets of the past, thrilling to the discovery of new evidence. And while working in the archives, I could legitimately delay the daunting task of actual composition. Still, archival work prompts sudden insights or connections that I quickly write down. I used my usual four-color pencil to distinguish among my "ideas" and various categories of quoted or paraphrased text.

Einstein had willed his papers to the Hebrew University in Jerusalem (with which, I discovered, he had had anything but solidly harmonious relations), but they were still locked in big filing cabinets in the Princeton institute's attic, under the pleasantly authoritarian rule of Helen Dukas, Einstein's amanuensis from 1927 to his death in 1955.* At the archive I met Abraham Pais, the Dutch-born physicist—during the German occupation saved by a wonderfully brave "Aryan" family—who was himself preparing the first of his important works on Einstein, whom he had known and worked with at Princeton; Pais had also known my uncle Otto. He was sparklingly bright and deeply complicated by turns, bubbly and sad-sardonic. I was grateful for his encouragement.

Immersing myself in the huge Einstein archive, I found a few nuggets, especially in the correspondence between Einstein and Fritz Haber, who in important ways was his fraternal opposite: they were good friends with almost

---

*At about this time, the project of publishing *The Collected Papers of Albert Einstein* was launched, one of the major scholarly editorial ventures of our time. In 1984, I joined its Editorial Committee and have been associated with the project and its sometimes turbulent history ever since. The first volume of a projected twenty-five or thirty appeared in 1987.

antithetical styles and politics. I could hear echoes of Einstein's actual voice, expressing his views and suggesting their emotional source. For the rest, I delved into the published Einstein literature, which in the 1970s was mostly focused on his science. "Ordinary" historians had not yet concerned themselves with Einstein (or other modern scientists) as important public figures. Some of Einstein's essays on political-moral issues had been published, as had a few biographies. But Einstein "the man" wasn't yet a popular theme. I was lucky again to have stumbled upon a wonderfully rich, largely untilled field.

Conversations with colleagues and friends were essential to me, key among them my uncle's student, the Nobel laureate I. I. Rabi, a Columbia colleague. Rabi was a phenomenon of brilliance and incisive judgment. And, like Pais, he encouraged me despite my scientific ignorance. But however hard I worked, I felt I was in way over my head. It was one of the hardest assignments I had ever given myself. There were many moments of panic: I can still recall the precise spot near the Princeton institute where I first thought that temporary suicide might be an enticing solution.

I called my lecture "Einstein's Germany," meaning the Germany as it existed and the Germany as he had experienced and imagined it. I came to realize that Einstein felt attraction to and revulsion from Germany—attraction to its uniquely congenial scientific community and an affinity for German culture; revulsion from the authoritarian style of its society and from the militarism that at its most unrestrained in the Great War brought the country to ruin.

As a teenager, Einstein left Germany, and in his mid-twenties, in the patent office in Bern in 1905, he wrote the five papers that revolutionized modern physics and cosmology. Max Planck, then the preeminent scientist in Germany, was the first to recognize the genius of this unknown clerk, and in 1912, together with Fritz Haber, Planck sought to entice Einstein with an unprecedentedly generous offer to come to Berlin, then the Mecca of theoretical physics. He accepted. (Some years later, I discovered that an estrangement from his wife and a secret love affair with his cousin and, later, second wife, weighed heavily in favor of his return to Germany.)

Three months after he arrived, the war broke out; he witnessed in disbelief the nationalist frenzy, and was appalled to see his colleagues extol the war as some kind of divine test, a path to purification and salvation. He thought it was a senseless, criminal slaughter from the very beginning. In November 1915, asked for his views, he explained his opposition to the war and concluded, "But why many words, when I can say everything in one sentence and moreover in a sentence which is particularly fitting for me as a Jew: Honor Your Master Jesus Christ not in words and hymns, but above all through your deeds."

The war proved him right; the nation's wild leap to pan-German madness and the subsequent defeat left it stunned and starved, the unity of 1914 shattered, and, in the shadow of the Bolshevik Revolution, the threat of civil war all too real. But Einstein quickly rallied to the newly proclaimed, improvised Weimar Republic, warning at the same time against revolutionary extremism.

A few weeks after the war ended, a British expedition, observing the solar eclipse, announced that Einstein's predictions of general relativity had been confirmed. "Almost overnight Einstein became a celebrated hero—the scientific genius, untainted by war . . . The new hero appeared, as if by divine design, at the very moment when the old heroes had been buried in the rubble of the war." Einstein's instant fame enraged some of his colleagues and many of his countrymen, the more so as he now openly championed causes—liberal internationalism, pacifism, and Zionism—that were repellent to anti-Weimar elitists. He was in Pasadena, California, when Hitler was appointed chancellor, and he never returned to Germany. For him, Hitler *was* Germany.

The relations of Christians and Jews in Germany was a central theme in Einstein's life: while enjoying collegial hospitality in Berlin, he had also experienced hostility, and he resented the discrimination against fellow Jews. Treating this theme of Christian-Jewish relations allowed me room for the correction of facile generalities, such as the then current "summary judgment about German Jewry, about their putative self-surrender, their cravenness, or their opportunism. These judgments . . . are likely to do violence to the past and to the future: the myth of yesterday's self-surrender could feed the delusion of tomorrow's intransigence." I also quoted Einstein himself, the celebrated early Zionist, who in 1929, when Arabs attacked Jewish settlements in Palestine, warned Chaim Weizmann against a policy of self-centered toughness, against Jewish "nationalism *à la prussienne*." "If we do not find the path to honest cooperation and honest negotiations with the Arabs, then we have learned nothing from our 2,000 years of suffering, and we deserve the fate that will befall us."*

I ended on an avowedly private note: "Greatness in any guise is not in vogue today, not in my discipline and not in our culture . . . We are uncom-

---

*When I sent David Landes a reprint of my Jerusalem lecture, he replied with interesting comments on the Zionists who in the 1920s pleaded for greater collaboration with the Arabs: they were the ones who "loved the Arabs best and understood them least." "They simply weren't listening to what the Arabs were saying, which was: 'Jews, go home.' The problem was, where was home?"

fortable even with the rhetoric of greatness, devalued as it so often has been. I would simply say that I find it inspiriting to look upon great peaks, as from an alpine village, and contemplate the distant mountains—cold, awesome, unattained and unattainable, mysterious." A metaphor for my belief in greatness and a private bow to Sils Maria—and the two may in fact be related.

In March 1979, shortly before I went to Jerusalem for the Einstein symposium, Raymond Aron and I walked to an exhibition in West Berlin commemorating the centenary of the births of Einstein, Max von Laue, Otto Hahn, and Lise Meitner. We passed bombed-out squares and half-decrepit mansions in the once-proud capital, talking of that earlier profusion of genius. Aron suddenly stopped at a crossing, turned to me, and said, "It could have been Germany's century." In a terrifying way, it *had* been Germany's century, and its failures had been the beginning of Aron's and my political education. The end of Germany's century had also brought us the Berlin Wall, in whose shadow we were walking.

★

CHAPTER 7

THE FOURTH AND
FORGOTTEN GERMANY

I KNEW SOMETHING about life on the other side of that hideous wall. In fact, I came to know the German Democratic Republic, my fourth Germany, better than many West Germans did, though my intrigued acquaintance with it was minimal. I watched it from afar, crossed it in a sealed military train in 1954, and spent many weeks inside it just before and just after the Berlin Wall was built in 1961. The GDR had the allure of the forbidden and the familiar: forbidden because it was a communist state that Western nations didn't even recognize until the early 1970s, and programmatically anti-American; familiar because it was German, especially familiar because it was a German police state. I felt bizarrely at home there precisely because I wasn't, once again an enemy in the country of my language. In many ways it was reminiscent of the first dictatorship I had experienced as a child. There was the same pageantry extolling power and achievement, the same relentless invocations of noble ideals (this time peace and democracy), and the same relentless campaign against a demonized enemy (this time the fascist-capitalist-imperialist "wreckers"). And I sensed the same pervasive atmosphere of fear, with the party, visible and invisible, all powerful against its presumed all-brutal enemies.

The German Democratic Republic, often and justifiably called the second German dictatorship, lasted more than four times as long as the Third Reich. But there are important differences: the citizens of the GDR never had a choice in a free election; the Red Army and its minions imposed the regime on the people; and the terror of its repressive Soviet-type tyranny was exerted mostly at home, and it did not wreak worldwide destruction. Life in the GDR was never easy, never prosperous — except for the select few high operatives of the regime, the *Nomenklatura* and other profiteers. I knew that many East Germans had made their outer and even inner peace with the regime, but I felt that they paid for Hitler's war more fully and in more crippling ways than the West Germans had. Hence I felt a certain abstract sympathy for them, the more so as I detested their government.

Toward the end of the war, in 1944, when the Allies agreed on the division of a defeated Germany into Allied zones of occupation, the Soviet zone comprised territories that stretched from the Baltic Sea to the ancient states of Saxony and Thuringia — with agrarian lands to the north, centers of industry in the middle, with Leipzig and the devastated Dresden, too. This zone, effectively controlled by the Red Army, expanded Russia's empire into the heart of Central Europe. And it became the German Democratic Republic when that state was formally established in October 1949, in response to the creation of the Federal Republic.

Like West Germany at its creation, East Germany was a state with very limited sovereignty. And unlike all the other Soviet satellites, it wasn't recognized by the Western powers and thus lacked a certain legitimacy; worse, it was the only one with porous borders. Berlin was an escape hatch for people from all the countries behind the iron curtain, where the Soviet Union kept a tight grip. So the East German regime outdid itself in proclaiming eternal friendship with Russia, its big brother. The Russians had to reciprocate, and yet in the early postwar years they kept clamoring for a different solution to the German problem: a unified, disarmed, potentially pro-Soviet German state. Stalin's famous "note" of 1952 proposing free, all-German elections to create a neutralized, unified Germany was the last official gasp of this policy. As we have seen, neither Adenauer nor his Western partners were prepared to sacrifice the FRG's integration in the West for this gamble.

From the very beginning of the occupation years, the Russians touted Stalin's wartime pronouncement that "the Hitlers come and go, the German people and state remain." By insisting they were the true champions of German unity, they hoped to win support among "their" Germans, but at the same time, necessity and revenge dictated a policy of exacting German reparations, including the dismantling of industrial plants and shipping them to Russia. This meant that relations between the GDR and the Russians were far more complicated than we perhaps assumed at the time. After the collapse of the GDR in 1990, we came to know much more about its structure and policies than we had known before, for it was a singularly opaque regime—though we tried to learn about it from published accounts and personal impressions.

The GDR defined itself in reference to Germany's Nazi past. The regime's main slogan and claim to legitimacy was its "anti-fascism," putative proof of its credibility being the fact that its first leaders were men who themselves had been victims of National Socialism. Many of the new functionaries had been incarcerated by the Nazis: Walter Ulbricht, effective head of the GDR, was a stolid veteran of the Communist Party in the Weimar years who had spent the last decade of his exile in Moscow (many of his German comrades there perished in Stalin's purges in the late 1930s); even before they had captured Berlin, the Russians had flown him, together with a handful of other young comrades, back to Germany. There he was supposed to organize the faithful, that is, veterans of pre-Hitler communism, most of whom had languished in German camps.

Ulbricht was a Stalinist by principle and character, a ruthless dictator within his own party who carefully prescribed a "cult of personality" despite its manifest unpopularity. He and many of his collaborators thought of themselves as faithful followers of Marxism-Leninism, fighters in the final struggle for a socialist future. Ulbricht's principal goal was to "construct socialism" at record speed and regardless of human cost. He continued in this policy even after Stalin's death, in March 1953, when Stalin's successors warned him against taking too relentless a course that would only encourage the already sizable exodus from the GDR. East Germany lost many of its most highly skilled people, but at least they were rid of potential malcontents or opponents.

Ulbricht and his fellow Communists early on duped and coerced some of the Social Democratic leaders in the Soviet zone to form a united party. "Anti-fascism" was the rationale for this enforced fusion of the two "Marxist" parties that in Weimar had been rivals, even enemies, a division that had paved the way for fascism. The argument, superficially plausible and heavily dosed with historical amnesia, was that a united socialist party would forever bar a feared fascist revival. Against the bitter opposition of Social Democrats in the western zones, but under fierce Soviet pressure, the eastern SPD, under the lamentable leadership of Otto Grotewohl, agreed in April 1946 to join the Communists. (When I first met Ralf Dahrendorf in 1957, I learned that his father, Gustav, a Social Democrat, had decisively opposed this merger in Berlin in 1945, when it was first attempted. His stand infuriated the Soviets, putting him and his family in immediate danger. Allied officers spirited them out of West Berlin to safety in a western zone, out of reach of kidnapping Russians.) The new Socialist Unity Party (SED) had various complements, anti-fascist mass organizations and even semi-independent political groupings or parties that became disguised servants of the new regime in East Berlin; their illusory freedom was intended to give substance to the regime's claim to democracy. But the promised equality between Social Democrats and Communists in the SED was quickly quashed; Ulbricht created and led a Leninist party, where subservience got the name of "democratic centralism."

In the late 1940s the Soviet zone seemed very remote to me; I had no friends in East Germany, no direct contact with it. But the emergent repressiveness of its regime was clear: why else did students and teachers at Berlin University in the Soviet sector in 1947 fight for and take considerable risks to create a "Free University" in West Berlin? By then the perfidy of the other Soviet-imposed regimes in Eastern Europe was clear; we noted that whatever "progressive" social measures were being taken—whether in education, property relations, or the creation of new elites—those countries enjoyed none of the basic freedoms and neither a free press nor free speech. A new wave of purges in 1948–1949, larded with "anti-Zionist" charges, made clear that the Soviet regimes throughout Eastern Europe were making a mockery of law and civic rights.

For many of us there was a measure of regret at the breakdown of the old wartime alliance and apprehension of the consequences. It wasn't just that we remembered how much we owed to the heroic Red Army. Anti-fascism still had its own appeal and importance: we had battled the fascist threat of the 1930s and 1940s, but surviving foes remained in Franco's Spain, in some South American dictatorships, and among Nazi exiles there. (*Fascism* had become the preferred communist term, since it didn't have the exclusionary German connotation that *National Socialism* did, quite aside from its not letting a shadow fall on the ideal of socialism.) In the Soviet zone, "anti-fa" was at once a moral commonplace and a more or less hidden political program: to eliminate the base on which fascism had allegedly grown, it was necessary to expropriate the large landowners and to nationalize heavy industry.

It is odd that both left and right quickly emptied *fascism* of all historic meaning. On the left, and not only in the GDR, the word was used indiscriminately to malign all enemies, to demonize the Federal Republic, which as a capitalistic society was believed ipso facto to be sliding back toward it. And on the right, at least in the United States, it was used for similar purposes, as in the McCarthyite label "premature anti-fascist"—as if there had been a time when one could be legitimately profascist! To reduce fascism to a slogan confounds democratic thought and practice. *Anti-fascism* meant many things to many people, but originally it was meant to signify opposition to fascism's destruction of all law and decency.

Accident sparked my first study of East German developments. When I was still at Columbia, before I left for Cornell, Columbia's then new president, Dwight D. Eisenhower, had founded the American Assembly, where outstanding American leaders met to discuss the great issues of the day, hoping their deliberations would "inform government and the general public." Averell Harriman, the millionaire diplomat who was soon to become governor of New York, had given Columbia his palatial family home, Arden House, some fifty miles north of New York, as luxurious facility for this worthy effort.

The American Assembly's opening meeting, in May 1951, was devoted to an examination of U.S.–West European relations, the subject at the heart of a bitter postwar American debate, which the Korean War only intensified. Isolationists, mostly Republicans, pressed for something akin to a Fortress America—a defense of the continent by air and sea, with minimal land troops outside the country—while others urged that America should be principally concerned with Asia; most Democrats and some Republicans, especially the much-touted "Eastern Establishment," insisted that the defense of Western Europe was integral to America's own. President Truman's appointment in 1950 of General Eisenhower as supreme commander of NATO forces in Europe had been the most compelling evidence of American resolve to preserve the Western alliance. In February 1951, Eisenhower returned briefly to the United States, consulted with the president and Congress, and appealed to the nation in a way that should resonate today: "I have been given a job in Europe that is difficult enough, but it would be rendered impossible of execution unless I know that the bulk of opinion, the great overwhelming public opinion of the United States, were in support of what I am trying to do."

Eisenhower was scheduled to return from Europe to open the Assembly, but Truman's decision in April 1951 to relieve General Douglas MacArthur of his command in the Pacific because he was "unable to give his wholehearted support to the policies of the United States Government and the United Nations in matters pertaining to his official duties" complicated matters. The dismissal, a triumphant affirmation of civilian control of the military, enraged the American right, and Senator Robert Taft declared that Truman's action "has led the world to believe we are looking in the direction of appeasement." The Senate was investigating the dismissal. It was not a propitious time for Eisenhower to return to the States. Would he have wanted to go to the Hill to answer questions about MacArthur's dismissal? Silence was preferable.

Meanwhile a few of us at Columbia were charged with preparing background material for the Assembly: Henry Roberts was asked to draft an analysis of the principal issues for U.S.-European relations, and I was to prepare a chronological description of events and plans concerning our postwar relations with Western Europe and the USSR. To work with Henry was wonderful good fortune: he had that all-too-rare gift of the historian whose knowledge of past complexity makes his vision of the present clearer. He was also exceptionally gentle, wise, and judicious—a model stylist and a quietly demanding mentor. The Soviet coup in Rumania in 1945, which he had witnessed, gave him an early sense of Soviet behavior in Eastern Europe; while insisting that the Soviets may have acted not according to a fixed blueprint but by improvised response to their perception of Western policies, he saw the overall pattern of domination emerging. Yet he rejected the notion of inevitable conflict or war. I worked closely with Henry, and remember fondly how at the end of many an afternoon I would repair to his house for what we called a quick "thimk" [sic], the planned ten minutes often becoming nicely longer than that. His wife, Deborah, a woman of great intelligence and moral fervor, was most hospitable. She had also been with the OSS, never disclosing what she had done. I do believe she knew more about Sicilian sewers in 1943 than a normal graduate student in French literature could be expected to know.

In the end I delivered something like a mini-survey of the six postwar years that had transformed our perceptions and our world, years that had been so incredibly full and tortuous! We had gone from celebrating a common victory over Nazism with our erstwhile Soviet ally to the reasoned fear that the expansionism of Russia, once more perceived as a totalitarian foe, might erupt in a conflagration worse even than the last war. I tried to convey a sense of the openness of the future, but believing that the best way of avoiding catastrophe was to be aware of the threat.

The clearest lesson I learned from doing this work was to see developments in East Germany in their full cold-war context. I wrote that "the spirit of Yalta" had been broken almost at once, principally by Soviet actions. The Yalta agreements had called for democratic regimes in Eastern Europe, but the Soviets wanted "friendly" governments in the countries they liberated from Germany, and when they discovered that free elections produced independent, potentially hostile regimes, they resorted to the gradual imposition of what they called "peoples' democracies," characterized by one-party rule and by the expropriation of large landed estates and businesses. Democratic principles were flouted, freedom of speech was suppressed, and terror complemented propaganda. This was a complete disregard of earlier Soviet pledges of genuine democratic rule. And since all this was true in the Soviet zone of Germany, it cast doubt on the official line that the USSR favored German unity. At a minimum, Russia wanted to hold on to a subservient East Germany; a maximum goal was a unified, neutralized Germany to be lured, ultimately, to its side.

I quoted the British Labour Party executive on the fall of Czechoslovakia: "No clearer demonstration could be possible, that Communists consider as enemies all those who do not surrender unconditionally to their slightest whim." *Whim* was a weasel word for the ruthless pursuit of Soviet power. On the other hand, this steady, methodical, brutal consolidation of Soviet power had encountered defiance in Yugoslavia, where Marshal Tito had successfully broken away from Soviet domination.

Our background papers were assembled and distributed to the Assembly, which met on May 21–25. The participants were an illustrious group, including Harvey Bundy, John Cowles, John Kenneth Galbraith, David Lilienthal, Henry Luce, Jacob Potofsky, Mrs. Ogden Reid, Arthur Sulzberger, and Thomas Watson. Keynote speeches were given by Lewis W. Douglas, former U.S. ambassador to Great Britain; Senator Paul Douglas, defender of Truman's European policy; and Senator Robert Taft, who argued the isolationist position, adding, however, that "Russia is much more of a threat to the security of this country than Germany ever was," and warning that "to make a modern nation completely ready to fight a war tomorrow at full speed . . . would completely end all freedom here at home."

Thereafter the group was divided into roundtables, each with a chairman and rapporteur. As rapporteur to the roundtable chaired by Donald McKay, a historian of France from Harvard, I had to prepare summaries of its sessions. After Henry Luce forcefully denounced the idea of recognizing the People's Republic of China at one early meeting, McKay ordered me to fetch from another roundtable Nathaniel Peffer, a Columbia Sinologist and vociferous proponent of recognizing the new communist government in China. A great contretemps ensued. (It took another two decades or more for the United States to recognize the PRC!)

The various groups debated the wisdom of the administration's European policy in the context of the Soviet danger, which was deemed to overwhelm all else, but discussed the whole range of issues, especially the possible expansion of NATO to include the FRG, and the putative primacy of Western Europe as against East Asia as our principal region of engagement. Our group acknowledged the immediate danger of "Soviet imperialistic aggression," from which

Western Europe had to be protected. "A third world war is not the solution and might result in the destruction of modern civilization," but the fear of such a war should not divert us from defending freedom. The other groups had similarly ominous assessments.

In my chronology, I sketched the main lines of the divergent developments in the two Germanys, but paid special heed to the GDR, about which we knew so little. The USSR was tightening its control over all its satellites in Eastern Europe, East Germany emphatically included. The latter had become a society, at once collectivist and replete with anomie, in which people were whipped into a constant state of political frenzy, a mobilization of emotion that was followed by enforced impotence of action. The constitutionally guaranteed rights of free press and assembly were dead letters, and orthodoxy suppressed whatever dissidence remained, whether in church or press or education. One might have once believed that Germany's Soviet protectors would allow a different type of society to emerge, cognizant of German traditions and conditions, but by now, after the Czech coup in 1948 and the new round of purges of "Titoist deviationists and Zionist sympathizers," it was clear that Moscow intended to tighten its rule even more brutally, with uniform policies transmitted by more or less subservient local servants. At the time, I may not have been sufficiently aware that the implicit anti-Semitism of these purges extended to the GDR, where, however, the racist undertone was much muted—a reticence dictated by the memory of Nazi times. Nor did we sufficiently realize that Ulbricht and his lieutenants were not so fully subservient as they appeared: they tried to assert a measure of independence, often wishing to follow even more radical measures than Moscow prescribed. Ulbricht brought his own paranoia to policy—and his own penchant for brutal suppression. Victims of the brown dictatorship excelled as perpetrators of a red dictatorship.

The cold war's intense cultural propaganda escalated in line with actual clashes. Western efforts were directed at Germans in particular, at Europeans generally, but the charge that Communists had a blueprint for world domination—as had the Nazis—had been long implanted in the American mind, and it eased the demagogic efforts of Senator McCarthy (far from alone in exploiting this theme). On the other side, the Soviets vowed to expose and oppose the capitalist-fascist-imperialist West. Soviets had genuinely thought that the end of the war would usher in another capitalist depression, with high unemployment and new recruits to communism. Reality turned out differently. The Western economies grew stronger, partly because American leaders understood after 1945 what they had failed to grasp after 1918: that economic and political development were inextricably connected. It is hard to develop a new democracy at a time of economic misery.

The GDR never ceased intoning its major line: the Federal Republic, riddled as it was with ex-Nazis, was an imperialist-fascist power constituting a constant and grave threat to the "democratic" Germany. That there *were* former Nazis in important positions in the FRG was a gift to left-wing critics; for example, Hans Globke, Adenauer's state secretary, had written the commentary to Hitler's Nürnberg laws. At the time, we didn't know how many ex-Nazis were flourishing in anti-fascist East Germany as well. The two Germanys were locked in their own miniature cold war, replete with rhetorical vilification and various forms of espionage.

And yet at the same time, in both parts of Germany there was initially the expectation for reunion—at first a genuine sense that this division couldn't and shouldn't last, later a ritualistic invocation of solidarity. The two Germanys were in competition, with the western part from the beginning being the stronger one, its economy growing dynamically, its society relatively free, its borders open. In contrast, the East Germans were cut off, their planned economy geared to the production of capital rather than consumer goods, and their standard of living—an increasingly important measuring stick for success— much lower than the Federal Republic's. Everything in the GDR had to be oriented eastward, its economy integrated in Comecon (the Soviet bloc's Council for Mutual Economic Assistance), its politics under close Moscow surveillance. The East German drive to expropriate and banish private enterprise in any form produced a ready group of aggrieved and discontented citizens, many of whom fled to the FRG: this loss of enterprising people was a gain for the FRG and a boost for its economic miracle.

Considering the handicaps, the East Germans' own economic progress, when it began some time later, was impressive, and celebrated as an economic miracle itself. Among the Soviet satellites, it became the economic leader; and the more the East Germans boasted of success, the more their socialist neighbors resented this new German arrogance. In Warsaw, Bonn was far more popular (and important) than East Berlin. Even in the 1960s it was a bit early for Ulbricht to be lording it over Poland or Czechoslovakia, but the German habit of feeling superior to Slavs reemerged; we now know that Ulbricht's ambition to have the GDR be a model of socialism grated on Kremlin rulers, too. The SED leader knew how to feign docility, but in reality he seemed to have developed a new version of an older German style: servility mixed with arrogance, to which he added the assurance that Marxism, after all, was a German product. To boot, he was a rigid person, humorless and dogmatic.

So the two Germanys gradually grew apart. Germany's much-touted nationalism wasn't strong enough to preserve much of a common identity. Many West Germans were busily shedding their nationalist passions and embracing a new Western European identity; they developed a certain unacknowledged indifference to their "brothers and sisters" in the east, while the GDR's propaganda mills never ceased attacking the imperialist-capitalist aggressors in the west, seen as endlessly trying to sabotage the GDR's efforts to build a true socialist, egalitarian society. The GDR might lag behind the "materialistic" West with its consumerist greed, but its very austerity bespoke moral superiority.

There were of course organizations in the Federal Republic that concerned themselves with "all-German" issues, some of them also propagandistically inclined. Both Protestant and Catholic churches in West Germany kept contact with their harassed and impoverished brethren in the GDR, where prescribed atheism challenged all Christians. Here, too, was a certain continuity with Nazi times, though the Nazis had disguised their atheistic inclinations, and pseudo- or near-pagan Christians had rushed to their support. The East German regime instituted blatant party analogues to Christian sacraments such as confirmation, and party doctrine replaced religious instruction in schools. German youths were once again clothed in party uniforms, and their party loyalty, especially their non-Christian commitment, was rewarded. Stubborn adherence to Christian faith was penalized—all this in territories that had once been the heartland of the Reformation.

The workers' rebellion of June 17, 1953, shook this self-confidently atheistic, socialistic regime, for it demonstrated clearly that Ulbricht's policy for constructing socialism—which favored the state-directed creation of heavy industry over consumer goods in a society of repression and deprivation—bred discontent. (Weeks before, the government had raised workers' production quotas, ignoring Soviet warnings that to make still greater demands was risky.) The regime had to call on Soviet tanks to put down this first open defiance, and though there were to be many such heroic efforts elsewhere in Eastern Europe, this was the only one in East Germany until 1989. June 17 was a signal event in the postwar era, and though it was sometimes politically exploited in West Germany, it was powerfully important. Bertold Brecht wrote his own satirical judgment of the party's response to the uprising, suggesting that the government, disappointed in the people, should dissolve it and elect a new people.

MY FIRST IMMEDIATE EXPERIENCE of the GDR, or rather of its capital, was a year later, during the summer of 1954, when I was teaching at the Free University and had my cursory foray into East Berlin which earned me High Commissioner Conant's rebuke for its brevity. Thereafter, I went to see some people in East Berlin in connection with my work, and Peggy and I repeatedly took advantage of East Berlin's fabled theaters of socialist drama. I saw a production of Schiller's *Don Carlos*; the Grand Inquisitor's deathlike face bore a clear resemblance to Adenauer's gaunt visage, and the famous plea *"Sire, geben Sie Gedankenfreiheit"* [give us freedom of thought] — for which line the Nazis had banned the play — received hesitant applause, a moment of defiance in the dark.

I also repeatedly visited the stately, spacious Karl Marx Buchhandlung on Stalinallee, where one could buy inexpensive editions of the great "classics of socialism" and translations of acceptable foreign works. The SED-controlled publishing enterprises produced a great flow of authorized books at low prices, hoping to leave no comrade behind. And in the secondhand section one could find "bourgeois" editions of old classics at bargain prices: I bought an old four-volume edition of Herder's *Werke* with a modern stamp on the flyleaf: FROM THE GHETTO LIBRARY — no place specified. A grim irony: the works of an Enlightenment philosopher taken from the ghetto, perhaps the one place where he might have been read in the old spirit.

I also purchased a big volume entitled *Deutschland*, translated from the *Great Soviet Encyclopedia*. Its editors, Jürgen Kuczynski and Wolfgang Steinitz, noted that this "most comprehensive scientific work in the history of humanity" had been raised to a "still higher level" in its 1950 edition, as decided by the Soviet Union's Council of Ministers. Of contemporary historical writing, it reported, "After the destruction of Hitler's Germany by the Soviet Union, German historians have gained wider perspectives in free scientific research . . . However, reactionary ideas are once again prevalent in West German historiography, as Anglo-American imperialists conduct a policy of dividing Germany so as to allow the revival of fascism and militarism in West Germany."

Stalinallee was East Germany's proudest emblem, the old Frankfurterstrasse, destroyed by Allied bombs, rebuilt in a garish display of fancy housing for "the workers" that was in fact allotted to the regime's high elite. I asked myself, Is this pretentious ugliness, this fancy slum, really the ultimate fulfillment of the communist society? Can the Communists be unaware that this showpiece of the "proletarian" world actually embodies their society's cruel inegalitarianism, with its provision of pseudo-luxury for only the few while promising to the many? At run-down lunch places, I met with "people of the new type," the East German version of the Soviet "new man," and I found them vaguely hostile. Was I being excessively harsh? Did childhood memories of one regime and aversion of the new one becloud my impressions? I was dimly aware of the danger.

My initial response now troubles me: Perhaps it was excessively affected by conventional cold-war assumptions, by an unconscious transfer of my old anti-Germanism to this new deformation. Perhaps I saw only what I was programmed to see. Certainly the public tone in East Berlin was pompous and oppressive, but did I then realize the psychological effect of the disparity between East German austerity and West German consumer extravagance? I had other conflicting thoughts: when, on a U.S. military bus, I visited the huge Soviet war memorial in East Berlin with its towering statue—World's Fair style—of a Soviet soldier clutching a Russian child in one hand and a sword smashing the swastika in the other, I half admired it. Was I yielding to a whiff of political nostalgia? Certainly it was true that without the Soviet Union, Hitler might have won the war. The inscriptions in the memorial hall, with its coffin of the unknown soldier, recalled the struggle against the "fascist hordes," and the cliché jolted me back to the present. It was a powerful monument not only to the Russian dead but to the death of many hopes and illusions.

That the early GDR appeared to some people as a temptation, as the promise at last of a peaceful, socialist Germany came home to me most vividly during that same summer of 1954, when I spent most of an entire night in Munich arguing with my childhood acquaintance Peter Hacks, now a playwright, over his plan to move to East Berlin: he was certain that the East was freer than the West, and he wanted to live the socialist dream and work with Brecht's Berliner Ensemble. Brecht—who in 1947 had fled to East Berlin from his American exile to escape the investigations of the House Un-American Activities Committee—was proof of American unfreedom, he said. I tried to dissuade him, arguing that life under one dictatorship should have been enough for him, but my impassioned counterarguments availed nothing; he immigrated to East Berlin. And it did seem that the Ulbricht regime knew how to celebrate art as a weapon in the class struggle against imperialists, and it lavished support on writers and artists, provided of course, they were loyalists.* That evening with

*In 1949, the year of Goethe's bicentennial, Thomas Mann, having left his American exile and comfortably settled in Switzerland, remaining equally aloof from both Germanys, made a special appearance in Goethe's town, Weimar, now in the east. And he was never a critic of the GDR as he had been of Hitler's Germany.

Hacks left me frustrated, and more convinced than ever that America's strident right-wing anticommunist crusade was helping its enemies—whatever else it was doing. I still hold this view, which in recent years has become unfashionable in American intellectual circles.* In any case, Hacks made his move in 1955, Brecht died a year later, and Hacks became the GDR's best-known playwright—alternating unpredictably between being the regime's propagandist and its critic. His historical plays were successfully staged in West Germany as well (and one of them was produced in New York, with Uta Hagen in the principal role). He was a gifted writer, also delightful in writing wittily didactic children's stories, fifteen volumes of them! By the 1980s he had lost faith in both Germanys, which he thought had declined into cultural barbarism. He died in 2004—controversial and contrarian to the end.

For the next few years I had no contact with the GDR, though my interest in the other satellite countries of Eastern Europe continued to grow steadily. The excitement of Khrushchev's secret speech to the Twentieth Party Congress in February 1956, denouncing Stalin's crimes and his cult of personality—though never published in the Soviet Union, a translation was published by the State Department in June 1956 and came to be known to millions—ushered in a year of brief rejoicing and lasting grief: in the fall of that year the Red Army crushed the heroic revolt in Hungary, and Polish efforts at liberation failed.

Henry Roberts and his Columbia colleagues published documents of that period in a book called *National Communism and Popular Revolt in Eastern Europe*. I have never forgotten, and I often ended my Columbia lectures with, Adam Wazyk's "Poem for Adults," published in Poland in 1955, a magnificent appeal for truth and against

> *the vultures of abstraction [that] pick out our brains,*
> *when students are enclosed in text books without windows . . .*
> *We make demands on this earth,*
> *for which we did not throw dice*
> *for which a million perished in battle:*
> *for a clear truth,*
> *for the bread of freedom,*
> *for burning reason,*

*In November 2001, in response to my inquiry, Peter Hacks described for me his father's political attitudes: "Until 1933 he was a Trotskyite and after Hitler a failed [*gescheitert*] Trotskyite," and added that he wished his father had helped in the building of the GDR. This was a marvelously ambiguous Pickwickian remark: as a Trotskyite, his father would have been liquidated in the GDR.

for burning reason.
We demand these every day
We demand through the Party.

As I tried to explain to my students, people deprived of freedom, such as those in Eastern Europe, often understood freedom better than those who enjoyed it or who had it but didn't enjoy it because they devalued it, thinking (like Marcuse) that Western freedom signified "repressive tolerance."

Ulbricht, being a hardliner by conviction, was suspicious of the post-Stalin experiments such as Khrushchev's "thaw" in the USSR, and of the turmoil rocking other parts of Eastern Europe in the 1950s. One prominent German dissident, Wolfgang Harich, was tried and imprisoned, and others suffered a similar fate, but intimidation hastened another form of protest, expressed in the steady flight of East Germans to West Germany via Berlin. This was solid evidence of opposition to Ulbricht's regime. The GDR sought to staunch the flow by punishing family members who stayed behind, but even this did not deter people.

The Soviets recognized the danger to the GDR of this constant outflow, and Ulbricht clamored for an end to West Berlin as a bridge to freedom. In November 1958, Khrushchev delivered his ultimatum; either the Allies would agree to a peace treaty that would settle the Berlin question or the Soviets would sign a unilateral peace with the GDR, which would then have the means of annulling Allied rights in West Berlin. Was he bluffing, or was he willing to risk war over Berlin?

I could watch the drama from close quarters when I spent my sabbatical of 1960–1961 in Paris, working on Bleichröder. David Landes and I needed hugely important material in German state archives that were now located in the GDR. Access to these had rarely, if ever, been granted to American scholars, and one needed multiple permits, including a visa from the GDR. Before going to Paris, I had checked with the head of the East European section of the State Department, and he had assured me, "You won't get in, but if you do, there is nothing we can do for you."

From Paris, I wrote the director of the German archives, one Dr. Lötzke, for permission to work in them; six weeks later, he replied that he had forwarded my inquiry to the archival division of the Ministry of the Interior. It was all very frustrating, so Landes and I went to see Georges Castellan, a French historian who had become a (sympathetic) specialist on the GDR. He lived in an impeccably bourgeois apartment, as many prominent *gauchistes* of the time did: Parisian comfort made it easier to await the inevitable triumph of the proletariat. Castellan knew us as "bourgeois" historians (if not worse), but he saw no reason why the East German regime should bar us. He referred us to a special committee on Franco-German exchanges, run by a Roland Lenoir. (*German* in this instance signified only East Germany.) After many months, and thanks to him, the two permissions were granted.

I knew that the trip would yield more than its principal objective, for I would be able to spend time in a country different from all other European countries, on my first visit to a Soviet satellite. (Visits to East Berlin were different: after all, Berlin was still under some Allied rule.) Landes and I arrived at Tegel Airport in West Berlin on April 17, 1961. Our East German contact person, Dr. Werner Richter, and his wife, picked us up: Richter was a man roughly of our age, a short, round, lively fellow, alert, outgoing, and humorous. At the time he was a high functionary at Humboldt University (as the University of Berlin was now called), and as such came with car and chauffeur. (I suppose he brought his wife along because, though crossings to West Berlin were easy, they were discouraged, and this bit of official business gave her a rare chance to see the place.) He gave us a tour of the heart of East Berlin: near the Wilhelmstrasse, the old center of power, we could see the remains of the Bleichröder Bank. Richter gave us some East German money, took our passports so as to obtain our visas, and settled us in at the HO Hotel Berliner Bär. We carried our bags up three flights because the elevators didn't work. The next morning at breakfast, I noted a good many old and young people, but our generation was barely represented: later I was told that there were as many seventy-five-year-old men as forty-two-year-olds in the GDR, the younger cohort having been decimated by war and emigration.

Everything was at once strange and familiar, and every detail caught my interest. I suppose we were unusual: Americans were a rare species. I reported as much as possible to Peggy in Paris, though I knew a censor might read the letters. I used deliberately mocking terms of praise, describing as "wonderful" what at the same time I hinted was wretched. David and I found traces of the past in the archives, but I was fascinated by the weird, often indecipherable present, every detail a part of a mosaic at once ancient and very modern.

The next morning Richter took us to the Potsdam archive, normally a short drive straight through the western part of the city. But to avoid the many delays at various border controls, he chose a route around West Berlin, a longish trip that allowed for a useful talk. (On the way back, Landes and I took a train that made a similar detour; this train line took so long that irrepressible East Berlin wits called it "the Sputnik," after the Russian earth satellite that had first orbited the earth three years before.) Potsdam, the old garrison city and seat of Frederick the Great's palace, Sans-Souci, had become a shabby town, a ghost of its once honored past, frozen in time, it seemed, with ancient cobbled streets uncrowded by cars, but carrying an occasional horse-drawn delivery carriage, its stately villas in socialist decay. It was a town of widows and of a large Soviet garrison.

Richter introduced us to Dr. Lötzke, who seemed amused or embarrassed when I thanked him for allowing us to work there (clearly he hadn't the authority to make the decision himself). We agreed on a modus operandi: we would not only work in the several archives but also order microfilms of what we needed; in return we would send the archives microfilms from our own Bleichröder archive. A number of young archivists were most helpful; with one of them, a Dr. Brather, I corresponded for some years (a contact recently renewed), and just about every conversation we had was revelatory. For one thing, people wanted to talk, and I was a rare animal, speaking their language, knowing their past, yet critical of most of their diverse views.

David and I worked furiously and productively in the—usually cold— reading rooms, where helpers brought us trays with files; some of these documents yielded hints that turned out to be central to my work. I wasn't sure that the promised microfilm would be reliable, so I took extensive notes as well with my trusty four-color pencil. It was an odd existence: in the archive, we found clues to life in the Bismarckian period, while outside were clues to an obscure, half-closed present.

In the director's room during our first interview, I noticed a woman in attendance, silently alert and unfriendly. I thought her the party representative. It turned out that she had more clout than the others, and on the second day, she arranged for us to have quarters in Potsdam, a rare privilege. So we moved from the East Berlin hotel to a well-known *Pension* for generals' widows. The caretaker was an expellee from Pomerania, complaining bitterly about life's difficulties: you couldn't get help, that is, servants, and if you did you had to pay them a lot *and* they had to eat at your table. She was an unreconstructed German nationalist, every word and gesture true to her class and age, and she was filled with pity for German suffering. She allowed me to make a call to Paris. (The operator asked the purpose of my call and my nationality; about the latter she exclaimed in astonishment, "We have people like that, too?") When we said good-bye, the landlady asked how old I had been when I left Germany: "Twelve," I said. "Oh, then such a short time here." I replied, "It sufficed."

At the end of the week, Dr. Brather and I took a three-hour walk. We visited Sans-Souci—with Frederick the Great's study!—and its rundown garden, where in a corner, behind some wooden barriers, I spied Christian Daniel Rauch's famous equestrian statue of the king, a landmark of prewar Berlin. Other bronze statues of Frederick's generals were also strewn about, more or less abandoned amid the weeds and uncut grass. I thought, So that's what you did with your past, cast it aside, put out of sight, as a mere remnant of the "feudal" past that communism has at last expunged. I remembered Edmund Burke's injunction to the French: "respecting your forefathers, you would have been taught to respect yourselves." (In later years, the GDR began to claim some of the old Prussian patrimony.)

Peter Hacks wrote about that past—one of his best-known plays dealt with Frederick the Great—for he wanted to use historical events for dramatic-pedagogic purposes, his inspiration being no less than Shakespeare and Goethe. I saw him in his small apartment far from the center of East Berlin. It was our first meeting since I had implored him not to migrate to the GDR; after a few moments of amiability, we settled down to an acrimonious exchange. By this time he had experienced the vagaries of communist cultural policies and encountered many successes and difficulties. I believe his work was more often produced and certainly better paid in West than in East Germany, so capitalist loot came to sweeten his life of socialist penury. (Brecht had shown the way.) But he divorced his personal disappointments from his political principle: to him and to his even more bellicose wife, the world was "objectively" divided into two camps, reactionary and revolutionary, and this opposition determined everything else. They were Marxists for whom the struggle between socialist and capitalist systems was fundamental; the moral superiority and ultimate historic victory of socialism, derivatives of Marxist-Leninist dogma, were articles of faith. For the sake of that certain future you put up with present-day deprivations. Life in the GDR was dull, he acknowledged, but it was still much better than in the West.

Hacks remained a dedicated Communist all his life, at times a critic of the regime, most of the time its champion. He knew about the West's deficiencies but nothing about its virtues, such as freedom of thought and movement; nothing could for a moment shake his commitment to what I thought of as a Marxist straitjacket. He was stubbornly consistent to the end: in 1990, he found himself in absolute opposition to a reunified Germany, for in his view the FRG had simply annexed the GDR. This conceit of dividing the world into two camps, the good and the bad, did not die with the demise of communism. It shapes the rhetoric and action of the ideologues governing the sole remaining superpower.

That night I encountered even more wondrous dogma. Landes had maintained friendly barter relations with Jürgen Kuczynski, the prolific economic historian of Marxist orthodoxy: Landes sent Kuczynski American detective stories, a passion of his, in return for serious works on economic history. Kuczynski's life is a fascinating tale of a talented servant and survivor. As a young man, he had visited the United States and the Soviet Union, imbibing high culture everywhere. He joined the German Communist Party in 1930—during its Stalinist suicidal phase, when its principal enemy was not the Nazis but the Socialists—and in his memoirs, which appeared in 1972, he declared that after joining, he did nothing that hadn't been approved by the party: "To quit the party would have appeared to me tantamount to quitting life, quitting humanity." In 1936 he fled to England, where he continued to write books on the conditions of the working classes under capitalism, a project his well-known father had begun, and toward the end of the war, the U.S. Strategic Bombing Survey recruited him to help investigate "fascist" war production. He wanted to be sent to Germany as soon as possible after the war so that he could begin work "for the party." And for the party he continued to write an astounding number of books, many of them scholarly accounts of the "everyday life" of the German people. (In volume 4, published in 1982, the first nine citations come from Stalin, Lenin, and Marx-Engels. Perfect conformity.) After 1990, he managed to accommodate to the new regime and to confess, at least in print, all manner of previous errors. A bon vivant, he died at the age of ninety-five.

After all our socialist meals, it was a gustatory pleasure to get a kind of German smorgasbord, which is what the Kuczynskis served us in their capacious apartment in an old Berlin building. After dinner, in their book-filled living room, I made some banal remark about the miseries of the century beginning in 1914 with the Great War. Mrs. Kuczynski dropped her knitting and pronounced that the war had been a good thing: after all, it had led to the end of the old bourgeois world. I switched to a neutral subject, genuinely admiring their huge collection of books. "My husband's third library," she said defiantly. I fell into the trap and asked about the first two. The first the Nazis stole, she explained; the English had taken the second when she and her husband left Oxford after the war. I was skeptical about this second story, but asked her about the first. That library was the most valuable one, she explained, including the handwritten protocol of the first meetings of the Internationale in the 1860s. She volunteered that they knew where these treasures were: the Nazis had stored them in the east, where they had fallen into Polish hands. Innocently, I asked whether some exchange couldn't be effected. "How could we ask our poor Polish comrades, after all they suffered, for a return of these objects?" I thought that the "poor Polish comrades" might happily exchange some German documents for other works or archives, but remained silent, and she returned to her knitting, like Mme. Defarge in Dickens's *A Tale of Two Cities*. Perhaps she was adding my name to those deserving of the guillotine. Oddly, her husband said little, though he was a learned and amusing person. I thought him a perfect example of an almost avuncular *debrouillard* in hard times. He knew how to calibrate his political utterances, while she was "a true believer"; nothing could shake her Moscow-centered faith, with its prescribed hatred of capitalism. Much later I heard the credible rumor that in Oxford she had been a Soviet spy.

Communist dogma could feed on the latest news: Landes and I arrived in East Germany on the day of the Bay of Pigs invasion, and the East German propaganda machine went into high gear. Headlines screamed about American aggression; posters and "spontaneous" mass rallies in defense of Castro were held everywhere. HANDS OFF CUBA! signs were the mildest form of attack. It was a most unpleasant sensation to witness this vilification while being ignorant of the true course of events. We now know that a reluctant Kennedy was pushed into this misadventure by Allen Dulles and the CIA; the official version at the time was that Cuban freedom fighters had landed in Cuba with no U.S. involvement; but the truth came out quite quickly, and Kennedy rightly rued his faith in the CIA and the Pentagon. It was a clear defeat, and an embarrassment, a boon to the enemies among whom we happened to be. "Cuba" came up in private conversation all the time, but the Soviet invasion of Hungary in 1956 didn't come up except when I referred to it.

Our next stop was Merseburg, a small provincial town near Halle, to which the Nazis had evacuated the huge holdings known as the Prussian State Archive, now in an old insurance building. On the train and at some stations, we saw masses of Soviet soldiers; in East Berlin there had hardly been any. There was a clear Russian presence in Merseburg as well: the station abutted Yuri Gagarin Platz, named in honor of the first cosmonaut's space trip, in April 1961: socialism triumphant in space, while on earth, primitive, desolate, yet somehow pleasingly old-fashioned. The town was the seat of the Leuna works, the GDR's largest industrial plant (despite wartime destruction and Soviet dismantlement, despite major losses in key personnel), successor to a Nazi factory that had produced synthetic fuel.* The smell of brown coal, reminiscent of my

---

*By odd coincidence, Fritz Haber had used his position during the Great War to have Leuna built, and already in the 1920s it had been Germany's largest chemical factory. Its official name was now VEB (the people's own!) Leuna Werke Walter Ulbricht, which suggested its importance. Leuna was unsurpassed in the level of its pollution, and I read of one asthmatic apparatchik whom the regime banished to Merseburg—for extra suffering.

childhood, hung heavy over the city—even over the gorgeously blooming lilacs we passed on the way to the archive. Landes and I had been put in a Hotel zur Goldenen Sonne, neither golden nor sunny, a ruin of a building; the sink in our room regularly emptied into a pail.

In the archive we were treated with great courtesy. Our requests would be brought promptly to us, but only five files at a time. One day a Soviet historian showed up, and he clearly could work without restrictions: a heap of files was instantly placed at his table. Amusing to see the subservience in action. We ate lunch at the Leuna canteen, where head archivists and managers mingled with a huge number of workers: potatoes with a heavy sauce and a slight admixture of sausage, no salad, and certainly no fruit—a caricature of a German meal, at a risibly low price. I eventually found jars of Bulgarian cherries, the only fruit available, in the one store in town, and devoured them in our room. Despite this seemingly egalitarian austerity, the GDR's standard of living was—or was claimed to be—the highest in the eastern bloc. When Landes and I were invited once to the director's house for Sunday afternoon coffee and cake, Landes talked of our Western world, including the stock market, and Dr. Weltsch was amazed at its opportunities. He knew capitalism only as the enemy, its sole known feature being exploitation; we complicated the picture.

The archive was rich, the work immensely productive, but a trial nevertheless. While we worked away in this godforsaken place, some of the French generals in Algeria staged an armed uprising against de Gaulle and his policy of ending the brutal war there by accepting Algerian independence. When they threatened to carry their rebellion to Paris itself, the East German papers reported that the rebels had taken Corsica and that Paris feared a parachutist invasion. I wanted to return to Paris—out of great curiosity in the unfolding history, but Landes was appalled at the idea of my desertion; his work ethic was incontestable. So I stayed.

It was unnerving that these momentous changes were taking place while we were isolated deep inside the GDR, cut off from access to Western sources. There was no way to get "straight" news: in the major hotels of big cities one could at least buy some foreign newspapers, usually days old, but not in Merseburg. I would occasionally call my cousin in Switzerland and thus get details as the drama continued. Eventually I heard of de Gaulle's address to the French nation and French troops, speaking of "a quartet of retired generals . . . [who] possess a certain expeditious and limited skill" and who must be crushed. "I forbid any Frenchman . . . to carry out any of their orders . . . French men and women, help me." This masterful speech was an almost instant success: the coup collapsed, some generals surrendered, and others went underground. (On my return to Paris, I had a message that a French writer-acquaintance of Corsican origin and connections and right-wing views wanted to see me at once. We met at the Deux Magots, and he told me the "inside story," of which I remember but one detail: the CIA had spawned the plot. For left and right, the CIA was the great satanic power, at the heart of all conspiracy.)

My visa for East German travel was restricted to the three districts of Berlin, Potsdam, and Halle. (The GDR had abolished the ancient *Länder*, such as Saxony and Thuringia, in another break with the past.) But just outside the permitted area and close to Merseburg was Naumburg, with its thirteenth-century early Gothic cathedral and twelve celebrated life-size stone statues of saints and local rulers, most wonderfully the magnificent Frau Ute, with her beatific, mysterious smile. I was eager to see the cathedral and to visit Pforta, a famous old school that Nietzsche had attended. Nietzsche's presence in Naumburg was not much acknowledged then, though a Nietzsche house-museum has been established since.

I decided to ignore my travel restrictions and go to Naumburg—only to find the cathedral closed for restoration. I finally located the home of the custodian and pleaded with him that I had come three thousand miles to see the cathedral and Frau Ute; he yielded and allowed me an illicit visit. A photograph of her hangs in my bedroom.

By the time I had seen all I wanted to see in Naumburg, it was night, and I boarded the local train to go back to Merseburg. I sat alone in my compartment in the train—which had a steam engine such as I had last seen some twenty-five years before—and stared out at the occasional dim lights from a village or small town. The old-fashioned countryside was shabby; the atmosphere was somber, with faded inscriptions from earlier times; the rhythm of things slower, more congenial. What was I doing on this night journey in forbidden and forlorn territory? What was I doing in Central Europe, at once so much more familiar to me than Americanized West Germany and yet so foreign?

The Kuczynskis and other loyalists spoke of the next great task: "to industrialize the peasant," to push collectivization further, to destroy the mind-set of the individual farmer and his tie to the earth and his own work. Dr. Richter spoke of the need to enter the cybernetic age, to make up for technological backwardness. Many people complained of material conditions, so clearly below Western standards, but a surfeit of posters boasted of great leaps forward and of collective enterprises over-fulfilling their quotas. Rallies, posters, uniforms were all signs of mass mobilization at a time of political impotence. Censorship was present but largely invisible; East Germans had crude views of the "enemy" but individual interest in the "foreigner." There seemed little interest, scholarly or otherwise, in National Socialism. Indeed the very term was for obvious reasons avoided.

I was struck by a sign I saw outside a Lutheran church in Merseburg: THE CHURCH: A CANDIDATE FOR MUSEUMS? NO, ALIVE! And from inside I heard the defiant sounds of a choir singing Luther's great hymn "A Mighty Fortress." The church seemed like a place of non-accommodation and refuge—so different from what it had been under the Nazis. I knew that the GDR had embarked on a fierce anti-church campaign, and in my eagerness to find resistance, I probably mistook an exception for the rule, for the churches in the GDR were mostly conformist, and some pastors may have believed in the regime's slogan "The Church in Socialism," that is, a church that accepted socialist principles and practices. It took several decades more before the East German churches did become havens for a peace movement and dissent.

East Germans hadn't asked for this regime; it had been imposed on them. Opposition to the regime was dangerous, and flight involved an implicit, harsh bargain: one sacrificed home and all that went with it for freedom and the chances of economic betterment. Common sense would tell one that the young and adventurous were the first to leave while, for various reasons, the others would stay behind. Would-be political opponents also left, as Poles or Hungarians were virtually unable to do. Thus East Germans who remained in the GDR were predisposed quietly to acquiesce to the regime or to resort to the earlier German pattern of "inner emigration," mixing outward conformity with inward aloofness; they certainly had no tradition of civic courage to fall back on. All too many Germans had been docile under National Socialism, whereas one could almost subsume Polish history under the rubric of heroic, if sometimes futile, resistance.

The people of the GDR had to make their arrangements; some may have been genuinely fired by the promise of socialism; most may have grumbled but were grateful for the slow improvement in living standards. To boot, people could appreciate the social services the state made available—medical care, full employment, educational opportunities, especially for those coming from underprivileged strata. Socialist society's trumpeted egalitarianism was visible—canteens and kindergarten for working mothers, cheap (though unavailable) cars. The regime made access to culture easy: cheap editions of German classics, inexpensive tickets to theater and concerts. As in the Soviet Union, the party would from time to time allow a sudden burst of greater freedom, but at all times covert and overt censorship set strict limits. The sting of adversity gave cultural life in the GDR a certain excitement.

In the East German regime's effort to indoctrinate, it had an obvious model: the USSR gave propaganda huge importance, as the Nazis had. And indoctrination in every totalitarian regime begins with the child and penetrates all of education. The differences between West and East Germany were striking; children in the east were schooled at an earlier age (partly because their mothers were working); access to universities was eased for the children of party loyalists and workers. Class distinctions faded; workers were rewarded with communal vacations; and in an effort to reward achievement and perhaps to strengthen competitive passions, the regime awarded an abundance of medals and decorations. The Soviet Union was the model in all this, though reminders of Nazi practices were hard to miss. The "dacha" culture of East Germany, with its visible and invisible privileges, combined the old and the new, a bit of the brown with a red patina. I noted especially another distinct copy from the Soviet system: the richly funded Academy of Sciences, whose academicians enjoyed special privileges (cars and chauffeurs!) and better working conditions than university professors. And the GDR way of investing in excellence was exemplified by its often corrupt support of sports.

Though I heard complaints about shortcomings, I rarely heard any expressed longing for freedom, whether of thought or of movement. I assumed there was a small cadre of functionaries and true believers, and then most everybody else: people who, grumbling, had made their peace with the regime, passively wishing for better conditions. I didn't sense any great longing for German reunification either. And how could there be, when the GDR was building up its own identity, in which socialism was central and its moral and material superiority over the capitalist West was gospel? People had given up on reunification in any foreseeable future; it had become a chimera. Or, put mischievously, they had privatized the hope: in ever greater numbers they made their private arrangements for reunification by crossing into the other Germany.

When President Kennedy and Premier Khrushchev met in Vienna in early June 1961, the latter wrongly thought he scented weakness, since the Americans had recently been so humiliated by the failed operation in Cuba at the Bay of Pigs, and so he moved aggressively on the Berlin question. On June 10, he published the aide-mémoire he had given to Kennedy: a repeat of the 1958 ultimatum threatening a separate peace between the USSR and the GDR that would automatically jeopardize or end Allied rights in West Berlin—the one that for three years had been followed by inaction. Kennedy understood the immense gravity of this new Berlin crisis and privately mused that a wall might go up. He also thought that if there were to be a third world war, it would start over Berlin, for he saw that the mass exodus of East Germans was threatening the very existence of the GDR—an intolerable prospect for its regime and for its Soviet protectors—and he knew that the surrender of West Berlin's freedom or of Allied rights would be an unacceptable injury to American power and prestige, quite aside from the political consequences for him at home. But nuclear war would be catastrophic. In sum, Berlin had become militarily indefensible and politically indispensable.

On my way home that summer, and because of the sudden topicality of Berlin, I was asked to give various talks in oddly different places. One was at Nuffield College, Oxford, at a seminar chaired by John Plamenatz, a great scholar of Marxism, who was amused at my remarks about the poverty of Marxist thought in the GDR. I warned against ignoring what was happening in East Germany, against believing that it was, as one writer had called it, "the disappearing satellite." And in September, I spoke about this again, at a church dinner in Rochester, Vermont, our summer home. In the discussion after my talk, a stranger identified himself as coming from Vermont's big city, Burlington, and he vehemently objected to everything I had had to say about the two Germanys: Wasn't it true that there were more Nazis in the Foreign Office in Bonn now than had been the case during the Third Reich? I concluded that the Vermont branch of the Communist Party had delegated a member to heckle me, which I thought flattering. (But the subject was not a trivial one: in the spring of 2005, Joschka Fischer, then German foreign minister, asked me to help prepare a historians' commission to investigate precisely this issue of ex-Nazis in the postwar German foreign service.)

With each passing week in that summer of 1961, tensions increased. Many escapees from East Germany were leaving because of economic stringencies imposed by the regime, while others fled out of *Torschlusspanik*, a fear that the escape hatch might soon be shut. I wrote to Hajo Holborn that I feared the Berlin crisis could precipitate a nuclear war: was there not the possibility of some form of negotiated solution? I don't think I knew how far I wanted the United States to go to avoid a military confrontation, but probably I balked at the idea of incineration over Berlin. In late July, Kennedy gave a masterful speech, indicating his readiness to negotiate, adding, however: "But we must also be ready to resist with force, if force is used upon us."

Two weeks later, the East Germans, backed by a reluctant Soviet Union, came up with their defiant alternative: on August 13, they erected the first barriers between East and West Berlin. The menacing, ugly, full-scale thirteen-foot wall—with a death strip studded with landmines before it, and East German soldiers on watchtowers with orders to shoot—was to follow forthwith. (We now know that Ulbricht had been relentlessly pressing the Russians to take action. In 2003 appeared Hope Harrison's fine book *Driving the Soviets up the Wall*—the title conveying the thesis.)

Ulbricht and Khrushchev had "solved" the Berlin problem but not on their original terms; Kennedy's unprovocative resoluteness had saved the world from a nuclear nightmare, but at the time the apprehension among West Berliners was extreme, and at first the United States did little to assuage it. Willy Brandt was enraged. Was the Wall, horrible as it was, in separating families and ending all contacts within the city, merely the first of a series of steps that would destroy their freedom? The United States sent additional troops to West Berlin; in October there was a confrontation over the rights of American military personnel to enter East Berlin; American and Soviet tanks faced each other at Checkpoint Charlie. But it was clear that the Russians were being far more prudent than the East Germans, and West Berliners were reassured by American resoluteness. The U.S. commitment was reaffirmed, and two years later, Kennedy's appearance in Berlin occasioned an outburst of pro-American enthusiasm such as had never occurred before or since.

By the summer of 1962, I knew I needed to return to the GDR archives, but my direct efforts to get renewed permission stalled. In August, I returned to M. Lenoir of the French-German committee in Paris, asking for his help again. In my presence, he called the ministry in East Berlin, and while he talked I glanced at a timely propaganda brochure, "La Question de Berlin." When he finished, I offered to pay for the call; he said it had been a collect call, but perhaps I would wish to buy the brochure, which was only five hundred *anciens francs* (about one dollar). I thought politesse demanded no less. He took the bill, smiled, and said, "I just wanted to show you we take money from both sides." Everything was settled, and at my request he even arranged for me to stay at Leuna's socialist-posh Walter Ulbricht Guesthouse.

I arrived in the GDR in September, and this time my visa extended to the whole country. In Merseburg, I again enjoyed the eagerness with which young archivists wanted to help and talk with me; one explained that he and others chose an archival career in order to avoid the dogmatism that governed academic historical work. On my last day, one fellow asked whether we couldn't have a beer together that evening. I invited him to join me, and eventually four young men showed up at the Walter Ulbricht Guesthouse, where we sat in the dining room surrounded by East German apparatchiks, some in uniform. My guests spoke loudly and critically of various aspects of GDR life, and I, well trained from earlier times, suggested we might take a walk to get out of earshot of the others. They rejected that idea and continued their laments. I understood their views of the present situation, I told them, but didn't the original *idea* of socialism have any meaning for them? The most articulate of them asked whether I knew what socialism really was. I obliged him by pleading ignorance. He explained in a deliberately loud voice, "Socialism is the rational and scientific effort of a united and heroic people to overcome difficulties— that don't exist anywhere else."

In Merseburg, I could indulge my weakness for political jokes, one product that was in plentiful supply in Eastern Europe. The Berlin Wall was often mentioned, its official name being "the great anti-fascist wall" and its stated function to protect the democratic part of Germany from NATO imperialists; odd, then, that the Wall's death zone was on the eastern, not the western side. One joke captures the irony: a film producer comes to Ulbricht and asks for a twenty-four-hour breach in the Wall in return for which he will hand over millions of hard currency. Why does he want this? UFA (the once great German film company, its studios in the GDR) is planning a film on the vast migrations in Europe at the end of the Roman Empire and needs a shot of a mass migration. Under dictatorships, jokes serve as safety valves, as *Ersatz* for action.

During this visit, I thought I sensed a slightly different atmosphere, a greater openness at a time of worsening economic conditions: could it be that the deadly NO EXIT sign of the Wall actually removed the need to contemplate flight, the end to an enticing, terrifying temptation? Once confined in the prison, some were eager to rise within it and to grasp new opportunities; others retreated into sullen resignation. The Wall rescued East Germany from dissolution; what had been regarded as provisional was now permanent. And it made certain truths unavoidably clear, one being that the regime was deeply unpopular. I often remarked, especially after 1989, that National Socialism hadn't needed a wall: ordinary or extraordinary Germans had had no great passion to leave the Third Reich. At the same time, the Wall, having cut off most inter-German communications, further diminished West German interest in the other Germany.

At the Potsdam archive in the Orangerie of Sans-Souci, I discovered that the police records of pre-1914 Berlin included records of the Bleichröder clan, a glorious find! But I had appeared at that archive without permission, and soon a gruff guardian, dispatched from the central archive, ordered me to leave instantly and report first to the state office in another part of Potsdam for permission. I refused, saying it was my last day and that I needed to finish my work. I didn't stir, and he took a seat next to me in the small reading room. I finished early, as it happened, and asked the archivist if they had records at hand of the village of Gütergotz, where Bleichröder had bought a large estate from the renowned Prussian field marshal von Roon. The archivist looked, found nothing, but offered me something about a neighboring town; I said I had never heard of it. Impossible! the man said. Before the war it had housed a huge and well-known automobile assembly plant. I said loudly, "Now dismantled by Anglo-American imperialists?" There was laughter all around. GDR agitprop often complained about Anglo-American destruction, but everyone knew who the real despoiler was. At closing time, I observed to my "guardian" that surely he had a car, and since I didn't know how to get to the train station, could he take me and thus make sure that I left Potsdam? He did.

I relished leaving the GDR, but that second trip deepened my interest in this strange and contradictory place. It *was* a different world, and Conant had been right in insisting that I should see as much of it as possible. I tried to soak up what I could, to make sense of my many fleeting impressions. I probably saw things through different prisms: on the surface, I saw the red version of a brown past, a strange mixture of the old with the "progressive" patina of Prussian socialism: the visible celebration of the (privileged) rulers of this new state of workers and peasants, the goose-stepping, glorified soldiers. At another level, I sensed that outside East Berlin, the country seemed more German than modernized West Germany; the private language was old-fashioned, as were the cobbled streets with only the occasional car, the slower tempo. Underneath the banners and slogans, beneath a prescribed uniformity, was a world of shabby authenticity. But I also saw our cold-war clichés confirmed: the omnipresent agitprop with its crude self-satisfaction about material triumphs and its brazen mendacity about the West.

At every step, I saw and felt that this was a German police state; we all knew that the GDR had staged Soviet-style purge trials, as the other satellites had, and had initiated some on their own. We knew the regime imprisoned and expelled people at will, and we knew of the terror and the censorship. But in these first visits, my greatest failure was to underestimate the power of the secret police, the Stasi, and not to grasp to what degree the rather appealing aspect of what was called "the niche society"—a society of close relations among families and friends—was continually threatened by informers and denunciations. Knowledge of Stasi pervasiveness, far more numerous and technically more sophisticated than the Gestapo, came later.

I didn't have the time or patience to study the GDR's orthodox presentation of the German past, which was so different from the diverse interpretations I was learning about in West Germany. It was clear that the GDR laid claim to every radical or revolutionary tradition in German history (a rather meager treasure) beginning with Thomas Münzer, Martin Luther's radical contemporary, a firebrand on the side of the peasant uprisings that Luther had condemned and for which Münzer was hanged. East Germans were taught to venerate Münzer; a late "hero" was Ernst Thälmann, Weimar's last leader of the German Communists, killed by the Nazis in 1945. Antifascist slogans and books abounded, but the structure of National Socialism wasn't studied in East Germany, nor its means of domination—and the reasons for the omission were obvious. In the early postwar years, the historians' guilds in both West and East Germany had met jointly, but that source of possible bourgeois contagion had long since been forbidden. The two Germanys had radically different pasts.

I was intrigued by this repulsive regime under which so many Germans had to make their home. After my first visit, I went to Budapest for additional research in the national library, and I sensed at once that this was a different, freer atmosphere! In a crowded city park, I talked with a Hungarian poet who denounced Kadar's regime. I asked if voicing his vituperative commentary about what we called goulash communism, given its relative affluence, was a safe thing to do. Torture had been abolished, he replied, and he would rather face a few years in prison without the threat of torture than suppress his thoughts. Memorable! I hadn't heard anything like this in East Germany.

I came back to New York with far more curiosity than knowledge. I realized that any view of the Soviet bloc as monolithic needed amendment, for distinctions remained, some of them consonant with national traditions. And I was eager to explore the contradictions I had encountered. Yet my West German friends and colleagues had little or no interest in hearing or talking about the GDR. Their lack of interest suggested just how profound was the unacknowledged estrangement. East Germany officially preached fear and loathing of the West, whereas in the West, citizens seemed oblivious to the "other Germany."

When Arthur Schlesinger in the White House asked me for a report on East Germany that summer, I wrote about "the virtual collapse of the agricultural sector" there, due, I had been told, to peasant resistance to further collectivization. I mentioned the many complaints I had heard—both from Communists and from critics of the regime—about the GDR's political backwardness and

cultural stagnation compared with Poland and Hungary, and even with the Soviet Union. Poles and Hungarians especially had devised slightly more open,
more livable forms of communism. Hungarians, in fact, worried that their
regime's reformist tactics might only encourage Ulbricht in his hard-line policies, which in turn might risk some great popular upheaval, bringing about Soviet insistence on more repressive policies for them all. (Later on it became
clearer that the East German regime was always urging Moscow to adopt the
harshest course—out of fear that any effort at a more relaxed, freer system
might imperil its rule, perhaps also out of old German illiberal traditions.) East
Germans, I wrote, had given up on the prospects of reunification. "They realize that they are far more isolated, far more cut off, than any other European
satellite. This they resent very bitterly." This partial sense of inferiority was
to last for the entire history of the GDR, even after it could boast of its economic superiority among satellite countries. Neither they nor the Hungarians
wanted to hear from Radio Free Europe and other groups that communism
was bad and their living conditions intolerable. They knew that well. What
they wanted to know about was the best of what was going on in the West:
"These people have an immense vitality and intellectual hunger," and deserve
serious fare.

I wondered if the East German regime's longing for international recognition might offer an opportunity for a bargain: Allied recognition of the East
German state in exchange for tangible concessions, such as a land corridor to
Berlin? Actually, this was implausible: Ulbricht would never have made that
kind of concession, and Adenauer implacably insisted that the FRG spoke for
all Germans.

In lectures that I gave in America that fall, I noted that while the Berlin Wall
deflected West Germans' interest in the people behind it, East Germans watching West German television could see every night how the western half of the
country was prospering materially, and in the glow of a Western embrace. (I myself had watched de Gaulle's triumphant tour through West Germany in the
summer of 1961, as he saluted the greatness of the German nation. No responsible German leader had dared to address this recently debased, defeated, and
divided people in such a fashion. It was as if de Gaulle, solidifying a formal
Franco-German reconciliation, had spoken a historic pardon.) East Germans
had to be aware of the Federal Republic's growing integration into the West,
while they weren't allowed to go to Paris or Florence and had to make do with
Budapest or Leningrad where, by and large, they met with disdain and mistrust, since in the "socialist camp," the GDR carried the full burden of accu-

mulated anti-German feelings. West Germans, however, whom Soviet-bloc governments might attack and whom no one prescribed as "brother," were treated with friendly respect (the D-mark helped). The GDR citizen had become "the ugly German."

So I urged people to have greater contacts with East Germans, which might help to bring about a gradual relaxation of their repression and isolation. Their regime had built a physical wall, but one should thwart the wish to inflict a similar wall around the minds of its people. I did my best to keep up my own contacts, corresponding with two of the young archivists I had met and with the old concierge-type in the Merseburg archive; I would send books to and exchange information with the former; the latter was an avid stamp collector.

In January 1964, I received a letter from one of those archivists about Kennedy's assassination: "The shock here was particularly great and persistent because for us America is the symbol of freedom and tolerance." He went on to say that he had been reading Norman Mailer and Thomas Wolfe. Even more important: at Christmas, thanks to new regulations, he and his family had been able to visit his mother-in-law in West Berlin for a day, and had her meet her new grandchild. East Berlin, he wrote, had changed unrecognizably for him after the joy of this (brief) freedom. He thought these emotions would have political consequences. A couple of months later, he wrote that the GDR did not permit books to be received from the outside without prior permission of the ministry: "It is depressing if one has to see how one is deliberately cut off from all cultural and intellectual life in the world." He was interested in my teaching: "Here we know nothing about conditions there, except for the clichés that the ruling class has a monopoly on *Bildung*. How is it in reality?" He read reports about economic conditions in the United States, about the five million unemployed and yet, incomprehensibly, a growing economy: "Here we don't have a single unemployed; to the contrary, there is a labor shortage. Yet our economic development is anything but satisfactory." He wrote other outspoken letters, referring once to the "iconoclasts" who had recently destroyed the ancient royal palace in Potsdam. (While writing this book, I heard from a colleague of this correspondent, who wrote scathingly about him, suggesting he had turned informer to the Stasi and amassed enough wealth to buy a villa in Berlin—a whiff of the East German system of denunciation, perhaps the most degrading aspect of life in the GDR.)

My other correspondent asked for a small favor: would I make sure the address on the envelope indicated his status as "pensioner" because then he would be exempt from having to pay duty on the things I sent him. He complained that his pension was so low that he had to go on working. "The earlier generous pensions don't exist anymore." To another colleague I sent a copy of my *Varieties of History*; he hinted that he could add "tragic-sad supplements" for the section on "History under Modern Dictatorships." I was surprised at the occasional openness of these letters.

I kept up my few contacts and then, in 1966, on my sabbatical in Oxford, when I wanted to show my family some scenes of my European childhood, we saw something of East Germany again. Poland refused to give me a visa because my passport listed Germany as my country of birth and Breslau, now Wrocław, as my city of birth. (To declare Poland my native country struck me as ahistorical and absurd: I had been born in Germany and didn't speak a word of Polish. I appealed to the Polish embassy: would a Pole born in prewar Lvov, annexed to the Soviet Union in 1945, put in his Polish passport that he was born in the USSR? No answer.) So a visit to Wrocław was out, but we could drive from Berlin via the GDR to the Czech mountains. However, our East German visas allowed transit solely on the autobahn, with no detour. I drove off the highway at the exit ramp to Dresden, for at least a distant glance at that once-magnificent city, at which point the car stalled; I was fearful about having to deal with hostile authorities when I was clearly in the wrong, but the car recovered. Still, helplessness even in a minor dose like that is a memorable moment. When we reached the GDR-Czech border a few hours later, the German border police nearly stripped the car, looking for some poor East German who might be hiding there. It took an exasperatingly long time, and when everything had been searched, a mirror attached to a long stick was wheeled underneath the car for a final look. I asked why and, receiving no answer, said I assumed it was to inspect the car's cleanliness.

Crossing into Czechoslovakia made me feel almost free in comparison — another childhood memory revisited. I noticed that in the familiar villages of what had once been the Sudetenland every inscription that might remind one of the German past had been rubbed out or chiseled away—and only the marks of erasures remained. I could understand the motive but had mixed feelings about it. My memories were unshakeable. We drove on to Prague, and I could show my children the ancient synagogue where I had once prayed to escape the Nazis.

On that same European trip, and back in Berlin, I crossed over to East Berlin with my son. On our return, leaving East Berlin, the East German border guard was going to confiscate Fred's camera because he hadn't declared it upon entering. I insisted that there had been no such instruction, and the guard countered that it might have been "phrased badly." I shouted back, "It wasn't phrased at all!" We exited without incident—and with the camera. These were minor, minor skirmishes, but each such exchange, I suppose, was pleasing to me as an attack on the present regime—in memory of an earlier one.

In the next few years, I had no reason to return to the GDR; I visited East Berlin with some regularity and I followed news reports, such as they were. Busy watching the student movement in France and West Germany, which had no echo in the controlled east, my revulsion of the regime deepened when its troops helped to crush Dubcek's efforts at reform in Czechoslovakia in 1968. "Communism with a human face," as Dubcek's plans were called, was anathema to Ulbricht, one of the staunchest advocates of military action against the reforming Czechs.

And still Ulbricht was not a Kremlin favorite: the Soviets soon tired of his arrogance and his demands for toughness against the "class enemy." In the spring of 1971, Brezhnev spurred on the SED to force Ulbricht's retirement. Erich Honecker, nineteen years his junior, became his successor, a man who had risen in the Communist Party at the end of Weimar and for ten years had been incarcerated by the Nazis; after 1945 he had steadily moved up in the SED.

Honecker began with a domestic policy of limited relaxation, a belated copy of Khrushchev's "thaw." For a time artists and writers were allowed somewhat greater license. Astoundingly realistic accounts of life in the GDR had already appeared: the best-known writer was Christa Wolf, whose *Divided Heaven*—a sensitive, candid novel of love in the divided country—had appeared in 1963. All in all, one could see that there was astounding talent in East Germany, though much of it no doubt was crushed or exiled. Its written and spoken language (not the party lingo) was a pure, even old-fashioned German, free of the Anglicisms that had crept into West German speech. That was the decided judgment of the remarkable novelist Uwe Johnson, self-exiled from the GDR, whose works explored both Germanys. (I met him in New York in the late 1960s; he chose to settle in England.)

At the same time, however, Honecker called for the full realization of communist orthodoxy at home and virtually eliminated whatever was left of private enterprise. By 1973—this was after the Basic Treaty of 1972 had been signed, after the early successes of Brandt's *Ostpolitik*, after the GDR regime had finally obtained some international standing—he proclaimed that East Germany had achieved "real existing socialism," a phrase that was quickly ridiculed and oft-invoked. East German policies became ever more schizophrenic: the state had to give up or at least moderate its once-favorite target for attack, the "revanchist-imperialist" FRG, which now was providing it with much-needed material help, yet the peace-loving people of the GDR also had to be "shielded" from contacts with the West. The propaganda machine contrasted socialist gains in "the first workers' and peasants' state in German history" with West German suffering and capitalist malfeasance.

The newly recognized GDR now began to claim more of the German patrimony: the SED admonished historians to deal with all aspects of German history, not just with the heroes of revolutionary movements. East German historiography was subject to strict control but nevertheless minor latitude was allowed: as in most dictatorships, one could compose useful monographs provided that the requisite quotations from Marx and Lenin adorned the text. (Fortunately the great forebears had covered vast areas of human knowledge, hence intellectual genuflection was relatively easy.) Still, all serious dissent led to prison or expulsion.

As in all communist countries, the past in East Germany was subject to frequent revision, but in this as in other fields, the GDR bore a special burden, since East German historians had to compete with West German colleagues, themselves split as to method and political perspective. In the West you could choose, but in the East the party through a multiplicity of institutions dictated one version. In the two Germanys many rival German pasts emerged.

The GDR had a special category of trusted *Reisekader*, or travel cadres, people whose loyalty was assumed to be solid. If for professional reasons they were invited to hostile countries, they could accept the invitations—always provided that their families stayed behind. In 1975 my friend David Calleo invited an East German historian, Fritz Klein, for a semester to Johns Hopkins's Paul H. Nitze School of Advanced International Studies, in Washington. I knew Klein and his careful work on Germany in the Great War, since we were both critical defenders of Fritz Fischer's theses, so I invited him to lecture at Columbia, the first East German scholar to appear there. My students were astonished when, in assumed seriousness, I welcomed him as someone coming from a historian's paradise, adding that I was referring to the archival treasures of the GDR; as with any paradise, it's "very hard to get in." Klein talked dispassionately of East German work on German history, concentrating on the key question, the rise of Hitler, and basically rehearsing the Dimitrov definition of 1935: blaming monopoly capitalism for National Socialism.

After the lecture, I invited him back to my home, and over some whiskey I complained about that part of his lecture. He said that he had a special position in the GDR guild, which allowed him to speak rather freely about all matters except for the period 1928–1933. It was an astounding acknowledgment—but then to explain Stalin's insistence in those years that German Communists should regard the Social Democrats (or *social fascists*, in their vile vocabulary) as their principal enemies demanded pettifogging of extreme dexterity.

I didn't know at the time, and learned only from Klein's impressive autobiography, published after the end of the GDR, that he had been a party member from the very beginning of the regime and that on his return from abroad he was expected to report on all his contacts there. He tried to live a decent life, making concessions to the horrible regime in order to avoid still more appalling conditions. He was a controversial figure, the more so as he admonished historians not to derive the past from a priori schema, such as the ultimate victory of the Marxist-Leninist proletariat, but to mix the most scrupulous research with Marxist principles of interpretation. To call for adhering to the facts was itself daring in a world in which historic figures were routinely relegated to the status of nonbeings, "unpersons." Klein had also favored some openness toward West German historians, especially progressive ones—the very ones whom party sycophants most feared; reactionary historians, after all, "unmasked" themselves.*

While East German historians were reserved in dealing with National Socialism, West German historians saw it as a portal to all of German history. When in the 1970s in the West the Holocaust began to dominate collective memory and sensibility, and was solicitously studied and scrutinized in the East, mere clichés continued to suffice honoring "victims of fascism," martyrs of communism, "heroes of resistance," and Jews—but the latter were not depicted as the one group for whom savagery and death had been uniquely decreed. The GDR *Nomenklatura* included Jews, but a nonarticulated subterranean anti-Semitism existed as well, made manifest already in those 1948 trials for Zionist conspiracies. Here, too, was a kind of schizophrenia: though the regime officially opposed all racism and racial prejudice, the unexamined effects of National Socialism persisted in this respect, and so did some of the old German anti-Semitism.

Contacts between the two Germanys multiplied in the 1980s, on both the official and the private institutional level. I was struck in 1983 by the joint East-West celebrations of the five-hundred-year celebration of Martin Luther's birth. Meanwhile the Schmidt and later the Kohl governments found various ways of

---

*Klein and I have exchanged accounts of our divergent memories. He recalls an embarrassing moment at dinner at our house before the lecture; he had never had artichokes, hence was puzzled on how to tackle them, which I didn't even notice; in fact I had forgotten the dinner. But I remember our candid post-lecture conversation, which he had forgotten.

helping the GDR economically while quietly exacting concessions that benefited East Germans with regard to travel. In the GDR, party orthodoxy proclaimed a "peace offensive," which initially signaled an attack on the deployment of U.S. nuclear missiles on German soil, a controversy that roiled the FRG as well, as we shall see in the next chapter. By the late 1980s, younger party leaders in the SED realized that the GDR was in desperate need of reforms, an awareness facilitated by actual conditions but stimulated as well by growing dissent in the rest of the Soviet bloc. Meanwhile some groups in the GDR were trying to promote a reformist temper by usurping the slogans for peace.

The high point of official contacts between West and East Germany came in September 1987, when Chancellor Kohl received Honecker on a state visit in Bonn, according him full military honors. By this time, politicians from all the West German parties were trying to cultivate relations with GDR authorities, at the same time insisting that they had not abandoned hopes for reunification. The Social Democrats, now in opposition, carried on what Timothy Garton Ash has called "a second *Ostpolitik*," meaning intensive contacts with the SED, including a working group that in August 1987 produced a joint paper, specifying their common and divergent principles. Erhard Eppler headed the West German delegation, Otto Reinhold the GDR's. The SPD group hoped that such a paper might lead to an easing of human conditions in the East and accorded excessive faith in the Eastern reaffirmation of the principles of the Helsinki Accord. A few Social Democrats (and many conservatives) were shocked by this SPD-SED cooperation, claiming that it accorded additional and excessive legitimacy to the Communist Party, to the neglect of just barely emergent opposition groups. In that period I repeatedly ran into Otto Reinhold, rector of the Academy of Social Sciences of the Central Committee of the SED; he exuded a kind of reasonableness.*

Others did the same. In May 1988, Hermann Axen, a Weimar Communist and a Jew, survivor of Auschwitz and Buchenwald, now foreign policy expert of the SED's Politburo, was invited to a meeting at the Council on Foreign Relations in New York, which I chaired. He, too, exuded GDR peacefulness, and was well received by American officials. (I jotted down "genial survivor," but it turns out I was wrong about *genial*.)

---

*In August 1989, Reinhold sent me a copy of a letter he had written on my behalf to the GDR archives, asking them to support the work I was then doing on Einstein and Fritz Haber. The salutation read, "Esteemed comrades" and the letter ended "with socialist greeting"—a variant on the Nazi formula "with German greeting."

But I also encountered GDR functionaries who were remarkably open-minded and outspoken in their criticism of conditions in the GDR. In Munich, in 1988, the rector of East Germany's Academy of Public Law told me that the GDR "needed much change." Later I talked repeatedly with Rolf Reissig, a man in his mid-forties of proletarian background, a social scientist who wanted to move from analysis to actual reforms; orthodox apparatchiks again reprimanded him, this time for his contacts with Western colleagues. He had helped to produce the SPD-SED paper, which he thought encouraged dissent in the Politburo. During the brief reform period in the GDR he became Otto Reinhold's successor as head of the Academy of Social Sciences and later headed his own institute.

Thus one viewed the paradoxical situation of the East German regime softening its position toward the West while steeling itself against reforms as practiced in the East. The political class in West Germany began to take a positive view toward the entire East: trade with the Soviet bloc was blossoming while Western trade grew less robust. At the time, I worried "lest new conflicts in the west might upset one of the greatest achievements of the postwar era, i.e., the willing integration of West Germany into the West. The very term 'West' has lately lost some of its luster."

To me, then and now, *the West* stands for a set of ideas and institutions, for a certain period of history, for the Enlightenment and for liberalism *tout court*. And as I tried to show in the themes of my first book, National Socialism had been the triumph of Germany's long partial war against the West. Hence my absolute faith in Churchill's and Roosevelt's avowals that World War II would determine the survival of "Western civilization." But by now, *West* was important to me because it was also the term that embraced both the United States and Western Europe, that emphasized the commonality of their basic principles. A diminished commitment to the West struck me as dangerous.

On certain occasions such worries seemed justified. One, most poignantly, occurred at one of the most privileged encounters of my life. In the early 1980s, I helped a Polish philosopher, Krzysztof Michalski, to establish an Institute for Human Sciences in Vienna, where East European writers and thinkers could have a temporary home in the "free world" and meet with Western colleagues. Michalski had close contact with another Polish philosopher, Cardinal Wojtyla, and after 1978 we were all aware of his spectacular impact as Polish Pope. After a few years, Pope John Paul II invited Michalski to organize three-day seminars at his summer residence at Castel Gandolfo; to the third of these, modestly entitled "Europe and Its Consequences," I was invited to give a paper, "Germany and Europe," in which I tried to sketch the Europeanness of German culture, however divergent its political life.

The meeting was in late August 1987, in hot and glorious weather. We were a relatively small group, put up in a former nunnery near the papal palace, each in a small, stifling cell. The town itself, wonderfully located above Lake Albano, was dominated by the beautiful seventeenth-century papal palace where we had our meetings. On the late afternoon of the first day, the Pope descended a rickety staircase to join us before dinner, and insisted on mixing drinks himself. The atmosphere was relaxed and semiformal. Someone asked the Pope about the Vatican bureaucracy, and he answered with measured discretion. I asked him about its archives, that treasure for historians, and mentioned the wealth of hitherto closed material, such as Cardinal Pacelli's reports from Germany in the 1920s. (I deliberately didn't mention the later, more controversial period.) I hoped, of course, that he might say, "Go there on Monday and consult them!" Instead, he delicately changed the subject.

At the seminar there were excellent papers, and discussions in which the Pope took an active part. He sat apart, at a separate table from the U-shaped one around which the rest of us gathered, but his attentiveness to all the proceedings was evident. Czesław Miłosz and Leszek Kołakowski were there, and Timothy Garton Ash. In presentations by Cardinal König of Vienna, a benign and impressive person who had been the moving force behind Wojtyla's election, and by the physicist-philosopher Carl-Friedrich von Weizsäcker, the discussion was narrowly European, and the term *West* didn't come up, which meant the United States was not being included in the conversation. I objected, wondering if this omission was perhaps "an unconscious sign of European complacency." Are Europeans—and I meant Western Europeans—after their loss of global political domination, pleased to present themselves as an "island of virtue surrounded by these dreadful, monstrous superpowers"? I added that the very meeting we were attending had in part been made possible by America's rescue of Europe in the war, done not simply out of geopolitical interests but out of a sense of kinship with Europe. To speak of Europe and to leave out the cultural, moral dimension that the United States presented seemed false. Over coffee I repeated this point with Cardinal König and the Pope, urging that another seminar be devoted to themes directly concerned with America's place in the West. I felt this so strongly that the inappropriateness of instructing the Pope and cardinal didn't occur to me. They listened—with noncommittal kindness.

The Pope and I talked of Wrocław/Breslau, a city he knew well, and we talked again at dinner. He invited participants to join him on three different linguistic evenings, conducted in German, English, and Polish. Tim told me later that the Polish evening had been the most fun. I sat close to the Pope (with his aide, a Polish nun, between us), and when the subject turned to American education, I mentioned the vital presence of bright Asian students: at MIT, for example, some 18 percent of entering students were Asian. Loosened by papal wine, I added, "They have taken the place of the Jews"—to which the pontiff replied, "Yes, but they [Jews] still control the media and finance." I was stunned; did he really think that, or was his remark an echo of common prejudices of the past?

At the end of our three-day seminar, the Pope thanked us and elegantly summed up what had been discussed, speaking without a single note in front of him and switching at the precisely fitting moment from German to English to French. It was a moving experience, and at some point I recalled the story I had heard in Warsaw in 1979, when a loyal communist student had come home and said of the Pope, "He is the kind of person who makes you behave better."

There was a kind of magic to those days: the beauty of Castel Gandolfo, the old papal palace, the celebrated jaunty Swiss guards, the grand edifice on the outside, the classic simplicity inside. I remember the Pope in full health, as a wonderfully humane, pastoral presence, at once a kindly, deeply sympathetic person.

The cunning of history provided, at the same time, another person, another man encased in a hierarchy, who would have a transforming effect on the world and most especially on Eastern Europe. Mikhail Gorbachev had become secretary-general of the Communist Party in Moscow in March 1985. Some Westerners recognized at once that this was a new type of Soviet leader: open, witty, shrewd—cast in a different mold. (Even before his election, he had visited Prime Minister Margaret Thatcher—and charmed her.) A realistic Communist— if that isn't an oxymoron—he tried to see the world as it really was and not through ideological lenses. Gorbachev matched his promise of "radical political reform" with deeds: in December 1986 he telephoned the celebrated, embattled dissident Andrei Sakharov at his exile in Gorky, inviting him to return to Moscow. Sakharov—defender of human rights, critic of the Soviet invasion of Afghanistan—was a hero in the West and anathema to the KGB. "Gorbomania" soon spread in West Germany and in France. West European leaders recognized Gorbachev's novelty and welcomed it; Honecker could only shudder. In turn, his immobility and fear of change irritated the Russian leader.

Galvanized by his sense of the Soviet system's failures, of its need for utter renewal, Gorbachev undertook his program of *perestroika* (restructuring) and *glasnost* (openness); it was nothing less than "a revolution from above," though he of course didn't use this profoundly non-Marxist term. At home, Gorbachev cited the late critical writings of Lenin, claiming ideological legitimacy for his innovations.

It has always seemed odd to me that in recent decades many historians have belittled the role of the individual and focused principally on the power of the "anonymous masses." As if Lenin and Mussolini, Gandhi and Nehru, Kemal Ataturk and Mussolini, Hitler, Stalin, Roosevelt, and Churchill hadn't exemplified the enormous impact a single person could have on the world stage. And here were Gorbachev, the Pope, and Nelson Mandela! I may have erred on the other side. I may at times have neglected these "anonymous forces," but history is a drama of individuals, too, creatures of their times who shape those times.

Honecker and his men were skeptical about Gorbachev from the very beginning. Such functionaries were perhaps the last to understand, let alone favor, his reformist agenda, his impulse to change and thus salvage the Soviet system, then in decay. East German apparatchiks, many of them veterans or servants of two dictatorships, would have found it difficult to countenance a plan for openness. In time, GDR censors banned a reformist Soviet journal (*Sputnik*) and some new Soviet films; they "edited" Gorbachev's speeches: Germans to the defense of Marxist-Leninist orthodoxy! Or were they just miserably afraid of candor, afraid of their own people?

The East Germans *were* afraid—and for good reason. By the late 1980s, their economy was in decline and close to bankruptcy, but this was as yet concealed. They realized that they had failed to match the West's revolution in cybernetics. And, more important, they saw unrest and spreading dissent all over Eastern Europe. They were angry and afraid—and still convinced that they alone were protecting the holy grail.

I have one ever-present poignant memory of my visits to the GDR, a kind of accidental epitaph. Every crossing into East Berlin was adventurous. At Checkpoint Charlie, the procedures were ponderous, and the most unpleasant moment came at the window where one handed in one's passport, which disappeared to invisible quarters, leaving one waiting for an indeterminate time, feeling naked. Once, in the late 1980s, Alan Bullock, Shepard Stone, and I were at that checkpoint. (We had dropped off Marion Dönhoff at the place for West German visitors.) After the usual multiple waits and going through several barriers, we thought we were done—when out of the dark came a Vopo (that is, a member of the People's Police) with a flashlight, demanding that we open the glove compartment of the car. All other parts of the car had already been inspected, and as he shone his light into the glove compartment, he bellowed, "Any arms, munitions, or newspapers?"

The question was, I thought, a gift to someone like me, who had grown up with Heine's mockery of Prussian douaniers searching for contraband, bijouterie, and forbidden books: Fools, he thought, you search in vain. My contraband is in my head, awhirl with dangerous ideas and explosive books, and when I unpack that baggage, it will hurt you. Here in East Berlin, more than a century later, I was encountering the same old Germanic fear of contraband ideas that mock tyrannical power and exult in freedom. Heine was right—or it is our job to prove him right. No border guard, no wall, can forever shield repressive regimes from the power of subversive ideas, from the lure of freedom. That wretched Vopo was at once echo and portent.

✦

CHAPTER 8

GERMAN THEMES
IN FOREIGN LANDS

THE WORLDS OF DISSENT and resistance have always had a deep and immediate interest for me—as much in the German past as in the political present. For years I had been engaged with both in different ways. In the 1970s and 1980s, struggles against oppression were being waged in many places and with uneven success; related to the mounting protests, and overshadowing them, were the visible threats of different international conflicts. Moved by the dangers faced by the former, I was lucky enough to learn more about the latter. Present-day dramas impelled me to think about them in the light of the historic past, and my experience with National Socialism quickened the impulse to activism. Ambition and impatience did the rest.

When I poured my worries and reflections about the caesura in world politics marked by the Yom Kippur War into my essay "The End of the Postwar Era," that article opened my way to an unanticipated adventure, to travel to parts of the world I had never seen, where new impressions and old themes illuminated each other. Over and over again, I would find that the lessons of the German past had their own resonance around the world. Between 1977 and 1981, I made intermittent trips that propelled me into becoming *"un specta-teur engagé,"* in Raymond Aron's phrase.

Once I had completed *Gold and Iron*—my sixteen-year-long immersion in European politics and finance, German unification (1871) and expansion, the prominence of European Jewry and the new hostility toward them—I wanted to embark on something new, with a change of pace. I recalled McGeorge Bundy's interest in my ruminations about "the Postwar Era" and proposed to the Ford Foundation a study of relations between Europe's ex-dependencies and present-day Europe. I wanted to see if personal impressions and carefully planned interviews might, for this project, take the place of archives. Was my unorthodoxy encouraged by something that Hugh Seton-Watson, friend and wise historian, had written in one of his early books on Eastern Europe? He acknowledged, "My sources have mainly been people. Conversations with men and women of each nation, of various political views and social origin, give one in some ways a better picture than study of documents." Hugh, a most acute observer and judge, was ready to travel anywhere—provided the venue offered exceptional bird- and people-watching: the exotic in both man and beast appealed to him.

I had always insisted that German history be "Europeanized," but at some point I realized I was becoming perhaps excessively Eurocentric. And I certainly understood Europe's relative decline in world affairs, despite the creation of the European Community—a historic achievement that in itself had grown out of the awareness of Europe's self-destruction in two world wars. The half-continent had grown dependent on the United States, threatened by the Soviet Union, and challenged by the "third world." Europe was "on vacation," I said. Also, the gap between developed and developing countries was being recognized, it was not narrowing but, ominously, widening; the then head of the world bank, Robert McNamara, asked Willy Brandt in 1977 to organize an international commission of leading representatives from "north" and "south" to propose reforms. Meanwhile the "chattering classes," ever more mobile, flew off to luxury hotels for three-day international conferences about great questions of the day such as "east-west relations"—I attended a few myself.

But I wanted to catch a sense of Europe and its importance in the world for myself and from a different perspective. How was it perceived among peoples with prior, deeply ambivalent relations with colonial powers? I had huge curiosity about the worlds I didn't know, and in graduate school my appetite had been whetted by pioneering courses such as Europe's Overseas Expansion, a deeply controversial subject of the greatest magnitude, overlaid by the fiercest polemics. For years in my own lectures I had suggested that the experience of European domination overseas required a balanced assessment, that the primitive arrogance of its earlier rulers shouldn't be replaced by mere simplistic anticolonialism or liberal guilt. Europeans had behaved with unmatched brutality, wrapped in racist twaddle and hypocrisy, and terror and exploitation had been imperialist hallmarks; but these should not entirely obscure the now partly neglected but beneficent achievements of the European presence in the world. I also wanted to see how the two more recent world-historical processes of the postwar era, decolonization and the integration of Western Europe, coincided in logic and time.

The Ford Foundation made my project possible, and Columbia gave me eighteen months' unpaid leave beginning in January 1977—just as Jimmy Carter's administration succeeded Gerald Ford's. (Kissinger, departing secretary of state, and Zbigniew Brzezinski, incoming national security adviser, wrote generous letters of introduction for me.) I enjoyed the preparations for my trip, dipping into new subjects and consulting with friends and experts. When I mentioned my proposed itinerary to anthropologist Clifford Geertz, he exclaimed, "And you left out the most important country: Indonesia!" I quickly added it. The Ford Foundation supplied not only material and logistical support but a letter from Bundy that opened many doors. Others showered me with names, including bankers whom I had met via *Gold and Iron*. (I labeled them diplomats in mufti.)

So in April, Peggy and I set out on a globe-girdling trip that began in Algiers and ended in Tokyo; later that year we went to Argentina, Brazil, and Colombia. Even more important to my work as a Germanist were subsequent trips, under different auspices, to the Soviet Union, Poland, and China, listening and lecturing on German-European topics. At each stop I would receive an initial briefing from resident Ford representatives (what an able lot) and embassy people (with varying results). I would also check in with German representatives, official and private. I led the life of some kind of journalist or diplomat *manqué*, rushing about collecting dots, as it were, and at times even connecting them.

I thought I would focus on political matters, but in the end what most engaged me were universal questions of political freedom, of repression and resistance, of old forms of oppression and new forms of authoritarianism. I suppose I heard once again echoes of my childhood. For decades, I had been living in freedom, and the experience of visiting countries where freedom was banished or threatened, where people had to battle for a voice, set in motion a reciprocal process: I saw these new lands of unfreedom with German eyes, and the new countries in turn made me understand better the German past.

It was a propitious time: the Helsinki Accord of 1975 had established the Organization for Security and Co-operation in Europe, and its all-important "third basket," with its guarantees about human rights, became even more important with an American president who was truly committed to the defense of these rights. Much greater attention was now focused on this issue. "Helsinki

Watch" committees sprang up to monitor the nations' compliance with the new accords; these committees were of great help to dissidents, who invoked Helsinki when they tried to speak out. Some Americans on the right thought of "human rights" as a weapon to be used against the Soviet Union, while they remained blind to offenses in "friendly" countries. Marion Dönhoff and other European friends inveighed against American double standards and hypocrisy. Ever since the Jackson-Vanik Amendment of 1974 forbade the U.S. government from extending most-favored-nation status to "non–market economy" countries that denied their citizens the right to emigrate freely, the United States had been pressuring the Soviet Union on the issue of allowing its Jews to leave if they wished (most of them to Israel). With Carter and Brzezinski, this and other human rights issues acquired a new valence in American policy.

To satisfy myself (and the Ford Foundation), I published several articles based on my trips, but the greatest gain was the wealth of experiences that enriched my understanding. And I have preserved valued memories of people and places, of new friends and acquaintances. It's one thing to read about the inequalities in the world, and another to see the actual personification of issues—starving, begging children in Madras; Arabs enraged at Zionist intrusions or Israelis defiantly resolved to survive and expand—to talk to proponents of self-satisfied authoritarianism or, above all, to people taking great risks to oppose intimidation and repression, whether in Tehran or Delhi, Buenos Aires or Moscow. And there was an ironic twist: some of the dangerous or oppressive places I visited had in my childhood been considered possible havens for us from Nazism.

My semi-official interviews led me down corridors of power, while official entertainment brought Peggy and me into fleeting contact with the diplomatic and financial world, but most valuable were my encounters with men and women who were to varying degrees opponents of local authority. I was grateful for my brief immersion in hitherto unknown waters, meeting with writers, businesspeople, journalists, dissidents, politicians in and out of office or prison. I was intrigued to hear people in power converse with some restraint, and people out of power (some of whom were to assume major offices later) speak more openly. I was encountering talking archives, living sources. To see how a chance remark might unveil hitherto unthought of connections—all that was useful adventure, and a friendly memory has blocked out what must have been boring meetings.

I had wanted to start in Algeria, in quiet homage to Albert Camus and in open recognition of the country's special place in the third world, given the Algerians' triumph in winning their independence in 1962 after a brutal eight-year struggle. France itself was torn apart by the Algerian War: the revelations that the

French armed forces were habitually using torture against captured Algerians suspected of terrorism aroused an ever-fiercer storm of protest in France.

This potentially rich country seemed run down. It was like a shabby Mediterranean version of East European socialism. Yet the Algerians themselves, even those with close if complicated ties to France, thought it was Europe, rather, that was in decline and decay, and they "proved" this with demographic evidence: Algeria's population was one third that of France, but the birthrate in each nation was identical; hence France (and much of Western Europe) was a magnet for North African immigrants. So the long-term perspective pointed to an aging Europe, still an economic giant, but with what future? As a museum of past greatness? I heard about "the European disease," the ill health of a rich, self-indulgent, decadent culture.

I was also immediately confronted by the Algerians' hatred of Israel, expressed both in the censored press and in omnipresent scribbles and symbols on city walls. I thought about the tangled chain that connected these hatreds to earlier horrors: the Holocaust had made the Zionist claim to a Jewish state, to Israel, morally compelling and a physical necessity, but the Palestinians who in 1948 lost their homes were also its indirect and underacknowledged victims. The memory of the European mass murder made some Israelis intransigent vis-à-vis the outside world, especially vis-à-vis Arabs, and the consequences for the Palestinians fed the Arabs' rage—though the Arab nations left the plight of the Palestinian refugees virtually unattended. Mutually reinforcing suspicions and hatreds pervaded North Africa and the Middle East.

Next came Cairo—and another steep learning curve in a chaotic city. The American ambassador there, Hermann Eilts, gave me an initial briefing. President Anwar Sadat had all but ended Egypt's close ties to the Soviet Union and seemed embarked on a pro-Western course. (I knew that Helmut Schmidt held Sadat in high esteem.) I doubt that anyone except possibly people at the very highest levels of the Egyptian and Israeli governments could have predicted that within six months, Sadat would make his historic, unprecedented trip to Jerusalem. In my conversations there was no hint of a popular wish for such a radical departure.

I met with much-discussed politician Boutros Boutros-Ghali at his rather humdrum *Al-Ahram* newspaper office. He hammered away at what most galled him: America's hegemony, by which he meant not just its military power but the universal dominance of coveted American culture. He had little interest in the Soviet Union, noting that Communists in communist countries were unattractive; only in capitalist countries did they have any appeal. And the rich Saudi and

Gulf Arabs, with their villas on the Riviera and their indifference to their peoples' suffering, were contemptible. He had little hope for peace with Israel. He, too, stressed demographic realities: three million Israelis faced sixty million Arabs, with three million Arabs born every year. Israelis should learn to speak to their neighbors—in Arabic; if not, they would be thrown out, as the French settlers had been from Algeria. Egypt, meanwhile, he thought, was slowly turning into another Bangladesh. A cynical strain lightened his gloom and recalled to me the radical chic of Paris intellectuals among whom he once lived.

Some of the Egyptian writers and poets I met had been Nasser's prisoners, confined in what they called his concentration camps. But many of them feared as well the rise of a theocratic fundamentalism such as already existed in Algeria and—in mirror Jewish form—in Israel. My interlocutors included Tasheen Bashir, Sadat's former spokesman (a friend of my Columbia friend Edward Said), and Louis Awad, a poet and expert on Arabic literature.

Ten hectic days in Jerusalem and Tel Aviv followed, with a quick succession of interviews by day and visits with friends in the evenings. Israel was still shaken by the Yom Kippur attack, the third and costliest war it had fought since 1948. (A canard made the rounds that spoke to Israel's vulnerability: Prime Minister Golda Meir was supposed to have asked her commanders how Israel could win a war. There are two ways, she had been told: the natural way, that is, by a miracle; or the miraculous way, which would be by natural means.) I met with politicians, generals, and public citizens—though such is the mobility in Israel that quite a few have successive careers in all these realms. I saw the legendary tank commander Israel Tal, a small, compact person, who told me about his experiences fighting with the British army in the Western Desert in 1942–1944. Europe's greatest contribution now, he said during our two-hour conversation, would be "survival." To him, too, Europe seemed indulgently feeble, even craven in the aftermath of the oil shock. He inveighed against the "sinfulness" of its purely defensive strategy, a luxury that only a superior power could afford; others needed a clear retaliatory posture. We talked about the Yom Kippur War. Dramatically he produced a photograph of himself with General Gamassi, chief of the Egyptian general staff, taken on November 1, 1973, at the kilometer 101 marker; their immediate joint task was to arrange for supplies to reach the encircled Egyptian Third Army, but they had also talked of strategy and philosophy, of Egyptian society and world politics. Gamassi had warned Tal that the Israelis might occupy Cairo a hundred times and still not defeat the Arabs, then added that Egypt was ready to bring an end to continuous hostilities.

In an official report, Tal had written that the Yom Kippur War had left Israel in confusion, with the question "what are we being killed for?" causing division and "threatening the secret of our military superiority—motivation and morale." He insisted that there could be no military solution to the Arab-Israeli conflict. He laughed when I mentioned that Chancellor Schmidt had told a friend of mine, a Dutch industrialist, that he believed the Bundeswehr was now the world's second best army, Israel's being the best. The irony was inescapable: for centuries Germans had been so proud of their militiary prowess, so contemptuous of Jews as mere hagglers and cowards, and now this reversal. But I realized that opinions were changing: Germans, and Europeans, especially on the left, could handle Jewish victimhood more easily than Israeli power.

Israel was at peace, but it was in serious economic straits, and revelations about various scandals assailed its self-confidence. General Tal was right: for the first time, the country was deeply divided about its ultimate aims. Israelis recognized the dangers of their isolation, especially those who felt a special kinship to Europe, and almost all the people I talked to were deeply disappointed by what they took to be Europe's futile submission to oil-rich Arab states. They resented being lectured to by Europeans on the evils of annexationism: after all, the Europeans had been masters of competitive rapacity. Still, Europe was Israel's largest trading partner and the Federal Republic its most trusted supporter, next to the United States.

To many Israelis, including government officials, the Arabs' final aim seemed unambiguously clear: to extinguish Israel. A high official at the Foreign Office, whom I knew as a political philosopher in civilian life, deplored Europe's "mixture of impotence, dependence, and shallow moralism." An adviser to the prime minister told me he was certain that the Arabs sought the destruction of Israel and equally certain that Israel's continued occupation of the West Bank was injuring Israeli society and violating the spirit of Zionism. In private talks, deep division between hawks and doves confirmed my general impression that the latter were willing to talk about Israeli transgressions, but even benevolent foreign criticism fell on deaf and injured ears.

My last talk was with a former general who believed in the possibilities of peace but doubted that any Israeli government could persuade the people of the need for concessions: "Perhaps we need a de Gaulle," he said, "but none is in sight." Within weeks the general and Labor Party leader Yitzhak Rabin was succeeded by Menachem Begin, Likud's leader and ex-head of the terrorist Irgun organization, and it was Begin who welcomed Sadat to Jerusalem the following November. But the dream of an Israeli de Gaulle never faded—and was never realized.

At the airport when we left, Israeli security people were suspicious: who were these two people who had come from Cairo and were leaving for Tehran? I was myself uneasy as I left friends in this embattled country that was both strange and familiar for a country with a glorious past and a frightening present where I knew almost no one. But we were in fact received most hospitably in Iran.

David Rockefeller, whom I had frequently met at the Council on Foreign Relations, had arranged for me to see the Shah, who in turn let it be known that we would be his guests for our entire stay. Consternation on my part. I refused to be beholden to the Shah, but our embassy insisted that to refuse his proffered hospitality would be considered an insult. I suggested a compromise: I would accept the offer of an occasional official car, leaving me, morally speaking, "a little pregnant."

I met the Shah in a grand room in his huge palace, yet our actual conversation was easy, with only a note taker present, and the leader seemed quite candid. He was all too ready to talk about Europe, well informed about the political details of the current scene. Europe was sick and decadent, with all the sins of "a permissive society," he thought, though he praised "white" Christian civilization, while hinting at its earlier exploitative character, and claimed that its much-vaunted democracy was now speeding its decline. This implicitly justified the Shah's own repressive rule and huge military buildup. He was a convinced authoritarian, in any case. His father had regarded Kemal Ataturk, the Turkish modernizer, as a model; the son may have had similar inclinations—a modernizer who sought grandeur for himself and power for his country—but he was indifferent to the well-being of his people while he basked in the company of rich Westerners. European, especially German, entrepreneurs hungered after his profitable favors.

An American businessman drew a scathing picture for me of the enormous American military and commercial presence in Iran, to which he himself was closely attached. It amounted to some twenty-five thousand people, many of them "out to make a fast buck." He noted that licentious behavior toward women, offensive in any group, was especially galling for the mullahs and their followers.

Peggy and I had moments of escape, such as a flying visit to Isfahan, city of ancient and resplendent mosques, serene and Persian as against the boomtown feel of Iran's modern capital. When I asked to see something of the mountains north of Tehran, which I had heard about as a child, we were given a car and driver for a short expedition. On the way back, on a narrow, little-traveled road, we met an oncoming car traveling at great speed, which suddenly switched to our side of the road, clearly trying to push us off it and into disaster. Our driver swerved at the last minute, and insisted later that this had been a deliberate attempt aimed at an official car.

I was relieved to leave the repressive ugliness of the Shah's Iran and looked forward to India, where the Ford Foundation put us up at its own New Delhi guesthouse, in its compound at Lodi Park. People then liked to say that in the early years of Indian independence, there were four great embassies in Delhi: the American, the Soviet, the Chinese—and the Ford Foundation's, whose representatives drove from Lodi Park to Government House in horse-drawn carriages.

India, the world's most populous democracy, was in the grips of a terrifying test of its freedom. In 1975, Prime Minister Indira Gandhi, Nehru's daughter, alleging the danger of economic chaos, had imposed an emergency rule that suspended all constitutional safeguards; opposition leaders had been arrested and tens of thousands of citizens imprisoned without trial. But she had called an election for June 1977, assuming that intimidation would yield victory for the Congress Party; and during the electoral campaign the emergency rule was suspended. (The opposition to Mrs. Gandhi won the election—in which 60 percent of eligible voters cast ballots. By 1980, the corrupt, coercive elements had returned to power.)

A decade earlier an Indian sociologist, Kewal Motwani, had written to me saying that my *Politics of Cultural Despair* was of particular relevance to him and his country; he identified with the figures I had written about. But he said they had appealed to a doubtful past, whereas "I am able to appeal to the past that has been built during the last seven thousand years of India's existence and survival as a nation that has given birth to some of the towering personalities who have shaped human destiny: Manu, Buddha. The present situation makes me feel unmitigated despair . . . and since India is being highly pressured into the age of industrialism, urbanization, amassing of vast fortunes and corruption, will the [expected] totalitarianism be of the Nazi or fascist type, or will it be of a gentler nature?"

I knew that Indians could be insufferable in their condescension to the United States, I had heard moralistic lectures in New York, and I had met Foreign Minister Krishna Menon, who mocked America's "ostentatious affluence"—not without cause. Indians were critical of Soviet life, and of course their country excelled as the premier nonaligned nation, a role that Nehru himself had pioneered. There was more than a hint in this that to Indians the two superpowers were equally repugnant—though Soviet and American favors were equally solicited. In the course of the 1970s, the United States, aware that the Soviet

Union was supplying arms to India, began covertly to support Muslim Pakistan. (This was part of Nixon's policy of reaching out to China, Pakistan's ally.) In India, I often heard variants of the pithy complaint "We are prisoners in a sea of Muslims," which was further incentive for the Indian government to keep its distance from Israel, a state it hadn't recognized.

India seemed a wondrous example of opposites living cheek by jowl, of material and intellectual wealth in a sea of dreadful poverty and illiteracy. MIGs were heard overhead, while water buffaloes pulled lawn mowers below. I sensed the insane contrast of having the most sophisticated arms being assembled by workers in a society that was still in other respects primitive and disease-ridden. But there was also great pride in India's modern changes: Ambassador Daniel Patrick Moynihan's apocryphal remark that "in the belly of India is a modern France"—that is to say, some fifty million Indians in Delhi, Bombay, and other cities already lived in the modern technological world—was often cited. And he was right, as India's extraordinary technological sophistication revealed itself in the decades to come.

My most moving visit was with Romesh Thapar, an Indian writer, filmmaker, and publisher of *Seminar*, a journal that had been banned under the emergency rule, but in the preelection period was allowed to publish. We talked of the recent erosion of democracy, of which he had firsthand experience. He told me that the Indian prime minister's office had warned him that he would be strung up in Connaught Square unless he conformed. Earlier, Mrs. Gandhi had been a friend. Friends of pre–emergency days shunned him in the streets. So he devoted the first issue of *Seminar* during this preelection "relaxation" to a study of fascism; the lead article, "Symptoms," analyzed the fascists' rise to power in Europe and emphasized the speed with which a nation could slide from prefascist thought to totalitarian rule. "We resume publication with the issue which could not be printed following the imposition of pre-censorship . . . The brazen misuse of power and the violation of legal procedure . . . The jails have yet to deliver thousands of political prisoners, the opposition parties face harassment." All this, he wrote, threatened the future of India. What courage! He listed *The Politics of Cultural Despair* as providing evidence about the ease with which people can embrace fascism; I was pleased to see my book put to such good use.

Thapar has since died, but his sister, Romila Thapar, a well-known historian of ancient India, was a relentless foe of the Hindu nationalist government of the late 1990s, declaring, "This is Germany in 1933 for India," a remark that suggests once again that German remains the language of political disaster.

Peggy and I left India via Madras, a fiercely humid, dirty, and squalid city that seemed to provide an unbroken stream of begging children. I instantly felt that dignity is what was being denied those children, and I have never forgotten the desolate poverty there.

We visited the museum of the East India Company in Madras, where I was struck by the displays of the heavy woolen uniforms worn by the eighteenth- and nineteenth-century British soldiers and officials. The Raj hadn't been a mere exercise in luxury, in dominating and corrupting the natives, I thought. However sordid some of the motives, however perniciously racist the perspective, some of Britain's servants of imperialism had viewed their—often onerous—task as a self-sacrificing duty. India was all-absorbing. Surely it was the most important and mysterious place to study Europe's imperialism.

My trip—so instructive, so full of vague apprehensions—continued its all-too-rapid pace to Sri Lanka and Jakarta, where I succumbed to a high fever and exhaustion, and where the wonderfully kind, competent Indonesian woman doctor at the British embassy treated me; I saw her as representative of the universally beneficent effects of women's emancipation, something I had long understood in the Western world.

Then on to Singapore and Hong Kong—and everywhere a rush to superficial modernization, the engines of capitalism driven by natives and foreigners alike, skyscrapers overshadowing the indigenous architecture of old. East Asia was the fastest growing region of the world, and local masters and their Western friends insisted there was some necessary symbiosis of economic growth and "authority" (or, as I thought, repression). I questioned whether what was called "law and order" was not a form of preemptive terror, and some of my interlocutors replied that detention was not inconsistent with human rights. Shocking, I thought.

In talking with Prime Minister Lee Kuan Yew in Singapore, I again caught a glimpse of this new authoritarianism, with its system of carefully fostered—and corrupt—economic growth along with unabashed repression. These modernizing Asians ridiculed the European "sickness" (specifically the British "disease," with its trade unions throttling development), which they claimed led to Europe's willing dependency on the United States. It was here in Asia that I first encountered something like the later Thatcherite mind-set: professed faith in the virtues of hard work and economic individualism, and contempt for the welfare state that "coddled" the weak. This was a new version of social Darwinism—bloody-minded if economically effective.

Tokyo was our final stop. The Japanese economy was at the height of its power, geared to massive exports while invisible, almost invincible moats were

built around the home market. Yet the country felt insecure—given its total dependency on imported oil—and isolated. The United States was remote and
puzzling, Russia and China were close and ominous, and Japan's immediate
neighbors still resented it for its unbridled aggression and atrocities during
World War II. In a mood of worried isolation, the Japanese talked of reaching
back to their roots, of preserving and strengthening what was quintessentially
Japanese in their culture.

German models had been centrally important to Japan's modernization after the Meiji restoration of 1868. So the Berlin-Tokyo Axis had an old history, yet
for all its links to Germany, Japan had known how to evade Nazi demands: it
had refused to surrender some seventeen thousand German Jewish refugees in
Japanese-occupied Shanghai, for example, allowing them to survive in misery.
This seeming solicitude, I have been told, was born of the Japanese belief in the
myth of the *Protocols of the Elders of Zion*, ascribing to world Jewry unimaginable and mysterious power. Why add Jews to their list of enemies? This might be
the only good that came of this abomination, which seems to have everlasting
energies: the *Protocols* are now used to stir hatred in the Muslim world.

But when I visited Japan, the Japanese had "forgotten" about their wartime
cooperation with the Nazis and about their own version of blitzkrieg, their astounding victories and vile terror in Manchuria and other conquered lands.
Still, Japanese historians had an intense interest in German history, and in
serene, beautiful Kyoto, they asked me to lecture on the German past; at dinner
afterward, we talked in German, the most readily available common language.

AFTER FOURTEEN WEEKS OF TRAVEL, I returned to New York and Vermont, my mind bursting with first impressions and second thoughts: I had
learned or tasted so much, but all on the run. Trying to make sense of it all, to
condense and interpret my impressions, I turned with the usual anguish to
composing. At such a moment I recall what Oswald Veblen is supposed to have
said: "How do I know what I think till I have written it down?"

I had found much less bitterness toward the former European rulers than I
had anticipated; perhaps anti-imperialism was fiercer in the lecture halls of
Western universities than in the hearts of Indians or Indonesians. Many of the
"progressive" people I met wanted Europe to be less dependent on the United
States. (With regrettable insouciance, I wrote of "Europe" when I meant "Western Europe," as many of us did then, unconsciously and unconscionably forgetting Eastern Europe.) West Germans were everywhere an active economic

and cultural presence, both helped and hindered by the relative absence of a German colonial past. But the general attitude seemed to be: better the predatory powers of the past than the superpower of the present, whatever its beneficent record or pretense.

The Arab-Israeli conflict was a central issue everywhere. I worried that Israelis were confounding well-intentioned warnings from abroad with cravenness or reemergent anti-Semitism. Criticism from anguished friends deserved Israel's attention, not contemptuous dismissal. By the time I was writing, Menachem Begin was prime minister, and the danger of Israeli isolation seemed even greater. My concerns were confirmed the next spring when Sir Sigmund Warburg, a German refugee turned major London banker, wrote a letter to the *Times* that I thought an important statement of dissent from Begin's positions. Warburg explained to me privately, "I felt I should be a demonstrative nonconformist in deviation from the almost macabre silence practiced by so many Jews—both inside and outside Israel—who disagree with Begin but are fearful of the criticism which they would encounter in the Zionist hysteria community if they were to say publicly anything against Begin."

But my fear of creeping authoritarianism was my major theme. In too many countries rulers viewed modernization and repression as complementary. I mocked the notion of "smiling dictatorships," the very phrase an affront to the imprisoned victims of these regimes. I wanted it known that not only totalitarian dictators but also these modernizing repressive regimes were using torture, routinely excusing this most outrageous of all violations of humanity. "Our often pious generalities about human rights need at the core a specific statement of the minimal conditions that we think should be universally binding—such as the abolition of torture," I wrote. Grim reading today.

My article, duly improved by the gifted editors Bill Bundy and James Chace at *Foreign Affairs*, eventually appeared. It was not dispassionate—I suppose I am not capable of writing on present-day affairs in that mode; Bundy sent me a note saying that my piece was "contrapuntal" to the hard thinking presented elsewhere in the issue, which was devoted to "power." I suppose that was true: I was intrigued by the sites of power but content to keep my distance from them.

NO SOONER HAD I FINISHED the article then I set off, in mid-August 1977, for the second part of my Ford venture, this time to Argentina, Brazil, and Colombia. I prepared as I had before, by reading and consulting with colleagues, especially Albert Hirschman—by discipline an economist, by temperament and wisdom a *philosophe*, and someone who knew many of the keenest people in Latin America; his list of contacts was invaluable, the mention of his name magic.

Recent contradictory and connected events had shaken Latin America and the Iberian peninsula that had once ruled it. The murder in 1973 of Salvador Allende, the democratically elected, socialist president of Chile, an assassination committed with American connivance, had allowed for the establishment of General Pinochet's murderous regime of repression, with its wholesale violation of human rights. (Kissinger's seeming disregard of human rights, in Chile as elsewhere, has amazed me, with the two of us coming, as we do, from similar childhood experiences.) And in 1976, in Argentina, a military junta had deposed Isabel Perón and established a particularly ferocious regime, as military officers in Latin America were wont to do.* At about the same time, in Portugal, where the dictator António de Oliveira Salazar had died in 1970, a difficult transition period led to Mario Soares, head of the Socialist Party, defeating his communist rival in 1976—just as Kissinger wrote off Portugal as succumbing to communism. And in Spain, a successful transition to democracy after Generalissimo Franco was completed in 1975 under a restored monarchy, with Juan Carlos, by conviction and character a democrat, as first ruler. This was a blessing for a people whose wounds from the civil war had not been acknowledged, let alone healed. The West German government had contributed to these Iberian successes: under both Brandt and Schmidt it had discreetly but decisively helped democratic elements in both countries. Brandt's relationship to Felipe González, leader of the Spanish Socialists, was an espe-

---

*I had had but one remarkable experience involving Argentina. In 1950, I became rapporteur for a study group on Argentina at the Council on Foreign Relations; the country was then under the Perón dictatorship. My responsibility was to furnish a report as faithful to the proceedings as possible—five off-the-record discussions among leading experts, with significant political differences among them; the compensation was ten dollars a report. At one meeting our ambassador to Argentina, the formidable Spruille Braden, drew a grim picture of Argentina, blaming "the son of the bitch" who ruled the country for much of the misery. This was an epithet hardly ever heard in the genteel patrician atmosphere of the Council—and surely not one that the accredited ambassador would want recorded in a paper, however confidential. And so I upgraded the term—I think to *deceitful* or *malevolent*. Days later, the Council's director of meetings, George Franklin, gentlest of men, called me to his office to tell me of Braden's fury at being edited. On substance he was completely right: Perón's populistic dictatorship, with its fascist echoes and hospitality to fleeing Nazis, was a regime of terror. Later I learned that Peronistas had exploited Braden's hostility to bolster the dictator's appeal: "Either Perón or Braden." Braden recalled a dispatch he had sent from Argentina in 1937 "in which he expressed his fear that Argentina was heading toward imperialism, militarism, and sui generis fascism."

cially close, almost paternal one. There was historic justice here: Hitler had helped to put Franco in power, and now Brandt helped González turn Spain into a stable democracy. Latin Americans were very much alive to these two opposing models.

The prosperous part of Buenos Aires struck me as very European—European, too, in its mixture of fear and deceptive normality. Argentina, potentially so rich, had once more fallen into economic crisis, an event that instantly sharpened the class conflict rooted in the terrifying inequalities that marked so much of Latin America. Left-wing bands had been kidnapping and murdering people, and the new regime used exceptionally brutal means to extirpate this terrorism and its putative sympathizers. Thousands of suspects "disappeared"— tortured, murdered, and sometimes simply dropped into the sea.

Crossing the Plaza de Mayo en route to an appointment with the economics minister, José Martinez de Hoz, I saw heavily armed militiamen dispersing a group of women who were demanding to know the whereabouts of their "disappeared" husbands and children. This showed the difference, I thought, between a totalitarian regime and a brutal dictatorship; the former would never have allowed protest in the first place. I went on to my meeting, where de Hoz explained that his austerity program was reducing Argentina's annual inflation rate from 700 percent to a mere 120 percent! Argentines called this horror "the third world war," noting that wars of the future would be not among nations but within them. The guerrillas in Argentina, I was told, were disproportionately children of the rich, and disproportionately Jewish. These privileged children were prototypes of the idealistic murderers of our time: intelligent, resourceful, utterly ruthless, and capable of many atrocities. Their opponents were equally fierce—and much more powerful. The moderates in the military insisted on authoritarian rule, in turn supported by much of the business community, while Argentina's "respectable" elements allowed thugs to protect them in this "dirty war."

Some military commanders had the fierce mind-set of the French generals who had opposed Algerian independence. I bought a copy of Argentina's leading right-radical journal, *Cabildo*, which featured a eulogy of the Swiss bishop Marcel Lefebvre, whom the Vatican was shortly to discipline for his reactionary extremism, and it also advertised the works of Charles Maurras, the late French ideologue of fascist persuasion. Maurras's virulent attacks on democracy, Jews, and the modern world in toto inspired Argentina's militant right, which saw enemies everywhere, including of course, foreign enemies (such as Amnesty International, which was calumnied as crypto-communist). The left assumed that the Central Intelligence Agency was masterminding the counter-insurgency, that the official terror had been learned at the hands of North Americans.

The worst state terror was over, I was told, but the trauma remained: an economist told me that he still woke up at night whenever a car stopped in front of his house, still fearing a dreaded knock at the door. The chief remaining targets were intellectuals and professionals, particularly psychoanalysts (mostly Jewish) who were suspected of having helped or tutored the guerrillas. Argentina's four hundred thousand Jews had to decide whether the endemic anti-Semitism was a familiar but passing phase or a new and mortal threat. Leaders of various Jewish organizations told me that Jews successfully looked to the Catholic hierarchy for protection, but the Church was itself divided, with progressive factions but also right-wing elements that compounded traditional hatred for Christ killers with resentment of godless secularizers. I showed one wealthy Jewish industrialist a passage from Bertolt Brecht that I had cited in *Gold and Iron*: "Working out whether to get out today or whether you have still got until tomorrow requires the sort of intelligence with which you could have created an immortal masterpiece a few decades ago." Shocked, he muttered, "But that is my problem exactly." As it has been for so many the world over, it was hard for him to *choose* exile; to be forced into it may mean salvation.

I talked to various remarkable scholars; Argentina's universities had been purged, but important work was carried on in private institutes. Most of these scholars were housed in dilapidated quarters, living on government sufferance, and receiving exemplary support from Ford and other American foundations—running expenses, the occasional mimeograph machine—and, importantly, affective encouragement. The charter of the Argentine-based umbrella group for the social sciences in Latin America, CLASCO, defined its aim as finding "an intellectual space, autonomous and free, despite the prevailing conditions"—a veiled reference to the centers that had been closed down, the colleagues imprisoned, tortured, and even killed because of their political ideas. (In Eastern Europe, George Soros had begun similar efforts: providing dissident scholars and writers with material sustenance, knowing that conveying the moral message to them was equally important: You are not alone.) I thought of some of these researchers and writers, in their uncertain world, as the unsung heroes of Latin American scholarship, and it was a privilege to meet them, a source of hope.

When we left the faded splendor of Buenos Aires for the dynamic ugliness of São Paulo, we were going to a country with which for a long time I had had some personal connections. In the 1930s, Brazil had been a haven for German exiles, Stefan Zweig the best known among them. My mother's youngest brother, Friedrich, a plant geneticist, had headed a university institute in Piraci-caba, near São Paulo. (The last time I had seen him was in New York, after the 1964 military coup. I had asked him how he could live under a regime that practiced torture, and his angry riposte cited the communist threat: our argu-ment, I suspect, confirmed our earlier prejudices about each other; I minded his brusqueness and reactionary politics; he probably thought of me as a naïve, impertinent leftie.) He was retired by now and, together with his very "Aryan" wife, an admiral's daughter, had returned to Germany, but I hoped to see my childhood friend from Prague, Hanne Kubelka, with whom I had been corresponding.

I knew that Brazil, a country of huge potential wealth and appalling in-equality, had a history of instability and extremism, where the wealthy few con-fronted the impoverished, often illiterate many. In the 1930s, it had suffered both communist uprisings and a fascist movement strongly supported by the Nazis. Fascism and Nazism had powerful sympathizers in most Latin Ameri-can countries. Brazil nevertheless joined the war against the Axis and experi-enced spectacular if uneven economic growth under civilian leadership until, in 1964, the army toppled the government—to prevent, it was alleged, a radi-cal takeover or a drift to chaos; the United States had been officially sympa-thetic. By now, however, there were signs that Brazil might manage a peaceful return to civilian rule.

The common denominator for both the radicals and the reactionaries I met was discontent. Florestan Fernandes, a well-known radical sociologist, who had been purged from one university but was newly appointed at the Pontifical Catholic University, argued against mere reformism, believing that a naked class system would promote radical change. He struck me as a believer in *la politique du pire*—that delusionary policy that holds that the worse things go the better for radicals. I have often fought with these self-righteous "wreckers," who seldom realize how bad and irredeemable things can get.

The most appealing person I encountered in Brazil was Fernando Henrique Cardoso, an economist friend of Hirschman's who invited me to his home. Dis-missed from his university post in 1969, he had become the mentor of a major research institute, Cebrap, where I met some of his colleagues; they seemed to have a knack for combining American social science with a European bent for political theory and reflectiveness—an appealing mixture. This attractive, qui-etly brilliant thinker, recognized everywhere in the academic-political world,

dismissed the chic leftist position that Argentina and Brazil were fascist countries; he agreed that it was critical to maintain the distinction, however fuzzy, between fascism and authoritarianism, since the latter, after all, allowed hope for
change. Cardoso emphasized that the situation in Brazil was better than it had
been at any time since 1964. President Carter's stand on human rights, he
thought, would have a positive impact on many countries in the process of
change. His reasoned, liberal outlook was most appealing, and I wasn't the least
surprised when the Ford Foundation's local representative called him our
"crown jewel." (Ford helped finance Cebrap.) That six years later Cardoso
would be elected president of Brazil—I doubt that many people entertained
that possibility, and it never crossed my mind. But to quote a Hirschman title,
Cardoso's election confirmed "A Bias for Hope."

Our embassy wanted me to lecture at the Fourth Army headquarters in
Belo Horizonte. The whole trip was so full of anomalies that my appearance on
a military base did not strike me as very special, but perhaps that was presump-
tuousness on my part; certainly the topic I chose, euro-communism, was a
provocation.

Euro-communism was a novelty of largely Latin origin, a name invented in
1975 to depict the joint declarations of the Italian and Spanish communist parties (later the French joined as well) announcing their willingness to work with
all democratic forces and to accept multiparty political systems: this was a rejection of the Leninist principle that the Communist Party was the supreme authority. (The three parties also critized certain policies of Brezhnev's sclerotic
regime.) Euro-communism was fiercely controversial: to many it seemed a
dangerous ruse, to "realists" a nightmare, but I thought it deserved to be taken
seriously, with final judgment depending on actual behavior. For the time being it seemed at the least to be a challenge to the USSR, a plea for respect of
some human rights. All I hoped to do was to have the question of its importance debated, not instantly dismissed. My audience was quietly skeptical—
after all, they had been brought up to fight any and all forms of communism.*

The officers listened politely, not so Joseph Bloch in Rio de Janeiro, head of

*When I came back to New York, I found a letter of mid-August 1977 from Herbert Lüthy,
Swiss historian and one of the most acute, prescient observers, written from his vacation in
Tuscany, with euro-communism in his mind: "I'll confess it without shame, I am utterly Italy-
besotted like a romantic Teuton and Europe-optimist as I haven't ever been in the last fifteen
years. I feel really as if the whole Mediterranean world with all its Andreottis and Berlinguers
and Karamanlis and Juan Carlos and Suarez and Soares were flowing into our old Western
world, enriching, rejuvenating, enrapturing, and I rejoice at this historic turn which manifests
itself there (but beware of euphoria, everything can still go wrong)."

a huge publishing empire there. Bloch's Jewish family had come to Brazil in 1922 from Russia, in flight from communism. He invited me to speak to his "top people," again about euro-communism. Massively self-satisfied and arrogant, he was contemptuous of anything that diverged from his primitive McCarthyite anticommunism. During lunch, he quipped, "You are clever, but I have the experience." After my lecture, he repeated this remark in a crowded elevator, and I replied, "It all depends on whether one learns from one's experience."

My introduction to the German presence in Brazil began with a meeting with Hartman Schulze-Boysen, the newly arrived German consul-general in São Paulo. He agreed with me that the alliance in Brazil between big business and the armed forces resembled the business support for the Nazis in prewar Germany. He knew whereof he spoke: he was the brother of Harro Schulze-Boysen, leader of the anti-Nazi conspiracy known as *Rote Kapelle*, which had supplied the Russians with military intelligence in the early stages of the war; Harro had been executed by the Nazis in 1942. With his liberal outlook, his fierce concern for human rights, and his connection to the anti-Nazi resistance, Hartman Schulze-Boysen was not your run-of-the-mill diplomat.

But I understood Germany's truly astounding economic presence only when I saw Volkswagen do Brasil, a huge plant on the outskirts of São Paulo run by Wolfgang Sauer, its spectacularly self-confident CEO. VW had established this plant in 1952, when it feared that a Soviet takeover of West Germany might eliminate the home plant. It employed forty thousand workers, only eighty of whom were German. Sauer, with his perfect Portuguese, was a new type of empire builder: a man of unbounded energy mixed with a calculated social conscience; keenly aware of the juxtaposition of his ultramodern plant with the huts and favelas on the nearby mountainside, evidence of the prevailing poverty and illiteracy of most of Brazil. He was proud of his company's innovative social services and the vast apprentice system by which it trained its own workers. Some 120,000 people had gone through the system, a substantial part of Brazil's emergent middle class. VW was Brazil's largest taxpayer and probably biggest employer, giving it a potential power that, Sauer said, was left unexercised. (His rivals disputed this claim.) The humming of his huge enterprise reminded me of Undershaft's armaments factory in Shaw's *Major Barbara*, capitalism triumphant. At the end of our meeting, Sauer recommended that in the Federal Republic I should see Hanns-Martin Schleyer, head of the German Confederation of Industry, but German terrorists murdered Schleyer shortly thereafter.

In Rio, the day I met Hanne Kubelka began oddly: Peggy and I were staying at a hotel in Copacabana, and in the early morning, when I went swimming at a deserted beach, two powerful waves in quick succession knocked me down. In a lifetime of ocean swimming, which I adored, it was my only time of fear. I felt as if a friend had betrayed me. Back at the hotel, I looked for Hanne, expecting a slightly older version of the beautiful Hanne of 1938. Then a stately middle-aged woman appeared—another correction to fantasy. At dusk she took us to a place beneath the Sugarloaf, and we talked of our last meeting, in the Czech mountains in 1938. Odd: angst at sea in the morning, and in the evening a memory of the earlier worse childhood fear—and a sense that I had been saved both times.

The next day, a Sunday, Hanne drove us to her laboratory outside São Paulo. She talked of the obstacles on her way to international success, and of Brazil she said it was "the country of the future and always will be." We agreed that however different our early experiences had been, they had somehow steeled us. As we parted, we vowed in retirement to write a joint memoir about our common and divergent paths. We kept up an intermittent correspondence, but the project remained undone, and she died in 2001.

Colombia—the final stop of my trip—was certainly freer than Argentina and Brazil, but the fear of violence was palpable. Bogotá resembled an armed camp, with the elite living in fashionable, secured suburbs, and guards with dogs patrolling the streets. I learned most from Rodrigo Botero, economist and Hirschman's close friend. (A couple of years later he became a member of Willy Brandt's North-South Commission.) Bishop Alfonso López Trujillo, secretary-general of the Conference of Latin American Bishops, the very prototype of an austere old-style church diplomat, taught me more than he perhaps intended. He insisted that the divisions within the Church—between the radical and the reactionary wings, between followers of "liberation theology" and staunchly reactionary elements—were insignificant. Pope John XXIII and the *aggiornamento* were unimportant. (In April 2005, Cardinal Trujillo was an ardent and influential supporter of Cardinal Ratzinger's election as John Paul II's successor.) A young Jesuit priest, fresh from Santiago, Chile—from the front lines, as it were—told a different story: In the days before Allende's murder there, people had rushed to the Church in the hope that it might prevent General Pinochet's coup. The young priest confirmed that some Church elements, and not only in Chile, tried to defend human rights both by protecting individual dissenters and by propounding political demands.

After intense weeks in Latin America, I drafted another report, "Between Repression and Reform," which *Foreign Affairs* published in July 1978, and which was reprinted in *O Estado de São Paulo* and other Brazilian papers.* In it, I speculated that a return to civilian rule and attendant reform was likely—and it happened. I wondered also how democratic rule might be established and sustained, given the sharp inequalities in Latin America that fed class antagonisms. Might there be a halfway house to democracy, I asked, a stage like the liberal-constitutional phase in Western Europe in the early nineteenth century, a polity characterized by the rule of law, an independent judiciary, and the recognition of fundamental civic rights of free speech and free assembly? Much more would have to be done to correct injustices and to make greater civic participation possible. "A country without torture, without the threat of disappearance at the pleasure of the rulers, is a country with some hope. Ask any prisoner whether the abolition of torture or of arbitrary arrest is a negligible improvement, a mere 'formal right.'" Sobering thoughts today, as we see how under some conditions of fear, democracies, faithful or not to counting votes, seek to curb or forfeit liberal guarantees, which remain the most essential elements of a decent society.

"THE PAST IS A FOREIGN COUNTRY; they do things differently there." This wonderful opening of L. P. Hartley's novel *The Go-Between* is a common saying among historians, but I found the opposite was also true: foreign countries could illuminate the past. In the fall of 1977, I returned to Columbia, but luck gave me a chance to learn about other places, and Columbia and I reached a kind of tacit bargain: I would assume extra responsibilities while in residence, and the university would indulge my wanderlust for serious travel. Thus in the spring semester of 1979, I was able to take up a long-standing invitation as Élie Halévy visiting professor at the Institut des Sciences Politiques (the "Sciences Po") in Paris, a successor institution to a school established after France's defeat in 1870 and intended to prepare a republican elite for political responsibility.

---

*In 1981, Jacobo Timerman, the Argentinean publisher who had been arrested in April 1977, tortured, released two years later, expelled from Argentina, and flown to Israel, published his stunning work *Prisoner Without a Name, Cell Without a Number*. Timerman thought the horrors he endured were analogous to Nazi terror. On a visit to New York at the time, he was interviewed by a *New York Times* reporter who mentioned my article to him, which Timerman thought very sound, given how little time I had spent in Argentina. Claudio Veliz, from Melbourne, wrote to me, saying it was "a most thoughtful and perceptive examination of the state of these countries; it may well be one of the best articles published by an outsider . . . in a long time." But the real value of his letter was in the long discussion of "suppression of freedom" from the left, giving as prime instance his own experience of having founded an institute in Santiago, Chile, patterned after Chatham House, and having been systematically harassed by the Allende regime.

After Germany's defeat in 1918, and following this model, the Germans founded their Institute for Politics in Berlin, Carnegie-supported and with a distinguished faculty whose orientation was liberal-democratic, unlike that of the universities.

The name Halévy compounded the pleasure of the appointment, for he was one of my intellectual heroes. My first lecture included an elaborate *éloge* to Halévy, only to discover that the students neither knew about him nor cared! Still, to be Élie Halévy professor at Sciences Po was a dream, to which was added the perfect residence. I had cajoled Shep Stone into renting us his grand apartment on the Quai aux Fleurs, next to Notre Dame and across from the still unspoiled Ile St. Louis, with views that made staring out the window an inescapable temptation. I thought Shep was right when with his customary modesty he claimed his the most beautiful apartment in Paris. So we lived in this splendid place, and very happily I walked to Sciences Po to give my lectures, "European Fascism, 1914–1945," and a seminar on antibourgeois sentiment in the nineteenth century.

French literature on fascism was scant and much of it unsatisfactory: the French had yet to recognize that prefascist thought and fascist political movements had been especially strong in their own country, and they had not really come to grips with the Vichy regime. They had indulged in comforting myths and done much less than their German colleagues in this respect. I began by explaining that a great longing for a new authoritarianism, or Caesarism, had existed before 1914; that after the Great War and the Bolshevik Revolution, the Italian fascist movement emerged, differing from the older conservative nationalism because it aimed at mass mobilization, and affirmed and practiced its faith in violence; that its principal enemy was liberalism but that it benefited decisively from the pervasive and easily manipulated fear of Bolshevism. In the mid-1920s Nikolai Bukharin, the darling of the Bolshevik Revolution, had acknowledged an affinity of methods between Bolshevism and fascism. Since many French scholars were *gauchiste* and vaguely sympathetic to the USSR, my account of Stalin's failure to understand fascism, indeed the fact that his policies had given it indirect aid, aroused angry dubiety.

A close colleague of mine at Sciences Po, Raoul Girardet, was different. A historian of French militarism, austere, conservative, kind, and forbidding. A staunch French nationalist, he had been close to the Resistance during World War II, but as a fierce opponent of de Gaulle's "abandonment" of Algeria, as he saw it, he had been imprisoned. We taught some seminars together, and I learned more about French conservatism. When I was in doubt or trouble, I turned to Serge Hurtig—I thought of him as the virtual head of Sciences Po— who had arranged for my visit and was a perfect host.

Paris could be wonderfully stimulating and singularly lonely at the same time. I think the very beauty of the city made me feel sad at times. To talk history and politics with François Furet and Pierre Hassner, a prolific commentator on international questions, with Pierre Nora and Robert Marjolin, a student of Halévy's, an economist-administrator with Gallic reserve and charm (first head of the OECD); to be with old friends and make new ones—all that was exceptional enrichment.

I saw Raymond Aron mostly at meetings in Berlin, less often in Paris. He, too, was a philosopher-historian and political commentator, a liberal of the old school of Montesquieu and Tocqueville. There was a deeply appealing melancholic and sardonic brilliance to him. We talked of his studies in Berlin in the early 1930s, where he had witnessed Hitler's rise to power; he called it the beginning of his political education. There was a fierce independence to him. And to de Gaulle's notorious, deliberately ambiguous definition of Jews after Israel's victory in the Six-Day War as "a self-assured and domineering people," he, a non-practicing Jew and critical supporter of Israel, countered with shrewd analysis and protest.

At dinner at the home of another historian friend, I met the head of the Asian division of the Foreign Ministry. As so often, the subject of Israel came up, and since Holocaust, the American television series, was being shown on French and German TV, that subject was broached, too. The diplomat wondered if the death camps and gas chambers had actually existed; where was the evidence? he asked. Perhaps all this talk of the Holocaust was a Zionist plot. I still have a clear memory of that dinner—the placement of the guests around the table, the host's embarrassment, my fierce objections in my flawed, passionate French, and my inner conflict about whether or not I should leave the party. This was my only "social" encounter with a Holocaust denier, and I doubt that it could have happened in Germany. The next day the host telephoned me to apologize.

While still in Paris, I was asked to speak at a belated memorial symposium for Hannah Arendt, who had died in 1975. I had never been and am not now an Arendt fan (hence I am also skeptical of the Arendt cult), but I had met her several times and was impressed by her metaphysical fluency and European arrogance. In my remarks, I concentrated on The Origins of Totalitarianism, a courageous work for her to have written at a time when insisting on the commonalities of Bolshevism and National Socialism was frowned upon. In that regard, I likened her to George Orwell, which I thought was high praise. I had also read *Eichmann in Jerusalem*, but there I had been puzzled by what I thought was an excessive need to insist that everyone was in some respect guilty—Nazi villains and Jewish victims, too, albeit in unequal measure. (Only much later did we learn of Arendt's intimate relations with Martin Heidegger, an intellectual villain par excellence.) So I spoke of her as a *moraliste*, a cultural critic trained in German idealism under the tutelage of Karl Jaspers and Heidegger, who then experienced radical uprootedness and discovered how easy it was to be stripped of the normal attributes of life, citizenship, civil rights, and home. For her, politics was a moral drama, but her approach to it was ponderously philosophical, and, while at times poetic, it was rarely historical.

In March 1979, I found myself in Jerusalem, on my third visit to Israel, for the long-planned Einstein centenary celebrations. The city sparkled in the sun, with its clear and fragrant air, at once daringly modern and stunningly ancient, the two harmoniously coexisting. At first I hesitated to wander about in the Old City, reluctant to be a tourist among presumably hostile Arabs, but I slipped into the sense of security that Israelis themselves felt about Jerusalem, a city that was theirs to preserve with its mysterious and multivalent past, theirs to build something startlingly new. The status of Jerusalem as both a Jewish and a Muslim capital, and its significance as a Christian holy site, required delicate attention, which the Israeli government believed it was giving it. But how could one miss the not-so-subterranean resentments on all sides, and the violent differences among Israelis themselves?

The Aspen Institute and the Hebrew University had planned crowded festivities, at the heart of which was a three-day symposium on all aspects of Einstein's science and life, attended by all the important Einstein experts. I felt uneasy from the start. A familiar feeling of fraudulence welled up in me, more intense than usual. I have always liked being among my betters, which is at once uplifting and down-putting, ideal for fortifying self-doubt, but in this instance the subject and my colleagues seemed overwhelming. My worries mounted when just before the opening session, Klaus Schütz, West Germany's ambassador to Israel, whispered to me that Gershon Scholem, sitting in the row in front of me, was telling people that in the German edition of *Gold and Iron*, which had just appeared, all the German citations had been translated from the English, that is, they were not in the original. This was an outrageous and utterly false allegation, the more galling given that I had spent weeks and weeks supplying the German translator with every one of the original texts! But I think Scholem thought of my book as an invidious argument for assimilation, a defense of a German Jewish symbiosis, a notion against which Scholem had fought all his life, having moved in the early 1920s from Berlin to Jerusalem, where his studies of Jewish mysticism brought him worldwide acclaim.

Scholem chaired the session at which the Israeli scholar and my friend Uri Tal and I spoke. He began by delivering a lengthy speech of his own, introducing Tal and acknowledging me. It was an inauspicious start, but my paper was well received, and Scholem had to admonish the audience to stop applauding. (Erik Erikson thought I had been an excellent devil's advocate at what he called the canonization ceremony.) At the end, Scholem broke protocol by "forgetting" to hand me the Einstein medal that every speaker received, but since it was lying on the table in plain sight, I simply took it. At a reception at Scholem's home afterward, with *Kaffee und Kuchen*, I was intrigued that Scholem's Faustian bastion of books was housed in something that perfectly resembled a German academic home of long ago, more "German" than anything I had ever seen in postwar Germany. How different was the official reception given by Israel's president Yitzhak Navon, who, in disclaiming any expertise on Einstein, cited Felix Frankfurter's remark to Ben-Gurion about some American politician—"There are gaps in his ignorance"—and said he hoped this was true for himself.

I saw some of my old interlocutors. Shimon Peres, indefatigable reader, had sent me a note after having read *Gold and Iron*: "Hélas! We do not have gold, and the need for iron [is] so high." He felt a strong kinship with Europe, whose politicians he shrewdly assessed: Austrian chancellor Bruno Kreisky had done much for the Jews, Peres thought, but, given his Jewish self-hatred, no sooner had he done something for them than he had to undo it the next morning; Helmut Schmidt, on the other hand, had been a great behind-the-scenes helper in arranging for Sadat's visit. Peres was a very appealing person—a thinker, a brooder, and an election loser. No accident, I thought, that he spent time talking about the near impossibility of democratic leadership, especially in peacetime.

But was it peace? Israel's treaty with Egypt was about to be ratified, but given the PLO's confused structure, Peres foresaw ever-greater terrorism in the West Bank. And only weeks before, Iranian revolutionary forces had overthrown the Shah of Iran and seized the American embassy and its staff. General Tal, whom I met again, didn't think this was peace; Sadat couldn't conclude a genuine peace without a solution to the Palestinian issue. He thought that the world now looked upon the United States as "a paralyzed giant," as Hitler had assessed

France and England in the 1930s. Israel, he said, should return all the territory it had conquered in 1967, both for prudential and for demographic reasons: an enlarged Israel either would not be an egalitarian democracy, or it would be a democracy with an Arab majority. And it didn't need to fear a small Palestinian state hedged in between Jordan and Israel.

General Tal was tough, realistic, prescient, and daring. He showed me his reports of 1976 warning that the Shah's regime was unstable, that Israel should prepare to accommodate seventy thousand Iranian Jews, and that in a future war, Iran would be Israel's enemy, unlike its stance under the Shah. In the vast Defense Ministry where we met, he said he was pretty much alone as a dove in questions of long-range strategy, but he was tough in any tactical situation; he could even imagine undertaking preemptive strikes. (Israel bombed Iraq's nuclear installation two years later.)

Even the irenic Teddy Kollek, the Vienna-born mayor of Jerusalem, was worried about Israel's long-term future and angered by the gratuitous insults of its friends. On his way to the Middle East, President Carter had allegedly said he was going to visit three countries, showing pictures of their respective leaders: Sadat, Begin, and Kollek. And his later note of thanks had been addressed to "Teddy Kollek, Jerusalem, Jerusalem" as if the city were separate from Israel. Such "stupidities," Kollek thought, would only fortify Arab intransigence.

Isaiah Berlin had asked me to come to his hotel for more talks. Isaiah was *ein Wunder*: the limpid rapidity of his thought and talk, the burst of ideas, the aperçus of human and historic foibles! To talk with him was to imbibe distilled champagne. But I couldn't see him right away: his prior guest tarried, and I waited. Finally, Isaac Stern emerged, and Isaiah triumphantly bestowed cousinhood on us, a fictional relationship the two of us joked about in the years to come. Isaiah reminisced with me about his one meeting with Einstein, around 1945, when Einstein had accused him of being a cold warrior. It was easy in those days to misjudge a critic of the Soviet regime and to confound liberal hostility to tyranny with militaristic ideas about keeping the Soviet empire at bay. But on one point they would have agreed: Einstein had publicly denounced Begin and Jewish terrorism. Isaiah told me that on an earlier occasion he himself had refused to shake Begin's hand.

My last meeting was with Ambassador Schütz, formerly Willy Brandt's alter ego in Berlin and his successor as mayor. We sat on a bench in the Garden of Gethsemane, above the city, admiring its splendor, but worried. The treaty with Egypt could not mark a great change; since Israel didn't want to give up the West Bank, and even a Palestinian state, if ever created, couldn't accommodate all the Palestinians languishing in refugee camps. Meanwhile the lines at the American consulate in Tel Aviv were growing longer, as more and more Israelis pondered a once unthinkable new fate: emigration.

We talked of the close relations, political and especially scientific, between the Federal Republic and Israel. Ironically, Israelis seemed more tolerant of West Germans than they were of their fellow citizens of German origin. The fine novelist Amos Oz had just written an essay lambasting Israeli society and excoriating those who wished to establish "a replica of Berlin in Nahariya." The German Jews, *Jeckes*, had been a favorite target of scorn and satire for decades. Poor *Jeckes*: persecuted by the Nazis, ridiculed by their own people. Oz decried Israel's fall from the hopes of its early settlers: "Did we seek to shake history only to erect here a dubious imitation of a *petit bourgeois* township in Poland or Iraq? . . . Is not our society now divided between men who steal and cheat at worst, and at best who work beyond their strength to acquire things they don't really need, to impress people they don't really care about?" Perhaps Oz's anticapitalist diatribe was a prophetic exaggeration, but it certainly was a healthy sign of a society's capacity for self-criticism.

Israelis were beginning to examine their own history, confronting questions of Zionist terrorism at the end of the Mandate, and of atrocities against Palestinians, still talked about almost in whispers, at the time of the War of Independence. Excesses were there from the beginning.

As I left this time, I felt an even stronger affinity for the country—admiration for what its people had accomplished and sorrow at their continued embattlement. Perhaps Einstein had been right to speak of his loyalty to the tribe. I felt that I, too, belonged to the tribe—even after my grandparents had lost or renounced the faith. I was grateful that Israeli friends accepted me. It was another way of living in many worlds—and in none completely.

My Einstein lecture in Jerusalem elicited invitations to talk on Einstein at other enticing places where he himself had had historic encounters—and where often I discovered unfamiliar traces of his life. I went to Leiden and to the fabled hall in Berlin-Dahlem where Einstein and Haber had often met. And I lectured at the Niels Bohr Institute in Copenhagen, where in 1936 I had been parked in the garden while my parents consulted James Franck on their plans for emigration. This time I met Bohr's son, Aage, also a Nobel laureate, and widow, Margaret, a tall woman of striking beauty, the helper-friend to so many scientists in troubled times.

Lectures in Stockholm gave me a chance to talk again with Olof Palme, ex–prime minister and a leading figure in Social Democracy. Palme said of the

Soviets—this was at the height of Brezhnev's gerontocratic immobility—"Don't push them too hard; they'll reform without pressure." This remark played into my hope that euro-communism might shake Moscow's insistence on its own dogmatic infallibility. (Palme's murder seven years later was a terrible shock: the many political murders I have witnessed are calamitous reminders of how easily great promise is snuffed out.)

I went to Rome—splendid center of euro-communism—and had a round of talks with politicians and journalists from the key parties. I sensed the huge disparity between the heavy-handed Brezhnev style of repression and Italian finesse and flexibility, to say nothing of a deep-rooted humanity in Italian life that even Mussolini could not entirely destroy. Italy's communist leaders, I thought, were after power and genuine change, probably in that order, and they could both harm and benefit Moscow; I understood that their socialist critics were perhaps even more skeptical of their sincerity than the Christian Democrats, pondering the possibilities of a "historic compromise" between the two main parties.

I talked with Antonio La Pergola, a preeminent jurist and newly appointed member of the Constitutional Court of Italy, where we met. He worried that in the face of terrorism, still rife in Italy as elsewhere in Europe, the protection of civic rights and liberties would become increasingly difficult. It had been only a year since the "Red Brigades" had kidnapped Aldo Moro, former prime minister and a key Christian Democrat, held him hostage, and murdered him. La Pergola favored the creation of an international organization of lawyers and judges, so that the judiciary of one country would know it belonged to a family of like-minded professionals and would, in a sense, feel accountable to them. (If only such a body had existed in the 1930s, I thought, when German and Italian judges violated the laws they had sworn to uphold: they might have felt spasms of conscience when faced by international censure.) La Pergola was in the vanguard on this issue, for soon such organizations began to flourish. He also successfully pushed for a more active defense of human rights in the EU.

MY PARIS STAY BROUGHT ME PHYSICALLY and intellectually closer to that other half of Europe that I had scarcely seen. We European historians of course cared about the Soviet Union's restive East European satellites, and we listened intermittently to the Kremlinologists. But by and large we paid insufficient attention to Eastern Europe, a neglect that post–1945 politics and the Soviet bloc's self-insulation made easier. Now I was determined to go to Russia and Poland—not as a tourist but in my new "Ford mode," as an accepted interlocutor. I was keen to see for myself. And Paris was a perfect place to plan such a trip; for one thing, the city was full of East European exiles, as it had been so often in the past. Also, I knew about the many networks of American and Soviet academics,* especially of natural scientists concerned with nuclear issues.

I think it was Robert Legvold, Columbia colleague, astute observer of Soviet affairs, and facilitator of faculty exchanges, who recommended me to the Arbatov Institute for the Study of the U.S. and Canada, a kind of think tank in Moscow. Georgyi Arbatov, a member of the Soviet Academy of Sciences, was a privileged member of the *Nomenklatura*, with access to the good life in that citadel of non-equality. A formal invitation from the institute was a prerequisite for getting a Russian visa, but Soviet bureaucracy moved with frustrating slowness. Luck helped. In Paris, I met Warren Zimmermann, a career American diplomat who was then deputy chief of mission at our embassy, a tall cheerful man of astonishing wisdom, wit, and decency. (His equally tall wife, naturally named Teeny, was just as remarkable: wonderfully alive, direct, and forthright. They had previously been posted at the embassy in Moscow, where I later learned that Teeny had helped dissident writers in ways that really mattered most, taking action that most American diplomats were unlikely to do: she took their manuscripts to the outside world.) One thing I learned on these trips was that some of our Foreign Service officers were simply spectacular models of intellect and commitment, and Warren was one. He put me in touch with Yury Rubinsky, a veteran member of the Soviet embassy in Paris—a most unconventional person, a cosmopolitan and a Jew, in a way a throwback to earlier periods in Soviet politics—and he helped out. On May 24 a formal invitation arrived from Vitali Zhurkin, deputy director of Arbatov's institute, to be its guest for a week, when I could meet with specialists on Europe and international affairs: "I hope such exchange of views will be useful to us."

---

*I played a tiny role in one major effort. In the 1950s, Paul Kristeller, a renowned scholar of the Renaissance, a German-trained, German-exiled colleague at Columbia, invited me to lunch. He was a forbidding and austere person, and this gesture was unprecedented. He had just returned from an archival trip to the Soviet Union and wanted to bestow a confidence on me: in Leningrad, he whispered, were the papers of Napoleon's brother, King Jerome of Westphalia, unexamined. A find indeed: Didn't I want to use them? Well, they didn't quite fit into my Bismarck book, but a few years later, Henry Roberts and Frederick Burkhardt, then head of the American Council of Learned Societies, went on an official trip to the USSR to establish scholarly exchanges. At one point the Soviets bristled at the two scholars' requests for access to the archives, saying, "You just want to have people snoop around Soviet matters." Henry, recalling my story, countered, "Why, no, we want scholars to have a chance to see treasures like the papers of King Jerome." An agreement was signed, and Burkhardt assured me that I had earned a trip of my own. As for King Jerome's papers, I don't know what happened to them, but they served a good purpose.

I was aware that relations between our two countries had become rockier; hence for the Soviets, relations with Western Europe assumed even greater importance. The Russians were concerned about our visibly closer ties with China, while the Carter administration, internally often divided, was worried about Soviet adventurism in Africa and the harsh treatments of dissidents and of Jews seeking to emigrate. There were tense preparations for a Carter-Brezhnev summit on SALT II, which was to take place in July 1979. But by and large, détente was already somewhat frayed—well before the Soviet invasion of Afghanistan.

I knew that Arbatov's institute would set me up with official types, but my particular passion of course was to meet with those people who lived in the shadow world of outcast existence. Many French intellectuals were solicitous of their East European counterparts, the Polish ones especially, and Annette Labourey ran a Ford Foundation–supported organization, whose main purpose was to help East European (and Iberian) intellectuals spend time in Western Europe. Roger Errera, a *conseiller d'état* with a fervent concern for human rights, gave me a list of his friends in Russia and Poland, as did the marvelous expert on Russian literature Max Hayward, at St. Antony's College, Oxford, who probably knew the most about the Russian scene, and Marion Dönhoff, who had her own close connections. Aleksandr Nekrich, eminent émigré Russian historian, now at Harvard and co-author of *Utopia in Power*, sent me contacts, adding, "Please, don't mention my name over phone, but pass my warmest regards if you meet them '*unter vier Augen.*'"

Key was Efim Etkind, a recent Russian exile, a renowned literary critic and translator, former professor of literature at the Herzen Pedagogical Institute in Leningrad, now teaching at the Sorbonne. He was the perfect Russian *intelligent*, wise, ironic, and melancholic, with both suffering and a bit of mischief registering in his expressive face. A war veteran and cherished teacher, he had suffered under Soviet repression in its refined Brezhnev style. In 1964 he had been a defense witness at the trial of Joseph Brodsky, later refusing to abjure his defense; he was a friend of Alexander Solzhenitsyn and accused of safeguarding a samizdat copy of the *Gulag Archipelago* for him; he had written a letter "To Young Jews," urging them to emigrate from Russia—and all these activities were presented to the Academic Council of the Herzen Institute in 1974, where Etkind had taught for twenty-three years, as the work of an "anti-Soviet renegade" using "tactics of the enemy." At a meeting held to discuss Etkind's case, his letter of defense was read: "I have done all in my power to inspire in my pupils love for the poetic word, interest in the humanities, and respect for true cultural values." But institute members inveighed against him, while KGB agents watched and listened.* By secret ballot his colleagues unanimously voted his dismissal and cancellation of his title. He was expelled from the Writers' Union as well and left Russia that year. In a public declaration, Etkind explained what had been done to him, noting that his being a Jew had weighed against him, as "turbid floods of anti-Semitism are spreading once again through our land." (Such defiance had no analogue under the Nazi regime, I thought.) His colleagues' indecent conduct was due, he said, to "soul-chilling, brain-numbing, silencing familiar and insurmountable, shameful and terrible—fear."

Etkind came to our home in Paris, and I fell for him at once, the more so as both his expression and his unobtrusive kindness instantly reminded me of the Russian friend of my New York adolescence, Ossinka Blumenfeld. He offered to give me names of his friends, but only after I had received my visa. By then he was ill and sent his beautiful daughter Masha to see me instead; she added the names of some of her friends in Leningrad, and so I enjoyed two generations' worth of contacts.†

By mid-June, Peggy's and my papers were in order and we left for Moscow. I felt a kind of anticipatory passionate ambivalence, a mix of abhorrence and admiration. Fleeting images swept through my mind: of the Bolshevik Revolution, which for a brief moment had seemed to signal emancipation and artistic freedom but almost at once became a reign of terror and was finally transfigured into paranoid madness under Stalin; the eye-opening betrayal of the Soviet-German pact; Germany's savage attack in 1941 and the unimaginable suffering of the Russian people thereafter; the two-year siege of Leningrad, with its millions of people cut off from the rest of Russia; the power of the Red Army, which at desperate cost defeated the hitherto unbeaten Wehrmacht; and then, after the war, more betrayals, greater repression, dissidents, and samizdat. I had

---

*When I met Etkind, he told me an additional dramatic detail. Before the meeting, the institute's rector summoned a prominent institute member who had never been abroad and told him about a forthcoming conference in Paris, to which he would like to send him. And there was one other matter: the rector knew that he and Etkind were good friends, and while of course he would never expect him to denounce a friend, perhaps at the forthcoming meeting he might simply define the minimum expectations of a Socialist academic? The colleague did this—betrayal by bribery, and Etkind lost his position and presumably the colleague got to go to Paris.

†The last time I saw Etkind was in 1993, at breakfast in Potsdam, where he had moved in 1990, living in the shadow of Sans Souci; he was writing about the king's poetry. There I met his new German wife, whom he had met at the University of Oregon! They had a simple, elegant home, at once Russian and German, and I marveled at what seemed a perfect companionship. Later, I heard that she sustained him in his last days in the hospital, hiding from him that she was herself a cancer patient—both gallant to the end.

just devoured Nadezhda Mandelstam's peerless *Hope Against Hope*, an unsparing portrait of suffering: "We were all the same: either sheep who went willingly to the slaughter, or respectful assistants to the executioners." Of course, Russians were *not* all the same—and thoughts about the totalitarianism I had known and the one I was about to see swirled in my head. I suppose my very ambivalence suggested that in my innermost self I didn't quite equate the two regimes.

At Sheremetyevo Airport outside Moscow we were met by Gelya Gorelosa, a pretty young Intourist guide-companion whom the institute put at our disposal; her other connections I could only surmise. As she drove us to the city, she pointed to the simple memorial marking the spot in the suburbs where the German advance had been stopped in December 1941—a few miles from Red Square. The actual sight was so much more memorable than texts describing the event! If the Germans had gone but a little farther, the history of the world would have been fatally different. Passing the fabled Park of Culture and Rest, with trappings of the Revolution and pictures of Lenin everywhere, she took us to the Akademiske Hotel, designed for foreign visitors: a cold, primitive, but adequate place in the outskirts of the city.

Once settled, I wanted to telephone my contacts, and I knew how to do this: only from public pay phones on the street, making sure I wasn't being watched. Certainly Gelya couldn't help with the kopek shortages, and to collect them required minor skill. It was a curious existence, to be a privileged visitor in a shadow prison. Sometimes the atmosphere reminded me of scenes from childhood—and I clutched my American passport.

I didn't know what to expect at the Arbatov Institute, housed in a renovated mansion in the center of Moscow just behind Kalinin Prospekt, but I soon learned that I would have informal talks with some of its members on everything from the SALT negotiations (Strategic Arms Limitation Talks) and American "interests" in the cold war to questions about Europe and the origins of said war. On that first day, I spent ninety minutes with Arbatov, an intensely serious, reasonable person with a glimmer of irony; he spoke in nonideological language and eschewed the traditional communist clichés. Given my interest in Europe, he said, I had done right to come: "We are part of Europe." This became the underlying theme, but Arbatov kept suggesting that Europe, meaning France and Germany, was inching away from the United States: This was no doubt what the Soviets were wishing for and something they meant to exploit, but it was also a way of downplaying the doctrinal view of the inevitable conflict between capitalism and communism. This insistent note that "we are part of Europe"—a wish more than a political reality—was a kind of foreshadowing of what in a few years Gorbachev was to celebrate with his phrase "The Common House of Europe."

For different reasons Arbatov and I both were partisans of détente, but we sparred and disagreed. I wasn't any good on the fine points of SALT, but on the origins of the cold war, I could hold my own and then some. I insisted that Stalin's brutal behavior in Rumania and Poland in 1945–1947 had produced the very results he feared: an antagonistic United States that resolved to rearm. Then the cold war fed on itself, every move by one side heightening fear and distrust on the other. Neither side was blameless, but the Russians' oft-repeated charge that "vested interests" in the United States sought to undermine SALT and détente I deemed simplistic.

Only after the collapse of communism did I learn that Arbatov had been a watchful critic of the "Soviet system," as he called it, impatient with Russia's intellectual isolation, eager to see the world without the blinkers imposed by Marxist-Leninist ideology. Obviously he had to hide his innermost political views and his dissatisfaction with Soviet stultification. (His 1991 autobiography explained that he had spent his childhood in Germany, witnessing the Nazi seizure of power and the rise of anti-Semitism.) We now know that he also helped to protect some of his collaborators whose views officialdom distrusted. The institute had its ups and downs, maneuvering between rigidity and freedom, but on the whole it gave conciliatory advice to the Communist Party.

My first day at the institute passed well enough. Yuri Davydov, the institute specialist on U.S.-European relations, was a friendly person who also regretted America's alleged retreat from détente, which implied that "vested interests"—that phrase again!—in America benefited from bellicosity. Carter's strictures on human rights rankled with Davydov: "The U.S. is more interested in having every Russian read *The New York Times* at every corner than in settling nuclear issues," Davydov said. His line was that the Soviet and Western systems offered different roads to happiness: Russia may have had three thousand dissidents, but we in the United States had six million unemployed (another constant theme). That he and his colleagues basically saw the USSR as a permanently injured party, almost an innocent victim, seemed clear. My day ended with other appointments being planned, and also a seminar that I was to give on European and American politics. My interlocutors seemed well informed and relatively nonideological. The conversations were sharp, the tone collegial, albeit with occasional barbed comments, or taunts—I may have been readier with these than they.

After I finished at the institute, I went to a playground opposite our hotel, where I dictated notes into a tape recorder. I knew we were being watched. Once, a lightbulb in our hotel room gave out and pleas to the woman-spy who watched over our floor proved ineffective—but Peggy's and my complaining loudly to each other in the room brought instant results. There are advantages to being bugged.

My days in Moscow were carefully divided into interview sessions, some sightseeing and visits to museums, and then some special entertainment in the evening that Gelya arranged. But on most occasions I would beg off these last, feigning fatigue or a big headache, since the evenings were the only time when we could see the dissidents, the friends of our friends. They proved open and wonderfully trusting. I first would telephone them, trying to identify myself with minimum risk to the other party, and once a rendezvous was arranged, Peggy and I would navigate Moscow at night, by taxi or via the city's celebrated subway, wandering the ill-lit streets.

My first visit was to a friend of Etkind's named Samarii Izrailevich Velikovsky, a student of French literature and philosophy who worked at the Institute for the Study of the Labor Movement. The big picture of Solzhenitsyn that dominated his tiny study conveyed a clear, courageous message. Velikovsky's institute hired few Jews because they tended to leave, that is, emigrate; he told me that after Prague '68 everything had become harder because intellectuals were thought to be especially dangerous. Even dissidents came in many guises, he remarked, with those with right-wing views often carrying a heavy dose of anti-Semitism. But then that was an old affliction. As a Jew, he added, he had to be twice as gifted as others, and still he had no chance of getting a university job. He talked quietly, a sad but brave man, without self-pity: "It is all so difficult, but so is being deracinated, living in exile."

Even more memorable was another friend of Etkind's, the novelist Lydia Chukovskaya. We stumbled to the address given, and then, at the foot of the usual dank, ill-lit staircase, an old, inebriated guardian tried to prevent us from getting to her apartment. I brushed by him, rushed up the stairs, and outran him, so that we reached the apartment before he did. Once inside with Chukovskaya, we could hear him knocking at the door, panting and shouting. I felt guilty lest I had endangered her, but she reassured me that he was a habitual enemy.

Chukovskaya was a kindly, strong woman, then in her early seventies, who spoke little of her own life and suffering. But I knew she had been a close friend and ally of Anna Akhmatova and was an indefatigable defender of fellow writ-

ers, quick to speak out publicly, for example calling Solzhenitsyn's expulsion
from the Writers' Union in 1969 "a national shame." Later, she, too, was expelled. She wanted to know all about Etkind and the world outside—I suppose
I could be useful in that regard—so we talked intensely (I've forgotten in what
language: probably scraps of English, German, and French?) as if we had
known each other for a long time. Sometimes it is the simplest phrase that il-
luminates a whole era: Chukovskaya's own remark that "The murder of the
truthful word . . . was one of the blackest crimes committed by the decades," or
her goddaughter's poignant observation to me, a few days later, that "In my
generation, nobody had a father." Stalinist terror had preceded and followed
the German invasion, and tens of millions had perished—what families remained unscathed? People had endured so much and yet so many were still
battling. With Chukovskaya as with others, we spoke of the anti-Semitism once
again rampant in Russia, despite—or because—Jews remained in high positions. Jews painfully worried over the pros and cons of exile, knowing that even
the first steps in that direction brought immediate retaliation.

I visited another think tank, the Institute of World Economy and International Relations, like Arbatov's institute a part of the Soviet Academy of Sciences,
and similarly housed grandly, as befitted a center that advised the government
(apparently in greater ideological conformity than Arbatov's outfit). The German specialist there, Dmitri Melnikov (whose wife translated Heinrich Böll,
the West German writer best known among the dissidents), boasted of good relations with Germany, by which he, like most Russians I talked with, meant the
Federal Republic; it seemed that "their" Germany, the GDR, was the object of
malign neglect except as an economic partner, and even there, West Germany
was far more important. The West German ambassador in Moscow, Hans-
Georg Wieck, a fellow historian, confirmed this. Somewhere in the Russian
mind the old dream of combining German technology with Russian resources
was still alive. Meanwhile, Helmut Schmidt and the doddering Brezhnev were
exchanging friendly visits.

Suddenly it was the last day at the institute and I still had not given the seminar I was supposed to offer. Two more appointments had been arranged, one
with Andrei Kokoshin, a mere twenty-four-year-old, remarkably open and cheerfully cynical. I was told that he came from an old military family and was known
for his free manner. After a remarkable career in Komsomol, the communist
youth organization, he was regarded as a rising star. (By 1991, as one of Arbatov's
boys, he rose to the post of first deputy defense minister of the Russian Federa-
tion, and later became Yeltsin's national security adviser. Arbatov wanted to

train a generation of creative men who some day could become "real peace-makers," servants of their nation, and he was one.) He told me of his sociological surveys to find out what young Russians wanted, to plumb the causes and consequences of Soviet backwardness, perhaps as a prelude to the formulation of needed reforms. Like others, he regretted Western ignorance of Russia; the only modern writer we knew, he thought, was Solzhenitsyn. I said that we saw most post-Leninist art as being variations on the theme of smiling persons on tractors. He laughed. I then asked why, despite my daily inquiries, my seminar was forever being postponed and had now obviously been abandoned. Mischievously he replied, "Do you really think we want to confuse our people?"

My last talk was with another deputy director of the institute: "You have been here for a week now. What do you think is our major problem?" he asked me. "Unemployment," I shot back. Russians insisted this was an exclusively Western phenomenon, indeed our chief problem, but the long queues waiting for bread did not match Marx's definition of productive labor, I said. His semi-response was, "You are right. We do have problems in distribution." Like most of the institute people I met, he was a serious, even friendly sparring partner.

In Moscow, I made at least two mistakes. I spent more time on the present than the past, more time with people than with the relics of Russian history that I should have sought out in its churches and museums. And I think I categorized people too easily, assuming that my daytime appointments were with apparatchiks, however intelligent, and the nighttime clandestine conversations were with heroic dissidents. The reality was subtler: some of the official intelligentsia, in their relatively privileged institutes, were themselves silent doubters or quiet reformists, aware of the regime's shortcomings; some of the dissidents had had earlier illusions and moments of complicity, and at present some of them had sympathy for the less attractive anti-Western, anti-Semitic strains in Solzhenitsyn's writings. Not every foe of the Soviet regime was a liberal, far from it—neither within Russia nor without.

After a week in Moscow, we were booked on a routine flight to Leningrad, but Gelya took us to the wrong Moscow airport: a fitting signal of the pervasive inefficiency. No matter: Leningrad was a kind of heaven, a visit with no formal duties, so to the authorities we were tourists, put up in the elegant Hotel Leningrad, across from the battleship *Aurora* from which the first shots of the revolution had been fired. We marveled at the haunting beauty of Pushkin's city, of Peter the Great's window to the West, of the River Neva and its elegant bridges, the Admiralty, the Winter Palace, the New Holland canals, the Hermitage with its stunning paintings. What a contrast to Moscow! On a postcard with a picture of the famous equestrian statue of Tsar Peter, I scribbled a note to a friend: "Two men had dreams here. One of them left works of great beauty."

I did have an agenda in Leningrad: Masha Etkind had given me notes with the names of her friends: in almost every instance, "Masha sent us" was sufficient. (She was after all, remarkably beautiful and vivacious.) People opened up, and told us that the literary world without the Etkinds was bleak, as was the scene generally. Russia was ruled not by a meritocracy but by mediocrity, and there was little hope: most young people chose the soft careerist path.

The name of Lev Kopelev had appeared on every list that people gave me, beginning with Marion Dönhoff's. A celebrated writer, a specialist in German literature, and a moral hero among the dissidents, Kopelev had been a fierce and decorated officer in the war, but he had protested the Red Army's atrocities on German soil, behavior he deemed a violation of socialist honor. The regime thought his protest unworthy of Soviet patriotism, and he was repeatedly tried, then sentenced to nine years of prison and labor camps. Released after Stalin's death, he remained a critic from within, still believing in the ideals of the Bolshevik Revolution and ever ready to speak out against their perversion, tireless in defense of the persecuted. He had been expelled from the party in 1968, and in 1977 from the Writers' Union; his telephone was cut off, and now he was persona non grata, living without permission in a writers' colony near Leningrad named Komarovo, on the Baltic Sea.

One of Masha's friends managed to get in touch with him and fixed a time for us to visit him, although our visas didn't allow us to go outside Leningrad. Still, an Intourist car drove us to the sea, and we walked to Kopelev's simple wooden cottage in the forest nearby. A big, powerful man of sixty-two, with a full silvery beard and exuding exuberant vitality, greeted us. We had lunch, and Lev and I talked and talked—in German; his wife, Raisa Orlova, equally formidable, also a writer and an Americanist, spoke English.

After lunch, Lev, in kind solemnity, took us to Anna Akhmatova's grave, at a nearby clearing in the woods. The ninetieth birthday of the brave poet had just passed, and her grave was covered with fresh flowers; slips of paper with poems had been placed under the pebbles. It was a shrine, a celebration of poetry and a protest against a regime that had branded her as "bourgeois decadent." What love Russian poets and writers bear their forebears and their language! They must have been doubly hurt by what befell them, for their wounds were wounds inflicted on Russia itself.

Then Kopelev walked us back to the railroad station through thick birch woods. He talked of his youth, how as an adolescent he had known of Stalin's terror, of family friends who disappeared, and of how, nonetheless, on June 22, 1941, when he heard the news of the German attack, he had rushed from the attic to his parents' room, ready to enlist, shouting, "For Stalin, for Mother Russia!" He talked of the current scene: yes, there was growing anti-Semitism, but it had begun already during the war, and now old anti-Semitic myths were being refurbished (in a popular history book, Rasputin was a Zionist conspirator, the Rothschilds masters of the world). He thought Carter's human rights program was helpful, since every appeal or letter, every call from abroad, made a difference. For Lev, Etkind's removal had left "a terrible void." But some émigrés harmed the dissident spirit, such as the "Ayatollah Vermontski." This was the first time I heard this sobriquet for Solzhenitsyn, whose *One Day in the Life of Ivan Denisovich* Lev and Raisa had helped to get published in Russia. (The character of Levin in *The First Circle* is based on Kopelev.) He said he couldn't counsel young people whether to emigrate or not. He could tell them only what not to do: not to betray a friend, not to bear false witness. Simplistic? No. The temptations of betrayal are the traps of totalitarian rule, indeed of any lawless society.

Lev entrusted me with a message to Marion Dönhoff and to Heinrich Böll: he and Raisa were now ready to accept their invitation for a longer stay in West Germany. He hoped to get the necessary papers, though it was a difficult and unpredictable procedure.

My own experiences made me ask him whether he really thought he would be allowed to return to the Soviet Union if he traveled abroad. "Let me tell you a Jewish joke," he replied. "In a small town in a bygone era, a Jew visits his rabbi and tells him about his tubercular wife and their five children; he is unemployed and can't feed the family, but he has just been offered a job on condition he shave off his *pajes*. What should he do? 'A good Jew doesn't touch the hair on his face,' the rabbi replies. Two weeks later, in still greater despair, he returns to the rabbi. As he waits for him in the hallway he sees in a mirror the rabbi trimming his beard! The poor man repeats his desperate tale, and the rabbi repeats the prescribed answer. Hesitantly the supplicant tells the rabbi what he had seen minutes before, and the rabbi responds, 'Yes, I did trim my beard, but at least I didn't ask anyone's permission!'" Kopelev wouldn't ask whether he'd be allowed to return; he assumed he would be. His parting words to me: "I feel closer to Marion Dönhoff than to my Stalinist cousin." And he handed me a copy of his book that had just appeared in German: *And Created an Idol for Me*; it had been published in Russian by an émigré publishing house in Michigan and quickly translated into German. This memoir of a Soviet life (published in English as *The Education of a True Believer*), is a stunning account of early joys and later disillusionment. His inscription (in German) was: "To Peggy and Fritz in memory of an acquaintance which I hope will turn to friendship." It did. He left us at the station, from where the train would take us to the Finland Station. (The locomotive that pulled Lenin's train from the west to this famous terminus was on permanent display there, a counterpart to Lenin's embalmed presence on Red Square.)

I delivered Lev's message to Marion, and eighteen months later Lev and Raisa flew to Frankfurt. They had return tickets and expected to use them, but Soviet authorities soon stripped them of their citizenship. They settled in Cologne, where he became a professor of literature and prepared a multivolume history of the literary encounters of Germans and Russians through the centuries.

Our last moments on Soviet soil made clear the ordered suspicion that governed daily experience there. In the chaos at the airport, a middle-age man ahead of us in the line was made to open every item in every one of his many bags; the guards found two letters and studied them; they searched a plastercast statue looking for hidden papers, and all the while I worried that they might find Lev's book in our bags. Contraband in "socialist" countries was the printed word. But in the end, we went through easily; Zhurkin's letter of invitation cleared us, and our bags went unchecked. I felt relief as we boarded the plane for Warsaw: the visit had given me unique experiences of various kinds of beauty, of decency in adversity, but I was happy to leave this prison.

My feelings about Poland were comparatively simple: sympathy and wonderment. For centuries the country had a martyred history, often brought on by its reckless policies, but the harshest period of all had begun almost exactly forty years before, when its ancient enemies and totalitarian neighbors had partitioned it. It was the fourth partition of Poland in less than a century and a half. During the war, German occupiers killed three million Poles and three million Polish Jews—almost all of Polish Jewry—while the Russians inflicted similar horrors, albeit on a smaller scale. Both occupiers had set out to bar any future revival of Poland by murdering its elites and suppressing its schools. No country suffered so much or offered greater heroic resistance—by force against the Germans, as in the Warsaw uprising of 1944, and by stealth and a hundred subterfuges against the communist regime imposed after the war. And its national territory had shifted: after the Soviets annexed a large swath of eastern Poland to the Ukraine, millions of Poles fled their homes for new ones in territory to the west that had once been German. This new Poland became the linchpin of the nascent Soviet empire, as signified by the very name "Warsaw Pact," NATO's counterpart.

Polish Communists always harped on the threat of German "revanchism," of West Germans plotting to regain what they had lost at the Potsdam Conference, the lands east of the Oder-Neisse line. They didn't seem to worry about their "friendly socialist neighbor" the GDR, but they did worry about the Federal Republic, where ex-Silesians and other expellees fanned nationalist passions. It was for this reason that Brandt's *Ostpolitik* and Helsinki were so important. And I knew that what Brandt had done publicly others were doing privately — reaching out to Poles, cultivating contacts with them. I had long thought that German-Polish reconciliation would be uniquely difficult, but the process had begun.

Perhaps more than other peoples, Poles had to live by an imaginary, mythologized history, their past having been a bitter alternation between early triumphs and crushing defeats. And how could they interpret the most recent past? I reckoned they now lived in enforced schizophrenia: official dogma decreed that the USSR had been Poland's liberator and remained her protective model, but Poles *knew* that the Katyn murder had been a Russian crime, not a German one, and they *knew* that during the Warsaw uprising of 1944, the Red Army had camped on the outskirts of the city, waiting for the Germans to raze the city and kill its people. How could young Poles learn this truth when schools taught a mendacious version? It was one of my first questions, and the answer was almost always the same: the Church was the source of enlightenment.

But 1979 was an astounding year in the history of Polish Catholicism. The "Polish Pope" had just visited his homeland, a year after his election; some thirteen million Poles had seen him and prayed with him on his triumphal weeklong tour; they heard him speak of courage, of the inalienable rights of each individual, of dignity and of God. His was not a direct attack on communist ideology or repression but an affirmation of Christian faith. Communist rulers vanished from the screen. A true sovereign had appeared. He captured the imagination of the pious and the fervently non-pious, and especially of young Poles.

Poland's economy, on the other hand, was in deep crisis. The party chief, Edward Gierek, had initiated a program dubbed the Great Leap Forward, a kind of force-fed industrial modernization financed by huge Western, mostly West German, loans. Industrial goods took precedence over consumer supplies, so the black market flourished, with the dollar as an almost indispensable second currency. Workers, the backbone of the whole program, suffered deprivations and shortages. It was a drab scene, and people expressed a kind of sullen discontent.

Yet I sensed at once that Poland was far freer and more open than the Soviet

Union. It was a police state, of course, with surveillance and an ever-changing mixture of repression and reward. But servants of the regime talked quite openly and critically of conditions, while opponents expressed their pride in what Poland had achieved after the still palpable horror of the war. Warsaw itself was the symbol of Poland's defiant insistence on being itself. The Germans had leveled it, and then new housing had appeared—cramped, Stalinist, and ugly. Yet amid the utter devastation, the Poles had at once rebuilt the royal castle in the heart of the city and the old medieval and Renaissance quarter around it, too— stone by stone, building by building, in the original harmonious style.

My routine in Poland was simple, since I could meet with officials and private people in relative openness. As soon as I arrived, I called Stefan Nowak, an outstanding sociologist who had taught at Columbia. No subterfuges needed. He came to the hotel, and we sat in the main restaurant there. He drew a grim picture for me: the economic situation was hopeless, the party was split, hence no decisions could be taken. The Pope, he thought, was a clever, charismatic leader, and the Church a deterrent to any antiliberal crackdown. This was an early intimation of the unlikely fact that the Church—the Polish Church!—was shielding liberals. He thought conditions were even worse in the neighboring satellites.

It was in the old city, with its cobbled, narrow streets, with its splendid square and rebuilt royal castle, that I had some of my most memorable visits, beginning with Stanisław Stomma, a philosopher-jurist who was one of Marion's oldest friends. Home and host were pleasingly austere and old-fashioned. Stomma praised Marion's efforts on behalf of reconciliation between Germans and Poles, which had been, he said, one of his own hopes, even in the darkest days of the war and the cold war. For Poles, I reckoned, reconciliation with Germany was a dictate of political reason, for it provided a cultural-economic lifeline to the West. The great nightmare for them was a potential German-Russian rapprochement, and they watched warily as those two powers interacted.* I thought that perhaps it began to dawn on them that the pre-1939 policy of hostility to both powerful neighbors had been a suicidal luxury. The best of them tried to overcome their traditional distrust of Germans, realizing that the other neighbor-occupant was the immediate threat.

Stomma, a devout Catholic, was a member of a small circle of Catholic in-

---

*I relished one of Poland's greatest exports, its grim political humor, as in the answer to the age-old question whom the Poles should fight first, Germany or Russia, if the two neighbors were to attack simultaneously. Answer: "First Germany, then Russia. First business, then pleasure." Or the little newspaper ad in the rental section: "To exchange: sovereignty, little used, for better geographical location."

tellectuals in Kraków called ZNAK, which was tolerated by the regime and allowed four representatives in Parliament; in 1976, he had been the only deputy to abstain from voting on amendments to the Polish constitution—in effect, opposing them—specifying, inter alia, that the United Workers Party (communist) was the leading political force in Polish society. Like other prominent lay Catholics, he had also opposed the "anti-Zionist" campaign of 1968, which had culminated in the purge of remaining Jews in Polish public life. The Pope's visit, he thought, had changed the moral atmosphere.

The American embassy wanted me to have an interview with Bishop Dabrowski, secretary to Cardinal Wyszynski, but he was in seclusion outside Warsaw, recovering from the strains of the papal visit. His deputy and namesake, Monsignor Jerzy Dabrowski, received me in the primate's palace—the cleanest, most elegant palace I had seen in a socialist country. He was a shrewd, worldly cleric, considered a rising star in the hierarchy.

As soon as Dabrowski realized I wanted to talk about current political matters, he took me on a walk in the garden, presumably away from unnatural bugs. We talked about the Church's past and present—including Pope Pius XII, whom he thought a mysterious figure, difficult for the Church to reckon with. He agreed that radical elements in the modern Church had arisen in part as a repudiation of Pius XII's empathetic "understanding" of fascism. (I learned later that Pius XII, informed during the war of the Germans' systematic murder of Poles, said nothing in defense of his flock there. His silence should have a bearing on the never-ending controversy about his other great silence.) Both church and party had their internal disputes, for neither was monolithic, and relations between them were infinitely complicated. Some party factions silently welcomed a strong church as a weapon to ward off stringent demands from Moscow. Meanwhile the Church focused on teaching the nonparty version of Poland's past. It also favored the growing underground opposition because of its antitotalitarian stance, since the Church feared that spreading totalitarianism—not restricted to communism—was a threat to the faith. John Paul II, Dabrowski thought, was more than a "Polish" Pope: he meant to be a "Slavic Pope," affirming the spiritual value of Slavs, who, like Jews, had always been looked down upon.

One name appeared on every contact list I received—one person I was most eager to see: Bronisław Geremek, a historian of early modern France, head of the medieval section of the Institute of History of the Polish Academy of Sciences, and a key figure in the opposition. He had left the party in 1968 to protest the crushing of the Prague Spring. (I didn't know then that his father had been a rabbi and that he and his mother had been saved by a Gentile family.) I met him in his office, on the main square of the old city, and found him instantly appealing, wise, sharp, generous, and witty, marked by an unpretentious gravitas; his pipe somehow added to the amiable atmosphere. Our common language was French, his being perfect—no surprise, since he had lived and worked in Paris for many years and knew the French scene exquisitely well. After a few minutes, he suggested we go to a café on the square. I assumed that this was for the usual reason, so that we could talk more freely; years later, he mentioned, bemusedly, that I obviously hadn't noticed we were being monitored in the café, too.

He told me that the historians in his section at the academy—he had fourteen colleagues—could work nonideologically, but modern history was under stricter censorship. We talked of current problems: the way he saw it, the Polish economic situation was so bad, and the party itself so divided, that the government didn't dare move, either on the economic front or with regard to the opposition; at any moment a spark could set off a great conflagration, so the government dithered. The people's economic misery as a political solvent reminded me of Mirabeau's remark, made just before 1789, that "the nation's deficit is the nation's treasure." Geremek agreed that this might fit Poland as well.

The government stoked anti-German feelings because that unified people, Geremek thought. A West German election was about to pit Helmut Schmidt against the controversial CDU-CSU candidate Franz Joseph Strauss—if the latter were to win, and *Ostpolitik* to fade, that would be a boon for Polish Communists. (Schmidt won handsomely.) The more we talked, the more complicated it all seemed. Suddenly I grabbed a piece of paper, trying to express graphically my impressions of all this complexity. I drew five adjacent circles in a line, and said to Geremek, "If this extreme left circle is the opposition and the extreme right one is the party Central Committee, then there seems to be a connection between the opposition and the inner sanctum of the party through these intermediary circles or bodies." Geremek smiled, took his pen, and drew a line that directly connected the two end circles. "This, too, is possible, and it happens some of the time." I saved that piece of paper.

Finally he mentioned something called "the flying university," a group that regularly organized clandestine meetings of teachers and students in different places—church basements and homes—to discuss specific, often historical subjects. I was intrigued, and Geremek asked if I would be willing to give a lecture there. I thought this would be a great privilege and even suggested a topic: the lure of fascism. "Fine," Geremek said. "I'm the program director." What a country—where the head of the academy's Institute of History could double as the program director of an underground university! I remembered that Marion had referred to Polish conditions as surrealistic. They were indeed. Time didn't allow for me to lecture, but I learned later that the flying university had been patterned on earlier clandestine groups during the German occupation of Poland in the war, when all education beyond elementary school had been prohibited—slaves didn't need more. I became a Geremek enthusiast: he was a historian-activist who combined courage, wisdom, and humanity. I hoped that we would stay in touch, but I couldn't then conceive that our lives would continue to intersect.

That same day, I met Adam Michnik at another small café. Since he was a particularly "dangerous" member of the opposition—being the editor of an underground paper appearing more or less monthly, with a circulation of five thousand, and each copy read by about ten people—there was a conspiratorial air to our encounter. He had been many times imprisoned, he told me; being a Jew made him an especially enticing target. In the recent past he had been arrested for "only" forty-eight hours, because the police could legally detain a person for that length of time without trial. He made little of this—after all, he said, there was no torture for political prisoners. What a contrast between his intellectual toughness and political courage on the one hand, and his physical fragility on the other, made more poignant by his stutter. Michnik had been trained as a historian and had spent eight months in Western Europe; like many Polish writers, he followed Western books and debates and was intellectually and physically at home in Paris. He was now teaching postwar Polish history at the flying university; about one hundred students regularly attended his classes.

Michnik echoed many of Geremek's themes; they were friends and companions. He, too, thought that worsening conditions would precipitate political upheavals. He talked of his contacts with like-minded Czechs and Hungarians. All oppositional efforts needed money—perhaps Radio Free Europe could give them funds? I should mention this to Brzezinski, he said. I thought private money would be preferable. It was at about this time that George Soros was initiating his discreet, vital help in Eastern Europe. How ironic that the Polish underground was receiving help from the Pope *and* from a Hungarian émigré-financier. Détente, Michnik thought, favored East European dissidents and their hopes for reform. But how far could reforms go without provoking another Soviet crackdown?

He mentioned that his much-older brother had served in Poland's Stalinist regime right after the war, as had many Jews. Michnik's enemies tried to paint him with that Stalinist brush, a grotesque effort, since he was five years old at the time. In prewar Poland, he said, educated Jews felt an affinity for German and Russian culture and condescension or contempt for Polish culture. In turn, Polish anti-Semitism had a long history, and even now, he said, a clandestine anti-Semitic paper invoked the *Protocols of the Elders of Zion* as proof of a long-standing Jewish conspiracy. As we parted, Michnik told his quiet girlfriend to slip me the most recent issue of his paper, which she delicately did.

These two meetings, in what was generally a bracing atmosphere in a country of hopeful instability, turned me into a passionate Polonophile, as if Geremek and Michnik were typical Poles, as if most Poles had similar qualities of civic courage! I knew of course that this was a romantic delusion—itself a Polish disease. But I also knew that during the 150 years when Poland was partitioned and erased from the map, its people had been taught profound lessons in defiance. I left these two men, so gentle in character, so fervent in their fight for freedom, with admiration, perhaps even with envy.

Our embassy then sent me to Poznań to lecture, where I had never been. I found Posen—to use the German name for the city that had been Prussian for nearly two centuries—intriguing, with its still largely German face (it had not been destroyed in the war) but its very Polish life. From there I rented a car, and Peggy and I drove along unfamiliar roads to Breslau/Wrocław—my first return to my native city, on a visit I have already described. From Wrocław we drove to the Sudeten Mountains in a pilgrimage to my parents' and my past. We stayed in the village where my Brieger grandparents had spent their summers, and we ate at an old German mountain hut, which now resembled a socialist Howard Johnson. Above loomed the highest peak of the range, the Schneekoppe, marking the border between Poland and Czechoslovakia. I learned later that this was where Václav Havel had secret rendezvous with Polish dissidents. Nearby was the church where my parents had been married in 1919. A young pastor in blue jeans invited us in, telling me that the archives were intact, though there was no time to consult them. There were still headstones marking the German dead in the church cemetery: in most other places they had been knocked down or defaced, an early ethnic cleansing even of the dead. I was intensely curious about these ancestral places, now in altogether new hands. The countryside was familiar but I felt a stranger, a detached observer of a deep historic change. In any case my emotional attachment was to the Czech side of the mountains, where I had once briefly tasted freedom.

Back in Warsaw again, I met with a man close to Gierek, Mieczysław Rakowski, editor of *Politiyka*, the principal political weekly, whose striking, modish head topped a trim, heavyset body. He exuded self-confidence, a person at home in several worlds, a socialist bon vivant. He was what Germans disparagingly call a *Windhund*, the dog that sniffs whence the wind comes and turns accordingly. He had an awesome reputation as everyone's favorite "reformist" Communist, a clever dove tilting at hard-line troglodytes. As a Communist, he couldn't stray too far and he kept close contacts with the Russian masters; as a Polish intellectual, he cherished his ties to the West, especially those to Marion Dönhoff. The regime, he said, had modernized Poland's industrial sector but couldn't shake the people's old agrarian mentality: hence the inherent contradictions. He thought the Church was far more important than the secular opposition, which, being tolerated, had become marginal and predictable. The German question came up: Arbatov had hinted at the possibility of a reunified, neutral Germany, and Rakowski shuddered at this: no one could guarantee that Germany would remain neutral.

Our stay in Warsaw coincided with the American embassy's Fourth of July party, where party officials mingled with representatives of the opposition. Here was one place where they could actually talk to each other. And these opposition figures were intriguing. As Timothy Garton Ash later wrote, "By 1979, then, there was already the embryo of that alliance of workers, intelligentsia and Church, unprecedented in Polish history, unique in the Soviet bloc, unseen in the West, which was to grow into Solidarity."

I was immensely moved by Poland, hence delighted when the embassy asked me to come back the following June, in 1980. An ambitious program had been planned, with lectures and seminars in Warsaw, Thorun, Kraków, and Gdansk. According to the embassy's report about these meetings, "members of Stern's various audiences (among whom, many highly placed intellectuals) . . . reacted strongly. There were some heated exchanges and some telling points made by Stern."

In Warsaw I had another talk with Rakowski. As we said good-bye, I asked a last question: "Rousseau once said of the Poles that one day they would astonish the world again. When will this happen?" "Not this month, not this year," Rakowski answered, "but in this decade." I thought that was extraordinary: this clever analyst and semi-apparatchik acknowledging the likelihood of radical change within ten years! (I have searched since then for the source of the Rousseau quotation, which I had summoned from memory; I haven't been able to find it, but surely I couldn't have made it up?) But it happened a mere fortnight later! Workers at the Lenin Shipyard in Gdansk went on strike on

August 14, protesting the dismissal of a veteran woman worker. Their list of demands began with the right to organize free trade unions and to strike. Solidarność was born, a workers' movement in a "workers' state."

And a new hero was born: Lech Wałęsa, the leader of the strikers. An earlier organization of dissident intellectuals, the Workers' Defense Committee, KOR, instantly supported the strike, and sixty-four prominent Polish intellectuals publicly demanded a solution without bloodshed: "the place of all the progressive intelligentsia . . . is on the side of the workers." Two of the signatories were Geremek and Tadeusz Mazowiecki, the latter a courageous philosopher-intellectual and editor of a liberal Catholic weekly; the two of them immediately left Warsaw for Gdansk and became Wałęsa's indispensable advisers. A union of workers and intellectuals—an old Social Democratic dream! My enthusiasm for the union's revolutionary call to freedom was fired by my luck in knowing some of its key figures.

Solidarność soon became a mass organization with ten million members, and negotiations between it and the party ensued. There were frequent rumors that the Soviet Union was preparing to crush this Polish experiment, as they had the reform movements in Hungary and Czechoslovakia. The situation remained highly volatile for eighteen months; then, on the morning of December 13, 1981, General Wojciech Jaruzelski, president of Poland, proclaimed a state of martial law: the army was everywhere deployed, all civic rights were abolished, all communications were censored, and thousands of people were arrested, including advisers of Solidarność such as Geremek and Michnik. All resistance was crushed. The Poles insisted—extravagantly—that their own government was committing acts worse than those of the Germans.

I was stunned, and vented my rage in a letter to *The New York Times*: "The Polish march to freedom, now being brutally crushed, constituted one of the most daring and promising deeds of our century. I saw the quiet heroism of Poles reaching out for freedom . . . An internationally renowned historian, Bronisław Geremek, has been thrown into jail, as have long-time opponents of tyranny such as Adam Michnik, and many, many others . . . The West must realize that it's our hopes and our friends who are being crushed by a meticulously planned takeover that recalls the horrors of earlier fascist seizures of power." I thought the Roman Catholic Church in America should support their brethren's demand for the release of prisoners, and the American government should do likewise, "as should the financial community of the West, which alone has some immediate leverage on the—probably quite frightened—Polish junta that now governs the country."

Polish television had "exposed" Geremek's Jewish origins and his links "with revisionist-Zionist centers abroad." *Libération*, a French Catholic paper, commented that anti-Semitism was the only ideological cover Jaruzelski could muster. For the next weeks I worked with my old academic comrades from 1975, again led by H. A. Winkler, to help with packages of food—and protests. Brzezinski, who was no longer in the government, and I tried to raise money for support of the families of the victims. On Christmas Eve Zbig called; he had heard that a fellow prisoner had seen Michnik emerge from interrogation bloodied and nearly unrecognizable. I was distraught. (The report turned out to be wrong, but the danger was always present.) I saw one of Geremek's sons, who was in Brooklyn at the time; the other was briefly imprisoned along with his father.

In early January, I met Marion in Sils Maria. I remember the exact spot in that beautiful place where we had our one and only violent argument: she defended Jaruzelski's action on the grounds that it had prevented Russian intervention, which would have injured détente. I passionately objected. Nothing could justify the suppression of Polish freedom fighters, I insisted. Our disagreement ended in great anger. Eventually we dropped the subject, and our friendship remained unimpaired, as did her general deep attachment to Poles, who eventually came to understand her nonsupport of Solidarność. I think her well-intentioned desertion of Solidarność made me all the more determined to help it.

The following spring, the rector of Warsaw University proposed a generous exchange program with Columbia, which I welcomed, provided Geremek would be appointed as first exchange professor. Conversation ceased, but I pressed West German officials on the same issue. In August 1981, Arseny Roginsky, a Russian historian and son of a gulag victim, was arrested for having used forged papers to gain access to archives that were, illegally, forbidden to him. His real "crime" was his editing of *Memory*, the underground journal that collected evidence of what actually had happened in Russo-Soviet history as against the official distortions and lies. Two colleagues joined me in writing a letter to the *Times* protesting the arrest. We were making every effort we could to remind the Russians of their Helsinki obligations, and did so in the spirit not of cold warriorism but of outrage at the violation of human rights. Since the Western record on human rights was reasonably correct in those times, we could make these gestures with confidence. And at about that time I was asked to join a Helsinki Watch committee, and thus could follow the issues even more closely. But I knew well that remonstrating in New York was as nothing compared to the anguished experiences of decent people in the grip of malignant power. Yet at the very least we signaled public and private solidarity, and that presumably was worth something.

My encounters with Kopelev or Geremek, with men and women of quiet courage and steely faith, gave deeper meaning to my own sense of what the twentieth century meant in human history. Not only was it a memorable privilege to witness these dissidents, but it kept me attuned to that part of the world where civic courage was ever more successfully challenging repressive communism—itself in turmoil. One didn't have to be a Germanist to thrill to this kind of civic resistance, but I think to be one made it more poignant and special. We had a unique need for that kind of affirmation.

I MADE ONE MORE TRIP where German themes were central. In June 1981, I spent two weeks lecturing in the People's Republic of China. This was an unexpected boon for me. The United States had for decades refused to acknowledge the communist victory of 1949 in China or the existence of the People's Republic; a vehement "China Lobby," with its own reactionary political correctness, insisted that China consisted of the brave people on Formosa (as Taiwan was then called), to which a defeated Chiang Kai-Shek had retreated. The presumption that we were threatened by a single communist monolith was so deeply ingrained that American policy makers had been slow to recognize the Sino-Soviet split when it occurred in the late 1950s, and hence were wary of exploiting it. The Chinese, meanwhile, became fervently anti-Soviet, using the code words *hegemonic power* to characterize an imperialist Soviet Union that in post-Stalin times was, they claimed, betraying Marxist-Leninist doctrine. Simultaneously, Chairman Mao Tse-tung launched the savage "Cultural Revolution," one of the great totalitarian nightmares of the late twentieth century.

U.S. relations with the PRC had become a function of American domestic politics: the powerful right-wing taunt "who lost China?" and the McCarthyite persecution of the outstanding American diplomats and scholars who had understood the Chinese upheavals, further obstructed efforts at realistic appraisal. American ignorance and hostility paralleled paranoid Chinese isolation. Then, in the early 1970s, President Nixon, even as he expanded the Vietnam War, authorized the first secret contacts with the PRC, presuming that the enemy of my enemy is my friend. The question now became who, if anyone, could "win" China back? Nixon, with his unassailable credentials as a right-wing an-

ticommunist, could try his hand at so radical a venture.* Successive administrations slowly cultivated mutual contacts, and the Carter administration established full diplomatic relations in 1979; regular scholarly exchanges were
gradually set up.

That was the year that my own distant involvement in China began. At a
State Department meeting on future United States–China relations, Ambassador Averill Harriman declared that our new China policy was the single most
successful aspect of the administration's foreign policy, and I was charged with
writing comments about its implications for other parts of the world, especially
the two Europes. I urged that the administration "educate the public in the in-
tricacies of a dangerous friendship" and stressed the need for humanitarian
help to Cambodian refugees. The United States should push the Europeans to
do more. In December, in Washington, at a Chinese-American conference
about the Soviet Union, I met Huan Xiang, ex-diplomat and now vice president of the Chinese Academy of Social Sciences, an organization known to be
both a huge think tank and an arm of the Chinese intelligence services. He
suggested that I visit China, and six months later I received a formal invitation
from Liu Si-mu of the Academy's Institute of World History to lecture on European history, "including imperialism, National Socialism, the First World
War and appraisal of Otto Fürst von Bismarck-Schönhausen." In China, I
would be the guest of the academy; travel expenses would be covered by Columbia's Research Institute on International Change, which had received Ford
money for conferences in Beijing.†

I came to Beijing as a total stranger, knowing very little but aware that the
Maoist regime was inflicting monumental cruelties on its own people while totally insulating the country from the outside world. Foreign visitors were kept
from catching even a glimpse of ordinary Chinese life. I had read Simon Leys's

---

*In 1971, President Georges Pompidou of France had to cancel a speech he was scheduled to give at
the Council on Foreign Relations, but he received a few people from the Council, myself included,
at his hotel. He was asked whether he had discussed China with Nixon, whom he had just seen.
His response: "I won't speak for the President, but as for me, *premièrement la Chine existe*."

†Seweryn Bialer, a Polish-born scholar of Soviet politics, was head of the Research Institute. He
once told me of his Polish childhood and his survival in Auschwitz, his running a Polish
Communist Party training school after the war, and his leaving Poland in 1955. For a time, he
treated me as a confidant, and I helped him to get long-term support for his projected book on
the Battle of Moscow, for which he seemed uniquely qualified. In quick succession Bialer had
completed three important books on Russia and was a sought-after adviser. There was a mysterious, slightly forbidding quality about him, a misanthropic streak.

remarkable *Chinese Shadows*, a searing account of the brutalities of Mao's China, published in France in 1974 and America in 1977, in which he assessed the efficacy of the regime's policy of preventing "all natural human contacts, however brief, between foreigners and the Chinese people." Clifford Geertz, just back from China, had confirmed Leys's view. Now I could make my own comparisons with the USSR. Chinese officials seemed more open than their Soviet counterparts, but private contacts were almost impossible. In thinking about the role of chance in my travels, I wondered if other people pushed me into a kind of Felix Krull existence, assuming I was somebody I wasn't. Perhaps the Chinese thought I had important connections in Washington. If so, it was their mistake and my gain. Or perhaps I mistook civility and courtesy for true openness.

But Peggy and I were greeted by charm and courtesy from the moment we landed in Beijing. The venerable institute director said to me on the tarmac, with a knowing smile, "I read your speech at the San Francisco Historical Congress in 1975 in response to the Soviet presentation"—an instant reference to the common enemy. And yet, as we were taken to a university hotel near the huge Friendship Hotel on the outskirts of Beijing and I caught a first glimpse of the place, I thought it the most Stalinist city I had ever seen: bizarrely ugly, monstrously monumental, with Soviet-type mausoleums, Soviet-type apartment blocks, Soviet-type squares, palaces, avenues, and the endless parade grounds of communism. On the streets were huge crowds of people in blue denim uniformity, on foot, on bicycle, or on crowded, antiquated buses—masses in synchronized uniform and seeming purpose. Yet soon enough I came to realize that while the trappings were Stalinist, the spirit seemed more open than it had been in official Moscow. A fellow historian, Fengli Luo, was assigned to accompany us on trips in China everywhere, including the Great Wall, and he made it possible for me to have impromptu conversations (as on train platforms) with ordinary people, conversations in which over and over again the pain of the Cultural Revolution and of being uprooted during it came up.

Officially, visibly, the Chinese past was shrouded in the simplest communist orthodoxy. At the National Museum of History, the entrance was decorated with huge portraits of the Four Heroes: Marx, Engels, Lenin, and Stalin—the last not demoted, as he had been in the USSR, but still honored as the great modernizer. These portraits had originally hung over Tiananmen Square but now were mildly downgraded to the mere vestibule of history. And in the museum, history began in 1949; the many millennia of rich Chinese life before then were reduced to doctrinaire slogans—though I thought that in some collective unconscious, this history was still informing the deep pride and hope that gave the Chinese the strength to be so courteous to foreigners without ever being obsequious.

The pace of my visit was relentless: the very night of my arrival I had to lecture to a large audience of academy dignitaries, and perhaps a smattering of students on the assigned topic of National Socialism. So I spoke of Hitler's reign of propaganda and terror, the drill by which an impotent people was made to feel commonality and community. The translator, speaking with great fervor, electrified the audience, and afterward I asked him what he had done to make the audience react as it had. His response was swift: "You were talking about us! You were talking about the Cultural Revolution!" It was proof again that German history is ever relevant to political catastrophe. And the Cultural Revolution was on everyone's mind. While the top cadres of the Party had been sent off to plow fields and quarry stones, the young Red Guards had ravaged China's repositories of culture: its libraries, temples, and laboratories. (They were storm troopers by another name, probably with more license for spontaneous brutality than their German counterparts, who had been meticulous murderers on command.) Everyone had a tale of suffering, of brutal violence, of being uprooted and sent to the countryside, regardless of age and health.

I arrived at what seemed like a historic turning point: people suggested that the worst of the terror was over; their diverse remarks and recollections were often cast in identical terms. Was this a totalitarian repudiation of totalitarian madness?

In Beijing, Shanghai, and Xian, I kept coming up against the orthodox Chinese version of Marxism-Leninism, a creed that they charged the Soviets had abandoned. They seemed genuinely startled by some of the "facts" I mentioned in my lectures and took for granted. Did the German High Command really transport Lenin back to Russia? Did Stalin's fight against "social fascists" (that is, Social Democrats) really help the Nazis to power? Some of my interpretations explicitly contradicted their dogma about historical materialism and the fundamental role of the class struggle. They were uneasy about my saying that Jean Jaurès and Rosa Luxemburg would have been the most serious opponents of Lenin's dictatorship had they not been murdered. In Xian University, in front of hundreds of students, I argued that Lenin's doctrine of "revolutionary defeatism"—his wish that the carnage of the world war would continue until it finally produced a social revolution—seemed inhuman. And I argued that Marxism-Leninism had proved incapable of understanding the true nature of fascism, disregarding its psychological roots and therefore adopting suicidal policies that eased its path to power. Afterward, the president thanked me for such an "interesting presentation" with which he couldn't "entirely agree," hence his hope that I would soon return "for discussion." This was courteous self-protection, and I sometimes worried that perhaps my lecture had bordered on being a taunt, but the atmosphere remained cordial. The Russians clearly would never have unleashed such a subversive speaker on a Soviet audience — a difference in culture and self-confidence?

I was struck by how often and how fervently the "Jewish question" came up. Why, I was asked, the fanatical hatred of the Jews in Europe? Why so little Jewish resistance, except in Warsaw? I discussed anti-Semitism and pointed to the Soviet paradox: many of the early Bolsheviks, including of course the great "villain" Trotsky but also Zinoviev, Radek, and Kamenev, had been Jews, yet Stalin hated Jews. This astonished the Chinese. Their response seemed to combine lingering dogmatism and liberated curiosity.

In Shanghai, where I had been asked to lecture on Bismarck, there was but one critical question: Was Bismarck progressive or reactionary? We didn't think in these simple categories, I said. We accepted the historic gray. Perhaps we weren't clever enough to know what was progressive and what was reactionary. "Only the Chinese know that it was progressive to be with the USSR in the 1950s and even more progressive to be with the United States in the 1970s." They enjoyed my impertinence. Their anti-Soviet sentiment was ferocious — surpassing that of American "cold warriors" by far. Officials I talked to said they feared the Soviets had a master plan for world conquest, a pincer movement striking simultaneously at the Persian Gulf and the Straits of Malacca. They took the risk of war seriously, but as a Foreign Ministry official explained, "The Russians may come into China, but they will not be able to leave."

Chang Zhi-lian, a member of the institute and a specialist in French history, risked taking an exceptional step: he invited me to his home. Our guide had trouble finding it, but eventually we arrived at a closed compound that had once been part of the American Yenching University. Chang had one large room in a 1920s house, a single all-purpose room crammed with books in several languages, decorated with pictures of Chou En-lai, the brilliant, nimble Mandarin statesman, and Lu Hsun, the respected if rarely read writer who was critical of all power, even revolutionary power. The room was cozy but austere — although Chang possessed a telephone, a major, and rare, status symbol much costlier than his rent.

He had an additional room across the hall that he had given to his daughter and son-in-law. Normally a daughter would move to her husband's family, but that family had three sons—the more desirable gender—and no extra space. During the week, his grandchild lived at a city kindergarten while his daughter and her husband worked in a factory; the child came home for weekends. Chang said he liked this arrangement (it was consonant with Chinese policies generally, the authorities favoring family separations). "I am pleased that my family no longer has intellectuals." This was the proper thing to say, but was it true?

We talked about history and historiography; Marxism-Leninism was prescribed, anchored in the constitution, and no deviation allowed from it, though students could read books of foreign, even non-Marxist, historians. Chang's father had been a bureaucrat, a Mandarin, a founder of the University of Shanghai, and the owner of forty thousand books, which the family gave to Beijing Library. During the Cultural Revolution, Chang and his wife had been sent to the countryside to till the fields, expiating the sins of privilege. He had assumed that he would never return to the university, but by now he had a special position again; in earlier times he had been to Paris and the United States; he had studied with Hajo Holborn at Yale. His greatest hope was to visit America again, where he had siblings.

The present liberal phase, he believed, would be followed by many zigzags, two steps forward, one step back. I left him, thinking he was a superb *débrouillard*, a survivor, a man of outward conformity, and very different from the dissidents I had admired in Moscow and Warsaw. A few years later, he showed up in New York.

My last few days in China happened to coincide with a carefully planned and executed reinterpretation of Chairman Mao, the Great Helmsman. Mao had previously been exculpated of the sins of the Cultural Revolution, but after intense intra-party debate, a new authoritative judgment was at last issued. The earlier dictum that the so-called Gang of Four had been solely responsible for the horrors, of which Mao had been unaware, was abandoned; the new judgment insisted that Mao's *thought* remained the inviolable guide to revolutionary practice, but that his *thinking* in the last years of his life had often been erroneous. I loved this distinction! Mao remained the source of all truth, the leader above all others.

Hours before our scheduled visit to his tomb, I received the only embarrassed call of my time in China: did I know that such a visit required formal attire? Properly dressed in bourgeois finery, we were pushed to the head of the line waiting for a glimpse of the embalmed proletarian. Like many a Chinese emperor, Mao rests in his (Leninist) tomb, part god, part man.

————

I HAD GONE ON ALL THESE JOURNEYS as a German and European historian, and I returned as such, enriched by catching a glimpse of other cultures and political systems. I had seen German themes set in different forms, and with their resonance in mind I returned to the German past and present. (German themes can be subversive: in 2005, my book *Einstein's German World* was translated into Chinese, with a new introduction emphasizing the relevance for the Chinese of Einstein's hatred of economic inequalities, of militarism, of every type of coercion, and of his full and heartfelt support of human rights.) And what remained in my mind and heart was the human inspiration and civic decency I encountered everywhere. To see that in a corrupt and cruel world, there were (and still are) people who would risk all to preserve or resurrect a measure of freedom and decency was both exhilarating and humbling.

And in every country, I encountered the divisive place of the past in the present. In some countries, the intense controversies over the interpretation of the past were open; in others the fight against prescribed mendacity had to be waged covertly. Under tyrannical rule, a censored past is omnipresent—and worthless. Hence the historian, if given a chance, must intrude with banished truths or questions. I came to these countries aware of one of the great catastrophes in recent world history. The basic text for any nation in political crisis was still written in German. The German past had resonance everywhere, and not least in the Federal Republic itself, as it, too, entered a new political era.

CHAPTER 9

★

THE GERMAN QUESTION
REVISITED

THE FEDERAL REPUBLIC CAME OF AGE in the 1980s, a decade of rapid change, when the unexpected triumphed. A visible, early signal of its new importance came in January 1979, when a summit meeting in Guadeloupe of what had once been the Big Three of the West, the United States, Britain, and France, now included the Federal Republic, represented by Helmut Schmidt, himself no stranger to assertiveness. With its exuberant economy, it was often called Europe's "paymaster" because of its disproportionately large contributions to the European Community. But how would this modest role endure, considering that it was now the most powerful country in Europe west of Russia — and one with the greatest grievance: a nation divided?

Naturally, Germany's new prominence stirred old fears. In 1979, I heard Europeans speak again of "the unquiet Germans," a phrase that had been used in the interwar years to express anxious dubiety about German intentions. "The German question" — whither Germany? — was reemerging in world politics and in the minds of the Germans themselves. The past and present aspects of this question were dialectically linked in the most obvious way, since when Germans thought of the future, neighbors remembered the past. How Germans themselves would come to understand their past would be a measure of their national health.

At home, the Federal Republic could be regarded as a success story, in many ways a triumph of luck and prudence. For all its problems and shortcomings, its society was stabler and more prosperous (and less class-riven) than under any previous regime. Its democratic institutions were strong, and its political culture was more attuned to the West than ever before. And it had strung together a complicated network of foreign relations: in defense matters it was dependent on the United States, a relationship bolstered by trade and by myriad ties of private friendships; in Western Europe, it was most closely aligned with France, and to the degree that Europe operated constructively, it did so under a Franco-German condominium as had been exemplified by the introduction of the European Monetary System in 1979; the SPD's *Ostpolitik* meant closer relations with the USSR and the Soviet bloc, many more and bigger economic ties with the East, and more flexible German-German relations.

In the prevailing atmosphere of détente during the 1970s, West Germany's multiple and potentially conflicting interests had been manageable—one reason that West Germans, even more than other West Europeans, were always keener on détente than were many Americans. But the Soviet invasion of Afghanistan in December 1979 put the very survival of détente at risk. The Carter administration—already in shock over the seizure of the American embassy in Tehran only days after the tumultuous events leading to the overthrow of the Shah of Iran's regime—responded swiftly, imposing economic sanctions on the USSR and openly contemplating additional ones. But the European powers were reluctant to abandon the comforts of relaxation in their Soviet affairs; while they resented their security dependency on the United States, they shrank from the costly effort of creating their own credible defense. Endless debates on burden sharing didn't improve matters. Europe, I thought, had grown too strong for its own weakness.

Even before Afghanistan, urgent questions of defense were on the agenda. In 1977, Helmut Schmidt had warned that the Soviet deployment of SS-20 missiles, with their multiple nuclear warheads that could reach any target in the FRG and beyond, needed a NATO response, by which he meant, presumably, new U.S. nuclear weapons based in Europe. But this prospect was anathema to the growing European peace movement. Nonetheless, in December 1979, NATO adopted what it called a "dual-track decision," which provided for just such an American deployment unless the Soviet Union would withdraw their advanced weapons.

I had been alerted to some of these developments, and the subterranean shifts that accompanied them, during my travels and during my year in Paris. I poured my thoughts and apprehensions into an article, "Germany in a Semi-Gaullist Europe" (it appeared in *Foreign Affairs* in the spring of 1980), in which I made my case for why the German question had returned to world politics, and why transatlantic relations were so troubled. Soviet aggression and expansionism—and not only in Afghanistan—were producing new tensions.

In April 1981, Marion Dönhoff set forth a theme she was to repeat often in the years to come: for Washington "détente is dead," and she feared that West European criticism of America's saber rattling could bring about American complaints that the Europeans were veering toward neutralism, which in turn would fuel anti-Americanism in Europe. The danger of such an escalation of distrust was real, but Europeans also feared American weakness as much as American strength, and they saw weakness in what Schmidt in his milder moments called "America's abdication of fiscal leadership or responsibility." Europeans complained about inconsistencies in American policy and questioned the nation's dependability. I found some of this carping dangerous, but it was true that America must, as I wrote, recover its credibility, "not measured by military means alone, but by the implementation of an energy program that goes beyond rhetoric and minutiae, by the adoption of an economic strategy that will effect radical reforms. Nothing would sustain and benefit the alliance more than a domestically strong America; nothing would endanger it more than an enfeebled America. Credibility, too, begins at home."

Meanwhile the German question was roiling Germans themselves. Where were they going, and did they realize that whatever policies they adopted or path they followed, the past was an unmasterable burden for them? How Germans dealt with that burden was a kind of seismograph of the German spirit, an indicator for the future.

The past, summoned by various commemorations, such as the fiftieth anniversary, in 1983, of Hitler's accession to power and the fortieth anniversary, in 1985, of his end and of Germany's defeat, divided the present. Fiercely opposing memories had harmed German politics before; the way Germans chose to remember the traumas they had caused and suffered vitally affected their very health. Nor could they enjoy the luxury of imagining that their controversies were insulated from public opinion internationally: when they fiercely disputed their past—in its foreshortened version, the Third Reich—it became an international datum. I was drawn into the many public discussions about the German past, and my experiences in countries still in the grip of terror and tyranny—from the Soviet Union to Argentina to China—certainly made me realize again that "the past isn't dead," in Faulkner's celebrated phrase. "It's not even past."

AT HOME IN THE UNITED STATES my own life took an unexpected turn. In April 1980, Columbia's new president, Michael Sovern, a clever, decisive master of law and politics whom I had first met during our troubles in 1968, asked me to become the university's provost, with special responsibility for the arts and sciences. Nothing had prepared me for this assignment but passion for the place and a sense that the faculty should participate in its governance. To take on this new responsibility was a full-time commitment—though I managed to keep up and even enlarge my connections to Europe at the same time.

I thought I knew Columbia well, but I quickly discovered my ignorance of its complexities. (When I began in July, Sovern was on holiday, so I was responsible when at the very beginning and by pure chance, I had to deal with a crisis in our medical school; ties made during that emergency grew into close friendships—a pleasing chance for someone like me who had grown up in awe of the white coat.) I soon grasped what seemed to me an unacknowledged truth: people referred to Columbia and universities like it as "private" institutions, and, of course, they were private as compared with the large public state institutions, but given the growing ties of such private institutions to the federal and state governments and to foundations, I came to realize the ambiguity of the old conceit.

To learn the exigencies of budgeting—on the run—was hardest, but some mixture of principle, intuition, and uneasy bluff, plus the advice of a few reliable colleagues, helped to see me through. I had to learn to contend with bureaucracy and its petty frustrations; at moments of greatest exasperation I reminded myself that this was but an assumed identity. I was amazed at what I should have anticipated: the turf battles among administrators, great conflicts about space and resources among Columbia's many schools. (If they had nuclear weapons, I thought, they would use them.) And I learned more about scholars' foibles—often a euphemism for disguised self-interest—and lost some happy fantasies about academic life in the process. I fancied myself a servant of the faculty, but I remarked to David Riesman that it was difficult being a servant to people who no longer knew how to treat servants. Still, the heart of any university is its faculty, and my favorite activity was to help attract new and retain old talent at Columbia.

My most pleasing assignment was to help Columbia College become coeducational, an overdue and most desirable change. At the time, women enrolled in Barnard College, a separate entity within Columbia and with its own faculty—a school determined to keep the privilege of women's education to itself. There were two ways for Columbia to proceed: by obtaining Barnard's agreement or by acting unilaterally to attract its own women students. We negotiated for more than a year, and I thought of a quid pro quo by which Barnard would be given greater autonomy in making its faculty appointments. By 1982, and with Barnard's agreement, Columbia College finally admitted women—and both institutions have lived happily ever after.

By now, I have forgotten the humdrum routine and the disappointments of my provostial work, but I remember my pride in representing the university, my severely limited authority notwithstanding. During those years Marion Dönhoff once came to see me in my office in Low Library (in which I had placed some of my Poelzig furniture) and, as we left and crossed "my" campus, she observed, "You have the position and attitude of a Prussian *Landrat*," meaning the local authority, in the old Prussia, who had great power over the cherished lands placed under his care.

My new involvement in American academic life as a provost may have made me a more desirable figure for various West German groups to turn to when they wanted to hear an American voice. One quite early encounter had unforeseen consequences. In June 1981, I stumbled on a tiny notice in *The New York Times* that Hoechst, Germany's biggest chemical company, had invested seventy million dollars in support of a new molecular biology research program to be conducted at Massachusetts General Hospital. I was astounded: since when did German companies sponsor large-scale research abroad? I wasn't altogether surprised when a few weeks later, the central West German organization of scientific foundations invited me to a suddenly organized meeting of scientists and administrators from government, universities, and industry to discuss the best means for promoting excellence in the sciences. Since the subject was close both to my heart and to my provostial work, I accepted eagerly. It was soon apparent that the conclave was meant to ponder why Germans were no longer at the top of the scientific heap.

What an array of German talents was at that symposium! We met in September 1981; the place had symbolic meaning: the Villa Hügel, a richly appointed extravaganza in Essen that had once been the center of the Krupp empire in the Ruhr. We tried to define true scientific achievements and agreed that the best of these consist of convincing solutions to what are perceived as burning issues and/or that offer new perspectives for further research. West Germans acknowledged that their country lagged behind the United States, Japan, and Britain: we discussed likely causes for this and possible reforms. Certainly increased bureaucratization attendant upon the vast expansion of universities created obstacles. There were probably enough research funds available; the question was how and by whom they should be allocated. A Swiss sociologist-administrator, Walter Ruegg (a fellow critic of student radicalism), argued that good science could be promoted not only by giving grants but also by rejecting mediocre projects, that reducing funds might actually have beneficial consequences. I agreed: I had often thought a prize should be created for a project voluntarily abandoned.

Konrad Bloch, the Nobel laureate and Harvard professor of chemistry, was the only other American in attendance. He, too, was a refugee. A most engaging and generous person, he was born in 1912 in Neisse, a small Silesian town where some of my ancestors had come from and which had produced other notable scientists, including Rudolf Nissen. Bloch was one of many natural scientists I have met who lived fully in the "two cultures" and were masters and lovers of art and literature. How limited many of us humanists are by comparison! Observing that "any society of comparable cultural and economic status produces roughly the same proportion of individuals of exceptional, native talent and intelligence," he argued that institutional frameworks and climates are most likely responsible for differences in accomplishments. The most important prerequisite was intellectual freedom, free choice of research, but the closest and fairest relation between teacher and student was also vital. Teaching "is not only information transfer . . . it ignites the sparks that attract receptive minds into creative endeavors." He was implicitly characterizing the best of the American tradition.

I could understand the Germans' nostalgia for their past greatness and regret for the relative absence of cherished peak achievements in the present. At one point, Bloch and I looked at each other in silent wonderment: Couldn't the Germans see the one quite obvious cause for their nation's decline? Do you expel some of your best talent with impunity and without consequences? Why this silence among these utterly enlightened participants? It was an astounding reluctance. Perhaps the subject was too embarrassing to mention, the point too obvious to make? Bloch and I exchanged glances, and though we later spoke of it to each other, we didn't raise it then.

My participation at that meeting led to other invitations. And I became connected with the many groups, private complements to official contacts, organized by people who understood the centrality and precariousness of German-American relations. For Americans, the German connection was different from the old, oft-disappointed love affair with France, different from the "special relations" with Britain, underwritten as they were by reciprocal interests and age-old condescensions. The Federal Republic *was* different. The transition from enemy to dependent ally, even friend, had been so swift, and while the realities of elemental common interests were obvious and oft invoked, the divided, divisive memories of the unique and incomprehensible evil of the Nazi past were ever present.

As an Atlanticist, I believed as a first principle that the European-American connection was vital to our collective security and precious to American civic health. I found Soviet repression and aggression an abhorrent threat, but I also knew that the cold war could not be won by military means alone, and I favored the various forms of engagement with Russia, the Helsinki process, and all the arms-control efforts. Bolstering West German liberal democracy, which in turn required as honest an assessment of the German past as possible, was another commitment. Private wish and public weal happened to coincide.

At the time, I was astonished at the opportunities I was given to deepen my transatlantic connections, but in retrospect I can see how I easily became one of the "usual suspects." In 1981, I became a trustee of the German Marshall Fund, an American foundation born of Willy Brandt's generous decision to commemorate the Marshall Plan and designed to promote transatlantic projects. And what a splendid group the trustees were, including Walter Heller, Carl Kaysen, and David Ginsburg! Two years later Shepard Stone put me on the board of the Aspen Institute in Berlin, a meeting place he had created especially for East-West contacts, made lively by his uniquely provocative, stimulating bonhomie. Marion Dönhoff, of course, was on the board, as were Alan Bullock, Paul Doty, Edzard Reuter, and other well-placed internationalists. Shep was a celebrated figure in Berlin; I once toasted him as "the nongoverning mayor of Berlin." The patron saint of German-American relations was John J. McCloy, who had been the first American high commissioner in Bonn. He was a founding father of the American Council on Germany, in New York, another institution at which I gave occasional talks.

In all these groups—the normal quotient of boredom notwithstanding— not only did I learn a lot about German conditions but I also had the chance to formulate my views more or less spontaneously, often without the terrifying prospect of seeing them in print. I later came across a remark of Leibniz's that relieved me: "By myself I can't think of much, but when someone else says something I can think of something better."

The German American groups were but one part of a rapidly growing international network, composed of well-known internationalists and new, younger people, too. Perhaps there was an excess of high talk and high living— I often mused that some of the world's great hotels lived off world crises, real or assumed. But I note now that in the new century the decline of these public-minded efforts has perhaps added to international estrangement, while the corporate world has taken up the slack in the luxurious conference métier, serving narrower interests at higher costs.

These institutional connections went along with my ever-expanding personal ties to Germany. The Countess was still my closest German friend and occasional facilitator. Some of her friends became mine as well. Ralf Dahrendorf, in the meantime, had moved to England, though our regular talk about German affairs continued. But I came to know new colleagues, journalists, and public figures, men and women who in one way or another worked at the intersection of German history and active politics. There were so many meetings! I now realize how great was my private wish that the two parts of my life—European and American—should exist in harmony.

Wishing for harmony, I became a truffle hound for trouble, sensing that beneath the relatively amiable surface lurked discordant moods. Also, the hard issues became ever more urgent, above all NATO's dual-track decision of 1979 to allow for the installation of American medium-range nuclear missiles capable of reaching targets in the Soviet Union. The peace movement, which in West Germany included many SPD members, grew stronger and more vehement as the nation weighed the prospect of yet more nuclear weapons on German soil.

Ronald Reagan's election in 1980 didn't improve matters. The European press was full of wonder that a second-rate Hollywood actor could become leader of the free world, this seemingly naïve and ignorant man who saw the Soviet Union not simply as a military threat and ruthless rival but also as the embodiment of all that was evil in the modern world. For Reagan, the Soviet Union showed what happened when one subjected individuals to the state and abandoned all morality. Reagan's initial impulse was simply to assert America's superior military power, and he boosted defense spending as the essential part of a tougher policy against what he called "the evil empire." Europeans who believed in détente were anxious, and peace activists seized on Reagan's decision to reactivate plans, abandoned by President Carter, to develop a neutron bomb as evidence of the United States' new militarism; critics quickly dubbed this bomb, which was supposed to intensify radiation in a narrow range while reducing the blast effect—effective especially against tank formations—"the capitalist weapon," lethal to people but not to property.

In March 1981 another Biennial American-German Conference, this time held in Princeton (the strong German delegation included Marion Dönhoff and two leading Social Democrats, Klaus von Dohnanyi and Horst Ehmke, along with others representing different views), offered an early opportunity to assess the new administration. I warned against focusing overmuch on military security, on what was above ground rather than what was deeply rooted, that is, the peoples' desire for security; Reaganism had a strong cultural aspect, I thought— I was already troubled by what was to evolve into America's "culture wars."

A few months after the conference I wrote, "The more we [Americans] emphasize military force, the more the voices of dissent rise . . . To Europeans the increase in [American] overkill capacity is an irrational act, an absurdity; they know that we have enough to kill and be killed a hundred times over again. *Their* historic experience in this century has been the experience of brute and futile power, blindly spent and blindly worshiped." But I noted that that same European experience might foster quiescence in Europe. I wasn't blind to some early symptoms of such trends in Europe—I had already talked about Europe being "on vacation," taking leave of its historic responsibilities and in danger of losing its sense of destiny, settling down to its political decline and its neglect of its own security needs.

Meanwhile, and not unrelated, the West European nations had built up a magnificent welfare system, with health care, decent pay, and long paid vacations for their workers—benefits that far exceeded what most American workers enjoyed or Europeans had anticipated. In the Federal Republic, unionized workers could often count on six weeks of vacation, which even American managers couldn't dream of. Was there a subtle link between the vacations from history and the vacations from work? In what the French called the postwar *trente glorieuse*, West Europeans had invested in social peace and reconciliation, and this historically understandable tendency sometimes struck Americans as fomenting a temper of appeasement. Within a few decades, it became evident that such largesse cut into the Federal Republic's economic competitiveness, while deeper inclinations toward political abdication encouraged ill-tempered American polemic about "Old Europe's" pusillanimous self-indulgence. People on both sides of the Atlantic taunted Europeans with charges of insufficient manliness. But was I wrong to write about a Wilhelmian quality in America—something like the strident militancy and political ineptitude of the Kaiser's pre-1914 imperial Germany?

In West Germany, the peace movement continually gained strength through the 1980s, which the Soviet bloc thought would help to undermine the Western alliance. Storms of protests erupted, with peace marches on the streets, disputes in the media, prayers in the Protestant churches—so appallingly militant during the two world wars but now sturdy supporters of the antinuclear campaign. In March 1982, the Evangelical Academy of Tutzing—a renowned international meeting place on Starnberger Lake, near Munich—convened a symposium on "securing peace through disarmament." My much-admired acquaintance Hildegard Hamm-Brücher, at this point state secretary at the Foreign Office, opened the meeting; the large international cast included William Luers, U.S. ambassador in Prague; Christoph Bertram, brilliant director of the Institute for Strategic Studies in London; and a Soviet delegation that consisted of, among others, Leonid Samyatin and Vitali Zhurkin, my old acquaintance from the Arbatov Institute.

In his opening address the Nobel laureate physicist-philosopher Carl-Friedrich von Weizsäcker made a magisterial appeal to three audiences—the Church, Russia, and America. Disarmament alone would not bring about peace, he said, threatened as it always was by the fears of rival nations; only the awesome nuclear weapon had so far maintained an unstable peace. He gave qualified support to the peace movement, but warned that if it ended up weakening NATO, it would heighten the risk of war. The first requirement, in any case, was the removal from Europe of all intermediate-range nuclear weapons. "Like many Europeans," he said, "I am deeply disturbed by the foreign policy of today's American administration." His even-handed criticism of all principals made it clear that continued disarmament efforts were the only immediate pragmatic option.

I had been asked to respond to the presentation of Eugene Ivanov, deputy chairman of the Soviet Society for Friendship with Foreign Countries, who talked of the role of public opinion and argued that the peace movement, aroused by the renewed American effort to launch and win an arms race, would force governments to adopt saner policies. In the Soviet Union, he claimed, peace activists enjoyed the backing of the state, recalling that Lenin's first act was to issue "the peace decree."

The sanctimonious hypocrisy of Soviet protestations of peace along with Soviet aggression infuriated me, as did the repeated insinuations that American economic interests were the main threat to international concord. To rebut all these avowals of Soviet innocence from birth, from Lenin's first peace decree to the unwavering commitment to "peaceful coexistence," I cited Lenin's many assertions about the inevitable war against the bourgeois enemy, which justified all means, including deceit, subversion, and murder. I referred to his *Left-Wing Communism: An Infantile Disorder*, a radical text that had never been repudiated. And as to the military buildup in the United States, with the consequent alarming neglect of domestic needs and programs, it had, after all, been either provoked or made credible by Soviet aggression in Afghanistan and Poland, in Central America and Africa. "The invasion of Afghanistan was not an American invention." Also, Americans too had a peace and antinuclear movement, perfectly consonant with their democratic traditions of national self-criticism. I cited a recent speech of George Kennan in which he called "for an immediate across-the-boards reduction by fifty percent of the nuclear arsenals . . . of the two superpowers," and warned against "the almost exclusive militarization of thinking and discourse about Soviet-American relations that now commands the behavior and utterances of statesmen and propagandists on both sides." Kennan had welcomed the worldwide peace movements, knowing that they would also "attract the freaks and the extremists . . . [It] will wander off in many mistaken directions."

What worried me was the worldwide temptation to see the two superpowers in some kind of moral equivalency—a false and injurious notion. I knew all about the West's flaws and its often self-righteous bellicosity, but the distinction between an errant, misled free society and a world of totalitarian repression was absolute and should be made unambiguously clear to our "neutral" audience. In the West there were countervailing forces, and leading figures, such as the great scientist Hans Bethe, warned against the grotesque buildup of nuclear arsenals on both sides. I taunted the Soviet representatives with an implicit comparison: the heroism of five dissidents in Moscow in 1968 protesting the occupation of Prague demonstrated the same heroic resolve as five million Americans had shown in their denunciation of Vietnam as an immoral war.[*] After the meeting I wrote Warren Zimmermann, then counselor at the U.S. embassy in Moscow, "It was interesting to see the Soviets and the Americans woo the German soul. I am pleased to report that my talk was the only one that the Soviets did not applaud."

But Tutzing had congenial moments, none more important for me than a long conversation with Weizsäcker, for he was struck by a casual remark I had made about the possible affinities between the old German tradition of cultural

---

[*]Within weeks of our meeting, the American peace movement showed its strength; in June 1982 a half million people gathered in Central Park in New York protesting the arms race. And the protests continued. Establishment figures and well-known moderates voiced their dismay. In January 1984, Averell Harriman charged that "three years of nuclear irresponsibility" had increased the threat of nuclear war. At the same time, John Oakes, one-time senior editor of *The New York Times*, wrote: "President Reagan's consistent elevation of militarism over diplomacy creates a clear and present danger to the internal and external security of the United States. Presidents have been impeached for less."

pessimism and the present-day peace movement. Later on I sent him my book on cultural despair and soon received a remarkable letter from him, three single-spaced pages at once philosophical and personal. He resumed our earlier conversation, rebutting any notion of a new, left-wing nationalism in Germany. Nationalism—alien to him in any case—had always been much weaker in Germany than in other countries, he thought, and the Nazi period had been one of overcompensation; after 1945, German nationalism needn't be feared by anyone. But his skepticism about the peace movement was confirmed by my idea that it echoed some of the themes of German cultural pessimism.

He told me he had found the discussion of the American peace movement important precisely because it illuminated the difference between American and European attitudes, which latter expressed the wish to be excluded "from the mortal conflict between the two candidates for world hegemony as an instinct for survival." Since Europe would be "the natural battleground in the first phase of the Third World War," obviously "an active peace policy" was needed, but it required the stability of existing alliances; German or European neutralism "was a totally unrealistic dream construction."

Weizsäcker also wrote to me about my book, and told me that in his youth he had read works by my three authors—Lagarde, Langbehn, and Moeller van den Bruck—but after a while "discovered he could be a contented person even if he didn't grasp what these men wanted." Yet my book had shown him that their ideology had greatly influenced German politics. The next passage jolted me. Though he never had the slightest interest in Nazi ideology, Weizsäcker wrote, "Nonetheless, I was very much tempted after 1933 to join the movement in some way or another. That had nothing to do with the ideas these people had but solely with an elemental reaction to what . . . has been called a pseudo-outpouring of the Holy Spirit in 1933. If I try to analyze retrospectively what it was that affected me at that time and what did not, I . . . conclude that . . . the views of the Nazis were idiotic but the rise of the Nazis was a symptom of a process they did not understand themselves. It is this process I am trying to trace." As have I—the Nazis didn't understand the world-historical process of which they were the meanest symptoms.

He questioned what he thought was my argument—that German rejection of Western cultural development bespoke the way to national folly—and noted that as a four-year-old in the First World War he had experienced the ambivalence of this development. Yes, of course, the Germans were wrong to want to exclude themselves from Western development, "but as critics of it they might have intuited something valid."

I treasure that letter. In subsequent walks and conversations I could tell him that I myself had often insisted that German questions about modernity had been vitally urgent and the answers at times fatal.

The letter reached me at a time when for some quite specific reasons I was once again pondering the possible relations between Protestantism in unacknowledged decline and the rise of National Socialism. That very year, and in a different context, I had lectured on "the silent secularization" of German Protestantism, a term I coined analogous to the medical diagnosis of an unnoticed heart attack as being a "silent heart attack." The Enlightenment's attack on the Church or on faith, which the *philosophes* often dismissed as superstitious, hadn't convulsed the German scene, but in the nineteenth century there had been a falling away from religion and a simultaneous endowment of the secular—the state or science or culture—with awe and sanctity. I had suggested that National Socialism, only dimly conscious of what it was doing, appealed to uneasily secular people with its pseudoreligious rhetoric and ritual. And here was a much-respected German philosopher acknowledging that he had been moved by this very element in National Socialism! For this candid engagement in 1982 and subsequent conversations I am still grateful.

THE DEPLOYMENT OF PERSHING MISSILES on West German soil continued to be a most divisive issue in German politics. Schmidt, who privately shared the peace movement's abhorrence of nuclear weapons, didn't waver in support of the NATO deployment, but he faced great opposition in the country and within his own party; he warned the SPD that if judgment of what was possible were to yield to passion for what was desirable, political disaster would follow. But Schmidt's coalition partners also became restive, and as economic conditions worsened, the right wing of the Free Democrats, with its faith in the untrammeled market, was demanding cutbacks in social welfare that Social Democrats considered unacceptable. Prominent Free Democrats had long flirted with the idea of changing partners and allying with the CDU, even if their electoral mandate connoted an unambiguous commitment to the social-liberal coalition. Count Otto von Lambsdorff, finance minister in Schmidt's government, remarked in July 1982 at a dinner in New York that he wanted an end to the coalition soon. (I have a cordial acquaintanceship with Lambsdorff, a German Baltic aristocrat and ardent Atlanticist. His wife once smilingly told me that her maiden name was Quistorp; she knew I recognized the name, for a hundred years earlier Bleichröder had had to rescue her ancestors from complicated insolvency!)

In October 1982, Schmidt arranged to lose a parliamentary vote of confidence, knowing that the onus for the coalition breakup would fall on the Free Democrats. FDP and CDU deputies then elected Helmut Kohl as his successor. Hildegard Hamm-Brücher, a true liberal, was one of the few FDP leaders to protest the switch, which bore, she said, "the odium of injured constitutional decency . . . and offends morality." The social-liberal era had lasted for thirteen years—almost as long as the entire Weimar Republic. Its very existence had fortified democracy at home and strengthened the Federal Republic's standing abroad.

With Schmidt's departure, I thought, as I wrote at the time, "the West lost its most experienced, its most effective, and, in the eyes of many, its most attractive statesman . . . He may well have been the last of the remarkable postwar chancellors . . . The end of his government signals the beginning of a period of instability." I think I was right about Schmidt and wrong about the prospective instability. Helmut Kohl's new coalition was to cling to power for sixteen long years.

Helmut Kohl had joined the CDU as a young man and risen in its ranks; he was a consummate politician. I first depicted him as a man whose chief virtue was the absence of known vice, but by the time he left office, both his virtue and his vice had become manifest. I had met him in New York; he was friendly to a fellow historian but struck me as astoundingly provincial. He was strongly pro-American where the Republicans—newly in power under President Reagan—favored CDU conservatives like him. Kohl was joining the new rulers in Britain and the United States—Margaret Thatcher having become Britain's redoubtable prime minister in 1979—whom I considered to be radical ideologues in the guise of conservatives. Kohl was much closer to being a genuine conservative, i.e., socially conscious and pragmatic. Another difference was that in turning to the right, Thatcher and Reagan could indulge in superpatriotic celebration of "the shining city on the hill" or of the powers of the Royal Navy to liberate the Falkland Islands, whereas Chancellor Kohl had to operate within a framework where invocations of the past stirred up angry controversy.

By use of an unusual constitutional maneuver, Kohl was able to call for a new general election in March 1983. Economic conditions were deteriorating in West Germany, and unemployment was high. Running against the record of the preceding social-liberal regime and promising "more market, more mobility," Kohl scored a significant gain for his party, but I was struck by the ugly tone in his campaign: the style of German politics, and not just the substance or clash of material interests, is always of special interest. CDU leaders accused the peace activists of "treason" and branded the SPD candidate, Hans-Jochen Vogel (Bernhard's brother), as "Andropov's candidate"—yet another instance of conservatives insinuating that the Socialists were dangerous "reds," cousins of Communists. Has anyone ever tried to assess the communist contribution to right-wing success?

Kohl's center-right government, given a solid mandate in March, was widely hailed as constituting a *Tendenzwende*, a transformation of policy and spirit. In November the Bundestag approved the stationing of the Pershings on West German soil—against the votes of the SPD deputies, who defied Schmidt's warnings, and of a new group in Parliament, the Greens. The Green Party had started as a congerie of disaffected, predominantly young activists of diverse political views, but they were at one in their passionate opposition to nuclear weapons and their defense of the environment.

I was intrigued by this new defiantly antiestablishment nonparty. In dress and demeanor, they seemed successors to the '68 generation. I wondered if there were analogues here to my cultural pessimists and antimodernists. Did the Greens perhaps signal a political reemergence of the German soul that had given us, at its best, "poetry and truth" (the title of Goethe's autobiography) and, at its worst, grief and tragedy? I assumed that at some point Greens and So-cial Democrats would form coalitions on the *Land* level, but their outrage at what industrial greed and poison had done to nature found them friends among old-fashioned conservatives as well.

Within the solidly pro-Western CDU were some outstanding figures whom I thought were much superior to Helmut Kohl. (Kohl may have agreed with my judgment, for he was ruthless in derailing them as possible rivals in the party.) Bernhard Vogel was one, now minister-president of Rhineland-Palatinate, a position that Kohl had once held. Kurt Biedenkopf, general secretary of the CDU, a man of astonishing breadth, energy, and ambition, was by his very qualities someone whom Kohl had to try to relegate to the margins of power. Over many years of friendship, I saw both men regularly, in their country and mine; we carried on a continuous conversation—about almost everything.

I had friends in most of the German political parties, but my basic sympa-thy was with the Social Democrats, for historic reasons and because of my be-lief in progressive liberalism. I remembered their courageous opposition to Hitler. In the postwar era the party had made huge mistakes, but its best lead-ers—Ernst Reuter, Willy Brandt, and Helmut Schmidt—were models of effec-tive decency. On the issue of the Pershings, I could understand the Brandt wing in its opposition, but sided with Schmidt in his realistic appraisal of European needs and alliance solidarity.

MY TERM AS PROVOST ended in June 1983—three full and instructive years. Post-provostial life was for some years difficult, professionally and privately. What major work would I turn to? I had become uncertain about my projected but oft-interrupted book on Europe. But since my focus stayed on Germany it doesn't seem incongruous that already in November 1982, a month after Schmidt left office, I mused to Marion that perhaps I should try to write about him. A few months later, in New York, I had a two-hour conversation with him and his wife, a woman of precise curiosity and generous spirit. Less distant than he, conveying warmth and support with few words, Loki always showed me exceptional friendliness.

Our conversation began with his asking how many copies *Gold and Iron* had sold, and showing me an outline of his own projected book, *Encounters* (*Begegnungen*). I told him Burckhardt had used that title. He wanted to write about some of his important contemporaries, including artists and philosophers. He asked me if he needed a literary agent. I told him Kissinger had one, and he shot back, "I can't imagine anyone savvier in business than Henry." (The book, *Weggefährten*, appeared in 1996.)

I confessed to Schmidt that I already had serious second thoughts about my project: it had taken me sixteen years to do Bismarck, and I was too old to embark on anything so ambitious. It was dangerous, moreover, for a historian to deal with a living person: our perspective demanded distance. Schmidt brushed all that aside, pointing to his own archive and to the many contemporaries I could interview. We left it that I would visit him in June to discuss the matter further.

We ranged widely in that first long conversation. He spoke scathingly of the Carter and Reagan administrations. America was the most generous and vital nation, he thought, but it had lost its capacity for leadership. He was especially critical of American incomprehension of the problems of the developing world. I realized as we talked that his own ministerial career had begun when the United States was mired in Vietnam; he seemed uninterested, hence uninformed, about domestic American politics: he dismissed Lyndon Johnson but admired Nixon for his "opening" of China; of course Nixon was a crook, but what of it? This was a familiar European view. Schmidt was less philosophical than on earlier occasions, but the clarity of his thought and the fierce certainty of his judgment were as striking as before. Perhaps his celebrated roughness was a shield that protected an inner sensitivity.

In June 1983, I went straight from the provost's office to Marion's home in Hamburg, my base while working for ten days in Schmidt's archive. On the first day, Schmidt received me in his simple and light-filled modern house. He had helped to design it, including a bar in a nautical style; I noticed the rich library, ranging from the classics to the most contemporary literature, and the striking rugs and paintings.

I had known from earlier conversations with or about him that as a student in Hamburg in the mid-1930s he had turned against the National Socialist regime when it declared Emil Nolde a "decadent" artist. In his archive, I found a letter he wrote in 1968 to his friend the writer Siegfried Lenz, saying that as a seventeen-year-old he had thought Nolde the greatest German artist of the twentieth century, and the sculptor Ernst Barlach another favorite; so these two "banished" artists helped to shield Schmidt from the temptation of Nazism. It was odd that so many Germans, proud of their *Bildung*, were not similarly enlightened.

He had been an officer in the Wehrmacht, keeping secret the fact that he had a Jewish grandmother, a prerequisite for the certification as "Aryan" he needed for permission to marry. In fact, he didn't speak of this grandmother until much later, when in the Bonn Republic a Jewish grandmother was as much of an asset as she once had been a dangerous liability. Schmidt was attuned to music, painting, and literature but wore his *Bildung* lightly. I had to think of Weimar's most distinguished statesman, Gustav Stresemann, whose trusted assistants regularly hunted for requisite citations from the classics.

Schmidt had been given the sobriquet Schmidt-Schnauze, or "Schmidt the Lip," because of his cutting rebuttal in 1958 of arguments favoring West German atomic weapons. He told me that he had always relished the nickname as an honor. I suppose he knew that his quick intelligence was a deterrent to potential critics, to the *Dummköpfe* who, he thought, peopled the world. In a letter to Marion, he wrote, "in many realms Brandt seems to think leadership to be something almost indecent, certainly something undemocratic," but Schmidt himself thought that authority didn't derive from office or election, but had to be won and preserved by oneself. He admired strong, intelligent personalities, such as Anwar Sadat.

He brought me to a small hut in his garden, hastily erected to house his archive, where he gave me free rein among the intimidating mass of some 182 files of his own writings and at least 200 other files, which, judging from spot-

checks, seemed somewhat haphazardly assembled from his various offices beginning in 1953. Some files were classified by country, others by subject; there
were also records of his weekly *Kleeblatt* (four-leaf clover) discussions in the
chancellor's bungalow with his four closest advisers. The archive was alarmingly large, but from the start I had the impression that it was far from complete; there was no archivist on board to guide me. I thought this was a
presidential library *in nuce*, incomplete, presumably lacking some classified
material that had to be left in Bonn. Yet rooting around was exciting—I believe
I was the first historian he had allowed to do this—and full of suspense.
Schmidt was a genuine writer and also a man of marginalia, of comments
scribbled on documents, usually in his recognizable green ink. Time was short,
but I made as many exploratory forays as I could, with that uncanny, unsettling
combination of informed hunch and luck that guides archival work, a combination one can't ever trust or feel confident about.

At first I turned to Schmidt's correspondence, arranged, if I remember correctly, by subject and chronology. In letters from the 1950s and early 1960s, the
theme of German reunification dominated: Schmidt knew there was no immediate hope for it, and thus, unlike many in his party, he had supported West German rearmament and NATO membership, short-run obstacles to reunification.
NATO was an indispensable anchor, he thought, but those on the other shore
had to be remembered: as he put it in a letter in 1961, it was unacceptable to
think of East Germany as having been permanently deputized to carry the burden of the lost war. As chancellor he wrote that reunification would not be a return to yesterday's Germany but a move forward to a different tomorrow, to a
unified nation in a state form that couldn't be imagined yet. I don't think he
ever wavered in his faith that the two Germanys would someday in some way
be peacefully reunited. We often talked about the Polish model: "We Germans
should learn from the example of our Polish neighbors," he would say. It had
taken Poles 120 years to regain their full statehood.

One exceptional find was a private letter Marion had written to Schmidt in
October 1974, some five months after he assumed the chancellorship. In her
spare, candid style, she referred to a meeting of their "circle" the night before,
a circle that included Richard von Weizsäcker, a rising star in the CDU firma-
ment. Schmidt might be interested in Weizsäcker's appraisal of him and hers
as well, she said, because "when one has climbed to the lonely heights of top
leadership, where the air grows ever colder and the responsibility weighs ever
more heavily, one gets gradually pushed into a quarantine ward"; this had happened to everyone from Kaiser Wilhelm to Willy Brandt. "If your stance is pes-

simism, it would be bad, but doubts and occasional anxieties are good, are important, are the prerequisite of reflection and humanity. Only those who believe they are without fault and can do everything are free of them." So far, she added, almost everything had worked out well for him. But success is due "never only to merit but always also to grace, and whoever does not heed this, the gods destroy." It is in that spirit, she thought, that the Club of Rome was important. (The Club, founded in 1968 by an international group of early environmentalists, had attracted huge attention in 1972 with its report on *The Limits to Growth* predicting disaster if the heedless exploitation of natural resources continued unabated.) "The members realize that the spiritual background of our crisis lies in [our] immodesty and presumption." Immense material wealth had created all manner of new problems of welfare. Her ending: "This is no letter, only a marginalia!"

Those ten days in Schmidt's archive were wondrous. I thought of Portia's three caskets. Which of the hundreds of files should I open? Where were the greatest treasures? I tried to pick strategically, but I was often disappointed, and did not have enough time to pursue the sudden, sometimes thrilling find. One of Brandt's and Schmidt's underreported achievements had been their help to Spain's and Portugal's Socialists, when those countries found themselves in transition, threatened with communist takeovers; and I found reports of Schmidt's conversations with Mario Soares, leader of the Portuguese Socialists, the principal topic being how to get money to help them. There was a minute of a conversation with Pope Paul V in which Schmidt emphasized the congruence of Catholic social teachings and the 1959 Godesberg program of the SPD, while the Pope spoke of his high esteem for the German people, who, he thought, spiritually remained a single entity (an odd remark, given the prescribed atheism in the GDR). The Church and the Pope, Schmidt remarked, thought in longer temporal terms than politicians, with their day-by-day focus. The Pope replied, "God grant that it should be so!" And there was substantive correspondence with Schmidt's favorite philosopher, Karl Popper. Such a full life!

Given Schmidt's special feeling for the Poles, I fastened on the fascinating, but fragmentary, files dealing with German-Polish relations. There were memos of key talks, hints of ongoing discussions, but no coherent record and large gaps. I thought to myself that even for a mere article on Schmidt's relations with Poland the papers were inadequate, and much else that one would need was presumably inaccessible.

And yet it was so tantalizing! As chancellor, Schmidt had become quite close to the Polish party leader Edward Gierek, during whose rule Poland's indebtedness had quadrupled without a significant improvement in the standard of living. Between 1972 and 1980, when Gierek was deposed, the two men had official and private meetings, with parallel discussions going on at a lower plane, and these talks were not restricted to the difficult bilateral issues (one of which concerned the Germans still living in Poland, particularly in Upper Silesia and the Masurian lake country: the West German government demanded free movement for any of these who wanted to leave, and German-language instruction for those who wanted to stay). Poland considered the Federal Republic the most likely proponent of its interests at the EEC in Brussels; and Schmidt warned it that the Soviet Union's tactical nuclear superiority in Europe, by virtue of its SS-20s, threatened Poland as much as it did the West, for a Federal Republic intimidated by Soviet power would be of less use to Poland.*

I also found a record of a conversation between Schmidt and Mieczysław Rakowski in late May 1979, which was roughly when I had seen Rakowski in Warsaw. To Schmidt, Rakowski acknowledged that economic conditions in Poland were wretched: "Without deep changes in the system, we won't manage." Meanwhile the Church formed the real opposition to communism in Poland, and the election of Cardinal Wojtyla to the papacy gave Poles a new self-confidence; Gierek wanted to reconcile Church and party. But papers in Schmidt's archive for the most critical period, from the beginning of Solidarność in 1980 to the proclamation of martial law in December 1981, were scant. There was nothing on Schmidt's lamentable lapse, when on December 13, happening to be with Erich Honecker in East Germany, he made an anodyne statement about the proclamation. Polish officials had warned him about the difficulty of meeting the strikers' demands, and Germans and Poles were worried about the threat of Warsaw Pact intervention, which Schmidt was sure would harm European security overall. After martial law was imposed, Rakowski appeared yet again to "explain" its necessity, and to warn against Western protests or sanctions: Western demands for the release from prison of pro-Solidarność Poles were futile, he said, because they were the very people who deliberately wished to lead Poland into a catastrophe—by which he meant, I suppose, that they were willing to risk a confrontation with Russia. Like Marion, Schmidt kept his distance from Solidarność, a grave misjudgment, in my view.

*Schmidt retained his close ties to Gierek. Several years later he told me that if he, private person though he now was, ever heard that Gierek, then under house arrest, were in any danger, he would fly to Warsaw and demand to see him; if prevented, he would do all he could to embarrass the regime.

There were accidental surprises, little treasures I stumbled upon, such as a copy of a letter from George Kennan to Marion Dönhoff of April 24, 1977: "But I am not at all happy about the state of affairs in Washington. The cold warriors now have the bit in their teeth; they enjoy powerful support both in Congress and in public opinion generally, not to mention several of the great lobbies (above all, the Jews and the AFL-CIO). The press and Mr. Carter would find it hard to oppose them." I suspected he was referring to right-wing Republicans who were then already benefiting from the rise of the neoconservatives, a circle of fiercely anti-Soviet writers, pundits, and ideologues (many of them ex-Trotskyites, and now extremely censorious of liberals whom they thought insufficiently anticommunist) such as Norman Podhoretz and his wife, Midge Decter, who were pressing for yet greater U.S. military power vis-à-vis the Soviet Union, for freer Jewish emigration from the USSR, and for increased support of Israel. Worry over Israel cropped up in unexpected places. On one occasion Schmidt referred to Prime Minister Begin as a man of hatred, but he warned me at the same time against writing about the end of the irenic Zionist dream: "It could become a self-fulfilling prophecy." In June 1980, for another example, Schmidt and Nahum Goldmann, one-time president of the World Jewish Congress—known as a statesman without a state, and in 1951 the initial negotiator with Adenauer for German reparations to Israel—had met to plan a dinner for Goldmann's eighty-fifth birthday. I found the minutes of the conversation, written by an old acquaintance of mine, Otto von der Gablentz. Beyond planning for the dinner, they talked policy: Goldmann, a cunning charmer, thought the FRG should pay four hundred million deutsche marks to Israel as a final restitution—eighty billion had already been paid or promised. Israel, he went on, was plagued by internal ills and corruption, and would soon have to declare bankruptcy; the extreme Orthodox were preparing for civil war. Pierre Mendès-France had said to him he no longer believed in peace in the Middle East and warned, "In ten years there will be no Israel." Jews, Goldmann added, were "a people one can admire but one cannot love. They are wonderful when they are persecuted. They are impossible when they have it good. Then their chutzpah comes to the fore." Such calculated candor! Schmidt asked him if there were any respected Israelis who understood something about the economy. Goldmann replied that there were, in the universities, but Begin thought "professors are a misfortune for the world," to which Schmidt replied, "For once he is right."

But here I was, a professor, working in the Schmidts' garden, and the Schmidts were wonderfully hospitable. On one of my last days, they came to the archive, he to say that he had to travel, she to say that when I finished I should come up to the house and have a drink. We talked about various things, but above all about Poland. I told her I had tried to concentrate on the Polish file, knowing how important Poland had been to her husband's work. "It came from the heart," she said.

After Hamburg, I went for a short respite to Sils Maria, and there, on a favorite mountain slope, I scribbled some notes, thinking that I would write the article on Schmidt and Poland after all, stressing that Schmidt's reputation as a *Macher*, or operator, a relentless doer, neglected his controlled passions, his broad and informed interests, his political ethic. Perhaps I could add something about his French policy, how he had made the FRG a major voice in the world largely via his French connection, and how he had continued Brandt's *Ostpolitik*, which was really "*Deutschland-Politik.*"

But I had many other commitments and deadlines. Worse, my earlier doubts came back. The historian should stick to the past, or at least I should stick to the German past, the more so as that past—especially the Nazi past— was once again such a prominent and divisive issue. Germany would not have been divided nor Israel created had it not been for Hitler's Germany and its bid for world hegemony. So I reluctantly gave up the idea of writing about Helmut Schmidt and sheepishly informed him of my retreat. He was generous, and over the next two decades our association grew ever closer.

IN THE 1980S, RETICENCE ABOUT THE PAST gave way to competitive commemorations: Chronology commanded a public awareness of the past's centrality; collective memory, fed by the media, became almost obsessive. The fiftieth anniversary of the rise of National Socialism and the fortieth of its defeat made public commemoration a spontaneous imperative. It was also a time when the generation that had experienced the Nazi "triumph" confronted a generation that had been born during or after what had turned into tragedy. Great ceremonies stimulating public memory brought with them great controversy. The question that had haunted some of us for so long—how was it possible?—now seized and divided a larger public. I brooded about changes in the landscape, and various invitations gave me a chance to address new issues.

In 1983 joint East and West German commemorations celebrated the five hundredth anniversary of Martin Luther's birth. I thought the collaborations were an important signal of changing attitudes. It seemed to me that the two Germanys were tacitly acting as one nation. Pastors in both parts who embraced the peace movement were trying if not to repudiate then at least to atone for Protestant subservience to the state, particularly during Nazi times. Luther had been both revolutionary and profoundly conservative, and his church could always claim that his doctrine of "Christian freedom" concerned a spiritual essence while it simultaneously demanded or allowed for unconditional obedience to the secular authorities, instituted by God. Now here was the atheistic East German state collaborating for the moment with the Church to celebrate the great reformer previously vilified as the lackey of princes, coconspirator in the suppression of the peasant revolts of the 1520s, a class enemy. But the GDR embraced the heartland of Luther's life and of Reformation history; its attention to Luther chimed in with its effort to reclaim more of the German and Prussian heritage. I was struck that Pope John Paul II acknowledged Luther's deep religious nature, while the Communists acknowledged his "objectively" progressive role: ecumenical recognition at last!

In that same year two conclaves on German-American relations took place in the United States, one celebrating the founding in 1683 of the first German colony in the new world, at Germantown, Pennsylvania. Despite the officially upbeat mood at the meeting, I cautioned that the earlier overexuberance had waned; the new German-American relationship was a sober one, with interests and perceptions diverging and suspicions mounting. Some West Germans viewed President Reagan's rhetoric as at best imprudent and dangerous, while some Americans complained that the West Germans were ungrateful, potentially unfaithful, and politically myopic. When the conference papers were published, the president of the Federal Republic, the Christian Democrat Karl Carstens, came to the United States to mark the occasion. President Reagan gave him a state dinner, to which Peggy and I were invited, a privilege I hadn't anticipated.* But it was the portrait of John F. Kennedy that I saw in the White House that brought tears to my eyes, a reminder that once there had been greatness and high spirits there.

The second conference was organized in September 1983 by James Billington of the Woodrow Wilson Center in Washington: "German-American Relations and the Role of the Federal Republic in Europe and the World." Two incidents at the margin of the meeting were memorable for me. After one presentation, Midge Decter rose and, her voice dripping with sarcasm, reminded

*The dinner had a comic aftermath: thereafter, the White House, regardless of incumbent, sent me an official Christmas card, a minor privilege I shared with about a hundred thousand other people. Then, during George W. Bush's first term, a million cards were sent out, and I was dropped off the list. Who, I wondered, edited the lists—and at whose expense? The removal was more flattering than the inclusion.

us of the existence of the GDR, which she believed we were ignorant of, and thus were slighting a great threat to American interests. I remembered that she had recently become an instant expert on Germany; German friends had told me about a celebrated "junket" (her word) she had gone on in West Germany with mostly Jewish intellectuals, and how she had made a special request to see "a concentration camp"; she was taken to Dachau, where, she reported, she found gas chambers and ovens; my friends had told me that the group's ignorance had matched its arrogance.

I was interested by this encounter with Midge Decter. Three years earlier, just after Reagan's election, she had invited me to join a nascent group, the Committee for the Free World, that would fight liberal orthodoxies, ever-spreading "totalitarianism," and totalitarian ideas expressed within the democracies. I was uneasy about this group, despite some of its sponsors whom I respected, such as Brzezinski; I feared that their immediate enemy was what they construed as liberal or left-wing orthodoxy. So I had written Decter a reasoned letter declining to join the group, explaining that "the examples of Spain, Portugal, Greece, Poland, and Hungary make me hesitate to accept a statement that the Western democracies face 'a growing threat to their continued viability.'"

My apprehension was justified, for it became ever clearer that the neocons were illiberal ideologues, convinced, inter alia, that their stance on defense and détente was uniquely right and uniquely patriotic. Donald Rumsfeld was a cofounder of the committee, which—we now know—was heavily subsidized by Richard Mellon Scaife, the well-heeled patron of radical right-wing causes. In the 1950s, I had encountered Irving Kristol, another and somewhat appealing early neocon, at the Hofstadters' and the Trillings'; Dick had rebuked him in the 1960s for his illiberal views, and Irving claimed a decade later that neocons were liberals "mugged by reality." Wasn't *mugged* a code word for crimes imagined as being committed by black prowlers in the cities? (I had long suspected that the neocons' break with liberals contained a racial element, and this was confirmed by their attack on affirmative action.) But if "reality" had "mugged" them, it had also greatly enriched them. Their march to wealth and power over the next few decades deserves a Balzac as chronicler; he could use the amiable Richard Perle as a key figure, combining greed with hard-edged moralistic "realism." It was a great failure on the part of American moderates to pay so little heed to the carefully orchestrated buildup of the neoconservative position, and to be too self-confident about our own intellectual and political position.

A happenstance incident at Billington's conference left me with a permanent gain. During a coffee break, I fell into an intense conversation with an "observer," a wonderfully alive woman, petite in stature, sparkling in manner, a German American scholar of modern literature whose name was Ernestine Schlant. As we chatted in the vestibule of the center, a hugely tall person came up to her and hugged her: it was Bill Bradley, saluting his wife. This was an encounter that was to lead to new political connections.

In March 1983, Reagan had furthered his military plans by announcing a "Strategic Defensive Initiative" (popularly known as Star Wars), that would focus on a complex nuclear defense of North America. Would this mean that an invulnerable America might neglect its commitments to NATO and, consequently, to the defense of the Federal Republic? The old suspicions about European unpreparedness meanwhile grew in America, about West German "ingratitude" and the danger of German "self-Finlandization," an infelicitous reference to a country recognized as neutral. These and other difficulties welled up during the many public events of that decade of commemoration, and the German question went on being debated, with a certain éclat.

In 1983, West Berlin—Richard von Weizsäcker its mayor—organized a three-day symposium, held in the old Reichstag building, on Germany's path to dictatorial rule. Weizsäcker, the younger brother of Carl-Friedrich, already had a distinguished political career. The philosopher Hermann Lübbe, in a much-noted paper, argued that the very incompleteness of de-Nazification after the war had been a cardinal element in the success of the Bonn democracy; a thorough de-Nazification, which so many of us had hoped for, would have made political outcasts of millions and created resentful Weimar-type enemies of the new regime at its start. I thought this an important emendation, but not an excuse for the egregious cases of culprits kept in important posts.

As an "interlocutor" on a different panel, I called for greater attention to the way Germany's elites had responded to Hitler—mostly favorably; one needed to study both the continuities in German history and the possible alternatives to Hitler's rise to power. The published record of the proceedings noted that some of my remarks aroused amusement (*Heiterkeit*) in the audience of a thousand people. Perhaps I injected a somewhat different tone, mischievously tentative, playful and ironic into the otherwise ponderous discourse. I hope the lighter style did not disguise the depth of my engagement.

That summer, the University of Tübingen's renowned Evangelical-theological faculty wrote that it wanted to award jointly to the philosopher Hans Jonas and to me its annual Dr. Leopold-Lucas Prize for outstanding work in theology and intellectual history that also promoted understanding among peoples. (Jonas had published a pioneering study of gnosticism in 1934, much influenced by Martin Heidegger; thereafter he lived as a refugee in Palestine, Canada, and finally in the United States, where in 1979 he published a treatise on ethics in our technological age.) Leopold Lucas had been a biblical scholar and rabbi, deported to Theresienstadt, where he died in 1943; his widow was murdered in Auschwitz. Would I accept? (A prior recipient had been Léopold Sédar Senghor, the poet-philosopher who had been president of Senegal.) I was astonished by this letter out of the blue—and accepted gratefully. The ceremony was set for June 1984, but the dean asked early on for the title of the formal lecture I was expected to give. Time and occasion, I thought, demanded some reckoning with National Socialism, a broad sketch for a town-and-gown audience; the title "National Socialism as Temptation" suddenly occurred to me, echoing in some mysterious way my earlier ruminations—in this instance, perhaps, my reaction to Weizsäcker's extraordinary letter. I now see that the title already signified a provocation, suggesting as it did that National Socialism was not a regime of terror imposed on Germans, as so many Germans still liked to believe, nor was its success due to Germans' being congenital authoritarians, as others argued; it also moved away from the then popular notion of National Socialism as a local variant of a general "totalitarianism," a category that minimized national and historical characteristics.

I found myself with a promising title and empty sheets of my habitual yellow legal pads. The substance and argument evolved slowly and painfully, the more so since I was writing this lecture in German, one of my first major efforts in my native language. I spoke the langue, of course, and enjoyed doing so, but formal training had stopped when I was twelve years old. In a way I had to relearn the language, and in the process may have found my own voice in German: an amalgam, perhaps, of older German prose to which I added a lighter American tone.

But content was of course the principal challenge. I first looked for the voices of that time, especially unfamiliar ones in letters, diaries, and books, revealing the views and conduct of the elites with regard to National Socialism both before and after Hitler's coming to power. I started with the premise that National Socialism, whose triumph was so often explained in purely material or political terms, had had its powerful psychological appeal. Its pseudoreligious garb, its promise of a national rebirth, of a *völkisch* community led by a self-proclaimed savior who would redeem the country by eliminating its corrupters—Marxists, Jews—and their poisonous influence on German life, was a key element. So National Socialism was a temptation—in the sense of the first definition of the term that the Oxford English Dictionary gives: attraction to evil. A fearful and humiliated people seemed prepared to believe that the road to the salvation they craved had to include fearsome, violent means. I had experienced Germany in its frenzied state of exaltation, fear, and terror, and unarticulated memories of childhood may have informed my study, but so ingrained was the historian's ethos of distrusting the subjective that the pertinent memories returned not then, as I was preparing the lecture, but only now, with this writing. I was looking for "hard" evidence on a most elusive subject. Still, my passionate personal concern did creep in.

It was easy enough to see that National Socialism was an unabashed mixture of "idealism," with its adherents ranting against materialism and egoism, and nihilism, with its hatred poured on Jews and Marxists and its contempt for ineffective liberals. It was easy to see its exaltation of ancient military virtues and plain force. But how could so many Germans have believed that the Nazis' simplistic and ominous program was the way to a national rebirth, to a moral cleansing, to the creation of a people's powerful community? I was interested in the Germans' wish to believe, in their voluntary choice of Nazism, dissatisfied as I was with the idea that terror had simply subdued them. (George Lichtheim, one of the best observer-historians of the time, in his *Europe in the Twentieth Century* [1972] described the Nazis' appeal to all classes, especially to the peasantry, but concluded, "For all that the new regime had to be imposed by wholesale terrorism, the murder or imprisonment of thousands of opponents and the establishment of a secret police dictatorship unparalleled outside Stalinist Russia.") Of course, intimidation and terror existed and material interests were at work, but so were intellectual presuppositions and psychic needs and hopes. It was these things I wanted to ferret out.

I had some hunches. Weizsäcker's letter to me had confirmed my early apprehensions and pointed me in new directions. In his diary, Thomas Mann, for example, wrote that Hitler was "a tin god" who had "become a religion for millions," with the irrational winning over of a "horrendously overstimulated population in a state of national orgasm." Mann foresaw that vindictiveness and megalomania would end in another war.* Shortly before his death in 1929, Stresemann had spoken of Hitler's "satanic genius." Many were beguiled by this

---

*I sketched Mann's political odyssey, with its symptomatic quality. Germanic chauvinist in the Great War, he recouped quickly, rallying to the republic in 1922, almost at once recognizing the dark forces in National Socialism, and after its triumph, he chose to live abroad, reluctant to have himself associated with "the emigrants." Preserving his contemptuous distance from National Socialism, he had moments of doubt: was there perhaps some good in it, thoughts that he was ashamed of? Mann's ruminations, confided only in his diaries, exemplified the ambivalence of so many Germans; there were the many followers and the few opponents, often in "inner emigration," but there were also many in neither camp, uncertain, changing with time and events, often outwardly conformist, but with moral or prudential unease. After the purge of 1934, Mann became the most consistent and authoritative voice of anti-Nazi thought.

"tin god" and "satanic genius," enthralled by faith in salvation as some transcendental release from existing pain and uncertainty, as guaranteed by one "savior," speaking in tongues but backed by a host of followers. Hitler's demagogic powers and his movement's dramaturgy were key, and in both of these, the pseudoreligious element was central, being a psychological lure and a license to suspend reason and judgment. (Oddly, I didn't go into Hitler's hysterical, hypnotic oratory, which I had heard in my childhood and which powerfully shaped the tone of official speech in the Third Reich.)

Providence, Hitler always claimed, had lifted him from obscurity, anointing him the redeemer of his fallen country, which he would rid of its godless, insidious aliens and lead to an invincible *Volksgemeinschaft*, poised to regain its position in the world and conquer the indispensable *Lebensraum* for the Aryan *Volk*. He appealed to his people's readiness for sacrifice on behalf of national greatness and pride. And this transfigured politics of National Socialism, with its uniforms and flags, its hymns and sacred martyrs, created a dramatic alternative to dull, divisive bourgeois politics. The Nazis defined themselves as a dynamically new movement, yet their practiced self-presentation harked back to old church and army rituals. Slogans of conquest came to life in their meticulously staged mass rallies: politics turned into mass delirium, transporting the lonely, apathetic individual, fearful of public life, into a community of dedicated fighters for ultimate greatness.

Of course "conditions" favored the chiliastic turn, and I recalled the known traumas of a lost war, inflation, and depression, as well as all the intellectual antecedents, including the latent anti-Semitism of the churches and Germany's long-cherished antipathy to "the West." Nietzsche's dictum seemed stunningly relevant: "Weariness that wants to reach the ultimate with *one* leap, with one fatal leap, a poor, ignorant weariness that does not want to want anymore: This created all gods and other worlds."

Yet from the very beginning, some Germans had instantly recognized the demonic dangers in National Socialism. I thought of Paul Tillich, the Lutheran philosopher-theologian who belonged to a circle of "religious Socialists" in Weimar and became the first "Aryan" to be dismissed from his academic position in the spring of 1933. Other theologians, too, spoke with varying degrees of apprehension, among them Rudolf Bultmann and Dietrich Bonhoeffer, who after deepest reflection chose resistance and suffered martyrdom.

The German elites' voluntary submission to the Nazis may have felt at the time as an embrace, a collective rejoicing, an experience of unreflective solidarity. National Socialism represented order, authority, decisiveness, and radiant self-confidence: a political *Gesamtkunstwerk*, a Wagnerian transformation into a nation humming in work and spirit. Whatever their motives—genuine enthusiasm, careerism, or preemptive cowardice—they were swept up in an even more intoxicating delirium, from which, I hastened to add, some believers awoke, and which they even repudiated.

Submission or surrender to the new regime meant implicit abandonment of old traditions and acceptance of or indifference to state terror. Because of course there was instant terror, wielded against thousands of political opponents who, if Jews, were treated with special cruelty. Yet with only a few exceptions, the German professoriate, for example, shamefully betrayed both the hallowed principle of academic autonomy and their own colleagues, accepting the dismissal of Jews and "non-Aryans" from academic posts and all other public offices. Yet while the risks of nonconformity varied, in the first months it required perhaps no more than *Zivilcourage*; voicing dissent was only minimally dangerous. I cited a few instances of established dignitaries who made gestures of private decency while making public compromises, noting that at a time of manipulated hysteria, "a refusal to say yes was no small thing."

I tried to substantiate the notion of "temptation" among the elites, this irrational leap to something mysteriously and dangerously enticing, not in the spirit of *tout comprendre, c'est tout pardonner*, since to pardon is not the historian's task; nor was it my predisposition. In fact, writing this lecture tapped into and reawakened a huge anger in me, overshadowed by deep puzzlement. I knew that many Germans had been torn, uncertain, and wavering in 1933, and I could readily confess that I didn't know how I would have behaved, only how I would have wished to behave. I relished the ironic formulation by which I acknowledged that I had been spared the National Socialist temptation "not through any special virtue on my part but because I am a full-blooded non-Aryan for whom temptation was forbidden." When I gave the lecture, the audience responded visibly, uneasily, at my mocking mix of Nazi diction with private self-doubt, as they did to my recalling "how enthralled my schoolmates were by the Hitler Youth, how appealing and binding that communal experience had been, and how painful exclusion could be."

In composing the lecture, I felt afresh that I had experienced the drama of National Socialism with a certain frisson; its pageantry of march and music, of strutting self-confidence, had impressed and appalled me. I had been shielded from temptation not only by decree but by knowledge and fear of Nazi murder and intimidation, and by parental example. And yet by what satanic trick do I still know by heart the lines of the party's Horst-Wessel anthem? I suppose that my equally strong memory for the words and tunes of "La Marseillaise" and the "Internationale" is an antidote.

And what of the Germans who resisted National Socialism, the Socialists and Communists who went underground, the diverse men and women in the 20th of July plot against Hitler? Perhaps one could examine the collusion of the many in light of the heroism of the few. The latter's belated willingness to risk their lives to free their own country and Europe from a reign of terror had a human and historical significance unparalleled in German history. My views probably grated on people on the right and left, the former still suspecting the resistance of treason and the latter uneasy about excessive regard for an often nondemocratic elite. But however debased the behavior of Germany's privileged elite, I didn't think they were monsters. You didn't have to be a monster to have supported National Socialism.

Still, I think I made unmistakably clear my plea for immediate resistance to incipient tyranny; there is a fatality in waiting for a riper moment, when resistance might demand martyrdom or end in futility. I knew that this failure was not a German fault alone, and in my final printed version of the lecture, I quoted C. Vann Woodward's description of the American South, still dominated by Jim Crow in the 1930s: "Few were able or willing to speak out. Those who did seemed to me to speak in too mild a voice. The thing was that they lived under powerful inhibitions."

I finished my lecture, but even now, some twenty years or more later, I still feel that the triumph of National Socialism retains something inexplicable, and it gnaws at one's professional and private conscience. That a man and a movement so unambiguously mean-spirited and malevolent should have appeared as salvation to millions, Hitler as Providence's deputy? I suppose there will always remain a large residue of puzzlement.

Thet lecture had an afterlife for me, for it may have augmented my unanticipated role in Germany as a foreign historian-observer with a native touch. I didn't solicit this part, but I relished the ever more frequent contacts and my growing circle of German friends. I was increasingly living in two countries — a life-enhancing, life-complicating development.

I hadn't thought of immediate publication of the lecture — to me, the distinction between the spoken and the written is awesome — but the dean of the theological faculty at Tübingen, Otfried Hofius, insisted that our texts be published at once, and entitled *In Dark Times*. Jonas had given a profound and moving talk, "The Concept of God After Auschwitz." Hofius and I went over my manuscript, and his editorial interventions improved it. He didn't like one particular construction I had used, and the third time he tried to change it, I demanded an explanation as to why. He replied, "It hasn't been used since Luther's time!" I told him that if it had been good enough for Luther, it was good enough for me. Inwardly, I was amused that my boyhood German was Luther-tainted.

"National Socialism as Temptation" was, then, my first exploration of a subject I would return to: the drama of human behavior in the face of terror, and the moral atmosphere of the German tyranny. When I expanded it for English publication, I added an epigraph from Edmund Burke: "No passion so effectually robs the mind of all its powers of acting and reasoning as fear. For fear being an apprehension of pain or death, it operates in a manner that resembles actual pain." So the ideas in it informed my subsequent work, and I was pleased to hear echoes of it in the later work of other scholars. Since I have had my measure of brickbats or, worse, oblivion, it was satisfying to see Robert Gellately, a foremost scholar of the Nazi period, in his *Backing Hitler: Consent and Coercion in Nazi Germany* (2002), conclude: "In writing this book I was constantly reminded of the phrase in one of Fritz Stern's essays on 'National Socialism as Temptation.' He suggests how even the most educated Germans found reasons for supporting the system, and were less regimented, cajoled or forced than we often assume."

More recently, the theme of National Socialism as a political religion has become downright fashionable, perhaps excessively so, at the expense of careful political-cultural history. I don't know if anyone else before me had invoked the notion of "temptation" with regard to National Socialism (though, in 1977, *The Totalitarian Temptation* appeared, Jean-François Revel's polemical, ill-tempered book on pro-Stalinism in contemporary Europe), but it gained currency. Since I always try to place the German instance in its European context, I regret that I said too little about National Socialism's admirers abroad, the conservatives of many professions and occasional intellectuals who marveled at its dynamic character, who "understood" its anti-Semitic efforts while regretting its excesses. On my travels, I had seen that the temptation went beyond Germans—and today, an ignorant, sneaking regard for National Socialism may be more pervasive than we realize, certainly more powerful abroad than in Germany itself.

While I was at Tübingen, the university's president, Adolf Theis, and I had several private conversations, and a remark he made left a lasting imprint on me: in reply to my observing that present-day Germany's striving for a greater place in world politics had, unlike earlier efforts in 1914 and 1933, received little notice, he said, "And that may be our chance." Then he asked me to come back and give the *Festvortrag* at a private ceremony for Theodor Eschenburg's eightieth birthday, to be celebrated in an old Swabian castle, Urach. (Eschenburg had had a remarkable career: in the 1920s in Tübingen he was head of a right-wing student association, while being close to Gustav Stresemann; at the beginning of the Third Reich he engineered, for unclear reasons, entry into and then exit from the SS; after the war, he became a professor in Tübingen, formally in political science, though by inclination he was a historian, and became an adviser-critic to various FRG governments, a frequent contributor to *Die Zeit*, and a friend of Marion Dönhoff's.)

On that second stay in Tübingen, I also visited Hans Küng, the Catholic theologian there whose challenges to Pope John Paul II's dogmatism had brought the Vatican's wrath down upon him; he had been removed from the Catholic faculty. We met on the veranda of what I remember as his ultramodern home; he was dressed in an impeccable white kind of zoot suit. I told him that William Bundy of *Foreign Affairs* had agreed with my notion to ask him for an article about the Pope. Küng's instant answer was, "Yes, if I can compare the Pope and Reagan."

IN 1984, AT THE FORTIETH ANNIVERSARY OF D-DAY, Chancellor Kohl wished, most insensitively and unsuccessfully, that West Germany be allowed to join the nations that had been wartime allies in their celebrations in memory of the Normandy landings. And then, a year later, just before the anniversary of Germany's unconditional surrender on May 8, he insisted that President Reagan and he jointly visit a military cemetery in Bitburg; he clung to that demand even after it was pointed out that members of the notorious Waffen SS were buried there. Secretary of State George Shultz counseled Reagan against this plan, but Kohl declared that his chancellorship was at stake. It was clear he wanted the American president not only to acknowledge publicly what many people had come to feel implicitly—that Germany's present was detached from its terrible past—but, more, to achieve an amnesty for the dead. And the undisturbed, unhistorical Reagan went along, declining only Kohl's additional request for a formal handshake at the site. If proof of the centrality of symbolic politics was needed, this would serve. Bitburg was another signal that "the German question" had reappeared: that the Nazi past still cast a shadow over the Federal Republic in world politics.

Non-Germans concerned about German intentions were reassured, how-

ever, by Kohl's continued fidelity to Europe, and Europe was in an important
constructive phase, with Greece, Spain, and Portugal joining the European
Community, reclaiming the European patrimony denied to them by earlier
dictatorships. "Europe" was obviously more than Brussels and EEC regulations, more than economic benefits, and that "more" was rightly defined historically and culturally. In various milieux, I happily addressed the historic
roots of European commonality, which were sometimes seen more clearly
from afar than from within a European nation. And I had felt European, after
all, long before it became a political project. The child in me probably rejoiced
as well, for Europe remained a favorite, partial home, imbued with a special radiance. I don't think I ever lost the sense of surprised pleasure at appearing under French or other continental auspices—to say nothing of my feelings when
in 1985 the aged Harold Macmillan, vice chancellor of Oxford University, presented me with an honorary degree.

Bitburg also confirmed and intensified the Germans' own reckoning with
their past, which had become an international enterprise as a matter of course.
And the scholarship involved underscored the degree to which West Germans
had turned to the West, whether to include the work of American and British
historians—Gordon Craig or Alan Bullock were landmarks of modern German enlightenment—or simply because key debates and controversies about
the past had an international cast. The real work was of course still done alone
in one's study, a continuous exercise in what many Germans consider a prerequisite for all work: *Sitzfleisch.*

Richard von Weizsäcker, whose election in May 1984 as president of the
Federal Republic brought a new voice and authority to the country, had been
scheduled well before the Bitburg controversy to speak at the solemn joint session of Parliament on May 8, the fortieth anniversary of Germany's unconditional surrender. When he fulfilled this ceremonial task, he delivered not just
an implicit rebuke to the impropriety of Bitburg but something much more: a
magisterial reckoning with the German past and the present, delivered with
a quiet, penetrating dignity reflecting his moral authority compounded by his
official position.

"We must find our own standards," he said. "We are not assisted in this task
if we or others spare our feelings. We need and we have the strength to look
unblinkered at the truth—without embellishment and distortion." The day
called for remembrance of *all* the suffering caused by war and tyranny: "We remember especially the six million Jews who were murdered in German concentration camps" and the sufferings of all peoples in the war, "above all the

countless citizens of the Soviet Union and Poland who lost their lives." Only then did Weizsäcker also speak of German soldiers killed, of German victims of terror, civilians lost in air raids, of Germans wounded and crippled, of millions made homeless. "If nations had been able to survive this inhumanity and annihilation, then it is first of all thanks to the women," he said.

Weizsäcker insisted that "the genocide of the Jews is unique in history." And every German, he added, was likely to have witnessed Jewish suffering. The moral and material ruins that Germans had faced at the end of the war had been German induced: "We cannot separate May 8, 1945, from January 30, 1933." In its brief life, National Socialism—"having whipped up and exploited mass hysteria"—had wrought the catastrophe.

He knew that most Germans did not want to face this truth—or indeed any truth that reminded them of Germany's primary responsibility for the war. But invoking Jewish tradition, Weizsäcker insisted that remembrance was the only path to reconciliation: "Those who don't want to remember past inhumanity will be vulnerable again to new dangers of contagion."

Young Germans should realize how much had been achieved since 1945. He alluded to hopeful signs of the present; the two separate German states contain one people, "feeling at one in the will for peace." He noted Gorbachev's conciliatory words, adding that whatever our concerns regarding human rights in the USSR, we wish for "friendship with the peoples of the Soviet Union."

Marion and I watched the speech on TV. Weizsäcker's unflinching, eloquent, and somehow consoling words were extraordinary: they were words that Germans and non-Germans could live by. His unsparing analysis of the past, and his moral tone and eloquence gave his speech its great emotional power. We both thought it the most important speech given in postwar Germany. It was the reckoning of a genuine conservative—at the right time and occasion.

Days later, Weizsäcker, to whom I had sent a copy of my "National Socialism as Temptation," wrote me: "Your lecture uncovers in a severe and yet unwounding fashion important reasons for the rise of National Socialism. It not only helps better to understand what took place, but also emphatically warns of the dangers that always exist, such as insouciance regarding emerging and slowly mounting discontent and the more or less irrational search for alternatives to a superficial and inadequate political present." He had read the lecture, he said, "with liveliest interest and gratitude" while preparing his own speech.

These various commemorations of 1985 triggered a new round of German soul-searching about the past. The unspoken intent of the Bitburg pageantry and then Weizsäcker's articulate candor marked two poles of this new confrontation, and they both cast shadows. The third meeting of the Evangelical Academy in Tutzing, which I attended in March 1985, dovetailed with another set of anniversaries—of Germany's unconditional surrender, of the Yalta and Potsdam conferences—and the program included a discussion of "Forty Years After Potsdam." The Soviet representative, Nikolai Portugalov, foreign affairs adviser to the Central Committee and a German specialist, a man of broad competence, led off. The charge that the creation of "socialist" regimes in Eastern Europe had violated the Yalta agreements was a historical falsification, he insisted. "The Soviet Union bears no responsibility for the confrontation imposed on her in the late 1940s which from the beginning was intended to revise the war's consequences [*Kriegsergebnisse*]." Portugalov argued that the Soviet Union, despite its grievous wartime losses, had always pressed for German unity; it was the West that had chosen division. He accused the United States of "brutally stopping" détente, and demanded a return to the Helsinki spirit, when Europeans first understood their continent as a "common house." It was a clever Soviet ploy to talk only of different social, but not political, regimes, as if the issue of political freedom were not the key one.

I answered that although the United States was not blameless in the origins of the cold war, it had been primarily responding to the imposition of communist regimes on the nations of Eastern Europe, a development that had *not* been foreseen at Yalta. Portugalov lectured me that these regimes had been the result of great social revolutions. In turn, I pointed to early examples of Soviet coercion, such as Vishinsky's arrival in Bucharest in February 1945 to lead the brutally engineered change in Rumania's government. I recalled the stiff notes FDR had sent to Stalin after Yalta, warning against Soviet expansionism in Eastern Europe, by which, I said, the Soviets had gambled away a huge reservoir of sympathy earned during the war. Of course, there were areas of historical uncertainties, subject to disputes, but the fact that the Soviet archives were hermetically sealed, like the Vatican ones, made resolution more difficult. American archives, on the other hand, were gradually becoming available to historians, who were long practiced in the criticism of national policy.

Another panel discussed Stalin's surprise note of March 1952 proposing free elections leading to a unified, neutralized Germany. Portugalov insisted that this had been an "authentic" Soviet effort to solve the German question, which the West had wrongly dismissed. We knew, of course, that most Westerners at the time had believed the note to be a sham, a maneuver to disrupt the Federal Republic's integration with the West. I argued that the secrecy of Soviet decision making had strengthened our suspicions of the disruptive aims of Stalin's note. We still didn't regard it as "authentic." Asked to speculate about the future, Portugalov said he thought that the restoration of a German nation-state such as had existed after 1871 or in 1937 was impossible. I countered that only men moved by religious or materialistic faith would declare something "impossible." I thought it was only improbable. I could imagine a slow dissolution of the two blocs over decades as the ideological enmities waned.

That evening, the academy's director insisted that Portugalov and I should have a private chat, and in my mind's eye I still see where we sat during our brief, intense time together. Portugalov, very much at home in German culture and in private rather genial, talked about the issues dividing Russia and America, and warned that the former would never tolerate further deployment of nuclear weapons in Europe. I told him that I didn't believe the United States would desist, unless the Russians withdrew its Euro missiles. He became quite heated, and finally exclaimed, "If you push us too hard, we'll send another Stalin note, only this time it will be genuine [*echt*]." I was amused by the blatant candor with which he contradicted in private what he had proclaimed in public. For that, I told him, you'd need a daring young leader, and his instant response was "We'll have one." A week later, the Kremlin leader, Konstantin Chernenko, died, and within hours Mikhail Gorbachev was general secretary of the party. Portugalov had surely known about Gorbachev's imminent rise, but I was astounded. Seweryn Bialer, in his fine *The Soviet Paradox: External Expansion, Internal Decline* (1986), noted that in Chernenko's last year a "minicult of personality" had formed around Gorbachev, a premature anointing unprecedented in Soviet history. Soviet leadership had drifted for years, but Gorbachev was a new generation, and, to boot, a man of high intelligence and vision. Five years later, Gorbachev did send "another note," but it was of a kind no one could have predicted.

ONE YEAR LATER, Ernst Nolte, a German historian with a metaphysical bent, published an article in Germany's foremost daily on "the past that won't go away." He initiated yet another passionate controversy, wrongly labeled *Historikerstreit*, or historians' conflict. The chief protagonists weren't historians.

Nolte's article reproduced a speech he had prepared for a symposium from which he had been disinvited. His argument was involuted, but the motive was clear: if the past wouldn't go away, at least let it be seen less darkly. Moreover, it was only the National Socialist past that hadn't been put to rest as "history."

And there were "interests" behind the insistence on keeping it alive—chiefly the desire of the young to rebel against their fathers and the desire of the persecuted or their descendants to preserve their exceptional and privileged status.

It was a horrendous breach of decency and common sense to suggest that "interests" kept alive the memory of what most of the world regarded as the greatest crime in modern history, but Nolte's argument went further: the Bolsheviks in the early 1920s had already committed the crimes that the Nazis later practiced, he argued; only the technological details of the genocide had been different. Hitler had read the accounts of Soviet mass murder and mass deportations. Thus Nolte's insidious questions: "Did National Socialism, did Hitler, carry out an 'Asiatic' deed perhaps only because they thought of themselves and their kind as potential or actual victims of one? Was therefore the Gulag archipelago more primary [*ursprünglicher*] than Auschwitz?" He was insinuating a thesis that "relativized" the crimes of National Socialism, that treated them as copies not as originals, implying far lesser guilt. To do so in the form of seemingly naïve questions was itself offensive.

Nolte's record gave his cunningly disguised apologia added weight. A student of Heidegger, Nolte was schooled in metaphysics and later had turned to history, a subject he taught in a *Gymnasium*. An injured hand kept him out of wartime service. One of his first books, *The Three Faces of Fascism*, I knew well, having reviewed it for the *Journal of Modern History*, comparing its fusion of philosophical and historical thought to Hannah Arendt's *Origins of Totalitarianism*. (Nolte was weak on the Action Française, strong on Mussolini, by whom he seemed fascinated, and masterly on Hitler, but I thought the book uneven, and questioned his central thesis that fascism dominated the epoch of the two world wars, conditioning all other events. There were also "serious flaws of method and of style." I thought the book "exceedingly, and unnecessarily, difficult and demanding." Still, it was a "deeply original analysis of a central facet of our historical experience.")

In time I got to know Nolte, visiting him in Marburg, where he had become a professor of history (the Marburg faculty included some of the few left-liberal or Marxist historians teaching in Germany); we had common interests and friends, most notably Hajo Holborn. Nolte was a remote, rigid, and learned person, but he intrigued me, and we kept in touch. In 1967, I offered him help in obtaining a visiting professorship in the United States. In 1969 he complained to me that extremists had taken control of the state Ministry of Culture: "Still, I don't plan to capitulate before this violent dogmatism and in the end I don't believe the state will simply collapse under the attack driven by the *ressentiments* of a few octogenarians and the activism of many of the young." For him, 1968 confirmed all his suspicions of left-wing conspiracies and, like many paranoid people feeling themselves attacked, he provoked his assumed enemy. In 1973, he had accepted a call to the Free University in Berlin, and for his first seminar at this most radically left-wing university he chose as a subject the Spanish Civil War, not his specialty but one calculated to detonate ideological bombs. The academic upheavals of the 1960s had driven him into a much more reactionary position.

I took him at first as a naïve academic—he had the air of the stereotypical German philosopher—and for a while I wrongly assumed that he didn't know what he was doing, that he was more a metaphysician than a historian. But every successive book of his disabused me of this amiable illusion, for with each one he "relativized" the Nazi period more, seeing it in a congenial cold-war mode as a response to Bolshevism. Later he argued that Chaim Weizmann's statement at the outbreak of war in 1939 that Jews were on the side of the Allies must be read as a declaration of war, hence explaining Hitler's war on the Jews. Nolte copied me on his angry correspondence with American colleagues, and I gradually ceased my contact with him.

Nolte's article in 1986 unleashed a storm. Jürgen Habermas, outraged by Nolte's insinuations and their political implications, fired off the first vehement reply. Others joined the fray, statements and counterstatements crowded the media, and soon the polemics acquired an ugly tone, with ad hominem attacks and muttered innuendos about motives. The antagonists weren't debating evidence or adducing new information; the fights were over questions of uniqueness and comparability—were the Soviet crimes or those of Pol Pot in Cambodia at least as heinous as those of the Nazis?

Hans-Ulrich Wehler, one of the most engaged and knowledgeable of West Germany's historians, wrote that the dispute was about arguments that aimed at absolution, at minimizing German responsibility, which was the wish of many conservatives in the Kohl era—quite aside from the glorifier of the Wehrmacht or the occasional though completely marginal Holocaust denier (more active and successful in France, England, and Lincoln, Nebraska, than in the Federal Republic).

Shortly after Nolte's article appeared, I wrote him that "I was deeply disturbed by it." He wanted full details, because he had just written that he doubted that his critics were still capable of reading correctly or arriving at objective assessments; he didn't want to think this of me. This was flattering, but I was deep in other work and deadlines and therefore content to watch from afar as my historian friends Hans and Wolfgang Mommsen, Kocka, Eberhard Jaeckel, and others fought the good fight. Their exemplary work helped greatly to create a fragile liberal consensus on how to teach and live with the past. It remains a matter of delicate balance: to focus excessively on the Third Reich at the expense of the history of earlier centuries is a dangerous distortion.

The *Historikerstreit* came to a temporary end when President Weizsäcker addressed the annual meeting of German historians in 1987. His speech was conciliatory in tone, unambiguous in substance: "Auschwitz remains unique," he said. "It was perpetrated by Germans in the name of Germany. This truth is immutable and will not be forgotten." He warned against "relativizing," against forgetting that Germany "was led by criminals and allowed itself to be led by them." Efforts to bend or banish this simple truth have never ceased in Germany.

IN 1986, MY INTERMITTENT PUBLIC ROLE landed me in a brouhaha with *Der Spiegel*, an episode that offered me a glimpse of life with the West German media. In early April, terrorists said to come from Libya bombed a disco in West Berlin, a favorite of GIs. Two people were killed, and 155, more than a third of them Americans, were wounded. Colonel Qaddafi's Libya had harassed American interests for some time, and the Reagan administration wanted to show that it was anything but a paper tiger. On April 14, President Reagan announced an air attack on Libya in "self-defense . . . a mission fully consistent with Article 51 of the UN Charter." American planes, starting from U.S. bases in England, bombed two cities in Libya, killing thirty civilians, including Qaddafi's daughter. (France had denied overflight rights, but then France had long cherished a special relationship with North Africa.)

The American attack caused an uproar everywhere. This "retaliation" seemed to fit Reagan's style, with its militarization of foreign policy and its steady increase in arms spending. On April 15, Swiss TV interviewed me about the whole affair, and I criticized this "global unilateralism," regretted the ensuing stress within NATO, and suggested that Reaganite politics was reminiscent of the worst of Wilhelmine foreign policy. But I also warned against European passivity and indifference. Two days later, *Der Spiegel* asked me for an interview. (In the intervening days, I spoke with experts at the State Department, who assured me that no one at State except for Secretary Shultz had been consulted on the bombing.) The *Spiegel* correspondent and I instantly agreed on the ground rules, which included a promise that I would have to authorize the final published text of the interview.

Opening question: Is this the worst crisis in Allied relations since 1945? I thought not but that the flare-up was grave nevertheless. The discrepancy between American expectations and Europe's performance was growing: "Actually Europe today is too strong to be so weak." Europeans resented the American tendency to simplify, and, I said, Reagan was an extraordinary example of a simplifier. Americans feared another "Munich," most especially the neoconservatives, who suspected Europeans of an appeasement mentality. It would have been better to have had an Allied policy on Libya, imposing tough sanctions and installing an international tribunal. European passivity encouraged Reagan's unilateralism. And I commented that the United States had been driven reluctantly into the position of a world power in 1917: "There has never before been a democratic world power."

Europeans regarded the American mixture of realpolitik and idealism as dangerous and hypocritical, said the *Spiegel* reporter. True, I agreed: the United States, certain of its exceptional stance since its birth as a republic in a world of old monarchies, has pursued its interests with missionary zeal and given its policy a religious cloak.* The *Spiegel* man said that the Foreign Ministry in Bonn worried that Reagan might be harder to contain than Qaddafi— to which I responded with a question of my own: would Bonn merely worry and carp, or would it promote a closer relationship among its European partners? After all, Reagan didn't want a war with Libya or Nicaragua; his rhetoric was far more bellicose than his actions; he wanted to show strength and toughness so that the world wouldn't slither into another war, to show strength without the risk of a new Vietnam.

It all went as agreed: I received a copy of the transcribed interview, made minor corrections, and signed off on it. Silence followed. Then, after a curious delay, I received the published version: I immediately detected eight major changes, of which the most egregious one was in the last line, which now had me saying that President Reagan wanted to show strength even "at the risk of another Vietnam." Most of the changes were politically motivated, I was sure, since my positive comments about the United States and criticisms of Europe had been deleted.

Enraged, I called the *Spiegel* interviewer, who was himself alarmed at what

---

*As so often, I was reminded of the anecdote from the mid-nineteenth century, when French and British interests in the Middle East clashed. The French ambassador came to Lord Palmerston, foreign secretary, to say that France accepted the British demands. Departing, he begged leave to make a personal remark: "We French are used to the fact that you English will always pull the ace of trumps out of your coat sleeve, but what we can't get used to or accept is that you always say that God put it there."

he called a "catastrophic" mistake, saying I had been treated unfairly. At his request, I sent him a draft of a letter I was writing to the editor about these serious "distortions." Next, I spoke to the Washington bureau chief, who agreed that either my original letter or another mildly toned-down version of it that we compromised on would be printed. But this didn't happen. Instead, I received a letter from *Spiegel*'s lawyer, Fried von Bismarck, who claimed that the editors had already acknowledged that the "chain of admittedly unhappy circumstances" had led to the alterations; rather than print my letter, *Spiegel* would print a correction of their own, concerning the last line.

By this time I happened to be in Europe, and Marion Dönhoff, outraged on my behalf, urged me to consult a lawyer myself and recommended *Die Zeit*'s law firm, Senfft, Kersten and Schwenn. (German newspapers, I learned later, had a penchant for blackening one another's names; I think Marion rather relished the likely fight.) In the meantime, I learned from a *Spiegel* editor that the Hamburg editor responsible for the interview had been guilty of similar slanting in an earlier situation. Things now seriously heated up. Heinrich Senfft was not only a prominent, trial-happy lawyer but a radical critic of FRG conformity. He informed Fried von Bismarck that I had given him, Senfft, power of attorney, that *Der Spiegel* had a contract with me that had not been fulfilled, and that he, Senfft, wanted to know in three (!) days whether to start judicial proceedings.

By now Senfft was far more exercised than I, and reported that this threat to *Spiegel* had "produced a Chernobyl panic" in its editorial offices and that Bismarck had told him that he had neither written nor approved the letter he had sent me but merely, under pressure, had signed it. Ever a Bismarck—a great-nephew of the chancellor—he asked Senfft if the matter couldn't be handled "through money." Senfft responded indignantly. We realized that for *Spiegel* the matter was critical: if their modus operandi in this case became known, they would have great difficulty obtaining other interviews. By now, I was on holiday in Sils Maria. Senfft warned me that Rudolf Augstein, fabled founder and editor of the magazine, would telephone me; he feared that Augstein would use his legendary charm and exploit "my so agreeable courtesy" to dupe me. I was forewarned. Augstein did call, and began by saying, "Herr Stern, you don't know how much I admire you." I instantly returned the compliment, adding that mutual admiration had nothing to do with the matter. Augstein acknowledged that *Spiegel* was in the wrong, that a court trial between the magazine and me was "unthinkable," that the whole affair was after all much worse for them than for me. We reached no agreement, and the matter then reverted to the redoubtable Senfft. On June 12, he got them to promise to print my original letter and to be responsible for thirty thousand deutsche marks for expenses incurred—the entire sum correctly went to his firm, and I felt vindicated! On June 23, *Spiegel* published my original letter, detailing at length all the omissions and distortions of the original interview. The whole episode had lasted two months, a tiresome and richly rewarding affair by turns. Some of the German antics were amusing; all were instructive. To best *Spiegel* was wondrous. To learn how to deal with interviewers has been of lasting benefit.

AT THE TIME OF THE *HISTORIKERSTREIT*, I was invited to undertake several other projects. (As Isaiah Berlin said about himself, I am like a taxi, I have to be hailed.) I had accepted to give the main lecture in October 1986 on the seventy-fifth anniversary of the Kaiser Wilhelm Institute for Physical Chemistry (after World War II renamed the Fritz-Haber-Institut). The life of my godfather Haber was the prescribed subject, which demanded extensive archival research, but it was also a festive celebration that unexpectedly embroiled me in an immediate political storm. Hours before the very formal occasion, I was handed a polemical brochure that members of the institute had composed, attacking the institute's involvement in military-industrial enterprises and identifying Haber as the worst offender, inventor in 1915 of the gas that was used by the Germans as a military weapon on the western front. My prepared text acknowledged the horror of gas warfare and mentioned that the great pacifist Einstein had deepened his friendship with Haber after the war, but then I interpolated some further warnings against polemics that ignored all historical context. Afterward, I was struck that most of his life Haber had suffered abuse and worse from right-wing chauvinists—and now, posthumously, he was being denounced by self-righteous left-wing pacifists.* Haber's two children from his second marriage were in the audience: a public occasion with a private undertone.

My new public role in the Federal Republic grew. In February 1986, Horst Ehmke, vice chair of the Social Democratic Party in the Bundestag, inquired if I would be willing to give the annual Bundestag speech on June 17. The Adenauer government had established June 17 as West Germany's sole national holiday, honoring the uprising in East Berlin on that day in 1953, which had

---

*In 2005, a new flurry of attention to Haber occurred in New York. Sensationalist American media reports made him the inventor of Zyklon-B, ignoring everything else about him. A mediocre book, hyped by publicity from the publisher, started off this caricature, which seeped into plays, television, movies, and even into publications of New York's fine guardian of German Jewish history, the Leo Baeck Institute.

been crushed by Soviet tanks. This "Day of National Unity" was marked by solemn ceremonies in the Bundestag, often used to vent anticommunist slogans and conjure up visions of unity. For most West Germans, June 17 was just a spring holiday, the original purpose all but forgotten.

Why me as a speaker? Why me as the first foreigner to speak at this symbolic, nationally televised event? I was flattered, of course, but puzzled and apprehensive as well. I consulted friends. Worried about the inappropriateness of an American speaking on such an occasion, I also asked some of the European experts at the State Department, who for no memorable reason strongly warned against it. Henry Kissinger thought it would be entirely appropriate and useful, on the other hand; at some point in the future, he said, the United States would have no reason to oppose German unification, and the State Department's opposition merely reflected a fear that I might say something unkind about a communist regime with which we had to cooperate (typical Kissinger on State Department bureaucracy!). German colleagues and friends encouraged me; Marion Dönhoff, skeptical at first, argued in favor. And so I accepted—only to discover that the invitation had been premature! Custom decreed that the major parties take turns in inviting a speaker, and that year the CDU was pushing for a candidate from the FDP, its coalition partner, whose choice, ex-president Walter Scheel, indeed became the speaker for 1986.

Scheel's eloquent speech reflected liberal premise and realistic politics: Germans no longer expected reunification anytime soon, he said, but it would come within the framework of a new peaceful European order, with open borders and respect for human rights. At such a point, would one expect that the GDR and the East European countries would "kindly adopt our value system and abandon theirs? That only they would change their system, and we wouldn't even have to think about ours?" (He couldn't have dreamed that that's exactly what would happen five years later!) Scheel was strong in his demand for a new peaceful order and a new solidarity, all the more imperative after the disaster at Chernobyl in April of that year, when a nuclear reactor in that Ukrainian town's nuclear power plant exploded in flames, killing dozens of people and irradiating possibly hundreds of thousands more; this tragedy had brought home humanity's collective jeopardy.

In the summer, Ehmke wrote to me again, saying that the invitation to me had now been decided upon without controversy. Ironic, he thought, that Scheel's speech had appalled the CDU's right wing. Philip Jenninger, CDU president of the Bundestag, now extended a formal invitation for 1987, which, worriedly and disregarding other deadlines, I accepted.

I had my usual dilemma: to prepare a major speech in German while attending to full-time teaching and various other commitments. But two things I knew: June 17, 1953, should be celebrated as a German revolt for *freedom*, and Germans should honor the uprising and its victims. I wanted to reach the citizens of the GDR as well; I knew that subtle shifts between the two entities were taking place, that contacts between the two Germanys were multiplying, as was the aid, open and veiled, that the West was extending to the east, which was notably in decline. One remarkable form of aid was the Federal Republic's policy of buying the freedom of political prisoners in the GDR; the price per individual varied, though by now it was hovering at around DM 96,000. All in all, the total amount of voluntary ransom paid by the West German government amounted to close to DM 3.5 billion for nearly 38,000 GDR prisoners — an impressive, and depressing, amount.

I read earlier speeches given by various public figures on June 17 and noticed that, before Scheel, the custom had been to denounce what Reagan called "the evil empire" and cast doubt on détente. But I thought that this kind of tough talk did nothing to improve the lives of East Germans, most of whom didn't need to be told about an "evil empire"; those who did would dismiss such talk as "imperialist" propaganda. (The official GDR line was that the uprising in 1953 had been the work of imperialist agents and West German "wreckers.")

Early on in my preparation, I stumbled across the fact that Ferdinand Freiligrath, a once-celebrated German poet whose sympathy for radical causes and for the proletariat forced him into many years of exile, had been born on June 17, 1810. I pounced on this, knowing that Freiligrath's name would be instantly recognized in West Germany, while his "class" poetry was still read in East Germany. He could serve as a key witness to my argument that June 17 should be understood as part of a recurrent German fight for freedom. With great pleasure I lost myself in his life and milieu, in a partly unconscious escape from the difficult, less tractable issues of current German politics. By June, I had a text, which Felix Gilbert read, and to which Ralf Dahrendorf, who happened to be in New York that spring, gave a superb final edit.

And so I flew off to Bonn, anxious and uncertain. I was deposited in a hotel, where a bouquet from Hans-Jochen Vogel awaited me in my room, and then I was taken to the Wassermühle (Watermill), the temporary but resplendent home of the Bundestag. That evening I spent with Carl Duisberg, a career diplomat then attached to the chancellor's office, and his wife, a congenial couple whom I had met earlier. I discovered that Duisberg was the grandson of a chemist-industrialist with whom Fritz Haber had had close if ambiguous relations. The Duisbergs gave me what I most needed: a quiet rest, sympathetic, supportive, and undemanding company, and Frau Duisberg served an exquisite *Mohnkuchen* (poppy seed cake), the only Silesian specialty I missed.

The next day, Jenninger led me into the legislative chamber, where Bundestag deputies sat across from the speaker's podium and the government bench; Kohl, together with Foreign Minister Hans-Dietrich Genscher and most of the Cabinet members were present, as were most members of the upper house, the Bundesrat. To the right sat deputies of the CDU and the FDP, to the left those of the SPD. (In the January 1987 election, the CDU had lost seats and now held 223; the FDP had gained and now counted 46 seats, while the Social Democrats had 186. Spectacular gains had been made by the Greens, now counting 46 deputies, all of whom were absent, having earlier decided that the June 17 ceremony was an event hijacked for nationalist-conservative purposes.) The session opened with the formal announcement that President Weizsäcker had taken his seat in the visitors' gallery.

Of course I was nervous. I am nervous before any public lecture, and in this instance I think I was in a daze, half listening to Jenninger as he proclaimed that June 17, 1953, had marked a revolt for unification. My mind wandered. I remembered my son's parting words: "How would your parents have felt about this occasion?" But then, as in most instances, once one starts to speak, there's no time for feelings; the mind fastens on the text, the eyes occasionally focus on the audience. Yet I was so intent on my text that I didn't reach out to the audience as one usually does on more informal occasions. The audience, of course, was right in front of me, and perhaps I cast an occasional glance at the government bench. But in writing the speech I had several other audiences in mind, especially the listeners in the GDR, where most people could receive West German TV.

From the start, I defined this day of commemoration as one honoring a major instance of the German struggle for freedom. The memory of its many victims "should neither be forgotten nor misused." I alluded to my own experiences and to my wonderment, having been driven out of Breslau as a boy, at speaking to this house: "I had many dreams and hopes, but I doubt that it would have occurred to me that I would one day address a German parliament . . . It is one of the towering achievements of the Federal Republic . . . that today for the first time in German history it is generally accepted . . . that a freely elected parliament is an indispensable component of a free polity . . . In your invitation and in my presence there remains much that is unexpressed;

it cannot be otherwise." I thought of the alterations in them and in me that had been prerequisites for this occasion.

Some points I made unambiguously clear, others perhaps by suggestive indirection. "In German history there has rarely been an unproblematic national holiday," I said (this is still true today), and I quoted the SPD leader Herbert Wehner, who in July 1953, during the debate establishing the holiday, had said, "I found it deeply stirring that over and over again one cry arose: We are *workers* and *not slaves*." To which I immediately added, "Perhaps some of you are mindful that the people of the German Democratic Republic have had a much harder life than their more fortunate compatriots." *Perhaps* — more hope than certainty on my part.

The demand for justice and for popular sovereignty was inextinguishable, I claimed. "The uprising of that day must take its place in German history as one of those great moments in which people resisted violence and inhumanity. This uprising pointed to the future, even if many of the interpretations offered immediately after the event were misleading. It was not an uprising for reunification."

I also recalled "the cruel acts" committed "by Germans and upon Germans" in the epoch of the two world wars. I referred to President Weizsäcker's speech of the year before, on May 8, which "virtually everyone abroad received . . . with admiration and gratitude. Many of us hoped that his was the authentic voice of the Federal Republic, perhaps even of the silent suprastate nation. It would be presumptuous on this day to do more than express thanks, also from someone who lost close relatives at Auschwitz." At this point, there was an interruption of applause, which surprised me. Did I suddenly, fleetingly realize that this wasn't a ceremonial but a political talk? Further applause added to the drama. My reference to Weizsäcker had a subtext: people *abroad* had hoped that he had spoken for the FRG, but had he? And my formulation of two states but one nation was, I think, an unusual recognition of a disputed reality.

At another point, I alluded to the obvious "division of Germany," and I went on to say, "I come from a Germany that no longer exists and that will never exist again." My family had escaped from Breslau at the beginning of unimaginable forced resettlements — of Germans evicted in the east, and of Poles similarly displaced to the west to live in formerly German territories. In an effort to put pain in context, I added, perhaps too abruptly, "An undivided Germany brought unspeakable misfortune to other peoples and to itself." I cited earlier German historians who had made analogous judgments. I thought it was important to recognize German suffering as well as that of other peoples, and I regarded the reference to German responsibility as obvious shorthand. I insisted that the June 17 revolt, crushed by Soviet tanks, had not been a failure: the East German uprising should be put in universal, not only national, terms, and seen as a harbinger of later uprisings in other communist countries—just as there had been successful revolts for freedom and against dictatorships in Spain, Portugal, and Greece—triumphs of democracy in which the Federal Republic had been subtly helpful. For all our sense of crisis, we must realize "that more of Europe today lives in freedom than has been true before—and freedom is wonderfully seductive!"

In the "other German state," I went on to say, there are those "who, quietly, keep alive the meaning of June 17. They deserve our respect . . . [W]e should honor the clear, courageous voices from the other German state that demand human dignity and human rights. These voices often come from the Church, a Church for which the teachings and the example of Dietrich Bonhoeffer are still very much alive," a reminder "of the victims of another never-to-be-forgotten moment of German resistance."

A self-indulgently large part of my talk dealt with Freiligrath, a poet remembered more widely for his democratic-emancipatory commitment than for outstanding literary gifts. A passionate voice for the downtrodden and oppressed, Freiligrath in 1851 had to flee into exile, where he encountered Karl Marx and Heinrich Heine, and with whom he had short, quarrelsome friendships. I cited Freiligrath because he exemplified the historic fact of a common European life and culture, which made it easier for him and for others like him to spend decades in exile. In exile, as Heine understood, burns the passion of true patriotism, the longing for a home that would be free of repression and censorship. Not many in my immediate or distant audience would have been familiar with these thoughts or experiences, and some might also have felt uneasy about my frequent invocations of Heine.

Freiligrath was meant as a felicitous frame: I wanted to give June 17 its historic pedigree; it was not merely a courageous revolt against immiseration, but a heroic moment in the continuous pursuit of freedom. The liberal or radical hopes of 1848 that had animated Freiligrath had been crushed, and when German unity finally was achieved, it came under very different auspices. Germans were dealing with "a past that grows more remote, but does not fade away and shouldn't fade away"—my reference to the rhetoric of the *Historikerstreit*. The world, I reminded them, viewed the Germans' presentation of their past "as a kind of seismograph for German consciousness generally."

I spoke briefly about relations between the two Germanys, though it was not for a foreigner to judge an ongoing process of seeking greater commonality, greater closeness. "The FRG should never forget that history has sentenced it to be a model of a liberal polity: in order to preserve itself, to honor the victims of the past, and to give hope to people in the other Germany." It should do all it can "to lighten the load of those others, to defend and strengthen human rights." In the last forty years respect for German achievements in culture and science had been restored, and yet worries about West Germany's sense of political responsibility remained. I reminded West Germans of the earlier commonality of Europe and also of their responsibility for the other Germany, so near geographically, so far, I feared, psychologically.

Throughout, I suppose, the subtext was a question: when you Germans dream of reunification, are you thinking primarily of unity or of freedom, of a Germany without a wall dividing the country or of the actual liberation of all your citizens? In German history, unity and freedom often appeared as joint goals, but at the critical moment, the former took precedence over the latter. I wanted to reassure East Germans that their muffled voices pleading for freedom were heard, that they too belonged to Europe, and I hoped that West Germans would use their material leverage to afford those East Germans greater freedom to travel, to improve their lives as much as possible.

I suspected that West Germans might be tempted to rethink basic tenets of world politics: "An enticing wind from the East comes at a time of disillusionment with the West"—I had in mind Eastern blandishments, on the one hand, and unease about the United States, on the other. I ended by insisting that Germans had to retain their ties to the West and had to remember the "common political culture of the West, where values of a free and pluralistic society are anchored constitutionally." After all it was in the West that the hopes of the young Marx for an emancipatory, humane society were most likely to be realized—I had the GDR audience in mind here.

The immediate response of the Bundestag audience was amazing to me: the official protocol of the session records thirteen interruptions for applause and, at the end, "prolonged applause" in which, the press noted, Chancellor Kohl joined, contrary to custom. I don't remember whether at the time I was aware that at some points the interruptions seemed more enthusiastic on the left, more hesitant on the right; a retrospective view of the TV film made me realize the occasional unevenness. But the interruptions gave the occasion the atmosphere of a political speech, somewhat disguised in poetic drapery.

We all then stood to sing the national anthem, that is, the third verse of "Deutschland, Deutschland über Alles," a paean to peace, freedom, and justice. I was filled with contending, fleeting emotions: this was the hymn I had learned to abhor, and I had never thought that I would freely join in singing it, that Haydn's stirring music, originally composed for Austria and so malignly misused for Germany, could be heard as a song of pride and peace.

Afterward, at a reception given by Jenninger, I felt at first depleted and then in something of a daze from all the enthusiasm and the stir around me. It was a very political atmosphere, with members of all parties shaking hands and muttering kind words. I remember Bernhard Vogel's smile and handshake, his friendly appreciation modified by the remark "A little too much Freiligrath." (I knew he was right.) Jenninger led me to a corner table to talk with Kohl and Weizsäcker, both of whom were complimentary. (There was an unarticulated distance between the garrulous Rhinelander and the reserved Swabian, with Kohl dominating the conversation and carrying on about his children in American universities. Such different men!) Weizsäcker said, "You didn't make it easy for your audience," which at the time I took to be praise, but perhaps it was splendidly ambiguous! And when it was all over, my friend Hermann Hatzfeldt, Marion's nephew, who had come to Bonn to hear the speech, drove me back to his historic castle at Crottorf, where I could unwind with friends. The extraordinary day ended with Hermann and me watching excerpts of the speech on the evening news, quietly celebrating with rare wine.

The next morning was a different world: West Germany's conservative newspapers reported on the "appalling mistakes" in a Bundestag speech given, as most of them noted, by an American historian and Jewish refugee. "In his much-noted speech the 61-year-old Jew, who in 1938 had fled from Breslau with his parents, also spoke about the political development of the FRG," one said. The front-page headline of Die Welt was "Stern's Speech Encounters Criticism." "Jenninger corrects his assertion that the uprising was not for reunification." (Well, Jenninger had spoken first, so he couldn't have "corrected" me.)

It was merely two of my sentences that had caused the storm: the one in which I said that the 1953 uprising had been for a better, freer life, not for reunification; and the one about an undivided Germany having brought suffering to Germans and the world. Die Welt's editorial insisted that for a long time now most people had understood that the East German protests against exacting working conditions were quickly followed by calls for "freedom, democracy and reunification." The Frankfurter Allgemeine Zeitung was outraged: a front-page report and commentary thought it "scandalous" that this year's Bundestag speaker, an (unnamed) American, had tried "almost desperately to distract people from the theme of reunification." It focused on my criticisms of the

German past and said not a word about my emphasizing the German struggle
for freedom, my assertion that the Federal Republic was the most successful
polity in German history, or my tribute to the East Germans who were quietly
preserving the spirit of the revolt. The charge was that I had "judged Bismarck's
unification entirely negatively," indeed that I had an altogether negative view
of the German past and present. But the *FAZ*'s own voice was almost restrained
compared with the readers' letters that appeared over the next month.

One of the first referred to my alleged "not for reunification" theme, saying
that "it is wrong and documents in stupefying fashion his historical ignorance
and simultaneously his anti-German manipulative designs." Others suggested
a motive for the uproar: my (insufficiently nationalist?) statements obviously
reflected the views of the party that had invited me. Evidently, I was a convenient intermediate target in a bitter attack on the SPD. One writer, referring to
Kohl's having joined in the applause, charged that this showed that the FRG
remained "an [American] satellite." A deputy from the North-Rhine West-
phalian Parliament, angry at what I had said about the dangers of an "undivided Germany," insisted that a reunified Germany in a peaceful European
order would be "a blessing" for all Europe, especially impoverished Eastern
Europe and the USSR—"the exact opposite of what Fritz Stern as German-
Jewish expellee expects."

The public debate continued. A left-liberal paper (*Frankfurter Rundschau*)
reprinted my speech with a subhead: "The Jewish historian F.S. pleads for a
commemoration in present-day perspective." A brief introductory note identified me as an "American professor of history" whose speech had provoked critical comment "in conservative circles." Correct! But why the characterization
as "Jewish"? I found it peculiar, my first reaction being that they had used the
term unthinkingly, as a way of identifying an American with a special background, or as a hint as to why conservatives had a special reason to be critical?
Or was it a matter of pride: to boast that the Bundestag had invited so strange,
so burdened, yet so familiar a person to speak? It was puzzling to have this
come from a friendly party: I doubt that the *Rundschau* thought that my Jewishness determined my views, which in any case the paper itself didn't object
to. Perhaps this all suggested how unassimilable the question of Jewishness remained. On the other hand, at lunch the next day, Count Lambsdorff mentioned to me that Genscher had asked him if any other country would have
invited a foreigner to speak at its national holiday. Genscher was right to ask.
The Germans were unique, with a unique past, and some of them resented

that this unique past was so often presented by foreigners with an uncomfortable claim to intimacy.

The mostly accusatory debate in the *FAZ* letters column continued, and on July 13, a Bundestag member protested that the newspaper had reduced the speaker to "an unperson" by withholding his name while regularly referring to the "scandalous" content of his speech: "I have rarely seen [except in the radical right-wing papers] a Jew of German origin be so unqualifiedly put down [*abgemeiert*]." The writer had heard almost all the June 17 speeches in the last decade, and "none has so deeply impressed as Fritz Stern's." Still, the negative letters continued—and soon a book about the *Historikerstreit* repeated their allegations, calling my comments about the revolt in "Mitteldeutschland" (a right-wing code word for the GDR, signaling a claim on further German territories *east* of it) historical falsification, and identifying me twice as someone from Columbia, "the seat of exile for the Frankfurt School." Guilt (or undeserved praise) by association? Kind souls sent me a flier from a Marburg student fraternity with a banner headline, "Germany Is Greater than the FRG"; it claimed that the high point of historical distortion about June 17 had come with my speech, and lamented that no member of Parliament had walked out in protest against this "defamation." Right after the speech, Herbert Hupka, CDU head of the right-wing revisionist League of Silesian Expellees, invited me to their forthcoming annual meeting. It was an ambiguous gesture: was I invited to be celebrated as an ex-Silesian or to be vilified as traitor? I declined.

The immediate comment of the liberal-centrist *Süddeutsche Zeitung* was that the speech "offered Germans unpleasant truths," and that the "not for reunification" sentence causing discomfort showed "that this view, known for so long, still hasn't penetrated the minds of all CDU politicians." The clearest support came from Theo Sommer on the front page of *Die Zeit*; he thought the attacks on my speech suggested that West Germans were "becoming neurotic," and reminded readers that the Berlin workers had demanded that Ulbricht go, not that Adenauer come: "Why rob the revolt of its dignity? It was a beacon for freedom, not for German unity."

There were many private commendations. A friend and colleague wrote on the same day, praising a "liberal, decisive speech which the whole House applauded, if not on all sides equally long or powerful. That not nation and unity, but freedom, democracy, the West and human rights constituted the fundament—that was the political message." Exactly my intention. Others welcomed the speech as putting paid to "the legends" about the origin of June 17.

My memory today is that the sixty-one-year-old Jew was taken aback by the distortions, these belated salvos from the *Historikerstreit*. I was concerned that I had done my friends and the SPD a disservice, yet the authoritative rebuttals to the criticism reassured me. Hans-Jochen Vogel wrote me an all-too-complimentary letter, and none of my CDU friends seemed the least troubled about the controversy. What seemed to stick in peoples' minds was not the controversy but the fact that I had been the only foreigner to address the Bundestag on June 17.

The speech eventually appeared, in translation, in *The New York Review of Books*, with an introduction by Timothy Garton Ash, from whose subtle and unexcelled knowledge of life and dissent in Eastern Europe I had learned much. He agreed with my placing the events of 1953 in line with earlier German demands for freedom and as the first in a line of revolts in Eastern Europe. He said of the judgments expressed in my two controversial sentences, "Both . . . might rationally be questioned . . . Nonetheless, these rational objections hardly explain the vehemence and—one is bound to say—the venom of some of the reactions to Professor Stern's remarks." I think I had wanted to impress on the West Germans that freedom was the highest good and the protection of human rights their special responsibility. I should have pushed my thoughts further; the East German call for free elections in 1953 would almost certainly have ended Stalinist rule, culminating in some form of unification.

In retrospect I must confess I am astonished that in writing the speech, I didn't myself stumble over these two sentences. My main concern probably was not to allow conservative Germans to appropriate the heroism of the workers or of GDR citizens—as if all they wanted was reunification. It was reassuring to read Gordon Craig, the American scholar with the most balanced view of German history, cite my controversial remarks, noting they caused "a storm of protest, although these things were indubitably true, or perhaps *because* they were true and the politicians did not want to be told the truth by a historian qualified to report it."

The "patriotic" anger still erupts with astounding regularity and ferocity. A single instance: In 2002, Henning Köhler's hefty history of Germany since 1890 was published, in which he attacked the left-liberal followers of Habermas in the *Historikerstreit*, claiming that they had emphasized the singularity of Auschwitz in order to legitimize the permanent division of Germany, seeing it as just penalty for past sins. In that connection he adjudged my interpretation of the June 17 uprising "a remarkable failure of judgment for a historian," showing a tendency to reinterpret history and "altogether deny the will to unity." He mocked Weizsäcker's speech of May 8 and elevated me, along with the well-known writer Sebastian Haffner, to the status of "unification-deniers" (*Einheitsleugner*) in the Federal Republic.

I had every reason to be grateful for the invitation to the Bundestag: it had been an instructive and moving occasion, and the continuous attacks were instructive as well. It was a revelation to hear the rather wretched tone of German debate at first hand, to get a whiff of the *ressentiments* and latent concerns about ex–German Jews. There is an old German proverb, *"Viel Feinde, viel Ehre"*: Many enemies, much honor. Well, I was beginning to collect adversaries in Germany.

By the mid-1980s it wasn't only the German question that concerned me. There was also—and once again—an ominous version of the American question: how was the ever-growing international power of the United States affecting the country at home? What of changes in society and polarized views about a domestic agenda, above all changes in our political culture, our spirit, putting our liberal democracy at risk? There was plenty to worry about, and as usual my priorities were clear: one becomes more fully American when insidious dangers threaten the republic.

By 1986, American politics were roiled by the revelations that Reagan's administration had arranged secret arms deliveries to Iran, profits from which went to the right-wing Contras in Nicaragua, who were fighting the liberationist Sandinistas. This Iran-Contra scandal not only involved secret dealings, contravening acts of Congress, but compromised the highest office: men closest to the president were found guilty of lying, of claiming in their defense that patriotism trumped truth and respect for the law. Reagan, rightly dubbed "the Teflon president," reigned on, invulnerable; amiability and simplicity shielded him. In many ways it was a time of respectable recklessness.

It was President Reagan himself who made me switch into an activist mode. During the Republican Convention in New Orleans in August 1988, Reagan pledged "every fiber" of his being to support George H. W. Bush's candidacy on the Republican ticket, so as to defeat the Democrats, who, he charged, were "liberal, liberal, liberal"; he pretended that it took great courage merely to invoke the "dreaded L-word." His speech was the lead story in *The New York Times* of August 15. The minute I saw the paper and read the article, I began scribbling a response—I still have the penciled notes I made on the front page. To have the president lead the presidential campaign for his successor with a charge against liberalism—at a time when "liberals" were already the favored target of neocon intellectuals—struck me as hugely dangerous. My anger made me turn the scribbles into an op-ed piece, which appeared on September 4 in the Sunday *New York Times*. Liberalism—one of "America's noblest traditions," I insisted, often defined as a state of mind—had "transformed the world . . . [I]ts greatest victory has been the American Revolution; its greatest pronouncement, the Declaration of Independence; its greatest bulwark, the Constitution of the United States and the Bill of Rights." It had "stood for freedom against tyranny. At its best . . . a force for change and progress, seeking the institutional defense of decency. At its worst, it has been class-bound or it has entrusted the largeness of its spirit to the narrowness of bureaucratic power." In America's liberal premises the world had seen "the best promise of the West."

I questioned whether Reagan could claim to be a protagonist of conservatism, "that great and complementary tradition that has always insisted on certain principles, among them respect for the sanctity of law, national and international; respect for an independent judiciary, chosen with the utmost scrupulosity, rectitude in speech, and, above all, fiscal responsibility and prudence." Reagan was a popular, even charismatic front for a new right-wing radicalism. My hope was that in the election people would remember that "the best of American public servants have been liberals and conservatives simultaneously or by turns" and that we would build on that heritage "to shape a better future."

Everything I cared about I put into that little article: I had studied the calamity of anti-liberalism in Germany, I had opposed that same spirit among the left in America and Europe in 1968. I knew about the flaws and shallow optimism of some forms of liberalism, having learned from its great critics, from Nietzsche to Lionel Trilling. I wasn't a partisan of a political program, but a believer in the liberal spirit, a voice in defense of a unique historic legacy.

I was pleasantly surprised by the letters I received in response, the great majority in support. On the other hand, Norman Podhoretz published an article to correct "the eminent historian" who didn't know that liberals had themselves to blame for their loss of popularity, since they had capitulated to the radicals of 1968, abandoned their earlier support for containing communism in favor of "a pervasive sympathy with Marxist-Leninist revolutionaries in the Third World," and supported reverse discrimination (that is, affirmative action). This was pathetic, but such distortions went on feeding the antiliberal spirit in America, with dire consequences, and even the neocons may some day rue their attacks.

The response that meant the most to me was an unexpected letter from C. Vann Woodward. To quote from it here is to transmit an eloquent and balanced voice of that time: "Shame on all American historians that they had to wait for a colleague in European history to rise to the defense of their tradition, their country, their credo, their very calling under vile attack from a vulgar re-actionary. My consolation is that none of them could have done it so well . . . In the academy itself it is still the intimidation by the left that inhibits use of the word—not the right. As in the days of the terror, as you say, the threat comes from both sides."

I was overwhelmed, but I quickly wrote to thank him; we corresponded, and I raised the idea of putting an ad in the *Times* "simply on the word 'liberal' and its history and abuse . . . probably without endorsing any candidate."

I went to see Vann in New Haven, a man of unassuming wisdom and hu-manity, of passion modulated by irony, generous and forceful. He had been one of Dick Hofstadter's closest friends, and that made for a special bond between us. We agreed that an ad would be useful, so we prepared a text, reaffirming "America's liberal tradition" and regretting that the president "has taken the lead in vilifying one of our oldest and noblest traditions. We are deeply con-cerned about the erosion and debasement of American values and American traditions that our country has long cherished. In the past and at its best, liber-alism has sought the institutional defense of decency . . . Liberal policies re-quire constant scrutiny and sometimes revision. Liberal principles—freedom, tolerance, and the protection of the rights of every citizen—are timeless."

Our next task was to collect signatures—and money! A full-page ad cost forty-eight thousand dollars. I spent six weeks on these two efforts, having vol-unteered to attend to practical matters. We started with obtaining the signa-tures of the presidents of Harvard, Johns Hopkins, and Pennsylvania (later Donald Kennedy of Stanford joined as well), plus the director of the Institute for Advanced Study in Princeton. Members of the Kennedy administration—Bill and McGeorge Bundy, Robert McNamara, Arthur M. Schlesinger, Jr., and Donna Shalala—signed on, as did well-known names from the academic and public worlds, though we excluded people in or seeking elective office. Some worthies for good reason gave money but not their names; others were sympa-thetic but unhelpful. Richardson Dilworth, a distinguished investment banker, once a member of the Rockefeller Brothers Fund, a philanthropist—and a Re-publican!—agreed to look at what we had to say, and we talked about it. "I agree with every word of your statement, and I won't give you a penny," he said. Why not? "Because it won't do any good. What this country needs is a great ca-tastrophe." My instant response: "Mr. Dilworth, I come from a country that had a great catastrophe. That's why I think it's better to act beforehand." Roughly 15 percent of the signers were people who had come to the United States as refugees from Europe.

Meanwhile, in the presidential campaign, George H. W. Bush kept attacking his opponent, Michael Dukakis, as a liberal—at a time when fewer and fewer Americans defined themselves as such. When I delivered the ad to the *Times* in late October, we had slightly less than the required sum, but our credit was good, and it appeared on October 26, a week before the election. The ad created a stir, was widely reprinted, and on October 30, Dukakis for the first time in the campaign announced, "I'm a liberal in the tradition of Franklin Roosevelt and Harry Truman and John Kennedy." This was pathetically late and feeble.

The White House, we were told, was troubled, and refused comment. "Old cons" as well as neocons were outspokenly angry: on the day before the election, William Buckley fulminated against "40 or 50 worthies, whose political inclinations are merely suggested by naming three of them, John Kenneth Galbraith, George F. Kennan and Arthur M. Schlesinger, Jr., respectively one Socialist, one unilateral disarmament hound and one left-of-center partisan on any issue save any issue in which any Kennedy is right of center." Two days later, Marion Dönhoff's front-page column in *Die Zeit* said, "This has never happened before in America: a whole page in the *New York Times* with a sharp attack on the president, signed by 60 personalities with no immediate connection to the electoral campaign, among them three Nobel laureates . . . Sad, if the chief of the Western world has to be reminded of the fundamental principles of its existence—but thank God there are guardians of these values who are not asleep." If only we had been ready a week sooner! But the effort made clear to me what fired my passion as a citizen. The German past had shaped me; a liberal America had saved me.

THAT THE DENIGRATORS OF LIBERALISM—George H. W. Bush and Dan Quayle—won the 1988 election was a disappointment, to put it mildly, but the resurgence of liberal hopes in Eastern Europe, an unexpected simultaneous development, deflected regret into cautious rejoicing. By February 1989, representatives of an utterly discredited Communist Party in Poland sat down with representatives of Solidarność at what was to become the symbol of the peaceful revolution: a round table. A few months later, Tadeusz Mazowiecki, a dissident intellectual, Catholic patriot, and committed Europeanist, became prime minister, with four Communists in his cabinet. In June, in Budapest, Imre Nagy, the murdered hero of the Hungarian revolt of 1956, was officially reburied as a national hero.

The communist regimes in Poland and Hungary thereafter cautiously re-treated, yielding power in fact and doctrine. Sparks of resistance appeared everywhere, for the revolutionary discontent was contagious and jumped across national borders. Though for a time the communist regimes in Eastern Europe retained the brute force to reclaim power, they had lost legitimacy, even in the eyes of some of their own servants. Soon, on city streets everywhere, more and more people clamored for an end to one-party rule, to the secret po-lice, and to penurious isolation. I kept thinking of Václav Havel's memorable phrase that people wanted to "live within the truth." I knew that they had had enough of squalor and mendacity.

The sheer speed of the radical changes during that amazing year of 1989 was astounding, and one had to worry how it would all end; we remembered the Soviet tanks in Budapest in 1956 and Prague in 1968, and in that very spring came the massacre at Tiananmen Square in China. Would it really be different this time? I hung on every new development with hope and appre-hension. Above all, I wanted to be there, actually to witness what was unfold-ing as a dramatic revolution. It was hard to watch it from afar. Extraordinary events were happening in the places of my childhood; there had been all the wretched occasions when I had been glued to the radio—but this time was dif-ferent; there was the promise of liberation!

Much depended on the Soviet Union, of course, and especially on Mikhail Gorbachev, who represented something radically different in the Kremlin, and whose much-touted vision of a "Common House of Europe" would, I hoped, make him hesitate to order another brutal crackdown.

By May 1989, East Germans were demonstrating their opposition by exit-ing—via Hungary, to which, it being a fellow socialist country, there was easy access and which had opened its borders with Austria. All the socialist coun-tries had agreed to abide by one another's exit rules, so the Hungarian author-ities were obligated to send back East Germans caught trying to make this escape to Austria, but they were reluctant to do so. We now know that they were acting out of humane conscience, and with the Federal Republic's knowledge and tacit support. The flow steadily increased. The East German regime, of course, saw all this as Hungarian treachery.

By the fall of 1989, some thirty thousand East Germans had reached West Germany via other socialist countries; the Wall had lost some of its utility, if none of its ugliness. All this caused alarm in both Germanys: neither had an in-terest in seeing the East German state decline into some kind of dependent old folks' home. Many in the Federal Republic, preferring the comforts of détente to the risks of liberation or revolution, feared for the loss of "stability" in Europe. Yet East Germans were exiting in ever-greater numbers, encouraging those who stayed behind to raise their voices in mounting protest, while GDR loyalists were divided and in disarray. We were witnessing an enactment of what Albert Hirschman has called, in his great analysis, the dialectical relations among "exit, voice, and loyalty."

For months, East German churches had been holding peace vigils—hewing, ironically, to the regime's own line of East Germans being apostles of peace. The Nikolaikirche in Leipzig had started this process, and by the fall, the vigils were being held all over the country, with candlelit processions on the streets of people demonstrating for peace. The processions grew ever larger, and the police repeatedly dispersed them. The demands grew bolder.

In mid-September, encouraged by the Polish examples, some GDR citizens founded a civic organization called Neues Forum, demanding an open dialogue with the SED, with the aim of securing freedom and justice. Admirable new leaders emerged, among them Jens Reich, a molecular biologist, and his wife, a physician. Civic organizations multiplied, and this great awakening found physical expression in large demonstrations everywhere. Soon millions were participating, and the chants became more defiant: the slogan "Wir sind das Volk" (We are the people) implicitly repudiated the party's claim to represent the people, and by November, even more portentously, "Wir sind ein Volk" (We are one people) appeared. The people's grievances were many, and the accumulated anger at the insidious power of the regime's omnipresent secret police was huge, further inflamed by the knowledge that local elections in May had been obvious frauds. Peoples' hopes were for a "better," a truly democratic GDR, and for unification.

Erich Honecker, steeled in Stalinist discipline, was determined to preserve his rigid command system. But the party's younger leaders understood the need for immediate reform—for example, Hans Modrow, the party leader in Dresden, known for his integrity. So the SED was split between hard-liners who viewed the opposition as the work of imperialist agitators to be suppressed by force, and realists who knew that the regime was materially and morally close to bankruptcy.

With great historic irony, the pompous official celebrations of the fortieth anniversary of the GDR and the spontaneous protests coincided: on October 7, 1989, the party staged a gaudy festival while the police used force to suppress massive demonstrations; Gorbachev, in East Berlin for the celebration, privately affirmed that policy decisions affecting the GDR were made in Berlin, not Moscow. For reform-minded East Germans, he was now a hero, but what no one outside the innermost Kremlin circle knew was that he had already insisted in 1986 that the Soviet Union had to respect the diverse experiences of East European nations. "It is impermissible," he had said, "to think that we can teach everyone. No one gave us that right." (Modesty worth remembering!)

On October 9, a huge demonstration was planned in Leipzig, and no one knew whether the demonstrators might be massacred, as in Tiananmen Square only four months earlier; few knew that the party had rushed extra blood supplies to local hospitals in case of trouble. But nearly a hundred thousand perfectly disciplined Germans, determined to shun violence, demonstrated peaceably. The powerful, last-minute intervention of Kurt Masur, conductor of the Leipzig Gewandhaus, enlisting party officials such as Wolfgang Berghofer, mayor of Dresden, helped to prevent police suppression. These younger party men, wishing to maintain a socialist system cleansed of corruption of men and nature (the country had become the world's second worst ecological disaster area), were strong enough to intervene and prevent bloodshed locally, but they were too far from central power to salvage the state.

A week later, the Politburo ousted Erich Honecker himself, who had lasted as chief of party and state for sixteen years, replacing him with the lackluster Egon Krenz, a less doctrinaire functionary mouthing vague notions of reform. The party threw their hard-line functionaries overboard—and made concessions, but it was too little and too late. The pace was being set in the street: millions of East Germans, alternately emboldened and enraged, went on marching in peaceful demonstrations, while thousands fled to the West.

West Germans watched this unexpected turmoil on the other side of the Wall with apprehension, worried lest somehow their own normal lives might be perturbed. So many West Germans had come to settle for the allegedly temporary division of Germany and were content to see the lot of the Easterners improve, if possible. But would the influx of GDR refugees continue to grow? How would the FRG cope with onrushing change? For me, looking at it from New York, the burning question was whether communism could really be toppled, freedom attained, and the prisons emptied—all without bloodshed. In those tense, passionate weeks in the fall of 1989, I hung on newscasts, completely caught up in the drama. As the unprecedented became routine, it seemed as if political miracles would never cease.

Luck forced me to try to put this drama into historical perspective. In late October, I had to prepare a speech for a Columbia ceremony on November 1, and as a title I had chosen "The Common House of Europe: An American Perspective." At a time of cautious, uncertain jubilation, I wanted to suggest the connections among seemingly separate processes that were all pointing to a new Europe, and I began in cheerful provocation: "Since the unread Hegel is popular these days"—I was thinking of Francis Fukuyama's essay "The End of History"—"I use his terminology to say that the 'world spirit' has once again found a temporary home in Europe." East Germans were challenging their regime: "not since 1848 have Germans appeared on the stage of history so spontaneously, so daringly, and—to all appearances—so successfully." I wanted people to appreciate the enormity of what was happening. These Germans "were the ones who paid for the lost war, paid for it by deprivation and repression, by unrelieved drabness; they suffered while their rich cousins in the other Germany prospered." This was my blinkered view, my first summary judgment of the citizens of the GDR, undifferentiated, infused with sympathy for the underdog. I spoke as if these protesters represented most of the people, almost as if they could redeem the well-practiced conformity of earlier decades. I also warned that West Germans might not be too eager to share their prosperity with their long-lost cousins.

Meanwhile, Western Europe also stirred with a new vitality. The historic changes occurring in the East were coinciding with a new vitality in the West, as evident in the project for a reformed European Community, a region with open frontiers without border guards. These paradoxically congruous developments—nationalist affirmation in the East, supranationalism in the West—had their exemplary figures as gigantic upheavals always do: the Polish Pope, Gorbachev, and, to a lesser degree, Jacques Delors, president of the European Commission. Gorbachev's ambiguous term *Common House of Europe* carried a subliminal and mischievous message: implicitly it excluded the United States, as the old term, *the West*, had not. Indeed, Gorbachev explicitly warned about "the threat [that] emanates from an onslaught of 'mass culture' from across the Atlantic." I was full of hope, perhaps in some sense even proud of Europe's recovery, but I ended in cautious defiance: "For the moment, the one thing that it seems safe to say is that there is no common house of Europe, and that we are a part of it."

My friend the English historian David Cannadine, who was in the audience, unbeknownst to me told Robert Silvers at *The New York Review of Books* about my lecture. Silvers decided to publish it, and gave me a deadline of November 9 to complete the text for publication. I spent that day making final revisions. As dusk fell, the phone rang. It was a local television station calling: "The Berlin Wall has fallen," the reporter said. I was transfixed, feeling a mix of incredulity, apprehension, and elation. I knew that this world-transforming event—for once a benevolent surprise—marked a historic caesura. Germany was back on the global agenda. It wasn't clear what would happen next, but for the moment East Germans were dancing on the wall and the death strip to freedom had been cleared. The spontaneous joy on both sides of the Berlin Wall made me think of the last act of *Fidelio*, of prisoners let out of their cells, but this was an unparalleled, irreversible opening to freedom.

The Berlin Wall had been breached inadvertently, after a GDR minister had given a befuddled version of plans for less restrictive travel policies for East German citizens. But seeming accidents have the power to shape history: the thousands of East Berliners who streamed across the border that night gave accident its historic meaning. Willy Brandt found the perfect words for the occasion, "what belongs together, comes together."

Almost at once, in wonderment, I realized that this amazing excitement was occurring on November 9—the date with the heaviest historic legacy in Germany—when, in 1918, millions of Germans had taken to the streets clamoring for an end to the war and demanding a more egalitarian future, when the Kaiser had fled, when the old regime had collapsed in bankruptcy and a republic was proclaimed; when, in 1923, Hitler had staged his attempted coup d'état in Munich, whose failure he had turned at once into his first great publicity stunt (in the Third Reich, November 9 was a holiday, commemorating the Nazis who had been killed in that abortive Putsch, an annual party-pagan rite of martyrdom); and when, in 1938, the Nazis had organized *Kristallnacht*, unleashing their sadistic fury against Jews while most Germans went about their business. What a trick of fate to have the only successful, peaceful revolution in German history fall on that unforgiving day!

November 9 was also the date of my father's death. History had been so hard on his generation, but perhaps this November 9 marked the end of the era that had begun with its unparalleled violence in 1914; now a peaceful revolution was perhaps ushering in a new time. In fleeting euphoria, I thought that my grandchildren would live in a better world. I was at my most unhistoric— and yet I still believe that 1989 was the brightest moment in Europe's darkest century.

CHAPTER 10

UNIFIED GERMANY:
A SECOND CHANCE?

THE *ANNUS MIRABILIS* OF 1989 ended on triumphant notes: soon after the Berlin Wall was breached, the Czech dissident-playwright Václav Havel, having returned to Prague from house arrest in rural Bohemia, helped to found a new club, Civic Forum, and within days his group called for the end of the communist regime in Czechoslovakia. Havel, who had written about the power of the powerless and the yearning of people "to live in the truth," became his people's hero, and by December, the Prague Parliament, cowed, elected him president of the republic — a worthy successor to Thomas Masaryk, the philosopher-historian who had been its first president. The Prague of my childhood liberated — and by so magical and humane a leader!

Almost simultaneously, in East Berlin the East German Parliament abrogated the constitutional provision that gave the Socialist Workers' Party the leading role in the state. And on Christmas Day, in the shadow of the dismantled wall, Leonard Bernstein conducted the Berlin Philharmonic together with East German musicians in Beethoven's Ninth Symphony with its "Ode to Joy": what better way to celebrate Germany's first successful revolution?

But jubilant high drama couldn't resolve the staggering problems the two Germanys confronted. What would happen to them — and to a European order that for half a century had been built on the division of Germany? How would the two states constitute their new relations? And what would happen to the GDR and its communist regime, wounded, tainted, but still in power? We in the West had been fed the fable that the GDR was the eighth or tenth largest industrial economy of the world, not realizing how much it was being propped up by ever-increasing subsidies from the West. In fact, East Germany was in terminal bankruptcy, and its citizens sensed it, so they continued their trek westward; more than a thousand a day crossed the now open border. At first they were welcomed with open arms and material help.

In late November, I was supposed to give various lectures in the Federal Republic, and there I felt firsthand people's excitement and confused uncertainty. I was shocked when I first heard some West Germans mumble mournfully about their past decades, "Thank God for the Wall." Life had been simpler before, when one hadn't had to face directly the human problems of the GDR, when heartfelt laments about long-lost brothers and sisters sufficed, along with an occasional Christmas package. I had one particular concern about this that I presented to a Munich audience: given the huge imbalance between the two German states and the evident dependency of one on the other, I worried lest West German tutelage would relegate East Germans to renewed nonage. The latter's experiences and hopes should count as well, I argued. The new order, whatever it might be, should not consist only of West German models or commands. Reciprocal give-and-take made practical, but above all moral and psychological, sense.

At the end of November, I had my first chance in those heady days to talk again with Otto Reinhold and Rolf Reissig, respectively rector and (much younger) deputy rector of the Academy of Social Sciences of the SED's Central Committee (in fact, the party's think tank), whom I had known for some years. Representatives of the opposition and Werner Krusche, a leading figure of the Protestant Church in East Germany, were also present. (This was at an Aspen meeting in Berlin.) The discussions replicated the drama of the GDR in miniature: at formal sessions, Reinhold and Reissig seemed in essential agreement—to have a "roundtable" between party and opposition, with the former surrendering its claim to sole leadership, accepting democratic electoral and media laws, and allowing for the introduction of some market-economy features—but privately Reissig, who was that rare breed a socialist realist, spoke to me of the need for more radical reforms and asked me to see him in East Berlin to discuss these possibilities. (I didn't yet know that in early November he and a few of his colleagues in the academy had actually argued for the dismantlement of the Wall. And regretfully I didn't have time to accept his invitation.) Only a few weeks later, the academy's staff demanded Reinhold's resignation, and Reissig became his successor. (Eventually all the institutes of the East German Academy of Sciences were closed, and Reissig founded his own institute.)

A bombshell landed in the middle of our sessions: on November 28, Chancellor Kohl surprised the Bundestag by presenting a ten-point program designed to lead gradually to Germany's reunification within a new "peace order." (We now know that Nikolai Portugalov, my one-time sparring partner and German expert on the Soviet Union's Central Committee, a week earlier had told Kohl's principal aide, Horst Teltschik, that the USSR—while still hoping that the GDR could be saved by Gorbachev-type reforms—was certainly opposed to *rapid* unification; Kohl thought his plan for *gradual* unification might therefore be more acceptable.) Kohl recommended further easing of travel regulations between the two Germanys, and he promised additional economic aid to the East on the condition that fundamental, irreversible changes in the GDR's political and economic system were adopted: "We do not want to stabilize conditions that have become untenable." Free elections in the East would lead to new forms of cooperation, to confederate institutions and eventually could lead to one parliament. All of this would have to be embedded in all-European agreements and security considerations. Ultimately one state would emerge, he said, but no one "knows today what a reunited Germany will ultimately look like." Vague as Kohl's ten points were, they clearly and for the first time acknowledged that the ultimate aim was the nation's unification. Kohl himself thought it would take at least a decade.

His pronouncement electrified the world, the more so as he had prepared his program in absolute secrecy, not even informing Foreign Minister Genscher beforehand. Nor did Kohl warn his foreign allies; President George H. W. Bush, his most important and influential partner, was the only head of state to be informed while the speech was being given. Kohl was mixing statesmanship with ruthless party-political interests, for his eyes were firmly on the elections of 1990. He ran roughshod over putative CDU rivals and tried to pulverize the opposition by depicting the SPD as insufficiently patriotic. In December, U.S. Secretary of State James Baker alerted President Bush of worries that Kohl's "domestic political interest is leading him too far, too fast on the issue of unification; he is tapping emotions that will be difficult to manage." Baker was right. At a moment of supreme importance for Germany and Europe, Kohl's obedience to the presumed imperatives of his own career belittled the occasion.

Kohl's plan obviously required negotiations with the four Allied powers that still had residual rights and, most important, troops on German soil; the Soviet Union had half a million soldiers in the GDR. The United States, cheerfully distant and basically confident that the country had become "America's Germany," could take a more relaxed stance, but Kohl's correct insistence that even a unified Germany would remain in the Western world heightened Russia's anxieties. And the European nations, especially those that had experienced German terror at firsthand, had every reason to be apprehensive about a still larger, still more powerful Germany. Considering their inevitable anxieties, I was appalled that the ten points had said nothing reassuring about Poland's western border, a moral requisite, it seemed to me. Later, Kohl asserted, lamely, that only a unified Germany could make a final declaration on that issue. But in fact he was reluctant to upset the politically organized Silesians and other expellees who at the very least wanted recognition of their loss of home and perhaps also compensation. Still it would have been politically prudent to give Poland minimal reassurance that Germany would abjure any form of revanchism, the more so as Poland's new leaders supported Germany's unification, a position that was actually exceedingly unpopular in their country.

While Kohl's pronouncement suggested that the GDR would dissolve gradually, its citizens set a more rapid pace. The great exodus continued, while the outrage of those who stayed behind was fed by new revelations of how their "socialist" leaders were living in capitalist comfort, in sealed-off compounds, with swimming pools and Volvos, with Western luxuries and their own medical services. In January 1990, crowds stormed the Berlin headquarters of the Ministry of State Security, the Stasi, detested, omnipresent bastion of the old regime, and there they began to destroy its secret records until members of the civic opposition restrained them, knowing these records were requisite material for a future reckoning with the regime. The Stasi may well have been the world's most perfect institution for corrupting a people—much bigger than the Gestapo had ever been, less brutal but more insidious. More than a hundred miles of Stasi files remained, exhibits of the Stasi's fiendish means of surveillance and intimidation, and of the aid it had received from tens of thousands of citizens whom it had recruited to spy on friends and family. Morale plummeted as anger and disillusionment spread.

Karl Marx predicted that at some advanced stage of socialism the state would "wither away." I can't think of a modern state withering away, but perhaps the GDR, with its retrograde stage of socialism, came closest to the experience. At the roundtable, party and opposition were debating reforms, and the SED did indeed abjure its claim as the state's supreme authority, dismantle its dictatorial structure, and even adopt a more congenial name, Party of Democratic Socialism (PDS); it also found a new leader, a Berlin lawyer named Gregor Gysi, who in earlier years had defended key dissidents. Gysi, a descendant of a prominent Jewish family, was in appearance and demeanor antithetical to the earlier apparatchiks, being informal, witty, spontaneous, and clever, often too clever by half. Radical changes were now occurring routinely—from the top and from below, in the open and secretly. Popular anger at continued Stasi operations led to open outbursts, while delicate negotiations between the regimes in Bonn and East Berlin went on secretly; the key negotiator on the western side, acting with great tact and firmness, was Claus Duisberg, in Kohl's chancellery.

Party and opposition in East Germany agreed to hold elections in March for a new East German parliament, a free election being itself a novelty. Nazi and communist regimes had of course held elections—the trappings of democracy had been deemed indispensable, as were the foreordained results—but most East Germans had never experienced a free election. The PDS campaigned for a reformed but semi-independent separate state, while the East German leaders who had inspired the civic movements advocated something different from a capitalist FRG or a pseudosocialist GDR: a sociopolitical system that would combine capitalist efficiency with greater social justice and a more egalitarian structure. Meanwhile, the West German parties—CDU, SPD, and FDP—organized and financed their eastern analogues, and focused on the issue of how to achieve unification.

Bonn's Basic Law of 1949 had specified two ways: new *Länder* could accede at once by accepting the Basic Law or they could accede after a new constitution had been adopted. Kohl, having forged a coalition of several groups in the east called Alliance for Germany, a thinly veiled CDU organization, campaigned for the quick route, promising that in the unified Germany "blooming landscapes" would replace the impoverished, ecologically desolate disaster area that was the old GDR. He didn't present the citizens of either Germany with a bill for this dream project, and did not call on them for any sacrifice. (Helmut Schmidt, out of office, burst into a meeting at *Die Zeit*, where since 1985 he had been co-publisher, and vowed, "Now is the time for a Churchillian blood-sweat-and-tears speech!") Willy Brandt, who received fervent welcomes when he campaigned for the Social Democrats in the east (the most effective campaigners, it has to be said, were westerners), urged the slower path, because it would allow for East German participation in planning for the new nation. Kurt Biedenkopf, who took part in the campaign, too, noted in his diary a week before the election that no political party was living up to the requirements of the "historic moment." He was right. Neither CDU nor SPD used the moment for a realistic reckoning: Kohl was eager for a quick unification but ignorant of the true conditions in the GDR; the SPD knew more and wrongly thought a slower pace would be feasible.

The polls forecast a left-wing victory, with the SPD considered the favorite. But the results, with more than 90 percent of eligible voters casting ballots, were a stunning reversal of expectations: Kohl's "Alliance" carried the day, receiving 48 percent, the SPD 22 percent, the PDS 16 percent, other parties the rest, and the coalition representing the civic movements just under 3 percent. In short, most East Germans were tired of socialist promises and practices, they wanted an end to experiments, and they wanted what they imagined the other Germans had. The proletariat wanted the fruits of capitalism—and wanted them immediately (and literally "fruits": they wished for bananas, and the well-fed West Germans mocked them for this). Forty years of deprivation had been enough. Only the actuality of a Marxist-Leninist state, only what was called "real existing socialism," could have driven Leipzig workers to vote for the CDU. They cast aside their own true reformers and moral proponents of change and renewal—this fate befell reformers elsewhere in Eastern Europe, too. Reformers had cleared the way to the promised land, but "practical" politicians—with access to huge campaign chests—supplanted them. Regrettably, the reformers' early defeat forecast their later marginalization, when their presence in public life would have made a difference.

After the March election, East Germany's first and only democratically elected government was installed with Lothar de Maizière as minister-president. Maizière was a modest Berlin lawyer, a defender of dissidents, and an activist within the Protestant Church who had gone into politics more out of duty than ambition; he was a violinist by passion. Like many other politicians in the dying days of the GDR, Maizière was accused of Stasi connections, but these charges were quickly proven wrong. As a church activist he was bound to have had some contacts with the ubiquitous state security, but that was all. I thought it another minor political miracle that such remarkable political figures appeared on the scene: especially Maizière and Gysi—a Huguenot descendant and a Jew—representatives of the two tiny minorities that had once had a huge, beneficent influence on the flowering of old Prussia.

With the German question on the front burner and Germanists in demand everywhere, my own life began to change—in mood and actuality. My first impulse would have been to go to East Germany to teach, to help students grapple with the realities of their past and present, to challenge the distorted simplicities they had inherited. I would have liked to follow my friend Biedenkopf, who right away went to teach law part-time in Leipzig, heeding Kurt Masur's plea, "We need you." I may not have understood enough about the economic deficits of the GDR, but I did know about its deficits in the historic-intellectual realms. I thought it would be thrilling (and useful) to help East German students grasp the complexity of their history. I would have learned about the process of un-learning! East Germany's self-image was one of heroic exceptionalism, of being the embodiment of all that was progressive in German life, and this myth had to be corrected. Nietzsche once said that the attraction of attaining knowledge was heightened by the shame one had to overcome. The Soviet Union had ac-knowledged the difficulty in reordering the past: Gorbachev's regime had can-celed all history examinations in the USSR for a year. I can't think of a higher compliment to the centrality of history than its decreed suspension.

At the time, many of us were asking ourselves, "What is to be done?" I had a long dinner with George Soros in the spring of 1990 in which he told me about his projected Central European University in Prague, another daring initiative of his political philanthropy, at once effective and admirable. Gere-mek and I discussed similar questions in Warsaw in June. He put it so simply: historians are needed, he said, because truth is needed.

Circumstances made me stay full-time at Columbia, but there was much to be done. I urged my colleagues on the board of the German Marshall Fund to bring East Germans to the United States on programs similar to those that had given West Germans such great opportunities in the post-1945 era. The ex-periences would be different, of course: the earlier cohorts came from a devas-tated and bankrupt country to a victorious and self-confident America. Our own country had little of its earlier optimistic faith, and GDR citizens were now of a different generation from the survivors of National Socialism, but still, it was imperative to give them a chance.

The specter of a reunited Germany troubled many people, especially in Europe, but when I was asked to interpret the continuing drama and speculate about its possible ending, I told people I thought that the liberation of the East Germans and the creation of a united Germany, firmly anchored in Europe and the West, deserved all our support. Not everyone agreed. In retrospect I am pleasantly surprised that my views sustained a tone of optimistic equanimity.

And some of Eastern Europe's leading dissidents, including those who had themselves suffered from German barbarism, affirmed their trust in a new democratic Germany and took risks to effect a reconciliation with it. When in early January 1990 Václav Havel said, "We have a duty to apologize to the Ger-mans who were expelled [from our country] after the Second World War," his

communist opponents pounced on this allegedly non- or anti-national position, but I celebrated it, and in an essay in *The New York Times* called it "a magnanimous gesture"; Eastern Europe needed to free itself from Soviet orthodoxy
not only in the present but about the past, too. The expulsion of Germans from
the Sudetenland had been "executed under often brutal conditions," and it
had harmed not only Nazis but anti-Nazi Germans. (I mentioned a Sudeten
German friend as an example: an opponent of Hitler who had died during the
extrusion—this was Gret Kubelka.) "Apologies are necessary conditions for a
new Europe," I thought, and I also mentioned East Germany's official apology
for having participated in the Warsaw Pact actions against the Prague Spring in
1968, as well as the Soviet Union's acknowledgment in 1989 of the illegality of
its invasion of Afghanistan in 1979. To create a new and better order would require each country—and I included the United States—to face its past hon-
estly, neither succumbing to exaggerated guilt nor indulging in amnesia. In
1990 apologies had not yet become routine and meaningless gestures. But I received unforgettable hate mail for that piece. Slovaks wrote to tell me that all
Czechs were "pigs" and only Slovaks had opposed Hitler—a patent untruth. A
rabbi was enraged that I could mention a single Sudeten German woman who
had died: Had I forgotten about the six million Jews killed?

A few weeks later I was summoned to discuss the place of the German past
in assessing a German future—and in surprisingly august company. In late
February 1990, the British embassy in Washington asked if I would accept Mrs.
Thatcher's invitation to come to Chequers for what her private secretary,
Charles Powell, said would be "a very informal talk" with a few experts about
the lessons to be learned from German history that would help in dealing with
German reunification in the present, and with the future united Germany as
well, "and how we can assure that unification strengthens the stability and security of Europe." The meeting in late March was to be treated as "strictly
confidential."

I accepted—how could I turn down the chance to meet the British
prime minister, and at Chequers, fabled residence of British prime ministers,
Churchill's retreat, the British "Camp David"? The list of participants was
daunting: Gordon Craig was the other American, along with three British
historians—Lord Dacre (Hugh Trevor-Roper), Norman Stone, and Timothy
Garton Ash—and the journalist and former director of Radio Free Europe,
George Urban.

When Gordon Craig and I met in London on March 23, we were given
Powell's memo about the next day's meeting. The opening session would be on

the German past: "What does history tell us about the character and behavior of the German-speaking people of Europe? Are there enduring national characteristics? Have the Germans changed in the last 40 (or 80 or 150) years?" The prime minister would "tap the wisdom of each individual participant for this." The second session would deal with "Germany's future role in Europe and what changes this might require in our diplomacy."

Mrs. Thatcher received us graciously, and at lunch I sat next to her husband, Denis Thatcher, whom it was difficult to converse with. She, on the other hand, sparkled in a slyly flirtatious way, exuding charm and boundless self-certainty. Foreign Secretary Douglas Hurd and Powell, the note taker, were typically reserved.

The prime minister ran the meeting, asking each of us for an opening statement. My quickly scribbled notes indicate that my first item was "Anglo-German antagonism: greatest injury to the promise of the twentieth century." I talked about the antagonistic reversal of relations in the late nineteenth century, when imperial Germany had surpassed England's industrial strength and challenged its naval power (largely for domestic and prestige reasons), and then, in the horror of the Great War, the way each nation identified the other as the mortal enemy. The millions of dead and mutilated left a divided legacy: for some, the fervent wish "never again" to wage war; for many, a deep distrust of English hypocrisy on the one hand and German ambition and aggression on the other.

I added that misunderstandings might have bolstered this antagonism. The British never forgot that Chancellor Bethmann Hollweg, on receiving Britain's declaration of war on August 4, 1914, with its emphasis on Germany's violation of Belgian neutrality, had said, "All this for a scrap of paper," which led Britons to think that Germans regarded treaties as mere scraps of paper. I suggested the possibility of a different reading: Perhaps the Chancellor had been giving inept voice to his dismay that Britain was not remaining neutral as the Germans had hoped it would, and instantly realized the magnitude of the disaster. Perhaps it was more a lament than a judgment about treaties, a clumsy analogue to Sir Edward Grey's remark, "The lamps are going out all over Europe; we shall not see them lit again in our lifetime."

Of course the German past was a heavy, inescapable burden, but it was of limited relevance to the present situation, we historians all thought. It made for fear among Germany's neighbors and for violent conflicts among Germans. But Germans had changed; the Federal Republic now had a responsible, Western-oriented political class, and its earlier traits of anxious aggressiveness had largely disappeared. While reunification would pose huge problems, Germany would in the end master them.

We "experts" pressed this view the more as we discovered the depth of the prime minister's suspicion and dislike of Germans. The historically minded Iron Lady was imperturbably opinionated: the Germans, she was certain, would exploit their newly gained power to dominate the European Community and carry out their old self-assigned mission in Eastern Europe. Her question as to when they would march east again sprang from deep conviction; the Germans had all sorts of virtues, she said, such as discipline and hard work, but they were dangerous by tradition and character. Her skepticism and distrust seemed unshakeable. (Hurd's occasional intervention suggested a far more open mind: he was a realist unburdened by excessive prejudice.)

At the end, thanking us, the prime minister clapped her hands in a school-girl gesture, mischievously promising us, "I'll be so nice to the Germans! I'll be so nice to the Germans!" Kohl was to visit London a few days later, and I thought to myself that both leaders represented some of the less appealing features of what they themselves would have called national characteristics. In fact, Mrs. Thatcher had no choice but "to be nice," but she was grudging all the way. In her memoirs, she admitted, "If there is one instance in which a foreign policy I pursued met with unambiguous failure, it was my policy on German reunification."

At a teatime break, chance put me next to Mrs. Thatcher and slightly away from the others, so we had a brief chat. I said that if she felt as she evidently did about the Germans, I would assume she would try to revive something of the old *entente cordiale* between France and Britain. She let me have it about the French, who were quite hopeless, she said, and she threw in the Italians, too, as being frivolous and unreliable, adding, "The only people you can trust are the Dutch." I said carefully, "Prime Minister, that may not be quite enough."

When we left and repaired to our cars—after a round of drinks she had mixed herself and after she had shown us copies of some of our books, which she claimed to have read—I said to Tim Garton Ash, "The only word she didn't use was *Hun!*" The anti-German feeling ran deep, and her unspoken assumption may have been Churchill's view that the Hun is always at either your throat or your knees. These long-cherished prejudices were immune to reason.

Mrs. Thatcher couldn't slow down the process of German unification as she hoped: it had developed its own dynamic. But in Europe, she wasn't alone in her skepticism. François Mitterrand in France was equally reluctant to see a larger, more powerful Germany as neighbor—he may have agreed with François Mauriac, who had famously said he loved Germany so much he wanted two of them. But Kohl engaged Mitterrand in pushing for a plan, called Maastricht 1992, which envisioned the transformation of the European Community into a still more cohesive European Union. Kohl hoped that moves toward greater European integration would ease the difficulties with German unification.

The disposition of the German question required Allied acceptance and German-German agreement. To prevent even the appearance of having the negotiations dictated by the Allies, the formula "two plus four" was invented, meaning that the two Germanys would deal with their internal problems, and the four Allies would agree on how to reconcile their residual rights in Berlin and regarding the stationing of troops with German expectations for self-determination. Kohl was obviously the key player in both sets of negotiations, and his finesse and sure-footedness at the time were impressive. His indispensable ally was President Bush, since American interest was in the continuance of a strong Germany tied to NATO and the European Community.

Kohl also had to establish a common currency, and over the opposition of the Bundesbank, he decided on a 1:1 exchange rate between the deutsche mark and the *Ostmark* for most transactions, thus vastly overvaluing the latter, which he found a politically convenient compromise. The full extent of the GDR's economic collapse may not yet have been apparent, but people sensed that the material costs of bringing East Germany into a viable united Germany, and of making it sufficiently prosperous to dissuade further emigration, would be huge. Thus to disguise the magnitude of the task proved an additional psychic mortgage. I didn't pay enough attention to these economic aspects at the time. I worried about the human or psychological issues: hunger could be appeased, I thought, but humiliation would rankle for longer. I was afraid that East Germans would come to harbor a sense of loss and resentment.

In June, I had a chance to visit Maizière at his Berlin home, which reflected his modest, austere style. (I have forgotten who arranged for this visit; I thought it a special privilege.) When I mentioned that I thought the psychological difficulties of unification would be even greater than the economic ones, he instantly agreed: "I don't want to bring seventeen million psychological cripples into the new Germany," he said. In December 1993, he told me that he had said to Kohl at the time of reunification, with his cutting wit, "I am sorry I didn't bring sixteen [sic] million infants [Säuglinge] with me." Both formulations suggest that Maizière sensed that West Germany wished East Germans to be psychologically submissive and meek.

There was something pathetically symbolic about the contrasting actors in this drama: Kohl with his bulky presence, his massive self-satisfaction, and his Rhenish Catholic bonhomie, and the slim, tiny figure of Maizière, the austere, even humble, Protestant. They didn't like each other, and Maizière's dubiety about the virtues of capitalism didn't sit well with the chancellor.

There were also outspoken German opponents of unification, Günter Grass the most prominent among them. He insisted that the country's division was a historic punishment, that Auschwitz constituted a moral bar to unification, and that the peace of Europe depended on Germany's permanent division. But, I wondered, why should one third of the nation pay the entire bill? Others, in both west and east, would have wanted a confederate Germany in which a reformed GDR with a mixed economy that showed a "third way" between capitalism and communism would live on for a while. I thought this a congenial impracticality. The GDR was past reforming: its people had run out of patience.

In these months of upheaval, I was asked to speak at many less august occasions than Chequers, and my message was everywhere the same, though the emphasis may have varied: confident analysis of unification when talking to non-Germans; when talking to West Germans, pleas to treat East Germans with tact and empathy. But I knew that many Europeans and Americans had deep reservations about an enlarged Germany. Still, these talks and meetings sometimes allowed for opportunities to speak "truth to power," if I may presumptuously use the cliché describing the citizen's rare chance to address and correct people at the top who confound power with knowledge. At what turned out to be my last Trilateral Commission meeting, in April 1990 in Washington, Secretary of Defense Richard Cheney lamented that every time Havel or Wałęsa spoke he lost two divisions—that is, that the decline in the communist threat in Europe encouraged congressional frugality. He was trying to be jocose, but I objected nevertheless: surely the political presence of Havel and Wałęsa was worth the difficulty, and anyway security should not be measured solely by the number of divisions. (Little could I have known that in a dozen years Cheney would be determining policies relying solely on the ruthless and often incompetent use of power.) And when in the same meeting, Count Lambsdorff proclaimed that "socialism had ruined eastern Europe" but that West Germany's economic strength could cope with the derivative challenges, I countered that not socialism but communism had done the wrecking. Soviet communism was a horrendous falsification of true democratic socialism, which in the nineteenth century, by organizing the proletariat and pushing for social reforms, had in the end saved capitalism. "Now I can think of something positive regarding socialism," said Lambsdorff graciously.

The prospect of German unification presented a special problem to American Jews, some of whom clung to a rigidly negative view of the country, though anti-German feeling had somewhat lessened over the years. West German officials had made special efforts to reach out to American Jewry, indeed to woo it, and by and large the work of reconciliation had progressed. Still, for many, Germany was considered the country of mass murderers, as Einstein had labeled it in 1953. Early in 1990, Edgar Bronfman, head of the World Zionist Organization, wanted to present the Jewish position on unification to the Bundestag, and asked for my advice. I was skeptical—*was* there a Jewish position?—and urged him to first present his qualified acceptance of unification to a Jewish audience in New York. Eventually he did address a German audience in Berlin, but with little resonance.

Later in the year, Ismar Schorsch, chancellor of the Jewish Theological Seminary in New York and a former doctoral student of mine, asked me to speak on German unification at the annual gathering of friends of the seminary, that year honoring Gershon Kekst, a benefactor and head of a public relations firm. I hesitated: Was this an appropriate topic for such an event? Did he know that I had been baptized at birth? Yes, he knew, he said, and I should speak freely.

So once again I talked about the consequences of 1989–1990: Ben-Gurion's remark of 1957, "The Germany of today is not the Germany of yesterday," I told them, had been amply confirmed in the intervening years. West German politicians and writers acknowledged German responsibility for Nazi savagery, and there was no German triumphalism (like the American triumphalism about "winning the cold war"). The victims of the past must be remembered, I said, though never exploited; their memory was sacrosanct. I added a cautionary note: to understand the Holocaust as the deepest moral warning was obligatory, but to cultivate it as a permanent claim against future German generations or to allow the memory of the Holocaust to encourage intransigence sounded a dangerous false note. Nor must we forget that Germans had had indispensable collaborators in their crimes. The very power of the German Jewish poet Paul Celan's oft-quoted line, "Death is a master from Germany," sometimes allows Germany's foreign accomplices to be forgotten.

I had expected dissent, but encountered none, either there or from most other skeptical audiences. Since by coincidence three of my books were being published in France in 1990, and another in Holland, I was asked for lectures and interviews in Europe, too. Everywhere, I talked about our apprehensions that should be qualified by our hopes; it was a different Germany in a different Europe. After all, in 1989, nationalism had shown its Janus faces: powerful and beneficent in inspiring dissent in Eastern Europe, ugly and bellicose in the disintegrating Yugoslavia.

In mid-July 1990, Kohl and Gorbachev hammered out a final agreement on Germany at Gorbachev's Caucasus retreat. A unified Germany would eventually have full sovereign rights, hence would be free to choose its alliances (that is, remain in NATO); Soviet troops would for a limited time remain in the GDR and Allied troops in West Berlin. The Bundeswehr would be limited to 350,000 troops, and Germany would renounce all nuclear and chemical weapons. The Federal Republic also authorized an immediate five billion deutsche mark credit to the USSR—later it granted even more—to help with the costs of building housing in Russia for troops returning from their East German barracks.

Meanwhile the two German states also reached an agreement. The pace of events had been set by the steadily worsening situation in East Germany: the exodus continued, and the economy languished as industry was beginning to lose its export markets to the east and the common currency allowed East Germans to buy West German goods so long desired and denied. Maizière pressed for speedy unification: by October 3, the GDR became a part of the Federal Republic under Article 23 of the Basic Law. The day was marked by solemn ceremony but without triumphalism. Germany's brief and only attempt at socialism (once an indigenous product!) passed into the dustbin of history. To achieve unification with Allied consent marked a great diplomatic success, but I thought none of this could have happened but for the courage of the East European dissidents and the millions of peaceful East German citizens who had taken to the streets—and because Gorbachev recognized that Soviet tanks neither could nor should preserve a tyrannical rule over foreign nations.

It was in the context of this evolving German success that an angry whimper from England caused a momentary stir. In July 1990, Britain's trade minister, Nicholas Ridley, Mrs. Thatcher's closest Euro-skeptic ally in the Cabinet, gave an offensively anti-German interview in *The Spectator*, in which he insinuated that a unified Germany would gain peacefully what Hitler had striven for by force (a caricature of Kohl with a Hitler mustache accompanied the text). Ridley was dismissed, and the whole flap was not taken too seriously in Germany, but it reflected the rift between pro- and anti-Europeans in Britain, especially among the governing Tories.

Ridley was bad enough—but worse was to come. A misleading record of our Chequers meeting with Mrs. Thatcher was leaked (apparently from the British embassy in Bonn) that made it sound as if her "experts" had shared in bashing Germany. Charles Powell's protocol of the meeting—which we had never seen—appeared in *Der Spiegel* and then in the British press. It read like the record of a conclave of anti-Germanists, which of course was the very opposite of what it had actually been. One sentence listed a catalogue of unattractive German characteristics that had been discussed, beginning with *Angst* and aggressiveness and ending with sentimentality. All of us were annoyed by the false impression created by this account and concerned lest our German friends believe it.

Tim Garton Ash was the first to respond, pointing out in a British newspaper that in actual fact "the weight of the argument was overwhelmingly positive," that all of us—who by no means held identical views—emphasized that the Federal Republic did represent something radically new in German history. "Each spoke his own mind. Fritz Stern said nothing that he would not have said—indeed, has said already—in his well-known publications." Ditto for himself. I added a rejoinder, and then in a long article for the *Frankfurter Allgemeine* (reprinted in *The Washington Post*) reiterated his point that the effect of Powell's summary had been the opposite of our hope to contribute to a better understanding of the radically new situation, of the profoundly different, and finally Westernized, new Germany. I wrote the article just days after Kohl had had his triumphant conversations with Gorbachev, which in substance confirmed West Germany's attachment to the West, but in style—for example, Kohl's keeping Bush in the dark about some details—hinted at German-Russian bilateralism. Did it have to be in the Caucasus that Kohl announced that "on the day of German unification all Allied rights will automatically cease"? Factually correct, but was it tactful?

Unification, I added, represented a second chance for Germany, a rare gift for nations as for individuals. Germany's first chance had been before 1914, when it was on the cusp of becoming Europe's preeminent power, but the outbreak of the Great War, inseparable from Germany's flawed political structure and its mounting chauvinist madness, wrecked that chance. Its second chance was to build on the success of the Federal Republic—this time in peace and prudence.

The phrase "second chance" stuck. The *Frankfurter Allgemeine* used it as the title of my article, and it has been frequently cited ever since; Germans sometimes introduce me as the man of the "second chance." I still think the term is appropriate, being at once celebratory and admonishing: a great gift had been bestowed on the country, and it required protection. The past should serve as a lesson.

THE PHRASE THAT I THOUGHT DEFINED a historic moment also encapsulated the deepest personal experience for me. I was myself reaching out for a second chance. In the early 1980s, Elisabeth Sifton, a renowned book editor and publisher, had sent me the galleys of a book for a comment; we developed an epistolary friendship—in the days before e-mail, letters were means of conveying intimate thoughts and confidences—and then we met. I had never encountered so magnetic and high-spirited a woman before, gifted in countless ways, with an inner and outer beauty. She was compelling and alive, with unceasing intellectual curiosity and spontaneous openness of response to life and art. She was half European herself, she understood and encouraged my European orientation, and her upbringing had fostered in her a forceful political commitment. Her mother was English, and her late father, Reinhold Niebuhr, was a famous theologian and social critic whose book *The Irony of American History* I particularly admired—quite aside from his abhorrence of Nazism and his tremendous help to European refugees. Mine and Elisabeth's interests and passions coincided, and it became an all-consuming love. Our lives became intertwined even as our tempers—and the force of circumstances—occasionally created storms. She has ever been and remains a life-sustaining, life-enhancing gift: my second chance.

My unconscious, I believe, did me a service by initially hiding from me the connection between my public expression and my private experience. I might have suppressed the remark about Germany's second chance if I had recognized immediately that its origin was related to a personal matter. Historians often find their life and work related, but we are also taught not to let the former intrude on the latter. In any case, my private life developed its share of stress. The process of divorcing Peggy was difficult, even if the final stages were entirely amicable. Separation or contestation doesn't come easily to me.

In the final months of provosting, in 1983, I had begun to have lower back troubles that kept getting worse, much as I tried to control them by exercise. By mid-1990, I found it hard to walk for any distance without great pain; after many tests, a diagnosis of spinal stenosis was made, and on January 15, 1991—which I remember because it was also the day the first Gulf War started—I underwent a laminectomy. I recovered quickly—so quickly that I could go to Sils

Maria that summer and do some decent hiking. (I was walking along Lake Sils in August when I heard the news that the coup against Gorbachev had collapsed!) Sils had long occupied a special place in my life, not only because its awesome beauty enhanced my memories of my parents and the past, when I had been with them in the Alps as a child, but also because it was a place of my own where I could meet and make friends and once again use my native tongue free of political distress. Alpine hiking had become a passion for me, and going to Sils had a double function: I could rest, recoup, and recover there, but the promise of it also became an imperative for doing hard work, the material prerequisite for the uniquely restorative Alpine weeks. My children share my feelings, as do Elisabeth and my grandchildren. It has become my second, elective home.

Less than a year after that holiday in Sils, I woke up one night with a throbbing chest pain, and—for all my much-vaunted medical genes—fell into the indulgent fantasy that I was merely suffering from an upset stomach. In fact I had had a heart attack, and by the end of the next day I found myself at Columbia's medical center and, with the help of a Columbia friend, in the care of Jerry Gliklich, a cardiologist born in 1948 in a town some sixty miles west of Wrocław! This splendid doctor has become not only my physician but a trusted friend: another kind of homecoming! And under his care, and with the wondrous support of Elisabeth and my children, I again recovered quickly; I was grateful that these two crises happened in the right sequence: the back operation allowed me to do the regular daily walking that a post-infarct life requires.

My very first question to Dr. Gliklich, when I was still in the hospital, prompted by my father's concern about the effect of high altitudes on heart patients, was whether I'd be able to go back to Sils Maria. He thought yes, and fairly soon. I at once felt better. In fact, in the summer of 1992, Elisabeth and I went for our two weeks in Sils, at the end of which—together with our French friends Roger Errera and his wife, Irene—we managed a seven-hour hike up to the awesome high point where the Lunghin Pass crosses the Septimer Pass, and then down along the stony Septimer path to the Bregaglia Valley, a path the Romans had built and Martin Luther had trod.

I BECAME EVER MORE INVOLVED in the life of the new Germany. An early trip to the ex-GDR was in May 1991, when the German Academy of Language and Literature, to which I had been elected in 1988, met in the well-chosen cultural mecca of Weimar. I found it overwhelming to see so many layers of

German history all at once: the Goethe House and the Schiller Museum; the quiet old cobblestoned town; the dilapidated buildings, torn posters, and brown-coal smell (which I rather liked) of the old GDR; and in the center, a broad street with new stores hawking Western goods. At one end of town one could visit the old ducal palace, richly appointed inside but its grounds a wilderness, and on the way to it one passed a large Soviet war cemetery.

The academy's formal sessions and papers were dutifully academic, but as so often, incidental conversations and shared walks in the interstices made the meeting worthwhile. The academy had invited a few East Germans to the discussions, but the West Germans paid little heed to what they had experienced and, finally, achieved; a local pastor said to me, "I felt like a liberator [*Befreier*], and now I feel like a loser [*Besiegter*]." The sentence stuck in my mind.

The enduring memory, however, was of a trip I took on my own, to Buchenwald, which lies only about five miles from Weimar at the top of a steep hill; the Jews who were seized on *Kristallnacht* in 1938 were made to walk or run up that hill to the camp. A neighbor of ours in Breslau, like most Breslau Jews, had been taken there, and I fell to thinking about what such an ordeal would have done to my father, with his health and spirit already shaken by the Great War. If he had had to endure this horror, my own life vis-à-vis the German past would have been unalterably different, I realized once again.

The cab that drove me to the camp went past the vast barracks for the Soviet soldiers still quartered there. The actual site on top of the hill and enveloped by beech groves (*Buchenwald*) was "romantic," with a dreamy view toward Weimar: it had been the Nazis' diabolical trick to place their barbarian excrescence next to the grail of German classical culture. At the camp, the huts still had communist labels, highlighting the communist heroes who had successfully organized an underground resistance group there; and some Nazi documents were on display, too, such as the lists of Jewish inmates, with their titles, doctor or *Privatgelehrter*, supplied. (But right after the camp's liberation in 1945, I learned later that day, the Soviet authorities had used it to imprison their "enemies," including old Social Democrats.)

As I left, shaken and inwardly silent, I saw a tourist bus disgorging French visitors, including a number of blacks, perhaps francophone Africans, and I wondered, what did they think of "Western civilization"? When I telephoned my son that night to tell him of the welter of emotions that had struck me, so much involving his paternal grandfather, he called the visit a pilgrimage, and perhaps it was: a pilgrimage to horror, with thankfulness for my family's escape, and for rare fortune at a time of deepest misfortune.

The likely pitfalls on the road to German unification—East Germans called it by different names, absorption at best, *Anschluss* at worst—seemed obvious. I had often said that the way Germans treat Germans, how governments treat their own citizens, is a likely indicator of a country's conduct abroad. In post-unification Germany this was an issue of central importance: how would the prosperous West Germans treat the poorer newcomers, and vice versa? The future looked both brighter and darker, freer and less secure. West Germany took charge of the major economic work—of privatizing, for example, the huge state-run and badly run industrial combines. On several occasions in the old West Germany, I spoke of the American experience, of Lincoln's magnanimity at the height of a terrifying civil war, but of how after the war that magnanimity was often betrayed by venal Northern carpetbagging and hostile Southern resistance.

Chancellor Kohl continued to obscure the massive expense of unification. Finally, in March 1993, the Bundestag adopted what was called a solidarity pact, levying new taxes to pay for reconstruction in the east and projecting a transfer of approximately 7 percent of GNP to the eastern *Länder* over the next decade, much of it for a viable infrastructure of new roads and telecommunication webs. But the creation of these essential aspects of a modern society couldn't make up for the massive unemployment ensuing when obsolete and sometimes overstaffed plants were dismantled.

Much more had to be dismantled, and the entire state apparatus—including its civil service, its teachers, and its judicial system—had to be vetted. Who should do this, and by what rules? The communist regime had depended on multitudes of subservient functionaries, but what choices had those people had, and how could one distinguish between time servers and local tyrants? How would one judge, or even find out about, the people who had somehow alternated between collusion with the terrible regime and acting decently on occasion? Only now was everyone in both east and west beginning to understand the full extent of the Stasi's villainy, its pervasive surveillance and corruption. Who were the truly guilty?

I suspected that West Germans who had been lenient in the 1950s with Nazi accomplices in the brown past would be harder on people with a red past, and I anticipated that de-Stasification would be more thorough than de-Nazification had been. On the other hand, a considerable group of untainted, competent West Germans free of any vindictiveness now could and did assume positions in the eastern *Länder*. I watched as two old friends, Kurt Biedenkopf and Bernhard Vogel, in their new posts as minister-presidents of Saxony and

Thuringia, respectively, became warmly acclaimed *Landesväter*. But it is not surprising that East Germans complained of being "colonized" and exploited, while West Germans complained of East German self-pity and ingratitude. (As one East German wit quipped, "If there is something worse than being exploited, it is *not* being exploited.") Tact was needed in the many realms of what West Germans came to call the *Abwicklung,* a bureaucratic term (once much used by the Nazis) to signify bringing a process to conclusion. I asked a friend who chaired one of the West German commissions assessing East German academic institutions and personnel why no neutral—a Swiss or an Austrian, say—had been asked to help adjudicate. It hadn't even occurred to the West German authorities.

In June 1993, a new group, called the German-American Academic Council, of which I was a member, had a meeting with Chancellor Kohl. At the end of a long discussion, I happened to ask the last question, which was my old one: might not the economic problems, staggering as they were, perhaps be more easily solved than the psychological ones? Kohl's long discursive answer ended with the remark, "The idea that everything was right with us and everything was wrong with them is idiotic!" I jotted down the phrase instantly, thinking, if only once he had said something like that in public! That was the tone that was most needed, and it was largely absent, as was any effort at moral-political education.

It saddened me that within only a few years disillusionment was replacing high expectations. Some Germans quipped that their country was more divided than ever, and while progress in the "new" *Länder* was manifest (many a desolate town or neighborhood was being spruced up; the sight and smell of new paint was cheering), I came to realize that the East Germans were succumbing to the anomie that is always attributed to those suffering from the early stages of harsh capitalism. The first signs of what was called *Ostalgie* appeared—nostalgia for the close-knit, familiar, shabby GDR, for the exemplary symbols of its social-security net, like its much-touted child-care centers (*Kinderkrippen*) that so handsomely allowed mothers to be part of the (relentlessly driven and underpaid) work force. The older generation began to cleanse its memory of the oppressive, boring aspects of the GDR and remember gratefully the parochial privacy, slowness, and predictability of its "socialist" life—in many ways more "German" than life in Americanized West Germany. In Berlin a leader of Neues Forum said to me, sighing, "Didn't we bring *anything* to this new country? Was there *nothing* that deserves recognition?"

Helmut Schmidt wanted to establish a private nonpartisan foundation, the Deutsche Nationalstiftung, to promote intra-German reconciliation within an integrating Europe; he financed this himself initially, later from foundation grants and donations. He invited me to join the senate of this new organization, made up of Germans from both east and west and three foreigners; its executive committee included Biedenkopf, Masur, Reimar Lüst, and Schmidt himself. The foundation has become a voice in nation building, determined not to allow national feeling to become again a passion exploited by the radical right. Its work has taught me a great deal. But its very existence testifies to the unsolved problems of German unification.*

Even in old democracies, politicians with their eye on the next election prefer flattering the public to educating it. I was dismayed, for example, at the simplistic history invoked in the United States to justify American triumphalism about the events of 1989. In his State of the Union speech in January 1992, President Bush declared, "By the grace of God, America has won the cold war . . . [We are] the kindest nation of earth . . . [T]he world trusts us with power . . . They trust us to be on the side of decency." Would it were so! I wrote at the time. The United States had done enough so that its leaders could have afforded to acknowledge the signal importance of the East Europeans themselves in toppling communism. Even a rhetorical overestimation of American power and character was morally repulsive and politically dangerous. I hadn't forgotten Bush's vilification of liberalism in the 1988 campaign, and I was troubled by the reigning political style: a Reaganite world had created a skewed vision of American greatness and a practice of unleashed greed—what Jacques Delors, president of the European Commission, called "capitalisme sauvage."

Accordingly, I was delighted by Bill Clinton's election in 1992. When Swiss television asked me for comments from Washington on the morning after the election, I didn't hide my elation at the Democratic victory; on camera (the interview took place on the rooftop of the AFL-CIO headquarters) I pointed to the White House behind me and said, "It's ours again!" I had another brief moment of celebration.

A few weeks later, I had a chance to report about Clinton in Germany: Joschka Fischer, then Hesse's minister for the environment, a Green in the first red-green coalition, invited me to lecture in Bonn at an ongoing series, "Germany: What Now," focusing on the new Germany's foreign policy. I had met Fischer before and found him appealingly unconventional and sharply intelligent. As I was sitting in my hotel room going over my scribbled notes just be-

---

*It also exemplifies the growing importance of private or corporate foundations in the new Germany, which have enriched the country's political and intellectual culture. They operate in often conscious emulation of American groups such as Carnegie, Rockefeller, and Ford.

fore my talk, I received a phone message that President Weizsäcker was planning to come to the lecture: it was hard enough to prepare, but this made it quite daunting.

Still, it was easy enough to stress my main point, which was that Clinton was an internationalist who would continue the special U.S.-German relations of his predecessors. I mentioned American satisfaction with Germany's technical support during the Gulf War and the German presence among the UN blue helmets in Bosnia. At home, I said, Clinton would have to deal with the various deficits he had inherited; I mentioned President Bush's solicitude for the newly powerful Christian fundamentalist groups, and explained the lamentable significance of his nomination of Clarence Thomas to the Supreme Court. But I also mentioned an earlier irritant in German-American relations: in December 1991, Kohl had made his precipitous decision, against the wishes of the European Community and the United States, to recognize Croatia's independence, a move that many feared would lead to Bosnia's declaring independence, too, which would provoke a Serb attack and plunge the Balkans into war. (Days after Bonn had taken this action, I happened to have seen Cyrus Vance—who had been President Carter's secretary of state and was now helping the UN effort to achieve a negotiated peace in the Balkans—and he told me of his shock when Foreign Minister Genscher had responded to his criticism by shouting into the telephone, "You are wrong, you are wrong!") Americans had also been dismayed by outbreaks of xenophobic violence, especially in the "new" *Länder*, though they also knew of the silent marches protesting such violence. The discussion that followed involved a good cross-section of Germany's political class. As the dignified Weizsäcker, participating purely as a citizen, walked out with the tieless, sneaker-clad minister and me, I thought to myself, This really is a new Germany!

EARLY IN THE MORNING OF JUNE 8, 1993, Richard Holbrooke telephoned me: Secretary of State Warren Christopher had just told him that President Clinton wanted to appoint Holbrooke ambassador to Germany, and Holbrooke wanted me to know this right away. (He had been told he would go to Japan, Asia having been his principal interest and competence as a diplomat, but Tokyo went to Walter Mondale.) Holbrooke asked for my help. His immediate question was how the Germans might respond to the appointment of an East Asian expert to Bonn. It would be easy to reassure them, I said: if they had any misgivings, one could say that Clinton's choice of an ambassador with global knowledge was a recognition of Germany's new global importance. Also, the value of an ambassador can be measured by his proximity to the president, and Holbrooke had been a campaign adviser to Clinton. The next day, an administration spokesman announced the appointment listing these two reasons!

Holbrooke and I had first met in 1969 in Princeton, when he was at the university's Woodrow Wilson School of Public and International Affairs, on leave from the State Department and I was at the Institute for Advanced Study. Our mutual friend the diplomatic historian and political scientist Richard Ullman, on the Princeton faculty, introduced us; I instantly took to the ebullient, experienced, and very knowledgeable twenty-nine-year-old. Holbrooke had entered the foreign service after graduation from Brown and looked for ways to serve the country in responsible positions; he wanted to devise policy and execute it. He thought practically, but he dreamed idealistically. Personal and national interests coalesced in his ambition: so young, so energetic, so clever, and so eager! And impatient too: "Cut to the chase!" could have been his motto. I was older, but he seemed smarter. We immediately agreed then that the Vietnam War was inimical to our national interest (he had been in Vietnam and had taken part in the Paris negotiations of 1968 between the Johnson administration and the North Vietnamese), and we went together to talk to Clark Clifford about ways to end the Vietnam nightmare.

After his year in Princeton, Richard asked to be director of the Peace Corps in Morocco; among his many attractive sides, he was a Francophile, however skeptical, and wanted to serve in a francophone country. (I have been told that when he asked for the job, the State Department official carefully rehearsed with him his swift career: college, foreign service, Vietnam, Vietnam negotiations in Paris, Princeton—all in just a few years. "Young man," he said, "if you want to keep up the momentum, slow down.") During Christmas 1970, my family and I visited him in Morocco, where I saw him as a forceful mentor of the volunteers. There was a proconsular touch to the post, or perhaps I imagined it: I had always been fascinated by the last great French proconsul in Rabat, Marshal Hubert Lyautey. I followed Richard's subsequent career as editor of *Foreign Policy*, successful apprentice in the financial world, assistant secretary of state in the Carter administration, then back to finance. (The ease of moving in and out of government service remains a distinguishing, at times corrupting aspect of American politics.) We saw each other quite often and exchanged books and manuscripts.

Days after his phone call, Holbrooke rang again with an extraordinary idea:

that I should go with him to Bonn as "senior adviser" to the embassy. I was stunned and delighted. The chance to serve the American government in my native country? To learn something about the actual conduct of diplomacy, and to be active in a different world? To a friend I said it was like having OSS experience without a war and at the end of a career. But I consulted experienced friends to make sure: Gordon Wright, superb French historian, who had twice served at the Paris embassy, summed it up kindly: "Good for the U.S., good for Germany, good for you." Warren Zimmermann, who had just resigned from the foreign service over America's passive policy in the Yugoslav wars, was similarly encouraging. But both men warned that the embassy staff would view me—an intruder with putative knowledge and special access to the ambassador—as a nuisance. German friends, especially Biedenkopf and Bernhard Vogel, were enthusiastic.

The burden of realizing this exciting prospect actually happen, of clearing the obstacles to it, fell on Holbrooke, who encountered some unease at the State Department, for he was proposing something unprecedented, hence uncongenial, to a bureaucracy. The idea, as I remember, was that I would receive official housing and per diems but not be on the official payroll. I also needed a semester's leave from Columbia, and Holbrooke marched off to George Rupp, Columbia's president, to request that he agree to what he came to call a "lend-an-eminent-professor program." (Soon he had to do it again, when Frank Wisner, ambassador to India, asked to have my colleague Ainslie Embree as his adviser, following the Holbrooke-Stern precedent.) I also had to go through security clearances. I was cleared to the level "up to and including secret." And there were occasional bad patches: Holbrooke was disturbed when Kissinger told him that a CDU functionary had warned him that I was sympathetic to the left wing of the Social Democrats. An American colleague, eager for the assignment, made the same point with malign purpose in a national paper. Then, days later, Kissinger reported that Kohl was "ecstatic" about my coming, and he himself became so supportive that eventually he told me that the whole thing had been his idea.

Early on, I had to choose between having a large office somewhere on the same floor as the ambassador's suite, or a small office right in it. I opted for the latter, which turned out to be the right place to be and most amusing, too. I declined an offer to live at the ambassadorial residence on the Rhine, though as it turned out I spent much time there; I felt Holbrooke and I ought to keep some distance, some privacy for both of us. So I was housed in a small apartment in "Little America," the American colony that had grown up in the early postwar years in Plittersdorf, an inclusive but isolated suburb of Bonn, with shops, a school, a social center, and a church. Elisabeth helped to move me in but then had to return to a new job in New York; I managed by myself, though it was a bit lonely at times. Plittersdorf's separateness from ordinary German life kept the embassy staff and their families too much among themselves. The embassy itself in Bad Godesberg was even farther from Bonn, a few miles up the Rhine, along with the residence, in a huge complex that had been built for U.S. occupation headquarters in the late 1940s. I soon discovered a wonderful path between the embassy and my flat in Plittersdorf, along the ever-busy river; taking my daily walk to and fro was among the happiest experiences of my diplomatic sojourn.

The embassy in Bonn was America's largest in Europe. To be a part of its staff, however temporarily and of however dubious a rank, filled me with a deep inner pleasure. Was it perhaps a second act of naturalization? What a great, mysterious feeling it was to be quickly accepted, to *belong* to this American team—even if at moments my special status also spelled exclusion. And it was a source of pride to represent the United States—the country of the Marshall Plan and the Berlin airlift; in Germany people still greatly appreciated McCloy and Acheson. And there was so much work to be done!

Holbrooke hit the ground running, ready almost at once not only to direct the embassy but to get to know the German scene and its key players, to represent American interests in as many ways and quarters as possible. He impressed his German interlocutors; I don't think they had seen an ambassador so vigorous and knowledgeable since the days of James Conant in the 1950s or Arthur Burns in the 1970s. Richard was in almost constant motion, meeting German officials and top people in business and media, speaking to countless groups, and doing everything at high visibility. I enjoyed watching him size up the country and the people. He was appalled by some of the rigidities of German life, and of the labor market in particular; he thought the economy was hobbled by all too many restrictive rules. In private he never tired of ridiculing the prescribed early closing hours for German stores, for example—then a maximum inconvenience for working people who were also shoppers, however protective the rule was of the stores' employees. I told him about the peculiarities of German capitalism, with its socially protective and commercially protectionist features.

From the very beginning Holbrooke was conscious of the permanent shrinkage of the American physical presence in Germany. GIs and their families had been welcomed in the old Federal Republic and had for decades been a major link between two cultures, so the agreed-upon reduction of U.S. troops and their total withdrawal from Berlin would leave a large vacuum. In 1990, U.S. military strength in Germany was 247,000; by late 1994 the level would be down to 83,000. At the same time, Congress mandated cuts in the diplomatic presence as well. For these reasons Holbrooke made every effort to strengthen nongovernmental ties between the two countries. (Shortly after he arrived in Bonn, without a wife or family, he introduced a secret weapon, his mother. "Mutti" had been born in Hamburg to a prosperous "non-Aryan" family that emigrated in the early 1930s. After the war she had often traveled to Europe but never to Germany. She now returned, Germans took to her, and her presence underlined Holbrooke's connections with the place, as did the photograph he prominently displayed at the residence of his grandfather in his imperial German uniform during the Great War.)

In our age of instant communication, ambassadors are needed less for diplomacy than they once were, and more for establishing these nongovernmental links and for creating the right image of the nation they represent. Richard was very good at both, and by introducing him to friends and acquaintances in German public and business life as well as in the academy, I could facilitate his efforts. We were an odd couple, perhaps: he fully conscious of the media, I insufficiently impressed by photo ops and ceremonial occasions. But we worked happily together at a relentless pace.

I had seen many of our embassies in transit and from a distance. But I hadn't realized before how much an embassy is a huge conglomerate that comprises representatives of almost all U.S. governmental agencies: not just the foreign service in the political and economic sections and administrative section, but at that time still, the U.S. Information Agency and others, each with a big staff, each guarding its own turf. And then there was "the Station," as the intelligence group was known.

Holbrooke ran a tight ship, conveying discipline and high seriousness. He conducted the weekly staff meetings (if and when he was in town) with an intriguing style. His radiant, cheery self-confidence brought occasional lightheartedness to the business. Each section head reported on immediate issues, and Holbrooke, ever probing, would quickly commend or reprimand, sometimes both in effective combination: "That cable of yours on the minor election in Saxony was fine, but you were late meeting Senator X at the airport, which is impermissible and must never happen again."

He wanted to whip the staff into shape, wanted the best of the foreign service regulars to do more and better work, and he tended to disregard the lag-

gards, whom in private he might scorn as "brain dead." On his arrival the political staff had given him a rather too elaborate written briefing that began,
"*Change* is the one word which best characterizes Germany and its politics as
you begin your ambassadorship." He covered this document with acerbic marginalia, and went in search of the smartest people he could find—alive, energetic, capable—to tell him more. He could be charming and encouraging, or
curt and even abrasive, but always focused on substance and on national interest, on Washington and its politics. He was a stickler for perfection, yet he
didn't govern by fear; temper tantrums were not his thing. But one had to be a
dolt not to notice his view of you: he didn't suffer fools gladly.

I had to learn on the run, while trying to avoid major faux pas. Holbrooke's
superb right hand, Rosemarie Pauli, often clued me in on the frequent, breathless changes of daily plan and purpose. The ambassador had an unshakeable
habit of being late, hence there was always a certain nervous expectancy—
though in between meetings he knew how to relax in his large office: shoeless,
feet on the desk, ear to the phone, eyes on CNN, offering world-historical
reflections enlivened by gossip in between his endless telephone calls. He was
a good judge of people, though in the rare cases when he was wrong, he was
very wrong. Of course he focused on Chancellor Kohl's office, the seat of government decision making, and excessively neglected the Foreign Ministry. In
that he was following Kohl himself, but the German Foreign Office minded;
Holbrooke had his critics, even in Bonn.

Within the embassy, he had his favorites. The "admin" officer, Donald Hays,
was a quiet magician who could handle any problem of logistics and mainte-
nance; he had to operate within the severe cost cuts that Congress had imposed,
and this at a time when the embassy was planning its inevitably expensive move
to Berlin. Congress had the notion that Germany ought to pay for this move—
after all, we had helped the country with its unification—and it was left to Hays
to persuade the Germans to give us "additional value" for our base closings, that
is, to reimburse us for the improvements we had installed at the bases we were
now abandoning. Hays handled delicate matters of state and recalcitrant problems of human and material wear and tear with equal, efficient imperturbability.

There was one person whom Richard treated with special attention—and
whose inscrutable face and sibylline remarks I found fascinating, even before I
knew all that Milton Bearden had done and represented. Officially he was
listed as "Counselor, Office of Regional Affairs," and when he gave me a
farewell present, he attached a visiting card imprinted "with the compliments
of the Coordinator and Advisor American Embassy Bonn." But everyone knew

he was "station chief," that is, the CIA chief at the embassy. For decades he had been a key CIA operative, most recently in charge of U.S. efforts to arm the Afghans in their struggle against the Soviet Union. In Bonn for more than a year, Bearden had already built up key contacts there, one of which was Kohl's flamboyant head of intelligence services, Bernd Schmidbauer, and his assistant, Rudolf Dolzer. (Schmidbauer, a one-time ecologist, ran extensive intelligence operations particularly in the Middle East, and he had close contacts in Iranian intelligence.) Bearden was shrewd and incisive, seemingly low key, with a charming French wife. At dinner during my first week in Bonn he told me how the Stasi had penetrated West German intelligence from the beginning; he thought that Germany was not yet "a real country," by which he meant not yet a full player in international affairs. Soon thereafter, Holbrooke and I had lunch at Bearden's remote residence—very remote, as I remember. I was a novice, eager to learn; everyone knew of the great and often nefarious power of the CIA, but I gleaned practical details I had not known before.

I talked to the station about German prospects and participated in some of their meetings. And I am grateful to Bearden for conversations we had as I was writing these recollections. At the time, I hadn't known that at the beginning of Holbrooke's tenure, Kohl was annoyed because he imagined that Clinton's people were instructing his likely opponents in the next election, for example Rudolf Scharping, minister-president of Rhineland-Palatinate. This paranoid notion that the opposition's campaign was being run out of the American ambassador's residence was totally unjustified, but Kohl's apprehension was communicated to Bearden, who in turn alerted Holbrooke; he advised Holbrooke to accompany the chancellor in America on a private visit, to a World Cup match in Chicago. In the meantime, I had a conversation with Biedenkopf in which he spoke highly of Scharping, who "intends to tell the electorate that the country needs change, a tactic in conscious emulation of Bill Clinton's campaign." How much personal contacts matter, and how hugely domestic politics intrude on foreign policy!

Around the embassy, I was an all-purpose character. The American and German press suggested that "the historian-in-residence" was "providing private lessons on the past to help Holbrooke read the future . . . [Stern's] herringbone tweed jackets and wild white hair stand out in embassy corridors trod by clean-cut young diplomats." (That is how *The New York Times* perceived it.) At our first country-team meeting, Holbrooke introduced me to the staff and, without warning, requested comments from me. Fortunately, the previous Sunday I had been impressed by a "cultural" event that I took to have a hidden political meaning, though it was not generally so interpreted.

It had to do with the election of a successor to President Weizsäcker, whose term was to end in 1994; Kohl had proposed Steffen Heitmann, an East German CDU man and hence apparently an ideal candidate. But it turned out that Heitmann came from a different, primitively nationalist, antifeminist world. He had once said, "We don't need lessons from the World Zionist Organization." That Sunday, I had watched a televised ceremony at the Paulskirche in Frankfurt, where Friedrich Schorlemmer—an East German pastor famous for his championing of the peace movement and his mantra-like call that swords be turned into plowshares—received the Peace Prize of the German Book Trade. Schorlemmer spoke with eloquent candor about the German past, recalling Auschwitz, and about the German present, hoping that East Germans would be allowed to retain some of what had been good in their society. I thought his speech was an implicit response to Heitmann, whose candidacy, I suggested, was dead. (In the end a genuine liberal-conservative, Roman Herzog, former judge of the FRG's Constitutional Court, became Weizsäcker's successor.)

At later staff meetings, I ventured further political prognostications: if the 1994 parliamentary election didn't produce a clear majority, a grand coalition was likely to be formed—under Wolfgang Schäuble, the CDU's parliamentary leader, I thought, since the SPD would serve with Schäuble, a fierce antagonist and a commanding intellect, but not with Kohl. These were guesses based on casual comments I had heard or on barely noticed incidents. I'd make such remarks sitting next to the ambassador, who would often turn to me for a comment on the historical context of some current question. But much more often, Richard and I consulted in private.

We had barely arrived in early October when Holbrooke quickly recognized Joachim Bitterlich, chief foreign policy adviser to Kohl, as a key contact, and he planned to go to Leipzig with him for a special commemoration of the "Battle of the Nations" in October 1813, the Allied victory over Napoleon's troops on their retreat from Moscow. Inconsequentially, I wondered out loud if it was wise for the new ambassador to Germany to join in celebration of a decisive French defeat, but more important, I cautioned Holbrooke against going to Leipzig, East Germany's *Heldenstadt*, without paying official tribute to the city's key role in the liberation of the east. He did it. (Bitterlich's wife is French, and he was reputed to be closer to French than to U.S. positions, and Holbrooke's weighing in was important.)

There were occasional major flaps, some of which I got involved in, others I would merely hear about. In my first days erupted the question of what would happen to the Berlin Document Center, the American repository of the personnel files of Nazi Party members—some eleven million!—that Allied troops had captured in April 1945; the files had yielded essential information for the Nürnberg trials. The Bundestag had clamored for a return to German hands of this unique treasure trove on Nazi history, and the U.S. agreement to do so was the more necessary as large thefts had occurred on the American watch. The archive obviously contained potentially explosive material about Germans still in public life. After prolonged negotiations, the two sides had drawn up an agreement for the transfer, and Holbrooke wanted me to vet it—to the initial annoyance, I discovered later, of the embassy's political section.

I had a historian's dismay at giving up such a treasure—those millions of pages!—and was somewhat suspicious of the well-known habit in German archives of finding reasons (such as "privacy" restrictions) for delaying or obstructing access to sensitive material. Still, the draft agreement envisioned that the United States would make and preserve copies of all documents (though some originals had nonduplicable important markings). I urged that the Germans should follow the United States' user-friendly access policy, but it was hard at that late stage to introduce minute new provisions, let alone to renegotiate. Later, David Marwell, director of the Berlin Document Center, gave me a tour of the vast complex where the papers were housed, originally a building used as a listening center under Goering's control. He showed me some prize possessions, and I saw the place humming with people microfilming documents.

What I didn't know at the time but learned recently was that the United States also had access to Stasi files concerning Stasi agents in West Germany, material that had been placed in Russian hands; how it ended up in American hands is not revealed. The story about this material has the German code name Rosenholz, and a Web site by that name gives further information. Sharing this material with German intelligence, Americans could help identify former Stasi agents, but Kohl was concerned lest the United States was holding back papers that might perhaps be useful to him in incriminating his potential opponents, such as Scharping.

I was in constant touch with all the different embassy sections, and I told my colleagues then that my key concern was the American presence in what had been East Germany, where for forty years anti-Americanism had been part of education and of party orthodoxy. American diplomats seemed slow to realize what needed to be done there, and I took every opportunity to go to the old GDR for lectures and interviews. My lectures dealt with the German past and the American present; my rewards were East German stories, including often chilling accounts of Stasi intimidation; one woman told me that she feared her political activities in the late 1980s might lead to her arrest and to the seizure of her children by the state—and it was a perfectly justified fear.

In Leipzig for November 8–9, the fifth anniversary of the fall of the Wall, I was asked to participate in a peace prayer commemorating *Kristallnacht* at the Nikolaikirche. After the service, a candlelit procession to the site of the old synagogue was followed by a memorial service in the Thomaskirche, with music by the Leipzig "Synagogalchoir." At the synagogue, we were met by a gang of angry "anti-fa" youths who for unclear reasons tried to label our procession profascist. Dinner was at the Auerbach-Keller, place of wild celebration in *Faust*. What a kaleidoscope of impressions of past and present! And all on my father's death date.

Bernhard Vogel, now minister president of Thuringia, asked me to inaugurate a series of lectures in the Staatskanzlei, a baroque masterpiece in the *Land* capital of Erfurt, under the title "Friends from Abroad about Germany from Within." Erfurt is a historic gem, where I was given a tour of the Augustinian monastery where Martin Luther had studied, with his cell and the monastery's rich library. I stumbled there on some nineteenth-century anti-Semitic tracts (and a pictorial representation of Luther's pilgrimage to Rome, made across the Alps via the Lunghin Pass and Castasegna, the route that Elisabeth and I had recently walked, rather more comfortably, from Sils Maria). I also went to the old Baltic port of Rostock, where Soviet walls still blocked off some of the city's access to the sea. For each visit, regional USIA offices prepared my program, and the pace was fierce, but the many informal contacts made it all worthwhile. Here was my chance to learn for myself and help others "unlearn."

Memorable was a rushed visit to the Center for Research into Contemporary History in Potsdam, where my friend Jürgen Kocka had asked me to talk informally with his collaborators there. The center faced an uncertain financial future, and any outside recognition would help. For this private session Kocka expected some off-the-cuff reflections on the two German dictatorships, implicitly raising the confounding comparison of them, a subject still raw and often shunned. On arrival, I discovered a group of fine scholars and former GDR citizens, including Jens Reich, Fritz Klein, and Joachim Gauck: the cast was very different from what I had been led to expect.

I sketched some similarities between the two regimes, stressing that while the roots of National Socialism had indeed been deep in German history, the GDR also had been more than a foreign imposition, that it had roots in Germany's earlier working-class movement and in Weimar history. I knew that East Germans rightly insisted that their regime had not been responsible for starting a war or for genocidal murder. But in both systems there had been terror, tyrannical disregard for the law and for human rights, and the foulest means of surveillance, and in both systems there had been true believers and all too many people who readily served the regime in power. And there were multitudes who combined public accommodation with retreat into a private sphere with quiet grumbling—and perhaps acts of human solidarity. But the second German dictatorship was explicable only as a consequence of the first; without the Soviet victory over National Socialism, a German communist regime was almost unimaginable.

I worried out loud that the Stasi files, of which Gauck was the official custodian, were occasionally, often illicitly, used for political purposes. Gauck was convinced that all Stasi collaborators must be hunted down and prosecuted; he violently objected to Adam Michnik's advice for Poland—amnesty, not amnesia—which Marion favored and I could understand. (Gauck later visited me in New York once and referred to Marion and Helmut Schmidt as "enemies.") He vehemently demurred, saying that neighboring ex-communist states envied the Germans for having files in which one could identify those who were culpable.

Then, when it suddenly occurred to me to ask if it made sense to speak of "the early GDR as temptation," as I had spoken of National Socialism, tempers really exploded. Many participants denounced the very idea and insisted that the East German communist regime had always been viewed as a foreign excrescence. A few others angrily demanded: Why only the *early* GDR? There had been believers in the ultimate goal of an egalitarian, just society all along, and for them the temptation was to believe that that distant goal required present sacrifices. I certainly hadn't anticipated that my question would show how deep and alive this issue was in the minds of East and West Germans alike, with opposing views on each side. I myself could understand why people had fallen for the temptation, but my position was clear: one dictatorship sufficed.

On occasions like these, whether in the east or the west, I spoke as a historian or political commentator, not in any diplomatic guise. My basic text was the same, though in different places I would give it different emphases. I worried about the progress of Germany's inner unification, and I saw some confirmation of my fears about western tutelage, the more so since unemployment was at least twice as high in the east as in the west. Where were those "blooming landscapes" that Kohl had promised? I expressed hope and worry; the success or failure of Germany's "second chance" depended on reciprocal understanding and acceptance, on a measure of inner pacification.

At times, Holbrooke would assign me to a command performance as a historian in action. In October a large delegation from the United Jewish Appeal visited Germany, I believe for the first time. (The embassy was monitoring a draft German law dealing with the restitution of property in East Germany originally lost as a result of Nazi persecution. The Conference on Jewish Material Claims Against Germany had well-founded objections to aspects of the draft, and lobbied for changes.) At their banquet in Berlin, I talked about the need to understand the German Jewish past in all its complex ambivalence, with its rich creativity in the years before Hitler, when German Jews were allowed to excel in so many realms in a culture of discrimination; it was not in American or Jewish interests to hobble Germany's present efforts to come to terms with its many pasts.

The principal speakers, however, chose a very different tone: they fastened on the danger of neo-Nazis and right-wing extremists, and their theme was "We will not be quiet." Well, they weren't quiet that night or on other occasions: they seemed to sit in simplistic judgment of Germany's past and present. I jotted down in my diary "moral arrogance." I worried that my reaction perhaps reflected some kind of German Jewish subservience, an insecure fear of angering German Gentiles, or was it a justified concern that the stance of American Jews was counterproductive? Days later, I had a long talk with Isaiah Berlin about this; he, too regretted the conduct of official American Jewry in Germany. On a subsequent occasion, I asked Holbrooke if he couldn't suggest to these official groups that they might adopt a bit more reserve or tact, if only out of enlightened self-interest; his dismissal was swift and decisive. In private, I wondered if the Holocaust, which in some ways was related to the Germans' earlier paranoid anti-Semitic fears of putative Jewish power, had not in the end augmented Jewish power by giving Jews greater moral authority and a temporary immunity to criticism.

However absorbing German domestic issues were, I also had to assess how Germans operated internationally. The use of the Bundeswehr, the strongest army in Western Europe, in "out-of-area" operations had been constitutionally circumscribed, but in 1994, the Federal Constitutional Court relaxed these prohibitions, and in the first Balkan war, the German army offered various forms of support and surveillance flights over Bosnia. What would Germany's future participation in NATO be? Kohl, a convinced European, saw that working toward a still-closer European union would appease the fears aroused by German reunification. But Germany also had obligations to protect the newly liberated countries of Eastern Europe, to be their de facto facilitator as they sought entry to the West. Kohl was also a committed Atlanticist and, like his predecessors, had to balance his European engagement with his basic pro-American outlook. Deservedly he earned the respect of all his partners.

Inside the embassy, I was learning a lot about the sometimes suddenly explosive problems of American foreign policy, and I was learning it on the run, piecing together bits of information from day to day. At one point, the United States and Britain were angry when German officials received the head of Iranian intelligence, insisting that maintaining the Iranian connection was in large part to help Israel gain the release of one of their men. Policies toward Iran were an intermittent point of dispute.

Holbrooke and Strobe Talbott, then deputy secretary of state with special expertise on Russia, planned another first—an American-German-Russian conference to be held in Bonn, to work on greater U.S.-German coordination on policies toward Russia and the new government of Boris Yeltsin. In November, Talbott came to Bonn to meet with Bitterlich and a strong German delegation, as well as with his counterpart, Russia's deputy foreign minister. At Holbrooke's dinner, I celebrated the moment when former enemies and former allies could bury many hatchets: here was the promise of a new era. (I don't think this initiative survived Holbrooke's departure in the summer of 1994.) On that occasion and later, I strongly seconded Talbott's view that the countries that geography had punished by putting them between Germany and Russia needed special protection, even at the risk of Russia's initial opposition. The United States had established "a partnership for peace" with several East European nations, but I thought this a rhetorical flourish without much substance: membership in NATO, however unpalatable to Russia, had to be the ultimate solution.

NATO enlargement became an ever more urgent and controversial problem. Talbott recognized "that virtually everyone I knew from the world of academe, journalism, and the foreign-policy think tanks was against" it. Some years after I had returned from Bonn, in October 1996, at a dinner after a lecture Talbott gave at Columbia's Harriman Institute, the question of NATO enlargement, which he had merely touched on in his formal remarks, became a raging dispute. George Kennan, the then ninety-two-year-old dean of Russian analysts, called the Clinton plan for NATO enlargement a "strategic blunder of potentially epic proportions." All others weighed in on the same side, as Talbott recalls: "Only one participant spoke in favor . . . and it was, significantly, the only one whose field was Central Europe rather than the former Soviet Union. It was Fritz Stern . . . Why, he asked, did not the Poles, Czechs and Hungarians deserve security and consideration every bit as much as Russia, especially since they had far more reason to worry about being attacked by Russia than the other way around?" In January 1997, Talbott saw Kohl, fearing "the worst." Instead "Kohl's own version . . . began with a simple assertion of equity . . . in effect, the argument Fritz Stern had made in November."*

Holbrooke, never shy about breaking custom, had another idea: the U.S. embassies in Paris and Bonn should have closer ties, and he engineered the first-ever visit of some of the top Bonn embassy officials to their counterparts in Paris. (The fact that his friend Pamela Harriman was ambassador in Paris made it easier. At one point, as Richard was explaining a German position, Pamela interjected, "You haven't gone native, Dick?"—a frequent enough *déformation professionelle*.)

At the beginning of the joint session of the two embassy staffs, I was supposed to review current Franco-German relations; some American diplomats regarded too close a Bonn-Paris axis as a potential threat, but I argued the opposite, suggesting that post-1945 Franco-German reconciliation after centuries of intermittent enmity was of world-historical significance. I referred to Thomas Nipperdey's magisterial history of modern Germany that opened, "In the beginning was Napoleon." (Bearden told me later that he often cited that remark.) Actually, I began with Richelieu's principle of *raison d'état*, which established a French tradition of nonreligious, nonideological foreign policy, then sketched French political and cultural dominance from Richelieu's day until the emergence of a powerful united Germany in the aftermath of the Franco-Prussian War of 1870–1871; I suggested that only with the record in mind of the subsequent horror of the Great War and its aftermath, the Second World War, could one assess the immense achievement of the Franco-German entente in our own time. Though most of the staff probably wanted to know more about the last meeting between Kohl and Mitterand, they were indulgent, even attentive, and in the end peppered me with questions. The subject of Franco-German reconciliation was familiar to me, but the setting was novel: I wasn't used to having Renoir and Cézanne paintings as a backdrop. And Holbrooke and I stayed at the ambassador's residence on the rue du Faubourg–St. Honoré, the old Rothschild palais. On that cold, gray November weekend I felt "at home"; after all, I had spent years with the Rothschilds!

Then there was yet another first: Holbrooke organized a dinner at his residence in Bonn, to which he invited the chancellor: this had never happened

*Strobe Talbott, *The Russia Hand: A Memoir of Presidential Diplomacy* (New York: Random House, 2002), pp. 220, 226.

before. Kohl dominated the evening (the only person who dared interrupt him was Hans Tietmeyer, head of the Bundesbank), while the guest of honor, Henry Kissinger, was uncharacteristically quiet. Kohl was an amiable and expansive raconteur, offering the occasional revealing aside—amiable but misanthropic, rather contemptuous of people, explicit about his belief that you could never expect people to be grateful, and occasionally making crude sexual allusions. (As I was writing this book, I was told that at Kohl's bidding, Bitterlich had urged that I be dropped from the guest list, presumably because I had made some critical remarks about him, though not during my embassy tour. Holbrooke refused.)

Also at the dinner were Generals Charles Boyd, deputy commander in chief of the U.S. forces in Europe, and Klaus Naumann, chief of staff of the Bundeswehr. Both were extraordinary: Boyd had been for years a POW in Vietnam, a man emanating deep personal authority; and Naumann was a steely, wise, and open officer, the epitome, in a way, of the citizen in uniform.

As so often in Bonn (and in life), a small episode that evening led to a whole different adventure. General Naumann passed me a note during dinner reminding me of a conversation we had once had about his plan for an exhibition honoring the fiftieth anniversary of the 20th of July coup against Hitler: "I would appreciate it if you could help us in opening doors" in the United States, he wrote. A few days later, I visited him at the Ministry of Defense (most of its installations near Bonn remained there, even after the government moved to Berlin, since it was a safer location). Smiling, he said he could ask his friend John Shalikashvili, chairman of the U.S. Joint Chiefs of Staff, but thought that given Shalikashvili's Ukrainian background, I might be the better intermediary. Amusing! In any case, I wanted to help, thinking it was propitious for the Bundeswehr to celebrate the men who, breaking their oath, had tried to save their country. The exhibit was mounted at the Bendlerstrasse, in the very place where Stauffenberg and the others had been executed and where I had gone to hear them honored in 1954; it was a pleasure to work with Naumann to arrange to have the exhibit come to America, and it deepened my own relations to this signal event, which had meant so much to me for so many years.* Naumann and I developed a warm personal relationship.

---

*I facilitated bringing the exhibit to the Library of Congress in Washington in the summer of 1994, where among others Klaus von Dohnanyi, son of one of the most admirable of the resisters, gave a superb eulogy. Nevertheless, *The Washington Post* and other papers thought the Library was the wrong place for such an exhibit. Subsequently the exhibit went to Columbia University and to West Point, where I encountered the immense seriousness with which the cadets wrestled with the issue of breaking an oath in order to obey a higher command or necessity.

Through all those almost five months in Bonn—the longest stay in Germany for me since I had left in 1938—I had a full life in and out of the embassy, in my office and on the road, with Richard and alone. I felt as if I were living in both my countries, trying to bring them together, in fact and in my head. I liked my double role. And it was useful to connect with men whom later I encountered as friends in the United States—Wolfgang Ischinger, for example, then political director of the Foreign Office, as profound as he was sympathetic, and the only diplomat I know who is also a licensed ski instructor. (Later he became German ambassador in Washington.) And another diplomat, Dieter Kastrup, whom I met at a diplomats' dinner that was both special and somehow representative: Carl Duisberg, Kohl's special aide in German-German relations and an old acquaintance of mine, had invited me and some of his colleagues from the Foreign Office. During a pause in the dinner table conversation, Kastrup, in what struck me as a slightly provocative and ironic tone, asked me pointedly, "And what is it exactly that you do at the embassy?" Surprised, I replied, "I tell them what you [Germans] were, what you are, and what you could be." After that facedown, Kastrup and I became close acquaintances, and when he subsequently became German ambassador to the UN we saw each other quite often in New York. He was a remarkably sharp, impressive observer, and his unobtrusive grace in helping his wife, who as an adult had lost her eyesight, touched me from my very first encounter with them.

I also got to know diplomats from other countries, and I discovered that many of them were historians by avocation, sprinkling their conversations with historical analogies as they encouraged me to talk of the German past. So for those brief months I moved in a new milieu, each occasion slightly different, but all of them lively. I felt at times that I owed the pleasant occasions to an overestimation of my role at the embassy and my knowledge of Germany, but I enjoyed all of them.

When I think of my old and new German acquaintances—Ischinger, for example—I would in English call them "friends." But in German, this would be presumptuous and misleading. Americans more easily and quickly transform strangers into friends. In German, there are many gradations; you talk of a close acquaintance, *ein guter Bekannter*, which is more distant than a friend, before you say *mein Freund*, though nowadays one moves more readily to a first-name basis. I feel comfortable with both customs: the American better serves a liberal polity, but the German expresses a certain depth and lends an extra note to the human comedy.

A further gradation of German intimacy comes in the use, with a friend, of

the second-person singular: the move to the informal *du* is or used to be special. The Countess and I were friends for years, using first names, before she
suggested one day, "Why don't we use *du?*" Once established and drunk to, it
felt natural. This familiar mode has now become much more frequent among
younger German friends. (Germans also have, or had, the custom of "breaking" with friends, demonstrating the end of a friendship by a refusal to shake
hands. And the German cult of friendship, its effusive expressivity, can easily
degenerate into sentimentality.)

But whatever the custom or language, friendship *is* the great treasure. Helmut Schmidt contemplated entitling the book he wrote about people close to
him *Friendship*, but he chose *Companions on Life's Way* (*Weggefährten*) instead. Still, he included his thoughts on friendship, one of its criteria being a
need for honesty and truthfulness, a sense each friend must have that he can
rely on the other to speak his mind freely. Schmidt signed a January 2004 letter to me, "your friend."

When I left the embassy after almost five hectic months (though arrangements were made whereby my association with it continued sporadically for a
while), Holbrooke organized a farewell party for me. Days before, President
Weizsäcker had summoned me to his office and greeted me, "You are not welcome . . . because you are leaving!"—a memorable formulation. Richard spoke
most generously about me, and in return my thanks were heartfelt. In the characteristic high spirits of such an event, especially a Holbrooke event, I said I
had but one wish for the splendid staff: "If Don Hays could cut the ambassador's phone line for half an hour a week, it would already be a great gain."
They roared with laughter. Milt Bearden gave me an envelope, with the injunction not to open it till I got home: his gift was a (declassified) report written in July 1955 from the Office of Intelligence Research on questions
concerning a "Reunified Neutralized Germany." His note read, "Almost 40
years old, but kind of fun to read. Warmest regards."

On one of my last solitary walks from the embassy back to my apartment,
roughly an hour along the footpath by the Rhine, with the rolling hills of the
Siebengebirge on the other side (nestled in it the historic Petersberg, now the
government guesthouse), and the river itself—so alive, so peaceful—with
barges and boats of various European nations going to and fro, a sudden feeling of deep contentment came over me: this was the kind of German landscape, serene and beautiful, that my parents had been attached to. I had never
felt this kind of sympathetic contentment before, and it seemed as if I understood my parents better. I felt their innermost loss as perhaps I never had be-

fore. For a brief moment I was here in their stead, filled with imaginary glimpses into their world. Heine's "Loreley" came to mind, that beautiful German lyric that even the Nazis couldn't expunge, having to declare its Jewish author "unknown."

> *I do not know what haunts me*
> *What saddens my mind all day*
> *An age-old tale confounds me,*
> *A spell I cannot allay.*

At that moment of strange elation, the many sides of the past welled up in me. I realized just how special my American stay in Germany had been, bringing the two parts of my life together. It marked a new stage of reconciliation, on the surface and within myself.

LIFE AT THE EMBASSY had been an exhilarating adventure; it also suggested that historians have their usefulness in practical life. But after four months of life on the run, I was glad to return to "normality," to life in New York, richly enhanced by Elisabeth—who had been able to come to Bonn a few times and who had followed events there via frequent phone calls. And I returned to Columbia, to that often exasperating institution that had been my home for so long and about which I felt mixed gratitude and obligation.

I can perhaps gauge the measure of my attachment to Columbia by my instinctive efforts to help it when it was in trouble, which was often. Over the years, Columbia changed, as it seemed to become larger and less collegial. But teaching was my calling, and also a prescribed route to learning: a largely joyful, breathless effort to keep up with my subject and my students.

Still, in 1996, at the age of seventy, I decided to retire. American universities had been forced to give up the ancient custom of compulsory retirement, and I knew there was a fear that some professors would hang on forever, to the detriment of the younger generation. I didn't want to set a bad example—and fifty years of teaching sufficed. (Actually, I continued teaching till early 1998.) I must have introduced thousands of undergraduates to the history of modern Europe, and even now I meet strangers who tell me they were students of mine long ago. And to help graduate students cope with what William James called the Ph.D. octopus had been of special, often rewarding importance to me;

many of my graduate students went on to distinguished careers, and many stayed friends—in turn giving me all manner of help and support.

I began one of my last lecture courses on German history by saying, "There is no such thing as 'German' history"—a provocative way of insisting that German history can be grasped only as part of European life. Intermittent nationalist delirium may have beclouded this truth, but at all times, and certainly in the modern age, German life was in continued formative connections to the rest of Europe: German politics, culture, science, and material development were inseparable from Europe—in conflict at times, in reciprocal creativity at other times, always in decisive exchange. I always treated German history that way, so it was odd that I made this programmatic plea so late in my career. Mine was not a political bow to Brussels but a simple account of "wie es eigentlich gewesen," to use Ranke's injunction to try to depict the past "as it actually was."

My ties to Columbia and to the academic world in America and abroad persisted even after my retirement. In 1998, Columbia awarded me an honorary degree: I was delighted that Kofi Annan and Lauren Bacall were fellow honorees that year, making us "classmates." And Columbia will remain "home" even posthumously: my papers (and the papers of my parents) will be there.

Even before retirement, I became involved in Holbrooke's dream to create a permanent cultural presence in Berlin to take the place of the American troops who for half a century had protected and enriched the city. He began thinking of an American Academy in Berlin where gifted Americans could work for up to a year and by their very presence enhance German-American ties in the capital. We had talked about this scheme at the embassy, and I had conjured up a German analogue: after Napoleon's devastating defeat of Prussia, the philosopher-statesman Wilhelm von Humboldt urged the king to found the University of Berlin and thus "replace by spiritual means what had been lost physically."

With his customary energy, Holbrooke mobilized Henry Kissinger and Richard von Weizsäcker as co-chairmen, raised funds in both countries, and found an ideal home: a splendid villa in Berlin's fanciest site, on the lake called Wannsee; in the decade before Hitler's rise to power, the villa had belonged to Hans Arnhold. In the interim years the villa had been used for various purposes, but Stephen Kellen, Arnhold's son-in-law, had a keen private interest in it since his wife had spent years of her childhood there. Stephen was now president of Arnhold and S. Bleichroeder in New York, the bank I like to call "mine" since I had written the history of its illustrious beginnings. The Kellens proved most supportive of Holbrooke's plan. After a sound selection committee for fellows had been established, I, too, joined the board and watched the academy grow in stature and influence—the more so when official relations between the two countries deteriorated and a subliminal German suspicion of America, buried under feelings of admiration and gratitude, was inflamed by George W. Bush's administration in Washington, which acted in arrogant unilateralism. The academy owes its existence to many benefactors, but it is amusing to think that it all began with Walter Mondale's wish to go to Tokyo, the prerequisite for this last Holbrookian invention in Germany, and blessed by Bleichröder's ghost. Accidents, brilliantly exploited, make history!

At President Clinton's request, Holbrooke returned to Washington in 1994 as assistant secretary of state for European affairs, and a year later he was chief negotiator to end the war in the former Yugoslavia. Working overtime in Dayton, Ohio, on these impossibly difficult negotiations, he had to cancel a major speaking engagement in New York at the fortieth anniversary of the founding of the Leo Baeck Institute. At the last minute I took his place, but praised the reason for his absence, saying that "by his intelligence and energy, by his tough realism, by his diplomatic skill and intuitive apprehension [*Fingerspitzengefühl*]" he was an ideal peacemaker. I indulged in a historical fantasy:

> He should have been sent to Belgrade in July 1914 after the murder of the Austrian archduke. He would have told the Serbs to accept the Austrian ultimatum and cheat later. He would have shuttled to Vienna and told the Austrians that it would be madness to go to war, that the Germans were pushing them into this adventure, that their empire wouldn't survive it. He would have gone to Berlin and warned the Germans that to go to war over an Austrian archduke when within their grasp was the peaceful supremacy in Europe was to play Russian roulette—and by thus instructing the most immediately concerned powers, he could have avoided the First World War. In which case neither he nor his Hungarian-born wife nor I would be here in the United States.

MY OWN INVOLVEMENTS with my fifth Germany grew steadily. Short visits and longer stints at Munich and Mainz universities gave me platforms from which to watch and address German affairs. Germans have a flair for quick alterations of mood, but the swing from euphoria in 1989 to anxious disillusionment was astonishingly swift. (The Germans have an untranslatable phrase for their swift changes of mood: *"Himmelhochjauchzend, zu Tode betrübt,"* literally, hyperjubilation and mournful sadness.) The country was formally united but mired in an alarming mixture of melancholy and self-pity. A certain angry arrogance crept in as West Germans complained that the reconstruction of East Germany was too expensive, that their brethren were failing to carry their own weight, while many East Germans went on feeling colonized, condescended to, and exploited. Of course, life in the old GDR gradually improved—for some, probably for many; perhaps they were suffering the pangs of what we call the revolution of rising expectations.

In politics, Helmut Kohl pulled off another electoral victory in 1994, though with a narrower margin than before. He campaigned as "unity" chancellor while insinuating that his red-green opponents lacked patriotism. When he decided to run again in 1998, I thought that the man who had rightly attributed much of his success to being underestimated now overestimated himself. He lost, and his great achievements were tarnished by revelations that he had been implicated in unsavory details of a CDU campaign-finance scandal. He will be remembered as a good European, and as the unifier of his country, but he was nonetheless a divisive unifier.

Gerhard Schröder, a pragmatic Social Democrat, now became head of a red-green coalition, with Joschka Fischer as his foreign minister. (To think that Fischer, a violent radical of the '68 days, was now Germany's most popular politician! It was odd to imagine him in the historically staid and formal atmosphere of the Foreign Office.) The new government decided to participate in NATO's efforts to stop Serbian aggression and to protect human rights in Kosovo. If reds and greens had been in opposition, they might have voted against sending German soldiers to war, out of loyalty to their pacifist principles, but Schröder and Fischer were able to persuade their parties that the presence of German troops in the Balkans as peacekeepers and not as brutal conquerors was yet another step in the full realization of Germany as a responsible power.*

To be a witness to and participant in things German kept involving me in various tasks of multiple reconciliations: Germans had to be reconciled among themselves, between east and west, with their neighbors, with all the victims of

---

*In 2005, when this red-green coalition collapsed, a so-called great coalition, CDU-SPD, took its place, with the Christian Democrat Angela Merkel as Germany's first woman chancellor, while Matthias Platzeck became head of the Social Democratic Party. Merkel and Platzeck had grown up in the old GDR, and I thought their ascension to power was an implicit recognition of the talents that had been liberated in the old East, which, properly understood, should contribute to the true unification of Germany.

their past atrocities, Jews foremost, and with their own ever-disputed past. By profession and, I suppose, by temperament I was a partisan of reconciliation as a means of strengthening democracy, and I was particularly keen on German-Polish reconciliation as a political and moral imperative. (Given my Breslau-Wrocław connection, this too had its private side.) Germans began to ask me to speak at formal occasions about my own past, wishing, I suppose, to have a witness and interpreter of past events, and in the process I began to see myself somewhat more clearly as from a distance, slightly more conscious of private reasons for public engagement.

This was true in my scholarly work as well: after the embassy, I returned to my intended double biography of Fritz Haber and Albert Einstein, fraternal opposites, their dual story that of a discordant friendship and of the great tensions and temptations within German Jewry. Back I went to the archives, to the poisoned golden age of Germany before 1914, to Germany's "first chance," the catastrophic end of which both Haber and Einstein experienced. But I was distracted by complementary excursions: I became an itinerant memorialist for other great German scientists, among them Paul Ehrlich and Max Planck. When I was asked to address the formal commemoration of the fiftieth anniversary of Max Planck's death, it gave me a chance to learn about another life of science shadowed by private and public tragedy: Planck lost one son in the Great War; another, Erwin, was murdered by the Nazis as a putative accomplice in the 20th of July plot. I ended my speech—before an intimidating array of the German establishment—by saying that Planck had lost two sons to "the German delirium," and that the murdered son should be remembered along with the honored father. But I also had to deal with Planck's inner conflicts regarding the Nazi regime; it was hard to be an old-fashioned German patriot, used to serving the state, *and* to preserve one's decency. I tried to use these opportunities to combine efforts at conciliatory comprehension with unvarnished admonition; and perhaps the Germans were using me to say things that were still too painful or delicate for them to express.

I became ever more interested in what had been a network of scientists of the Haber-Einstein generation. The scientific work of these men had been studied, but not their lives and not their public influence. Next I added Chaim Weizmann to the scientist-statesmen I studied, when I gave the annual Weizmann Lecture at his institute in Rehovot. Elisabeth and I had a week in Israel in 1994, spending some time on the peaceful grounds of the institute, a world-class center of collegial research, and the rest touring the country, including the West Bank, where we were struck again by the clash between nature's severe beauty there and the harsh conditions of the Israeli occupation.

Still, the Oslo Accords aroused hope for a resolution of the Arab-Israeli conflict, a hope that was devastated when in 1995 Yitzhak Rabin was murdered by a fanatical Jew, driven to his despicable act by the relentless right-wing vilification of a general who had become committed to this chance for peace. I was at once reminded of the 1922 murder of Walther Rathenau, Germany's Jewish foreign minister, whom nationalist fanatics had killed after the political right launched a hate campaign against him as a "traitor"—and I wrote about the parallel of the two tragedies, born of nationalist fanaticism, with dire world-historical consequences. A year later, I was asked to speak about this parallel at a Tel Aviv symposium celebrating the opening of an institute named in honor of Rabin and dedicated to the study of Israeli history. The chosen topic for the occasion: "The Modern State and Political Assassination."

So Elisabeth and I returned to Israel on a sadder trip than the last one, but enlivened by our friends the philosophers Avishai and Edna Margalit; Avishai delivered the opening lecture at the conference. The tensions among the Israeli scholars and public figures in attendance were palpable from the start, but they erupted openly only at the very last panel, devoted to the consequences of Rabin's murder for Israel today. The one word I caught—it was used repeatedly—in the torrents of impassioned Hebrew, haltingly translated, was *Kulturkampf*, referring to the vehement disputes among the Orthodox, Reform, and secular Jews of Israel. Once again an echo of German history became an urtext for political fatalities in other civilized countries.

My essay on Rathenau renewed my brooding about Weimar and the accidents of its existence. In 1998, again at one of my favorite places for quiet work, the Netherlands Institute for Advanced Study, I accepted an invitation to speak at the long-running seminar on socioeconomic history at King's College, Cambridge, directed by Emma Rothschild and Gareth Stedman-Jones. I had admired Emma for years, and keeping with a conceit that the quality of the lecture should aim at matching the quality of the sponsor—or, put more prosaically, because I often write for a particular person—I worked especially hard on the paper I prepared for her seminar, which ended up being about "Death in Weimar." In it, I explored the grief that so colored life in the early years of Weimar, when death and mutilation were so pervasive, and I also focused on the fact that some of the Weimar Republic's key defenders died at a relatively young age—Rathenau himself, but also (from natural causes) Max Weber, Ernst Troeltsch, Friedrich Ebert, and Gustav Stresemann—while Weimar's enemies lived on to their eighties and nineties in unacknowledged senility. Once more I explored my interest in the crossroads of biography and history, in the place of accidents; at the time, I was reading a new book by the Hungarian writer Péter Nádas, which had as one major theme the importance in our lives of what *hadn't* happened, and I thought at once that this was true in history, too.

In 1998 my book *Einstein's German World* appeared, its centerpiece a very long essay on Haber and Einstein. As epigraph for my introduction, I cited something from a 1945 letter written to a Dutch physicist friend by Lise Meitner, the Austrian-born physicist who had been Otto Hahn's major (and underacknowledged) collaborator until she was forced into exile as a non-Aryan: "You ask about my attitude to Germany . . . I can best express it metaphorically: I feel like a mother who sees that her favorite child has gone hopelessly astray." This, I thought, was the briefest, most poignant expression of the feelings that many German Jews harbored about their former home.

WHEN I WORKED IN BONN IN 1993–1994, I met Poland's ambassador in Germany, Janusz Reiter, a young Polish journalist who had matured in the underground opposition during the 1980s. (He had been one of Marion Dönhoff's first Polish "finds," whom she brought for a time to *Die Zeit*.) Propelled by the Polish revolution into this high post, he was a linguistically gifted, historically minded diplomat, critically open to Western ideas and institutions. One of the thrills of post-liberation Europe was finding so many young men and women such as Reiter who, rising quickly to positions of responsibility, filled them so well. In Poland's case, it was all the more remarkable: their elders had either fallen victim to German and Russian barbarism, which had tried to expunge the nation's elites, or been tainted by some form of accommodation and complicity. Yet this new generation seemed braced, not damaged, by the memory of earlier tyrannies. (In 2005, Reiter became Poland's ambassador to the United States!)

Reiter was dedicated to finding ways of reconciling the many peoples in his country and in Germany who had lost their homelands, and in the summer of 1995 he organized a public meeting in Berlin where the painful issue of "Lost Homelands" could be discussed. He asked me to put the issue in its European historical context, though I suspect he wanted me to reflect on my own experience. The panelists who joined me included Marion Dönhoff and the German and Polish ministers of the interior, both of whose families, like the Countess's and mine, had lost their homelands (and both of whom happened to have been born on the same day). Of course, for centuries Europeans had experienced expulsion and loss, though recent instances had been particularly violent. After 1933, Germans had been expellers and expellees by turn. The pain of expulsion was palpable, as evident in the words to describe even less traumatic losses: homesickness, *mal de pays*, *Heimweh*. We all agreed that the political exploitation of private grievances wreaked horror, but also that the experience of starting anew, while not forgetting the past, could be exhilarating.

To define what I thought should be the spirit of the meeting I quoted Marion's credo that "the highest form of love is to love without possessing," and mentioned the remark of that splendid Swiss historian Herbert Lüthy, who had written that a new peaceful order in Europe would require people's "capacity to mourn without hating." By simultaneously acknowledging one's own and the other's pain, a sense of commonality and harmony might take the place of hatred. At the meeting, speakers and audience seemed to fuse passion and reason, experiencing a sense of relief and excitement that these issues could be aired publicly for the first time in decades.

The next day, Ambassador Reiter insisted on driving Elisabeth and me to my native city, which he knew was our next stop. So instead of the planned train trip to Wrocław, we drove along Hitler's autobahn, which I had last traveled in August 1938, right after my parents, sister, and I got our U.S. immigration visas. What an extraordinary way to return, with Poland's ambassador (and our friend) taking us back for my first visit to Wrocław since the end of communism, when I could show Elisabeth the site of my happy, painful childhood. Wrocław still bore all the traces of wartime destruction and socialist decay that I had seen in 1979, but the huge efforts at rebuilding were astounding. What life pulsated in the city! And with what honesty Poles now acknowledged that Wrocław had had its centuries of German life! What pride they took in its earlier distinction! Wrocław was being given back its history, and I felt that I was too.

In the spring of 1996, we returned to Wrocław when I received the annual Silesian Cultural Prize there, established after 1989 to honor a person of Silesian birth or residence. The prize money came from Germany and the local festivities from the Poles; the two nationalities took turns proposing names. Given my philo-Polish predisposition, I was especially pleased to have been chosen by the Poles. The festivities took place in the beautiful baroque auditorium of the university, the Leopoldina, and the biggest surprise was that Bronek Geremek came to give the *laudatio*.

My son, Fred, joined Elisabeth and me on this trip, and together we visited the places of my childhood. Fred had been exceptionally close to my parents and had grown up with my mother's many stories of her life in Breslau, so he could connect present places with those happy recollections. After a festive official lunch, he confided to Reiter's assistant that if there were time he knew I would like to visit the nearby mountain village, Zobten, where for a few years my parents had sublet a weekend house; the assistant mobilized the district governor's car to take us there. I couldn't find our erstwhile house, but the trip, in glorious weather, was splendid anyway. We walked on paths across peaceful fields and pastures, marveling at the orchards with their trees heavy with cherries. Returning to the car after our stroll, I discovered that the driver had picked a bunch of cherries for me, giving me back the tastes of my childhood. I can't forget that gesture and the fleeting feelings of some deep contentment, the kindness of the present linked with the better memories of the past.

Later that summer my daughter, Katherine, and her family came with me to Wrocław. Katherine, a fellow historian, had been equally close to my parents, and she, too, along with her husband and children, could now connect the tales from her childhood with actual physical places. She found the city grander than she had expected and was fascinated by the way it harbored two cultures. Both Fred and Katherine had a great appetite for seeing the partly vanished sites of my family's European life. They understood.

Those were years of almost euphoric reconciliation, of spontaneous reaching out to truth and to neighbors, of enacting an affective counterpart to Germany's long-delayed recognition of the border it shared with Poland. Then, gradually, relations frayed again, and Poles were disappointed that Germany became less of a champion of its cause in Europe. It is so easy to fall back on ancient prejudices, on nationalism — easy and destructive.

BY THE MID-1990S, GERMANS THEMSELVES were confronting new controversies about their past. Younger scholars were relentless in uncovering the pervasive culpability and complicity during National Socialism, the moral indifference to evil that had often been born of careerism and greed. The fact that citizens of other countries (think only of Austria) behaved no better did not remove the primal stain: Germans had been the mobilizing perpetrators of malignity.

Hitler's Willing Executioners: Ordinary Germans and the Holocaust, the work of an American political scientist, Daniel Goldhagen, created a furor when it was published in 1996. Goldhagen's answer to the question "why did the Holocaust occur?" was simple: it was German anti-Semitism, inasmuch as

Germans had for centuries embraced an "eliminationist mind-set" and had wanted to express it in action. That was Goldhagen's "analytical framework," followed by an "empirical" part in which he reconstructed three specific, gripping episodes of the Holocaust that showed the bestiality of "ordinary" Germans, mostly older men, few of whom had been Nazis. Goldhagen's inference was that almost any other German could have taken the place of any of them. The book was an indictment of a whole people, such as had often appeared right after 1945. Historians in America and in Germany—many of them the very ones who had done so much to uncover the specific horrors of the Nazi regime—criticized Goldhagen's sweeping generalities, but the public in both countries enthusiastically bought his book.

I found Goldhagen's contemptuous attacks on his critics among liberal German historians—who themselves had often enough been denounced by German nationalists—odious. So I joined the fray by writing in *Foreign Affairs* a fairly vehement critique of the book, its promotion and reception, its virtues and flaws. I was troubled by its moral and historical reductionism, its disregard for context and nuance. German anti-Semitism didn't come in one "eliminationist" form, and it had its own history, its own ebb and flow, all of which Goldhagen omitted. Even the Holocaust had a specific historic context, which was not exclusively German: it took place in the long night of organized bestiality, at the very nadir of Europe's brutalization in the aftermath of the Great War. I also noted Goldhagen's unscholarly attacks on his critics—in one case, his attempt to silence one. I may also have harbored a prudential concern that his primitivism might mobilize German antipathies to America and to Jews. I received brickbats in response, including a long, angry response from the author, but also grateful commendations. Gordon Craig thought it was "the best article I have read on the book and controversy. I am glad you came to the defense of the German historians for whom Goldhagen had nothing but contempt."

In 1999, I was able to return to the subject in less charged, pleasanter circumstances when I was asked to lecture on Jacob Burckhardt in his native city of Basel. (I was put up at the frayed Hotel Euler, the very place where, in January 1934, Fritz Haber, having talked to my parents about plans for their emigration, succumbed to a heart attack. I had trouble sleeping that night.) I wanted to restudy earlier remarks I had made about Burckhardt's critical views of modern Jewry; I suggested as my title "On the Use and Abuse of Anti-Semitism for Life," an obvious allusion to Nietzsche's famous essay "The Use and Abuse of History for Life." The guardians of Burckhardt's legacy who were my hosts were taken aback, so I offered the less provocative "Burckhardt, Nietzsche, and the Temptations of Anti-Semitism." But the audience at the lecture sat up when I mentioned my original title: there *had* been "uses" to anti-Semitism; to be a nineteenth-century critic of Jews was a way to identify with ancient "virtues," to remonstrate against modernity and the debasement of true values in the pursuit of profit and tawdry materialism. "Anti-Semitism" in Burckhardt's time—itself a neologism of the 1870s—ranged from mild social prejudice to politically motivated violence and rabble-rousing, but none of it could be understood except against the background of the Jewish minority's astounding rise in Western and Central Europe, a story probably without analogue in European history. Above all, I wanted to distinguish between Burckhardt, who in private correspondence uttered his critical remarks against Jews, and Nietzsche, who encountered in his private life some of the fiercest anti-Semites of the day and denounced them all, recognizing the power of their *ressentiment*, a poison whose deadly force he was one of the first to understand. This was a delicate subject for the Basel patriciate, and a vigorous discussion ensued.

THE 1990S BROUGHT ME into even closer and more regular contact with Germans, and partly through a succession of extraordinary surprises. In 1994, I was elected to Germany's Orden pour le Mérite, a self-perpetuating body of forty German and forty foreign scientists, scholars, and artists. I was not alone in being astonished and awed by this honor; most members acknowledge it. Felix Gilbert, for instance, said at his public induction that, thinking of his predecessors, he wondered, "What am I doing here?" My feelings, *a fortiori*. Like all new members, at my first meeting, I had to give an informal account of my life and work, and I mentioned Theodor Mommsen's warning that anyone who needed more than four hours' sleep wasn't suited for a historian's career, as well as Ranke's notion that historians get better with age. I hoped I might yet justify their choice. George Kennan, Gordon Craig, and the great physicist Victor Weisskopf were among the other American members, and since I delight in being able to admire—a pleasure balanced, I think, by the pain of well-developed self-doubt—I rejoiced in being among their company.

The Orden invites its members and their partners to semi-annual meetings, and on those occasions we have chances for informal chats on all manner of topics across disciplines, interspersed with lighthearted banter and bonhomie among men and women from many countries and fields. Thus trips to Germany and to Europe multiplied; six to eight transatlantic flights per year became almost routine. Odd: the Germany of my childhood had made me into a European; the Germany of my later years helped to bring me back to Europe.

In October 1998, the prolific German writer Martin Walser, whom I had met several times at Orden events, since he, too, is a member, received the Peace Prize of the German Book Trade, a prestigious award established in 1950. (Martin Buber, Theodor Heuss, Paul Tillich, and, more recently, Václav Havel and Jorge Semprun, have been among its recipients.) The prize ceremony, with the president of the Federal Republic and many politicians and other public figures almost always in attendance, takes place in the old Paulskirche in Frankfurt, no longer a church but a venerable landmark as the seat of Germany's first democratic parliament in 1848. Walser used the occasion to address issues of memory, with explicit references to the Holocaust that implicitly touched on a projected Holocaust memorial in Berlin.

Walser insinuated that writers who continually reminded Germans of their "shame" did so in part to absolve themselves of complicity in the evil past, to prove their own innocence or superior moral judgment, and did so because they wanted to wound "all Germans." In recent decades, he said, Germans were being reminded every day of their "ineradicable shame." Could it be that the "intellectuals" and "critics" who engaged in this censoriousness felt themselves uplifted when they did this, closer to the victims than the perpetrators? (Like Ernst Nolte, Walser softened his insinuations by asking rhetorical questions, by not naming names. But most people knew whom he had in mind—Grass, Habermas, and other "critics.") Nobody doubted the existence or horror of Auschwitz, he acknowledged, but to be confronted with it constantly and to have the shame instrumentalized was offensive. He confessed that he was driven to "looking away." "Shivering with boldness," he declared that Auschwitz should not be used as a means of intimidation or as a "moral cudgel" with which to punish all Germans. Perhaps, he asked mischievously, there was such a thing as the banality of the good?

The immediate response to the speech was positive, but within days, charges and countercharges dominated the German newspapers. Ignatz Bubis, head of the Council of German Jews, angrily denounced Walser, and so did many other commentators; the controversy quickly escalated, gaining venom and losing substance, as often happens with public debates in Germany. Walser responded with truculent anger; Bubis called Walser's defenders, even those who merely said he had the right of free speech, anti-Semites. The newly elected chancellor, Gerhard Schröder, who had originally been critical of the projected Holocaust memorial in Berlin, announced that after Walser's speech it was impossible to oppose it. The unanticipated consequences of Walser's ex-postulations were remarkable.

I thought at first that Walser hadn't quite known what he was doing, though surely he had meant to be provocative—but that interpretation was hard to sustain. A writer as exquisitely attuned to language and nuance as he would have had to be aware of the likely responses. Bubis declared that his life's work of reconciliation had been in vain; the clever, dreadful Marcel Reich-Ranicki, a literary critic of Polish Jewish origin, who had extraordinary sway as a kind of culture czar in Germany, claimed that Walser's speech confirmed his sense that Jews had become fair game again. The ugly furor lasted for months.

The issue of course will never go away, but I thought Walser's speech and the ad hominem attacks that followed it lamentable. Meanwhile, in the heart of Berlin, the controversial memorial to the murdered Jews was being built, a permanent reminder of a unique crime, committed by Germans in collusion with many others. And the Walser controversy coincided with a serious shift in European views of Israel—on the left, growing anger at Israel's occupation of the West Bank and Gaza; on the radical right, an intensification of the usual anti-Semitic animus. Some Jews, in turn, conflated all criticism of Ariel Sharon's Likud government with anti-Semitism—even when that criticism merely paralleled the views of Israeli critics. It became hard to imagine that there might come a time when Germans could speak of any aspect of Jewish life with ease.

But avoidance of painful truth was not an option. In 1999, I spoke of "The 'Subtle' Silence and Its Consequences," the phrase coming from Nietzsche, writing about what Goethe might have thought about Germans and the "profundity" often attributed to them: "But he never pronounced clearly on many things around him, and all his life he was good at maintaining a subtle silence; he probably had good reasons." What a wonderfully ironic, iconoclastic thing to say!

I was not alone in raising this theme. Also in 1999, Hubert Markl, president of the Max Planck Society, had declared at its fiftieth anniversary: "Those who think that fifty years after the end of the war . . . the time for such introspection [about past conduct] has passed . . . are misguided. All that has passed is the time for silence born of shame and remorseless suppression, for keeping quiet so as not to wound, and the immediate postwar era's will to forget." By now Nietzsche's phrase is often invoked in debate. (That same year, I chose it as the title of a collection of my essays published in Germany.)

Soon the issues surrounding Walser's speech touched me directly. In the spring of 1999, I was attending a public forum in Weimar organized by the

Deutsche Nationalstiftung to reassess the Weimar Constitution, drafted eighty years earlier. (I argued that it would have been a reasonable democratic charter for a democratic society; Germany at the time was far from democratic.) Next came a meeting in Berlin at which some of the major participants in the Walser debate were trying to heed Schröder's plea for reconciliation. (A few months later, Bubis died, embittered, and by his instructions, he was buried in Israel.) On returning to my hotel that night, I was given a message to call regardless of the hour a Mr. Ulmer of the German Book Trade. His question: would I accept the Peace Prize for 1999, for which the jury had unanimously recommended me?

I was stunned. I am no stranger to fantasy, but this possibility had never occurred to me; a historian had never before been selected. I called Elisabeth to tell her the news, but wasn't allowed to mention it to anyone else until a formal announcement had been agreed upon. In my happy daze, I suddenly remembered that the day was also the eightieth anniversary of my parents' wedding.

For a brief time, the prize changed my life. Once the news became public, many people and writers thought it an appropriate response to Walser's provocation the year before. I had to wonder if I owed the honor to Walser, if I had been selected as a kind of antidote to him. I was later assured that this was not the case, but in any event, life became a turmoil, and briefly I was turned into a public figure.

Herr Ulmer visited me in New York together with Eberhard Jaeckel, fellow historian and member of the jury, to discuss the selection of the laudator, the person who introduces the winner, who explains and justifies the choice. Ulmer suggested two or three names of splendid Germans, and asked for my ideas. I was flattered by his suggestions, but I had my heart set on Bronisław Geremek, my friend and fellow historian, and by now Poland's foreign minister. I thought the chances were slim that he could or would agree—all the greater the pleasure when I heard that he had accepted. Quite aside from my private feelings, his presence would manifest multiple reconciliations.

The Walser controversy obviously heightened interest in whether and how I would respond to that debate. I wondered myself, and preparing my acceptance speech proved particularly recalcitrant: I had to mix the historic and the personal, and I sensed that this was perhaps the best occasion I would ever have to voice my hopes and admonitions—and all this within a very precise time limit.

The occasion itself, on Sunday, October 17, combined excitement and the pleasures of old friendships. Geremek and I were driven together to the

Paulskirche, which was surrounded by police and by camera teams, for the audience at the televised Peace Prize ceremony includes not only publishers and writers but political figures.

A long line of officials—headed by Petra Roth, the charming CDU mayor of Frankfurt, and the president of the Federal Republic, Johannes Rau, and ending with Geremek and me—processed together into the great hall. Ulmer read the official citation, which was about my having promoted peace by establishing bridges of understanding among different periods and peoples, fairly depicting "the always controversial historic presence of Jews in German . . . life," and prescriptively addressing questions about the German present. Next came Mayor Roth, who emphasized the importance of literary accessibility and echoed some of my hopes for and concerns about the new Germany. She also delighted me by quoting an answer I had once given to the "Proust questionnaire"—that famous series of questions about one's values and experiences, much cherished by magazine editors—in which I described my favorite activity as "hiking with occasional illuminations" [wandern mit Einfällen]. I had been thinking of Sils Maria, but she most generously suggested that it would appear that I was quite often on the road. Would that it were so!

Geremek's speech was an eloquent defense of history as a vital antidote to the temptations of forgetting the past. He began with Paul Valéry's remark that history is one of the most dangerous poisons that the chemistry of the brain has invented. Having cited the French historian and Resistance martyr Marc Bloch, who had said that history could be compared to a knife with which you could cut bread and you could kill, Geremek covered the main themes of my work with empathetic precision, and said I cut bread. I was especially pleased by his saying, "Fritz Stern doesn't hesitate to speak the truth about Germans and about Jews, and precisely such truths that today could be painful for Germans, but also for Jews." Amid the ovation he deservedly received, we embraced, and I took my turn.

After giving heartfelt thanks to the organizers and above all to Geremek, I was happy to note that he was the first major historian since Tocqueville to be a foreign minister. And I thought that the prize being awarded a historian for the first time was an honor to the discipline itself and a recognition of the historian's responsibilities. I recalled that when I first heard about being awarded the prize, in April, Europe and America had stood at the edge of a new kind of war in Kosovo, the policy a decision of a democratic alliance unwilling to tolerate brutal inhumanity. "The military defense of human rights is a new phenomenon." Similar cases were likely to occur, and we needed unambiguous guidelines for such actions: "Responsibility should not rest solely with the world's only superpower."

When I talked about an active, prudent foreign policy for the new Germany, I stressed that its prerequisite remained the urgent moral task of internal reconciliation. Yet the estrangement between East and West Germans seemed to be growing. "There should be no room in this Germany for second-class citizens or for people who think of themselves as such. There have been enough second-class citizens in history. I have experienced this myself." This remark, at once a political provocation and a private confession, brought the first interruption for applause: I could feel the political atmosphere intensify in the hall. I noted that Ruth Dreyfuss, president of the Swiss Federal Council, had recently evoked the proper spirit for our times for dealing with the past when she acknowledged that she thought of her country "with gratitude and pain." If a Swiss citizen rightly said this, how much truer must it be for others, and especially for Germans.

Auschwitz would, "unavoidably and for all time," remain the symbol of German inhumanity. In Primo Levi's harrowing account of his existence there, he wrote that, on his arrival, he saw an icicle outside the barracks window and, driven by desperate thirst, reached for it, but a "heavy guard prowling outside brutally snatched it away from me. '*Warum?*' I asked him in my poor German. '*Hier ist kein warum*' (there is no why here), he replied, pushing me inside with a shove." This was the primary question, I said. Job asked: "How long wilt thou not depart from me, not let me alone till I swallow down my spittle? Why hast thou set me as a mark against thee, so that I am a burden to myself?" This denial of "why" was the authentic expression of all totalitarianism, revealing its deepest meaning, a negation of Western civilization. But it also should remind those of us who live in fragile democracies that authority should never be divorced from accountability. Too many Germans, too many people in the twentieth century, failed to ask "why?" The hallmark of our century might well be "they didn't want to see or know."

In conclusion I tried to account for my continuous concern with Germany. It wasn't only that National Socialism had been the decisive element in my political education, or that in childhood I had seen how German democrats fought for freedom and lost, or that after 1945 many of them returned to the task of building a different country. It was friends who had given me a spiritual connection to Germany, and I mentioned only one to stand for all, Marion Countess Dönhoff, "whose gift of friendship has been at once liberating and decisive for the course of my life." (The *Frankfurter Allgemeine Zeitung* reprinted my entire speech the next day, omitting only this one sentence about the editor of a rival paper! Marion was angry at this, rebuked them, and mentioned it in a brief essay about me. So much for my hope for a more liberal culture of conflict!)

German-American understanding was a dictate of history, politics, and my own life. My last lines were: "I am a citizen of one country, but my love belongs to two languages, equally endangered, one common culture, equally neglected. My gratitude belongs to the country in which my children and grandchildren can be raised in freedom. For the fact that I sense this gratitude so keenly and that I have experienced friendship as so vital a gift—for this I thank the country that once forced me into exile and with which I have forged new ties."

A standing ovation of many minutes greeted my exhausted, puzzled self: I can't recollect my precise feelings at that moment—humbled, numbed, empty. But my spirits rose with the affectionate greetings of old friends and of my son, Fred, and with the truly festive air. After leaving the hall, when we were all together in a room with friends and officials, sipping champagne and chatting before lunch, I relaxed. Elisabeth whispered to me, "Are you happy?" and I rejoined, "If not now, when?"

EPILOGUE

THE YEAR 2002 WAS EPILOGUE: sad and ultimately healing, a kind of closing of a life's circle. Just before New Year's Day, Marion Dönhoff telephoned me from Crottorf, where she was spending Christmas with her nephew Hermann. For several years she had been in failing health, with recurring bouts of cancer—afflictions she bore stoically. I had visited her in Hamburg earlier in the winter, and when I had seen her one evening, champagne had dulled the pain of her now-paralyzed arm, but the next morning brought renewed excruciating agony. Now she wanted to know when I would be returning to Europe: in March, I said, to Warsaw, "our city," for a book presentation plus a symposium with Geremek and Michnik. "I think I'll be better," she said, "and I'll come, too."

Over the next weeks I called her regularly, as I had before; in February, she had a fall in her home and was taken, comatose and unconscious, to the hospital. A fortnight later, she awoke and, cognizant of her now gravely weakened condition, demanded to be taken to Crottorf. When I learned this I planned to see her there when I got to Europe. After my meeting in Warsaw, I went to Sils, and the very next day Hermann called. Marion had died early that morning: realizing that the end was near, she had told the night nurse, "Call Hermann," and then died peacefully.

So now I went to Crottorf for her burial. When I got there, Hermann wanted me to say good-bye to her and took me to the castle's private chapel, where her simple wooden coffin lay on a wooden block, a few flowers on top. At the service in the great hall, a pastor friend of Marion's gave a brief sermon, family and friends sat in three or four rows, dressed in black: Dönhoffs and Hatzfeldts of four generations, Weizsäcker, Ted Sommer, Dahrendorf, Kissinger, and Christa Armstrong, her old friend from East Prussia. We walked behind the hearse to the village cemetery where, in the Dönhoff corner, one of her brothers had also been buried. Clouds suddenly parted, and a brilliant spring sun lit the scene: the open grave beneath a linden tree, birds singing, and each of us—including her crusty housekeeper with Marion's mischievous dachshund—approaching it, bowing, and dropping a sprig and a handful of soil on the coffin. We took leave of her in the austere tradition into which she had been born: one of quiet human decorum and nature unspoilt. Then we returned to the castle for a simple meal, with children underfoot and many private conversations. It was calm but exalted, perhaps the last time that her friends and family would be together.

A few days later, in Hamburg, of which Marion had been an honorary citizen, there was a state funeral for her in the city's largest Protestant church. Hermann had asked me to be one of the four eulogists, speaking for Marion's friends; city officials picked me up early, and for a while I sat alone in the reserved pew at the front, alternately uneasy in the present and sunk in the past. The others gradually came to the pew: Helmut and Loki Schmidt, Chancellor Schröder and President Rau (though only the latter spoke, protocol forbidding both chancellor and president to speak at the same public occasion). Weizsäcker spoke, then Schmidt, representing *Die Zeit*, and I followed him, saying once again what I had written before: "If there was one place in Germany that again was home for me, it was in her house and company, in everything she said and didn't say." When I returned to my seat, Helmut and Loki Schmidt clasped my hand in unspoken comfort. Yet Marion felt then, and remains, a steady presence in my life: Elisabeth once casually called her "your spiritual mother," a new thought but apt. In ways I can't express, she, as no other person, reached to the child in me and treated the adult as friend and intellectual companion.

Chance seemed to decree that the older I got, the more often I would be reminded of my childhood, even physically. In the autumn of that same year, the University of Wrocław was to celebrate its three hundredth anniversary, and the Polish authorities wanted to make it a truly international event.* The university

*The university had had a typical Central European history. The Habsburg emperor Leopold had founded a Jesuit institution in Breslau in 1702, the date that had always been regarded that of the university's birth. In 1756, Frederick the Great's conquest of Silesia brought the university under Prussian-Protestant rule. And in 1811, after Prussia's collapse in the face of Napoleon's new

senate identified the institution as "heir and progressive custodian of many traditions and cultures," committed "to the ideals of openness, tolerance, peace and understanding between peoples as well as the complete return of the renewed Republic of Poland to Europe"—pious words, but given that Poles in the communist period had denied the city's German past, the words expressed a new spirit. And in planning for its anniversary, the university was assisted by a German Polish Society of Friends of Wrocław University, founded by a Hamburg physician, Norbert Heisig, a native of Breslau; it was hoped that both Germany's and Poland's presidents would attend. The university asked me to speak at the ceremony, and I was delighted to accept; I suggested "The Recovery of Europe" as my title, vaguely pleased with the double meaning: the recovery of the *idea* of Europe after the murderous excesses of nationalism and the *actuality* of (Western) Europe's material recovery after 1945. My somewhat haphazard choice helped to determine the theme of the festivities—"the intellectual unity of Europe"—which was doubly appropriate given the current debate over EU enlargement. To me the very idea of having a native boy as principal speaker—obviously in English, the new world language—was wondrous.

As was the occasion itself. By noon on November 15, precisely three hundred years after the opening of the first institution, the two presidents arrived, and to the strains of Chopin's great A major *Polonaise*, an enormous academic procession moved into the beautiful baroque Leopoldina. The bearer of the university standard was at the head, followed by faculty members, deans, Senate members, the visiting rectors of other Polish universities—all in their ermine-decorated velvet gowns and caps, a different color for each faculty—and Wrocław's rector at the end. When we were all together at the front, the choir sang *Gaudeamus igitur*. No German university could have mustered such majesty: 1968 had put paid to all that.

After presidents Rau and Kwaśniewski had spoken, Austrian, Czech, and Hungarian representatives joined in extolling the mission of a university in a newly peaceful Europe. I also celebrated the uniqueness of the occasion: the presumption of peace in all of Central Europe for the first time. Though we knew "of the violence, the unleashed sadism of the past century," though "in

---

armies, the then Prussian king and his chief minister, Wilhelm von Humboldt, refounded the university as part of the nation's cultural renewal in the Prussian era of reform, and this was the institution my great-grandfathers, grandfathers, and parents had attended. After 1933 the university became super-Nazified. Then, in November 1945, Polish scholars and professors from the University of Lvov, a city now annexed to the Soviet Ukraine, moving westward several hundred miles as so many thousands of Poles had had to do, refounded their faculties in Wrocław.

space we are closer to Auschwitz than to Immanuel Kant's Königsberg . . . in spirit I know the opposite is true."

I spoke not only as a native son but also as an American, of course, and I told the audience that American historians had understood the commonality of European history even when Europeans themselves were divided into hostile camps, frozen in national narrowness, when national differences mattered more than a shared past. We were the ones who taught "Western civilization," a term that appropriately included the history of Europe's most prominent offspring in the new world. But all of us together could now celebrate a free university, remembering that from 1933 to 1989 it had served and suffered under two totalitarian regimes, very different but alike in their suppression of freedom and dignity. Disappointments and new dangers confronted us, "and no country, my own emphatically included, is free of fundamentalist intolerance." But we should remember that nonviolence had been the essential element in 1989. In that context, I mentioned Gandhi's legacy, quoting his response to the question of what he thought of "Western civilization." It would be a good idea, he is supposed to have said. So our task remained to turn the idea into a reality, preserving the ideals of an enlightened Europe. And a spirit of humility would be appropriate, I added, thinking of my own country.

A lively discussion ensued, with the two politicians and me taking questions from others, and at the end of it we all moved to the university church, where Beethoven's Ninth Symphony was performed—fitting in itself, and the "Ode to Joy" sung in German by three Polish choirs, made me choke up. Finally we walked down to the river and watched the most spectacular fireworks emanating from the other side of the Oder, multicolored flares lighting up the night sky.

The next afternoon was a second ceremony, when the university awarded me an honorary degree. When I went down the hall toward the rector's office, I noticed on the walls various portraits and displays that featured, inter alia, pictures of earlier honorands (among them, to my delight, the great liberal John Stuart Mill) and of Breslau's Nobel laureates, including Haber, Ehrlich, and Otto Stern; so the university's Polish masters accepted a continuity of honor with the old German traditions of the place.

In the rector's office, an eighteenth-century gem, with wall paintings and sculptures of striking beauty, I met my official academic host, the university's oldest historian, an ex-rector himself. I had met him before, on an earlier visit to Wrocław, and I hadn't been surprised to learn that he had had a somewhat dubious—that is, conformist—record during the communist years. Now he reminisced with me about his time as rector, and mentioned having spoken for another honorary-degree candidate once, the philosopher Leszek Kolakowski—difficult, he said, because he had had such "a curved existence." Was this a snide reference to Kolakowski's initial attachment to and subsequent early break with the communist regime? The adjective struck me as memorable, the remark insidious.

I was formally robed in black gown and velvet cap, and we set off in the same, if somewhat smaller, academic procession to the same glorious aula, with me walking (shakily) at the end, just in front of the rector, whom I had come to like greatly, a modest chemist with considerable wisdom. A chair on one side of the three-tiered platform had been designated for me, with a microphone in front of it. I had been given no instructions as to what would happen: I felt alone. The gowned Polish academic dignitaries were mostly behind me, and in front, a full hall, a reassuring Elisabeth surrounded by hundreds of Germans and Poles.

After a women's choir sang "Gaude, Mater Polonia," the rector announced gravely that at the suggestion of the faculty of history and pedagogy, and after the positive concurring evaluation of the Senates of the University of Warsaw and the Adam Mickiewicz University in Poznań, the Senate had decided to award me an honorary doctorate. I tried to listen to a halting translation of the citation, given first in Latin and then in Polish, on an ill-functioning earpiece, but in a way it didn't matter that I couldn't understand: I was in a trance. Only another musical interlude brought me to myself, and I thought again of my parents, saw them in my mind's eye, felt the pain of their lives even more than the joys, and was lost in clouds of thoughts and pictures, deep and unspecific feelings. Was this happening to me, and why?

I had jotted down some words of thanks on a yellow pad, words to explain why this honor touched my innermost being. I read the notes, but then I spoke spontaneously from the heart about my complicated feelings for this place "in which I was nurtured and from which I was expelled." And I read from the memoir I had written for my children about coming back to Wrocław in 1979, when I went to my grandmother's villa and the then-occupant, an ex–cavalry officer, showed me what had been my grandmother's living room, where—to my astonishment—the walls were covered with drawings of concentration camp inmates, and before I could say anything, he opened his shirt and showed his tattoo: "five years at Auschwitz, Birkenau, and Buchenwald," he had explained. And on a table, near where my grandmother used to sit, was a wooden statue of Father Kolbe, who in the camp had volunteered to give up his life in order to spare another's, and whom Pope John Paul II on his visit to Auschwitz had specially honored. On the balcony overlooking the garden where I had played as a boy we shook hands: "the transfer of a claim, gratefully and joyfully carried out by me—as if suddenly, for one brief moment, all the tangled past made sense; I told him I was glad he was there . . . [A] sudden moment of happy, grateful acceptance: in that mad world, something had gone right."

That spontaneous feeling of something being right filled me on this occasion, too, a ceremony of reconciliation. I wished the university in its new European setting all possible success and good fortune; the fireworks were like symbols of its brilliant ideas, old ones and those yet to come. I turned to the place of honor: "Rector Magnificus, you have given me back a part of my past, and I thank you from the bottom of my heart."

The procession moved out, and the rector and I marched at the end. As we talked together, he said he had been moved by my remarks; his father had been imprisoned at Auschwitz and Neuengamme (a horror camp near Hamburg). He hoped, he said, that I would now consider myself a member of the university—a distant home?

He *had* given me back a part of my past. I had always wanted to be fair and loyal to that part of my past that linked me to my parents and their world before it was destroyed, to honor what was right in it, to understand its destruction. I had returned from whence I came. I had touched a world that had formed me. It felt right. It still does.

ACKNOWLEDGMENTS

THIS BOOK HAS A HISTORY and it began in Europe. In 1998 I was spending several months at the Netherlands Institute for Advanced Study, where the rector, my fellow historian Henk Wesseling, decided I should give the lecture at the year-end ceremony—on any topic. He brushed aside my pleas regarding my other commitments with the counsel: "Make it personal." So I spoke about "Five Germanys I Have Known," and NIAS published the talk. A closed chapter, I thought.

Back in the United States, I showed the text to a few friends, including Roger W. Straus, president of Farrar, Straus and Giroux. Roger saw the lecture as the seed of a book and proposed that he publish it. I signed up for what I thought would be a short-term task, but a book develops its own long-term demands. I owe the book to Roger, and I regret that he didn't see its completion.

I had the good luck to have Rebecca Saletan as my first editor, wise and admonishing, until the day she left for new responsibilities at another house. Eric Chinski nobly assumed a heavy, undigested legacy, and with literary shrewdness and great pedagogic humor gave the project new life. The reader—and I—owe his sense of parsimony a great debt: existing pages, like the deleted ones, bear the imprint of his semi-indulgent judgment.

Friends were indispensable. Lionel Gossman, a literary universalist, read early chapters, noting stylistic infelicities and spotting the big and still only partly developed themes. He understood my intent, a boost to my morale. When the text was almost complete, I asked three friends and colleagues for a critical reading: Ralf Dahrendorf, with his incisive comments, revived a collaborative tradition between us, going back nearly a half century; the comments of James Sheehan and Jürgen Kocka were deeply helpful extensions of countless conversations we have had. Roger Errera in Paris also gave me additional advice and encouragement. My debts to these and many other friends, accumulated over decades, are large. I hope the book in general is a testimony to the friendships that have formed my life.

I have had indispensable help in the intellectual work of ordering family papers and related chores: Carleen Roeper helped immeasurably at the beginning, Jocelyn Wilk patiently ordered disordered papers, and Jonathan Shainin with good humor and expertise prepared the final manuscript.

The book is dedicated to my children: their love and support have been an inestimable gift. By being firmly anchored in the United States, they sustained my forays into familiar, foreign lands.

Elisabeth Sifton, my wife, has been a life-enhancing presence for me throughout: her spirit, blithe and critical, has inspired my work. She understood my new ties to my old country and shared in them. She was at my side with profound and prescient help, and her occasional candid exasperation served as a much-needed spur. My gratitude to her is joyfully unbounded.

Fritz Stern
New York, April 2006

INDEX